Shojiro Nishio   Akinori Yonezawa   (Eds.)

Object Technologies
for Advanced Software

First JSSST International Symposium
Kanazawa, Japan, November 4-6, 1993
Proceedings

Springer-Verlag
Berlin Heidelberg New York
London Paris Tokyo
Hong Kong Barcelona
Budapest

Series Editors

Gerhard Goos
Universität Karlsruhe
Postfach 69 80
Vincenz-Priessnitz-Straße 1
D-76131 Karlsruhe, Germany

Juris Hartmanis
Cornell University
Department of Computer Science
4130 Upson Hall
Ithaca, NY 14853, USA

Volume Editors

Shojiro Nishio
Department of Information Engineering, Osaka University
Suita, Osaka 565, Japan

Akinori Yonezawa
Department of Information Science, University of Tokyo
Hongo Bunkyo-Ku, Tokyo 113, Japan

CR Subject Classification (1991): D.1-4, H.2

ISBN 3-540-57342-9 Springer-Verlag Berlin Heidelberg New York
ISBN 0-387-57342-9 Springer-Verlag New York Berlin Heidelberg

This work is subject to copyright. All rights are reserved, whether the whole or part of the material is concerned, specifically the rights of translation, reprinting, re-use of illustrations, recitation, broadcasting, reproduction on microfilms or in any other way, and storage in data banks. Duplication of this publication or parts thereof is permitted only under the provisions of the German Copyright Law of September 9, 1965, in its current version, and permission for use must always be obtained from Springer-Verlag. Violations are liable for prosecution under the German Copyright Law.

© Springer-Verlag Berlin Heidelberg 1993
Printed in Germany

Typesetting: Camera-ready by author
45/3140-543210 - Printed on acid-free paper

Symposium Chair
Takuya KATAYAMA (JAIST)

Program Committee Co-Chair
Shojiro NISHIO (Osaka University)
Akinori YONEZAWA
            (University of Tokyo)

Finance Chair
Kokichi FUTATSUGI (JAIST)

Local Arrangement Chair
Yoichi SHINODA (JAIST)

Symposium Series Committee Chair
Mario TOKORO
            (Keio University/Sony CSL)

Executive Committee Chair
Koichiro OCHIMIZU (JAIST)

Publicity Chair
Takuo WATANABE (JAIST)

Sponsored by
JSSST(Japan Society for Software Science and Technology)
JAIST(Japan Advanced Institute of Science and Technology)

In Cooperation with
ACM SIGSOFT, Japan ACM SIGMOD
IEEE Computer Society(TCSE), IPSJ

Preface

This volume is the Proceedings of the International Symposium on Object Technologies for Advanced Software (ISOTAS). Currently object technologies are attracting much attention in diverse areas of research and development for advanced software. Object-oriented programming holds great promise in reducing the complexity of large scale software development, and recent research in this field opens up new paradigms for parallel and reflective computing. Object-oriented databases are expected to serve as a model for next-generation database systems, by overcoming the limitations of conventional data models. Furthermore, recent research in software object bases is aimed at developing a uniform approach to the management of software artifacts produced in the software development process, such as specifications, manuals, programs, and test data, which traditionally were managed in a very ad hoc and arbitrary manner.

Active research and experimentation on object technologies in these diverse areas suggest that there are some underlying, fundamental principles common to a wide range of software development activities. The first of the JSSST (Japanese Society for Software Science and Technology) international series of symposia focuses on this topic. The aim of this symposium is to bring together leading researchers in the areas of object-oriented programming, object-oriented databases, and software object bases. We hope to promote an understanding of object technologies in a wider context and to make progress towards the goal of finding better frameworks for future advanced software development.

The Program Committee received 92 submissions from 18 different countries in Europe, America, Asia, and Australia (including 31 domestic submissions). Each submission was reviewed by at least three members of the Program Committee and sometimes by external referees. This volume contains 25 contributed papers and 6 invited papers presented at the symposium. The contributed papers were selected by a highly competitive process, based on referee reports and painstaking deliberations by members of the Program Committee.

We would like to thank all the people who made the symposium possible, including the object technology researchers who submit their works to this symposium and all those who contributed their expertise and time in reviewing the submissions.

August 1993   Shojiro Nishio, Akinori Yonezawa
                                                 Co-Chairs, Program Committee

Program Committee Members

Co-Chair: Shojiro Nishio (Osaka University)
　　　　　Akinori Yonezawa (University of Tokyo)

Tsuneo Ajisaka (Kyoto U.)
Mehmet Aksit (U. of Twente)
Malcolm Atkinson (U. of Glasgow)
François Bancilhon (O$_2$ Tech.)
Klaus R. Dittrich (U. of Zurich)
Kokichi Futatsugi (ETL/JAIST)
Yutaka Ishikawa (ETL)
Hyoung-Joo Kim (Seoul N. U.)
Roger King (U. of Colorado)
Tok-Wang Ling (N. U. of Singapore)
Nazim Madhavji (McGill U.)
Ole L. Madsen (Aarhus U.)
Oscar Nierstrasz (U. of Geneva)
David Notkin (U. of Washington)
Koichiro Ochimizu (JAIST)
Atsushi Ohori (OKI)
Junichi Rekimoto (NEC)
Motoshi Saeki (Tokyo Inst. Tech.)

Edward Sciore (Boston College)
Etsuya Shibayama (Ryukoku U.)
Shinji Shimojo (Osaka U.)
Yoichi Shinoda (JAIST)
Alan Snyder (Sun Microsystems)
Ikuo Takeuchi (NTT)
Katsumi Tanaka (Kobe U.)
Mario Tokoro (Keio U./Sony CSL)
Hideyuki Tokuda (Keio U./CMU)
Katsuyasu Toyama (NTT)
Takuo Watanabe (JAIST)
Grant E. Weddell (U. of Waterloo)
Peter Wegner (Brown U.)
Jack Wileden (Univ. of Mass.)
Kazumasa Yokota (ICOT)
Masatoshi Yoshikawa (AIST, Nara)
Roberto Zicari (J.W. Goethe U.)

External Reviewers

Yoshiji Amagai
Takasi Arano
Shigeru Chiba
Laurent Dami
Birgit Demuth
Fabrizio Ferrandina
Yoshihisa Fujinami
Stella Gatziu
Andreas Geppert
Kohei Honda
Yasuaki Honda
Atsushi Hori
Takashi Imaizumi
Dirk Jonscher
Kiyohiko Kajihara
Kazuhiko Kato
Hiroki Konaka
Shinji Kono
Kazushi Kuse
Dong-Ik Lee
Mong Li Lee
Ling Liu
Munenori Maeda

Hidehiko Masuhara
Satsohi Matsuoka
Jeff McAffer
Akira Mori
Katashi Nagao
Ataru Nakagawa
Chisato Numaoka
Markku Sakkinen
Ichiro Satoh
Stefan Scherrer
Masato Suzuki
Naohisa Takahasi
Akikazu Takeuchi
Hee Beng Kuan Tan
Kenjirou Taura
Takao Tenma
Ken Wakita
Toshimasa Watanabe
Shigeru Watari
Raymond C Welland
Shuichiro Yamamoto
Kenichi Yamazaki
Yasuhiko Yokote

Contents

(Invited Paper) Uniting Functional and Object-Oriented Programming
John Sargeant 1

Traces (A Cut at the "Make Isn't Generic" Problem)
Gregor Kiczales 27

Gluons: a Support for Software Component Cooperation
Xavier Pintado 43

TAO: An Object-Orientation Kernel
Kenichi Yamazaki, Yoshiji Amagai, Masaharu Yoshida, Ikuo Takeuchi . . . 61

Change Management and Consistency Maintenance in Software Development Environments Using Object-Oriented Attribute Grammars
Katsuhiko Gondow, Takashi Imaizumi, Yoichi Shinoda, Takuya Katayama 77

Design of an Integrated and Extensible C++ Programming Environment
Kin'ichi Mitsui, Hiroaki Nakamura, Theodore C. Law, Shahram Javey . . . 95

Metalevel Decomposition in AL-1/D
Hideaki Okamura, Yutaka Ishikawa, Mario Tokoro 110

Definition of a Reflective Kernel for a Prototype-Based Language
Philippe Mulet, Pierre Cointe 128

Kernel Structuring of Object-Oriented Operating Systems: The Apertos Approach
Yasuhiko Yokote 145

(Invited Paper) Object Database Systems: Functional Architecture
François Bancilhon 163

Maintaining Behavioral Consistency during Schema Evolution
Paul L. Bergstein, Walter L. Hürsch 176

An Object-Centered Approach for Manipulating Hierarchically Complex Objects
Ling Liu 194

Towards the Unification of Views and Versions for Object Databases
Kwang June Byeon, Dennis McLeod 220

Abstract View Objects for Multiple OODB Integration
Qiming Chen, Ming-Chien Shan 237

An Object-Oriented Query Model Supporting Views
Suk I. Yoo, Hai Jin Chang 251

(Invited Paper) Refactoring and Aggregation
Ralph E. Johnson, William F. Opdyke 264

Transverse Activities: Abstractions in Object-Oriented Programming
Bent Bruun Kristensen 279

Dynamic Extensibility in a Statically-Compiled Object-Oriented Language
Jawahar Malhotra 297

(Invited Paper) Managing Change in Persistent Object Systems
Malcolm P. Atkinson, D.I.K. Sjøberg, R. Morrison 315

An Object-Oriented Pattern Matching Language
Marc Gemis, Jan Paredaens 339

CLOG: A Class-Based Logic Language for Object-Oriented Databases
Siu Cheung Hui, Angela Goh, Jose Kolencheril Raphel 356

(Invited Paper) Name Management and Object Technology for Advanced Software
Alan Kaplan, Jack C. Wileden 371

Constraints in Object-Oriented Analysis
Stefan Van Baelen, Johan Lewi, Eric Steegmans, Bart Swennen 393

Integration of the Tool (AWB) Supporting the O* Method in the PCTE-Based Software Engineering Environment
Sai Peck Lee, Collette Rolland 408

Minimizing Dependency on Class Structures with Adaptive Programs
Karl J. Lieberherr, Cun Xiao 424

First Class Messages as First Class Continuations
Ken Wakita 442

A Typing System for a Calculus of Objects
Vasco T. Vasconcelos, Mario Tokoro 460

A Type Mechanism Based on Restricted CCS for Distributed Active Objects
Yasunori Harada 475

(Invited Paper) Adding Implicit Invocation to Languages: Three Approaches
David Notkin, David Garlan, William G. Griswold, Kevin Sullivan 489

Requirements and Early Experiences in the Implementation of the SPADE Repository using Object-Oriented Technology
Sergio Bandinelli, Luciano Baresi, Alfonso Fuggetta, Luigi Lavazza 511

Object-Oriented Formal Specification Development using VDM
Amarit Laorakpong, Motoshi Saeki 529

(Invited Paper)

Uniting Functional and Object-Oriented Programming

John Sargeant[*]

Department of Computer Science
University of Manchester
Manchester M13 9PL
Tel: +44 61 275 6292
Fax: +44 61 275 6236
js@cs.man.ac.uk

Abstract

United Functions and Objects (UFO) is a general-purpose, implicitly parallel language designed to allow a wide range of applications to be efficiently implemented on a wide range of parallel machines while minimising the conceptual difficulties for the programmer. To achieve this, it draws on the experience gained in the functional and object-oriented "worlds" and attempts to bring these worlds together in a harmonious fashion.

Most of this paper concentrates on examples which illustrate how functions and objects can indeed work together effectively. At the end, a number of issues raised by early experience with the language are discussed.

1 Introduction

Modern computers are parallel. Most programming languages assume they are serial. There is an obvious need to advance beyond data parallelism and threads packages (useful though those are). However, the various forms of implicit parallelism explored during the 80s (functional, and/or parallel logic, concurrent object-oriented etc. [McG+85, Nik88, Agha86, Yon90, Am87, UeCh90]) have, by and large, made little impact on real use of parallel machines. One problem has been lack of convincing demonstrations of performance (although this is changing - see below). An equally important reason, in the author's view, is that many such languages have been too narrowly focussed, and have not incorporated the best of modern programming language technology.

UFO is not a narrow "single paradigm" language. It has been influenced by a number of disparate language styles, leading to an interesting, and potentially very useful, synthesis. The main influences are as follows:

1.1 Dataflow languages, especially SISAL

SISAL [McG+85] is a pure functional language with strict semantics, primarily geared towards numerical computation. It can be classed as a dataflow language, in that the

---

[*]During the early work on UFO, the author was supported directly by the Department of Computer Science. Recent work has been funded by Science and Engineering Research Council grant GR/J 11089.

underlying computational model is a parallel dataflow one. Sequencing is by data dependence only; parallelism is the default.

A great deal of work has been done on optimising SISAL for conventional supercomputers, and recently substantial numeric SISAL programs have been shown to run faster on multiprocessor Crays than Fortran versions [Cann92]. Functional languages need not be inefficient, at least for such applications. However, SISAL is quite a limited language (e.g. it has no polymorphism, data abstraction, or higher-order features; multidimensional arrays have to be represented as arrays of arrays). An update, SISAL2, has been defined [Bo+91] which addresses some, but by no means all, of these limitations.

The original idea behind UFO was to create a language based on SISAL which could be used for a wider range of parallel applications, by adding objects to encapsulate updateable state. In fact, UFO has gone well beyond this original idea, but still has a subset which (apart from syntactic differences) is very similar to SISAL.

1.2 Object-oriented languages, especially Eiffel

Issues of software reliability, reuse etc. are even more critical in parallel programming than in the old sequential world. It rapidly became clear that UFO must have good encapsulation and abstraction mechanisms, and a flexible static type system. A survey of object-oriented languages rapidly showed that Eiffel [Mey88, Mey92] was closest to what we were looking for. In particular, the Eiffel type system, with its elegant combination of genericity and inheritance looked like a good starting point.[1]

The UFO type system is therefore heavily influenced by Eiffel, although currently the rules for redefinition on inheritance are more restrictive, in order to avoid complex global validity checking. Unfortunately, to someone brought up in the functional/dataflow world, Eiffel looks extremely imperative and serial, and so the runtime semantics of UFO are very different.

1.3 Pure lazy functional languages, notably Haskell

Modern pure functional languages, for which Haskell [Hud+91] is now the standard, are characterised by higher-order functions, lazy evaluation, and strong static type systems with marked similarities to that of Eiffel.

Initially, UFO allowed constant function values, but not full higher-order functions, as it was feared that the latter would over-complicate the type system. Early experience showed that a partial parameterisation mechanism was useful, and gave no particular problems. Examples appear below.

Lazy evaluation, however, was never an option. Although it improves the expressiveness of a pure functional language, lazy evaluation is incompatible with the presence of updateable variables, as the execution order is almost impossible to visualise. Furthermore, the semantics require normal order evaluation, which is sequential. To exploit parallelism in a lazy language, it is necessary to do strictness analysis, in much the same way as it is necessary to do dataflow analysis to extract parallelism from an imperative language. It is still unclear how successfully this can be done. The effect of lazy evaluation can be simulated in UFO for those applications which really benefit from it.

---

[1]The author is firmly of the opinion that static typing is a Good Thing, except for a few specialised applications. By definition, the end user never sees static type errors, but may well see runtime ones! This prejudice has been strengthened by early experience with UFO, as explained in section 6.2.

A further difficulty with laziness, at least in its most general form, is that it conflicts with dynamic binding. In order to dynamically bind on an object (i.e. the first argument to a function), it is necessary to evaluate it. Few programmers outside the pure FP community are likely to regard laziness as a higher priority than dynamic binding. Compromise solutions are possible, such as using lenient, rather than lazy evaluation, or restricting laziness to certain data structures, although such compromises are rather against the spirit of pure lazy FP.

Another interesting aspect of Haskell is its type classes, which are a systematic way of dealing with overloading, and a first step towards "proper" classes and inheritance. For instance, there is a type class Eq which includes all types with equality defined, and it has a subclass Ord of types which also define ordering. Type classes can be used to impose constraints on generic types.[2] For instance, the type of a sorting function is:

```
sort :: Ord a => [a] -> [a]
```

"sort is of type list of a to list of a provided a is an instance of Ord". The ordering operators (< etc.) can then be used within sort in the knowledge that any actual type provided will have implementations of them.

However, the actual implementation of the operations is concentrated in the instances (actual types) at the leaves of the class hierarchy. It is not possible to inherit from an instance, and so the normal OO practice of incrementally adding implementation down the hierarchy is not possible. This is very restrictive and UFO has a more conventional inheritance mechanism.

1.4 Concurrent object-based languages, particularly ABCL

In concurrent object-based languages, such as early actor languages [Agha86], POOL [Am87], ABCL [Yon90], and HAL[HoAg92], a computation is expressed as a network of communicating objects, each of which manages its own local state. The design of UFO was particularly influenced by ABCL.

There are considerable similarities between UFO (stateful) objects and ABCL objects; they provide mutual exclusion on method accesses, so ensuring coherent updating of the instance variables. Incoming messages/method calls are queued if necessary. An object may continue to execute a method after it has returned a result, and may in some circumstances accept another message before it has returned a result. An object may selectively accept some messages and not others.

However, the differences are substantial; the model underlying ABCL is one of communicating sequential threads. As a result there is a distinction between different sorts of message passing ("past", "present" and "future") which is unnecessary in UFO. ABCL also has a notion of pre-emption ("express messages") which relies on the existence of such threads, and seems inappropriate (and hard to implement) for UFO.

More recently, it has become clear that there are interesting similarities between HAL[HoAg92] and UFO. Unlike earlier actor languages, HAL does have inheritance, and it also has a single-assignment update scheme very similar to that of UFO.[3]

---

[2] Readers familiar with Eiffel will notice a similarity to constrained generics.

[3] The traditional actors' primitive "become" is rather different from that described below, as it updates the whole state at once.

2 Functional UFO

This section describes a purely functional subset of UFO, showing how classes and inheritance are useful things to have, even in a pure functional language, and how these object-oriented notions can peacefully coexist with higher-order functions. The description is informal, via a series of small examples.

2.1 Why functional?

The recommended style for writing UFO programs is to remain within the pure functional subset unless there is a clear reason to introduce stateful objects. This is in sharp contrast to the very imperative style usually adopted in OOP. The reasons for this are as follows:

- Functional programming is very simple; there is no need to distinguish between a copy of an object and a reference to it, for instance. Solution composition[4] is simply expressed as function composition.

- Parallelism is implicit, and relatively easy to exploit, as parallel calls cannot interfere with each other.

- Parallel functional programs are guaranteed to be deterministic; the result cannot depend on evaluation order.

- Functional programs are relatively easy to reason about formally. This allows simple program transformations (between serial and parallel algorithms, for instance), and allows a class of compile-time optimisations (e.g. common subexpression elimination and dataflow loop "vectorisation" [BoSa89]) to be done more easily for general cases.

- Functional programming has some neat abstraction and encapsulation mechanisms, particularly higher-order functions to capture common patterns of recursion.[5]

The efficiency argument against (strict) functional languages is no longer valid for most applications, as most of the sources of inefficiency can be removed. Sharing analysis can drastically reduce the number of copies made of data structures, as the SISAL results show. Many higher-order functions can be transformed out. Garbage collection is present in most object-oriented languages anyway. The remaining inefficiencies are almost certainly balanced by the ability to exploit a small amount of parallelism in almost any application, and are overwhelmed for highly parallel applications.

Given all this, it is perfectly reasonable to write substantial programs (compilers, for instance) entirely in the pure functional style. However, the author is not a True Believer in pure functional languages: some problems are simply best expressed using stateful objects. Some parallel algorithms (for instance bounded search algorithms) may be much more efficient if stateful objects are used.

---

[4]Not problem decomposition, if we believe in object-oriented design!
[5]In fact, some object-oriented languages have comparable facilities, blocks in Smalltalk, for instance.

2.2   A simple list class

Many of the features of functional UFO can be illustrated via a simple list class, whose definition begins as follows:

```
** Functional list class
class List[Alpha]( private h: Alpha; private t: List[Alpha] )
  head : Alpha is
    nullcase : error( "Head of null list!\n" )
    otherwise : h;

  tail : List[Alpha] is
    nullcase : error( "Tail of null list!\n" )
    otherwise : t;
```

The first line after the comment declares both the `List` class, and a constructor function `List( h, t )` which can be used to build instances of it. `Alpha` is a type variable: as in Eiffel (and Haskell) the component type of a list is arbitrary, but it must be consistent within a particular list. `h` and `t` are stored as instance values (not instance *variables*: their values cannot be updated), but since they are declared private, a client of the class cannot access them directly. This implements data abstraction, here used only to provide "protected" `head` and `tail` functions which attempt to fail gracefully if the list is empty.

In contrast to most languages, `null` is not a special value with its own type, or with no type at all; each class has its own distinct null value.[6] This allows methods to be called on null objects; null is detected by the `nullcase` clause, if present, otherwise a default nullcase signals an error. This not only allows more graceful failure in cases such as the above, but also frequently allows recursive algorithms to be written more neatly, as the next few examples will show. Every class also has an associated error value, generated by the `error` function.

The rest of the list class is as follows:

```
  map ( f: Alpha -> Beta ): List[Beta] is
    nullcase : null
    otherwise : f(h) :: t.map( f );

  foldr ( op: (Alpha, Beta) -> Beta; id: Beta ): Beta is
    nullcase : id
    otherwise : op( h, t.foldr( op, id ));

  filter( p: Alpha -> Bool ): List[Alpha] is
    nullcase : null
    otherwise : if p(h) then h :: t.filter( p ) else t.filter( p ) fi;

** Append
  operator ++ ( other: List[Alpha] ): List[Alpha] is
    nullcase : other
```

---
[6]This can be implemented as a pointer to a "null implementation" of the class.

```
       otherwise : h :: (t ++ other)
end ** class List

** Cons
operator :: ( h: Alpha; t: List[Alpha] ): List[Alpha] is List( h, t );
```

map, foldr and filter are standard higher order functions. map applies function f to every element of the list, producing a new list. foldr "folds" up the list (from the right, or far, end) by combining successive elements using the binary operator op, to produce a single result element. Filter returns all the elements of the list which satisfy some predicate. Such functions encapsulate common patterns of recursion, and are heavily used by functional programmers to avoid messy explicit recursions.

The reader will have noticed two different function call syntaxes, the "functional" style:

```
f( arg1, ... argn )
```

and the "OO" style:

```
arg1.f( arg2, ... argn )
```

these are interchangeable via a trivial syntactic transformation, and the programmer is free to use whichever is more natural for a particular case.

Infix operators, here cons (::) and append (++), may also be defined. cons is defined outside the class itself because the class is implicitly the first argument to every method defined within it, and the list is the second argument to cons.

These functions (apart from ::) show how the base case of a recursion is typically to a null value, and this is caught by nullcase. Without this, every user of map would need to remember to test for null. For instance, map itself would have to be written:

```
map ( f: Alpha -> Beta ) : List[Beta] is
  f(h) :: if t.is_null then null else t.map( f ) fi
```

In most FLs, map, foldr and filter are defined only on lists. However, the concepts of mapping, folding, and filtering apply to arbitrary collections. UFO allows function names to be overloaded on the first argument type (i.e. the class type when the function is defined within a class).

There is no separate interface declaration for a class, since a simple tool can be used to extract the interface information, which is as follows: [7]

```
** Functional list class
class List[Alpha]( h: Alpha; t: List[Alpha] )
  head: Alpha
  tail: List[Alpha]
  map ( f: Alpha -> Beta ): List[Beta]
  foldr ( op: (Alpha, Beta) -> Beta; id: Beta ): Beta
  filter( p: Alpha -> Bool ): List[Alpha]
```

---
[7] This idea is directly stolen from Eiffel.

```
  ** Append
  operator ++ ( other: List[Alpha] ): List[Alpha]
end ** class List

** Cons
operator :: ( h: Alpha; t: List[Alpha] ): List[Alpha]
```

map provides an opportunity for parallelism, as all the applications of f can be made in parallel and are guaranteed not to interfere with each other. We will see later that this guarantee is maintained even if the elements of the list are stateful. An example of the use of map in the prototype UFO-in-UFO compiler is to apply a typechecking function to a list of definitions:

```
class Topdef ** Top-level definition class
  typecheck : (Topdef, List[Error]) is ...
end

** To typecheck a list of Topdefs...
check_all( defs : List[Topdef] ): List[(Topdef, List[Error])] is
  defs.map( Topdef|typecheck )
```

Since typecheck may be overloaded, it is necessary to disambiguate it. On a normal call, this is done according to the type of the first argument. When used as a function value, this is not possible. It would be possible to infer the type (easily in this case, since the type of defs gives it away) but in general this inference is very complex in the presence of inheritance. It was decided to require all global function values to be explicitly disambiguated, using the *type name* Topdef|.

In fact, the typechecking function has a second parameter which carries context information, e.g. the global namelist. It would be possible to have a separate mapping function for this case, but this would rapidly get messy. The standard functional programming solution to this is to allow functions to be partially applied (i.e. to too few arguments). So the example is actually written:

```
defs.map( Topdef|typecheck( _, cxt ) )
```

where since typecheck has type

```
( Topdef, Context ) -> (Topdef, List[Error])
```

the result of the partial application is a function of type:

```
Topdef -> (Topdef, List[Error])
```

as required for the map. Note that, since the first parameter is omitted in the partial application, explicit disambiguation is still required. A further example of partial application appears later.

2.3 Inheritance

In UFO, classes with inheritance can be used even in pure functional programs. The prototype compiler is such a program and uses classes and dynamic binding extensively. Using static typing along with dynamic binding ensures that there is always an appropriate method to call at runtime. This argument is eloquently argued by Meyer in [Mey88].

A simplified fragment of the compiler will illustrate class definitions and inheritance:

```
deferred class Expression( spec: TypeSpec) inherits Treenode
print: String is deferred
typecheck( cxt: Context ): (Expression, List[Error]) is (self, null)
end

class IfExp( ... condexp, thenexp, elseexp : Expression )
          inherits Expression

  print is
     "if "    ++ condexp.print ++ "\n"
  ++ "then "  ++ thenexp.print ++ "\n"
  ++ "else "  ++ elseexp.print ++ "\nfi\n"

  typecheck is
    { new_cond, cond_errs = condexp.typecheck( cxt );
      new_then, then_errs = thenexp.typecheck( cxt );
      new_else, else_errs = elseexp.typecheck( cxt );
      ** Check condition is a boolean and result types are compatible
      result_type, compatibility_errs
                  = check_compatibility( new_then.spec, new_else.spec );
      type_errs = need_boolean( new_cond.spec ) ++ compatibility_errs;
      ** Combine the errors from the various checks
      combined_errs = cond_errs ++ then_errs ++ else_errs ++ type_errs;
      return (IfExp( result_type, new_cond, new_then, new_else ),
              combined_errs )
    }
end ** Class IfExp
```

Recall that ++ is append, here overloaded and used on both lists of errors and strings.

A deferred class[8], such as Expression, is one which serves as a superclass for other, concrete, classes but can't itself have instances. Individual methods of a deferred class may be deferred, like print, in which case the implementation is left entirely to subclasses, or a default implementation may be provided, as in the case of typecheck. The idea of typecheck is that it takes an expression, and a context and returns a new expression decorated with types, and a list of any errors found.

The parameters to a class (e.g. spec for Expression) are stored with the class as instance values. Unless they are declared private, these instance values can be accessed by code outside the class, in the same way as parameterless functions e.g.:

---

[8] Also known as a virtual class, or abstract class, in other object-oriented languages

```
t = some_exp.spec
```

IfExp is a concrete subclass of **Expression**. Typically, the class parameters for a subclass are an extension of those for its parent. This is indicated by the ... notation in the header.

print simply constructs a string representing the expression, in UFO syntax. This recursively calls other print functions on the component expressions. The appropriate print function is called at runtime by dynamic binding. The fact that there *is* an appropriate print function is guaranteed at compile time by static typing.

The body of **typecheck** is a *block*, which provides an inner scope, and contains a series of value definitions for local names such as **condexp_out**. These are *not* assignments; each name is given a value exactly once. The result of a block is the expression following **return**. The first part of the result of **typecheck** is an **IfExp**, built by calling a *constructor* giving actual values for the class parameters. Since the result type of **typecheck** is the tuple type (**Expression, List[Error]**), the result of type (**IfExp, List[Error]**) is valid.

2.4 Dynamic binding vs. pattern matching

The only real conflict between functional and OO styles concerns the way in which selection is done. Modern functional languages rely heavily on pattern matching. It is intuitively appealing, and allows simple, concise definitions, and reasoning by case analysis. It is traditionally regarded as a Good Thing by functional programmers: "Pattern matching is one of the cornerstones of an equational style of definition; more often than not it leads to a cleaner and more readily understandable definition than a style based on conditional equations...it also simplifies the process of reasoning formally about functions" [BiWa88, p. 37].

For instance, map in Haskell is written:

```
map [] f = []
map (h:t) f = f h : map t f
```

and the expression example might be written:

```
type Expression = (Exp, TypeSpec)

data Exp =   ConstExp String
           | IfExp Expression Expression Expression

...

print (exp, spec) =
  case exp of
    ConstExp str -> str
    IfExp condexp thenexp elseexp -> .... etc
```

Data types are defined by a combination of type synonyms (often for tuple types like **Expression** above) and algebraic data types. Operations on them are defined by pattern matching and explicit selection using case expressions. As we have seen, the same effect is achieved in UFO by using named selectors (i.e. public instance values) for components of structures, and selection between alternatives is done by dynamic binding.

Pattern matching conflicts with data abstraction because, in order to pattern match on a data structure, its concrete representation must be known. Programs which use pattern matching heavily are painful to change, since changing a data structure causes missing cases and broken patterns to be spread across the program. Many, but not all, of these are detected statically. The trend among functional programmers seems to be to rely less on pattern matching and to program named selectors.

Dynamic binding gives better adaptation to change, since when a new subclass is added the additional methods required are localised within that subclass. Existing selectors are not affected, and missing cases can be detected statically as deferred methods not implemented in all subclasses.

In the current version of UFO, the special case of matching an empty list, or other null object, is handled by the `nullcase` construct or by explicitly testing with `is_null`. Other cases are handled by dynamic binding.

The above argument is an extension of that presented by Meyer against case statements in [Mey88]. However, there is evidence that this is not the whole truth, and this issue is re-examined in section 6.4.

2.5 Functional loops

One further feature of functional UFO needs to be explained, as it has an important analogy in the behaviour of stateful objects. There are sophisticated facilities, based on those in SISAL, for dealing with functional arrays and loops. This is essential for numeric, and other array-based applications. The basic idea is that, rather than manipulating arrays by individual updates, loops are used to create whole arrays monolithically. For instance, the version of `map` for arrays is:

```
map( a: Array[T]; f: T-> U ): Array[U] is
  for x in a do y = f(x) return all y od
```

Loops are typically generated from arrays (`for x in a`) and produce arrays; the expression `all y` yields an array containing the values of y from all the loop cycles. In a loop such as the above, all the bodies may execute in parallel. In general, there may be data dependencies between the loop cycles. For instance, the following loop generates an array of n random numbers in the range 0 to 1:

```
rands( init_seed: Int; n: Int ): array[Real] is
initially
  seed = init_seed;
  i = 0
while i < n do
  new seed = (13849 + 27181 * seed) mod 65536;
  new i = i + 1;
  rand = new seed / 65536.0
return all rand
od
```

Despite the presence of **new i** = i + 1, and similarly for **new seed**, this is still pure functional, referentially transparent, code. i and **new i** are distinct values. The only "assignment" allowed is the single definition of **new i**. This *single assignment rule* is characteristic of dataflow functional languages, which have to deal with numeric problems and so frequently use loops rather than recursion.

An alternative way to write the example is:

```
rands( init_seed: Int; n: Int ): array[Real] is
initially
  seed = init_seed
for i in [1 to n] do
  new seed = (13849 + 27181 * seed) mod 65536;
  rand = new seed / 65536.0
return all rand
od
```

The effect of a more conventional **for** loop is obtained by having a syntax for arrays containing arithmetic progressions: [1 to n] is the array [1, 2, ... n].

3 Asynchronous Communicating Objects

Some problems, particularly in a parallel environment, are not best expressed in the pure functional style. UFO therefore has stateful objects, and a crucial aspect of the design is the effort to minimise the problems this causes, both by the way the runtime behaviour of objects is defined, and in the type system.

3.1 A simple example

The following defines a random number generator class:

```
stateful class Random( init_seed: Int ) is
  { initial seed = init_seed }

  ** Return a random real number between 0 and 1
  proc nextrand : Real is
  do
    new seed = (13849 + 27181 * seed) mod 65536;
    return new seed / 65536.0
  od

  ** Return a random integer between lower and upper
  proc rand_between( lower, upper : Int ): Int is
  do
    range = upper - lower + 1;
    return lower + trunc(!nextrand * range)
  od
end ** Random
```

A stateful class typically has one or more *instance variables*. It may still have functions, which may refer to the current values of those variables, but it will also have *procedures* which may update them. The body of such a class starts with an *initialisation block*, which gives initial values for the instance variables.[9]

Procedure calling is distinguished by the use of !, rather than the dot used for function calls. The body of a procedure is similar to the body of a loop, and this similarity is deliberate. The single assignment rule applies, in that each procedure body may update each instance variable at most once. The distinction between **seed** and **new seed** is exactly that in the loop example.[10] Of course, in this case, it does not maintain referential transparency, as calls to a Random object's **nextrand** procedure may occur from anywhere with a reference to that object, in a nondeterministic order. What it *does* do is to allow parallelism to be exploited within the body of a procedure, while maintaining internal consistency with respect to the instance variables; all references to **seed** within the same method invocation will see the same value. This scheme removes the need for any statement sequencing even within procedure bodies; *sequencing is still by data dependence only*.

This, of course, leaves the problem of how interference *between* method calls to stateful objects is prevented. Each stateful object has a FIFO queue for the methods (both procedures and functions) called on it. When it gets to the head of a queue, a method "locks" the object, and takes a (reference) copy of any instance variables to which it refers. As the method executes (in parallel, constrained only by data dependence) it will assign new values to those instance variables which it updates. Once this (statically obvious) set of assignments is made, the object is unlocked.[11]

This very weak sequencing has several consequences:

- A function call locks the object only transiently, to take copies of any instance variables to which it refers. It therefore causes very little sequentialisation and cannot cause deadlock.

- A procedure call unlocks the object at the earliest possible moment, when coherent access to the instance variables is guaranteed. The call may not return its result until much later.

- Conversely, it is possible for a method to return a result before it has terminated, since it may make procedure calls which do not return values necessary to produce the result. This and the previous property are usually considered characteristic of a "concurrent object-oriented" language.

- The distinction between "synchronous" and "asynchronous" method calling or message passing is rather meaningless in this context, since we are not dealing with communicating sequential threads at the language level. An implementation in

---

[9]It may also define constant instance *values*. These differ from parameterless functions in that they are created once when the object is created, rather than being repeatedly evaluated. In functional UFO, this only matters semantically in terms of termination properties, but if an instance value refers to a stateful object, the difference is critical.

[10]This idea is not as novel as we first thought. Arvind's managers, dating from 1978, work the same way. However, he used explicit merging of input streams. HAL also has it.

[11]This implies that the implementation of a procedure may need to take copies of any new values to which it still needs to refer.

terms of such threads will need to make some calls asynchronous in order to preserve the semantics. In general, such an implementation will need to ensure that it creates no spurious data dependencies which could cause deadlock; even a sequential implementation will need to operate in a pseudo-parallel manner.

- Since locking exists only for long enough to ensure coherent access to instance variables, and sequencing is only by data dependence, it follows that the only way that deadlock can occur is by cyclic dependencies between instance variables. The hope is that this should be relatively easy to reason about.

3.2 Introducing extra sequencing

The main problem with this approach is that it leaves the programmer with too little control over sequencing in some cases. Examples where this may be a problem are:

- If we want to ensure coherence of a whole substructure referred to ¿from an object, not just the instance values. This is the traditional "granularity of locking" problem: UFO provides a very fine granularity, ¿from which coarser grain solutions may be programmed.

- If we want to ensure that one event "happens before" another, even if they are not data dependent. Controlling the order of display in a user interface might be an example.

- If we want to reason about some fairness property of an algorithm, not just termination/deadlock freedom, or if an unconstrained solution has too much nondeterminism to be reasoned about effectively.

The following, very artificial, example shows how extra sequencing is achieved.

```
stateful class counter( init: Int )
  { initial count = init }

  proc inc( n: Int ): Void is do new count = count + n od

  read : Int is count
end

sillyadd( a, b: Int) : Int is
{ c = Counter(0);
  c!inc(a); c!inc(b)
  return c.read;
}
```

sillyadd is intended to return a + b, but since statements are not sequentialised, the read may occur before either or both increments. The key to fixing this, while retaining weak sequencing, is to notice that, once a set of method calls to the same object are queued, they are sequenced, so it is only necessary to control the order of queueing, *not* to wait for termination. The extra sequencing is achieved by *introducing extra data dependencies*. The syntax for expressions and method calls is extended as follows exp2 'after' exp1

call ['ack' name]

The **after** clause delays the evaluation of exp2 until after that of exp1. The **ack** clause returns the named value *when the call has been queued*.[12] So the example is fixed as follows:

```
sillyadd( a, b: Int) : Int is
{ c = Counter(0);
  c!inc(a) ack inc1; c!inc(b) ack inc2
  return c.read after (inc1, inc2)
}
```

Note the use of a tuple to collect acknowledgements. Of course this only works because of strict evaluation.

Unlocking of an object can be delayed simply by introducing an extra variable (called, by convention "unlock") which is not assigned until the required conditions have been met.[13] This can be used to control granularity of locking.

3.3 Conditional message acceptance

In the above example, the method using the counter controlled the order in which it queued messages. It is more in line with object-oriented philosophy to allow an object to control its own queue as far as possible. UFO, like other concurrent object-oriented languages, therefore has *conditional message acceptance* (CMA). A procedure may specify a new message acceptance list.[14] The next method to execute on the object will be the first in the queue which is on the list.

Consider the simplest possible stateful class:

```
stateful class Loc[T]( )
  { initial val = error:T }

  read is val;

  proc write( v: T ) : Void is do new val = v od
end
```

This behaves as a simple, updateable store location, and can be implemented very efficiently as such. It obviously needs to be used with extreme caution in our highly parallel world!

A safer sort of variable location is one which behaves like a location in an I-store in a dataflow machine [ArTh81, SaKi86], i.e. it is written once only, and reads queue until the write has occurred:

---

[12] No assumption is made about the hardware receiving messages in the order they are sent. However, on a machine where this is true, the implementation can optimise out some of the explicit acknowledgements this construct requires.

[13] A smart implementation may notice that "unlock" is a write-only variable, and so not bother to store it!

[14] A function may not do so, because it would be altering the state of the object.

```
stateful class ILoc[T]( ) inherits Loc
  ** val and read unchanged
  { initial accept = << write >> }

  proc write( v: T ) : Void is
  do new val = v; new accept = << read >> od
end
```

The pseudo-variable **accept** determines the current set of acceptable messages. Its type is a special type **Message_acceptance_list** (doing it this way ensures that updating the list has the same consequences as other updates - a function can't do it, for instance. It also allows the list to be set conditionally). Initially, only writes are accepted, so reads are blocked until a write has been done. In this very primitive I-store location subsequent writes are blocked for ever. More sophisticated versions can be obtained by inheritance, eg:

```
stateful class ILoc_with_extract[T]( ) inherits ILoc
  ** Initialisation and read as before

  proc write( v: T ) : Void is
  do new val = v; new accept = all but << write >> od

  proc extract : T is
  do new accept = << write >> return val od
end
```

extract doesn't bother to "delete" **val**, as the next thing to get in will be a **write**.

On a machine with hardware support for I-store style operations, these classes can still be transformed into something very efficient.

CMA provides a general conditional synchronisation mechanism, arguably cleaner than (for instance) semaphores. In doing so, it complicates the, previously very simple, story about deadlock given above. The queueing mechanism becomes more complex, although research in implementing similar constructs in, for example, ABCL [Yon90], suggests that this is not a serious problem.

4 The Type System

UFO has strong static typing with genericity, overloading, and inheritance polymorphism. There are enough mandatory type declarations, and the rules about redefinition on inheritance are sufficiently conservative, to ensure that only relatively simple type checking (with only trivial inference) is required.

The type system is not the subject of this paper, but one aspect should be mentioned, namely the way in which it gives safeguards in the handling of stateful objects.

Two requirements are imposed statically:

4.1 Any reference to an updateable object can be detected statically

This is based on the fact that only objects of stateful classes can be updated. A *class type* is a type of the form $C[AG_1..AG_n]$ where C is the class name and $AG_1..AG_n$ are actual types corresponding to the generic parameters (if any) in the class definition. The class C is said to be the *determining class* for the type. In what follows, the distinction between classes and types is sometimes blurred for brevity.

An *updateable type* is defined as follows:

- A class type whose determining class has procedures.

- A class type with an instance value of updateable type.

- An array whose base type is updateable.

A generic type is not considered updateable, even though it could be instantiated to an updateable type, because the updating procedures cannot be used in that context.[15]

One restriction is required. Normally, if C and D are class types, and D inherits from C, then D conforms to C. However, if D is a stateful class and C is not, the conformance no longer holds. Such inheritance is still legal, and can be used to reuse implementation, but a reference to a C cannot at runtime actually refer to a D.

4.2 A function may not modify its arguments

This is not merely a parameter passing convention. We require that, if an object is passed to a function, no part of the structure referenced ¿from that object can be modified by the function. This enables the programmer and the implementation to reason about functions much as in a pure functional language, even in the presence of stateful objects.

This is achieved as follows. For an updateable type T, there is a corresponding type Readonly[T], defined as follows

- If T is a class type $C[T_1..T_n]$, Readonly[T] is C'[Readonly[T_1]..Readonly[T_n]], where C' is the class obtained by deleting all procedures of C and converting the types of all instance values and variables of C to be Readonly.

- Array[T] becomes Array[Readonly[T]]

The idea is as follows:

1. When a value of updateable type T is passed as an argument to a function, it is statically converted to Readonly[T]. This means that the function can't directly update it, because its procs have disappeared.

2. T conforms to Readonly[T] (so that the argument passing works), but Readonly[T] does not conform to T. This prevents a Readonly[T] from being converted back to an ordinary, updateable, T, in various sneaky ways, e.g. by passing it through an "identity function" returning a T or binding it to a value name of type T.

---

[15]Constrained generic types, discussed below, will however be considered updateable if the constraining type is updateable, since in that case the procedures of the constraining type *can* be used.

So, for instance in the random number generator, both **nextrand** and **rand_between** must be declared as procs. **nextrand** modifies **seed** directly. Within **rand_between** the call **!nextrand** would be illegal if **rand_between** were a function, because it is equivalent to **self!nextrand**[16] and **self**, as a Readonly[Random] could not be an argument to **nextrand**.

Although this is expected to make reasoning about functions easier, it does not provide full referential transparency.

1. A function may return a result of updateable type, so that calling such a function twice with the same arguments is different from sharing the result of one call. This can be prevented by a static restriction, but such a restriction would be overly severe.

2. Since functions can create and manipulate stateful objects, they may have non-deterministic behaviour. In some cases, this is desirable. For instance a function taking the intersection of two large sets using some clever parallel algorithm might reasonably return the elements of the result set in a nondeterministic order. There is no way that the type system can be expected to distinguish "reasonable" from "unreasonable" nondeterminism.

5 Further Examples

5.1 Dining philosophers

The following is a solution to the classic dining philosophers problem using a boring but sensible solution from [BA82]: only four of the philosophers are allowed in the room at once.

```
** Enumerated type with one element, for signalling completion.
enum Signal { sig }

class Philosopher( doorman: Doorman; lfork, rfork: Fork )
  proc live is
  do
  while true do
    thought = think( ... );
    permit = doorman!enter after thought;
        { f1 = lfork! pickup;
          f2 = rfork! pickup;
          eaten = eat(f1,f2);
          { lfork!putdown; rfork!putdown; doorman!leave } after eaten
        } after permit
    od
  od
end
```

---

[16] As far as the type system is concerned. The reason for omitting **self** is to avoid going through the queuing mechanism again.

```
class Doorman()
{ initial occupants = 0;
  initial accept = all
}

  proc enter: Signal is
  do
  new occupants = occupants + 1;
  new accept = if occupants == 4 then << leave >> else all fi
  od

  proc leave is
  do
  new occupants = occupants - 1;
  new accept = all
  od
end ** Doorman

class Fork()
{ initial accept = << pickup >> }

  proc pickup: Signal is
  do
  new accept = << putdown >>
  return sig
  od

  proc putdown : Signal is
  do new accept = << pickup >> return sig od
end ** Fork

proc dining_philosophers : Void is
do
bouncer = Doorman;
fork =
  for i in [0 to 4] do f = Fork return all f od
philosophers =
  for i in [0 to 4] do
    p = Philosopher( bouncer, fork[(i) mod 5], fork[(i+1) mod 5] );
    p! live
  od
od
```

Exclusive access to the forks is provided by CMA. Since the philosophers lead rather serial (as well as tedious) lives, several uses of **after** are required. The block:

```
{ lfork!putdown; rfork!putdown; room!leave }
```

may be evaluated in such a way that the call to `leave` may be executed, and the next philosopher enter the room, before the forks have been put down. However, since the forks will be put down eventually, no deadlock can occur.

The uses of the dummy signal value may seem artificial, but in a realistic application, the forks would be resources required by `eat`, and `eat` and `think` would be computations returning results.[17]

5.2 Futures

A final example, illustrating inheritance, higher-order functions, and CMA, is a class which represents an arbitrary future (or thunk or closure).

```
class Future[T]( f : Trigger -> T ) inherits ILoc
  ** val, read and write as for ILoc, although direct writes will never
  ** be accepted.
  { initial accept = << force >> }

  proc force is do new val = f(trig); new accept = << read >> od
end
```

`Trigger` is simply an enumerated type with one element called `trig`. A suitable f can be generated by partial parameterisation, eg:

```
trig_rands( init_seed: Int; n: Int; t : Trigger ) is
    rands( init_seed, n )
...
future_rands = Future( trig_rands( 12345, 100, _ ) )
```

This can be used to build lazy lists and so on. There is therefore no need to include a special future construct in the language.

6 Experience so far, and Outstanding Issues

6.1 Language development and implementation

All UFO project software is written in UFO if at all possible, to maximise experience with using the language, and display confidence in its suitability for general applications. A minimal subset of UFO (UFO0) was initially implemented in Haskell, and then used to write a bootstrap UFO0-in-UFO0 compiler, which generates C. This has since been extended to implement fuller versions of the language.

During this process, it became clear that the full semantics for stateful objects, as described above, is quite difficult to implement serially with reasonably efficiency. The problem is not the need for pseudo-parallelism per se - it would be no problem to use a standard threads package - but that a naive implementation would generate many small threads and be very inefficient. A version with slightly different semantics, called UFOS, was therefore designed, to meet the needs of short-term development. UFOS can be

---

[17]Non UK readers may wonder why the Doorman is called `bouncer`. A bouncer is a large gentleman who stands at the door of e.g. a nightclub and "bounces" any undesirable customers.

implemented within a single serial thread. The main restriction is that there is no CMA, and there is a (rather obscure) class of programs which would work currently under full UFO semantics but which will deadlock in UFOS.

The compiler is currently written in purely functional UFO. Its performance is quite acceptable: about 3000 lines/minute on a Sun IPX. In fact the C compiler takes about 3 times longer to compile the generated C (which is about 3 times bigger). Some tests on smaller programs suggest that UFO is about 3 times slower than C on symbolic applications (list processing etc.). Currently there is no optimisation and garbage collector is very simplistic. Interestingly, the cost of dynamic binding is not significant, at least in the compiler. A dynamically bound call involves an indirection through a table, but in fact typically only about 10% of calls in the compiler are dynamically bound. This was a surprising result, since the compiler makes heavy use of inheritance and redefinition. However, in practice it spends most of its time crunching lists and strings.

A number of other issues have emerged during this development work, some of which are discussed in the following sections.

6.2 Some evidence for the benefits of static typing?

During recent development of the compiler, the author has attempted to systematically record and classify all errors discovered, in order to find what sorts of errors occur frequently, and in particular what proportion of errors are caught by the type checker. The results below represent development of about 2K lines of code, and a number of redesigns of complex sections of the compiler.

By definition, such an analysis underestimates runtime errors, as there are almost certainly bugs which have not yet emerged. However, it is unlikely that the numbers of these are large compared to the numbers below[18]. An attempt has been made to make the numbers as objective and meaningful as possible. For instance, as far as possible, multiple instances of the same error (e.g. the same misspelling of an identifier in several different places) are only counted once. However, it is difficult to be totally consistent across all the situations which arise, and there is inevitably some subjectivity in how errors are counted and classified.

The static errors were as follows:

Syntax errors: 45.

Non-existent names: 36. These were the cases where mis-remembered or mis-typed names resulted in references to names with no definition. Although these are flagged by the type checker, they were recorded separately, since they would be caught statically in most dynamically typed languages too.

Type errors: 96. These consisted mainly of providing the wrong arguments to functions. It is worth noting that two of these errors were actually not caught statically, due to a bug in the previous version of the compiler. These each required half a day of painful debugging to find.

The runtime errors were as follows (in ascending order of unpleasantness):

---

[18] I certainly hope not!

Wrong answers: 60. Since the output of the compiler consists of error messages or C code, "wrong answers" consist of spurious or garbled error messages or the wrong C code (mostly the latter). Most, although by no means all, of these were easy to find and fix.

Crashes: 11 . The majority of these were calling of deferred methods. It is possible to check for the possibility of this statically, and therefore eliminate it from production code, although it is useful to allow code to be compiled without implementing every deferred method. The rest were the result of calling methods on null objects e.g. running off the end of a list. Note that with typed nulls and the `nullcase` construct, it is possible for the programmer to control what happens in this case. The other possible source of crashes is arithmetic errors, although this has not yet happened in the compiler. Segmentation faults etc. cannot occur in (a correct implementation of) UFO.

Loops/out of memory errors: 0. These are potentially the hardest errors to track down. They occurred several times during development of the initial Haskell version of the compiler, due every time to accidental setting up of mutual recursion between local variables. This cannot happen in UFO, as local variables are subject to definition before use; mutual recursion can only happen between methods, and then one expects to have to think about base cases.

The author feels that the results of this experiment so far have been encouraging. About 2/3 off all errors are caught statically, mostly by the type checker, and the runtime errors which remain are mostly of a benign nature. The latter feature is probably due as much to the functional programming style as to the type checker, though. Furthermore, the use of unidirectional type checking rather than unification-based type inference has resulted in error messages which are usually straightforward and easy to understand. It is also easy to continue checking after an error is found without causing cascades of spurious errors; the technique is to propagate an unknown type, which matches anything, after an error.

The experiment will continue through further development of the compiler and the construction of other applications of UFO. The author would like to encourage users of other modern languages to try similar experiments.

6.3 Towards more flexible static type systems

Proponents of untyped or dynamically typed languages often claim that the penalty for static typing is a lack of flexibility and generality in the code which can be written. Certainly this is true, to some extent, in all existing statically typed languages, even UFO. The question of how to make static type systems more flexible is an interesting and complex one.

One approach is to think in terms of constraints on type variables, and therefore on types containing variables. In general, the more constrained (or more specific) the type of an object is, the more operations are valid on it. For instance, there are often more methods defined on a class than on its parent.

An example of the approach is the constrained generic type, as in Eiffel. A type variable may be constrained to conform to some type:[19]

```
V <- T
```

Whereas very few things can be done with a value of an ordinary unconstrained generic type, in the constrained case, whatever `V` is bound to must be a `T`, so any method valid on `T`s may be used. Constrained generics will be added to UFO fairly soon.

However, this is not the only possible constraint. For instance, consider a conditional expression:

```
if cond then e1 else e2 fi
```

It is not necessary for the types of `e1` and `e2` to be the same, or for one to conform to the other, provided there is some type to which they both conform. The result type of the expression will then be the most specific such type, or *least upper bound*. If no such type exists, a type error will result. So, another possible constraint on a type variable is

```
V <-> T
```

(`V` is compatible with `T`), i.e. (the value bound to) `V` and `T` must have a least upper bound. This is a weaker constraint than conformance, and the set of valid methods is correspondingly smaller, i.e. those methods defined on the least upper bound type.

Other sorts of constraints may be considered (e.g. equality, inequality, statefulness). However, this raises a number of questions:

- What sorts of constraints are useful?

- Under what circumstances do unique least upper bounds always exist when they "ought" to exist? Clearly, multiple inheritance would cause a problem here, for instance.

- If variables may have multiple constraints, there needs to be some notion of ordering of constraints, and the definition of type equality needs to take account of this.

The author hopes to collaborate with someone with a background in formal type theory in order investigate these ideas further.

6.4 Pattern matching vs. dynamic binding revisited

One of the most interesting results of the experience so far is a growing realisation that the case against pattern matching (and for dynamic binding as the only selection mechanism) is much less clear cut than the earlier discussion (section 2.4) suggested.

Evidence for this comes firstly from the way explicit selection mechanisms are creeping back into the language. There is already a `case` expression, and a facility to define enumerated types, as it is extremely unwieldy to define a bunch of classes merely to distinguish between characters, say, or between values whose *only* characteristic is that they are distinct.

---

[19] In Eiffel the arrow is the other way round, but it seems to me much more natural this way, rather as if V was a value drawn from a set T.

Another practical observation is that it is sometimes necessary to check what the class of an object is, in order to know enough about it. This is analogous to the **class** method (which is quite frequently used) in Smalltalk or the "reverse assignment attempt" in Eiffel. Basically, some operations need to know the structure of more than one object at once, and if this structure is hidden, a rather unwieldy message-sending protocol has to be set up, which effectively uncovers it incrementally. A good example of this is type equality checking. Consider the following simplified definition of typespecs, first as a Haskell datatype:

```
data Btype = IntType | RealType | CharType | BoolType

data TypeSpec = BasicType Btype
              | ArrayType TypeSpec   -- component type
              | UnknownType
```

Defining, say, type equality on this structure by pattern matching is trivial:

```
eqtypes UnknownType    _                 = True  -- Unknown matches anything
eqtypes _              UnknownType       = True
eqtypes BasicType bt1  BasicType bt2     = bt1 == bt2
eqtypes ArrayType sub1 ArrayType sub2    = eqtypes sub1 sub2
eqtypes _              _                 = False
```

In UFO, typespecs are represented as an inheritance hierarchy:

```
deferred class TypeSpec

class BasicType( bt: Btype ) inherits TypeSpec
class ArrayType( subtype: TypeSpec ) inherits TypeSpec
class UnknownType inherits TypeSpec

eqtypes( t1, t2: TypeSpec ): Bool is ** Left as an exercise...
```

The reaser is encouraged to spend a few minutes thinking about how **eqtypes** might in fact be implemented in UFO. Note that the hierarchy is in a sense isomorphic to the Haskell data type. However, there is other information contained within the **TypeSpecs** (e.g. how they are printed in UFO concrete syntax or represented in C) which is not part of that data type. Perhaps it makes sense to regard this "bare bones" view of an inheritance hierarchy as a first class part of the language, and therefore provide a general pattern matching construct e.g.:

```
eqtypes( t1, t2: TypeSpec ): Bool is
case t1, t2 of
UnknownType       _                   : true
_                 UnknownType         : true
BasicType         BasicType           : t1.bt == t2.bt
ArrayType(sub1)   Arraytype(sub2)     : eqtypes sub1 sub2
otherwise                             : false
esac
```

Note that the third and fourth cases show two alternative ways of dealing with class parameters. This would subsume the current `case` and `nullcase` constructs, the reverse assignment attempt etc. To be a component of a pattern, a value would have to be publicly accessible (e.g. a public class parameter).

The difficulty with providing such a feature is that it might be used inappropriately, leading to unnecessary loss of data abstraction and to fragile programs. However, the author's current view is that at least a restricted form (i.e allowing the `BasicType` line in the example above but not the `ArrayType` line) would be useful.[20]

6.5 Other issues

There are a number of other issues which have not yet been addressed.

Modules. Since UFO allows functions outside of classes, it is not sufficient for the sole unit of modularity, and of compilation, to be the class definition. Instead, there will be a more conventional module system, rather similar to the clusters of Eiffel, but more closely tied into the language.

Multiple inheritance. MI provides more expressive power at the expense of more complexity. It is perhaps more important in a statically typed language than in an untyped one. For instance to give a type to something which is both comparable for equality and representable as a string, it needs to have descended ¿from appropriate classes (`Eq` and `Printable`, say) which may well not be on a unique path up the hierarchy. However, MI causes extra complexity in the type system (e.g. see the discussion of least upper bounds above). At present, it is not clear whether, or in what form, it should be introduced.

Inheritance and subtyping. Experienced OO programmers recognise that it is a mistake to regard inheritance for the purpose of reusing implementation as the same thing as subtyping. In fact, UFO already goes some way to correct this. Classes can be defined as *closed*, in which case they are not type-compatible with parents or children, although their code is still inherited.[21] The removal of type conformance of stateful classes to stateless parents is another example, but ideally there should be a more general way of distinguishing between implementation reuse and subtyping.

CMA mechanisms. The conditional message acceptance mechanism described above has the drawback that the acceptance criteria of existing methods may have to be redefined on inheritance because of the addition of new methods. An example of this is the redefinition of `write` in `ILoc_with_extract` (section 3.3). An alternative approach is taken in HAL, where the acceptance criteria are defined separately from the methods, as functions of the instance variables. This is arguably cleaner, although it involves introducing extra mechanisms, and is potentially inefficient as, in principle, all the acceptance criteria need to be re-checked after every procedure call. This tradeoff requires further investigation.

---

[20] The alert reader may have realised that once pattern matching is allowed, we are on the slippery slope towards adding unbound variables and therefore attempting Grand Unification. Mañana.

[21] The original motivation for this was efficiency, as dynamic binding is not needed for methods of closed classes. The standard `List` class is closed, for instance.

Error and exception handling. The whole area of error and exception handling is a subject for future research. Conventional exception handling mechanisms are well understood, but they assume that there is a single thread of control, or at least a model of communicating sequential threads. It is unclear what mechanisms are appropriate in the highly dynamic parallel runtime world of UFO.

Persistence. It is hoped that the issues involved in persistence will not be substantially different from those in existing languages, but this has not yet been demonstrated.

Computational models. The appropriate computational model for UFO is a form of extended dataflow, rather than one of communicating sequential threads. Such a model is currently being developed. A static version of the model will form the intermediate representation used by the parallelising compiler. A dynamic version could be used by a parallel debugging tool, and might form the basis of a real parallel implementation on a suitable machine.[22]

Formal semantics. Ideally, there should be a formal definition of the semantics of the language, and a formal development methodology to allow proofs of correctness.

Work is in progress in a few of these areas (notably modularity and computational models). For the rest, it is hoped that, after a few years' experience with UFO1, a review will take place with the aim of defining a UFO2 which addresses these issues, and any others which arise in the meantime. However, in the nearer future achieving real parallel performance for relatively simple cases is a higher priority.

References

[Agha86] G. Agha: **Actors: A Model of Concurrent Computation in Distributed Systems**, MIT Press Series in Artificial Intelligence, 1986.

[Am87] P. America: **POOL-T: A Parallel Object-Oriented Language**, in A. Yonezawa & M. Tokoro (eds), Object-Oriented Concurrent Programming, MIT Press Computer Systems Series, 1987.

[ArTh81] Arvind, R.E. Thomas: **I-structures: An Efficient Data Type for Functional Languages**, MIT/LCS/TM-178, Computer Science Laboratory, MIT., Cambridge, MA, 1981.

[BA82] M. Ben-Ari: **Principles of Concurrent Programming**, Prentice Hall, 1982.

[BiWa88] R. Bird, P. Wadler: **Introduction to Functional Programming**, Prentice Hall, 1988.

[BoSa89] A.P.W. Böhm, J. Sargeant: **Code Optimisation for Tagged-Token Dataflow Machines**, IEEE Transaction on Computers, 38(1), pp. 4-14, Jan. 1989.

[Bo+91] A. P. W. Böhm, D. C. Cann, J. T. Feo, R. R. Oldehoeft: **SISAL 2.0 Reference Manual**, tech. report CS-91-118, Computer Science Dept. Colorado State University, 1991.

---

[22] The first real parallel implementation will be on the KSR1 machine at Manchester, and that will be in terms of conventional sequential threads.

[Cann92] D. C. Cann **Retire Fortran? A Debate Rekindled**, Communications of the ACM 35(8), August 1992, pp 81-89.

[HoAg92] C. Houck, G. Agha: **HAL: A High-level Actor Language and its Distributed Implementation**, Proc. 21st International Conference on Parallel Processing, August 1992.

[Hud+91] P. Hudak et al: **Report on the Programming Language Haskell, Version 1.1**, Univerity of Yale tech. report, August 1991.

[McG+85] J. R. McGraw, S. K. Skedzielewski, S. J. Allan, R. R. Oldehoeft, J. Glauert, C. C. Kirkham, W. Noyce, and R. Thomas: **SISAL: Streams and Iteration in a Single Assignment Language**, Reference Manual 1.2, Manual M-146, Rev. 1, Lawrence Livermore National Laboratory, 1985.

[Mey88] B. Meyer: **Object-Oriented Software Construction**, Prentice Hall 1988.

[Mey92] B. Meyer: **Eiffel the Language**, Prentice Hall 1992.

[Nik88] R.S. Nikhil: **ID Reference Manual**, CSG memo 284, MIT Laboratory for Computer Science, 1988.

[SaKi86] J. Sargeant, C.C. Kirkham: **Stored Data Structures on the Manchester Dataflow Machine**, Proc. 13th Annual Symposium on Computer Architecture, 1986, pp 235-242.

[UeCh90] K. Ueda, T. Chikayama: **Design of the Kernel Language for the Parallel Inference Machine**, Computer Journal 33(6), 1990, pp494-500.

[Yon90] A. Yonezawa (ed.): **ABCL, an Object-Oriented Concurrent System**, MIT Press Computer Systems Series, 1990.

Traces
(A Cut at the "Make Isn't Generic" Problem)

Gregor Kiczales
Xerox Palo Alto Research Center*

July 26, 1993

Abstract

Object-oriented techniques are a powerful tool for making a system end-programmer specializable. But, in cases where the system not only accepts objects as input, but also creates objects internally, specialization has been more difficult. This has been referred to as the "make isn't generic problem." We present a new object-oriented language concept, called traces, that we have used successfully to support specialization in cases that were previously cumbersome.

The concept of traces makes a fundamental separation between two kinds of inheritance in object-oriented languages: inheritance of default implementation – an aspect of code sharing; and inheritance of specialization, a sometimes static, sometimes dynamic phenomena.

The Problem

Object-oriented programming languages have proven to be a powerful tool for making a variety of systems *end programmer specializable* [KL92]. That is, once the system has been written, compiled and distributed, a further programmer can modify or extend its behavior. This technique has played a critical role in the reflection and meta-level architectures community, where it has been used to "open up" programming languages [BKK+86, Mae87, Coi87, Fer89, FJ89, MCD91, KdRB91, CI93], operating systems [YTY+89, YTM+91, YMFT91], and even window systems [Rao90, Rao91].

A Simple Example

As an example of this style of using object-oriented techniques, consider a simple graphical editor that might be part of the standard toolset in a user interface library. It accepts a variety of graphical objects as input, display them on the screen, allow the user to edit them, and then returns the modified objects.

Using existing object-oriented languages — and a healthy dose of careful design and documentation — it would be possible to craft this system so that an end-programmer could extend its behavior, perhaps by adding completely new kinds of graphical objects,

---

*3333 Coyote Hill Rd., Palo Alto, CA 94304; (415)812-4888; Gregor@parc.xerox.com.

or more likely by defining new kinds of objects with behavior that is a specialization of that provided by default kinds.

Such an editor might provide, as part of its standard library, a class called `<line>`[1], whose instance are line segments that can be moved and resized freely. Given this, one might imagine that an end-programmer might want to extend the system, by adding a new kind of line segment, with the specialized behavior that its slope cannot be changed. Assuming a simple documented protocol between the editor and line objects, consisting of messages to get the end points of a line (`end-1` and `end-2`), and a single message to set both endpoints (`set-end-points`), something like the following would serve to extend the system with the new behavior:

> The concept of traces can be added quite naturally to a number of existing object-oriented languages. But in this paper, we present traces using a *very* simple Scheme-based object-oriented language. Its advantage, besides its simplicity, is that, in later parts of the paper, it makes it easier to understand traces and their relation to existing object-oriented concepts. An overview of this simple language can be found in Appendix A, but the key point to notice for the time being is that the body of a class is a procedure that returns a *list* of methods.

```
(define <fixed-slope-line>
  (class (<line>)
    (lambda ()
      (list
        (method set-end-points (new-end-1 new-end-2)
          (if (same-slope? (end-1 self) (end-2 self)
                           new-end-1 new-end-2)
              (call-next-method)
              (warn "Can't change orientation of line.")))))))
```

Having defined this new class of line, the programmer could then create instances of it, and pass those into the editor. They would have all the normal behavior of lines, with the exception that if the editor tried to change their slope — by calling `set-end-points` with arguments that changed the slope — the user would be warned that the slope cannot be changed.

Glass Boxes

This style of system design has been called by a number of names, including "glass-box abstraction" [Rao91] and "open implementations" [Kic92]. Underlying these names is an intuition is that the extensible system is a "box" into which one passes objects on which it operates. Unlike a black-box or closed implementation, the box is glass, or open, because it follows a well-defined protocol on those objects, and one can thus specialize its behavior by passing in objects which respond to the protocol in specialized ways.

---

[1] In this paper, we are use a naming convention in which class names are bracketed by "¡" and "¿."

While existing object-oriented languages have been a critical enabling technology for open implementations, there is an important class of problem that they have not handled well. Specifically, the case when the extensible system itself (i.e. the graphics editor), creates new objects internally, that must in some way derive part of their behavior from the objects that came in from the outside.

As an example, consider the case where the graphics editor has an operation that groups a collection of line segments together, to form a polygon. In the heart of such an operation, we would expect to find an instance creation operation that looks something like:

```
(make <polygon> 'lines (list  line-1   line-2  ...))
```

This code says to create an instance of the class <line> passing it an initarg[2] named line whose value is a list of the line objects that comprise the polygon.

The key point here is that the class of the resulting polygon is fixed in this code. That is, all polygons created will be instances of the class <polygon> — never any subclasses of it — and so will have the standard polygon behavior. But, it would clearly be desirable for programmers of subclassesof of <line> to be able to affect the behavior of polygons made up out of those lines. For example, the programmer of <fixed-slope-line> might want to prevent such a polygon from rotating, since that would change the slope of the line.

The question is how to arrange for the (internally created) polygon objects to inherit the appropriate behavior from the (externally created) line objects. There are two traditional approaches to this problem, neither of which has proven completely satisfactory: delegation and dynamic class selection.

Delegation

Using delegation [Lie86] the strategy would be to arrange for the line objects to be *parts of* the polygon object. The polygon would then delegate part of its behavior (i.e. some aspect of rotation) to the line objects, thereby allowing them to control it.

An initial approach in this case would be for the polygon to accept a rotate message, which would work in three steps: (i) asking each of the lines for its endpoints, (ii) calculating the new endpoints for all the lines, and (iii) asking each of the lines to change its endpoints accordingly.

But this doesn't work as well as one might like. It won't quite capture the behavior we are looking for, at least not without some work. Consider the case where only one of the line objects in a polygon is an instance of <fixed-slope-line>, and it happens not to be first one in the list of lines the polygon contains. Then, some the other lines will have had their positions changed before the fixed slope line is encountered. So, when the fixed slope line signals its warning message, some of the lines will already have been changed, and the polygon will be in an inconsistent state.

While the delegation protocol can be enhanced in various ways to deal with this case — for example, the polygon could save the old end-points and restore them if it runs into a problem with any of the lines — these sorts of solutions tend to become cumbersome.

---

[2]The term *initarg* is an abbreviation for the more cumbersome *initialization argument*.

The problem is that *a polygon is really more than a collection of lines*, and any attempt to treat it strictly as such will ultimately founder on that difference.

Dynamic Class Composition

The second approach recognizes the problems inherent in the first, and is based on having the newly created objects (i.e. polygons) be responsible for all their own behavior, but allowing the old objects (i.e. lines) to have a say in how the new object is created: specifically, a say in the class of the new object.

To use this approach, a message would be added to the protocol of line objects, asking them what class any polygons they contribute to should be. So, the code that creates polygons would now look like:

```
(let* ((proposed-classes (mapcar polygon-class all-the-lines))
       (class (most-specific-class proposed-classes)))
   (make class 'lines (list line-1 line-2 ...)))
```

Where the function `most-specific-class` is responsible for taking all the proposed classes and finding, or creating, the least specific class that is a subclass of all of them.[3] The polygon still receives the lines as an initarg, but only to read the values of the endpoints and then discards the lines themselves. Given this protocol, the programmer of `<fixed-slope-line>` could update their code as follows:

```
(define <fixed-slope-line>
  (class (<object>)
    (lambda ()
      (list
        (method set-end-points  same code as before )

        (method polygon-class () <no-rotate-polygon>)))))

(define <no-rotate-polygon>
  (class (<polygon>)
    (lambda ()
      (list
        (method rotate (degrees)
          (warn "Can't rotate."))))))
```

This approach works reasonably well, but it can become cumbersome if there are many internal creation operations, because a new message must be added to the protocol for each one. Moreover, it only works in languages like Smalltalk, CLOS and Self, that allow runtime class creation.

---

[3] It could, and often would be one of the proposed classes itself of course.

Traces

The idea of traces is based on recognizing what is good — and bad — about both of the traditional approaches. It takes from the dynamic class composition approach the realization that an object that is made up out of others cannot successfully delegate its behavior to the others, if *the sum of the parts is greater than the whole*. It takes from the delegation approach the simplicity of creating new objects out of old ones.

The key idea underlying traces is to formalize the notion that, as a computation proceeds, new objects are created, which often arise from (or are created by) other objects. We call the older objects (i.e. lines) *ancestors*, and the newer objects (i.e. polygons) their *progeny*. In addition, we formalize the notion of a *trace* which is a packet of behavior that can be attached to an object (i.e. line), and then automatically propagate to some of the object's progeny (i.e. polygons), where they install the appropriate specialized behavior.

The addition of traces manifests itself in two language constructs: A change to the object creation function, and the addition of a new construct to create traces.

The object creation function must be revised to indicate the ancestors of the object being created. To reflect the sense that it is the ancestors which produce the new object, we have changed the name of the object creation function to **give-rise-to**.[4] So, in the example we have been discussing, the creation of a polygon from a set of lines looks like:

```
(give-rise-to <polygon>
              (list  line-1  line-2 ...)
  'lines (list  line-1  line-2 ...))
```

The first argument, `<polygon>` is the class of the object being created, just as in the earlier calls to **make**. The second argument is a list of the direct ancestors of the object being created. The remaining arguments are initargs and values, just as in the previous calls to **make**.

A new macro, called **trace**, makes trace objects. The trace includes a specification of the path of progeny along which it should propagate, and what methods it should create when it is activated. A trace can be attached to an object using the **traces** initargs. The following code creates a `<line>` object, with a single trace that will propagate to just those progeny of the line that are instances of `<polygon>`. It will specialize those polygons, with a method on **rotate** that prevents them from rotating. (Note that for the time being, we are dropping the specialization that the line itself not be able to rotate — we'll return to that shortly.)

```
(give-rise-to <line>
              '()          ;The line itself has no ancestors.
  'end-1 ...
  'end-2 ...
  'traces (list (trace (<polygon>)
                  (lambda ()
                    (list
```

---
[4] We have considered retaining the name **make** for objects with no ancestors, but will not do so in this paper.

```
            (method rotate (n-degrees)
              (warn "Can't rotate."))))))
```

The **trace** macro has two parts. The first part, called the path, is a list of class names, the second is a procedure that returns a list of methods, just like the body of a class definition.

The path controls both the propagation and activation of traces. This trace has the behavior that it propagates only to instances of `<polygon>` and, when it gets there, since the remainder of the path is empty, it activates itself. Essentially, the path says that the trace should follow that list of classes in `give-rise-to` steps.

When a trace is activated, the method maker procedure is called to produce a list of methods, and these are *prepended* to the methods produced by the class itself. In cases where traces come in from more than one ancestor, their relative precedence is determined by the ordering of the ancestor list.

The following is an example of objects with multiple traces, and traces with longer paths, showing their behavior:

```
(define start
  (give-rise-to <object>
                '()
    'traces (list
              (trace (<a> <b>)
                (lambda () (list (method test () 'start))))
              (trace (<x>)
                (lambda () (list (method test () 'start)))))))

(define a (give-rise-to <a> (list start)))
(define b (give-rise-to <b> (list a)))
(define x (give-rise-to <x> (list start)))

(test a)    -->    ???
(test b)    -->    start
(test x)    -->    start
```

A More Elaborate Example

Traces make dynamic inheritance of behavior so much easier to handle that we have been able to open implementations of systems that were difficult to handle with previous techniques. As an example of such a system, consider a metaobject protocol (MOP) for a Scheme interpreter.[5] Such a MOP would has roughly three kinds of metaobjects:

---

[5]Note that in the MOP we will be presenting, the base language is Scheme, and the metalanguage is the simple object-oriented extension to Scheme we have been discussing. That is, the system is not metacircular.

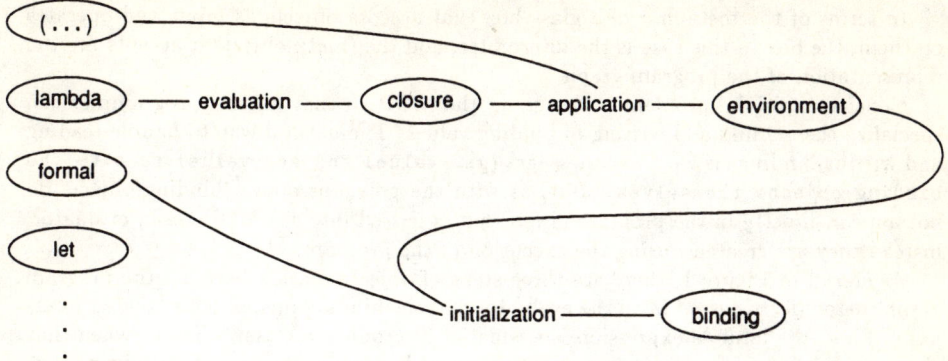

Figure 1: The rise of objects within the evaluator. On the left, are the metaobjects that represent the program text. These are created outside the evaluator and are dropped into it. The lines represent the rise of metaobjects from others within the evaluator.

- Metaobjects that represent the program graph, including **lambdas**, **formals**, **applications**, **lets** and **variable-references**.
- Metaobjects that represent Scheme runtime objects, including **pairs**, **numbers** and **closures**.
- Metaobjects that represent internal runtime state of the interpreter, including **environments** and **bindings**.

The MOP works in the usual way: a documented set of generic functions handles the evaluation of the program, building environment structure as it goes, and creating and passing Scheme data as specified by the program. So, for example, in the execution of the following code fragment:

```
(let ((make-counter
        (lambda (c)
          (lambda (x) (set! c (+ c x)) c))))
  (let ((c1 (make-counter 0)))
    (c1 1)
    (c1 3)))
```

First, the evaluation of the first **lambda** expression that begins on line produces a closure. When that closure is then called by the application on line 4, a new environment is created; it contains a binding for the variable named c, for which the initial value is 0. The closure then returned by evaluating (**lambda** (x) ...) is closed over that environment. When that second closure is called (the last two lines) and the **set!** is executed, it is the binding for c, created earlier, which is changed.

In terms of the metaphor of a glass box that accepts objects as input and operates on them, the box in this case is the interpreter, and the (meta)objects it accepts are the representation of the program graph.

Consider now the problem of designing the MOP so that an end programmer can specialize the reading and writing of binding values. The natural way to handle reading and writing bindings is with two messages (`get-value`) and `set-value`) sent to the binding objects themselves. But, as with the polygons above, binding objects do not appear directly in the program graph that is passed into the MOP-based evaluator, instead they are created during the execution of the program.

As shown in Figure 1, there are three steps of object creation between the program graph metaobjects passed in to the evaluator and the binding metaobjects created internally. First, the lambda expression is evaluated to produce a closure. Later, when that closure is applied to arguments a new environment is created. As part of initializing that environment, bindings are created. But somehow, the user of the MOP must be able to mark one of the lambdas in the program graph, since that is all they have their hands on.

Using traces, the designer of the MOP need only *document the ancestor relationships* as they appear in Figure 1, and then it becomes easy for an end-programmer to define bindings with specialized behavior. The following code creates traces that can be attached to lambda metaobjects, but propagate to that lambda's binding metaobjects and cause messages to be be printed when the binding is accessed:

```
(define make-noisy-binding-trace
  (lambda ()
    (trace (<closure> <environment> <binding>)
      (lambda ()
        (list (method get-value ()
                (call-next-method)
                (output self " was read."))
              (method set-value (new)
                (call-next-method)
                (output self " was set.")))))))
```

All the MOP user would then have to do is make sure that the appropriate lambda metaobjects given to the interpreter had such a trace. That is, these lambdas must be created by code something like:

```
(give-rise-to <lambda>
              '()
  'arglist ...
  'body ...
  'traces (list (make-noisy-binding-trace)))
```

In our implementation of this MOP, we have defined a special syntax that makes it convenient to create program graph metaobjects with traces from the text of a program.

This syntax, shown below, is the analog of the :metaclass option in CLOS and similar options in other MOPs that change the class of the program text metaobjects.

```
(let ((make-counter
        {(make-noisy-binding-trace)}
        (lambda (c)
          (lambda (x) (set! c (+ c x)) c))))
  (let ((c1 (make-counter 0)))
    (c1 1)
    (c1 3)))
```

Without traces, supporting this sort of end-programmer specialization in this MOP would have been truly cumbersome. The protocol would be more complex in that each object creation step would have to define explicit messages that determined the class of the object being created. End programmers would have to define numbers "container classes" whose only role was to participate in one-step of the object creation chain. The true code being injected in the system (i.e. the methods on **get-value** and **set-value** would end up becoming lost in the noise of the mechanism that gets them where they are going. By making the propagation of traces transparent, this program becomes radically simpler.

Specifying Trace Paths

In the formulation given above, the path a trace should follow is specified as the list of the classes it should follow in **give-rise-to** steps. This is simple, and is often good enough, but it suffers from one of the classic problem in object-oriented programming: it forces the designer of a protocol to represent any distinction among progeny that might be important to a trace as a difference in the class of the object being created, rather than some more fine-grained aspect of the individual object's state. This is essentially an instance of the dilemma of capturing a difference among objects in their class vs. in a slot.

A Protocol for Traces

To provide greater control over trace propagation and activation, we have made traces themselves be objects, with a simple, but powerful protocol that controls their propagation and activation. This protocol is driven by the **give-rise-to** primitive. As part of creating the new object, **give-rise-to** first collects the traces from each of the ancestors, then asks each one whether they: (i) want to propagate to the new object; and if they do, (ii) whether they want to activate at that object; and if they do, (iii) to produce a list of methods.

The protocol includes one message that applies to all objects and three that apply only to traces:

- **traces**
  This message is sent to all the ancestors specified in a call to **give-rise-to**. It returns a (possibly empty) list of trace objects.

- (**propagate?** *trace class . initargs*)
  This message is sent to all the traces of all the ancestors. It asks whether the trace wants to propagate to the new object. It returns either false, or a (possibly new) trace object which will actually be propagated.

- (**activate?** *trace class . initargs*)
  This message is sent to all the traces returned by **propagate?** It asks whether that trace wants to activate at this object. It returns either false or a trace object, which is the one that will actually be activated.

- (**make-methods** *trace . initargs*)
  This message is sent to all the traces returned by **activate?** It returns a list of methods.

A key point to notice is that because methods on the **propagate?** and **activate?** messages have access to the initargs specified in the call to **give-rise-to**, they can use a more fine-grained resolution than just the simple paths supported by the **trace** macro.

History Traces

As an example of using this protocol, we show the definition of a general-purpose "history trace," that keeps track of all the progeny (direct and indirect) of the object it is installed on. It does this by propagating across all **give-rise-tos**. At each progeny, it installs an **initialize** method that records the new object on the growing list of progeny. Note that each individual history trace keeps track of its own progeny, and if one object happens to be the progeny of more than one trace, there are no bad interactions, it simply appears on both lists, as do all of its progeny.

```
(defclass <history-trace> (<simple-trace>)
  (let ((*all-progeny '()))
    (list
      (method all-progeny () *all-progeny)

      (method propagate? (c . ignore) self)   ; go everywhere
      (method activate?  (c . ignore) self)   ; activate everywhere

      (method make-methods (class . initargs); ignore args
        (list
          (method initialize ignore
            (call-next-method)
            (setq *all-progeny (cons self *all-progeny))))))))
```

Inheritance Reconsidered

A language with traces changes the familiar object-oriented notions of inheritance in two important ways: First, it adds a sense of dynamic inheritance and second, it leads to a programming style in which there is a sharp distinction between inheritance of code in the default implementation and specialization performed by end programmers.

Dynamic Inheritance

A language with traces, has the traditional static inheritance among classes, but it also has *dynamic* inheritance of behavior from ancestors to progeny. In fact, the progeny paths along which dynamic inheritance can take place are much more important to the end programmer than the static inheritance, since we don't allow the addition of methods to a class once it has been defined. The documentation of a system written using traces always includes those progeny paths, perhaps in a form something like that shown in Figure 1.

Just as it is possible to build automatic tools for browsing class graphs — that is static inheritance — moderately sophisticated code analysis techniques should make it possible to build automatic tools for browsing the dynamic inheritance of a program.

It is important to note that this dynamic inheritance is different from that found in languages such as Self. In those languages — where there is no notion of class — it is true that prototypes are constructed dynamically, as are "instances" of them. But, any given object is cloned from a single other object, from which it takes all of its the behavior. This is different than the behavior of give-rise-to in which the class specifies the bulk of the new objects behavior, and traces on the ancestors provide specialization. Also note that, in traces, ancestors don't necessarily have the behavior they give to their progeny. They are instead simply carriers of that behavior.

A New Programming Style

In our use of traces, we have developed a programming style in which the end programmer specializing a system never defines subclasses of the supplied classes. Instead, they always use traces, even when the object they want to specialize is one they are creating directly.

Returning to the example of the fixed slope line, the end programmer using this style would not define a new class called <fixed-slope-line>. Instead, they would simply create an instance of <line> with a trace that activates itself immediately and supplies the appropriate behavior. The complete definition of fixed slope lines, using traces, is then:

```
(define make-fixed-slope-line
  (lambda ()
    (give-rise-to <line>
                  '()
      'traces (list
                (trace ()
                  (lambda ()
                    (list
                      (method set-end-points ...))))
                (trace (<polygon>)
                  (lambda ()
                    (list
```

```
                (method rotate ...))))))))
```

This style is attractive in that it provides a strong syntactic distinction between code that defines a default implementation, which is mostly written using classes,[6] and code that specializes existing code, which is entirely written using traces.

Performance

We have not yet developed a high-performance implementation of a language with traces in it. Traces have been so useful in our work on metaobject protocols that we have been happy to pay the costs associated with our very simple unoptimized implementation. We believe that we can nonetheless make make some simple observations about the performance possibilities for traces.

In some sense, traces can be seen as "lighweight classes" with `give-rise-to` performing dynamic class composition. Seeing it this way makes it clear that something like traces could be layered on top of a languages like Smalltalk, CLOS or Self. In CLOS and Smalltalk, `give-rise-to` would do dynamic composition of classes. In Self, the whole thing could probably be built using Self's ability to directly manipulate vectors of methods that form objects. Method dispatch would just be the host language's method dispatch. This approach would likely result in good performance for method invocation, at the expense of potentially terrible performance for some calls to `give-rise-to`.

Arranging for traces to have fast method dispatch *and* fast object creation could be much more difficult. Potentially sophisticated flow analysis will be required, to allow the compiler to infer what traces might actually arrive at each `give-rise-to`. We are deferring any such effort until we have much more experience working with traces, so that we can have a better sense of how to invest our energies.

Summary

We have presented a new object-oriented language concept, traces, together with a concrete embedding of that language in a simple object-oriented extension to Scheme. Traces require two additions to existing object-oriented languages: an explicit notion of ancestor-progeny paths, and trace objects, which are carriers of behavior that can follow those paths. This provides us with a powerful way to open up certain kinds of systems that were difficult to handle with previous object-oriented languages. Traces also provide us with two critical distinctions in programs: first between static and dynamic inheritance; and second, between inheritance of behavior in the default implementation and specialization by the end programmer.

Acknowledgments

The concept of traces arose out of discussions with members of a group working on a MOP-based Scheme compiler. Over the past several years, this group has included: Hal

---

[6] Even code defining a default implementation might use traces, to capture default dynamic inheritance of behavior.

Abelson, J. Michael Ashley, Jim des Rivières, Mike Dixon, John Lamping, Anurag Mendhekar, Luis Rodriquez, Erik Ruf and Amin Vahdat. Brian Smith contributed numerous insights regarding object individuation criteria. Discussions with Craig Chambers, Dan Friedman, Chris Haynes, Satoshi Matsuoka, Mario Tokoro and Akinori Yonezawa, helped form the idea into a workable language.

A A Simple Object-Oriented Language

To simplify the presentation, this paper presents traces by starting with a new and very simple object-oriented language. This appendix presents an overview of that starting point.

The language is a variant of Scheme, with objects added. To do this, we have added: *objects, selectors, methods* and *classes*. An object is simply a list of methods, a method is a pair of a selector and a procedure. A class is a linguistic convenience for producing a list of methods that comprise an object. (Users can, and sometimes do, make the list of methods directly without a class.)

A regular Scheme application, whose head is a selector, is called a *message send*. The first argument, which must be an object, is searched for its first method that matches the selector, and that method is then run.

As an example of using the language, consider the following definitions of the classes <position> and <line>. These are the definitions that are assumed to be part of the default library provided by the graphics editor discussed in the body of the paper.

The class <position> defines immutable cartesian positions, that support two messages, pos-x and pos-y, to access the x and y coordinates of a position. The class <line> defines a line segment, of which the two endpoints are represented by position objects. Line objects support operations to access each of the endpoints, and to set the two endpoints together.

```
(define pos-x (make-selector))
(define pos-y (make-selector))

(define <position>
  (class (<object>)
    (lambda ()
      (let (*x *y)
        (list
          (method initialize initargs
            (set! *x (getl initargs 'x))
            (set! *y (getl initargs 'y)))

          (method pos-x () *x)
          (method pos-y () *y))))))


(define end-1 (make-selector))
(define end-2 (make-selector))
```

```
(define set-end-points (make-selector))

(define <line>
  (class (<object>)
    (lambda ()
      (let (*end-1 *end-2)
        (list
          (method initialize initargs
            (set! *end-1 (getl 'initargs 'end-1))
            (set! *end-2 (getl 'initargs 'end-2)))

          (method end-1 () *end-1)
          (method end-2 () *end-2)

          (method set-end-points (new-end-1 new-end-2)
            (set! *end-1 new-end-1)
            (set! *end-2 new-end-2)))))))
```

The **method** macro is like Scheme's **lambda**. It returns a method for the selector that is its first argument (evaluated when the method is constructed). The rest of the args of a **method** form are just like the args to a **lambda** form: the parameters to the method and the code body.

Within the body of a method, **call-next-method** can be used, as in CLOS, to call the next method for that generic-function in the object's list of methods. Also note that the lexical variable **self** is bound within the body of a method to the object that was the first argument to the generic function.

The object creation primitive, **make**, takes a class and initargs as arguments, just as it does in CLOS. After the object is created, it is automatically initialized. Methods on **initialize** receive all the initargs passed to **make** and can process them as they like. The convention is for methods on **initialize** to always invoke **call-next-method**. (Bottoming out at the most general class, **<object>**.)

```
(define p1 (make <position> 'x 3 'y 5))         a positon
(define p2 (make <position> 'x 9 'y 5))         a positon

(pos-x p1)                                      returns 3

(define l1
  (make <line> 'end-1 p1
               'end-2 p2))                      a line

(set-end-points l1                              rotate and resize
                (make <position> 'x 0 'y 0)
                (make <position> 'x 10 'y 10))
```

Each time an instance of the class is created, the class's method maker procedure is called to produce a new list of methods. The resulting list is stored in the new instance, as its list of methods. If the class has superclasses, the methods from all the classes in the class precedence list are appended. In the starting point language, `make` is implemented as:

```
(define make
  (lambda (class . initargs)
    (let* ((cpl (class-precedence-list class))
           (methods (apply append (mapcar make-methods cpl)))
           (object (make-object methods)))
      (apply initialize object initargs)
      object)))
```

A final point is to note that this very simple semantics means that no special support must be provided to distinguish slots, methods, internal slots, internal methods, class slots etc. Ordinary lexical scoping can be used to handle all of these, and with more power than is commonly found in existing object-oriented languages.

References

[BKK+86] D.G. Bobrow, K. Kahn, G. Kiczales, L. Masinter, M. Stefik, and F. Zdybel. Commonloops: Merging Lisp and object-oriented programming. In *OOPSLA '86 Conference Proceedings, Sigplan Notices* 21(11). ACM, Nov 1986.

[CI93] Shigeru Chiba and Yuuji Ichisugi. Open c++. In *European Conference on Object Oriented Programming*, 1993. to appear.

[Coi87] Pierre Cointe. The ObjVlisp kernel: A reflexive lisp architecture to define a uniform object-oriented system. In Pattie Maes and Daniele Nardi, editors, *Meta-Level Architectures and Reflection*, pages 155–176. North-Holland, 1987.

[Fer89] Jacques Ferber. Computational reflection in class based object oriented language. In *Proceedings of the ACM Conference on Object-Oriented Programming Systems, Languages, and Applications (OOPSLA), New Orleans, LA.*, SIGPLAN Notices 24(10), pages 317–326. ACM, October 1989.

[FJ89] Brian Foote and Ralph E. Johnson. Reflective facilities in smalltalk-80. In *Proceedings of the ACM Conference on Object-Oriented Programming Systems, Languages, and Applications (OOPSLA), New Orleans, LA.*, SIGPLAN Notices, 24(10), pages 327–335, October 1989.

[KdRB91] Gregor Kiczales, Jim des Rivières, and Daniel G. Bobrow. *The Art of the Metaobject Protocol*. MIT Press, 1991.

[Kic92] Gregor Kiczales. Towards a new model of abstraction in software engineering. In *Proceedings of the IMSA'92 Workshop on Reflection and Meta-level Architectures*, 1992. Also to appear in forthcoming PARC Technical Report.

[KL92]   Gregor Kiczales and John Lamping. Issues in the design and documentation of class libraries. In *Proceedings of the Conference on Object-Oriented Programming: Systems, Languages, and Applications*, 1992. To Appear.

[Lie86]   H. Lieberman. Using prototypical objects to implement shared behavior in object-oriented systems. In *OOPSLA '86 Conference Proceedings, Sigplan Notices* **21**(11). ACM, Nov 1986.

[Mae87]   Pattie Maes. Concepts and experiments in computational reflection. In *Proceedings of the ACM Conference on Object-Oriented Programming Systems, Languages, and Applications (OOPSLA)*, pages 147–155, 1987.

[MCD91]   J. Malenfant, P. Cointe, and C. Dony. Reflection in prototype-based object-oriented programming languages. In *Proceedings of the OOPSLA Workshop on Reflection and Metalevel Architectures in Object-Oriented Programming*, 1991.

[Rao90]   Ramana Rao. Implementational reflection in Silica. In *Informal Proceedings of ECOOP/OOPSLA '90 Workshop on Reflection and Metalevel Architectures in Object-Oriented Programming*, October 1990.

[Rao91]   Ramana Rao. Implementational reflection in Silica. In Pierre America, editor, *Proceedings of European Conference on Object-Oriented Programming (ECOOP)*, volume 512 of *Lecture Notes in Computer Science*, pages 251–267. Springer-Verlag, 1991.

[YMFT91] Yasuhiko Yokote, Atsushi Mitsuzawa, Nobuhisa Fujinami, and Mario Tokoro. Evaluation of muse reflective object management. In *Proceedings of the 8th Conference of Japan Society for Software Science and Technology*, September 1991. (in Japanese, also available as a technical report SCSL-TM-91-019, Sony Computer Science Laboratory Inc.).

[YTM[+]91] Yasuhiko Yokote, Fumio Teraoka, Atsushi Mitsuzawa, Nobuhisa Fujinami, and Mario Tokoro. The Muse object architecture: A new operating system structuring concept. *Operating Systems Review*, 25(2), April 1991. (also available as a technical report SCSL-TR-91-002, Sony Computer Science Laboratory Inc.).

[YTY[+]89] Yasuhiko Yokote, Fumio Teraoka, Masaki Yamada, Hiroshi Tezuka, and Mario Tokoro. The design and implementation of the Muse object-oriented distributed operating system. In *Proceedings of the First Conference on Technology of Object-Oriented Languages and Systems*, October 1989. (also available as a technical report SCSL-TR-89-010, Sony Computer Science Laboratory Inc.).

Gluons: a Support for Software Component Cooperation*

Xavier Pintado

Université de Genève
Centre Universitaire d'Informatique
24, rue du Général Dufour
1211 Geneva 4
SWITZERLAND
e-mail: pintado@cui.unige.ch

Abstract

This paper presents *gluons* as objects that mediate software component cooperation. We discuss the advantages of encapsulating inter-component interaction inside a set of special objects. We present the design of a hierarchy of *gluon* classes that provide the support for the application domain independent part of component interaction protocols. As an example, we present the design of a financial information framework and we discuss the role that *gluons* play in the definition of the framework.

1 Introduction

Increasing software construction productivity by emphasizing reuse has been one of the main goals of the software industry. Object-oriented techniques have been acknowledged as a promising approach towards this end since they provide various mechanisms to support the reuse process. Among various lines of attack, our interest is in achieving reuse by building software systems based on the connection of reusable software components. Previous work on component connection has emphasized the direct connection of components[Ingalls88, Mah91] or the utilization of a language to express the patterns of cooperation between the reusable components [HelHolGan90, NieTsi91]. In this paper we explore an approach where such connections are mediated by objects.

The idea of interposing an object or a mechanism between two collaborating entities in order to increase the flexibility of the way entities can cooperate has old roots. Operating systems designers, for example, faced a similar connection problem when they attempted to provide interprocess communication. The *mailbox* concept provided increased flexibility for synchronization and buffering as compared to schemes relying on direct process communication. In the same way we believe that component connection can benefit from the increased flexibility provided by a communication mediator object.

---
*This research was supported in part by REUTERS (EUROPE) S.A.

This paper introduces *gluons* as objects that mediate object collaboration. In the next section we discuss the role communication mediator objects can play in an object-oriented environment. Section 3 describes the design of *gluons*, their structure, and their functionality. In Section 4 we present a financial information environment for which the connection of components relies on *gluons*. Section 5 concludes with general remarks and discusses new directions for future work.

2 The role of communication mediator objects

Our approach promotes a view of software design whereby component collaboration is achieved by the exchange of services. The main difference between collaboration through component connection and service exchange is that component connection implies a fixed relationship between the cooperating objects, while service exchange provides additional flexibility by interposing an object, the gluon, between the provider of the service and its clients. In such a framework the communication mediator object acts as a vehicle for the exchange of services provided by software components much in the same way as money mediates the trade of goods and services.

Figure 2 provides a schematic representation of a communication mediator object. The schema portrays the essential features of a communication mediator object (CMO). A CMO mediates the cooperation between a *server* and potential client objects. A CMO is associated with one server with which it keeps a link through reference rs. Any other object can ask for the delivery of the services provided by the *server* by sending messages (e.g. m_1, m_2, m_3) to the CMO. Upon receipt of messages, the communication mediator object sends a set of messages to the *server* so that it delivers the requested service. The messages that are actually sent to the *server* depend on the specification of the communication mediator object as we shall discuss in a later section.

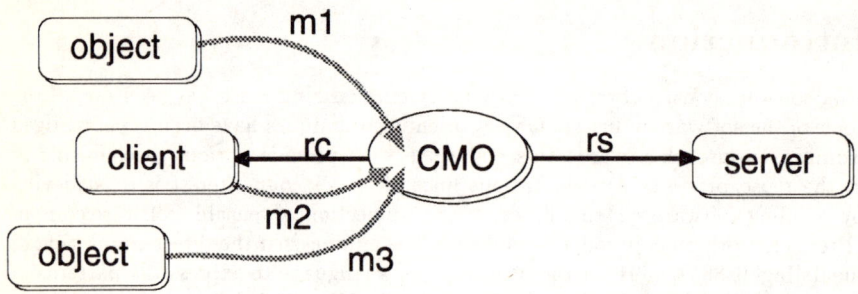

Figure 1: Schematic representation of a communication mediator object.

In the general case, there is no fixed relationship between the CMO and the client objects; any object can potentially be a client and the CMO does not keep references to the objects that issue requests for service. The acquaintance of a CMO with client objects only lasts the time of a service exchange. Therefore, a CMO establishes an asymmetric relationship between client objects and *server*, which is typical of a client/server relationship. However, the framework provides a kind of CMO that keeps a reference to a second object rc, called the *client* so that upon receipt of a message, the communication mediator sends messages to both the *client* and the *server*. This kind of CMO allows for the definition of symmetric patterns of interaction between objects.

Making such an object responsible for inter-component communication can serve various purposes, and we now discuss some of the advantages of this technique.

2.1 Encapsulation of Protocols Inside Objects

Protocols define the rules that allow software components to communicate. They represent common agreements which software components obey so that they are able to interact. Although much energy has been devoted in studying the design of reusable software components, little has been said about protocols and the role they play in the reuse process. Helm[HelHolGan90] proposes *contracts* as a means to specify patterns of collaboration between objects. *Contracts* are written in an ad hoc language that specifies the constraints to which the participants of a *contract* must obey. A more rigorous formalism for the specification of object interaction can be found in [Arapis91]. Procol[Laffra92] is an object-oriented programming language with provisions to specify protocols inside objects. Protocols are specified in the form of augmented regular expressions that are parsed at execution time when instances of the object receives a message. One can, for example, specify that whenever message m_1 is sent to object X then it should be followed by the invocation of method m_2 of the same object.

We think that protocols should not be embedded inside the reusable software components as in Procol. Rather, because they represent communication agreements they should be defined outside the reusable components as in *contracts*. Our approach consists of encapsulating protocols inside a communication mediator object. Doing so has two main advantages. The first advantage is uniformity. If software components and protocols are both objects, they can be managed, retrieved, and manipulated with the same mechanisms. In particular, protocols can be stored in the same software information base as the reusable software components allowing for the same retrieval mechanisms to be applied to both; also, reuse tools such as the affinity browser[PinTsi88, PinTsi90, GibTsi90] can be exploited to explore the relationships between them. The second advantage is the possibility to rely on inheritance to build new protocols by incremental refinement of existing ones. Communication mediator objects should allow for grouping of sequences of methods invocations (i.e. message sequences) in such a way that objects' interactions involving more than the sending of one message can be expressed in a flexible way.

We observed, from our object-oriented design experience that the reuse of protocols is at least as important for reuse as the reuse of software components. This observation occurs naturally when we notice that, in fact the two issues are strongly related. It is indeed, difficult to design reusable software components independently of a specific development framework. A common pragmatic solution consists of respecting a global design discipline. Most of the times this discipline is informal and is limited to a naming convention that attempts to associate the same message name to operations with similar semantics. Although conformance to a naming convention seems necessary for reuse, it does not seem sufficient. Our approach focuses on protocol reuse both at the design and at the implementation level. Focusing on protocol reuse at the design level is not new. Reuse of protocols is indeed a common practice in the electronics industry, and, interestingly, the choice of an interaction protocol is done, in general, prior to other design decisions. We follow a similar approach by first defining the set of interaction protocols that are typical for a particular application domain. These protocols, once encapsulated inside communication mediator objects constitute a first layer of compatibility constraints to which software components should comply. By emphasizing on protocol reuse we avoid, to a large extent the effort of object standardization since the only prerequisite for two software components to be interaction compatible is that they obey the same protocol.

2.2 Dynamic Connection of Software Components

To allow for the dynamic connection of software components in a flexible way, the compatibility requirements between software components should be verified at runtime[1]. More precisely, component interaction should obey two requirements. The first requirement is that, independently of their static types, the components should be able to participate in a specific interaction if they comply to the protocol that defines the rules of the specific interaction. Second, the verification of a component's conformity to a protocol is performed when the interaction is triggered. Communication mediator objects, as they have been outlined in Figure 2, obey both requirements. They provide a generic vehicle for communication between objects of any statically defined type.

One issue related to dynamic connection of software components is software reliability. What happens if the user tries to connect components that do not comply to a common protocol? Can we have both reliability and flexibility? CMO's offer a specific solution to these questions. A communication mediator object in charge of verifying that the candidates to the interaction comply to the protocol it defines. If, for example, an object sends a message to another through a communication mediator and the receiver is unable to respond to it then the mediator stops the interaction by not forwarding the message further since it would generate an error. CMO's play a central role in the dynamic connection of software components. First by providing the support for the connection. Second by encapsulating a protocol. Third by verifying that the components are compatible with the protocol.

2.3 Reconcile interfaces

With communication mediator objects it is possible to conceal, to some extent, interface mismatches between components inside the communication mediator object. It is easy, for instance, to perform parameter conversion, and to convert method names. More sophisticated reconciliation strategies can also be performed by communication mediators. One example is the negotiation of parameter types. Imagine software components that deal with dates and provide methods to set dates. A date can be expressed in many different formats and data types. Moreover, different components may provide different method names to set dates. It is possible, in such cases to have the communication mediator select the method (and data type), from a set of alternatives to which a component can respond, then make the necessary conversions and finally set the date. These examples provide some intuition on the central role that communication mediator objects

---

[1] There is a running debate between the supporters of statically typed object-oriented programming languages (e.g. Eiffel, C++), and those that believe in the benefits of languages for which type checking is performed at runtime (e.g. Objective-C, Self, Smalltalk). The former emphasize software reliability and argue that it is impractical to build production quality software that may stop execution after a runtime type violation. The latter stress the flexibility provided by weakly typed languages and the impact they may have on the design of reusable software components.

can play at adapting interfaces and protocols from different frameworks. Communication mediators can provide to some extent functionality similar to the Common Object Broker[OMG92].

2.4 Support for Distributed Strategies

Object-oriented distributed systems can take advantage of an uniform concept to specify distribution mechanisms. For example, *proxies* are by their very nature communication mediator objects since they act on behalf of another object to which they grant the access to services from other objects. Communication mediator objects can also be useful at supporting systems interoperability by assuming the responsibility of performing necessary conversions without modifying the communicating components. They can also be instrumental in defining fault-tolerant strategies by encapsulating the transparent access to alternative service provided by other objects residing either in the same machine or in other machine. Yet another example is the utilization of communication mediators to specify starting points for concurrent threads (i.e. fork points). These are a few examples of how communication mediator objects can be utilized to conceal distribution allowing the construction of distributed systems from software components that have not been designed specifically for such environments.

2.5 Controlled Access to Software Components

Communication mediator objects can be instrumental at providing controlled access to software components and resources. Controlled access may be important for security enforcement by restricting service access to authorized users. Controlled access can also play an important role at supporting pricing strategies for reusable component utilization. For example, a user of an application could be billed the services provided by the software components of an application through a software clearinghouse that would be in charge of collecting fees for different software components developers. In this context the connection object plays the role of a capability-based component connector.

2.6 Summary

Fundamentally a communication mediator object provides two things. The first is a level of indirection in accessing services provided by software components. This level of indirection allows for the exchange of services between components, replacement strategies, and dynamic connection of objects. The second capability provided by communication mediators is the provisions for encapsulation of sequences of messages that can be triggered at a later time. That is, they allow protocol encapsulation.

3 Anatomy of gluons

In our framework communication mediator objects are called gluons because they serve as glue for the connection of reusable software components. Their distinguishing feature is that they are aimed at establishing collaboration relationships between software components. As other objects, gluons are organized in a hierarchical inheritance structure in order to express specialization relationships. Currently, the gluon hierarchy is defined as shown in Figure 3.

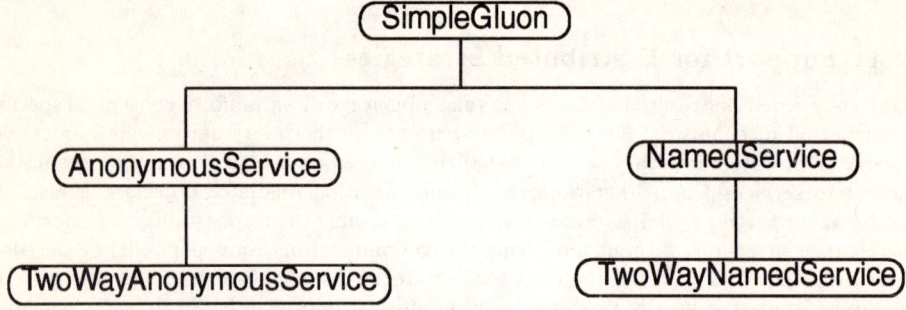

Figure 2: Application domain independent Gluon hierarchy.

The simplest gluon can be found at the top of the hierarchy. `SimpleGluon`'s offer forwarding capabilities; upon reception of a message, a gluon forwards to the object that is in charge of delivering the service. Forwarding a message represents the minimal functionality of communication mediator.

The classes on the left branch of the hierarchy allow for anonymous requests for service delivery. That is, instances of such classes behave like tickets: they grant the rights to a service provided by an object without naming explicitly neither the method (or the methods) nor the object that provides the service. Any object can ask for the delivery of the service, provided it can send a message to the gluon that mediates the service.

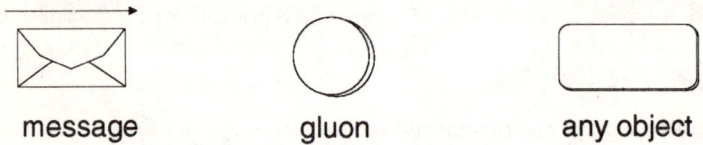

Figure 3: Meaning of the symbols utilized in the diagrams.

The classes on the right branch of the hierarchy differ from those on the left side by the fact that the services are named: an object can ask for the delivery of a service provided it knows which message triggers the execution of the service. Named invocation is similar to message sending. The difference resides in the fact that the knowledge of the objects that participate in the service is encapsulated in the gluon. Therefore, the object that requests the service does not necessarily know who delivers it and who benefits from it.

The hierarchy we discuss here represents the classes of gluons that do not depend on a specific application domain. They offer the basic support that allows, by parametrization, and subclassing, the definition of protocols and inter-object communication patterns appropriate to a particular framework or application domain.

3.1 SimpleGuon

The behaviour of `SimpleGluons` is depicted in Figure 4. Whenever a `SimpleGluon` receives a message it tries to forward it to an object that has been assigned as its server. This is true, of course, for the messages to which the gluon cannot answer itself (see Table 1, for `SimpleGluon`'s interface).The request for service succeeds if the server can respond to the message, otherwise the invocation has no effect and the gluon returns.

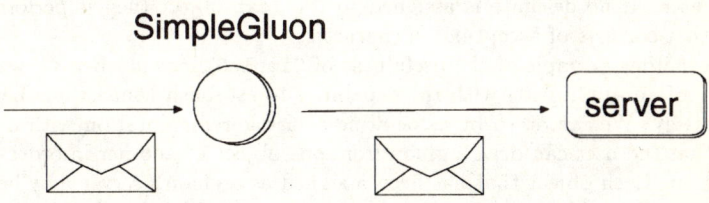

Figure 4: A `SimpleGluon` can receive a message from any object and it will try to forward it to an object that has been assigned to it as its server. If no server object has been assigned then the message has no effect other than rising an undelivered condition on the gluon.

The server is the object that provides the service requested. In fact an object sends a message to a gluon in order to have a service performed by another object; that is, a gluon acts on behalf of its server. The gluon plays, therefore, the role of a broker; that is, it mediates a transaction. An instance of `SimpleGluon` responds to any message to which its server responds to, and, if another server object is assigned to a gluon the set of messages to which it responds changes accordingly.

Method Signatures	Description
`setServer:`(objId)server	assigns a server to the gluon.
(objId)`getServer`	returns the object that has been assigned as the gluon's server.
(int)`error`	returns the error code. This code is reset before the reception of a message.

Table 1: SimpleGluon's Interface

Despite its simplicity, a `SimpleGluon` can serve various purposes. For example, with a `SimpleGluon` we can express delegation in the sense defined in[NeXT90]. The delegation mechanism allows classes to be tailored by assigning to an instance of the class a delegate object that acts on the behalf of the object for certain activities.

The delegation mechanism works as follows: when the object receives a message invoking one of its methods, if the method belongs to the subset of those that have declared delegable by the class designer then the object tests whether a delegate has been assigned to it. If not the object performs its default action. If such a delegate exists the object eventually performs some action and then invokes the corresponding delegate's method (the method with the same signature). When the delegate exits from the execution of the method, the control returns back to the delegator. If the delegate does not provide a method with the same signature then the delegator acts with its default behaviour.

The NeXT `Text` class provides an interesting practical example of the usefulness of delegation. A small subset of its methods are delegable. Typically the delegate implements methods like `textWillChange:`. This method would be invoked by the delegator after the user attempts to modify the text but before the text objects accepts the modification. In this way it is possible, for example, to filter all the control characters typed by the user. If no delegate is assigned to the `Text` object then it performs its default action that consists of accepting all characters.

Yet another example of the usefulness of `SimpleGluons` is when we want to provide the user of an application with the capability to establish connections between objects interactively. We can do so by associating a visible representation with a gluon in such a way that the user can drag a gluon from one object to another in order to establish a connection. Each object that has been assigned as a gluon's server may be interactively connected. The only requirement for the interaction to take place is that the server object responds to the message. If this is not the case, or if no server is associated with the connected gluon, the result is that nothing will happen. In this case the gluon acts both as a vehicle for establishing the connection and as a mechanism of dynamic matching for methods.

To summarize, a `SimpleGluon` establishes a many-to-one relationship between a server object and any other object that can send a message to the gluon. Upon receipt of the message, the `SimpleGluon` forwards the message to the server if the server object can respond to it.

3.2 AnonymousService

`AnonymousService` inherits from `SimpleGluon` and so it displays the same forwarding behaviour as the `SimpleGluon`. Additionally, it provides a capability that allows an object to request the delivery of the service by anonymous invocation. By anonymous invocation we mean that any object can invoke the service mediated by an `AnonymousService` instance by simply sending the message doIt to the gluon.

The `doIt` message sends to the server object the sequence of messages it finds on its message stack, starting with the message at the top of the stack. The messages can take parameters and return values. The values for the parameters are popped from the top of the stack and the values returned by the messages are pushed on top of the stack as well. The set of methods defined in `AnonymousService` can be found in Table 2. Each time a new message is pushed on top of the message stack, the gluon verifies that the server can respond to it. If not the message will not be added to the stack. The same verification is performed each time there is an attempt to assign a new server object to the gluon. If the new server does not respond to all the messages on the message stack, the stack is cleared by sending a clearParameters message to self.

`AnonymousService` instances establish a many-to-one relationship between a server object and any other object that can send a message to the gluon, that is, the client. If the message received is `doIt`, the service provided by the *server* is defined by the set of methods that have been placed in the message stack.

Figure 5 depicts schematically the anonymous request for service mechanism.

`AnonymousService` gluons act as tickets. Because service request can be anonymous,

Method Signatures	Description
doIt	this method triggers the delivery of the service; that is, the sequence of messages in the message stack is sent to the server object.
clearMessages	empties the message stack.
(SEL)popMessage	pops the message at the top of the message stack.
(SEL)pushMess:(SEL)m	adds a new message at the top of the message stack.
clearParameters	empties the parameter stack.
(SEL)pushParam:(void)p Type:(char)type	allocates space for a new parameter on the top of the parameter stack.
(void)popParameter	pops the parameter at the top of the parameter stack.

Table 2: AnonymousService Interface

Figure 5: The anonymous request for service mechanism provided by an AnonymousService instance. Upon reception of the doIt message, the gluon sends to the server the sequence of messages stacked on the gluon's stack.

the client does not need to know what is the service provided. Also any object can request the delivery of the service and the gluons can be exchanged between software components granting to its owner the rights to the service it defines.

These gluons are specially useful when we want to send a predefined sequence of messages to an object without defining who is going to trigger the execution. In such a case the object will be assigned as the server of the gluon and the sequence of messages will be pushed on the message stack. The gluon can now be circulated (e.g., sent inside a message as a parameter), and the service can be requested by any object that can interact with the gluon.

3.3 TwoWayAnonymousService

The gluon classes discussed so far establish a one-to-many relationship between the object that has been assigned as the server of the gluon and the other objects that may eventually send a message to the gluon. These objects become clients of the gluon whenever they ask the gluon to deliver the service provided by the server. The relationship between the client and the server is asymmetric in the sense that a gluon knows the server that provides the service but is not aware of who is its client. The interaction asymmetry can be illustrated by the situation where someone picks a phone number at random on a telephone directory and makes a call. The caller knows to whom he is speaking[2] but the callee has no way of knowing the interlocutor, and even worse, he cannot call back. That is, communication is one-way.

TwoWayAnonymousService, on the other hand provides a symmetric interaction mechanism by assigning both a server and a client (see Table 3 for **TwoWayAnonymousService** interface). **TwoWayAnonymousService** defines interaction relationships that are one-to-one as shown in Figure 6. The class inherits the message and parameter stacks of its

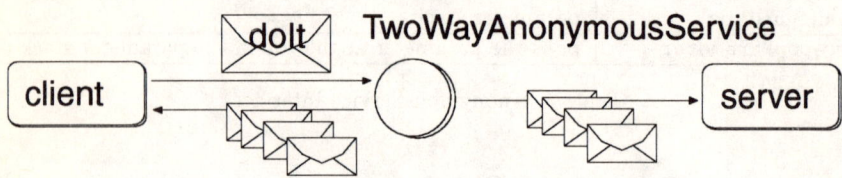

messages on the message stack

Figure 6: The anonymous request for service mechanism provided by a **TwoWayAnonymousService** instance. The gluon establishes a relationship between a client object and a server object. When the message **doIt** is sent to the server, messages on the message stack are sent to the server, to the client, or to both.

superclass. But because a message can be sent either to the client or to the server there is a tag associated with each message that specifies its destination (i. e., client or server).

Method Signatures	Description
(SEL)setClient:(objId)client	assigns a client component to the gluon.
(objId)getClient	returns the client associated with the gluon.

Table 3: TwoWayAnonymousService Interface

TwoWayAnonymousService gluons allow for the encapsulation of an activity between two objects. The gluon carries the definition of the activity so that it can be triggered at a later time.

3.4 NamedService

A **NamedService** class provides functionality similar to the **AnonymousService** class except for the way services are requested. While **AnonymousService** instances deliver the service whenever they receive the **doIt** message, service delivery for **NamedService** instances is triggered by a specific message that needs to be specified when the protocol is

---

[2] Assuming there is a one-to-one relationship between a phone number and the person that answers the call. Of course, this assumption is not realistic in general but is acceptable for this example.

encapsulated into the gluon (see Table 4). Therefore, clients need to know the name of the service in order to invoke it.

Method Signatures	Description
setServiceSignature: (string)messSignat	sets the signature of the message that a client should send in order to request service. When the message is received the sequence of messages in the message stack is sent to the server object.
(SEL)getServSignature	returns the signature of the message the gluon should receive in order to trigger service delivery.
clearMessages	empties the message stack
(SEL)popMessage	pops the message at the top of the message stack.
pushMessage:(SEL)mess	adds a message on top of the message stack.
clearParams	empties the parameter stack.
pushParameter: (void)par Type:(char)ty	allocates space for a new parameter of a given type on top of the parameter stack
(void)popParameter	pops the method on top of the parameter stack.

Table 4: NamedService Interface

NamedService gluons are useful whenever the invocation of a protocol should be named. In fact, a NamedService gluon acts as an extension of the *server* to which it adds a new method.

Typically, a software component can act as a server for a set of gluons that encapsulate an activity[3]. Indeed, because they are designed for reuse, software components often provide a rich interface for which most of the methods are not intended to be invoked alone, rather they should be integrated within a sequence of messages that together represent a coherent service. But the designer does not want to combine them inside new methods because that would reduce the flexibility in the way operations can be performed reducing thus the reuse potential of the software component and also because it is virtually impossible to anticipate all the usages of the component.

3.5 TwoWayNamedService

TwoWayNamedService behaves similarly to TwoWayAnonymousService except for the way services can be requested. TwoWayAnonymousService service requests are named in the sense defined in NamedService from which it inherits.

A typical usage of NamedService gluons is in reconciling software component interfaces. For example, if a software component A sends a message M to which no software component can respond to, and it is possible to find another component B, that although not responding to that message can provide similar functionality. Then a NamedService gluon can be interposed between the two components. The signature of the gluon's service is the signature of M, B acts as the server and A acts as the client.

---

[3]By activity we mean a sequence of object interactions.

3.6 Discussion

The gluon's inheritance hierarchy that has been presented is an attempt to define a family of protocol classes appropriate for software component interaction. Our design approach explores essentially two dimensions. The first dimension is related to the kind of connection relationship between the server and the client. This dimension describes, to some extent, the asymmetry of the interaction protocol[4] regarding the prerequisites the gluon imposes on both servers and clients. For example, any object can be a client of an **AnonymousService** instance since nothing is assumed in the protocol about the client. Conversely, the servers that can be assigned to such a gluon are restricted to those that can respond to the sequence of messages that make up the encapsulated protocol.

The second dimension is related to how services can be invoked or, more precisely, it describes to which extent the clients need to be aware of the services provided by the client. Anonymous invocation does not put any restriction on the objects that can issue a request for service but a named invocation implies the client's knowledge of the service name. Based on our experience we think that these are important dimensions in the definition of the framework independent part of a protocol since we found the gluon classes appropriate to express the desired connection semantics.

4 Financial Information Framework

We present in this section the architecture of a financial information framework for which a prototype has been built at the University of Geneva. Gluons play a central role in the framework since the interactive connection of financial analysis tools and data sources rely on them. The role of gluons is the encapsulation of a set of protocols for which most of them are specific to the financial application domain.

Component compatibility is based on protocol conformance; two components can interact if they comply at least to a common protocol which is encapsulated in a gluon. Protocol conformance defines equivalence classes in the sense that all the components that conform to a protocol belong to the same class of plug compatible components.

Real time access to financial data is a critical resource in financial decision making and, therefore, a financial framework should grant access to real time data sources. These sources can be external to the institution such as those provided by Reuters, Telekurs, and Telerate, or they can be generated inside the institution. The former typically provide market information from stock exchanges and economic news that may have an impact on financial decisions. The main constraint on these data is time; a few seconds can be critical for financial decisions. The latter can be either data that is directly related to the economic activity or it can be a by-product of the transformation of data from external and internal sources. User perception of a financial decision support system usually narrows down to two preeminent entities: information sources, and tools that display, retrieve, and transform data from those sources. Therefore, a desirable feature of a financial framework is the homogeneous integration of the various information sources since they represent the raw material on which the tools operate.

---

[4]In our implementation of a financial information framework we use a variant of the **SimpleGluon** that has multiplexer capabilities; that is, it maintains a list of the servers to which the received message is forwarded. In this case we can say that the SimpleGluon establishes a many-to-many connection relationship.

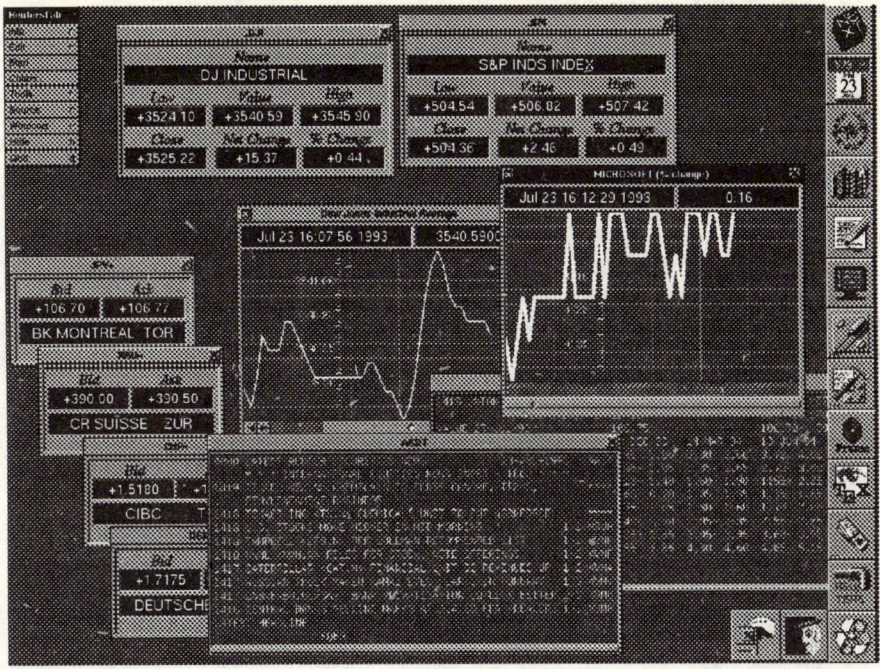

Figure 7: Display presenting some of the financial market monitoring tools available for the display of realtime information. Inspectors display real time values such as the Dow Jones Industrial and Standard & Poors indexes. Other windows display currency exchange ratios and informations about companies. The framework also provides a graphical class for the display of time series.

4.1 Real Time Market Data Sources

Our framework provides access to a real time financial data sources. The software component that mediates the access to it encapsulates a Reuters real time data feed. Although this is the only real time data source that can be presently accessed through the framework we tried to design the component in such a way that most of the major data sources available in the market can be accessed through the same component.

During the design phase we identified a specific class, we call it a dictionary, that plays an important role as a building block for the encapsulation of the data feed. A dictionary is a set of pairs (k, v), each representing an association between a key k, and a value v, where the key k is unique. We call such a pair a field. The number of fields in a dictionary is not fixed; fields can be added and deleted during the lifetime of a dictionary. There are no restrictions on the type of the key or on the type of the value, although for implementation reasons the type of the key is limited to a few simple types such as integers, and strings. Dictionaries offer two access mechanisms: direct access and ordered access. Direct access is important since real time constraints require $O(1)$ retrieval time complexity for a field. On the other hand values are often accessed sequentially in a predefined order. The definition of order is provided by a function that defines a total order over the fields by returning the relative positions of two fields. This function can be replaced at any time by another function that displays a similar behaviour.

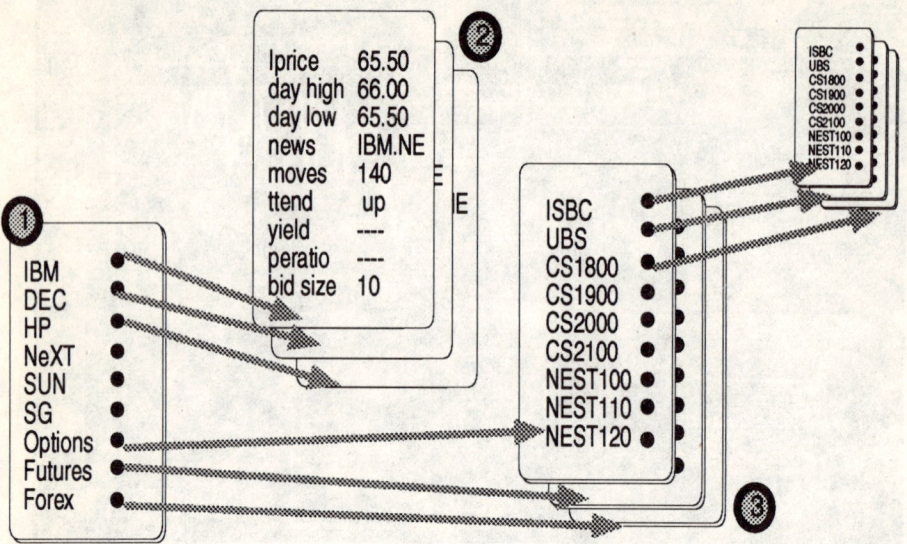

Figure 8: Structure of information container objects inside the real time server component (DataFeed). The data is contained in dictionaries. Dictionary 1 contains references to all the information updated in real time by the data source. The other dictionaries contain either values (2) or reference to other objects (3).

Figure 8 shows the internal structure of the DataFeed component. The first dictionary contains the list of all the items for which a real time update has been requested from the source (Figure 9 displays the DataFeed inspector). Each entry contains either a reference to another dictionary or a value (e.g., a stock price). The DataFeed component is in charge of:

- Creating and deleting the objects that contain the information. Objects are created dynamically after DataFeed receives a request for a new information item. DataFeed forwards the request to the data source and creates an empty dictionary object that will receive the information requested when it is available. An object is deleted when DataFeed receives a message instructing it to do so.

- Updating the dictionary objects that contain the information provided by the data source. The data source sends updates to the information items that have been requested. Updates arrive without further requests other than the initial request for the item. The rate of updates is unpredictable and thus the time to needed to locate and update a dictionary object should be independent of the number of information items for which a request has been issued.

- Granting data source access to other components by distributing dictionary objects upon request. Other components can access data from the source only by requesting these objects for which DataFeed is in charge of performing real time updates.

To summarize, DataFeed is a software component that manages the access to data sources and grants the access to other objects by exporting dictionary objects that contain the source real time information.

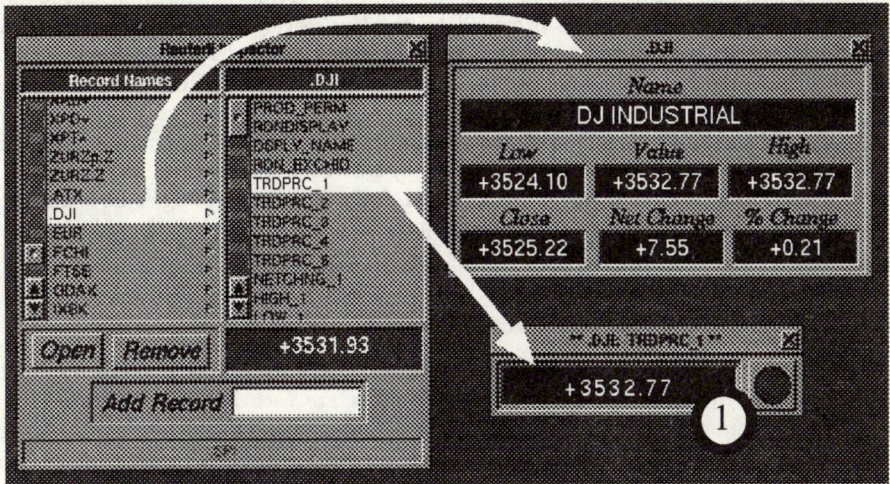

Figure 9: An inspector that displays information contained inside the DataFeed component. The selected item on the browser is the Industrial Dow Jones Index. The selection on the right column of the browser is the last index value available. Double clicking the browser items opens the corresponding inspectors. The single value inspector has a gluon attached to it (1).

4.2 Financial Analysis Tools and Dictionaries

Dictionaries play a central role in providing financial tools access to data sources. Indeed dictionary objects and field objects (objects contained by a dictionary) are the only objects through which software components can access the data sources encapsulated in DataFeed components. Dictionaries are the objects that carry the information and they provide the functionality that allows other components to retrieve the source data:

- Components can register for notification whenever a dictionary is updated. Dictionaries can be assigned both a component and a message. Whenever the dictionary is updated, the message is sent to the component.

- Components can retrieve any field of a dictionary by providing its key or its index. The field object performs the appropriate type conversions to the value before delivering it. Type conversions are necessary because values inside a dictionary are stored as strings of characters. There is a key server associated with each data source. Its role is to provide type information, names, and information describing the meaning of the values associated with the key. This means that, for instance, a price can be retrieved as a float, a double, or a string.

- Dictionaries can be assigned objects to which they delegate notification strategies, and display behaviour. It is indeed important that each dictionary displays itself according to the type of information it contains. For example, option market information should not be displayed as foreign exchange data. The meaning of the data associated with each key is provided by the key server associated with a specific data source. We decided that operations for which the behaviour depends on the source semantics should not be provided by dictionary objects. The delegation mechanism seems to fit quite well such a design goal. Different notification strategies are necessary to fulfil the various notification needs. For example, portfolio valuation does not need, in general, to be updated continuously but the display of a traders desktop should be updated in real time. Different strategies have different costs in terms of resources allocation such as network bandwidth and processor time.

4.3 Dynamic connection of analysis tools and data sources

Financial analysis tools are connected to other tools and to data sources through gluons. Typically, dictionary objects and field objects are each assigned as servers of a TwoWayAnonymousService gluon. Whenever a dictionary or a field are updated they send a message doIt to the gluon that triggers the interaction between the client (the tool) and the server, if any. If the server is a field, the client first sends a message to the server asking for the new value and sets the value on the client. Second, a similar exchange is performed to send the name of the value so that the client can identify it. This simple protocol allows for the majority of the connections in the framework since any component that accepts a named stream of values as input can be connected with this protocol. Examples are graphical tools that display time series, and simple alarms that monitor price changes.

Gluons associated with records encapsulate more sophisticated protocols. If we want, for example to connect an option valuation tool based on some model (e.g., Black and Scholes). When the user attempts to connect the tool to a dictionary object through a gluon, the protocol executes a few steps. First it tries to identify a dictionary object to see if it is compatible (i.e. it contains information about an option). In the second step it tries to negotiate the field it needs for the calculation. For instance, with the Black-Scholes model, the tool needs five parameters to perform calculations. If all the needed fields are present then the gluon performs the transfer and triggers the calculation. In this way it is possible to implement very high level connection semantics.

4.4 Implementation

The Financial Information Framework has been implemented on a NeXT platform under NeXTstep. All the code has been written in Objective-C and Postscript. Some of the dynamic capabilities of gluons rely on the dynamic dispatching of messages provided by the language and on the fact that Objective-C is weakly typed. Gluons could have been implemented in other languages as well but an implementation in a strongly typed programming language not providing dynamic dispatching of messages as, for example,

C++ would be fairly more difficult. Presently, the whole framework represents less than ten thousand lines of code. Such a small number is possible because we are developing with NeXTstep, an object oriented environment that allows for a high degree of reuse.

5 Conclusion

This paper presents gluons as objects that mediate object cooperation. We discuss a hierarchy of gluons that provide an application-domain independent basis for the construction of domain specific interaction protocols. Gluons seem to be specially useful whenever the patterns of interaction between objects are dynamically established. The paper provides an example of a financial framework where the user performs analysis on real time data by connecting tools and information sources both encapsulated inside objects. In this framework, gluons provide a very high level connection mechanism that is very close to the user concepts.

We plan to extend our work by first analysing in more depth the notion of interaction protocol and the kind of support that should be provided by a framework in order to improve the reuse potential. We plan also to design and develop financial analysis tools that take profit of new technologies such as multimedia. We are particularly interested in techniques for the visualization of financial data.

6 Acknowledgements

The driving force for the design and implementation of Gluons was the I.A.P. (Information Access Programme) project. The IAP project explores innovative concepts and mechanisms to access, retrieve, and visualize information. Number of people collaborated directly or indirectly in this project. First, Betty Junod from CUI, helped both with design and implementation. Gérard Clément from Reuters helped with information and unconditional enthusiasm during the endless discussions about the design of the system. Pascal Fuld, and Steve Higgins, also from Reuters provided invaluable information and support. Finally we would like to express our gratitude to Alex Horwitz from UNICIBLE both for the financial support and for his diligence in making things run smoothly.

References

[Arapis91] Constantin Arapis, Specifying Object Interactions, In Object Composition, Dennis Tsichritzis, ed., Centre Universitaire d'Informatique, June 1991.

[Arapis92] C. Arapis. Dynamic Evolution of Object Behavior and Object Cooperation. Ph.D. thesis, Centre Universitaire d'Informatique, University of Geneva, Switzerland,1992.

[BigPerl89] T.J. Biggerstaff and A.J. Perlis, Software Reusability - Vol. I - Concepts and Models, Frontier Series, ACM Press, 1989.

[Deutsch89] L. Deutsch, Design Reuse and Frameworks in the Smalltalk-80 System, in Software Reusability, T.J. Biggerstaff and A.J. Perlis editors, ACM Press, pp. 57-71, 1989.

[GamWeiMar89] Erich Gamma, Andre Weinand, Rudolf Marty, Integration of a Programming Environment into ET++, Proceedings of ECOOP '89, British Computer Society Workshop Series, Cambridge University Press, 1989, ISBN 0-521-38232-7.

[GibTsi90] Simon Gibbs, Dennis Tsichritzis, Eduardo Casais, Oscar Nierstrasz, Xavier Pintado, Class Management for Software Communities, Communications of the ACM, Volume 33, number 9, September 1990, pp. 90-103.

[HelHolGan90] Richard Helm, Ian Holland, and Dipayan Gangopadhyay, Contracts: Speifying Behavioral Compositions in Object-Oriented Systems, ACM Sigplan Notices, Volume 25, number 10, october 1990, pp.169-180.

[Ingalls88] D. Ingalls, Fabrik: A Visual Programming Environment, Proceedings of OOPSLA '88, SIGPLAN Notices, volume 23, number 11, november 1988, pp. 176-190.

[JohFoo88] R.E. Johnson and B. Foote, "Designing Reusable Classes," Journal of Object-Oriented Programming, vol. 1, no. 2, 1988, pp. 22-35.

[Laffra92] Chris Laffra, Procol, a concurrent object language with protocols, delegation, persistence, and constraints, Ph.D Thesis, Amsterdam, 1992.

[Mah91] Michael Mahoney, Interface Builder and Object-Oriented Design in the NeXTstep Environment, Tutorial Notes of CHI '91, available through anonymous ftp at nova.cc.purdue.edu.

[NeXT90] NextStep Concepts manual, NeXT Computer Inc., 1990.

[OMG92] Object Management Group (OMG), The Common Object Request Broker: Architecture and Specification, Object Management Group and X Open, OMG document 91.12.1, revision 1.1, 1992.

[NieTsi91] O.M. Nierstrasz, D.C. Tsichritzis, V. de Mey and M. Stadelmann, Objects + Scripts = Applications, Tech. Report, Centre Universitaire d'Informatique, in Object Composition, Dennis Tsichritzis, ed., June 1991.

[PinTsi88] Xavier Pintado, Dennis Tsichritzis, An Affinity Browser, in Active Objects Environments, ed. D. Tsichritzis, Centre Universitaire d'Informatique, 1988.

[PinTsi90] Xavier Pintado, Dennis Tsichritzis, Satellite: Hypermedia Exploration by Affinity, in Hypertext: Perspectives, Concepts, and Applications, ed. Jacques Andre, Cambridge University Press, 1990, pp. 278-288.

[Pintado91] Xavier Pintado, Fuzzy Relationships and Affinity Links, in Object Composition, ed. D. Tsichritzis, Centre Universitaire d'Informatique, 1991.

[RajLev89] Rajendra Raj, Henry Levy, A Compositional Model for Software Reuse, Proceedings of ECOOP '89, British Computer Society Workshop Series, Cambridge University Press, 1989, ISBN 0-521-38232-7.

TAO: an object orientation kernel

Kenichi Yamazaki   Yoshiji Amagai   Masaharu Yoshida
Ikuo Takeuchi

Basic Research Laboratories, Human Interface Laboratories
Nippon Telegraph and Telephone Corporation
Midori-cho 3-9-11, Musashino-shi, Tokyo 180, Japan
e-mail: yamazaki@nuesun.ntt.jp

Abstract

This paper proposes an object-oriented programming language framework that deliberately separates mechanism from policy. Mechanisms such as slot access and message passing are designed to have a natural semantics and to be efficient. Conventional and controversial concepts such as class, inheritance, and method combination, on the other hand, are classified as policy, and are left open to the user by providing so-called hook mechanisms. TAO is a language conforming to this framework and has only a few more than twenty primitives for object-oriented programming. This paper also gives examples illustrating how conventional concepts of object-oriented programming can be implemented on top of these primitives.

1 Introduction

Object orientation is a programming paradigm that addresses not only computation mechanisms but also ways of designing and constructing large programs. It also provides an ample capability for modeling the real world in computer memory. It is therefore being incorporated into a number of programming languages, databases, software design methods, and applications such as simulation and computer graphics. There are a lot of different object-oriented programming styles, however, mainly because there are different policies on how to abstract basic computation mechanisms into the higher concepts of program construction. Such a seemingly important abstraction as the concept of class, for example, is not necessarily involved in every object-oriented programming language. In some, a central role is instead played by delegation. And the question of how to provide inheritance is still controversial among designers of programming languages.

Designers of operating systems are in a similar situation because there are also basic mechanisms for process switching and interprocess communication, and there is policy on how to combine them to schedule a number of resources. Researchers in this field have found it important to separate mechanism and policy in order to make the kernel flexible enough to cope with various multiprocess configurations[Wulf81].

We think it is also important to separate mechanism and policy in object orientation. Here mechanism refers to the invocation of a method of an object and the access to the internal state of the object. Mechanism thus encapsulates an object and, more importantly, it supports efficient execution of the object behavior. Policy here relates to the abstraction of the mechanisms to have objects share code and to make programs well-structured. It supports modeling and program design in an object-oriented style.

A Lisp-based multiple-paradigm symbolic processing language TAO introduced in this paper proposes a set of primitives that provide efficient mechanisms for object-oriented programming together with other primitives for procedural, logic, and concurrent programming. TAO will be implemented on a dedicated symbolic processor called SILENT[Yoshida90].

The objective of the TAO/SILENT system is to provide both an exploratory programming environment and a real-time programming environment for such applications as robotics, object-oriented graphics, and intelligent computer network control. Because it is crucial that TAO/SILENT simultaneously provides both flexibility in programming and high-performance execution, mechanism and policy are deliberately separated, and TAO is designed so that a variety of policies can be easily and efficiently implemented on top of the primitives.

Although there are only a few more than twenty TAO primitives for object orientation, they will support a variety of object-oriented programming styles without loss of efficiency. In this sense, TAO can be deemed as a low-level machine language of the SILENT machine, a language that provides mechanisms only and leaves the making of policy to the user of the TAO/SILENT system.

In this paper we will describe the essential half of the small set of the object orientation primitives of TAO together with other basic TAO features, and we will use examples to show the capabilities of these primitives.

2 Design of the Object Orientation Primitives of TAO

The following are the design principles of the object orientation primitives of TAO:

1. *Simplicity.* The number of primitives should be as small as possible and the semantics should be as simple as possible. Subsidiary features that can be readily derived from the primitives are left to an extension of TAO.

2. *Efficiency.* Features which will affect the system performance are supported by TAO directly as primitives, even if they can be written in TAO using other primitives. Seemingly crucial features that are not used frequently, however, are not supported directly as primitives.

3. *Message-passing metaphor.* Generic functions and message passing are different frameworks for incorporating object orientation into Lisp. Although the generic function framework seems to be natural in the context of Lisp, it lacks modularity (the capability of coupling data and operations tightly in a module) because classes (data) and methods (operations) are separate from each other. Message passing, on the other hand, is a natural metaphor for denoting each object as fully encapsulated data with its own operations — especially if each object is considered as a concurrent object[1]. We therefore adopt message passing as a basic mechanism.

4. *Policy/mechanism separation.* The most fundamental and frequently used features are classified as mechanisms: e.g., message passing, method search, and slot access.

---

[1]Although TAO is equipped with a lot of concurrent and real-time primitives that can be used to enhance a concurrent object-oriented programming, we do not have enough space to discuss this topic.

Features that will serve as scaffolding for language extension are also classified as mechanisms: e.g., missing method handler and method found hook described later. These mechanisms are supported by TAO directly and efficiently. For example, we designed TAO so that slot access is a lexical variable access which can be compiled into efficient code.

Other features are classified as matters of policy that are left open to the user who extends TAO. These are features like class, inheritance, class variable, dynamic object, and method combination. Instead of making policy fixed in the language, TAO provides such scaffolding mechanisms to enable the user to make a variety of policies as desired.

5. *Not everything is object.* We do not conceive of every data type as an object, since such primitive data as, say, number 3, character #\a, and list (foo bar) could not be considered to be able to have its own internal state and operations individually, and they will of course have their own optimized internal representation. Hence we regard the object as one of the TAO data types, one that has its own internal structure.

Examples shown in this paper will be written in the bare TAO language. Ordinary users would not use the bare TAO directly, but would instead use a TAO extension with more convenient features and syntax sugar. We do not describe such syntax sugared features that are not substantial for this paper.

3 Forms and Operators

This section outlines some unique features of TAO that will be necessary for understanding the rest of this paper.

3.1 Separation of Expression and Form

"Program as data" is one of the most important and beautiful features of symbolic processing languages like Lisp. This feature, however, tends to cause semantic gaps between interpreted and compiled execution and to degrade performance when these executions are mixed. It is nonetheless important to allow "program as data" if we want to make object orientation truly powerful. If, for example, inheritance of methods is implemented by a sort of program synthesis where pieces of superclass's method code are copied into a subclass and embedded in the subclass's environment dynamically, the source code must be conveyed and manipulated directly. It is unreasonable, however, to keep the method code as an S-expression even when it is executed, since TAO is a lexically scoped language in order to make the optimizing compilation go as far as possible. "Program as data" suffers from the conflict between semantic clarity and execution efficiency.

Our solution is to separate written expressions and executable forms strictly as first-class data. That is, an expression should be *formulated* into a form before execution. Thus an expression like (+ 10 4) cannot be evaluated unless it is formulated. An expression *expr* is formulated by the form construct:[2]

   (form *expr*)

It returns the form for *expr*, which is executable in any lexical environment similar to the one where the formulation was done. Consider the following simple example:

---
[2] *Special form* of Common Lisp is in TAO called *program construct*.

```
(defun foo (expr)
    (let ((x 0) (y 1)) (eval (form expr))) )

(foo '(write (+ x y)))
```

When the function foo is defined, its body is formulated. The information of the lexical environment about the variable locations for x and y is attached to the form of (form expr). When the expression (write (+ x y)) is formulated, x and y are properly understood as local variables by referring to the attached information. And finally, the returned form is executed by eval.

Note here that the lexical environment where the form can be evaluated is not the *same* but *similar* to the one where the original expression was formulated, since the formulation attaches information that can be detected only by static analysis of the expression. We use the word *skeleton* to denote such a similar lexical environment, ignoring concrete values of the lexical bindings. The formulation can be thought as a simple compilation and a form can be thought as a compiled code segment. Note that an arbitrary piece of program can be formulated in this construct and only the form construct needs to keep the skeleton information at run time, which implies that most programs need not keep their skeleton information at run time.

A form is a first-class entity and can be *unformulated*, or transformed back to its original expression, by the function unform unless it has been compiled in an optimized fashion. The unformulation is useful when the user does meta-programming, reflective programming, and debugging.

Though "program as data" is no longer strictly true in TAO, it will be seen in the succeeding sections that the clarity of semantics and the execution efficiency are achieved. However, hereafter, we will use the terms *expression* and *form* interchangeably when there would be no confusion.

3.2 Operators

In addition to functions, TAO has *predicates* in the sense of Prolog. Both are called *operators* generically. There are also *amphibious operators* that behave either as a function or predicate depending on the context.

An anonymous function is created by the following forms, called function creating constructs, similar to conventional lambda expressions:

    (op <*param*> <*body-form*> ...) [3]
    (op* <*param*> <*body-form*> ...)
    (op@ <*param*> <*body-form*> ...)

An anonymous predicate is created by the following forms, called predicate creating constructs:

    {op (<*param*> <*guard*> <*body-form*> ...) ...}
    {op* (<*param*> <*guard*> <*body-form*> ...) ...}
    {op@ (<*param*> <*guard*> <*body-form*> ...) ...}

---

[3] An entity enclosed by triangular brackets is not evaluated as an argument.

Here *param* corresponds to the head pattern of a Prolog predicate, and the list of lists headed by *param* corresponds to a set of guarded Horn clauses of the same functor. (Precisely speaking, however, an anonymous predicate has no functor name.)

An anonymous amphibious operator is created by the following function:

    (amphibious *function predicate*)

Operator creating constructs op, op*, and op@ differ from each other in their scope rules. When we discuss the scope rules of operators, we call the operator's body *operator region*, or simply *region*.

An operator created by op is called a simple operator. In its operator region, no lexical binding outside the region can be referred to. In other words, no lexical environment outside the operator is enclosed in the simple operator. For example, the following form creates a simple function that calculates the average of two numbers:

    (op (x y) (/ (+ x y) 2))

An operator created by op* is called a dynamic operator. In its region, all outside lexical bindings can be referred to within the extent of these bindings. A dynamic operator corresponds to a lambda closure valid only if it is used in a downward *funarg* (function argument).

An operator created by op@ is called a *closure* and plays a central role in the TAO object-oriented programming. In its region, only part of outside lexical bindings can be referred to. Closures can be created in a restricted context. We will describe the closure in detail in Section 4.2.

Note that the same symbols like op and op* are used for creating both functions and predicates. Round parentheses and braces differentiate them.[4] Functions and predicates can be named globally by defun and defpred, respectively. They can also be named locally by labels and op-let[5].

Functions and predicates can be invoked by the following operator calling forms, respectively:

    (<*function*> arg_1 arg_2 ...)
    {<*predicate*> <arg_1> <arg_2> ...}

In TAO, unlike Scheme[Clinger91], the car of an operator calling form is not evaluated unless it is prefixed by an underscore sign, in which case it is evaluated to get the operator to be invoked. In any case, when the invoked operator is amphibious, round parentheses mean a function call and braces mean a predicate call.

An operator can be unformulated to its creating form's expression, so that the user can get the original expression of the method of an object [see Example (5) in Section 5].

The rest of this paper will omit the description on predicates, since their behavior is almost symmetrical to that of functions.

---

[4] The data type of a list denoted by a pair of braces is slightly different from the data type of usual lists.
[5] op-let is a simple extension of the flet of Common Lisp.

4 Object-Oriented Programming

Although simulating an object by a set of lambda closures is a well-known programming technique in Lisp, it does not implement a full-fledged object. Here we extend the concept of lambda closure so that it is qualified as an object that has its own identity, encapsulated data and operations, and message interface.

4.1 Objects

An object is created by the following program construct:

   (obj-let ((<*slot-name*> *slot-value*)...) <*body-form*>...)

This construct binds each variable *slot-name* to the corresponding initial *slot-value*, creates an object that encloses these variables, and then executes *body-forms* successively. The body of `obj-let` is called an *object region*. Variables declared by `obj-let` are called *slot variables*, or simply *slots*, and they have lexical scope and indefinite extent. Variables declared by `let` of TAO, however, have lexical scope but dynamic extent. In this sense, `obj-let` resembles the `let` of Common Lisp but differs from it in that `obj-let` creates a first-class entity, namely an object consisting of slot variables and other information. In the object region, the object created by `obj-let` can be accessed by a read-only variable `@`, and closures for the object can be created by the `op@` construct.

An object encloses all slots that are lexically visible from the creating `obj-let`. That is, if more than one `obj-let` is nested, the object created by each inner `obj-let` encloses all slots declared by the outer `obj-let` forms (including itself). For example, assume that two `obj-let` forms are nested as follows:

   (obj-let ((a 0))
       (obj-let ((b 0)) (!a 1))
       (write a))

Here the form (!*position val*) is almost equivalent to (setf *position val*) in Common Lisp. Let the object created by the outer `obj-let` be *A* and that created by the inner one be *B*. The object *A* encloses a, and *B* encloses a and b. The variable a of the object *A* and that of the object *B* are the same. Thus 1 is printed [see also Example (3) in Section 5].

The functions `slots` and `shared-slots` can be used to get the list of the pairs consisting of each slot name and its current slot value; `slots` lists the slots of the innermost `obj-let` only, and `shared-slots` lists the slots of the outer `obj-let` forms only.

Other system-defined data types such as numbers, strings, and processes can to some extent be regarded as objects because they can have a message interface in a restricted manner or can accompany an object to extend their behavior. This paper, however, does not treat those system-defined data types in detail.

4.2 Methods

As shown in Section 3.2, a closure can be created by the `op@` construct only in an object region. It can be attached to any object with a name. An attached closure is called a *method* and its name is called its *selector*. A closure encloses part of the lexical environment; namely, all slot variables, local operators bound by `labels` and `op-let`, and local macros visible from where the closure is created. Other lexical bindings, however, such as those created by parameter binding and by the constructs `let` and `block` are not enclosed.

A closure can be thought as a pair consisting of an object and a *closure skeleton* that in turn contains the information about access to the slot variables of the object but does not contain information about the slot values. In fact, the closure skeleton is a first-class operator that can be applied to an object as its first argument in addition to the arguments specified in the `op@` form. If it is applied to an object together with other arguments, it automatically checks whether the given first argument is akin[6] to the object where the closure is created [see Example (2) in Section 5]. In other words, borrowing the terminology of lambda calculus, a closure can be said to be created by "currying" of the closure skeleton and object. Thus we often say "closure encloses an object."

An attached closure, or method, can be invoked by one of the following message-passing forms:

$$[receiver\ (<selector>\ arg_1\ arg_2\ ...)]$$
$$[receiver\ \{<selector>\ <arg_1>\ <arg_2>\ ...\}]$$

The first form invokes a function closure and the second invokes a predicate closure of an object *receiver*. These forms can be interpreted as calling a function, or a predicate named *selector*[7] in the world of the *receiver*. For example, a multiple-world model in logic programming can be readily implemented by attaching predicate closures to individual objects each of which represents a different world. In this sense, the semantics of message passing is a natural extension of the usual operator call within the context of an object. For convenience, the parentheses in a function message passing form can be omitted:

$$[receiver\ <selector>\ arg_1\ arg_2\ ...]$$

A closure is attached to an object with a selector by the following function:

(`attach-method` *object selector closure*)

It should be pointed out that the object to which a closure is attached may differ from the object enclosed by the closure. When they are the same, the closure is called a *home closure* and only the closure skeleton is attached to the object. When the objects are not the same, the closure is called an *alien closure*. When an alien closure that encloses an object A is invoked as the result of message passing to an object B, it is executed in the environment of the object A, not B. The variable `@` in the body of the closure is bound to the object A. Calling an alien closure accomplishes the simplest delegation.

4.3 Information Sharing

Information sharing is an important characteristic of object-oriented programming. Some languages make information sharing possible by class and some do it by delegation.

---

[6] An *akin object* is described in the next subsection.
[7] If *selector* is preceded by an underscore sign, it is evaluated to get the actual selector symbol [see Example (5) in Section 5].

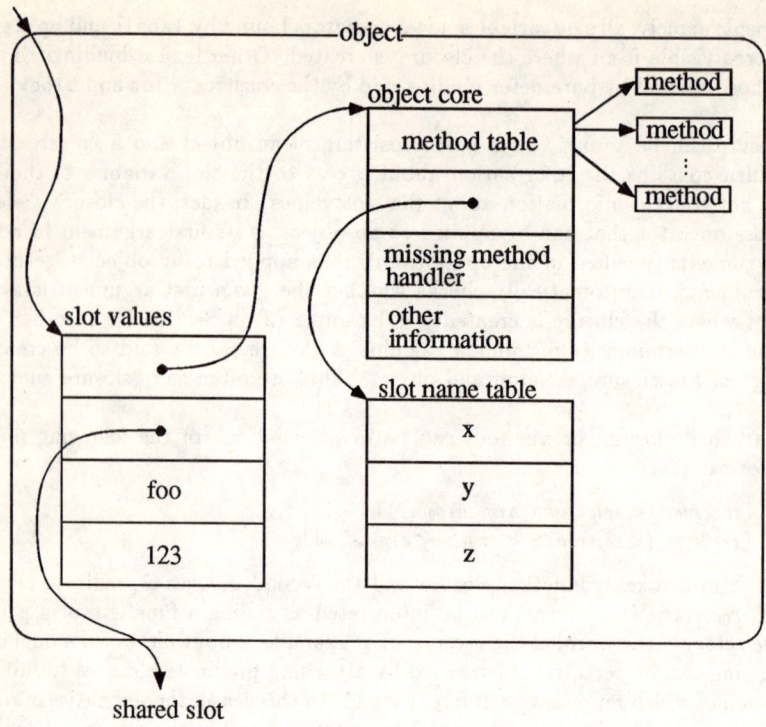

Figure 1: The internal representation of an object.

Because information sharing is a matter of policy, TAO provides no built-in class or delegation.

An object is represented internally as shown in Figure 1. It consists of a set of slot values and an *object core* which in turn consists of a method table, a slot name table, a missing method handler, and other information.

There are two types of sharing mechanisms provided: either, slot variables can be shared by nested `obj-let` forms as described before, or an akin object can be created by copying an object. And there are two types of akin objects: weakly akin objects are created by the function `new-obj`[8] and strongly akin objects are created by the function `copy-obj`. A weakly akin object has its own slot values and its own object core whose initial contents are the same as those of the original object's core. Note that methods themselves and the slot name table pointed to by the object core are not copied, but shared. Hence if a new method is attached to a weakly akin object, it does not affect the original object. A strongly akin object, on the other hand, has its own slot values, but it shares the object core with the original. Thus they always have the same set of methods and the same missing method handler [see Example (3) in Section 5].

---

[8] A weakly akin object can also be created by evaluating the same `obj-let` form more than once.

Since methods themselves are not copied, a message sent to an akin object is forwarded to the same object enclosed in an alien closure. Home closures in an akin object are still its own home closures because only their skeletons are attached to the method table. (However, a complete closure — that is, a pair consisting of the object and closure skeleton — will be returned if the user tries to get the method out of the object.)

4.4 Language Extension by Hooks

Classes and inheritance are also typical information-sharing mechanisms in conventional object-oriented programming languages. Although classes can be implemented by akin objects, inheritance requires another mechanism. Since inheritance is a matter of policy, TAO provides only a scaffolding mechanism for it. That is, TAO provides *hooks* that give the user a chance to extend the built-in method search. The user can trap the control flow, modify the program, and then resume the control.

To trap a message passing, a hook can be put immediately after method search. There are two types of hooks provided. The first one, called a *missing method handler*, is invoked when a method is not found. A missing method handler is attached to an object by the following function:

    (attach-missing-method-handler *object hook-operator*)

Although the missing method handler *hook-operator* is expected to be an amphibious operator, to simplify the following discussion, we focus only on function messages. Predicate messages are processed in a symmetric way. When a function message is sent and no method is found in the method table of the object, the function part of the handler is invoked. If no handler is attached, an error occurs. The *hook-operator* should have the following interface:

    (op@ (*hook-fn selector . args*) ...)

The argument *hook-fn* is #f (false) in most cases, and *selector* and *args* are respectively the original message's selector and arguments. The dot before *args* means that the rest of the arguments are bound to *args*. The value returned by this operator becomes the value of the original message-passing form.

The other type of hook, called a *method found hook*, is invoked immediately after a method is found. It should be hooked explicitly by the following form:

    (method-found-hook <*message-form*> *hook-fn*)

The *message-form* must be a message-passing form, and *hook-fn* should be a function of three parameters: *closure*, to which the found method is passed; *selector*; and the rest parameter *args*, to which all arguments of *message-form* is passed. If a method is found, *hook-fn* is invoked, and returns a value, which is in turn the value of the method-found-hook form. Because *message-form* is not executed automatically, the found method should be invoked explicitly in the body of *hook-fn*, if necessary. If no method is found, the missing method handler, if any, is invoked with *hook-fn* as the first argument of the handler. In the missing method handler, the user may call *hook-fn* explicitly as if a method were found in the original method-found-hook form.

5 Examples

In this section, we show small pieces of programs illustrating the power of the primitives described so far.

(1) A program that creates an object that has two methods:

```
(!aSpaceShip
 (obj-let ((x 0) (y 0))
    (attach-method @ 'distant (op@ () (sqrt (+ (* x x) (* y y)))))
    (attach-method @ 'move (op@ (dx dy) (!!+ !x dx) (!!+ !y dy) @))
    @ ))
```

Here the form (!!*fn* ... !*position* ...) is called a self-assignment and is roughly equivalent to (!*position* (*fn* ... *position* ...)).

The method that formulates and evaluates any expression in the object region can be defined as follows:

```
(!aSpaceShip
 (obj-let ((x 0) (y 0))
    ...
    (attach-method @ 'eval-in (op@ (e) (eval (form e))))
    @ ))
```

This method enables the user to attach a method after the object has been created as follows:

```
(attach-method aSpaceShip 'warp
    [aSpaceShip (eval-in '(op@ (p q) (!x p) (!y q) @))] )
```

The method `eval-in` formulates the given `op@` expression in the object region of `aSpaceShip`, evaluates it, and returns a closure.

(2) If the user declares closures in `labels` in an object region and then attaches them to the object, these internal methods can be called by each other lexically within the region; that is, no method search is needed.

```
(obj-let (...)
    (labels ((name1 (op@ ...))
             (name2 (op@ ...)) )
      (attach-method @ 'name1 #'name1)
      (attach-method @ 'name2 #'name2) )
    ...
    @ )
```

If the user wants to implement on top of TAO a typed object-oriented language like C++, in which most of method search can be removed, he would translate a message-passing form into a direct method-calling form roughly equivalent to

(_*closure-skeleton obj arg* ...)

because the method to be called can be detected at compile time. Note that the above direct method call does not involve cons cell consumption, whereas if closure-calling forms like

   (_closure arg ...)

were used, a closure would be consed every time a different constituent object is given.

(3) A simple class[9] with class variables can be implemented by nested `obj-let` forms as follows:

```
(!SpaceShip
 (obj-let ((number-of-spaceships 0))       ; class var definition
    (obj-let ((template
                (obj-let ((x 0) (y 0))     ; instance var definition
                  (attach-method @ 'distant ...)   ; method definition
                  (attach-method @ 'move ...)
                  (attach-method @ 'eval-in ...)
                  ...
                  @ )))
       (attach-method @ 'make              ; class method definition
         (op@ (x y)
              (!!1+ !number-of-spaceships)
              [(copy-obj template) (move x y)] ))
       (attach-method @ 'defmethod
         (op@ (name op@exp)
              (attach-method template name
                 [template (eval-in op@exp)] )))
       (attach-method @ 'eval-in (op@ (e) (eval (form e))))
       ...
       @ )))
```

The intermediate `obj-let` creates a class `SpaceShip` and the innermost `obj-let` creates a template of the instance. When the method `make` is invoked, it creates an object strongly akin to the template and send a message `move` to it. Then the strongly akin object is returned. The outermost `obj-let` serves as the container of a class variable `number-of-spaceships`. The method `defmethod` attaches a method to the template, so that all instances will have the same methods. The method `warp` can be attached as follows:

   [SpaceShip (defmethod 'warp '(op@ (p q) ...))]

(4) To define a class that inherits instance variables from another class, it is necessary to manipulate a program as an S-expression. Backquote and unquote facilities common to today's Lisps are used for constructing a program. Here we define a class `DisplayedSpaceShip` that is a subclass of `SpaceShip` defined in the previous example.

---

[9]This is too simple in many senses; for example, an instance cannot know its class. A practical class definition will be more complicated.

```
(!DisplayedSpaceShip
 [SpaceShip
  (eval-in
   `(obj-let ((super template))
       (obj-let ((template
                    (obj-let ,(nconc (make-slot-declaration
                                          [SpaceShip (eval-in 'template)] )
                                 '((color :red)) )
                   (attach-method @ 'move
                        (op@ (dx dy)
                             (display-erase x y)
                             (!!+ !x dx)
                             (!!+ !y dy)
                             (display-show x y color)
                             @ ))
                   ...
                   @ )))
            ...
            @ )))])
```

Note that the same variable name template is used in two different senses: the newly declared template denotes the template of the class DiplayedSpaceShip, and the other occurrences of template denote the template of the class SpaceShip. Note also that here the variable super denotes the superclass's template, not the superclass itself [see the next example]. The function make-slot-declaration returns the list of all instance-variable names with their values[10]. In this case, it returns ((x '0) (y '0)), and the variable declaration of the innermost obj-let form will be ((x '0) (y '0) (color :red)). Thus an instance of the class DisplayedSpaceShip will have three own slots (x, y, and color) and two shared slots (super and number-of-spaceships).

(5) There are a number of ways to implement the inheritance of methods. Here we define a missing method handler that searches superclasses and attaches the found method to the original class on demand. This may be the most efficient implementation.

```
(attach-missing-method-handler @       ; attach the following closure to self
    (op@ (hook-fn selector . args)
       (block
          (method-found-hook [super (_selector . args)])[11]
             (or hook-fn
                (op* (closure selector . args)
                   (attach-method @ selector
                       [@ (!!eval-in (unform !closure))] )
                   (exit block (_closure . args)) ))))))
```

---

[10] It can be easily defined by using slots described before.

[11] This intentional dot is the TAO way to pass a set of arguments to an operator in a lump as apply does in conventional Lisps. The user can write such a form as (+ x 12 . (cdr y)). Note that TAO is particular about rest-argument passing so that the only heap memory consumed is that which the user explicitly consumes. Note also that selector is evaluated here.

Assume that hooks like this one are attached to all classes. When no method is found in a class, its superclasses are searched by using the `method-found-hook` form. Since `hook-fn` is `#f` at first, the hook function is created by the `op*` form. If no method is found in a superclass one level higher, the missing method handler is invoked in a similar way: the argument `hook-fn` is the hook function created previously. If a method is found in a superclass, this hook function is invoked with the found method. It attaches the method, by using a self-assignment message,[12] to the object to which the message is sent originally, executes it, and exits the block in the first invoked missing method handler.

Method combination and multiple inheritance can be implemented by using similar (but more elaborate) techniques to get a method as an S-expression by unformulation, modify it, formulate it again to a form, and attach the resulting closure to the original object. The formulation, unformulation, and hooks again play central roles.

Those programming techniques assume that message passing occurs most frequently and that other sophisticated actions, such as attaching methods and defining classes, are much less frequent. Hence it is reasonable to let the user manipulate S-expressions directly for these infrequent actions and to expect that the performance would be degraded only a little. It should be noted again that examples above are written in the bare TAO language without any syntax sugar.

6 Performance Estimation

In this section, we evaluate the performance of message passing and slot access, which are the most crucial functions in ordinary object-oriented programs. The estimated times are calculated under the assumption that the machine cycle of SILENT is 30 nanoseconds[13] and its cache always hits.

Because of the method search, message passing requires more execution time than function call does. The method table is a hash table designed so that every search time is almost constant independently of the number of attached methods. SILENT provides a built-in simple hash instruction that enhances performance remarkably. According to a simulation, message passing requires about 370 nanoseconds more execution time than a direct function call requires. Here a direct function call means that a function body is invoked directly, so the function cannot be redefined dynamically or interactively. In comparing with an indirect function call, which is the default mode in prototyping, the additional overhead is only 220 nanoseconds on an average, which is 30 percent more overhead to the total time to invoke a function indirectly and return from it (but not including time for parameter passing and body execution). These additional overheads are small enough and the speed of message passing is comparable to that of function call. The invocation of the missing method handler is also fast: it takes only 140 nanoseconds more than method invocation. This rapid invocation will be important when a delegation-based language is made on top of TAO.

Slot variables are accessed so often that the access time is also crucial to the overall performance. Since slot variables in TAO are lexical, the access time is thus comparable to the access time for local variables: a slot variable can be accessed in 90 nanoseconds

---

[12] In this case, the value of the message-passing form is assigned to closure.
[13] This value may slightly change, since the SILENT hardware is not yet fully completed.

and a local variable is accessed in 60 nanoseconds (in typical cases). Slot access would be much slower if slots were not lexical.

7 Related Works

Self[Unger87] is a similar classless language in the sense that each object can have its own methods. If no method is found when a message is sent, the message is delegated to its parent object. To implement this feature in TAO, it is enough to prepare a slot for its parent and the missing method handler that forwards the message to the parent. Object Lisp[Byers87] is also a classless language but it is more dynamic than Self, which in turn is more dynamic than TAO. TAO is a highly lexical language, although it is by nature capable of supporting efficient dynamic computation. That is, TAO can cope with a wide range of "lexicality" degrees.

When comparing TAO with more complicated languages such as CLOS[Steele90] with MOP[Kiczales91], we should be careful because their goals are different. TAO provides only primitives and mechanisms for extension. More convenient languages will be constructed on top of TAO, and end users will program in those languages. CLOS, on the other hand, is a self-contained full-fledged language. Hence we compare CLOS and TAO from the viewpoint whether CLOS can be efficiently implemented on top of TAO. The basic mechanism of CLOS is a generic function. Since we prefer the message-passing metaphor as described in Section 2, it is impossible to straightforwardly implement generic functions in TAO. A generic function can be emulated by attaching a dispatcher (specializer in CLOS terminology) explicitly to each TAO function at a cost of performance degradation. The MOP features such as multiple inheritance and method combination can be implemented by using PCL-like techniques[Kiczales91]. Such a way of implementation, however, is feasible on any Lisp language and is not concerned with the object-orientation mechanisms of TAO. Flavors[Weinreb83], on the other hand, which has message-passing-based multiple inheritance and method combination, can be efficiently implemented on top of TAO by using hooks. The instance variables of CLOS are accessed dynamically by the function `slot-value` that can be used by anyone outside the object. The instance variables of TAO, on the other hand, are lexically scoped, giving our approach the advantage of encapsulation and efficient execution.

TAO resembles C++[Stroustrup86] in that both are highly lexical languages, but TAO is more flexible than C++ because it has hook mechanisms that give it fertile extensibility and because it is based on a powerful symbolic processing language Lisp as well as an elegant logic programming language Prolog.

8 Conclusion

We proposed a simple framework for object-oriented programming in a multiple-paradigm language TAO. Our framework separates efficient mechanisms comprising a basis of object orientation (such as objects, methods, and message passing) from policy, which determines the abstraction and utilization of these mechanisms. The concepts of object and method are designed as a natural extension of lambda closure, and the concept of message passing is designed as a natural extension of function call. Policy is intentionally left open to the user who wants to extend TAO. The object orientation primitives of

TAO, like the other paradigm primitives incorporated in TAO, thus become small and elegant but have nonetheless a potential for language extension and evolution. In this sense, TAO deserves to be called an object orientation kernel.

References

[Byers87] G. Byers, et al. *Allegro Common Lisp Manual*, Coral Software Corp. and Franz, Inc., 1987.

[Clinger91] W. Clinger and J. Rees (Eds.). Revised^4 Report on the Algorithmic Language Scheme, 1991.

[Kiczales91] G. Kiczales, J. Rivières, and D.G. Bobrow. *The Art of the Metaobject Protocol*, MIT Press, 1991.

[Steele90] G.L. Steele Jr.. *Common Lisp the language, second edition*, Digital Press, 1990.

[Stroustrup86] B. Stroustrup. *The C++ Programming Language*, Addison-Wesley, 1986.

[Unger87] D. Unger and R.B. Smith. Self: The Power of Simplicity, OOPSLA '87 Conference Proceedings, p. 227-242, October, 1987.

[Weinreb83] D. Weinreb, D. Moon, and R.M. Stallman. *Lisp Machine Manual*, Fifth Edition, System Version 92, LMI, 1983.

[Wulf81] W.A. Wulf, R. Levin, and S.P. Harbison. HYDRA/C.mmp: An Experimental Computer System, McGraw-Hill, 1981.

[Yoshida90] H. Yoshida, I. Takeuchi, K. Yamazaki and Y. Amagai. The Design of a List Processor SILENT, IPSJ SIG Notes 90-SYM-56, 1990 (in Japanese).

Appendix: Primitives for Object Orientation

	syntax	type	description
*	[receiver (<selector> arg...)] [receiver {<selector> <arg>...}]		message-passing form
*	(obj-let ((<slot-name> slot-value)...) <body-form>...)	pc	creates an object and executes *body-forms* in sequence
*	@		read-only variable representing self
*	(op@ <param> <body-form> ...) {op@ <clause> ...}	pc	creates a closure
*	(copy-obj *object*)	fn	creates a strongly akin object
*	(new-obj *object*)	fn	creates a weakly akin object
	(strong-akin? *object₁ object₂*)	fn	checks if objects are strongly akin
	(weak-akin? *object₁ object₂*)	fn	checks if objects are weakly akin
*	(attach-method *object selector closure*)	fn	attaches a method named *selector* to *object*
*	(method-found-hook <message-form> *hook-fn*)	pc	executes *message-form* with a hook *hook-fn*
*	(attach-missing-method-handler *object hook-operator*)	fn	attaches a missing method handler to *object*
*	(slots *object*)	fn	returns a list of slots
*	(shared-slots *object*)	fn	returns a list of shared slots
	(closure-obj *closure*)	fn	returns the object enclosed by *closure*
	(closure-skeleton *closure*)	fn	returns the *closure* skeleton
	(missing-method-handler *object*)	fn	returns the missing method handler
	(selectors *object*)	fn	returns a list of selectors
	(method *object selector*)	fn	returns the method named *selector* in *object*
	(slot-value <slot-name>)	pc	returns the slot value that can be assigned outside the object
	(attach-obj *x object*)	fn	attaches an adjoint object to a pseudo object *x* (e.g. process)
	(adjoint-obj *x*)	fn	returns the adjoint object of *x*
	(obj-put *object symbol value*)	fn	puts *value* whose property name is *symbol* to *object* core
	(obj-get *object symbol*)	fn	gets the value whose property name is *symbol* from *object* core
	(obj-remove *object symbol*)	fn	removes the property of *symbol* from *object* core

*: described in this paper, *fn*: function, *pc*: program construct

If the last argument of attach-*XXX* is _ (a special value that denotes an undefined value), then those functions are interpreted as if they were named detach-*XXX*.

Change Management and Consistency Maintenance in Software Development Environments Using Object Oriented Attribute Grammars

Katsuhiko Gondow   Takashi Imaizumi   Yoichi Shinoda

Takuya Katayama

Tokyo Institute of Technology
Department of Computer Science
e-mail: gondow@cs.titech.ac.jp

Abstract

In this paper, we consider describing software development environments (SDEs) using a computational model OOAG (Object Oriented Attribute Grammar) [Shi89] [SK90], which incorporates functions for managing changes and maintaining consistency. In SDEs, the change managenent and consistency maintenance are key issues and OOAG is suitable for describing them. Software objects in SDEs have many derived values, and software objects and their derived values have complex relations with each other. Careless human activities often cause inconsistencies among software objects and it usually costs a lot to recover them. OOAG provides declarative descriptions to re-compute automatically derived values based on change propagation and to check relations among software objects, which help recovering activities of programmers.

OOAG treats SDEs as aggregated active objects, i.e. tree structures, where software products are distributed. Managing changes of derived values and consistency among software objects are described over tree structures in declarative manner. Attributes associated with nodes are re-computed automatically, if necessary.

OOAG is a computational model with the following extensions to standard attribute grammars(AGs): (1) OOAG can change tree structures depending upon their attribute values. (AGs that have this function are called higher order attribute grammars [HM89] [TC90]). (2) OOAG can describe message passing which pastes temporary attributes and their attribution rules to the tree structure.

The aim of this paper is to show that our approach of treating SDEs as aggregated objects is natural and OOAG's features are suited for the task of describing change management and consistency control in structure-oriented software development environments.

1 Introduction

In this paper, we consider describing software development environments (SDEs) using a computational model OOAG (Object Oriented Attribute Grammar) [Shi89] [SK90], which incorporates functions for managing changes and maintaining consistency.

In SDEs, the change management and consistency maintenance are key issues and OOAG is suitable for describing them. Software objects in SDEs have many derived values, and software objects and their derived values have complex relations with each other. Careless human activities often cause inconsistencies among software objects and it usually costs a lot to recover them.

OOAG provides declarative descriptions to re-compute automatically derived values based on change propagation and to check relations among software objects, which help recovering activities of programmers. OOAG treats SDEs as aggregated active objects, i.e. tree structures, where software products are distributed. Managing changes of derived values, consistency among software objects in tree structures are described in a declarative manner. Attributes associated with nodes are re-computed automatically, if necessary.

Attribute grammars(AGs) [Knu68] underlying OOAG, introduced by D. E. Knuth, have been studied as tools for formal specification of programming languages and automatic-generation of compilers [Fal84]. In recent research, however, syntax-directed editors based on AGs have been considered useful in describing and generating interactive programming environments [RT89]. Declarative structures, separation of semantics and syntax definition, local description resulting in high readability and high maintainability, and clear description caused by functional computation of attributes are the positive characteristics of AGs.

Thus AGs can be effective tools for systematically describing, generating, and maintaining large scale software objects. But, AGs lack the function that describes dynamic semantics, which makes it difficult to apply it to object management systems. For example, Gandalf project [Not85] adopted action routine, not AGs for its language system. In order to guarantee high interoperability of large scale integrated systems, we have to exploit a new high level specification language that can describe them in uniform manner.

To describe SDEs and language system as a structure-oriented environment, we have introduced a computational model OOAG [Shi89] [SK90] [1], which combines AGs and object oriented programming paradigm, while preserving the advantages of standard AGs. OOAG are suitable especially for describing huge aggregated objects with message passing among them and change propagations rather than inheritance.

The main extension of OOAG is as follows:

1. OOAG can change tree structures depending upon their attribute values. (AGs that have this function is called higher order attribute grammars [HM89] [TC90]).

2. OOAG can describe message passing which pastes temporary attributes and their attribution rules, which is completely different from the approach of [DR85].

While OOAG in [SK90] can describe dynamic semantics using descending message passing based on 1-visit AG [DJL88], OOAG presented here can handle more flexible dynamic semantics. Higher orderness of OOAG allows tree structures to be modified incrementally by using attribute values or interacting with users via messages. This extension is concise and natural because static specification corresponding to standard AGs and dynamic specification by message passing are separated syntactically and semantically, and each computation of both specifications is functional. In the next section, Section 2, we present the principles of OOAG with a simple example, emphasizing this point.

Our basic idea using OOAG's features is to describe SDEs as aggregated objects. Each object is an active object where methods are attached, and interacts with its parent, siblings, and children objects by means of attributes and message passing. Objects appeared in SDEs are treated as uniform active objects of OOAG resulting in high interoperabilities. In addition to the ability of change management and consistency maintenance, OOAG can guide programmers

---

[1] [Shi89] discussed basic ideas of OOAG. [SK90] focused on attribute evaluation algorithm suited for OOAG.

when inconsistencies among software objects are detected, and can enforce organization of software objects on programmers. High readability and locality of OOAG make it easy to understand descriptions of the system resulting in high maintainability. In Section 3, we discuss these advantages obtained when applying OOAG to describing SDEs. In Section 4, a summary is presented.

2 The Principles of OOAG

Even if we apply AGs to any system requiring modifications of tree structures or changes to attribute values, its specification describes only consistent states of a system and lacks dynamic specifications of the system. There have been some experiments to add to AG, the ability to specify dynamic behaviors of a system. The Synthesizer Generator(CSG) [RT89], which is a generating system of syntax directed editors, provides cut-and-paste and tree-transformation operations while retaining the advantages of attribute grammars. Yet in our experiments, CSG turned out to be inadequate when applied to describe object management system or software development system, mainly because it cannot modify tree structures without human guidance. Instead of the approach used in CSG, we have extended AGs by introducing message passing mechanism of object oriented programming paradigm.

2.1 Attributed Trees as Persistent Objects

In OOAG, all attributed trees are regarded as objects. *Static specification*, which corresponds to standard AGs, defines internal objects, relations between attributes and so on. More precisely, static specification consists of the following:

1. Construction rules of the form **class** $X_0 \to R[X_1, \ldots, X_m]$

   These rules determine the internal structures of an object. X_0 is the object to be defined, and $X_1, \ldots, X_m$ are its internal objects. R is a label for the rule and is used as a constructor of the object being described.

2. Declarations of static inherited attributes, static synthesized attributes, static local attributes, and native attributes

   Declarations of static attributes are attached to X_i ($0 \leq i \leq n$), which form is $X_i(i_1, \ldots, i_p | s_1, \ldots, s_q)$, where $i_1, \ldots, i_p$ are static inherited attributes, and $s_1, \ldots, s_q$ are static synthesized attributes. Whereas static synthesized and inherited attributes are associated with object X_i, static local attributes are associated with construction rules. A declaration of static local attribute 'l' has the form '**local** l' and is put down with static semantic rules described below.

   Static inherited attributes and static synthesized attributes are considered as external interfaces of an object. Native attributes supersedes terminal symbols, and holds the object state. We also use the term 'native attributes' for internal objects X_i ($1 \leq i \leq n$), because internal objects also hold the object state. Native attributes are similar to instance variables in object oriented paradigm.

3. A set of static semantic rules

   These rules define the values of static synthesized attributes of an object and the values of static inherited attributes of the object's internal objects and the values of static local attributes associated with a construction rule if necessary. The form of each static semantic rule is $a = f(a_1, \ldots, a_r)$, where a is an attribute to be defined by $a_1, \ldots, a_r$, which are others' attributes in the description; and finally, f is a function on $a_1, \ldots, a_r$. A notation 'X.i' represents a static attribute 'i' of an object 'X' and a notation 'n' represents a native attribute 'n' or a static local attribute 'n'. Of course, dependency graph of static attributes over any tree must be acyclic to be computable. Note that X_i ($1 \leq i \leq n$) representing internal objects can appear on the right-hand-side of static semantic rules. It means that static attributes can be bound with tree structure[2] of any subtree as their values.

2.2 Dynamic Activation of Objects

A set of dynamic specifications which describe messages passing defines dynamic behaviors of objects. Dynamic specification consists of the following:

1. Activation rules

   They are in the form $in_1, \ldots, in_s \Rightarrow out_1, \ldots, out_t (s, t \geq 0)$, where $in_i (1 \leq i \leq s)$ is an input message and $out_j (1 \leq j \leq t)$ is an output message. All messages take the form $Obj : mesg\_name(i_1, \ldots, i_p | s_1, \ldots, s_q)$, where Obj is an object, $mesg\_name$ is a message name, $i_1, \ldots, i_p$ are dynamic inherited attributes, and $s_1, \ldots, s_q$ are dynamic synthesized attributes. Similar to static local attributes, a dynamic local attiribute declaration '**local** l' is put down with dynamic semantic rules described below.

   Dynamic attributes are temporary attributes attached to objects when messages are being passed among objects, and dynamic attributes disappear after all of them are computed. Obj must be one of $X_0, \ldots, X_n$, **self**. When Obj is X_0, source or destination of a message is the parent of X_0. In order to send to or receive from X_0 itself, a keyword **self** is used.

   Activation rules have the following meaning: the dynamic attributes and their dynamic semantic rules will be pasted to the object after the object receives all input messages from the specified objects, and output messages will be sent simultaneously to the specified objects. If no input messages are specified, these rules will be effective without receiving any messages. So dynamic behavior depending on the values of static attributes can be described. Dynamic attributes pasted by message passing will be evaluated according to their dependencies, so message passing and evaluation of dynamic attributes are basically independent. It means that message passing and evaluation of dynamic attributes are done asynchronously. We discuss this point later again.

2. A set of dynamic semantic rules

   Each dynamic semantic rule is in the form $a = f(a_1, \ldots, a_r)$, which has the same form as that of static semantic rule, with the exception that values of native attributes can be defined and dynamic attributes can appear in $a_1, \ldots, a_r$. The form to define values of native attributes is $(\mathbf{new}\, a) = f(a_1, \ldots, a_r)$ where **new** is a reserved keyword, which distinguishes new next values of native attributes from old ones. Values of native attributes are replaced by new values after evaluation of dynamic attributes is completed. This form permits structure tree to be expanded as a result of dynamic attribute computation. Note that the keyword **new** must not appear on the right-hand-side of dynamic semantic rules, because new values of native attributes cannot be accessed until evaluation of dynamic attributes

---

[2] In current OOAG, object trees bound by attributes are not attributed.

is done. OOAG is a sort of higher order attribute grammars since a structure tree may be stored in an attribute and an attribute value can be used to define the expansion of a structure tree during dynamic attribute evaluation.

In dynamic semantic rules, values of static attributes can be referred to and dealt with constants. Similar to static attributes, dependency graph of dynamic attributes must be acyclic.

Dynamic computation of an object is invoked by sending a message to the object. This message has appropriate values bound by dynamic input attributes[3]. The object that receives the message selects corresponding dynamic semantic rules, pastes dynamic semantic rules and sends messages to objects which appear on the right hand side of the activation rule. An object repeats the same actions when it receives a newly generated message. Dynamic computation of objects terminates when all values of the dynamic attributes are consistent with each other.

Dynamic specification presented here allows us to describe more flexible message passing than that of [SK90]. For example, ascendant message, and message passing among children can be described.

```
class X₀(...|...) → R[X₁(...|...), X₂(...|...)]
    /* ascendant message */
    X₁ : message₁(...|...), X₂ : message₂(...|...)
        ⇒ X₀ : message₀(...|...)
    /* message passing among children */
    X₁ : message₁(...|...)
        ⇒ X₂ : message₂(...|...)
```

2.3 OOAG Evaluation Loop

Computation of Object in OOAG progresses by evaluating static attributes and dynamic attributes by turns. We call this repetition **evaluation loop**(figure 1).

(1) At initial state, an object tree is just statically evaluated. That is, all values of static attributes in the object are consistent with each other, and there are no dynamic attributes.

(2) When the object receives a message, dynamic attributes are pasted while messages pass among its internal objects. Message passing will be also invoked without receiving any messages if there are activation rules with no inputs messages.

(3) Pasted dynamic attributes are evaluated according to their dynamic semantic rules. Native attributes are also evaluated, if necessary.

(4) After (3), old values of native attributes are replaced by new values.

If the values of native attributes are changed during (4), and there exists static attributes that depend on these native attributes, then the evaluation process of static attributes is executed for the entire attributed tree in consistent with the static semantic rules. Then, it starts all over again.

---
[3]Dynamic input attributes are dynamic inherited attributes or dynamic synthesized attributes.

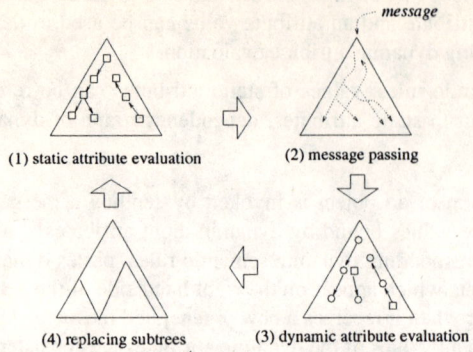

Figure 1: evaluation loop in OOAG

2.4 Simple Example

We will describe a simple example about program object 'P' and module object 'M'.

```
/* static specification of P */
class P(|executable)
  -> Program[M(|obj_code),M(|obj_code)]
  {
    P.executable=link(M$1.obj_code,M$2.obj_code);
  }

/* static specification of M */
class M(|obj_code)
  -> Module[ROBJ(|),cache,current]
  {
    M.obj_code = current ;
  }

/* dynamic specification of M */
  M:retrieve(revision,update|req_obj)
    case (in_cache(cache, revision))
      =>
      {
        M.req_obj = look_up(cache, M.revision) ;
        (new current) = if(M.update == true, M.req_obj, current) ;
      }
    otherwise
      => ROBJ:retrieve(revision|source)
      {
        M.req_obj = compile(ROBJ.source);
        (new cache) = lru_update(cache, M.revision, M.req_obj);
        (new current) = if(M.update == true, M.req_obj, current) ;
      }
```

Object P consists of two modules M in this example. The static attribute executable is maintained as values of the function link which links the object code of module M (Module M has the static synthesized attribute object_code in static semantic rule of P.)

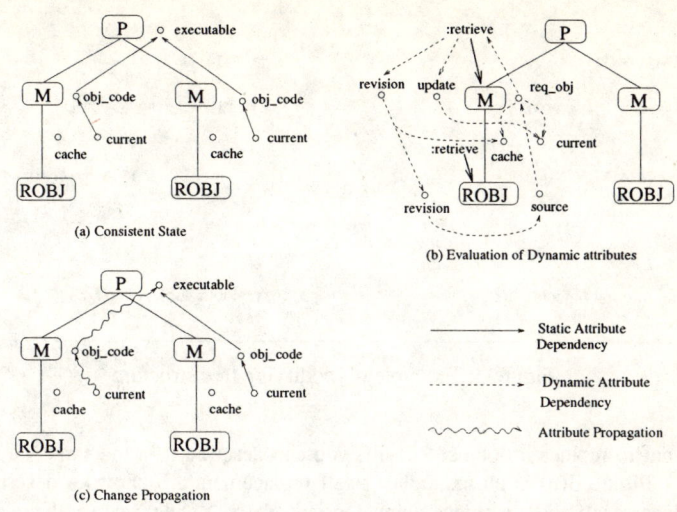

Figure 2: Behavior of object P

In the static semantic rule of M, it is declared that M has a component object ROBJ that is assumed to give version control services to the source text of the program. Two native attributes cache and current are also declared.

In the dynamic semantic rules of M, message :retrieve is implemented. This message will be sent with a revision number revision of the requested object code and a flag update to specify if retrieved object code is treated as the current object code of this module. If the object code corresponding to requested revision is in the cache (first case), it will be taken out of cache and treated as output of this message. At the same time, a value of update will be tested and a value of current will be replaced if true. If the object code corresponding to the requested revision is not in cache (second case), message :retrieve will be sent to ROBJ with requested revision number. The resulting source will be compiled to compute an output and cache will be updated. Then the flag update will be tested again and all necessary actions will be taken, if any. Note that whenever current value is changed, the static semantic rules compares a value of M.obj_code to current value and if they are different, it propagates the change to object P.

Figure 2 shows, of object P, (a) the quiescent state, (b) the evaluation of message :retrieve updating cache and current, and (c) the behavior of the object in change propagation.

2.5 Modification of Tree Structures

As mentioned above, it is required that attributed tree be modified during the computational process. In OOAG, by using the keyword **new**, replacement of tree structures are easily described in the same form as native attributes, since internal objects are treated as native attributes.

Figure 3(a) shows a description that an object X replaces A$1 and A$2 with a message's dynamic inherited attribute newobj, and an internal object instance A$1 respectively, when it receives message :replace_child.

```
class X                                    class X
  -> R1[A(|),A(|)]                           -> R1[A(|),B(|)]

X:replace_child(newobj|)                   X:replace_me(newA,newC|)
  =>                                         =>
  {                                          {
    (new A$1) = X.newobj ;                     (new X) = R2[X.newA',X.newC] ;
    (new A$2) = A$1 ;                        }
  }
                                             -> R2[A(|),C(|)]

     (a) replacing internal objects              (b) replacing object itself
```

Figure 3: Example of modifying tree structure

If you want to replace an object X itself, you can describe it in the same way as the child replacement. Figure 3(b) is an example of self replacement. It shows a description that an object X replaces itself with an object which consists of newA and newC (both are carried by the dynamic inherited attributes), when the object receives message :replace_me. The label R2 of construction rule is used as an object constructor in the description of the dynamic semantic rules. Note that the change propagation of static attributes will be invoked after the replacements of objects.

2.6 Object Sharing

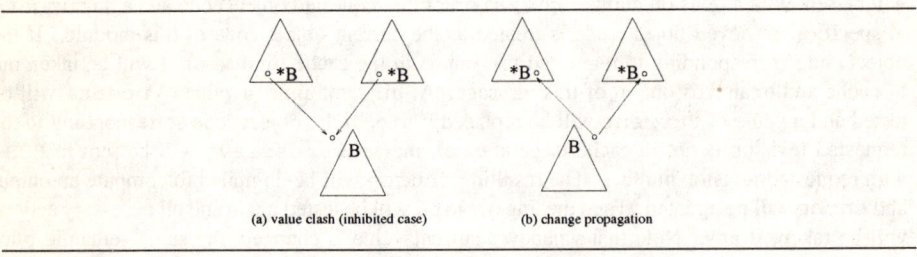

(a) value clash (inhibited case)   (b) change propagation

Figure 4: Named objects

We introduce *named objects* for sharing objects. Each object has an unique name in a system and can be accessed by its name. That is, name is an object identifier. Adding the symbol '*' to internal objects in construction rules specifies reference to a named object. A name of an object can be accessed by adding '&' to the object and the name can also be an attribute value. Any object that refers to a named object can not define the named object's static inherited attributes unless it is the parent of the named object, otherwise value conflicts will result (figure 4(a)). Unlike static inherited attributes, static synthesized attributes from named objects can be used in the static semantic rules as usual. In this case, changes of these static synthesized attributes caused by sending a message to a named object will also be propagated to all referring points (figure 4(b)). In dynamic specifications, there are no restrictions in using named objects. A message from an object A referring to an object B is treated as a message from a parent of B by B. When an object receives same messages from objects referring to it and its parent, these messages and their dynamic attributes are distinguished by their message's paths. That is, each message makes instances of dynamic attributes and pastes them. Consequently, programmers do not have to worry about message conflict.

2.7 Message Guarding

We mentioned above that the phase (2) and (3) in section 2.3 are completely independent, but actual computations of (2) and (3) are interleaved in current OOAG, because OOAG allows us to describe message guarding. Message guarding is a mechanism to control message passing depending on values of dynamic, static and native attributes. More precisely, message guarding is a multi-branch condition expression to choose output messages and dynamic semantic rules after all input messages are received. The form of message guard is as follows:

$$\begin{array}{l} \textit{input-messages} \\ \quad \textbf{case } \textit{condition}_1 \\ \quad \Rightarrow \textit{output-messages}_1 \\ \quad \{\textit{dynamic-semantic-rules}_1\} \\ \quad \ldots \\ \quad \textbf{case } \textit{condition}_n \\ \quad \Rightarrow \textit{output-messages}_n \\ \quad \{\textit{dynamic-semantic-rules}_n\} \end{array}$$

The *output-messages*$_i$ and *dynamic-semantic-rules*$_i$ corresponding to the first satisfied *condition*$_i$ are chosen. Any attribute except dynamic output attribute[4] can appear in message guarding. Moreover, message guarding restricts dynamic semantic rules to be computable as follows:

> Each dynamic input attribute appeared in both guard expressions and input messages must not depend on any dynamic output attributes in input messages.

For example, in the following dynamic specification;

class $X_0 \rightarrow R[X_1(|), X_2(|)]$
$X_0 : m_0(in|out), X_2 : m_2(in|out)$
case $(P(X_2.out))$
  ...
otherwise
  ...

$X_2.out$, which is an input dynamic attribute, can depend on neither $X_0.out$ nor $X_2.in$, but $X_0.in$ can depend on them, where P is a predicate function.

Message guarding make it possible to guide a message propagation to appropriate objects by referring to values of attributes. Message guarding is also useful to describe dynamic behavior depending on the values of static attributes, because a dynamic semantic rule will be effective without receiving any messages when no input messages are specified. For example, we can describe a behavior of an object, when some assertion fails

---

[4]Dynamic output attributes are dynamic synthesized attributes of X_0 or dynamic inherited attributes of X_i ($1 \leq i \leq n$).

$$\textbf{class } exp(|val) \rightarrow Div[exp(|val), exp(|val)]$$
$$\textbf{case } (equal(exp\$3.val, 0))$$
$$\Rightarrow exp\$1 : error(|message)$$
$$\{exp\$1.message = \text{"divided by zero"};\}$$

This script shows that an error message will be sent to the parent without receiving any messages only if the condition $(equal(exp\$3.val, 0))$ is true.

3 Using OOAG to Describe Software Development Environments

In this section, we discuss advantages obtained when using OOAG to describe SDEs.

SDEs used widely in the present are based on tree structured file system where both software objects and tools are scattered and they are loosely connected. File hierarchy tends to be constructed in a very ad hoc and arbitrary manner. This makes it difficult for programmers to understand the whole project and difficult to reuse software products for other projects, although tree seems to be a good structure that humans can manage directly.

As mentioned in section 2, declarative descriptions of OOAG consist of type definitions of aggregated objects (construction rules), definitions of static attribute computations (static semantic rules), and definitions of methods (activation rules and dynamic semantic rules). The collection of static attributes constitute a derived database of facts of aggregated objects. Message passing over aggregated objects is invoked by human activity or when some condition (message guard) is satisfied. Aggregated objects can be modified as a result of message passing.

Our basic idea using these features is to describe SDEs as aggregated objects. The advantages of this approach is as follows:

1. All conceptual entities like projects, teams, and so on as well as physical products like programs and manuals are treated uniformly as active objects.

    All objects appeared in SDEs have far more diverse types: integer, syntax tree, documenets, teams, and the entire project. We can treat all of them as uniform active objects of OOAG, which provide an unified perspective to SDE implementors.

2. OOAG can maintain derived values automatically.

    There are a lot of derived values in software objects. A compiled code of its source program is a typical derived value. Computing derived values by invoking tools as human activity may cause an inconsistent state among software objects.

    OOAG can keep derived values consistent by invoking tools automatically.

3. SDEs described in OOAG are active objects, which operate as an object management system in itself, since each object of the SDEs has access methods represented by dynamic specification of OOAG.

4. OOAG can guide programmers when inconsistencies are detected.

    Scattered software objects have complex relations with each other. OOAG can check them in the same ways as syntax-directed editors support, for example, the creation and inference of type declarations for used but undeclared variables. Human activities are required to repair broken relations if complex, creative judgments of programmers are needed. In these situations, OOAG can notify what has happened to programmers and help them by invoking an appropriate tool.

5. OOAG can enforce organization of software objects on programmers.

   Construction rules of OOAG enforce appropriate organization of software objects on programmers and OOAG can modify the structure of software objects incrementally by the progress of programmer's task. Proper repetition of structure modification helps programmers to guide the order of their activities, and relieves them from worrying about whether they obey their informal specification or not. Proper structure controlled by system make it easy to reuse software products, also.

6. High readability and locality of OOAG facilitate an evolution of the environment described above.

   Descriptions in OOAG are declarative, local, separated into structure definitions, relation management definitions, massage passing definitions. The declarativeness and locality of OOAG results in maintainability.

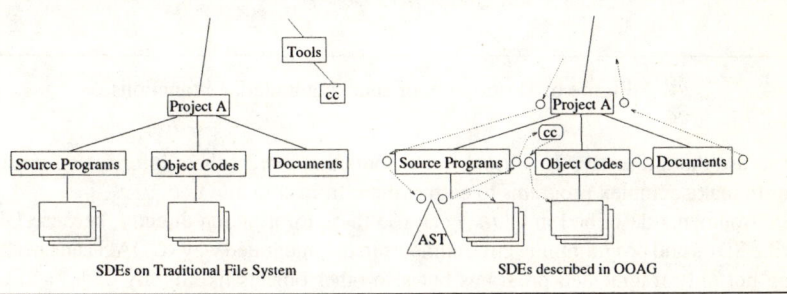

Figure 5: Conceptual Image of SDE described in OOAG

Figure 5 shows our conceptual image of SDEs described in OOAG. Attributed trees representing source programs are connected to other software objects by attributes and message passing definitions where their structure are strictly typed, while files and directories representing SDEs on file systems are loosely connected and untyped (managed in a very ad hoc and arbitrary manner). In SDEs using OOAG, each software object knows tools related to it as its methods. The environment is a derived database of software objects, which interact with each other by message passing.

In the following sections, We discuss further with several descriptions as examples.

3.1 Maintaining relations among software objects

A syntax-directed editor manages many relations in a program like a relation between a definition and a reference of function arguments. Structure trees representing programs in a syntax-directed editor (abstract syntax tree) contains a lot of such many useful information. But there are no

```
PROJECT(|)
    ->aProject[LIB(|def_func_table),
    SRCS(all_def_func_table|def_func_table)]
    {
        SRCS.all_def_func_table = append(LIB.def_func_table,
                                         SRCS.def_func_table);
    }

SRCS(all_def_func_table|def_func_table)
    -> Sources[SRC(all_def_func_table|def_func_table),
               SRC(all_def_func_table|def_func_table)]
    {
        SRC$1.all_def_func_table = SRCS.all_def_func_table ;
        SRC$2.all_def_func_table = SRCS.all_def_func_table ;
        SRCS.def_func_table = append(SRC$1.def_func_table,
                                     SRC$2.def_func_table) ;
    }

SRC(all_def_func_table|def_func_table)
    -> Source[FUNC_LIST(|def_func_table,ref_func_table)]
    {
        local undef_func_table;
        undef_func_table = check_undef_func(SRC.all_def_func_table,
                                            FUNC_LIST.ref_func_table);
        SRC.def_func_table = FUNC_LIST.def_func_table ;
    }
```

Figure 6: Description of checking undefined functions

ways to use them directly. It is usual to use tools that extract these information from program text or to make complex programs to extract them from structure trees.

Environments described in OOAG can use these information directly, because OOAG can describe SDEs and programming environments in the integrated way. OOAG can check relations among not only fragmented programs but also other objects like library codes and can repair them when their relations become inconsistent because of some changes. There are two ways to maintain these derived values: one is to compute them by invoking a message like 'make' to compile a source program, the other is to keep them consistent by change propagation. Dynamic semantic rules in OOAG supports the former case and static semantic rules in OOAG supports the latter case.

A program in figure 6 is an example of checking relations by change propagations, where it is assumed that a project consists of two source files and a library, and a source file consists of several functions like programming language C. SRC keeps used but not defined function names as a static local attribute undef_func_table. Adding, or removing functions causes OOAG evaluator to propagate these changes and to keep static attributes consistent.

SDEs should notify programmers when relations among software objects become inconsistent as human activities are usually required to repair them. Message guarding mechanism of OOAG is useful to describe these situations. Remember that a guard expression with no input messages means that the dynamic semantic rule will be invoked only if the guard condition is satisfied. For example, you might describe the following description in order to notify a programmer of undefined functions when a list undef_func_table in the figure 6 is not empty.

```
SRC(all_def_func_table|def_func_table)
```

```
-> Source[FUNC_LIST(|def_func_table,ref_func_table)]

case(NotEmpty(undef_func_table))
    => SYSTEM:notify(|person, message)
    {
        SYSTEM.person = SRC.programmer;
        SYSTEM.message = undef_func_table ;
    }
```

It is assumed that SYSTEM is a pseudo object representing an interface to the external environment. It might be good idea to implement programmers as pseudo-objects to send messages easily to an appropriate person in charge.

Of course, OOAG can maintain software objects by sending messages explicitly. In the next example below, the dynamic semantic rule will be invoked only if the condition (SOURCE.time>OBJECT.time) is satisfied when receving message make.

```
MODULE:make(|)
    case ( SOURCE.time > OBJECT.time )
        =>
        { (new OBJECT) = compile(SOURCE);}
```

That is, OBJECT will be re-compiled only if OBJECT is older than SOURCE when an object MODULE receives a message make.

3.2 Enforcing Software Object Organization

In UNIX[5] file system, programmers tend to organize their working areas in a very ad hoc and arbitrary manner, while files around the root of operating system are carefully arranged in good order. Guidelines on how to layout software objects often cause a lot of pains to programmers and are not effective as they are often inappropriate. Moreover, there are often several alternatives to organize software objects because of their complex relations and their evolutions.

Construction rules in OOAG provide types for structures underlying their working areas. These structures can be modified incrementally with the progress of their tasks, and guide their activities. The governed structures are easy for programmers to understand, and also make it easy to reuse software objects. This mechanism of OOAG provide a good perspective when the modifications are required.

In the next example (figure 7), a reorganization of documents and sources is described in the mechanism of modifying structure. An object PROJECT, which is assumed here, is organized into document part and source part separatedly at first, and then each document is required to be placed at the corresponding source program fragment. To satisfy this requirement, a programmer sends message ChangePattern2, which transforms the object into two pairs of source programs and its corresponding documents (figure 8). A with expression has the same meaning as 'with expression' in CSG. The syntax of a with expression is

> **with**($expression_0$){
> $pattern_1$: $expression_1$,
> $pattern_2$: $expression_2$,
>   ...
> $pattern_n$: $expression_n$ }

---
[5] UNIX is a trademark of AT&T Bell Labs.

```
PROJECT(|)
    -> Pattern1[ DOCUMENTS(|), SOURCES(|) ]

    PROJECT:ChangePattern2(|)
        =>
        (
            (new PROJECT) = with(PROJECT)(
                Pattern1[DocumentPair[doc1,doc2],SourcePair[src1,src2]]:
                Pattern2[ModulePair[src1,doc1],ModulePair[src2,doc2]] );
        )
    -> Pattern2[ MODULE(|), MODULE(|) ]

DOCUMENTS(|) -> DocumentPair[ DOCUMENT(|), DOCUMENT(|) ]
SOURCES(|)   -> SourcePair[ SOURCE(|), SOURCE(|) ]
MODULE(|)    -> ModulePair[ SOURCE(|), DOCUMENT(|) ]
```

Figure 7: Re-organization of sources and documents

The value of the `with` expression is the value of the *expression$_i$* corresponding to the first *pattern$_i$* that matches the value of *expression$_0$*. Figure 8 illustrates the modification of object when it receives message `ChangePattern2`. Of course, OOAG can describe more complex transformation in combination with message passing such as an incremental structure modification. Notice that modifying the structure causes static attributes to be re-evaluated in order to be consistent.

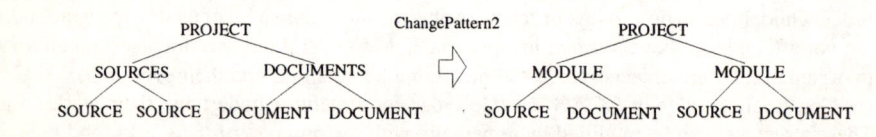

Figure 8: Re-organization of sources and documents

3.3 Environments as Object Management Systems

SDEs described in OOAG are objects which operate as object management system, because OOAG allows us to describe access methods like retrieval, insertion and deletion of objects represented by dynamic specifications.

Here is a description (figure 9) of file name retrieval as a typical example of retrieval using message passing. In this example, a message `find` is defined to make a list `path_name_list` which has all path names including file name `file_name`. Here it is assumed that file objects `FILE` are either directories (`Dir`) or plain files (`PFile`) and each plain file holds its path name and its file name as leaf native attributes `path_name` and `name`, respectively.

Message passing in this example might seem like a function call. But, as we mentioned above, descriptions of dynamic specifications are declarative, and message passing and evaluations of dynamic attributes are independent except message guarding. OOAG allows us to describe not only descent message passing but also ascent message passing, which enables 'overflow'

```
FILE(|)
   -> Dir[FILE_LIST(|),name]

       FILE:find(file_name|path_name_list)
          => FILE_LIST(file_name|path_name_list)
       {   FILE_LIST.file_name = FILE.file_name;
           FILE.path_name_list = FILE_LIST.path_name_list; }

   -> PFile[path_name,name,content,date,owner]

       FILE:find(file_name|path_name_list)
          =>
       {   FILE.path_name_list = if(FILE.path_name==FILE.name,
                                         list(FILE.path_name),list()); }

FILE_LIST(|)
   ->Pair[FILE(|),FILE_LIST(|)]

       FILE_LIST$1:find(file_name|path_name_list)
          => FILE_LIST$2:find(file_name|path_name_list),
             FILE:find(file_name|path_name_list)
       {   FILE_LIST$1.path_name_list = append(FILE_LIST$2.path_name_list,
                                                  FILE.path_name_list);
           FILE.file_name = FILE_LIST$1.file_name;
           FILE_LIST$2.file_name = FILE_LIST$1.file_name; }

   ->Nil[]

       FILE_LIST:find(file_name|path_name_list)
          =>
       {   FILE_LIST.path_name_list = list();   }
```

Figure 9: Retrieving file name

message in B-tree to be described for example. And we can also describe insertion or deletion as well as retrieval using replacements of native attributes.

4 Prototype system MAGE

Prototype object management system generator MAGE, intended to be used for verifying the feasibility of our approach, has been constructed. This is a successive system of OS/0 (Object System/ Zero) [SK90] and can handle new dynamic semantics presented in section 2. As shown in figure 10, the system consists of three parts. The system kernel and user defined object space are built on top of XLISP [Bet85] system. The OOAG object specification editor/translator are generated by The Synthesizer Generator system (CSG) [RT89], which translates OOAG specifications into executable xlisp programs. MAGE shell are also generated by CSG, which serves as a simple user interface to create instances and manupilate them. Graphical user interface including class/object browsers are built on top of Winterp [Nie89] system. Two major components of the system kernel are the definition of 'NODE' class, which implements functions common to all objects such as static/dynamic attribution algorithm, message passing manipulation, and the object scheduler (which emulates concurrency of multiple objects).

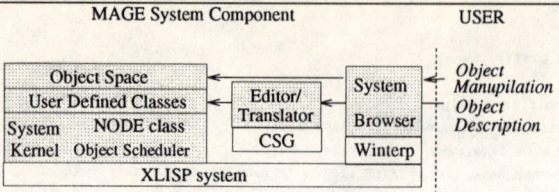

Figure 10: MAGE system component

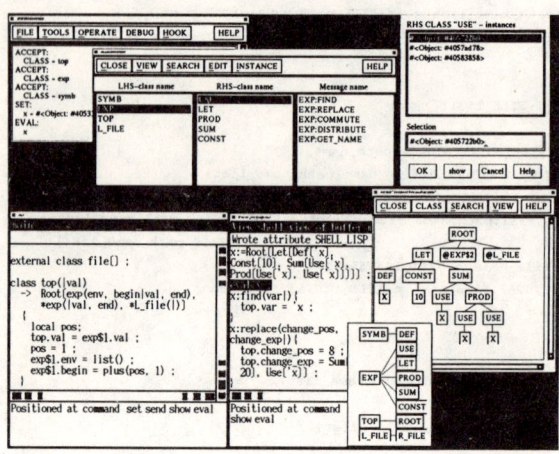

Figure 11: Screen snapshot of MAGE system execution

Figure 11 shows a screen snapshot of MAGE system execution. We summarize how to use MAGE system to help the readers understand the feel of it. First, the user invokes MAGE editor (figure 11, bottom left) to edit class definitions by selecting menus of system browser (figure 11, top left). This editor is a syntax directed editor generated with CSG, and provides static analysis. Class browser (figure 11, top middle) also provides it graphically. Then, he creates instances by means of MAGE shell (figure 11, bottom middle) and sends some messages to them. Graphical view of objects (instances) as well as values of attributes are given by object browser (figure 11, right).

On MAGE system, we experimented with relatively small descriptions including a configuration management system and we obtained good results. But since MAGE system is based on an interpreter language, its slow execution prevents us to perform large, practical experiments. Therefore, we are building new MAGE system written in an object oriented compiler language.

5 Summary

5.1 Conclusion

We have considered software develpment environments (SDEs) described in a computational model OOAG which is based on an AG that is extended with object oriented concepts. OOAG is one of the higher order attribute grammers and can describe dynamic semantics by means of message passing.

We showed the advantages obtained when describing SDEs as aggregated objects of OOAG. OOAG is a good tool to describe change management and consistency maintenance among complex relations of software objects especially. OOAG provides declarative descriptions to re-compute automatically derived values based on change propagation and to check relations among software objects, which help recovering activities of programmers. All objects appeared in SDEs are treated as uniform active objects of OOAG resulting in high interoperability. OOAG can also guide programmers when inconsistencies among software objects are detected, and can enforce organization of software objects on programmers. High readability and locality of OOAG make it easy to understand descriptions of the system resulting in high maintainability.

5.2 Future Works

HFSP (Hierarchical Functional Software Processes) [Kat89] [ST89] is an AGs based approach in describing software processes. In HFSP, a software process is described as a hierarchical decomposition of software activities, whose execution record is expressed as a hierarchical activity record called an execution tree. This execution tree does indeed corresponds to the software object tree described in OOAG. We believe that we can develop a good hybrid model of OOAG and HFSP for both software databases and software processes.

OOAG does not have a mechanism of inheritance that provides powerful abstractions for sharing similarities among classes while preserving their differences. In OOAG, a class is not even an object. [Hed89] makes an attempt to introduce a concept of class hierarchy into AGs, but this approach seems not to fit OOAG. We are now tackling this problem.

MAGE does not have mechanisms like an interface to persistent objects to generate practical environments. Also, we must experiment with OOAG by describing large, practical software development environments and running them on MAGE.

Acknowledgments

The authors would like to thank Takeshi Hagiwara for his appreciated endeavor in realizing MAGE system and his useful discussions. We would also like to thank Ivan Chung for reading the draft and making a number of helpful suggestions.

References

[Bet85] David Betz. *XLISP: An Experimental Object Oriented Language*, January 1985.

[DJL88] Pierre Deransart, Martin Jourdan, and Bernard Lorho. *Attribute Grammars: Definitions, Systems, and Bibliography*, volume 323 of *Lecture Notes in Computer Science*. Springer-Verlag, 1988.

[DR85] Alan Demers and Anne Rogers. Attribute propagation by message passing. *SIGPLAN NOTICES*, 20(7):43–59, 1985.

[Fal84]   R. Fallow. Generating a Production Compiler from an Attribute Grammar. *IEEE Software*, 1(4), 1984.

[Hed89]   Gorel Hedin. An object-oriented notation for attribute grammars. In *Proceedings of the European Conference on Object-Oriented Programming(ECOOP '89)*, 1989.

[HM89]   S.D.Swieerstra H.H.Vogt and M.F.Kuiper. Higher order attribute grammars. In *Proceedings of the ACM SIGPLAN '89 Conference on Programming Language Design and Implementation*, pages 131–145, Portland,Oregon, 1989. ACM.

[Kat89]   Takuya Katayama. A Hierarchical and Functional Software Process Description and its Enaction. In *Proceedings of the 11th Internaltional Conference on Software Engineering*, pages 343–352, 1989.

[Knu68]   D.E. Knuth. Semantics of context-free languages. *Mathematical Systems Theory*, 2(2):127–145, 1968.

[Nie89]   P.Mayer Niels. *The WINTERP MANUAL (Version 1.0)*. Hewlett-Packard Laboratories, Human-Computer Interaction Department, December 1989.

[Not85]   David Notkin. The GANDALF project. *The Journal of Systems and Software*, 5(2), May 1985.

[RT89]   Thomas W. Reps and Tim Teitelbaum. *The Synthesizer Generator*. Texts and Monographs in Computer Science. Springer-Verlag, 1989.

[Shi89]   Yoichi Shinoda. *On Application of Attribute Grammars to Software Development*. PhD thesis, Tokyo Institute of Technology, 3 1989.

[SK90]   Yoichi Shinoda and Takuya Katayama. Object Oriented Extension of Attribute Grammars and Its Implementation Using Distributed Attribute Evaluation Algorithm. In *Proceedings of the International Workshop on Attribute Grammars and their Applications*, Lecture Note in Computer Science. Springer-Verlag, 1990. 177-191.

[ST89]   Masato Suzuki and Katayama Takuya. Redoing: A mechanism for dynamics and flexibility of software process. Technical Report MS-TK-89-07-25, Tokyo Institute of Technology, 1989.

[TC90]   Tim Teitelbaum and R. Chapman. Higher-order attribute grammars and editing environments. In *Proceedings of ACM SIGPLAN '90 Conference on Programming Language Design and Implementation*, White Plains, NY, June 1990.

Design of an Integrated and Extensible C++ Programming Environment

Kin'ichi Mitsui[1]   Hiroaki Nakamura[1]   Theodore C. Law[2]
Shahram Javey[2]

[1]IBM Research, Tokyo Research Laboratory
1623-14, Shimo-tsuruma, Yamato-shi, Kanagawa 242
e-mail: mitsui@trl.vnet.ibm.com
[2]IBM Canada, Language Technology Centre
844 Don Mills Road, North York, Ontario M3C 1V7

Abstract

This paper describes a framework and some techniques used in the construction of integrated and extensible programming environments. To support programming in complex object-oriented languages such as C++, a database that contains semantic information on the source programs is essential. Tools in such environments should be constructed in a highly integrated fashion around the database. In addition, new programming techniques and the acquisition of knowledge through experience create a need for extensions. Such environments have to be designed so that extensions can be made easily. Thus integration and extensibility are key features of such environments.

1 Introduction

As C++ has become more popular and widespread, a strong need for sophisticated programming tools and environments has emerged, because the language is not only powerful but also complex. Many new types of tool that support C++ programming are based on semantic information extracted from source programs. Examples of such tools include style and coding convention checkers, code optimizers, program visualizers, and incremental compilers. Combinations of these new tools and traditional tools such as debuggers are also valuable. The extraction of semantic information from source code is not so simple as in conventional programming languages, because of complex name scopes and operator and function overloading. A full C++ compiler capability is necessary in order to extract such information, which is shared by various tools. These facts imply the need for a program database to store such information, and for some mechanism to integrate tools and the database. A simple tool integration scheme such as that seen in Unix is no longer usable in environments that support complex object-oriented languages.

There are several current research projects related to tool integration mechanisms. One is ECMA PCTE [Tho80], [1] in which integration is classified into three types: data

---
[1]Users may refer to a tutorial about PCTE and other integration issues in Ajisaka [Aji93].

integration, control integration, and user interface integration. In a fully integrated environment, tools share data representations, communicate directly with each other, and interact with users uniformly and consistently.

We are now developing a C++ programming environment that can support the tools described above. To achieve this goal, we have to realize all the types of tool integration.

To realize a fully integrated environment, we have taken an object-oriented approach. Fine-grained objects in the program database may behave differently depending on the various tools in which they are used. We separate the presentation from the tools. Presentation of the objects is managed uniformly by special tools named viewers.

A major focus of this paper is the extensibility of programming environments. C++ is evolving; its language specification is being enhanced. At the same time, know-how about C++ new coding techniques, idioms, and also pitfalls is being accumulated and shared among users [Cop92, MeJe91]. A requirement for programming environments is thus that they should be able to absorb these changes and knowledge rapidly. C++ programmers would like to be able to extend environments by themselves to reflect new knowledge and requirements, while software venders who are developing environments would like to produce enhanced versions quickly. Another requirement is that it should be possible to reuse these environments to support other languages and platforms. It seems quite reasonable first to design a small kernel of an environment and a mechanism for extending the environment, and then to attach all the functions using that mechanism, so that old functions can be replaced and new functions can be added easily. Extensibility is a key to the construction of environments, especially those that support languages like C++.

The issues facing us were as follows: what should be included in the small kernel mentioned above?; what should be the mechanism for extending it?; what is an appropriate granularity for extensions?; and are special extension languages necessary?

To solve these issues, we decided to use abstract base classes heavily to separate the specification and implementation of objects. The kernel is a collection of abstract base classes. Extensions will be made in two ways: by replacing implementation of objects to enhance them, and by adding new abstract base classes. To provide a mechanism for extension and to maintain proper granularity in extensions, we divide a single conceptual object into several physical objects. An object is dynamically extended in various tools in various ways. For extension languages, we decided to use the same language as that used to implement the base system, C++ in our case, because it is simpler and performs well. On the other hand, we have recognized the importance of special languages, particularly for ad-hoc query services to the program database. We describe an interpreter language plugged into our environment by means of our extension mechanism.

The rest of the paper is organized as follows. Section 2 summarizes research in this area and on these issues. Section 3 describes a framework and some techniques that we are using in developing our programming environment. Section 4 gives an example of the use of the framework. Section 5 describes some components that we have designed as applications of the framework. Section 6 describes the current status of our work, and Section 7 offers some concluding remarks.

2 Background

The need for integration in program development environments has been discussed in many papers [Har87, Rei90, Mah91]. Here we briefly review the related work.

The effectiveness of integrated programming environments has been proved by systems such as Smalltalk-80. These environments have succeeded in improving programmers' productivity. As a result of this success, many researchers and developers have been trying to build such environments for conventional languages.

In PCTE [Tho89], integration technologies are summarized as three basic steps: data, control, and user interface integration. Data integration forces all tools to share the same data representation. Control integration forces all tools to communicate with each other collaboratively, to support programming. User interface integration forces the user interface of each tool to have a consistent look-and-feel.

Since many of modern programming tools use common user interface management systems such as X Window and Motif, the user interface integration problem has been solved to some extent.

Field [Rei90] and Softbench [Oli91] were developed with a focus on control integration. Their purpose was to provide easy ways of integrating existing tools. In spite of some differences, they basically provided mechanisms for controlling messages among tools and defined message protocols. Existing tools are encapsulated or enhanced by a message handler so that they can communicate with other tools. This idea was successful and showed that existing tools can be integrated easily. However, the above environments did not manage data integration, because existing tools used individual internal data formats.

Cadillac [Gab90], whose product name is Energize, dealt with data integration. In Cadillac, the object server controls objects in the environment so that tools in the environment can share objects. However, the designers took a hybrid approach to tool integration; tools are not tightly integrated and do not access objects directly. Instead, they communicate with each other by exchanging messages with the object server, and access objects in the server by using object identifiers. Tools may have internal data that are duplicated in the server, especially when existing tools are integrated. Cadillac supports both a centralized object database service and a tool integration mechanism similar to those of Field and Softbench. Its designers introduced a mechanism for integrating external tools in a relatively tighter fashion. However, their mechanism for extending an object server's functions was unclear, although they said in their paper that they would provide an extension language.

Our focus is on developing a framework for building such object servers as that of Cadillac. We are aiming to provide really data-integrated and extensible programming environments. RPDE3's [Har87] objective is similar to ours: to ensure the extensibility and adaptability of such environments. Its designers developed several extended object-oriented technologies [HaOs90b, HaOs90a] to support extensibility and adaptability, while in this paper we describe techniques, applicable in implementing such environments, that use ordinary object-oriented programming languages such as C++.

Before describing our approach, we clarify what extensibility of programming environments means. The following are factors that we recognize as necessary for extensibility:

- *Well-defined interface for extensions.* Although this is a matter of course, it is very important to design a good interface through which extensions can access the system.

- *No impact on existing code.* The extension should not require modification of existing source code. It is very hard for extenders to maintain consistency when modifying source code written by others. A stronger constraint is that the extension should not require recompilation of existing source code. Sometimes, source code is not available.

- *Dynamic extension.* It is more convenient if (static) linking is also unnecessary for extensions. This can be implemented by using a dynamic loading mechanism for operating systems, in which, for example, some functions of program elements such as functions and variables are linked at load time or run-time. Incorporation of new functions or replacement of old functions is done without relinking.

- *Ease of extension.* Extenders may not have the source code of the entire system. However, the debugging of the extended part should not be hard. One way to ensure this is to provide a special extension language on a higher level than that used in developing the original system. Some debugging tools for such extension languages may be necessary.

3 Framework and Techniques

The tight integration approach that we have taken has several advantages. The user interface is highly uniform, not only in its look and feel, but also in the user interaction model that users have to learn. There is no duplicate functionality among tools. There is no duplicate information spread into tools. The system performs well even when tools have to communicate each other heavily.

However, we have to avoid making our system a huge, closed, monolithic tool. Such a tool could not survive long because it would be hard to maintain and incapable of absorbing new ideas. Hence, we have to design the system carefully.

This section describes our framework for building integrated and extensible environments, and some techniques for implementing the framework. Some of the techniques described here assume the use of strongly typed object-oriented programming languages such as C++ for the implementation. These languages have advantages as regards the performance and correctness of programs.

3.1 Object-based Approach

We have a central database for all objects that may be accessed by any tools or by any users in the environment. Objects are unique in our environment and exist across tool boundaries. Each object provides a collection of services. In data-integrated environments, sharing of data by objects is more suitable than flat data representation. Objects are abstract, so their physical representations can be replaced easily, which increases the extensibility of the environments.

There is another reason for using the object model as the basis of our database. Objects in our environment form a complex network of mutual references. Many computations performed in objects' services traverse that network. The object model can be directly mapped to efficient implementation of such computations.

Examples of objects in our program database include language elements such as C++ classes, functions, and variables; operating system resources such as files and processes; run-time elements such as stack frames and values of program variables; and others such as compilation units, source code lines for syntax errors, and break-points. These are *program* objects.

Other examples are view objects that manage the presentation of objects and viewer objects that manage collections of view objects. These are *presentation* objects.

Some objects in our environment can interact directly with users. Many objects are presented as rectangles on a screen. Users point to these areas and do something like pressing a mouse button to request a service. Then, objects respond and behave in a particular way. This is in contrast to traditional programming environments, in which coarse-grained tools provide services.

3.2 Request Handling by Objects

Each object that is allowed to interact with users manages requests from them. Simple styles of interaction include clicking mouse buttons on objects and selecting items of menus popped up by the object. More complex interactions use special dialogs to gather information necessary for performing requested services. These objects control users' input and initiate dialogs no matter what windows they are displayed in.

This is slightly different from Smalltalk-80's Model-View-Controller (MVC) model [KrPo88], because objects directly control user interaction by using menus and dialogs, and are shared by various windows.

3.3 Separation of Interface and Implementation

We separate the interface of objects, which specifies services, and the implementation of the objects, which defines the behaviors of the objects for the services. This information hiding is a well-known software engineering technique. Not all clients that request services access the implementation part directly. This allows extenders to enhance the system by replacing the body of services without affecting existing code, that is, the clients of the services.

Since we are using C++ to implement our environment, the above technique forces us to use abstract base classes to describe the interface for services of objects. Abstract base classes are never instantiated, whereas implementation classes always are. Figure 1 shows an inheritance hierarchy of abstract base classes and implementation classes. Services are defined by pure-virtual functions in the abstract classes, in which no data members are public to clients.

This technique also implies the possibility of dynamic loading of the implementation part. Since clients' code never assumes a particular physical memory layout of server objects or references to specific functions that provide services, there is no need for name linkage between clients and the implementation part. Note that we should avoid using "new" operators to create objects, because they directly access the implementation parts of the server objects.

The technique meets the second and third requirements for extensibility described in Section 2.

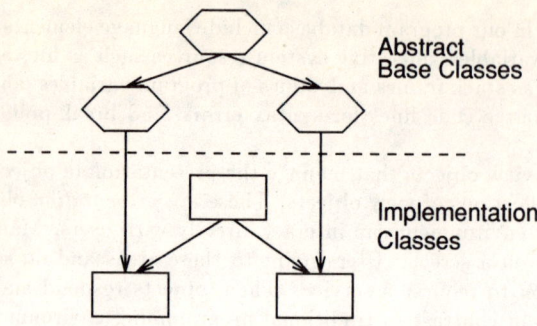

Figure 1: Inheritance Hierarchy of Abstract and Implementation Classes

3.4 Object Extensions

The services of a certain type of object may change according to the situations in which the objects are used. We call these situations *contexts* of objects. For example, a variable object may provide partially different sets of services in static analysis and debugging contexts.

After an object has been created, it has its own internal state, namely, a chunk of physical memory attached to it. If we want to extend the functions of the object, we may have to change the size of the physical memory. The implementation class of the object defines the physical structure of the object. We use the term *single class scheme* for the situation in which each object has only one implementation class. Single class schemes involve several problems.

First, attempts may be made to extend objects after they have been created. To reallocate memory for the object, a special mechanism is necessary. Second, if an object is extended in two irrelevant contexts, the object has to have a class that defines both contexts. This breaks the modularity of the system. In addition, the size of the amount of memory allocated for the object is the union of the memory needed for each. This may result in an unnecessary and unacceptable waste of memory, especially in our case, where a lot of fine-grained database objects are used in several contexts. Third, we cannot add new functions of objects as new abstract base classes without affecting the existing source code. For example, if we add functions to an abstract class, we have to modify its implementation classes.

For these reasons, we decompose a conceptually single object into several physical objects. Each object is initially designed with minimal services attached. Actually, it is impossible to provide all the possible services of objects from the beginning. New services of the initial object, which are provided in some context, are defined as a separate object, which contains a reference to the original object. We call the new object an *object extension*.

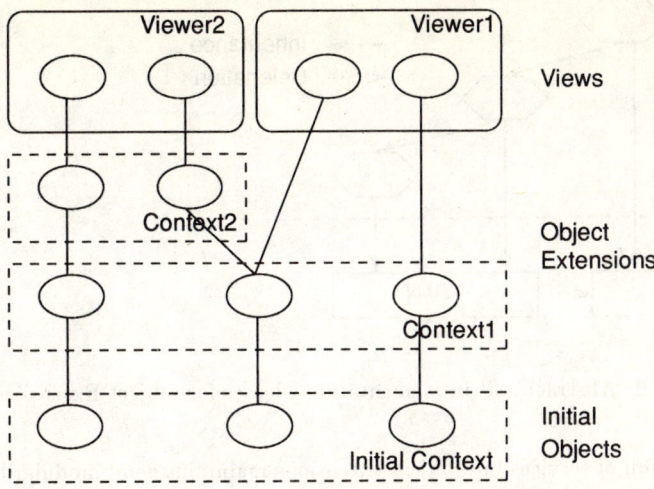

Figure 2: Object Extensions and Contexts

Figure 2 illustrates relationships among initial objects; their extensions, including views; and contexts. The ovals at the bottom of the figure are initial objects that have links to their extensions. Extensions may have further extensions. Objects and extensions are eventually linked to view objects if the objects are presented on a screen. Updates and deletions of objects are propagated through the links between objects and extensions. This is a natural extension of the MVC model. The dotted rectangles in the figure represent contexts. Contexts are also objects. A context maintains mapping between object extensions created in the context and their original objects, and manages the creation of object extensions. Clients ask a context object to retrieve these object extensions in the context, and never directly call "new" operators of classes that define the object extensions; as a result, the implementation aspect of these classes is completely hidden from clients, as mentioned in the previous section. Viewers can be seen as kinds of context, which manage view objects.

Services of object extensions and context objects are defined in abstract base classes, as mentioned in Section 3.3. Consequently, those who extend our environment may replace the implementation of these classes. In addition, they can add new functions to the environment by creating a new context and defining extensions of objects used in that context. Figure 3 shows classes for object extensions. In this example, a class of objects is extended to the right. Classes on the right inherit services from ones on the left. In implementation classes, requests for the services to the rightmost class may be delegated to the left or may be processed by the rightmost class itself. [2]

---

[2]This is similar to the delegation mechanism [Lie86], which can be implemented in C++ by passing the delegator object as a parameter of each delegation call [JoZw91].

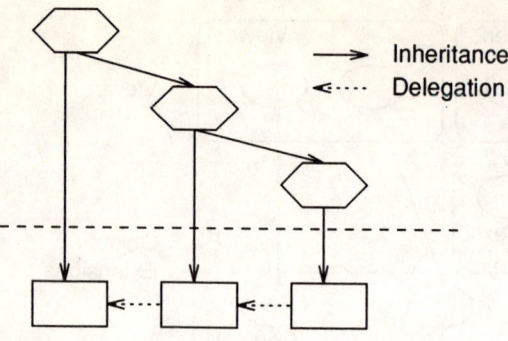

Figure 3: Abstract and Implementation Classes for Object Extensions

Decomposition of services into object extensions maintains good modularity; thus, it is an essential characteristic of extensible environments. This framework allows the entire system to be divided into a component that defines abstract base classes and components for contexts.

3.5 Viewers

Viewers have special contexts in which they manage view objects. There are three primitive types of viewers: *text*, *list*, and *graph* viewers. Although we may add some more viewer types, basically any information can be presented by these primitive viewers. This situation contrasts with that of traditional integrated environments, in which individual tools supports their own user interaction model, which may not be uniform. Thus, user interface aspects are separated from the notion of tools in our environment.

3.6 Interface with External Tools

We use contexts to implement interfaces with external tools. An example of this technique is support of external editors. Some editors such as Emacs have extension languages and can communicate with other processes by using them. The implementation bodies of editor objects such as text buffers whose interface is defined in the environment can be replaced with others that communicate with external editors. This technique essentially allows us to incorporate into the environment interpreters that process commands from/to external tools.

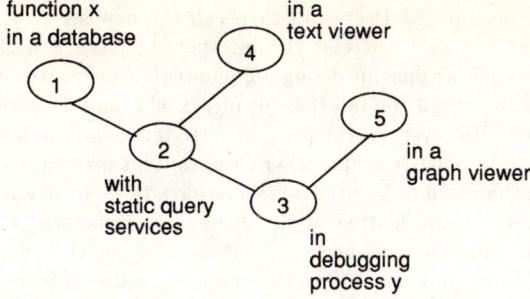

Figure 4: Decomposition of an object for function "x"

Another example is a command line query processor for the program database, which allows users and external tools to access the database by using operating system shell commands. Some more details will be given in Section 5.4.

This technique can be thought as an approach to meeting the fourth requirement for extensibility mentioned in Section 2, becuase interpreter languages usually relieve extenders of some burdens such as memory management, debugging, and slowness in development cycles.

4 Example

Figure 4 illustrates how the technique described in the previous section works. Suppose that we have the function "x" in our program database. The figure shows five decomposed pieces of the object. We use the numbers attached to the pieces to refer to them. Piece 1 is the core of the object, and holds static information such as references to other symbols. Piece 2 may support non-trivial query services such as finding special kinds of caller. Piece 3 knows about the dynamic aspect of the function; at least it must know about the location of the function in the process "y" in order to set a break point. Pieces 4 and 5 visualizes the function in each viewer.

To pop up a menu in a graph, piece 5 collects service items provided for users. The service items include ones from piece 2 such as static queries, ones from piece 3 such as setting break points, and view-related ones from piece 5 such as centering the node in a graph. Piece 4 pops up a menu similarly.

If we want to add new static query services, we may change the actual implementation of 2 without affecting the other pieces. Users can then call the new services, even in a debugging context. Another way is to extend the interface of piece 2 with the new services so that other pieces such as ones in debugging contexts can use the new query services. Then we may have to extend the interface of pieces 3, 4, and 5 as well, so that they can inherit the extension. However, all the previous interfaces and implementations are reused, and do not need to be rewritten. In either case, context managers that create implementation objects and maintain links between them have to be overridden.

If piece 1 changes its state, a notification of the change is propagated to all other pieces. For instance, if the function "x" becomes out-of-date, all the current views receive a notification so that they may respond to the change visually. If piece 3 changes its state, only the views within the same debugging context are notified of the change.

5 Components

This section describes the components and functionality of our environment. There are no separate tools in our environment. Instead, the same object may serve different functions in each component.

5.1 Program Database

Our C++ compiler populates a program database by using the results of syntactic and semantic analysis. Figure 5 shows a partial view of the abstract base classes that form the program database. Note that the classes in the figure can also be used for other conventional languages. Other classes that are specific to the supported language, such as C++'s "Class," are not included in the figure. The entire database forms a more complex graph.

Program objects in this database context store semantic information extracted from source code and provide simple query services used in other contexts.

The compiler replaces a part of the database when source files are recompiled. Objects in the database may change their internal state accordingly. For example, if a file that defines a certain "class" symbol is recompiled, the state of that symbol, such as references to base class symbols, may be changed. In addition, such objects may be deleted if they do not exist in source code. These changes and deletions are propagated to object extensions, and may therefore change the views in windows.

Object handling in the program database involves issues such as how to remove duplicates in separate compilation units and how to deal with the effects of macro changes. Another issue is how to implement an efficient persistent program database. Since these issues are beyond the scope of this paper, we do not give any further details of the program database.

5.2 Static Analysis

A static analyzer is a tool that helps programmers to understand programs, navigate through source code, check coding style and conventions, and so on. The services provided by language element objects in the static analysis context basically consist of navigating the program database objects and computing semantic information such as attributes of

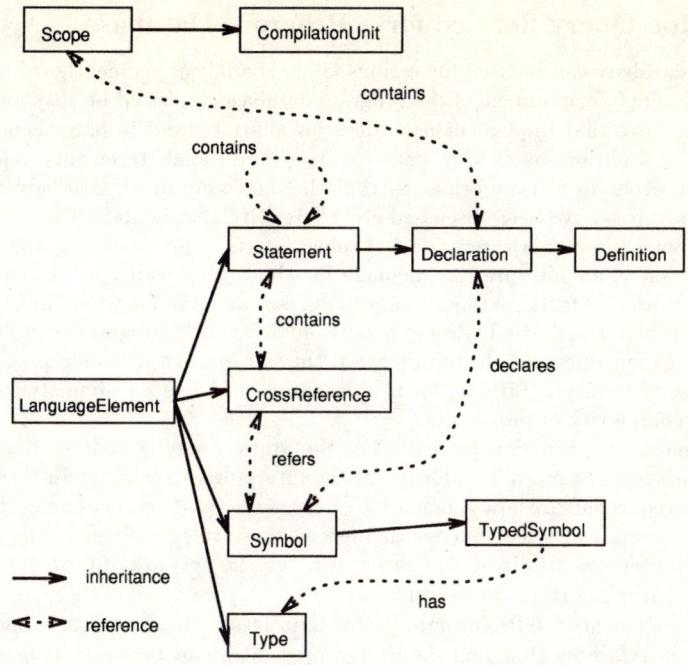

Figure 5: Program Database Classes (Partial View)

objects and relationships among objects. The results of this analysis are presented as views attached to these objects through various viewers.

Static analysis functions should be separated from database objects, because the former tend to be enhanced and extended as our knowledge about the analysis increases; if these functions all belonged to database objects, the services associated with database objects would be unnecessarily large and cause maintenance problems.

5.3 Dynamic Analysis

In addition to the debugging functions supported in traditional debuggers such as setting breakpoints on statements, inspecting the values of variables, and tracing stack frames, a combination of static analysis and debugging functions is more powerful than a union of both functions. For example, we can set breakpoints in all statements where a value is set to a certain variable. This means that a variable object in this context inherits services from the one in the static analysis context.

Some objects used in this context, such as breakpoints and stack frames, are specific to this context, while others, such as language elements, are extended from other contexts.

5.4 Ad-Hoc Query Service for a Program Database

The program database can be used for various kinds of analysis, as mentioned above. So that users can take full advantage of the program database, it should be easy for them to write ad-hoc queries that implement new ideas for analyses, and to plug them into the environment. In addition, users may want to write conditional statements dynamically in a session, in order to filter information that they have obtained. The advantages of having query services have been discussed elsewhere [GrCh90, LeMeRe92].

For the above reasons, we provide a Prolog interface for accessing the program database. Prolog is an interpretive language in which users can add or remove programs (called rules and facts) without compilation, so the cycle for trying out new ideas is remarkably rapid. In addition, Prolog is fairly high-level, so programs can be seen as collections of if-then rules plus facts. Figure 6 shows a part of a Prolog program that checks the Law of Demeter [LiHo89] for C+ programs, which is a coding style guideline to reduce the complexity of programs.

We implement this function by replacing the static analysis context described in Section 5.2 with one enhanced by addition of the interpreter capability. In this context, if an object is requested to show a menu for query services, it searches rules defined in Prolog so that users can select queries defined as these rules. When a user selects a rule, the interpreter executes it by navigating through the network of program database objects, and returns the result to viewers.

We have implemented a Prolog interpreter ourselves. This interpreter has a C++ programming interface so that built-in Prolog predicates can be easily plugged in. A similar idea is described by Levy et al. [LeHoJu90]. Unlike stand-alone Prolog systems, our interpreter directly accesses our program database and navigates through pointers in it to resolve goals.

5.5 User Interface

This component provides parts to implement a uniform user interface of our system based on the user interaction model.

Viewers are presentation parts in our environment. Components such as static and dynamic analyzers use these viewers for their user interfaces. Viewers themselves do not provide context-sensitive services; these are provided by objects projected onto the viewers.

A text viewer is basically a full-fledged text editor. A special feature of editors in tightly integrated environments is that language element objects are projected onto source code so that programmers can query or instruct objects directly in texts. A graph viewer displays program information, especially relationships among objects, in graph form. Objects in our environment form a huge network of relationships. The graph viewer is a tool for viewing this network by selecting the subnetwork that users are interested in. A list viewer displays the relationships more concisely than a graph viewer, in list form. An item in a list may have multiple columns.

Besides viewers, there are parts to compose menus and dialogs. Those who want to extend the system with new functions will use parts in this component to implement the input and output of the added functions.

```
% Law of Demeter: C++, class form strict version
%   In all member functions M of class C, use only
%   members of class C1 and its base classes.

preferred_supplier(C1, M, C) :- C1 = C.
preferred_supplier(C1, M, C) :- data_member_class(C1, C).
preferred_supplier(C1, M, C) :- argument_class(C1, M).
preferred_supplier(C1, M, C) :- call_constructor(M, C1).
preferred_supplier(C1, M, C) :- use_global_variable(M, C1).

data_member_class(C1, C) :-
    class_member(C, Member), typeof_variable(Member, Type),
    class_type(Type, C1).

argument_class(C1, M) :-
    typeof_function(M, ReturnType, NumArgs, ArgTypes),
    include_class_type(ArgTypes, C1).

call_constructor(M, C1) :-
    class_member(C1, Function), calls(M, Function),
    constructor(Function).

use_global_variable(M, C1) :-
    global(Variable), refers(M, Variable),
    typeof_variable(Variable, Type), class_type(Type, C1).

class_type(class(C1), C1).
class_type(reference(class(C1)), C1).
class_type(pointer(class(C1)), C1).
```

Figure 6: A part of Law of Demeter rules in Prolog

6 Current Status

The C++ programming environment described in this paper is currently being coded in C++ and developed on the AIX operating system with the X/Motif window system.

We are developing a reusable C++ class library that can be used in the construction of such programming environments, and that supports the framework described in this paper. The library includes classes for controlling Motif widgets, cyclic graphs, and text editors; classes for implementing the user interaction model including the window creation and the menu-command execution framework; classes for supporting object decomposition; and classes for supporting primitive debugging services. The user interface, database schema, and functionality of our environment are implemented by using the library.

7 Conclusions

We have explained our approach to the composition of integrated and extensible C++ programming environments, and described a basic framework and some techniques for implementing such environments.

We are building a C++ programming environment consisting of fine-grained objects. These objects provide various services in various tools. We separate the presentation aspect from the tools themselves, so that users can access the environment uniformly and consistently. Viewers are special tools that manage the presentation of various tools. We use abstract base classes heavily in the construction of the environment so that the implementation part of each object can be replaced easily. This increases the extensibility of the environment. We introduced the notion of object extensions, which are collections of objects decomposed from conceptually single objects. This notion was introduced to make extension of objects easier and more efficient. We also addressed the importance of providing query supports to allow users to take full advantage of our database. We explained a Prolog interpreter used for accessing the program database and for enhancing the static analysis tool of the environment, as an example of the extension of the environment.

We recognize that there are different types of user and levels of extension on the system. For those who want to try out new ideas regarding functionality of the system quickly, ease of extension is the most important consideration. Extension languages such as Prolog help them. Those for whom the performance is more important than ease of extension can use the idea of object decomposition and extension and code extensions in C++. Other users, like ourselves, may want to modify the database schema. They may also want to use the above idea to design a new schema that has minimal impact on other parts. However, this process may not be straightforward and is an open issue. The most difficult level of extension is related to the user interaction model. We spent much time on the design of the user interface, which indicates that the design itself is very time-consuming and difficult. We are regarding the user interface model as a core part of the environment, but not an extensible part.

Acknowledgements

The work described in this paper is being done jointly by people in the IBM Tokyo Research Laboratory and the IBM Language Technology Centre. The overall design is being discussed with Dave Penny, Tamiya Onodera, and Kazushi Kuse; we are using the NARC graph library written by Vance Waddle; the user interface class library is being implemented by Tsuyoshi Ohira, Akiko Kato, Paul Ng, and Neville Parakh; and the program database is being designed and implemented by Kazu Yasuda, Syoiti Ninomiya and Gary Keong. We would like to thank Dr. Tsutomu Kamimura for his comments and support. We would also like to thank the people in the IBM XL C++ compiler development team.

References

[Aji93] Ajisaka, T., "Open CASE Platforms," Computer Software, Vol. 10, No. 2, 1993 (in Japanese).

[Cop92] Coplien, J., "Advanced C++ Programming Styles and Idioms," Addison Wesley, 1992.

[Gab90] Gabriel, R.P. et al., "Foundation for a C++ Programming Environment," Proc. of C++ at Work-'90, 1990.

[GrCh90] Grass, J.E. and Chen, Y., "The C++ Information Abstractor," Proc. of 1990 USENIX C++ Conference, 1990.

[Har87] Harrison, W., "RPDE3: A Framework for Integrating Tool Fragments," IEEE Software, November 1987.

[HaOs90a] Harrison, W. and Ossher, H., "Extension-by-Addition: Building Extensible Software," IBM Research Report 16127, 1990.

[HaOs90b] Harrison, W. and Ossher, H., "The PlusPlus Object Definition Environment," IBM Research Report 16283, 1990.

[JoZw91] Johnson, R.E. and Zweig, J.M, "Delegation in C++," Journal of Object-Oriented Programming, Vol. 4, No. 7, 1991.

[KrPo88] Krasner, G.E. and Pope, S.T., "A Cookbook for Using the Model-View-Controller User Interface Paradigm in Smalltalk-80," Journal of Object-Oriented Programming, Vol. 1, No. 3, 1988.

[LeMeRe92] Lejter, M., Meyers, S., and Reiss, S.P., "Support for Maintaining Object-Oriented Programs," Trans. on Software Engineering, Vol. 18, No. 12, 1992.

[LeHoJu90] Levy, M.R., Horspool, R.N., and Junkin, M.D., "The Translation of Prolog into C++," University of Victoria, 1990.

[LiHo89] Lieberherr, K.J. and Holland, I., "Assuring Good Style for Object-Oriented Programs," IEEE Software, September 1989.

[Lie86] Lieberman, H., "Using Prototypical Objects to Implement Shared Behaviour," Proc. of OOPSLA '86, 1986.

[Mah91] Mahler, A., "Organizing Tools in a Uniform Environment Framework," Proc. of USENIX - Winter '91, 1991.

[MeJe91] Meyers, S. and Lejter, M., "Automatic Detection of C++ Programming Errors: Initial Thoughts on a Lint++," Proc. of 1991 USENIX C++ Conference, 1991.

[Oli91] Oliver, H., "Adding Control Integration to PCTE," Endres, A. and Weber, H. (eds.), Proc. European Symposium on Software Development Environments and CASE Technology, Lecture Notes in Computer Science, Springer-Verlag, 1991.

[Rei90] Reiss, S.P., "Connecting Tools Using Message Passing in the Field Environment," IEEE Software, July 1990.

[Tho89] Thomas, I., "PCTE Interfaces: Supporting Tools in Software-Engineering Environments," IEEE Software, Vol. 6, No. 6, 1989.

Metalevel Decomposition in AL-1/D

Hideaki Okamura[†]
okamura@mt.cs.keio.ac.jp

Yutaka Ishikawa[††]
ishikawa@trc.rwcp.or.jp

Mario Tokoro[†] [*]
mario@mt.cs.keio.ac.jp

† Department of Computer Science, Keio University
3-14-1 Hiyoshi, Kohoku-ku, Yokohama, Kanagawa, 223 Japan

†† Real World Computing Partnership, Tsukuba Research Center
1-6-1 Takezono, Tsukuba, Ibaraki, 305 Japan

Abstract

Research has shown that metalevel architectures and the concept of reflection are useful for modifying programming systems dynamically in a controlled way. To modify the system flexibly, it is necessary to represent various abstraction levels, from the programing language level to the OS level, as well as user's multiple views, such as the view where the distributed environment is transparent and the view where that is not transparent, in a programming system. In traditional reflective systems, it is, however, difficult to represent these aspects of the system because these systems are modeled by one metalevel. To overcome this problem, we have proposed a new reflection framework: Multi-Model Reflection Framework (MMRF), and implemented a programming system AL-1/D based on this framework. This paper gives a clearer definition of MMRF than in our previous paper. MMRF is a framework for decomposing a metalevel into multiple conceptual models according to the abstraction levels and user's views. These conceptual models may overlap each other in their functions and resources. The decomposed models should run concurrently because models represents system components running concurrently in a system. The definition of MMRF includes the conditions to enable models to run simultaneously without violenting consistently. The structure of a model includes information to decide whether or not these conditions are satisfied.

1 Introduction

To support a mechanism that can modify system specification, some researchers employ metalevel architectures and the concept of reflection. A reflective system has its own model that represents itself internally. The model can be modified by using the mechanism in the system such as reflective calls in a programming language. The system and model are causally-connected with each other. That is, if the system is modified, the modification is reflected in the model and vice versa. This mechanism enables users to modify the system dynamically by changing the model. In reflective object-oriented

---

*Also with Sony Computer Science Laboratory Inc. Takanawa Muse Building, 3-14-13 Higashi Gotanda, Shinagawa-ku, Tokyo, 141, Japan, mario@csl.sony.co.jp

programming languages such as 3-KRS[Mae87], CLOS[Kee89] and ABCL/R[WY88], object behavior can be changed by meta-objects. Reflective operating systems such as Apertos[Yok92] and Choices[CIM92] support a function for modifying OS features.

We want to customize following aspects of a system to modify the system more flexibly; (1) multiple abstraction levels, e.g., the language level and the OS level, (2) user's multiple views of the system, e.g., (i) the view where the distributed environment is transparent and (ii) the view where that is not transparent, and (3) independent and concurrent system components such as a message handler and a scheduler. If we try to incorporate this demand in the conventional reflective framework, the metalevel becomes unavoidably complicated, since the system has to be represented by one metalevel. Consequently, it is difficult for users to understand and modify the system.

Figure 1 shows a programming system model to describe the above-mentioned system aspects. This figure indicates a system representation from the viewpoint of the user who customizes the system.

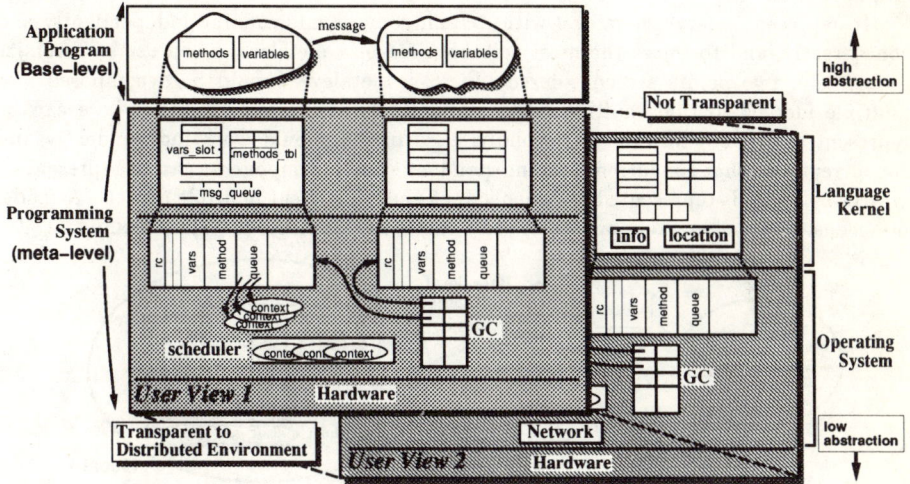

Figure 1: Metalevel in Programming System

In a programming system, there are some abstraction levels from the language level to OS level, as shown in Figure 1. At the language kernel level, an object is represented by system components such as a message queue, a variables slot and a method table. At the OS level, it is represented by memory segments and shared resources such as a scheduler, a memory manager (garbage collector), and networks. Users want to modify various parts in some abstraction levels according to the application characteristics.

For example, let us consider soft real-time application programs such as a multi-media system. Message priorities and time constraints are necessary for such programs. Some applications require efficient message handling, rather than support for priorities, when the programmer knows that multiple messages are not sent simultaneously in those applications. In another case, we need to modify an algorithm to enable it to handle messages after timeout, e.g. whether or not the execution of messages is retried; considering balance with communication costs. In soft real-time applications, users may want to modify the message handling policy from one without priorities to another which can handle priorities in the programming language level, and the scheduling policy related to execution after timeout at the OS level. Some users may want to modify at the language level without changing at the OS level, and vice versa. Others need to modify functions at both levels. Facilities for selection should be supported according to the abstraction level at which the users want to modify the system.

When these abstraction levels are defined as one metalevel, the range of the metalevel is broader than in traditional reflective systems such as CLOS. The metalevel in a distributed system is much broader.

Such a metalevel consists of many parts running independently and concurrently. For example, in the above-mentioned soft real-time applications, a message handler and a scheduler are running independently and concurrently. Moreover, users have multiple views of a system such as (i) the view where the distributed environment is transparent and (ii) the view where that is not transparent. The view of (ii) includes object locations and networks.

To represent a large metalevel with system components running independently and concurrently, and to select the most suitable part of a metalevel when users customize the system, two points are considered. First, a metalevel should be decomposed into multiple models so that multiple abstraction levels and user's multiple views can be represent easily and naturally. Secondly, each model should work independently and concurrently so that concurrent and independent system components can be represented. Object behavior is represented by independent and concurrent multiple models. A model may consist of system components at some levels to customize a system flexibly.

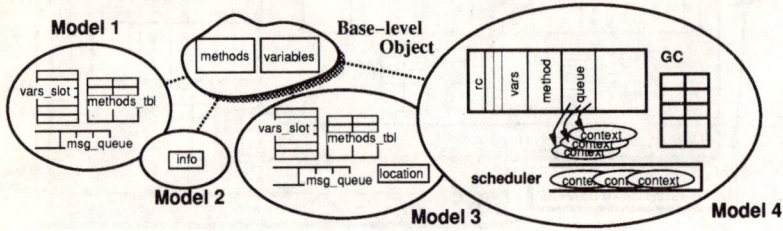

Figure 2: Multiple Models

Figure 2 indicates an example of the decomposition of the metalevel, shown in Figure 1, into multiple models . **Model 1** is used when users need to modify message handling policy at the language level. **Model 4** is used when the user need to modify the scheduling policy at the OS level. **Model 3** considers the difference in object location from that of **Model 1**. Multiple models also enable us to select whether the object location is transparent in a distributed environment.

However, some problems arise from the decomposition into independent and concurrent models and to design and implement each model by a software module. These problems are concerned with the consistency of models execution. Two kinds of consistency should be considered; *sequential consistency* and *concurrent consistency*. Sequential consistency means that a model can correctly represent the behavior of a base-level object. It is important to consider execution orders in a model, e.g. assignment execution is not permitted when an object has not yet started executing a method, etc. Concurrent consistency implies that conflicts can be found and avoided when shared system components in an object are simultaneously accessed by multiple models.

To solve above-mentioned problems, we proposed a new reflection framework; *Multi-Model Reflection Framework (MMRF)* and have designed and implemented a distributed reflective programming system *AL-1/D* based on this framework. MMRF has following characteristics:

- The metalevel can be decomposed into multiple models.
- A model consists of system components at one or more abstraction levels and user's views.
- Decomposed models can run concurrently to, and independently of other models.
- Consistency checking are supported to enable consistent execution.

One of our previous papers [OIT92] concentrated on the programming style in the AL-1/D system. That is, we presented some useful models on AL-1/D and described how to modify the system with those models. The definition of MMRF, however, was ambiguous. This paper describes the definition of MMRF, what structure of decomposed models is needed for consistent execution and how MMRF is introduced to AL-1/D. In Section 2, MMRF is defined. The definition of MMRF includes the structures of decomposed models needed for consistent execution. In Section 3, how MMRF is introduced to AL-1/D and how the system is modified are described. In Section 4, some issues pertaining to the implementation of AL-1/D are discussed.

2 Definition of MMRF

2.1 Overview

In MMRF, the metalevel is decomposed into models. In other words, the models composes the metalevel. A model is a conceptual unit. A model does not always represent an abstraction level and may consist of components at some abstraction levels. The definition of MMRF consists of (1) the definition of the entire metalevel before decomposition, (2) the definition of a model, (3) the condition for sequential consistency, and (4) the condition for concurrent consistency.

Object behavior is based on the concurrent object model [YT87]. The metalevel of an object consists of the "behavior" of an object and the "components" of the system that support behavior. Components include computational resources. Computational resources involve internal elements in an object such as a message queue and shared resources such as a scheduler.

The behavior of an object is represented by multiple state transition diagrams. Those state transition diagrams are used to check sequential consistency. A state is changed when an "event" occurs. For example, the action of "message sending" is represented by the state transition from state "running" to state "waiting" when the event is "message_sending". This description enables the system to check whether an event occurrence is correct in the current object state. For example, a behavior where a waiting object sends messages is not correct. In this situation, the system checks a state transition arising from a "message_sending" event when the object state is waiting. Multiple state transition diagrams enable the representation of some components running concurrently in the metalevel. That is, each state transition that exists on a different state transition diagram from another represents a separated concurrent execution. For example, the message handler and scheduler run independently and concurrently because the diagram containing state transitions for message handling is different from the diagram containing state transitions for scheduling. Figure 3 shows an example of message passing from object O_1 to object O_2.

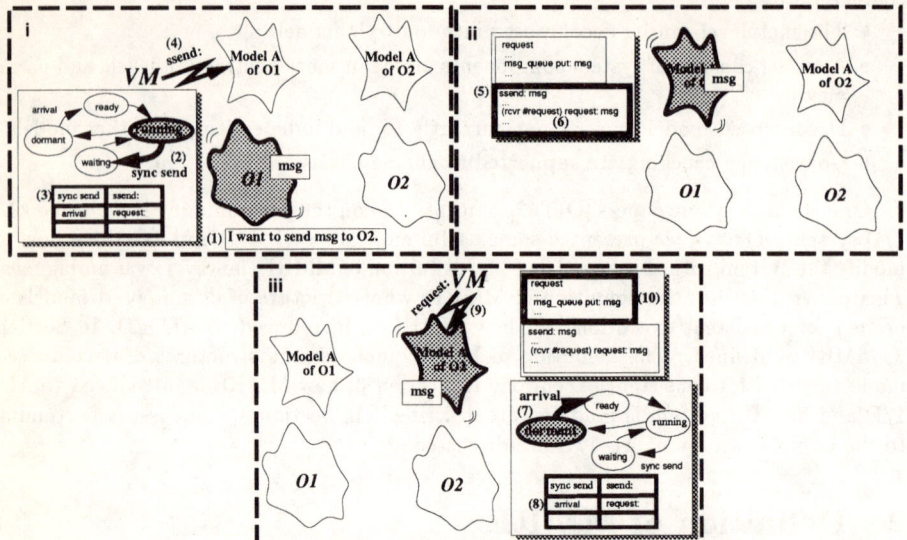

"VM" represents a virtual machine (system). Let us consider that O_1 and O_2 have **Model A**, with the same state transition and event definition. In (1), O_1 wants to send message **msg** to O_2. Then, in (2), the state of O_1 changes from *running* to *waiting* and event *sync_send* occurs. In (3) and (4), the system invokes **Model A** by action **ssend:**. In (5), the model of O_1 becomes active and executes action **ssend:**. In (6), the model of O_1 sends message **msg** to the model of O_2 with action **ssend:**. Then, in (7), the state of O_2 changes from *dormant* to *ready* and the event *arrival* occurs. In (8) and (9), the system invokes a model of O_2 in **Model A** by action **request:**. Finally, in (10), the model executes method **request:**, and O_2 execute message **msg**.

Figure 3: Message Passing on MMRF

2.2 Universal Meta

A *universal meta* defines the entire metalevel of a base-level object where the metalevel represents the behavior of the base-level object. This is like a "meta object" in traditional reflective object-oriented programming languages such as ABCL/R. The system components and the behavior of an object are included in the universal meta.

The universal meta u is defined as:

$$u \equiv < C, G, \Sigma, P >$$

Universal meta u consists of a set of system components C, a set of state transition diagrams G, a set of state variables Σ, and a set of pairs P of a state transition diagram and a state variable.

C is a set of components defined as: $C = \{c_i \mid 1 \leq i \leq n_1, c_i$ is a component in the system$\}$. A component is an metalevel object that supports execution of a base-level object in the system. For example, if the system includes a message queue, a method table, a scheduler, segment objects and so on, $C = \{message\_queue, method\_table, scheduler, segments...\}$. A component $c_i \in C$ may be defined by a set of components. For example, a component representing object segments at the OS level is defined by some internal components such as a message queue at the language level. This definition enables the representation of components at various abstraction levels. In this example, we represent segments such as $segments = \{message\_queue, method\_table, ...\}$.

G is a set of state transition diagrams defined as: $G = \{g_i \mid 1 \leq i \leq n_2, g_i \subseteq T\}$, where $\forall j, k(g_j \cap g_k = \phi, g_j \in G, g_k \in G)$. The behavior of an object is represented by multiple state transition diagrams. G represents the behavior of an base-level object. A state transition set $g_i \in G$ is an execution set whose member is running sequentially. In other words, actions on different state transition diagrams can occur simultaneously. For example, message handling and scheduling are executed concurrently, because they are on different sets of state transitions. $g_i \in G$ is a state transition diagram that is a subset of a set of state transitions T in the system. State transition $t_n \in T$ is defined as: $s_i \xrightarrow{e_k} s_j$, where $e_k \in E$, $s_i \in S$, $s_j \in S$. E is defined as: $E = \{e_i \mid 1 \leq i \leq n_3, e_i$ is an event which occurs in a system$\}$. S is defined as: $S = \{s_i \mid 1 \leq i \leq n_4, s_i$ is the state of a base-level object$\}$. $s_i \xrightarrow{e_k} s_j \in T$ indicates that the state of an object changes from s_i to s_j when event e_k occurs. A set of state transitions T is defined as: $T = \{t_n \mid t_n \equiv s_i \xrightarrow{e_k} s_j, s_i \in S, s_j \in S, e_k \in E\}$.

Σ is a set of state variables defined as: $\Sigma = \{\sigma_i \mid 1 \leq i \leq n_5, \sigma_i$ is a variable ranging over $S\}$. Each state transition diagram has a state variable that is bound to the current state of an object on the diagram. For example, an object has the state "running" for message handling, and another state "evaluation context in ready queue" for scheduling on different diagrams respectively.

When $s_i \in S$ is the current state on state transition diagram $g_k \in G$, the current state is represented by "$< g_k, \sigma_k >$ and $s_i = bound(\sigma_k)$". A pair $< g_k, \sigma_k >$ is a member of a set of relationships P between a state variables and a current state defined as: $P = \{p_i \mid p_i \equiv < g_i, \sigma_i >, g_i \in G, \sigma_i \in \Sigma\}$. $< g_i, \sigma_i > \in P$ means that σ_i is the state variable that has the current state on g_i. $s_i = bound(\sigma_k)$ indicates that state s_i is bound to state variable σ_k. The function $bound : \Sigma \rightarrow S$ returns the binding value of the argument of the function. The *situation* of an object represents the total state of the object and it is defined by a combination of states in multiple transition diagrams.

2.3 State Transition

State transition behavior is represented by the transition of bind relations. The transition rule is described as $e\frac{A}{B}$. $e\frac{A}{B}$ indicates the transition from A to B when event e occurs. A state transition from s_i to s_j when event e occurs is represented by $e\frac{s_i = bound(\sigma)}{s_j = bound(\sigma)}$. State transition behavior on universal meta $u = < C, G, \Sigma, P >$ is defined as:

$$e\frac{s_i = bound(\sigma)}{s_j = bound(\sigma)}$$

where $e \in E$, $s_i \xrightarrow{e} s_j \in y$ $(\exists y \in G)$, $u \in \Sigma$, $< y, u > \in P$.

2.4 Model

A *model* is a decomposed metalevel. This is a user's operation unit and a representation which is part of the base-level components and behavior. The system components, such as a message queue and internal data for a scheduler, may be changed simultaneously. Thus, a model is represented by a concurrent object. Model m_i named nm_i on the universal meta $u = <C, G, \Sigma, P>$ is defined as:

$$m_i \equiv <nm_i, \sigma_i, C_i, T_i, D_i>$$

Model m_i consists of a model name $nm_i \in N = \{nm_k \mid 1 \leq k \leq n, nm_k$ is a model name $\}$, a state variables $\sigma_i \in \Sigma$, a subset of components $C_i \subseteq C$, a set of state transitions $T_i \subseteq g$ ($\exists g \in G$), and a triple $<e, W, R> \in D_i$. D_i is defined as: $D_i = \{d_k \mid d_k \equiv <e, W, R>, e \in E, W \subseteq C_i, R \subseteq C_i\}$. $<e, W, R>$ means that when event e occurs, W is a set of components that will be modified and R is a set of components that will be read. Figure 4 shows an example of multiple models. In this figure, a universal meta u is decomposed into three models, m_1, m_2, m_3.

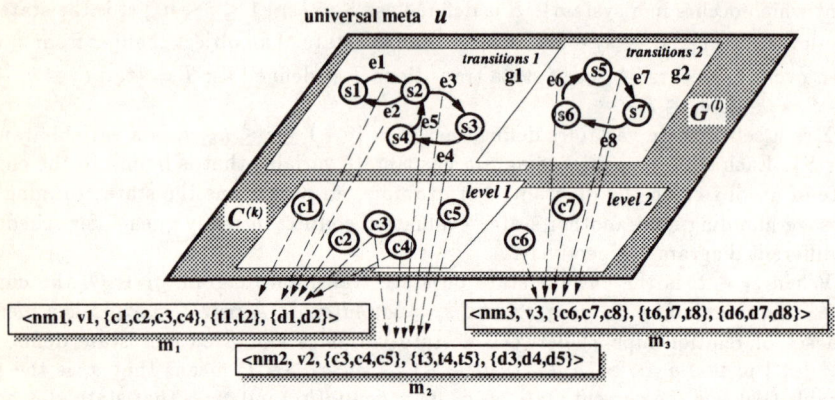

$t1 = s1 \xrightarrow{e1} s2$, $t2 = s2 \xrightarrow{e2} s1$, $d1 = <e1, \{c2\}, \{c3, c4\}>$, $d2 = <e2, \phi, \{c3\}>$ on m_1. $t3 = s2 \xrightarrow{e3} s3$, $t4 = s3 \xrightarrow{e4} s4$, $t5 = s4 \xrightarrow{e5} s2$, $d3 = <e3, \{c3\}, \phi>$, $d4 = <e4, \phi, \{c5\}>$, $d5 = <e5, \{c3, c4, c5\}, \{c3\}>$ on m_2. $t6 = s6 \xrightarrow{e6} s5$, $t7 = s5 \xrightarrow{e7} s6$, $t8 = s7 \xrightarrow{e8} s7$, $d6 = <e6, \{c6\}, \phi>$, $d7 = <e7, \{c6\}, \{c7\}>$, $d8 = <e8, \{c7\}, \phi>$ on m_3.

Figure 4: Example of Models in MMRF

2.5 Sequential Consistency

If a model correctly represents the behavior of a base-level object when an event occurs, the *sequential consistency* of this model is satisfied. The condition of sequential consistency is denoted in Condition 1. Model m_a is sequentially consistent, if and only if a state transition, which modifies the state from the current state s_i to any state s_j when event e occurs, is defined in m_a.

Condition 1 *Sequential Consistency*

When an event e in model $m_a = <nm_a, \sigma_a, C_a, T_a, D_a>$ occurs on universal meta $u = <C, G, \Sigma, P>$, m_a is consistent sequentially if and only if

$s_i \xrightarrow{e} s_j \in T_a$ and $s_i = bound(\sigma_a)$
where $T_a \subseteq g$ ($\exists g \in G$), $<g, \sigma_a> \in P$

□

It should be noted that the state is changed according to the definition in Section 2.3, when an event occurs.

2.6 Concurrent Consistency

The following examines the conditions where event e_1 and event e_2 can occur simultaneously. Condition 2 shows the condition for *concurrency condition*. Condition 3 shows the condition for *atomicity condition*. If both Condition 2 and Condition 3 are satisfied, e_a and e_b can occur simultaneously. The concurrency condition means that components shared by multiple models may be read by models at the same time but not modified. When a conflict occurs, m_a and m_b run according to the rules listed in Table 1. The atomicity condition means that the state of a base-level object must not be modified on two different state transition diagrams by two events that occur simultaneously.

Condition 2 *Concurrency between two models*

Event e_a in model $m_a = <nm_a, \sigma_a, C_a, T_a, D_a>$ and event e_b in model $m_b = <nm_b, \sigma_b, C_b, T_b, D_b>$ are satisfied by the *concurrency condition* if and only if the following condition is satisfied.

$(W_a \cap W_b = \phi) \land (R_a \cap W_b = \phi) \land (W_a \cap R_b = \phi)$

where $<e_a, W_a, R_a> \in D_a$, $<e_b, W_b, R_b> \in D_b$

□

Table 1: Action on conflict between models m_a and m_b

Conflict			Action
$W_a \cap W_b$	$\neq \phi$	(m_a writing, m_b writing)	m_b waits for m_a at reification
$W_a \cap R_b$	$\neq \phi$	(m_a writing, m_b reading)	m_b waits for m_a at reification
$W_r \cap R_b$	$\neq \phi$	(m_a reading, m_b writing)	m_b waits for m_a at reflection

Condition 3 *Atomicity in a model*

Let events e_a in model $m_a = <nm_a, \sigma_a, C_a, T_a, D_a>$ and e_b in model $m_b = <nm_b, \sigma_b, C_b, T_b, D_b>$ be satisfied with sequential consistency in universal meta $u = <C, G, \Sigma, P>$. e_a and e_b are satisfied by the *atomicity condition* if and only if

$g_a \neq g_b$

where $T_a \subseteq g_a$ ($\exists g_a \in G$), $T_b \subseteq g_b$ ($\exists g_b \in G$)

□

3 Programming System AL-1/D

AL-1/D is a distributed concurrent object-based programming system based on Multi-Model Reflection Framework. AL-1/D is available in six *basic models*. A user can perform meta programming and change the behavior of the base-level object. In this section, we describe how the metalevel in AL-1/D is decomposed into basic models and how the mechanisms of interaction among models are implemented in AL-1/D.

3.1 Overview of AL-1/D System

AL-1/D system is implemented on a bytecode interpreter and a compiler. The compiler translates AL-1/D source code into bytecode used as the instruction set for the interpreter. Bytecodes are derived from ConcurrentSmalltalk [YT86], although some codes for realizing reflective facilities have been added. AL-1/D systems are implemented in C++. An interpreter runs on a host. Multiple interpreters exist on multiple hosts, connected using UNIX TCP/IP protocols. The AL-1/D language is corresponding to what would be *Reflective Distributed ConcurrentSmalltalk*, but without the class hierarchy.

3.2 Definition of Universal Meta in AL-1/D

This section covers the definition of a universal meta in AL-1/D, based on MMRF. Object behavior is modeled by the *state transition*, the *components* from Definition 1.

A universal meta $u_{AL-1/D}$ is defined as follows:

$$u_{AL-1/D} \equiv\, <C_{AL-1/D}, G_{AL-1/D}, \Sigma, P>$$

A set of components $C_{AL-1/D}$ is outlined below:

$C_{AL-1/D}$ = { *message_queue, own_variables, method_table, info_table, meta_table, context_pool, object_state, evaluation_stack, sender_object, continuation, base_object, delegatee_object, temp_variables, context, segment, object_name, scheduler, gc, loader, file_handler, network, name_table, name_server, display, stdio, ...*}

The set of state transition diagrams $G_{AL-1/D}$ is shown in Figure 5. Table 2 lists the events in the state transition diagrams. The definitions of Σ and P are omitted because there is no space for description.

3.3 Basic Models

AL-1/D is available in six *basic models*; Operation, Resource, Statistics, DE, Migration, and System models. These models can be used to customize the behavior of an object in a distributed environment. Basic models are constructed based on MMRF. These six models are supported to enable concentration on the modification of the following features in the distributed programming system; language semantics, OS features, constraints between objects and the system, transparency in distributed environments, and the strategy of the migration mechanism.

In the following, we explain how basic models are represented, and what can be modified in basic models. This paper describes the Operation and Resource models, using sample programs. Other models are over-viewed. The use of these models is described in [OIT92].

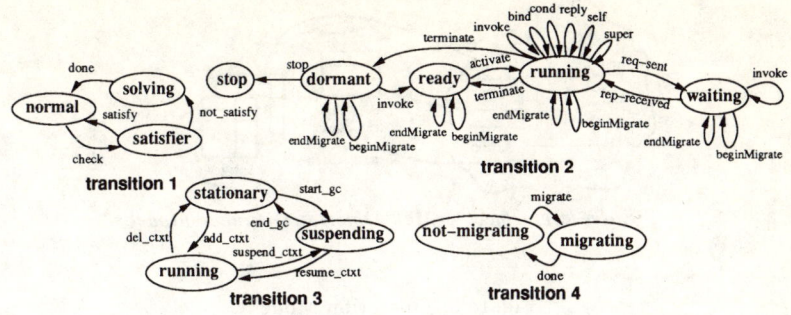

Figure 5: Default State Transitions of AL-1/D Object

Table 2: Default Events in AL-1/D

Event	Event Name	Event	Event Name
message arrival	event_arrival	answer arrival	event_answer_arrival
sync. message sending	event_sync_sending	async. message sending	event_async_sending
own variable binding	event_bind_ownvars	temp variable binding	event_bind_tmpvars
reply start	event_reply_start	return start	event_return_start
condition expression	event_condition	self call	event_self_call
delegatee call	event_delegatee_call	invoke a method	event_method_beginning
method ending	event_method_end	killed by GC	event_object_stop
exception handling	event_exception	timeout handling	event_timeout
migration	event_migration	before migration	event_before_migration
after migration	event_after_migration	stat check	event_stat_check
satisfied	event_stat_satisfied	not satisfied	event_stat_notsatisfied
running GC	event_running_gc	ending GC	event_end_gc
running context	event_add_context	ending context	event_del_context
suspending context	event_suspend_context	resuming context	event_resume_context

3.3.1 Operation Model

The Operation Model is used to modify the language operation semantics. In this model, OS features are invisible. A base-level object is represented by a message queue, its own variables, a method table, a name table, the state of the object, an evaluation stack, a continuation, a sender object and a template of the future object. Figure 6 shows an overview of the Operation Model.

The definition of the Operation Model based on MMRF follows.

$m_{ope} \equiv\ <Operation, \sigma_{ope}, C_{ope}, T_{ope}, D_{ope}>$
$\quad C_{ope} = \{message\_queue, own\_variables, method\_table, object\_state, evaluation\_stack,$
$\qquad continuation, sender\_object, name\_table, future\_template\}$
$\quad T_{ope} = \{running \stackrel{event\_sync\_send}{\longrightarrow} waiting, ...\}$
$\quad D_{ope} = \{\ <event\_message\_arrival, \{message\_queue\}, \phi>,$
$\qquad <event\_sync\_send, \phi, \{method\_table\}>,$
$\qquad <event\_bind\_ownvars, \{own\_variables\}, \phi>,$
$\qquad <event\_return\_start, \{evaluation\_stack\}, \phi>, ...\}$

The behavior of the model is specified by the methods of a meta object which represent the model. Table 3 lists the relationship between events and methods.

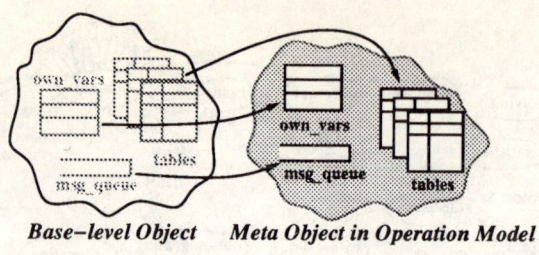

Base-level Object   Meta Object in Operation Model

Figure 6: Operation Model

Table 3: Events and Methods in Operation Model

event_answer_arrival	answer:from:	event_sync_send	ssend:message:
event_async_send,	asend:message:	event_bind_ownvars	obind:value:
event_bind_tmpvars	tbind:value:	event_reply_start	reply:to:
event_return_start	return:to:	event_condition	cond:true:false:
event_self_call	self:	event_delegatee_call	delegation:
event_method_beginning	methodBegin:	event_method_end	methodEnd:
event_object_stop	stop:	event_exception	exception:
event_timeout	timeout:		

The following example shows the definition of a meta object named **OpeExam**, that represents the Operation Model of base-level object **Example**. The **vars** statement defines the internal variables of **Example**. The default definitions of methods "**ssend:message:**", "**request:**" and "**obind:value:**" are also shown.

```
[ meta Operation OpeExam Example                [ method OpeExam
  (vars  messageQueue  /* message queue */             ssend: rcvr message: msg
         ownVars       /* own variables */       (rcvr meta: #request:) request: msg
         methodTable   /* method table */      ]
         nameTable     /* name table */
         state         /* state */              [ method OpeExam request: msg
         evaltop       /* evaluation stack */     msgQueue add: msg
         continuation  /* continuation */      ]
         sender        /* sender object */
         future        /* future template */    [ method OpeExam obind: pos value: val
  )                                               ownVars at: pos put: val
]                                              ]
```

"**ssend:message:**" defines the semantics of synchronous message sending. "**request:**" defines object behavior for arriving message. "**obind:value:**" represents the event which binds a value to an internal variable. When any meta object is defined explicitly, the default meta objects are defined and will contain the these methods. "**ssend:message:**" defines the event of the start of message sending. In this method, the method "**request:**" in a meta object of the receiver object is invoked. In "**request:**", the received message is queued into the variable **messageQueue**, representing a message queue. In "**obind:value:**", a value is inserted into its own variable slot, represented by the variable **ownVars**.

As shown in the following program, the method "`request:`" is modified so that a base-level object can handle messages with priorities. In this program, a received message is stored ahead of a lower priority message in the queue by a list operation, without changing the mechanism of the message queue.

```
1 [ method OpeExam request: msg
2   (vars list newlist)
3   list = msgQueue getFirst;
4   while (msg priority < list msg priority) do
5     list = list next
6   end;
7   newlist = List create value: msg;
8   list next: newlist;
9   newlist next: nil
10 ]
```

3.3.2 Resource model

The Resource model is used to modify OS features. In this model, the language layer is invisible. In the Resource model, environment elements related to a base-level object are the main concern. This model represents computational resources on a single host, not on a distributed environment such as a network. A base-level object is represented as a context object, a segment object, a scheduler and a garbage collector in the Resource model. Figure 7 overviews this model.

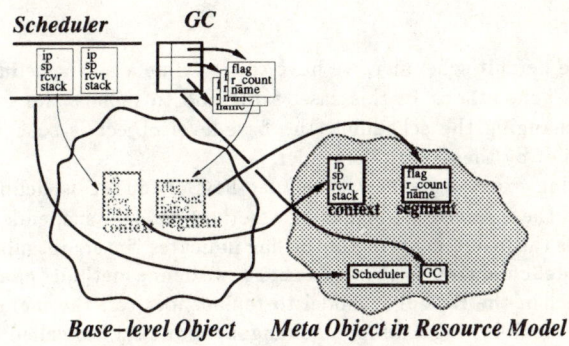

Figure 7: Resource model

The definition of the Resource model based on MMRF is given below.

$m_{res} \equiv <Resource, \sigma_{res}, C_{res}, T_{res}, D_{res} >$
  $C_{res} = \{context, segment, scheduelr, gc\}$
  $T_{res} = \{running \xrightarrow{event\_running\_gc} freezing, ...\}$
  $D_{res} = \{ \quad < event\_running\_gc, \phi, \{segment, gc\} >,$
    $< event\_add\_context, \phi, \{context, scheduler\} >,$
    $< event\_del\_context, \phi, \{context, scheduler\} >,$
    $< event\_suspend\_context, \phi, \{context, scheduler\} >,$
    $< event\_resume\_context, \phi\{context, scheduler\} >, ...\}$
  where $context = \{stack, tmp\_variables, ip, sp, ...\}$
    $segment = \{message\_queue, own\_variables, method\_table, ...\}$

The following example shows the definition of a meta object named `ResExam` which represents the Resource model of base-level object `Example`.

```
1 [meta Resource ResExam Example
2   (vars context    /* context object */
3         segment    /* segment object */
4         scheduler  /* scheduler object */
5         gc         /* garbage collector */
6   )
7 ]
```

The example below shows part of the definition of the `Scheduler` object. Method "add:" is invoked when a new context is generated. Method "run:" is invoked by the AL-1/D system periodically and performs context switching.

```
1  [ base Scheduler                         15 [ method Scheduler run
2    (delegation nil)                       16   (vars ctxt next)
3    (vars evaluator first last)            17   if (first != nil) then
4  ]                                        18     ctxt = evaluator get: first;
5                                           19     next = ctxt next;
6  [ method Scheduler add: ctxt             20     ctxt next: nil;
7    if (first == nil) then                 21     evaluator put: first;
8      first = last = ctxt                  22     if (next != nil) then
9    else                                   23       first = next;
10     last next: ctxt;                     24       last next: ctxt
11     last = ctxt                          25     else
12   end                                    26       first = last = ctxt
13 ]                                        27     end
14                                          28   end
                                            29 ]
```

To modify the default scheduler, we have to (i) define a new scheduler and (ii) store it in the variable `scheduler`. In this case, a method to replace the scheduler must be defined. After changing the scheduler, the base-level object is scheduled by the new scheduler instead of by the default scheduler.

In the following example, a new scheduler `NewScheduler` is defined. This object checks the flag of the inserted context in the method "add:", suspends the current context, and executes the inserted context if the flag indicates "interrupt mode", in lines from 7 to 10. To add `NewScheduler` to object `Example`, we define method "changeScheduler:" of the meta object in the Resource model to replace and call the meta object from another object. In the following example, "changeScheduler:" is called by the base-level object. After completing the meta object, reflection occurs and the new scheduler is used.

```
                                            16     last = ctxt
1  [ base NewScheduler                      17   end
2    (delegation nil)                       18 end
3    (vars evaluator first last suspend)    19 ]
4  ]                                        20
5                                           21 [ method ResExam
6  [ method NewScheduler add: ctxt          22         changeScheduler: sched
7    if (ctxt flag == #interrupt) then      23   scheduler = sched
8      suspend = evaluator get: first;      24 ]
9      ctxt waiting: first;                 25
10     evaluator put: ctxt                  26 [ method Example replaceScheduler
11   else                                   27   (vars newSched)
12     if (first == nil) then               28   newSched = NewScheduler create;
13       first = last = ctxt;               29   (meta: #Resource)
14     else                                 30      changeScheduler: newSched
15       last next: ctxt;                   31 ]
```

3.3.3 Statistics model

In the Statistics model, an object is modeled by statistical information related to the object itself and underlying resources, instead of by procedural modeling. The statistical information of the base-level object includes the *cpu time*, *memory usage*, and communication *blocking time*, while that of the underlying resources include such as load average, memory usage and communication usage. The scheduling priority in a local host and the load balancing strategy in the distributed environment are given by the constraints in the statistical information.

A meta object in the Statistics model holds this statistical information. By meta object programming in the Statistics model, a base-level object may control the dynamic configuration in a declarative fashion, i.e., may control the constraints programming.

3.3.4 DE model

The DE (Distributed Environment) model is designed to describe a distributed environment. Unlike the Operation model, the location of an object and remote host information, such as the CPU and communication load, are visible in the DE model. The semantics of remote communication and migration are described by a meta object of the DE model. The meta object keeps the location of the receiver object and three special objects called *nameserver*, *remoteinfo* and *network*. Each state change in the base-level object is expressed by interaction between those objects, to define the semantics of remote communication and migration.

The *nameserver* object is responsible for translating the unique identifier (UID) of an object to the object address (or location), so that it has a cache table for address translation. The *remoteinfo* object holds host information such as the CPU and communication load. Using this information, we may control the load balancing strategy, i.e., an idle processor or heavily loaded processor initiates load balancing.

3.3.5 Migration model

The Migration model describes how an object migrates to a remote host. A base-level object is represented by a meta object that consists of a *container* object and a *network* object. The container object is a movable representation of a base-level object. Unlike the DE model, the Migration model represents a low abstraction level, such as bit streams that are sent on a network.

When an object migrates to a remote host, the object is only moved by default. That is, even if the object has other objects, those objects are not moved. To decrease communication traffic, the base-level object can control which objects are moved to the remote host, using meta programming in the Migration model.

3.3.6 System model

The System model represents the components of the AL-1/D system that are related to the base-level object. That is, all components and all behavior are visible. The components are protected data that can be accessed as segment objects. The System model is used to modify the kernel of the AL-1/D system and to construct a model. The System model can be considered as being a representation of the default universal meta.

3.3.7 Programming with Basic Models

Application programmers can modify basic models as necessary to customize the system according to the characteristics of their application. For example, if there is a soft real-time application program, we need to customize objects in the application such that the message sending mechanism supports the timeout feature and the scheduler can handle interrupts asynchronously. In this case, we modify the contents of the method "ssend:message:" in the Operation model and replace the Scheduler object denoted by internal variable scheduler in the Resource model. Since these parts are independent of each other, these modifications can be made easily. The remaining four basic models are not considered and operate according to the default system definition.

3.4 Examples of Consistency among Models

This section provides examples of sequential and concurrent consistency among models.

Let us consider that the event of assignment to variables occurs when base-level object O is dormant; state **dormant** and when O is running; state **running**. When the state is **dormant**, the event is invalid because the state transition $dormant \xrightarrow{event\_bind\_ownvars} \beta$ (where β is any state) does not exist in the base-level object. On the other hand, when state is **running**, the event is valid because the state transition $running \xrightarrow{event\_bind\_ownvars} running$ exists. No assignment to variables occurs when no method is executed.

Next, let us consider the concurrency between the Operation and Resource models when the situation of object O includes state **dormant** in transition 1 and state **stationary** in transition 2 in Figure 5. In this case, state transitions by events event_arrival, event_add_context, and event_running_gc are valid because state transitions $dormant \xrightarrow{event\_arrival} dormant$, $stationary \xrightarrow{event\_add\_context} running$, and $stationary \xrightarrow{event\_running\_gc} suspended$ are defined in the Operation and Resource models. In Operation model $m_{ope} \equiv <Operation, \sigma_{ope}, C_{ope}, T_{ope}, D_{ope}>$,
$d_{ope} = <event\_arrival, W_{ope}, R_{ope}> \in D_{ope}$, where $W_{ope} = \{message\_queue\}$, $R_{ope} = \phi$.
In Resource model $m_{res} \equiv <Resource, \sigma_{res}, C_{res}, T_{res}, D_{res}>$,
$d_{res} = <event\_add\_context, W_{res}, R_{res}> \in D_{res}$, where $W_{res} = \phi$, $R_{res} = \{context, scheduler\}$ and $d'_{res} = <event\_running\_gc, W'_{res}, R'_{res}> \in D_{res}$ where $W'_{res} = \phi$, $R'_{res} = \{segment, gc\}$. $(W_{ope} \cap W_{res} = \phi) \wedge (R_{ope} \cap W_{res} = \phi) \wedge (R_{ope} \cap W_{res} = \phi)$ is satisfied by Condition 2. Thus, events event_arrival and event_add_context can occur simultaneously. On the other hand, $W_{ope} \cap R'_{res} \neq \phi$ because $segment = \{message\_queue, own\_variables, ...\}$. This is not satisfied by Condition 2. Thus, event_arrival and event_running_gc cannot occur at the same time and the Resource model waits for reification of the Operation model, based on Table 1 in Section 2.6.

4 Implementation

4.1 Reification, Reflection and Modification

Data is exchanged between a system and a model during reification and reflection. In AL-1/D, the values by which model components in the system are bound to the internal variables of a meta object when a meta object in a model starts invocation. When execution of a meta object finishes, the contents of the internal variables are reflected on the real system. In these cases, objects in the implementation language C++ are translated to objects in AL-1/D language, and vice versa. The AL-1/D interpreter ignores whether an object is meta or base-level. This is left to the compiler. When the AL-1/D compiler finds a definition of a meta object method, it generates *retrieve* bytecodes at the top of the method and *unretrieve* bytecodes before the return bytecode. Reification is performed by the retrieve bytecode. Reflection is performed by the unretrieve bytecode. When a meta object is invoked, a sequence of bytecodes, compiled by the AL-1 compiler, are executed on the interpreter. Any parts of object behavior that are not defined by the meta object are executed according to the default system definition. This mechanism enables the AL-1/D system to operate as fast as traditional object-oriented language systems such as ConcurrentSmalltalk, provided reflective features are not used.

When a model is modified, the behavior of its base-level object is modified because of its influence on a real system upon the termination of execution of the model. If a model in the virtual machine to which the modified model belongs is invoked. Subsequent to modification, reification occurs using system components. Concurrency control avoids conflict among models, as described later.

4.2 Sequential Consistency Checking

Execution of a model when an event occurs is represented by message sending and execution, because a model is represented by a meta object. A meta object is invoked by the AL-1/D system. Such an invocation of the meta objects is called *implicit* reification in [Mae87]. The AL-1/D system looks up in a table, called "event table", that maps between events and methods, and invokes a meta object by message sending.

Meta objects can also be invoked by events generated explicitly by users. This invocation is called *explicit* reification in [Mae87]. For example, an action where a receiver object accepts messages is generated by the sender object with message passing. In this case, it is necessary for the AL-1/D system to check whether the action is suitable for Condition 1 in MMRF. A table, called "state transition table", is used for checking. That table lists the relationship between events, and states after and before events. If the action satisfies Condition 1, the system reports an error.

4.3 Communication between Models and Objects

A model is represented by an concurrent object in AL-1/D. Some models in a base-level object can send messages to each other syntactically. That specification of AL-1/D results in problems, such as deadlocks. To avoid these problems, message passing between models that belong to a base-level object is not permitted, and an error is reported. Models are independent of other models. That is, one model is not a part of another model. Thus, this constraint is suitable for the definition of MMRF.

It is necessary, however, to provide a mechanism like continuations between models; there is the case where a model needs to be invoked after another model has been invoked. This is because a sequence of state transitions is represented by multiple models. For example, we may want the DE model to measure the number of remote messages and the Migration model to migrate a base-level object based on the result of the DE model. In AL-1/D, a *transition statement* can be used to describe such programs. This statement generates requests for state transitions. For example, "`state migrating: location`" is a transition statement for transition to the state `migration`. Transition statements can have arguments that correspond to those of the methods in a model invoked by that action.

4.4 Concurrency Consistency between Models

The AL-1/D system controls concurrency between models by examining Condition 2 in MMRF. That is, if a model is running when a method invocation request reaches another model and a base-level object includes both models, the AL-1/D system needs to examine whether the components of a base-level object are shared by both method invocations. The system uses a table, called the *accessed components table*, which stores components accessed by a method and controls concurrency.

The AL-1/D system provides users with another mechanism for concurrency control. Users can use either of two kinds of methods; the *state* and *non-state methods*. If a method in a meta object changes the state of a base-level object, the method should be defined as a state method. When a state method is invoked, all related meta objects and base-level objects are suspended, being only resumed only once the state method is completed. To support this mechanism, the *suspendMetas* and the *resumeMetas* bytecode are introduced. The bytecodes in the state method include a suspendMetas bytecode at the start of the method (before the retrieve code) and a resumeMetas bytecode at the end of the method (after the unretrieve code).

5 Conclusion and Remarks

This paper described the definition of the Multi-Model Reflection Framework (MMRF). A way of the decomposition of metalevel into multiple models, and conditions for sequential and concurrent consistency when multiple models are running simultaneously, are shown. To achieve sequential consistency, multiple state transition diagrams are employed to represent the behavior of a base-level object. To accomplish concurrent consistency, modified and read system components of a base-level object are kept in the models.

Using the examples of modifying message handling policy and scheduling policy in the programming system AL-1/D based on MMRF, we showed that metalevel decomposition is useful for users to customize a system that consists of some components running concurrently and independently. This example implies metalevel decomposition enables programmers to represent the concurrent behavior of a system naturally and to modify parts of the metalevel as necessary, without having to consider other parts or represent concurrency between modules in the metalevel. MMRF helps us to understand and customize the metalevel more easily than in previous reflective systems.

We also described how models are defined in the AL-1/D programming system and how AL-1/D is implemented based on the MMRF definition. There are six models, called basic models, in AL-1/D and the system components can be customized for various parts of the distributed system. Besides the modification of message handling and scheduling policy shown in this paper, programmers can customize which objects move with a migrating object to a remote host and so on. AL-1/D is implemented on Sun SparcStations, DEC stations, and SONY NEWS workstations, connected using UNIX TCP/IP protocols.

While it is true that MMRF is a general modular programming technique for the metalevel, it differs, however, in the following aspects. First, MMRF supports sequential and concurrent consistency checking when multiple models are running at the same time. This enables us to maintain the correctness of the base-level object behavior. Secondly, MMRF is not intended for system design but for customizing. That is, a model is not a physical unit for designing a system but a semantic one used to modify a system. For example, models can represent a set of operations at the language level, a set of shared resources, and so on. Thus, multiple models may share components of a base-level object or models may be independent of each other. Conceptually, models are similar to views in database management systems. The extracting and customizing of the necessary components in the programming system of MMRF corresponds to that of the necessary data in a database system.

References

[CIM92] Roy H. Campbell, Nayeem Islam, and Peter Madany. Choices, Frameworks and Refinement. *Computing Systems*, Vol. 5, No. 3, 1992.

[Kee89] S. E. Keene. *Object-Oriented Programming in Common Lisp: a Programmer's Guide to CLOS*. Addison-Wesley, 1989.

[Mae87] Pattie Maes. Concepts and Experiments in Computational Reflection. In *Proceedings of OOPSLA'87*, pp. 147–155, 1987.

[OIT92] Hideaki Okamura, Yutaka Ishikawa, and Mario Tokoro. AL-1/D: A Distributed Programming System with Multi-Model Reflection Framework. In *Proceedings of the International Workshop on New Models for Software Architecture'92 Reflection and Meta-level Architecture*, November 1992.

[WY88] Takuo Watanabe and Akinori Yonezawa. Reflection in an Object-Oriented Concurrent Language. In *Proceedings of OOPSLA'88*, pp. 306–315, 1988.

[Yok92] Yasuhiko Yokote. The Apertos Reflective Operating System: The Concept and Its Implementation. In *Proceedings of OOPSLA'92*, October 1992.

[YT86] Yasuhiko Yokote and Mario Tokoro. The Design and Implementation of ConcurrentSmalltalk. In *Proceedings of OOPSLA'86*, pp. 331–340, 1986.

[YT87] A. Yonezawa and M. Tokoro, editors. *Concurrent Object-Oriented Systems*. The MIT Press, 1987.

Definition of a Reflective Kernel for a Prototype-Based Language

Philippe Mulet, Pierre Cointe
Ecole des Mines de Nantes
3, rue Marcel Sembat
44049 Nantes Cedex 04
(+33) 40.44.83.87 - Fax (+33) 40.71.97.40
[mulet,cointe]@info.emn.fr

Abstract

We present the implementation of Moostrap, a reflective prototype-based language, the interpreter of which is written in Scheme. Moostrap is based on a reduced number of primitives, according to a previous work for defining a taxonomy for prototype-based languages.

Our purpose is to reify the behavior of any object through two steps: the slot lookup and its application. The first phase is reified thanks to *behavioral meta-objects*, and the second is managed by special objects, called *slot-executants*.

This kernel does not handle any implicit delegation at first. However, we introduce it, as a first extension of the basic language using a new behavioral meta-object.

Keywords: Prototype, Reflection, Primitive, Slot, Creation, Cloning, Delegation, Extensibility, Behavior, Meta-Object, Self, Smalltalk, Scheme.

1 Introduction

Our general area of research is the study of reflection in object-oriented languages (OOLs). We have previously defined a model of behavioral reflection expressing the computation of a message as the combination of a message lookup and a message application.

We have implemented and experimented this model in a newly defined prototype-based language, which bootstraps itself from a reduced set of primitives, and named Moostrap (standing for "Mini Object Oriented System Towards Reflective Architectures for Programming"). The purpose of this paper is to describe this reflective language.

Moostrap belongs to the family of prototype-based languages, a basic alternative to class-based languages. Indeed, we decided to free our language from classes, because they hardly deal with one-of-a-kind objects. Furthermore, we believe that classes interfere with the "emerging" notion of meta-objects [MDC92].

Initially, we realized a Smalltalk'80 implementation of the Self 1.0 prototype-based language [MR91], that we then extended to perform reflective computation [CMDM92].

Our purpose was also to add reflective facilities to control the computation rules of message sending.

In standard Self, prototype structure can be consulted thanks to *mirror* objects [CUL89]. These first-class objects are created explicitly to provide an interface between a prototype and its internal representation. Unfortunately, mirrors are not *causally connected* to the internal structure they only give a reading access to and are mainly used to create virtual slot-descriptor objects [MCD91]. In fact, mirrors are not supposed to play the role of behavioral meta-objects; we rather decided to introduce explicit meta-objects (to handle the lookup) and a new reification mechanism for slots (to handle the application process and to allow slot extension). This approach allowed us to roughly validate our scheme for behavioral reflection in the context of Self. However our explicit reification of slots was not nicely integrated to Self, and rather than changing the kernel of Self (and its virtual machine) we decided to design our own language and to implement its first interpreter in Scheme [Sch89].

This paper is divided into four parts. We first describe Moostrap as a prototype-based language, then we introduce the reflective model of this language. In a third part, we extend the kernel, thanks to reflective facilities, in order to add implicit delegation, a kind of inheritance between prototypes. Then we present some implementation details and conclude on our future work.

2 Moostrap: a Tiny Prototype-Based Language

The taxonomy of prototype-based languages, established in [DMC92], assumes that these languages are basically built on objects communicating by message sending and supporting cloning facilities. The classification is then made according to the following criteria: representation of information either unified as slots or separated as variables and methods, dynamic modification of object structures, ex-nihilo objects creation, explicit or implicit delegation, and handling of split-objects due to delegation.

According to this taxonomy, Moostrap is classified as a language where the prototypes store information as slots. It allows dynamic modification of prototype structures, creation of objects ex-nihilo empty or even with an initialized structure, but does not provide any mechanism of delegation. This is however supplied by implicit sharing between prototypes achieved by a primitive for adding shared slots.

2.1 Components of the Language

The set of primitives of Moostrap prototype-based language is deliberately kept small. Ex-nihilo objects can be created thanks to a special syntax; we only regard as primitives the following operations: cloning objects, adding slots to an object or removing them.

2.1.1 Ex-Nihilo Declaration of Prototypes

Prototypes are made up of slots. In Moostrap, the notion of slot corresponds to an association (`<name>` `<value>`), a type of dynamic binding. We distinguish two kinds of slots: data slots and function slots. Data slots are themselves divided into two categories: mutable and immutable slots. Function slots are immutable slots.

Data Slots
The distinction between mutable and immutable slots occurs at declare time, as in Self [CUL89], according to the following syntax:

(<name> = <value>) declaration of an **immutable** data slot.
> The value of the slot is computed at creation time, and cannot be changed afterwards. In fact, the slot produced by such a declaration is only a reading accessor to the data stored.

(<name> <- <value>) declaration of a **mutable** data slot.
> The value is used for initializing the slot, and can be changed afterwards at will. For such a declaration, the system builds in fact two slots, like in Self: a reading accessor (named as the declared mutable slot) that contains the real data to be stored, and a writing accessor (the name of which is obtained by adding the suffix ":" to the declared slot name), which is an assignment slot for updating the slot containing the data.

Examples:
- (x = 1) declaration of an immutable slot.
  It creates a slot named "x", used for reading the value of the binding (x 1).

- (y <- 2) declaration of a mutable slot.
  It creates two slots, named "y" and "y:", used respectively for reading or updating the value of y.

Function Slots or Methods
These slots contain function values, corresponding to standard methods in other OOLs. Their declaration uses the following syntax:
$$(<\text{method name}> (\text{arg}_1\ \text{arg}_2\ \ldots\ \text{arg}_n)\ <\text{expr}_1>\ \ldots\ <\text{expr}_p>)$$
The body expressions are evaluated sequentially, and the value of the last one gives the value returned by the method. In a method body, `self` is bound to the receiver of the message.

Example: `(greaterThan (n) (self > n))`
Method testing if the receiver is greater than its argument.

Declaring a Prototype
Creating objects ex-nihilo is allowed according to the following protocol:
$$(-\texttt{proto}\ <\text{slot}_1>\ <\text{slot}_2>\ \ldots\ <\text{slot}_n>)$$

Example:

```
(-proto (x <- 1)
        (y <- 2)
        (display () ((self x) display)("@" display)
                    ((self y) display)))
```

Declaration of a prototype made up with 5 real slots: two data slots "x" and "y", two assignment slots "x:" and "y:", and a method "display".

2.1.2 Message Sending

Message sending is the fundamental mechanism for invoking methods in Moostrap, and its syntax is defined as follows:

$$(\text{<receiver>} \text{ <selector>} \text{ <arg}_1\text{>} \ldots \text{<arg}_n\text{>})$$

Example: `(3 greaterThan 5) ---> false`

Extending Message Sending

Like Smalltalk and Self, Moostrap can be extended to provide conditionals using its only existing control structure, i.e, message sending. We introduce the notion of block, representing the evaluation of a sequence of expressions, which is delayed until the block receives the message "value".

$$(\text{-block (arg}_1 \text{ arg}_2 \ldots \text{arg}_n\text{) <expr}_1\text{>} \ldots \text{<expr}_p\text{>})$$

Example: *Method computing the factorial of its argument recursively.*

```
(fact (n) ((n = 0) ifTrueIfFalse
                    (-block () 1)
                    (-block () ((self fact (n - 1)) * n))))
```

Supposing that `hall` *object owns the* `fact` *method.*

`(hall fact 3) ---> 6`

2.1.3 Extending and Modifying Prototypes

We defined two primitives inspired by Self, to modify the structure of objects.

- Adding slots: `-addSharedSlots`.

  Use: `(anObject -addSharedSlots anotherObject)`

  It adds all the slots owned by `anotherObject` to the receiver `anObject`. Invoking this primitive results in having all the slots of `anotherObject` shared between `anotherObject` and `anObject`.

  Gathering in the same object several slots having the same name is not allowed, therefore the redundant slots of `anObject` are replaced by those of `anotherObject`.

- Removing a slot: `-removeSlot`.

  Use: `(anObject -removeSlot aString)`

  This primitive removes the slot named `aString` from `anObject`.

2.1.4 Cloning

Cloning is a fundamental aspect of prototype-based languages; it plays the same creation role as instantiation for class-based languages. The primitive `-clone` copies already existing objects. It creates a shallow copy of the receiver, i.e. the clone object is a set of new slots, sharing respectively the same values with the original object (cf. figure 1).

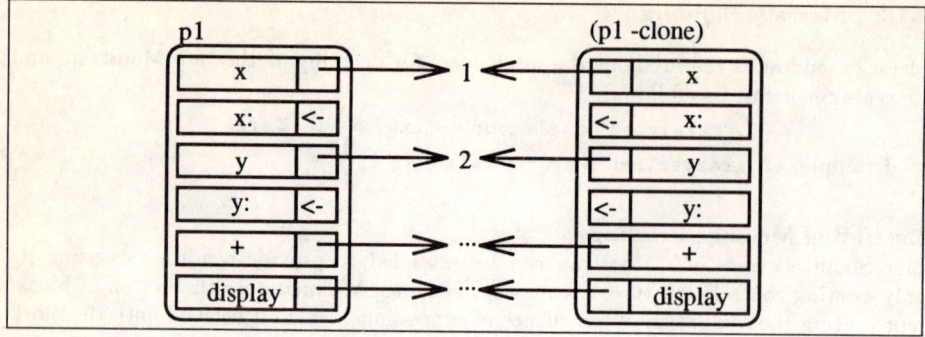

Figure 1: Relation between a prototype of a point **p1** and a clone of it.

2.2 Initial World in Moostrap

In the same way as Self or Smalltalk systems, the interpreter knows a small number of predefined objects, forming together the initial world of Moostrap.

- **hall** : *Main object in Moostrap.*

  The **hall** object is equivalent to the **lobby** of Self, and is used for referencing other "global" objects, via its slots.

  Unlike Self and its built-in implicit delegation, there is no inheritance in Moostrap at first. Therefore, **hall** is just a kind of global environment, like the **Smalltalk** dictionary in Smalltalk or the **user-initial-environment** in Scheme. Defining a global variable in Moostrap is adding by adding a slot to **hall**.

  Any expression typed at the top-level is evaluated in **hall** context, for example, in the expression (**self x**), the variable **self** is associated to **hall**. It is the same when creating ex-nihilo objects: any slot initialization is evaluated in the **hall** context.

  Example: (hall -addSharedSlots (-proto (lobby = self)))
  Adding a self-reference to **hall**.

  According to our interpreter, the **hall** symbol is a pseudo-variable, that refers to the main object. Pseudo-variables are special variables, implicitly bound by the interpreter, such as the receiver accessed by means of the pseudo-variable **self**.

- **true** and **false** : *Boolean objects.*

  In the same way as in Smalltalk and Self, booleans are used for implementing conditionals. The two pseudo-variables **true** and **false** denote the Moostrap's boolean objects. They could have been stored in two data slots of **hall**, but in that case, accessing the boolean **true** would have required the long and tedious evaluation of (**hall true**). True is also the result of the evaluation of an expression such as (0 = 0).

- **nil** : *Value of not initialized slots.*

`Nil` is the same as its equivalent in Smalltalk, or in Self. It is different from an empty prototype as returned by (-proto). It is also accessed via the pseudo-variable "nil", instead of being stored in the `hall`.

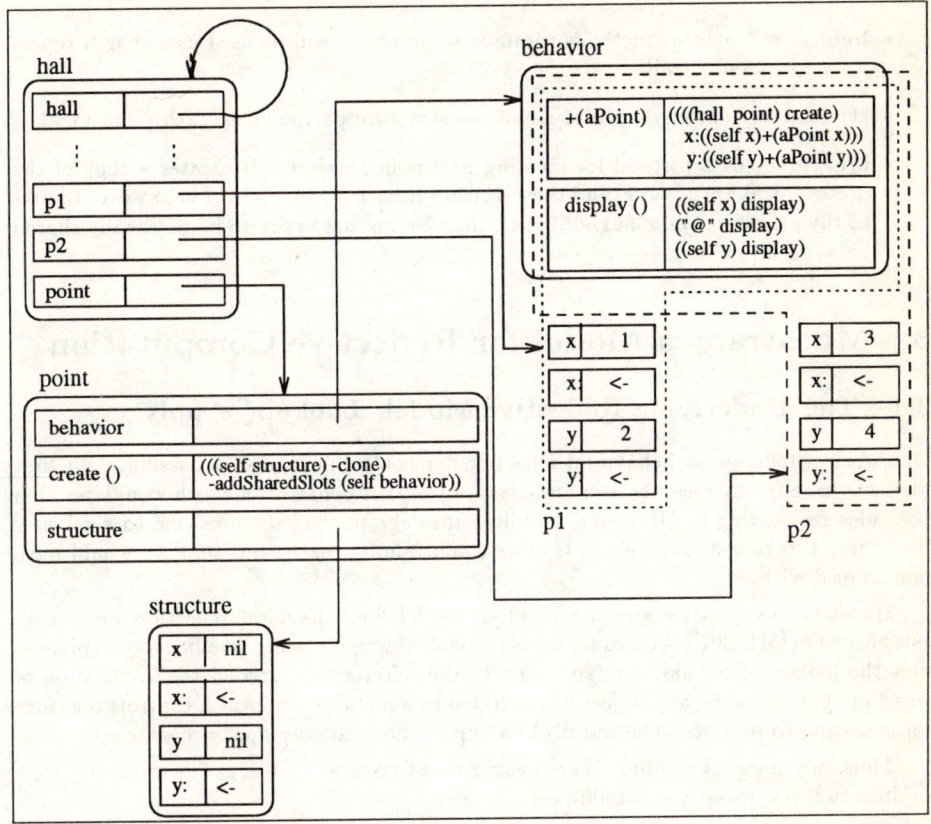

Figure 2: Representation of points based upon slots sharing.

2.3 Extending the Initial World: Modeling Points

To give a flavor of programming in Moostrap, we propose to model points. It will be also the opportunity to introduce how to share information in Moostrap by using the -addSharedSlots primitive.

In class-based languages, a point instance is generally represented as a pair of coordinates (x,y) sharing with all the set of other points, a behavior described in its class. In Self, there is obviously no class, but classes are partially simulated by repository prototypes called "traits". Then points can be defined as elementary prototypes, owning two mutable data slots "x" and "y", and sharing their common behavior by delegating to the same "traits".

At this point Moostrap does not yet support delegation. However, we can use slots sharing as a replacement to model points as in Self.

Figure 2 shows a proposal for implementing points. It consists in creating an object **point**, referenced as a global variable in **hall**. This **point** object comprises three slots:

- **behavior:** contains methods common to points, it will be used as a shared repository for points "traits."

- **structure:** contains a prototype of the structure particular to each point (x,y).

- **create:** holds a method for creating new points objects. It creates a copy of the prototypical **structure**, and then enriches it with all the slots of **behavior** (thanks to the primitive **-addSharedSlots**), thus forcing **behavior** to be physically shared between all points.

3 Moostrap: a Model for Reflective Computation

3.1 The Underlying Reflective Model: Lookup◯Apply

Our work is focused on behavioral reflection for controlling message passing. Our first idea was to reify any message as a first-class object, the behavior of which would describe the rules for solving it. However, handling message passing requires one to send new messages, also reified themselves, leading to an infinite regression, that we would have had to deal with.

Moostrap uses, as its starting point, a model for behavioral reflection previously established in [MDC92]. According to this model, message passing is reified as two phases: first the lookup of the slot corresponding to the selector, and second the application of this slot. Furthermore, any object is associated to a meta-object, which controls the rules for accessing to its slots. The result of lookup ought to answer **apply** messages.

Thus, any message sending (**receiver selector** arg_1 ... arg_n) is implicitly split up into two new messages as follows:

$$((\textit{meta-object}(\texttt{receiver})\ \texttt{lookup receiver selector})$$
$$\texttt{apply receiver}\ \textit{array-of}(arg_1\ ...\ arg_n))$$

Invoking a primitive (identified by a selector prefixed by "-") bypasses this reflective decomposition. Primitives are directly performed by the interpreter as global functions.

Example: (hall -lookup "clone")
   -lookup *returns the slot named "clone", located in* hall

3.2 The Lookup Phase: Behavioral Meta-objects

Every behavioral meta-object has to implement a method named **lookup**, used for describing and solving slot lookup. It takes as arguments the receiver of the message and its selector. Further, we will note it **lookup(rcv sel)**.

Any meta-object is a first-class object. As such, it must be described by a meta-object. This infinite regression of meta-links is stopped, just like for ObjVLisp, by introducing circularity in the meta-link [Coi87]. Some objects are their own meta-objects, and thus become meta-objects themselves. Henceforth, we will name them *circular meta-objects*.

3.2.1 The Basic Meta-Object

Moostrap's initial world includes a first circular meta-object, named `basic-meta-object`. This initial meta-object defines a basic `lookup(rcv sel)` method, searching for a slot in the only receiver. By default, all objects in the system are associated to it, especially for objects created ex-nihilo.

This `lookup` method either directly returns the slot found (by performing the primitive `-lookup`), or raises an error when it fails.

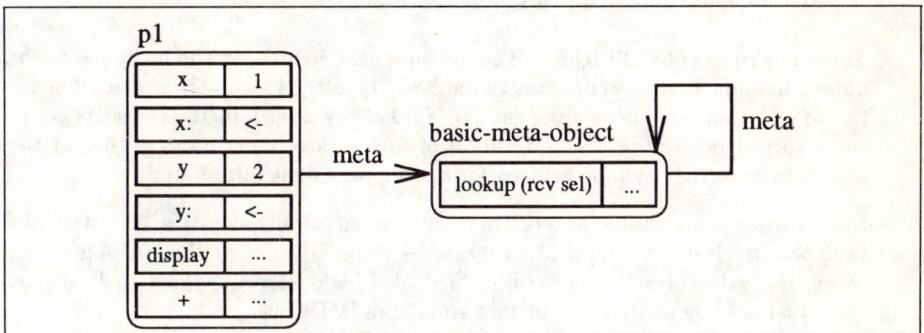

Figure 3: The meta-objects tower for point p1.

3.2.2 An Example of Lookup Reification

Continuing with our previous example of points, we are going to step a part of the lookup phases required for evaluating (p1 x).

The lookup phase is first delegated to the meta-object of `p1` (line 1), which is `basic-meta-object` (denoted `bmo` for compacting the following code). According to the reflective decomposition of message passing, a new `lookup` message is sent to the meta-object of `basic-meta-object` (line 2). And as `basic-meta-object` is a one, an infinite regression of lookup requests would occur unless taking care of it (lines 3 to ...).

```
1 ((p1 -get-meta-object) lookup p1 "x")
2   ((bmo -get-meta-object) lookup bmo "lookup")
3     ((bmo -get-meta-object) lookup bmo "lookup")
4       ((bmo -get-meta-object) lookup bmo "lookup") ...
```

This potentially infinite tower of meta-objects is stopped by the circularity of `basic--meta-object` (cf. figure 3).

This circularity is recognized by the interpreter which automatically bypasses the reflective lookup phase. Instead of resolving the lookup phase by jumping at the meta-

object level, the `lookup` slot of the meta-object is directly extracted (using primitive
-lookup) and then applied. For instance, the lookup phase raised for evaluating (`bmo
selector`) is handled as follows:

```
((bmo -lookup "lookup")     ; returns its own lookup method
    apply bmo selector)     ; uses it for returning the slot selector
```

Coming back to the semantics level, this technical solution simply expresses that a circular meta-object is self-described and can introspect. In particular it knows how its meta-object, i.e. itself, looks for slots.

3.3 The Application Phase: Slots-Executants

According to our reflective model, the result of the lookup phase is something that ought to understand an `apply` message. Three kinds of result can be considered:

- **Temporarily created object:** The lookup phase creates, on the fly, a descriptor object, holding an `apply(rcv args)` method. Thus the lookup phase can influence the application one, depending on the `apply(rcv args)` method associated to the returned descriptor.. The duration of life of these descriptors is that of the application, so they cannot be used for storing persistent information.

- **Slot value:** This case supposes that the content of any slot is a first-class object, able to deal with application messages (especially for methods). According to us, the value of a slot is polluted if it also includes its application behavior. Nevertheless, this approach is further studied in [MDC92].

- **Slot:** Instead of creating new objects on the fly, real slots are returned.

For efficiency reasons we have chosen the last solution. Because the receiver of a message is supposed to be an object, this solution raises the new problem of slot representation. Indeed, representing a slot as a first-class object would raise another infinite process. Therefore, although slots are not represented as first-class objects, they can be accessed, sent messages and even have their structure extended.

Consequently, the basic `lookup(rcv sel)` associated to `basic-meta-object` directly returns slots themselves.

3.3.1 Behavior of Slots

In practice, each slot is associated to a first-class object, called its `slot-executant`. An executant is a first-class object, taking into account the application phase of any slot, that uses it. It must implement a method named `apply` taking as arguments an array composed of the receiver and the arguments (also in an array).

Any time a non-primitive message (aSlot selector arg_1 ... arg_n) is performed, it is implicitly rewritten as follows:

$(slot\text{-}executant(aSlot)$ selector aSlot $array\text{-}of(arg_1 \ldots arg_n))$

Moostrap's kernel actually defines three slot-executants, one for each kind of slot (figure 4 illustrates their use):

- **data-slot-executant** is the executant normally associated to data slots. Its application method invokes the primitive `-apply-data-slot`, which consists in returning the content of the slot.

- **method-slot-executant** is the executant normally associated to method slots. Its application method invokes the primitive `-apply-method-slot`, which evaluates the body of the method stored in the slot, in the context of the receiver and arguments of the current message sending.

- **assign-slot-executant** is the executant normally associated to assignment slots. Its application method invokes the primitive `-apply-assign-slot`, which updates the content of its corresponding data slot.

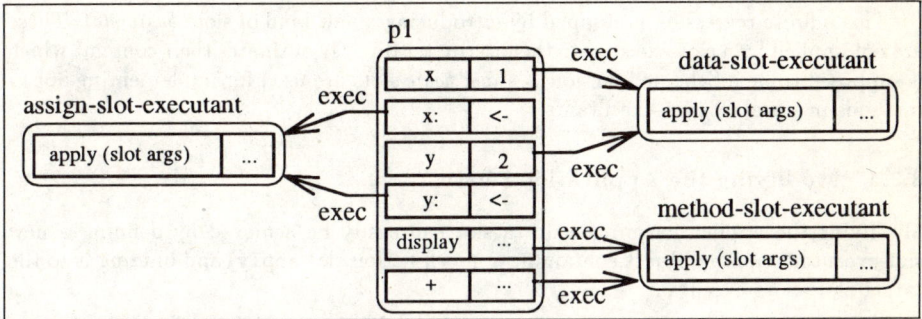

Figure 4: Executants associated to the slots of p1.

More generally, slots can be sent messages, automatically delegated to their slot-executant. Notice also that the two primitives `-get-executant/-set-executant!` allows a slot to access or change its executant.

3.3.2 Structure of Slots

A slot is not a first-class object, but even so we want to be able to modify its structure. Moostrap's prototypes are inspired by the three-level structure of frames [WH81]. In fact the representations of slots are decomposed into the following mono-valued facets:

- **name** containing the name of the slot.

- **value** containing the value of the slot.

Example: The slot (x = 1) is represented by two facets:
name associated to "x" and value associated to 1.

Here below are some primitives for handling the structure of slots, in order to add new facets or retrieve their value:

- **-add-facet** adds a facet to a given slot. It takes a name and a content as arguments. If the facet already exists, it is updated.

Example: Adding a facet to a slot for counting the number of its invocations.
((hall -lookup "x") -add-facet "counter" 0)
This slot is now represented as (name "x")(value 1)(counter 0).

- **-get-facet-value** returns the content of a facet, the name of which is taken as an argument.

Notice also, that unlike Self, where each slot-descriptor knows its holder, Moostrap's slots do not know the object which they belong to, thus allowing the physical sharing of slots between several prototypes (cf. the primitive **-addSharedSlots**).

3.3.3 Handling the Infinite Regression of Applications

The application process of a slot is delegated to its executant, which then executes its own method **apply**. This method is stored in a slot, delegating its application to an executant, and so on...

This infinite regression is stopped by introducing a new kind of slot: *basic slot*. These are not applied by a slot-executant: the interpreter directly evaluates their content, which is supposed to be a Scheme function[1]. Thus, *basic* slots are used for implementing **apply** methods in standard slot-executants.

3.3.4 Modifying the Application Phase

Modifying the application process for a slot can easily be achieved by defining a new slot-executant (i.e. an object containing a new function slot **apply**) and binding it to the target slot as its executant.

The following example shows such a situation. We improve the basic slot behavior, in order to count the number of invocations of a method slot. Therefore we create a new executant, named **counting-method-slot-executant**, as follows:

```
1  (hall -addSharedSlots (-proto
2      (counting-method-slot-executant = (-proto
3          (apply (slot rcv-args)
4              (slot -add-facet "counter"
5                          ((slot -get-facet-value "counter") + 1))
6              (slot -apply-method-slot rcv-args))))))
7  ((hall method-slot-executant) -addSharedSlots (-proto
8      (count (slot rcv-args)
9          (slot -add-facet "counter" 0)
10         (slot -set-executant!
11             (hall counting-method-slot-executant)))))
```

Line 1 to 6: We create the new executant, accessible from **hall** via the slot **counting--method-slot-executant**. It contains an **apply** method, assuming that the slot already owns a facet **counter**. The value of this facet is incremented, and then the method is applied primitively.

---
[1] In fact, *basic slots* are very close to *xmethods* in BOS [LS92].

Line 7 to 11: We extend the initial `method-slot-executant` in order to enrich the behavior of current method slots. They now can receive the message `count`, which adds to them a new facet `counter` initialized to 0, and then their executant is changed to the new `counting-method-slot-executant`. After this operation, they no longer behave like standard methods.

Now we can use it for counting the number of invocations of the `display` method of the point `p1`:

```
(((hall p1) -lookup "display") count)

(((hall p1) -lookup "display") -get-facet-value "counter")   --> 0
((hall p1) display)                                          --> 102
(((hall p1) -lookup "display") -get-facet-value "counter")   --> 1
```

4 Implementing a Model of Implicit Delegation

The functionality of Moostrap's kernel can be extended thanks to its reflective facilities, so as to add a model of implicit delegation.

4.1 A Model of Delegation

Delegation is an alternative to class-based language inheritance for prototype-based languages. A prototype can directly inherit properties from another object, referred by a delegation link. The idea is very simple: if a prototype does not know how to answer to a message, it asks to its "parents". Implementing delegation leads to change the algorithm of slot lookup in order to follow this delegation link.

In this section, we realize a single and implicit delegation scheme. That means that each prototypes can only have one direct parent. This parent is explicitly pointed out with a slot, named `parent`. Like in Self, the delegation is implicit since there is no need to qualify the location of inherited slots. The computation of messages automatically follows the pre-established delegation link.

Since behavioral meta-objects carry out the slot lookup, this model of delegation can be achieved in Moostrap by introducing a new behavioral meta-object, implementing a distributed lookup.

We define `SD-meta-object` (SD standing for single delegation), which performs delegation as a succession of elementary redirections. Each object will transfer the lookup to its direct parent if necessary. Thus from one object to the next the lookup is propagated through a delegation chain.

More precisely, the propagation of lookup is assured by sending the message `lookup` to the meta-object of the direct parent of the receiver. So, if the parent itself uses delegation, via its meta-object, the lookup may reach the next level, and so on... This model has the two following advantages:

- The mechanism is stopped as soon as an ancestor uses a meta-object, that does not perform delegation; for example `hall` is associated to `basic-meta-object`, so there is no delegation for it. In fact, it stops inheritance in an elegant way, unlike Smalltalk, where the superclass of `Object` is the non-class object `nil`.

- Several lookup semantics could be defined, and combined in the same delegation chain.

4.2 Definition of SD-meta-object

To define `SD-meta-object`, the first step is to create an empty shape, stored in a data slot, named `SD-meta-object`, in `hall`.

```
(hall -addSharedSlots (-proto (SD-meta-object = (-proto))))
```

The second step is to define a new `lookup` method:

```
1  ((hall SD-meta-object) -addSharedSlots (-proto
2    (lookup (rcv sel)
3      (let ((localLookup (rcv -lookup sel)))
4      ;Declaring local variables is allowed by using "let" constructions.
5      ;-lookup returns nil if the slot is not found.
6      ((localLookup -eq? nil) ifTrueIfFalse
7         (-block ()
8           (let ((father ((rcv -lookup "parent")
9                          -get-facet-value "value")))
10          ((father -get-meta-object) lookup father sel)))
11         (-block () localLookup))))))
```

More precisely:

Line 3: The local variable `localLookup` store the result of a first primitive lookup in the receiver (performed by the primitive `-lookup`).

Lines 6 to 10: When the requested slot is missing locally, the parent `father` has to be consulted. Its meta-object then receives a `lookup` message, and so searches at the parent level. Notice that sending the message "parent" to the receiver is prohibited, because it would enter an infinite regression of `parent` messages. Therefore, we have to use primitives to access it.

Line 11: On the other hand, when the requested slot is found locally, it is directly returned.

This process of successive redirections naturally ends as soon as a meta-object, performing no redirection, is involved. Furthermore, by construction, the root of a delegation chain does not use a delegation meta-object, but rather a more basic one, like `basic-meta-object`.

Finally we can mention that `SD-meta-object` uses implicitly `basic-meta-object` as its meta-object. It means that `SD-meta-object` cannot use delegation for itself.

4.3 Upgrading SD-meta-object for Enabling Overriding

This first version of delegation does not handle the access to overridden slots, like messages to **super** in Smalltalk, or (**call-next-method**) in CLOS. We can improve our delegation model, along the lines of Self's protocol, where such messages are performed by prefixing the selector with "resend.".

Handling resent messages is an additional variation on the lookup process. In fact, unlike standard delegating lookup, a resent message must be searched from the parent of the holder of the current method, let us call it the **sending-method-holder**. But in Moostrap, we do not have any initial information about the current **sending-method-holder**. However, reflective computation can overcome this lack of information.

Moostrap's reflective model expects the result of lookup to handle the message **apply**. At first, for efficiency reasons, we choose to answer with slots, enabling them to receive messages.

However, the lookup phase is very flexible. Therefore, instead of returning a slot entity, it can create, on the fly, return a slot-descriptor object, implementing its own **apply** method (cf. section 3.3). This object can store more information than a single slot entity, like the location of the found slot (its holder), and obviously a pointer to the entity corresponding to the initial found slot.

The transition from the notion of **holder** of a slot to the notion of **sending-method-holder** is made during the application phase of the lookup result. Indeed, the current **sending-method-holder** is the **holder** of the slot itself while the application phase is performed. This process is eventually recursively performed for internal computation in the current method. We thus create a stack of **sending-method-holders**, having for top the current one. Then the **apply** method will behave as follows:

1. The **holder** is pushed in the **sending-method-holders** stack.

2. The **slot** is asked for standard application, by sending to it the message **slot apply rcv args**.

3. The **sending-method-holders** stack is popped.

4.4 Revision of our First design for Points

We can take advantage of delegation to re-model points. We propose a new solution closer to the organization of prototypes advocated by Self and instituted by "traits."

According to Self, we define a prototype for grouping points "traits". Each point is created by cloning a first **prototype** of it, holding only mutable data slots "x" and "y", and a slot "parent", that explicitly references their "traits" object.

This **prototype** of point uses **SD-meta-object** as a meta-object, in order to inherit from the properties of the shared repository for points behavior.

Now, creating a new point only consists in cloning their predefined **prototype**, and initializing its coordinates. This implementation is illustrated by figure 5.

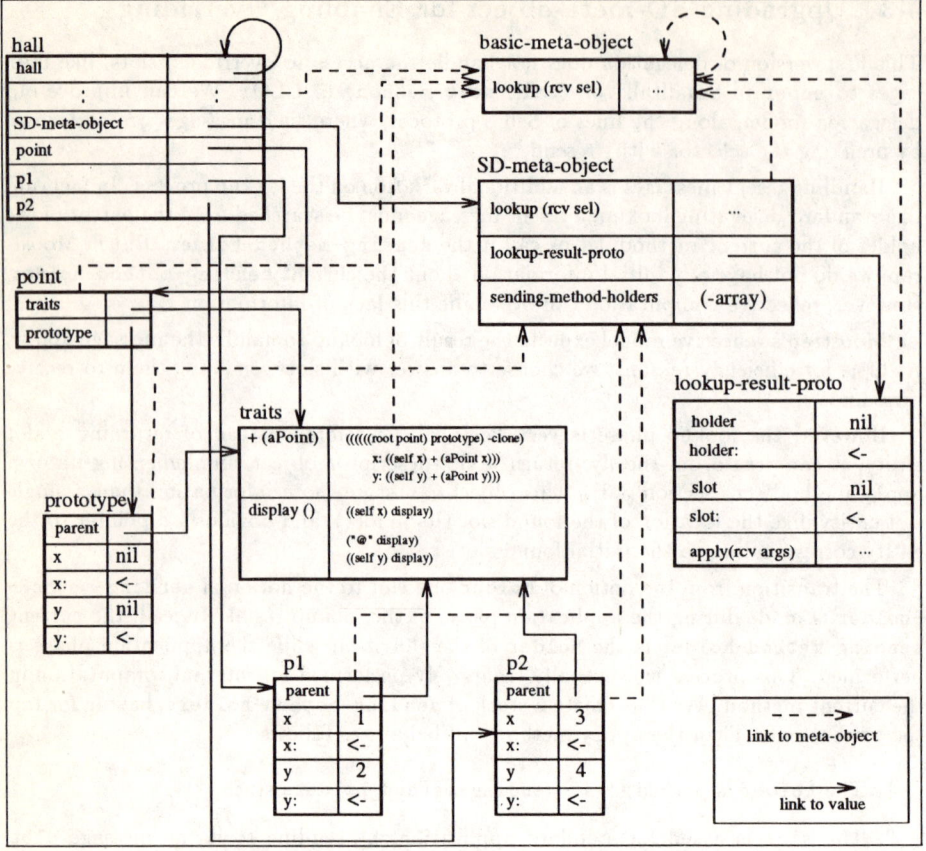

Figure 5: Using `SD-meta-object` for re-modeling points

5 Using Meta-objects to Handle Literal Objects

So far we have not mentioned literal objects often used like strings, numbers, arrays.

Since there is no delegation in the Moostrap kernel, the problem is to supply shared repositories to concentrate the common behavior for these basic objects. In fact meta-objects can play this role. The idea is to change the rules for slot accessing in order to perform the research - not directly at their level - but at the level of their meta-objects.

That leads us to introduce a new meta-object adapted to each category of basic objects. All these meta-objects hold common behavior and redefine the **lookup** method as follows:

```
(lookup (receiver selector)
    ((self -get-meta-object) lookup self selector))
```

Literal objects have no structure, and are fully described by their meta-objects. It is worth noticing that such meta-objects are very close to the notion of classes.

6 Conclusion and Future Work

Starting from this kernel, we are working in the following directions:

- By now, the whole model described in this paper is implemented. However, it requires substantial optimization for speeding it up. Nevertheless we do not want to limit the possibilities of Moostrap. For instance, messages sent to prototypes, associated to the `basic-meta-object`, could be basically handled for bypassing the reflective model; but then the basic `lookup` could not been modified...

- We are building libraries of examples, highlighting the contributions of reflective computation to OOLs. As such, we study different variations on the mechanism of delegation. In particular, we should propose a model for handling multiple inheritance.

- We intend to integrate structural reflection in Moostrap. In this way representation of methods could be reified. Then it would be possible for the lookup phase to answer a slot value that could handle an application message. This approach corresponds to the model described in [MDC92].

- The prototype-based language of Moostrap enables the building of split-objects [DMC92], but it still lacks mechanisms for handling the semantics of such distributed objects.

- We are also studying a new bootstrap process of Moostrap in order to integrate the delegation extension in its kernel.

- Furthermore, we are also studying alternatives to the standard semantics of message sending. In Scheme-like languages, the reflective approach leads to reify environments and continuations [JF92]. There are strong analogies between our prototypes and Scheme's environments (they can be considered as prototypes using implicit delegation). We want to study the correlations between these two languages, especially if we reify continuations in Moostrap, which would allow us to propose a new way of message sending.

Acknowledgements

We thank Jacques Malenfant and Christophe Dony for their contribution to the definition of a reflective and prototype-based model. A special thanks also to John Miller-Jones and Mike Clarkson for their comments on this paper.

Bibliography

[Coi87] Pierre Cointe. Meta-classes are First Class: the ObjVlisp Model. *In Proceedings of OOPSLA'87, ACM Sigplan Notices, pages 156-167.* Orlando, Florida, December 1987.

[CMDM92] Pierre Cointe, Jacques Malenfant, Christophe Dony et Philippe Mulet. Etude de la réflexion de comportement dans le langage Self. *Premières Journées Représentation par Objets (EC2), pages 213-224.* La Grande Motte, 1992.

[CUL89] Craig Chambers, David Ungar and Elgin Lee. An Efficient Implementation of SELF, a Dynamically-typed Object-Oriented Language Based on Prototypes. *In Proceedings of OOPSLA'89, ACM Sigplan Notices, 24(10):49-70.* 1989.

[DMC92] Christophe Dony, Jacques Malenfant and Pierre Cointe. Prototype-Based Languages : From a New Taxinomy to Constructive Proposals and Their Validation. *In OOPSLA'92, pp 201-215. ACM Sigplan Notices V.27 Number 17.* Vancouver, 1992.

[JF92] Stanley Jefferson, and Daniel P. Friedman. A Simple Reflective Interpreter. In *Advance Proceedings of the IMSA'92 International Workshop on Reflection and Meta-Level Architecture, pp 48-58.* Tokyo, 1992.

[KRB91] Gregor Kiczales, Jim des Rivières and Daniel G. Bobrow. The Art of the MetaObject Protocol. *The MIT Press.* Cambridge, Massachusetts, 1991.

[LS92] Sean Levy and Eswaran Subrahmanian. BOS: The Basic Object System, An Embeddable, Language-Independant Object System. Engineering Design Research Center, Carnegie Mellon University, 1992.

[MCD91] Jacques Malenfant, Pierre Cointe and Christophe Dony. Reflection in Prototype-Based Object-Oriented Programming Languages *In Informal Proceedings of the Second Workshop on Reflection Meta-Level Architectures on Object-Oriented Programming, OOPSLA'91.* 1991.

[MDC92] Jacques Malenfant, Christophe Dony and Pierre Cointe. Behavioral Reflection in a Protoype-Based Language. *In Int'l Workshop on reflection and Meta-Level Architectures, pp 143-153, A. Yonezawa & B. Smith (editors), RISE and IPA (Japan) + ACM SIGPLAN, JSSST & IPS.* Tokyo, 1992.

[MR91] Philippe Mulet, Fred Rivard. Ultimardrev Self: Réalisation d'un Interprète du Langage Self en Smalltalk 80. *Rapport du DEA LAP.* Université de Paris VI, 1991.

[Pae93] Andreas Paepcke. Object-Oriented Programming: The CLOS Perspective. *The MIT Press.* Cambridge, Massachusetts, 1993.

[Sch89] Revised 3.99 Report on the Algorithmic Language Scheme. *William Clinger and Jonathan Rees (Editors).* 1989.

[WH81] Patrick H. Winston, Berthold K.P. Horn. Lisp, Implementing Frames p.291-301. *Addison-Wesley Publishing Company.* 1981.

Kernel Structuring for Object-Oriented Operating Systems: The Apertos Approach

Yasuhiko Yokote

Sony Computer Science Laboratory Inc.
Takanawa Muse Building,
3-14-13 Higashi-gotanda, Shinagawa-ku,
Tokyo, 141 JAPAN
e-mail: ykt@csl.sony.co.jp

Abstract

This paper addresses the issues faced when constructing an operating system and its kernel with object-oriented technology. We first propose object/metaobject separation, a means of constructing an object-oriented operating system and its kernel. This method divides the implementing system facilities and applications into two types: objects and metaobjects. This paper presents the concept of object/metaobject separation and discusses why object/metaobject separation is required in terms of limitations in the micro-kernel and object-oriented technologies. We also discuss an example of using object/metaobject separation as implemented in Apertos. This paper then proposes mechanisms which efficiently implement object/metaobject separation. These are characterized by meta-level context management, and are implemented in the Apertos operating system. Meta-level context management is designed to reduce the overhead of control transfer between an object and its metaspace. Here, metaobjects reflectors, *MetaCore*, *Context*, and *Activity* are introduced to represent the metahierarchy of an object's execution. Finally, we present the evaluation results of the Apertos implementation, and discuss the relationship with previous work.

1 Introduction

Recently, object-oriented technology has become popular for the construction of complicated systems, enabling an operating system to again be constructed using that technology. Object-orientation encourages modularization, increases reusability and maintainability, gives users/programmers a single unified perspective of a system, as well as providing other advantages. Example systems are Chorus [Rozier *et al.* 88], Amoeba [Tanenbaum *et al.* 90], Clouds [Spafford 86], and Choices [Campbell *et al.* 91]. Also, micro-kernel technology is widely used for constructing operating systems. A micro-kernel defines minimum functions, on top of which richer system functions are implemented. Systems such as V-kernel [Cheriton 88], Mach [Accetta *et al.* 86], and the systems mentioned earlier all use this technology.

However, recent trends in the computing environment, such as mobile computing and massive-scale distributed computing environments, require a new technology that goes beyond micro-kernel and object-oriented technologies in the construction of an operating system. Although we can characterize this environment using several keywords, this paper focuses its attention on one crucial characteristic, i.e., open-endedness. That is, the system's behavior cannot be predicted from the system configuration time. The increasing scale and complexity of the system also forces users and programmers to reduce their demands on the system, lest it becomes impossible to accurately predict the number of entities, such as workstations, mobile terminals, devices, and activities. Further, due to a high degree of distribution, it is difficult for users and programmers to be freed from their dependence on the environment.

Micro-kernel and object-oriented technologies are limited to addressing the open-endedness property. A micro-kernel provides no policies other than the minimum mechanisms. However, we need a discipline with which policies or system services can be implemented on top of the micro-kernel. Also, since an object is open-ended, it changes its properties during its execution or lifetime. This sometimes requires the extension of the mechanisms provided by a micro-kernel. For instance, if an object provides a realtime constraint, a micro-kernel must provide a mechanism for realtime scheduling. The possibility of the extension of the micro-kernel weakens the advantages of micro-kernel technology.

Object-oriented technology addresses these issues in micro-kernel technology. We, however, encounter difficulties when we support objects in constructing operating system kernels. Even though object-oriented technology offers the advantages of encapsulation (or information hiding) for creating a unified interface between objects, we need a mechanism to break this encapsulation and support objects by operating system kernels in a uniform way.

This paper proposes object/metaobject separation, a means of constructing an object-oriented operating system and its kernel, which divides objects implementing system facilities and applications into two types: base-level objects (or simply objects) and metaobjects. An object is an entity that can be considered as being individual, i.e., it can be shared by another object. A metaobject is a member of a metaspace that provides an object with the optimal execution environment.

The term "meta" is defined in this paper such that:
- it is relative to a "base" (or the base-level of an entity);
- it provides a "base" with an interface and facilities to define the base-level abstraction and semantics that are available to base-level programming; and
- it is an environment in which an object is active.

In this respect a metaspace, in some senses, roughly corresponds to a virtual machine or an optimal operating system for objects. In terms of a virtual machine, a (virtual) instruction set is provided for objects, which defines a software architecture or a software model for object programming. For example, communication protocols between objects, such as synchronous, asynchronous, and realtime protocols, are defined by their metaspaces. In terms of an operating system, an object's execution environment is given by its metaspace, i.e., the metaspace supports an object as a cooperative entity with its environment. For example, if objects need to be scheduled in realtime, their metaspaces provide a realtime scheduler and memory management for that purpose.

In Section 2, we address the concept of object/metaobject separation and discuss why object/metaobject separation is required in terms of the limitations of micro-kernel and object-oriented technologies. We also introduce an example of using object/metaobject separation as implemented in Apertos. Section 3 proposes mechanisms that efficiently implement object/metaobject separation. These mechanisms are characterized by meta-level context management, and are implemented in the Apertos operating system. In Section 4, we present the evaluation results of the Apertos implementation. Section 5 then discusses the relationship with previous work. Finally, Section 6 concludes this paper by discussing the current status of the implementation.

2 Object/Metaobject Separation

As we mentioned in the introductory section, object-oriented technology is again becoming popular in the construction of operating systems. This is because it facilitates the implementation of complicated systems, including operating systems. Before presenting object/metaobject separation, we will discuss the definition of an object. Throughout this paper, we define an object as follows. An object is an entity which can be considered as being an individual. That is, an object is a unit to be shared by another object. Each object has a name (or an identifier) with which others denote that object, i.e., an object has an identity allowing it to be distinguished from other objects.

This basic property creates the following unique advantages. First, it encourages modularization. An object is a unit of protection, which prohibits erroneous and/or malicious access to an object. Actually, the internals of an object are accessed through its public interface as exported to other objects. Second, this property increases the reusability and maintainability. Since the internals of an object or the implementation of an object cannot be seen by other objects, an existing object can be replaced with a new one, if its interface is preserved. This is helped by class hierarchy in object-oriented technology. Finally, it gives users and programmers a single perspective of the system. An object is the only constituent of the system. When we denote a system service, the only entity we can see is the object.

Based on this definition, this section presents object/metaobject separation. Then, we discuss why object/metaobject separation is required, and discuss the limitations of micro-kernel and object-oriented technologies. Also, this section presents applications of object/metaobject separation.

2.1 Proposal of Object/Metaobject Separation

We introduce the notion of "meta" into operating system construction and application programming. That is, objects implementing system facilities and applications are "base" objects (or objects) or "meta" objects (or metaobjects). In detail, object/metaobject separation is defined as follows:
- each object is active in its own execution environment which is given by the group of metaobjects forming its metaspace; and
- a metaobject is an object cooperatively providing an interface and facilities for (the base-level of) objects to define object abstraction and semantics.

This is the principal definition of object/metaobject separation. We extend this below.

Here, consider the construction of a system supporting object-oriented programming. It is difficult to determine an object's granularity during system design. This is because there are three factors; a protection unit, a memory segment which acts as an information container, and an activity which is the thread of control; which should be independently considered and cooperatively designed. UNIX[1] is an example of a system combining these three factors. By introducing threads, the activities can be separated from these three factors.

Recently, the implementation of systems supporting object have shown a trend towards managing these three factors out of the kernel. Amoeba is an example in that its kernel knows nothing about an object. Since an object is a unit of protection, it is protected from others by capabilities managed by server processes. Also, a fine-grained object is protected from others by a programming language. The Amoeba kernel provides a memory segment, but a language system manages that segment for objects. Scheduler activation [Anderson et al. 91] and first-class user-level thread [Marsh et al. 91] are other examples to handle activities out of the kernel.

With the first definition, an object is free from the internal representation that is usually determined by the underlying operating system. This approach to the above three factors differs from that used in existing systems. Since an object is defined by its metaspace, i.e., an object's identity is given by that metaspace, the policy used to handle these three factors is determined by the metaspace. For example, a metaspace can define objects as an array of structures, but we can regard an element of that array as being an object from outside that object, because the only way to see that object, i.e., to invoke a method of that object, is to use a facility of its metaspace. In this respect, a metaspace shows the objects that are visible from outside the objects.

With the second definition, a metaobject represents a description of an object, i.e., an object's state and a group's state. In this respect, concurrent activities within a metaspace can be introduced to increase the availability of metaobjects up to implementation, and we can define these as concurrent objects [Yonezawa and Tokoro 87]. Also, it is possible for two or more metaspaces to share a metaobject, as a means of keeping common information among those metaspaces. This enables us to reduce the cost of negotiation between metaspaces to solve conflicts between them. By defining a metaobject as an object, the second definition implies that the system can be constructed by the hierarchical structure of objects and metaobjects.

In addition to this definition, we allow an object to change its relationship with its metaspace, i.e., an object can exchange its metaspace with another. This amplifies the advantages of object/metaobject separation. This also facilitates the implementation of object migration. Object migration is when an object travels to another metaspace. Object migration enhances the following capabilities of the system: system extensibility, software upgradability, environment support for mobile computers, environment-dependent system configuration, etc.

2.2 Issues in Micro-kernel and Object-Oriented Structuring

Recently, micro-kernel technology has been widely used to implement operating systems. It is beneficial for the independence of architectural (or hardware) heterogeneity of a system, because it defines the minimum set of system functions, i.e., it can be considered as being standard for inter-operability. It is, however, hard to extend the primitives provided by a micro-kernel when we need to support a new service which cannot be completed without kernel support. An example is a facility for realtime computing. RT-Mach has introduced a realtime facility to the Mach kernel [Tokuda et al. 90]. This is a

---

[1] UNIX is a registered trademark of AT&T Bell Laboratories.

crucial limitation on environments with property open-endedness, because new services that were not expected when the system was configured often emerge.

Micro-kernel technology is also helpful for the modular construction of operating systems. A micro-kernel usually supports a low-level scheduler, virtual memory management, and a mechanism for process communication. Additionally, many system services are implemented as independent modules (or processes in some systems) using this minimum set. It usually defines the basic abstraction of the system, for example in the Mach operating system, processes, threads, objects, and ports are provided by a kernel. In this respect, a kernel divides the system into two layers: one uses the abstraction implemented by the other layer (i.e., it acts as a kernel). Although micro-kernel technology increases the architectural independence of kernel software, it is not the best way of constructing an operating system. It says nothing about realizing independent modules, i.e., no guidelines or rules are provided by that technology. We need no longer be concerned about which services are implemented as modules or which functions are combined into a module.

Object-oriented technology can solve this issue to some degree. That is, it provides a discipline when designing modules, i.e., an object is an independent module, functions are classified by classes, and class hierarchy helps us to reuse existing functions. Also, object-oriented technology addresses the extensibility of the operating system in the sense that objects constituting the system can be dynamically replaced with new ones to support new services. The unified interface for an object helps us to replace an existing object.

However, object-orientation is not acceptable in the following case, because it creates a number of problems. That is, we have to overcome several difficulties when we consider everything as an object. Particularly affected are:

- the debugger, which needs to inspect the internals of an object;
- the object manager, which needs to access meta-data such as the representation of a message and an object's state information to deliver a message to the target and to control object activities; and
- the group manager, which needs to know the dependency between objects.

Since the private methods of an object are permitted to access its internals, we need a special method of exporting these to a debugger. Since meta-data is data that represents an object's state as well as a group's state, it can hardly be maintained by the object itself. If it is separately maintained by an object, it is difficult to keep meta-data consistent with the actual state of concurrently executing objects. Since dependency between objects is dynamically changing and determined according to the degree of global information, we need a way of keeping track of object-object interaction. These difficulties are caused by the object's basic property of being individual.

2.3 Contributions of Object/Metaobject Separation

Due to the issues raised in the previous discussion, we propose object/metaobject separation. Firstly, a metaspace is a collection of metaobjects and is dynamically constructed to be optimal for objects. That is, we can create a new metaspace for a new service. This has advantages over micro-kernel technology in terms of extensibility, and supports the open-ended property.

Secondly, since a metaspace can be a virtual machine devoted to objects, the architectural independence of objects can be achieved in that:

- when an object and its group change their property, we can move them to another metaspace (or a newly created metaspace) to satisfy that change; and
- we can create a new metaspace for a new system service that emerges dynamically.

In this way, the configuration of the system determined at system boot-up can be extended by creating a new metaspace and changing an object's metaspace. This increases the system's reconfigurability and extensibility.

Thirdly, object/metaobject separation can overcome some of difficulties highlighted in the previous subsection. That is, since a metaobject constituting a metaspace represents a description of an object, the internals of an object, the execution state of an object, the dependency between objects, etc. can be accessed through a metaobject. For instance, a debugger is implemented at the meta-level of an object to be examined.

Lastly, in object-oriented technology, there is no distinction between an object and its metaobject for that object. This distinction is crucial when designing complicated operating systems. Object/metaobject separation forces us to be aware of which objects are "meta" of other objects and which objects are running in which metaspace, both during programming and at run time. This clarifies the structure and the configuration of the system. Also, this distinction encourages us to design a new operating system for experimental purposes, which is augmented by the class hierarchy.

2.4 Example of Object/Metaobject Separation

This subsection demonstrates object/metaobject separation in the design of a virtual memory system, implemented in the Apertos operating system. In the design, the memory metahierarchy of the system, which is a metahierarchy dedicated for memory management, has been so designed as to obey the concept of object/metaobject separation. That is, the primary concerns of the virtual memory design are how the system is organized and who is responsible for managing the local storage of an object. Figure 1 shows our answer to these concerns. Here, a shaded rectangle denotes a metaspace, which is represented by a reflector presented later.

At the object-level, we can only handle objects. The internals of an object are protected by the system. At the meta-level of that object, the internals of the object, i.e, its local storage, are represented by several segment metaobjects. A specific property of an object's local storage is given by segment metaobjects. For example, when local storage needs to be managed with a specific page replacement algorithm, it is peculiar to an object's segment metaobject. Any area in memory can be managed inside a segment metaobject as a unit for page replacement. The correspondence between the memory chunk size in a segment metaobject and the underlying physical page size is taken by the memory metahierarchy. Also, in Apertos, several policies are provided as classes for constructing the virtual memory system. That is, a segment metaobject is created by a class which implements a property of an object's local storage. Note that, as discussed in [Yokote et al. 89], the class hierarchy and metahierarchy is orthogonal in Apertos.

Then, we introduce another metaspace for metaobjects to be objects. In the memory metahierarchy, page metaobjects are the "meta-"metaobjects of a segment metaobject. That is, the local storage of a segment metaobject is represented by page metaobjects at its meta-level. In a similar way, a specific property of a segment's local storage is given by page metaobjects. In Apertos, a page corresponds to a physical memory page, and a segment's page metaobjects are programmed not to move to secondary storage.

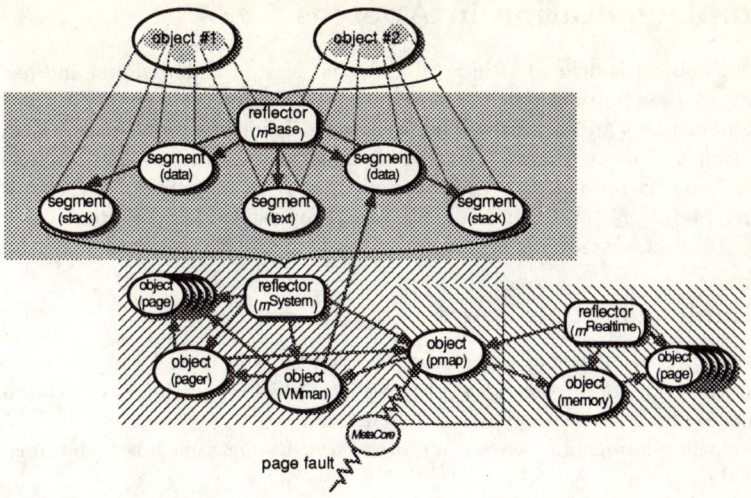

Figure 1: Memory Metahierarchy of the Apertos Virtual Memory System

According to the definition of object/metaobject separation proposed in Subsection 2.1, an object and its segment metaobject can change their metaspaces to others. In Apertos, this is used to create a dynamically reconfigurable and extensible virtual memory system. The configuration determined at system boot-up can be changed by creating a new metaspace which implements a new property of an object's local storage, and an object changes its metaspace to a new one. This means that an object's local storage is to be managed by a policy that is different to that of the original one. At any level of memory metahierarchy, a metaobject implementing storage management has independence of its metaspace. Hence it can be reconfigurable and extensible.

2.5 Summary

In this paper we claim that the (micro-) kernel of an operating system in an open system cannot provide the minimum set of functions on which system services are constructed, but should provide a means of encouraging object/metaobject separation. Further, object-orientation advocates using an object as an individual with identity and providing object/metaobject separation. Therefore, there are some difficulties in constructing an operating system and its kernel using object-orientation, hence we propose object/metaobject separation in which:

- an object is active in its own execution environment, which we call metaspace;
- a metaobject is an object constituting a metaspace, and cooperatively providing an interface and facilities for (the base-level of) objects to define object abstraction and semantics;
- objects and metaobjects have a relative relationship and are hierarchically structured; and
- an object can replace its metaspace with another.

These are the essential characteristics for addressing the open-endedness property.

3 Implementation in Apertos

An Apertos object is defined as in Section 2, that is, it is an individual and has identity. We make this assumption when implementing object/metaobject separation in Apertos. All metaspaces are constrained by this object definition upon their implementation. This section first discusses the issues of implementing object/metaobject separation in Apertos. We also present the Apertos implementation in terms of the introduction of reflectors, *MetaCore*, and *Context*. We then propose mechanisms that can efficiently implement object/metaobject separation. This is meta-level context management.

3.1 Implementation Issues

Since there are two types of objects in the system, objects and their metaobjects, the following two issues of implementing object/metaobject separation have to be considered:
- how a metaspace is created/constructed; and
- how the relationship between an object and its metaspace is maintained. In particular,
  - when an object interacts with its metaspace, or with a metaobject within that metaspace;
  - when a metaobject interacts with objects;
  - how an object interacts with its metaspace, or with a metaobject within that metaspace; and
  - how a metaobject interacts with objects.

First, we have to design the metaspace implementation. We have introduced a reflector that is a metaobject that creates a metaspace. We have designed it to be an object that interacts with a metaobject through a reflector representing its metaspace. Thus, an object explicitly invokes a metaobject with the facility provided in its reflector.

Then, we have to design the representation of an object given by its metaspace, i.e., a group of metaobjects. We have clearly separated the three factors discussed in Subsection 2.1. That is, a memory segment for an object as an information container is a metaobject. The storage of an object consists of several memory segment metaobjects in its metalevel, as presented in Subsection 2.4. Since we have designed an object as a concurrent object, a single activity is associated with each object. An activity as a thread of control is represented by a *Context* metaobject. To overcome the protection unit issue, we have introduced reflective object management. The details are discussed in [Yokote et al. 91a]. In short, compilers and class systems cooperatively provide optimal protection for an object.

Further, since there is an object running in kernel/system mode, we have to provide a mechanism for changing the object's execution mode. In some implementations, objects running in kernel mode are combined into a single module, usually called a kernel, and are invoked by issuing a system call instruction. Unlike those implementations, we have separated the execution mode (or protection) and the module so that a kernel-mode object can be created outside the kernel.

In these respects, the key is the efficient implementation of control transfer between an object and its metaspace. Table 1 shows the number of system call instructions (`trap` in MC68030 and `syscall` in MIPS R3000) executed for a specified operation. These numbers have been measured for the previous implementation of the Apertos kernel

Table 1: **Trap** Instruction Number upon Execution of a Specified Operation

operation	# of **trap**
Method invocation (call/reply round-trip, same metaspace)	4
Method invocation (call/reply round-trip, different metaspaces)	11
Memory segment creation (4KB segment)	44
Object creation (13KB text and 7KB data)	87

[Yokote 92]. The following subsection proposes the new mechanisms by which an object efficiently passes control to its metaspace.

3.2 The Apertos Implementation

The previous implementation of Apertos is described in [Yokote 92]. We have newly implemented the Apertos kernel based on that experience. The new implementation introduces the following special metaobjects:
- a reflector, representing a metaspace;
- *MetaCore*, located at each processor as a micro-kernel; and
- *Context*, virtualizing the underlying processor for representing an activity.

The following is designed to enable efficient implementation.

The Apertos kernel part is constructed as shown in Figure 2. In the implementation,

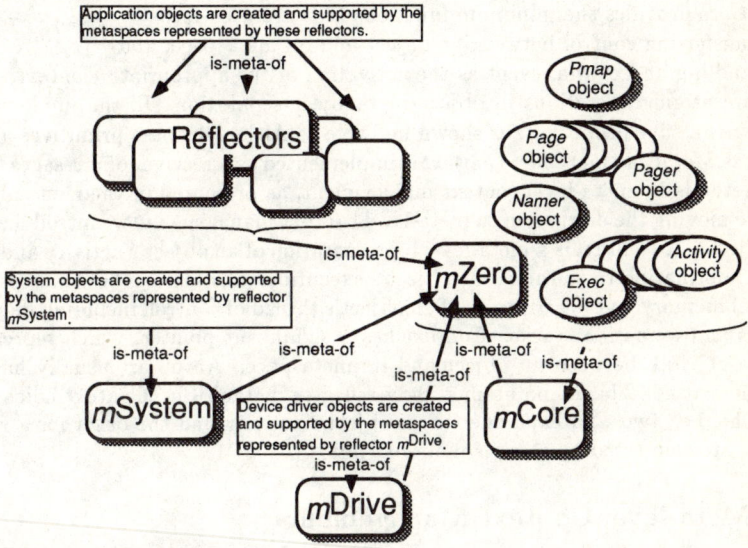

Figure 2: Structure of the Apertos Kernel Part

a metaspace is determined by the references created by a reflector to metaobjects. In the figure, m^{Zero} represents a metaspace consisting of metaobjects *Pager*, *Pages*, *Exec*, *Activity*, and *Namer*, and all of the reflectors in the system are supported by m^{Zero}.

Table 2: The *MetaCore* Primitives

primitive	description
M	causes the execution of *Context*, designated by the "is-meta-of" link. This causes object execution to stop. Execution is then resumed by primitive R.
R	resumes execution of any *Context* that has been stopped by M.
CActive	returns the reference to *Context* that is currently running.
CBind	associates *Context* with an interrupt. This takes an argument that includes a message to be delivered to an event handling object. When an event is raised, the active *Context* is suspended and its associated *Context* is immediately activated to execute the method of an event handling object.
CUnbind	removes the association made by CBind.

To have these metaobjects behave objects, the m^{Core} reflector is introduced. This represents a metaspace consisting of a single metaobject. In the current implementation, m^{Core} assumes the existence of the above metaobjects when Apertos boots, thus avoiding circularity in the memory allocation requests. m^{System} is the metaspace for system objects, including metaobjects implementing the virtual memory system and network protocol handlers. m^{Drive} is the metaspace for device driver objects, which provides facilities for device driver programming.

MetaCore provides the minimum functions that are used for:
- transferring control between an object and its metaspace; and
- handling an external event as the activation of the appropriate *Context*.

These are atomic operations in object/metaobject separation. In the implementation, *MetaCore* has five primitives, as shown in Table 2. Although these primitives are implemented as *MetaCore* methods, *Context* is implemented as a receiver of messages to handle those methods by meta-level context management, as presented in the next subsection.

Before moving the discussion to meta-level context management, we introduce *Context* metaobjects. A *Context* is a meta-level representation of an object's activity and contains enough information to continue the object's execution. *Context* contains no descriptions of virtual memory, but descriptions of an object's thread of control, including its processor registers and execution stacks. *Context* has a significant pointer, which represents the "is-meta-of" link between an object and its metaspace. An object usually has no link to its metaspace. This is maintained by a reflector metaobject. *Context* holds this link as a cache, i.e., two *Contexts*, one for an object's activity and the other for a reflector's activity, are connected by this "is-meta-of" link.

3.3 Meta-level Context Management

Since *MetaCore* is the only metaobject constituting the metaspace for *Contexts*, we can create *Contexts* within the address space of *MetaCore*. This, however, causes extra system call instructions, as shown in Table 1. A possible solution to this problem is to allow an object to transfer control to its metaspace without invoking of a *MetaCore* method. That is, *Contexts* are moved out of *MetaCore*, and to be created in any address space. This means that *MetaCore* is free from virtual memory management. Figure 3 shows a possible configuration of objects, their *Contexts*, and *MetaCore*. There are three

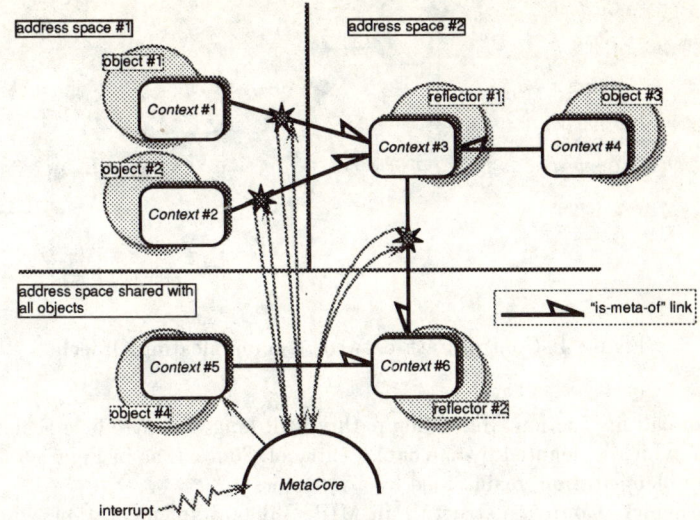

Figure 3: A Possible Configuration of Objects, *Contexts*, and *MetaCore*

address spaces in the figure, address spaces #1 and #2, and an address space shared with all other objects. An arrow denotes the "is-meta-of" link between two *Contexts*. For example, a metaspace of object #1 is represented by reflector #1, and this relationship is depicted by an arrow from *Context* #1 to *Context* #3.

Here, when two *Contexts* are in the same address space, there is no need to issue a system call instruction. However, when two *Contexts* are in different address spaces, a system call is still needed to transfer control to the metaspace, as marked with the star in Figure 3. It is complicated to implement a process marked with the star, which is divided into switching an address space to another and locating *Context* representing the activity of the reflector (i.e., the metaspace), because it needs the assistance of the virtual memory system. Also, since *MetaCore* is the only entity accessible from two *Contexts*, it has to provide a primitive to assist the process.

In meta-level context management, we made one assumption to restrict Figure 3. That is, two *Contexts*, one representing the activity of an object's execution and the other representing the activity of a reflector's execution, are assumed to be in the same protection domain. Thus, a system call instruction has to be issued only when the processor's execution mode is changed. Also, this implies that an operation purging the contents of the processor's cache and TLB is independent of switching *Context*. As a result of the above discussion, the control path between communicating two objects can be depicted in Figure 4. In primitive M, execution of the sender's *Context* moves to execution of the reflector's *Context*, representing the activity of the sender's metaspace. In primitive R, the reflector's *Context* execution moves to the target. During the processing of the gray area, it is possible to issue a system call instruction to change the processor's execution mode. That is, the latter half of processing primitive M or R may be initiated

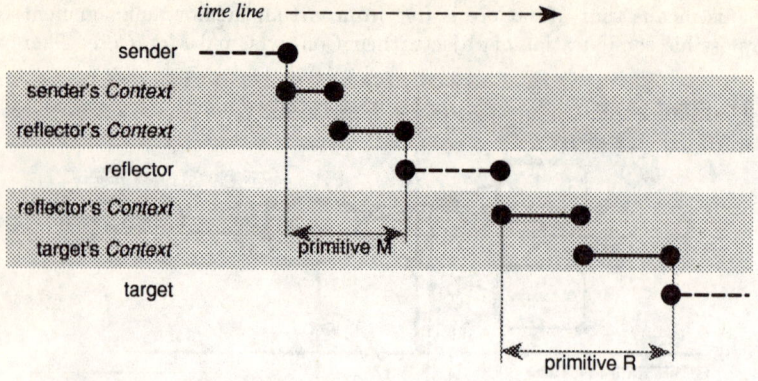

Figure 4: Control Path between Communicating Objects

by a system call instruction. Since this path is still long, we introduce a method cache mechanism, which is denoted by the `cache` entry of *Context*, as in Figure 5. This entry is, in this implementation, maintained by a reflector.

Figure 5 depicts *Context*'s structure in MIPS R3000 implementation, where the following information is maintained.

status: is the processor status for this *Context* execution.
cpu: stores the contents of the processor registers.
stack: denotes a memory segment that is used for an execution stack.
mode: is the execution mode. Two modes, user and system, are used.
mask: represents the processor's interrupt mask.
name: is an object identifier designating to this *Context*.
meta: is the "is-meta-of" link to *Context*, associated with the reflector of this object.
last: is a reference to the *Context* that most recently activated this *Context*.
state: represents the state of *Context* execution.
entry: denotes the object's method table to be used by primitives M and R.
urgent: denotes a method that is immediately invoked when an external event occurs.
cache: denotes a method of handling a method cache that shortens a path between communicating objects.

Here, we discuss metahierarchy for an object's execution, depicted in Figure 6. We introduce the *Exec* metaobject. It can be shared by all metaspaces. We also introduce the *Activity* metaobjects, which are a unit of scheduling in *Exec* and are used to manage an object's execution. That is, an object's execution, a thread of control of a method execution, is represented by an *Activity* metaobject at its meta-level. Even though we have already been given it by *Context*, metaobjects *Exec* and *Activity* make it higher, and provide mechanisms for the realtime scheduling for objects. Thus, when a metaspace uses *Exec*, *Activity* is the meta-level representation of an object's execution, rather than *Context*. In the implementation, *Activity* is defined as the data structure in the *Exec* metaobject, but it can be accessed as if it were an object. mCore, the metaspace for *Activity*'s execution, is responsible for this transformation. Also, *Activity*'s execution is represented by metaobject *Context* at its meta-level, i.e., mCore. As described earlier,

```
 1: class Context {
 2: protected:
 3:            CPUStatReg      status;
 4:            CPURegisters    cpu;
 5:            Temporary       stack;
 6:            CPUMode         mode;
 7:            longword        mask;
 8:            SID             name;
 9:            CName           meta;
10:            CName           last;
11:            mcState         state;
12:            EntryTable*     entry;
13:            Entry           urgent;
14:            MethodCache*    cache;
15: public: .....
16: };
```

Figure 5: *Context* Structure

Table 3: The Methods of Metaobject *Exec*

method	description
New	creates a new *Activity*.
Delete	destroys an existing *Activity*.
Run	starts the execution of *Activity* that has the highest priority.
Stop	suspends execution of the current *Activity*.
Top	changes the position of *Activity* in the queue.
GetActive	retrieves the identifier of the current *Activity*.
ChangeAttribute	changes the attribute of the specified *Activity*.

the metaspace for *Context* is the *MetaCore*.

Table 3 lists the operations provided by *Exec*. Metaobject *Exec* maintains the queue with priority. Users of *Exec* utilize the methods in the table to manipulate *Activity* in the queue. *Exec* itself has no scheduling policy, instead being merely a repository for *Activity*.

4 Evaluation

The results in this section have were obtained using Sony's NEWS workstations, equipped with a 20MHz MIPS R3000 processor, 20MHz R3010 floating point accelerator, 16MB of physical memory, and 64KB+64KB caches for data and instructions. When an object and its reflector are assigned to the same protection domain, i.e., they are in the same address space and in the same execution mode, no system call instructions are required. In MIPS R3000 implementation, *MetaCore* is very small, as listed in Table 4. Also, it is designed such that there are no memory allocation requirements inside *MetaCore*.

Table 5 shows the performance of the *MetaCore* primitives, which are invoked without using `syscall`. The numbers in parenthesis are the results with the previous R3000 implementation. Primitives *CActive*, *CBind*, and *CUnbind* are always used by `syscall`

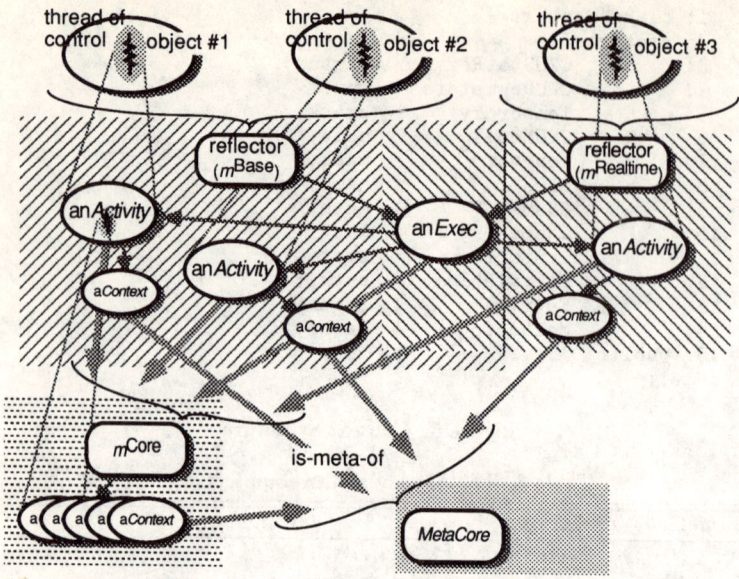

Figure 6: Execution Metahierarchy for an Object's Execution

Table 4: Size of *MetaCore*

text	initialized data	uninitialized data	total (bytes)
3808	224	3088	7120

to invoke them. Table 6 shows the use of `syscall`. In the table, ExceptionHandler shows the time interval between the occurrence of an interrupt and the starting of the handler. For this measurement, we used the `break` instruction. The following are the measured results for some operations provided by metaspaces (Table 7). In contrast to the previous implementation, thanks to meta-level context management, these numbers are improved two to five times.

5 Related Work

Object/metaobject separation is a new way of constructing operating systems. In terms of operating system structuring, many methods have been proposed, including layered

Table 5: Cost of *MetaCore* Primitives (w/o `syscall`)

primitive	cost (in μsec)
M	8.7 (21)
R	8.8 (20)

Table 6: Cost of MetaCore Primitives (w/ `syscall`)

primitive	cost (in μsec)
M	12.1
R	12.6
CActive	4.8
CBind	5.9
CUnbind	5.6
ExceptionHandler	17.1

Table 7: Cost of Operations Provided by Metaspaces

metaoperation	cost (in μsec)
call/reply roundtrip ($m^{Core} \leftrightarrow m^{Core}$, w/o method cache)	111
call/reply roundtrip ($m^{Core} \leftrightarrow m^{Core}$, w/ method cache)	12.4
call/reply roundtrip ($m^{Base} \leftrightarrow m^{Base}$)	193
call/reply roundtrip ($m^{Base} \leftrightarrow m^{System}$)	473
call (m^{Zero})	106
reply (m^{Zero})	110

structuring, hierarchical structuring, policy/mechanism separation, micro-kernel structuring, object-based structuring, open system structuring, and virtual machine structuring. Detailed discussions of these methods are given in [Yokote et al. 91b].

Object/metaobject separation can subsume these structuring methods. In contrast to policy/mechanism separation [Levin et al. 75], for example, we can implement an object as a policy module, and a metaobject as a mechanism module. However, this correspondence of object/metaobject separation to policy/mechanism separation does not correctly express the difference. That is, in the sense that a metaobject represents an object's behavior, it should be considered as being a policy module. The major importance is that metaobjects maintain a description of an object, and this is used to provide an optimal execution environment for the object, where there is a possibility of replacing a mechanism if it is not able to provide such an environment.

In contrast to micro-kernel structuring, object/metaobject separation does not divide the system into two layers. It allows us to construct an hierarchical structure of objects and their metaspaces. The ability to change a metaspace facilitates the implementation of object migration, as well as supporting mobile computers, embedded systems, and disconnected operations. Especially, since object/metaobject separation is more tolerant of environmental change than micro-kernel technology, it is advantageous in constructing robot control systems, as in [Brooks 86]. Further, the ability to provide an optimal execution environment for objects is an important capability for massively parallel computers, because the role of each processing element depends on the application. In this way, object/metaobject separation addresses the open-ended property.

Meta-level context management is comparable to the work on user-level thread management done by [Anderson et al. 91], [Marsh et al. 91], and [Druschel et al. 92]. Unlike these systems, however, threads are not managed by objects with kernel support. They are implemented as *Contexts* and are created in a metaspace. The dominant feature of object/metaobject separation is the independence of its objects from their metaspace.

6 Conclusion

Object/metaobject separation makes an object independent of its execution environment (or a metaspace) and encourages an object's metaspace mobility. The existing technologies, such as micro-kernel and object-oriented ones, are not sufficient to support an operating system and its kernel for an open system. We claim, in this paper, that an operating system should provide a means of encouraging object/metaobject separation.

The Apertos operating system is an example of implementing object/metaobject separation. We propose new mechanisms to efficiently implement object/metaobject separation, because the key to implementation is the interaction between an object and its metaspace. We devise a new technique to enable efficient implementation, i.e., meta-level context management. With this, we can reduce much of the overhead of interaction between an object and its metaspace. In the ideal case, for example, there are no system call instructions and the control path can be shortened between communication objects, maintaining object/metaobject separation.

Current status. The Apertos operating system is being implemented on Sony NEWS workstations, for which two processor architectures, Motorola's MC68030 and MIPS's R3000, are available. Thanks to the MIPS architecture [Kane and Heinrich 92], one notable feature of the implementation is that there is only one local kernel stack. This is also due to meta-level context management and the structure of *MetaCore*.

Apertos is also being implemented on i486-based PC-compatible computers. The kernel part of this implementation is already running and a simple GUI is available. The implementation of Apertos described in this paper (MIPS and i486 implementations) are available to anyone who is interested.

Acknowledgments

I offer my sincere thanks to Prof. Mario Tokoro, the director of the Sony Computer Science Laboratory Inc. He and I have been collaboratively investigating the conceptual design of the Apertos operating system. Also, I would like to thank the members of the Apertos project at Sony Computer Science Laboratory Inc. and Dr. Hideyuki Tokuda of Carnegie Mellon University. Several discussions with these people helped me to design the structure of the system, including the design of Apertos class hierarchy.

References

[Accetta *et al.* 86] Mike Accetta, Robert Baron, William Bolosky, David Golub, Richard Rashid, Avadis Tevanian, and Michael Young. Mach: A New Kernel Foundation For UNIX Development. In *USENIX 1986 Summer Conference Proceedings*. USENIX Association, June 1986.

[Anderson *et al.* 91] Thomas E. Anderson, Brian N. Bershad, Edward D. Lazowska, and Henry M. Levy. Scheduler Activations: Effective Kernel Support for the User-Level

Management of Parallelism. In *Proceedings of the 13th ACM Symposium on Operating System Principles*, pp. 95–109, October 1991.

[Brooks 86] Rodney A. Brooks. A Robust Layered Control System For A Mobile Robot. *IEEE Journal of Robotics and Automation*, Vol. RA-2, No. 1, pp.14–23, March 1986.

[Campbell et al. 91] Roy H. Campbell, Nayeem Islam, Ralph Johnson, Panos Kougiouris, and Peter Madany. *Choices*, Frameworks and Refinement. In *Proceedings of the 1991 International Workshop on Object Orientation in Operating Systems*, pp. 9–15. IEEE Computer Society Press, October 1991.

[Cheriton 88] David R. Cheriton. The V Distributed System. *Communications of the ACM*, Vol. 31, No. 3, pp.314–333, March 1988.

[Druschel et al. 92] Peter Druschel, Larry L. Peterson, and Norman C. Hutchinson. Beyond Micro-Kernel Design: Decoupling Modularity and Protection in Lipto. In *Proceedings of the 12th International Conference on Distributed Computing Systems*, pp. 512–520, June 1992.

[Kane and Heinrich 92] Gerry Kane and Joe Heinrich, editors. *MIPS RISC Architecture*. Prentice Hall, 1992.

[Levin et al. 75] R. Levin, E. Cohen, W. Corwin, F. Pollack, and W. Wulf. POLICY/MECHANISM SEPARATION IN HYDRA. In *Proceedings of the 5th ACM Symposium on Operating System Principles*, pp. 132–140. ACM Press, November 1975.

[Marsh et al. 91] Brian D. Marsh, Michael L. Scott, Thomas J. LeBlanc, and Evangelos P. Markatos. First-Class User-Level Threads. In *Proceedings of the 13th ACM Symposium on Operating System Principles*, pp. 110–121, October 1991.

[Rozier et al. 88] M. Rozier, V. Abrossimov, F. Armand, I. Boule, M. Gien, M. Guillemont, F. Herrmann, C. Kaiser, S. Langlois, P. Léonard, and W. Neuhauser. Chorus Distributed Operating Systems. *Computing Systems*, Vol. 1, No. 4, pp.305–370, Fall 1988.

[Spafford 86] Eugene Howard Spafford. *Kernel Structures for a Distributed Operating System*. PhD thesis, Georgia Institute of Technology, May 1986.

[Tanenbaum et al. 90] Andrew S. Tanenbaum, Robbert van Renesse, Hans van Staveren, Gregory J. Sharp, Sape J. Mullender, Jack Jansen, and Guido van Rossum. Experiences with the Amoeba Distributed Operating System. *Communications of the ACM*, Vol. 33, No. 12, pp.46–63, December 1990.

[Tokuda et al. 90] Hideyuki Tokuda, Tatsuo Nakajima, and Prithvi Rao. Real-Time Mach: Towards a Predictable Real-Time System. In *Proceedings of Mach Workshop*. USENIX Association, October 1990.

[Yokote 92] Yasuhiko Yokote. The Apertos Reflective Operating System: The Concept and Its Implementation. In *Proceedings of Object-Oriented Programming Systems, Languages and Applications in 1992*. ACM Press, October 1992. Also appeared in SCSL-TR-92-014 of Sony Computer Science Laboratory Inc.

[Yokote et al. 89] Yasuhiko Yokote, Fumio Teraoka, and Mario Tokoro. A Reflective Architecture for an Object-Oriented Distributed Operating System. In *Proceedings of ECOOP'89 European Conference on Object-Oriented Programming*, July 1989. Also appeared in SCSL-TR-89-001 of Sony Computer Science Laboratory Inc.

[Yokote et al. 91a] Yasuhiko Yokote, Atsushi Mitsuzawa, Nobuhisa Fujinami, and Mario Tokoro. Reflective Object Management in the Muse Operating System. In *Proceedings of the 1991 International Workshop on Object Orientation in Operating Systems*, pp. 16–23. IEEE Computer Society Press, October 1991. Also appeared in SCSL-TR-91-

009 of Sony Computer Science Laboratory Inc.

[Yokote et al. 91b] Yasuhiko Yokote, Fumio Teraoka, Atsushi Mitsuzawa, Nobuhisa Fujinami, and Mario Tokoro. The Muse Object Architecture: A New Operating System Structuring Concept. *ACM Operating Systems Review*, Vol. 25, No. 2, pp.22–46, April 1991. Also appeared in SCSL-TR-91-002 of Sony Computer Science Laboratory Inc.

[Yonezawa and Tokoro 87] Akinori Yonezawa and Mario Tokoro, editors. *Object-Oriented Concurrent Programming*. The MIT Press, 1987.

(Invited Paper)

Object Database Systems: Functional Architecture

François Bancilhon

O_2 Technology
7 Rue du Parc de Clagny
78035 Versailles Cedex, France
e-mail: francois@o2tech.fr

Abstract

Object database systems have now been on the market for about 4 years. They have evolved considerably and are now slowly converging to common and accepted overall architecture. The goal of this paper is to describe this architecture.

An object database system supports an object database model. This model can be decomposed into four different aspects: data, behavior, persistence and naming.

An object database system consists of a database engine supporting all or part of the database model. On top of this engine are implemented a number of language interfaces: an object definition language, an object query language and one or several programming languages. These programming languages can be internal or external. Internal languages are fully managed within the system, and are in general proprietary extensions of existing programming languages (C, Smalltalk, Lisp or C++). External languages are managed outside of the database system and are in most case standard languages (C++ or SmallTalk).

Introduction

Research on object databases (OODBS) started at the beginning of the 1980's with initial efforts such as [Copeland et Maier 84]. It became very active in the mid 1980's with projects such as Orion [Kim 88], Observer [Skarra et al. 86], O_2 [Deux et al. 91], Damokles [Dittrich 1986] and Iris [Fishman et al. 87]. At the end of the 1980's, a number of start-up companies were created (Versant, Itasca, Objectivity, Object Design and O_2) and joined the already existing object database companies (Servio and Ontos). As a result, seven products are now commercially available.

The products have been quickly maturing after several years of market presence. Production applications are being deployed in various areas: CAD, software engineering, geographic information systems, financial applications, medical applications, telecommunications (network administration), multimedia and MIS.

The Manifesto [Atkinson et al. 89] was written in 1989 when the arguments about object databases were still very confusing and when the need for a number of simple and clear rules was obvious. It played a reasonable role: as a pedagogical tool, it has been used to teach, present and explain most of the important concepts. As a marketing tool, it has been used by most vendors to claim compliance and present their product.

I have personally used it as teaching tool and found it adequate up to a point. It is a good tool for people who want to understand the *concepts*. It is not a good tool for people who want to understand what a system looks like, how is it *structured*. I have noticed that when I reach the point where I present the functional architecture of a system, the audience has a problem matching the actual 14 concepts of the Manifesto with the architecture of the system. Numerous questions arise, such as what happens to the DDL, do we still need a query language and what for, how does the system relate to C++, where should the methods be stored, what happens to the impedance mismatch, should we use standard or new programming languages, etc.

A few years ago, these questions had no common answers since all systems were very different, but as the field is maturing, as we understand better users needs and requirements and as systems evolve under customer pressure, there is a clear convergence among the systems concerning their overall architecture.

The goal of this paper is to clarify some of the architectural confusion by presenting this common functional architecture. It is thus purely pedagogical and contains no hard results.

1 Object database model

Standard data models (hierarchical, network and relational) are defined by a number of primitives that describe the structure of the data. Object databases require more than a data model: their models are more than the simple extension of traditional data models to a new paradigm. They actually cover a different dimension: they include dynamicity (operations are associated to objects) and deal with the distinction between persistent and non persistent data. This is why, instead of talking about a "data model", I talk here about an "object database model". This model includes:

1. a *data model* which describes the structural part of the information, *i.e.*, the data part of the objects,

2. a *behavior model* which models the dynamics of the data, *i.e.*, essentially the operations associated with the objects,

3. a *persistence model* which defines the way in which persistent and transient data is created and how it can eventually change its status,

4. a *naming model* which defines how one names and accesses the objects of the database.

I now present each one of these four categories. For each one, I recall the assumptions used in the relational data model. I also assume the reader somehow familiar with the data and behavior models, and I spend more time elaborating on the naming and the persistence models.

1.1 Data model

The data model specifies the structure of the data of the database.

In the relational model, the data model states that a database consists of a set of named relations, each one consisting of a set of tuples, each tuple having a set of named attributes with atomic values.

For an object DBMS, the data model supports the following concepts:

Complex object: This includes support for atomic objects such as integer, real, boolean, and string, support for the set (unique set and bag), tuple, list and array constructors. This also includes support for relationships between objects, whether it is a special concept or whether the tuple attribute construct is sufficient to support this feature. Relationships can be one way or two way, they can also be 1:1, 1:n or n:p.

Object identity: Objects have an identity of their own which allows them to be shared among other objects and to represent cycles in the object composition structure.

Classes/types: Objects of a similar structure are grouped together in classes and are characterized by a type.

Inheritance: Classes are organized in a class hierarchy. There is a partial order defined among classes which corresponds to the notion of specialization.

Logical to physical independence: A logical data model describes the conceptual schema and a physical data model provides hints (e.g. on data placement) or orders (e.g. on indices) to the object database engine. Physical to logical data independence is guaranteed, *i.e.*, the physical schema can change freely without requiring any modification of the application programs.

1.2 Behavior model

The behavior model specifies the operations attached to objects.

This part is simply absent in the relational model since it only deals with data and not with operations.

In an object DBMS, the model supports the following notions:

Encapsulation: Objects have a data part (specified in the classical data model) and an operational part consisting of a set of operations. Operations are described by their signature and their code is written in a programming language.

Classes/types again: Classes group objects of the same structure and with the same set of operations.

Inheritance again: More specialized classes inherit methods from their super class with the signature possibly redefined, they can also have their own specific methods, which will be in turn inherited by their subclasses.

Late binding and message passing: Since method code can depend on the actual class of the objects, it is possible that method name binding has to be done at run time.

Extensibility: The data and behavior model include a library of classes and objects. This set can be extended at will since the developer can add new classes and objects in the library.

Completeness: A complete application can be written in the programming language associated with the data model.

1.3 Naming model

The naming model specifies how to enter the database, how to name objects of the database and how to reach the information of the database. Names are used both by the query language which interrogates the database, and the method and the programming language. Thus, they have a strong influence on the way data is manipulated.

In the relational system, the naming model is simple: the names are those of the relations in the database and the only way to reach a tuple is by associative access to the relation (through a select-from-where clause).

In an object database, the structure of the data is more elaborate and there are two possibilities for the naming model:

Class extents: To every class is attached a collection consisting of all the objects of this class (the class extent). This collection has the same name as the class (or some name derived from it) and this set of names serves as the entry points in the system.

This exactly mimics relational systems: the equivalent of a relation is a class extent, the equivalent of a tuple is an object and the only way to access an object is through the associative access of a collection. It is however not consistent with the traditional model of naming in programming languages.

There is no need for declaring names, since they are derived from class declaration.

This has some influence on the query language: because the names only give access to collections of objects and not to any objects, the query language naturally uses this property and every query is in general of the select-from-where clause.

Named objects: Any object of any class can be named and can serve as an entry point in the system.

This approach is of course more powerful and different from the relational approach. It is consistent with the programming model of computation: one manages various types of data and the entry points in the system are the variable names.

An important property of naming systems is *class orthogonality:* a naming model has this property if any object of any class can be named. The class extent naming model is not class orthogonal (only collection objects can be named), while the named object approach is (every object can be named). The benefits of orthogonality in general are numerous: the system is simpler to describe, to document and to learn; it is better structured and easier to implement.

1.4 Persistence model

The persistence model explains how to program in the presence of persistent and transient data. Thus, it specifies how to create and delete transient and persistent objects. It also specifies how to change the status of transient and persistent objects.

In the relational model, the model of persistence is trivial: everything is persistent.

Object databases offer a richer model of persistence and deal with a universe where persistent and transient data have to be managed. The persistence model can be of several types:

1. *Systematic:* everything is persistent[1] (as in a traditional database) or everything is transient (as in traditional programming language).

2. *Class declaration based:* when the programmer declares a class, he/she states whether it is persistent (resp. transient). This can be done by an explicit key word, or by any other means (such as making the class a subclass of a special "persistent" class). Every object of this class is by definition persistent (resp. transient).

3. *Object declaration based:* when the programmer declares an object, he/she declares it as persistent (resp. transient) and the object is persistent (resp. transient) and remains so for its life.

4. *Object creation based:* when the programmer creates an object by a *new* command, he/she declares it as persistent (resp. transient) and it will remain persistent (resp. transient) for its life until deletion.

5. *Fully dynamic:* the status of persistence of object can change during its life; there are two ways to support fully dynamic persistence:

    - *By reachability:* The programmer defines some "persistence roots". Then, persistence is defined by the rule "every object reachable from a persistent root is persistent". All objects are created temporary, and to make them persistent, one must connect them (directly or indirectly) to a persistence root. To make a persistent object transient, one removes all the connections between this object and the persistence roots. In this case, there is no need for explicit delete[2]. This assumes some form of garbage collector to take care of the unreachable objects.

    - *By explicit command:* the programmer uses persist and unpersist command to change the status of objects during their life. This implies a subtle management of dangling references.

There are a number of desirable properties that the persistence model should satisfy:

Completeness: The system supports both persistent and non persistent data. Otherwise we limit the system to traditional databases (everything is persistent) or to programming languages (nothing is persistent).

Class Orthogonality: Persistence is orthogonal to classes, *i.e.*, every object of every class has the possibility of being persistent or transient. In other words, persistence or transience are not properties of a limited subset of classes. This property implies that the class system of the database (*i.e.*, the data model) and of the programming language are the same.

---

[1] I mention this solution just for the sake of completeness of the classification, since I do not consider that such a persistence model qualifies as an object database model.
[2] But vendor experience shows that developers request such a feature and every vendor will make it available sooner or later.

Transparence: Persistence is transparent, *i.e.*, persistent and non persistent data are treated the same way. Therefore the way of creating objects and of sending messages to them is the same for transient and persistent object.

Compatibility with the naming model: The model of persistence and of naming are compatible with one another. Every persistent object is reachable directly or indirectly via names (otherwise it is be impossible to delete an object!).

Of course, the most natural thing is to consider that names are the entry points of the database.

Support for referential integrity: References to objects must be valid after every database operation. This property is offered by the model of persistence by reachability: by definition every object referenced by a persistent object is persistent and thus every reference is valid. In any other model, one must insure referential integrity: all the other models support a delete statement and this can create dangling references.

2 Database engine

The database engine is a software module that provides all database functionality, and supports all (or part of) the object database model. Its interface is a library of functions (C or C ++ in general). It can be made visible and available to the application developer or it can remain an internal interface for system programmers.

This paper does not address the system and architectural aspects of object database engines. It should be mentioned however that the engine supports:

- indexes and data placement
- security
- concurrency
- recovery
- client/server[3]
- distribution

The object database model support given by the engine depends on the type of programming language support (internal vs. external, see Section 5).

- For external languages, it is sufficient to support the data model and the naming model. The engine provides low level access to each object structure, such as extracting the attribute of a tuple or scanning a set. It also accesses the database through the names. It can however ignore methods and the distinction between persistent and transient space.

---

[3]This assumes that the client/server split of the software is actually done in this module which is the case of most systems. This implies that all language processing (development and runtime) is done on the client workstation.

- For internal languages, the engine has to support the full object database model: not only the data model and the naming model, but also the behavior model (methods are stored in the database system and message passing is actually executed by the engine), and the persistence model (it manages the space of persistent and transient objects and their relationship). This implies a complete schema manager that can add/delete classes and modify them.

3 Object Definition Language

The object definition language is the equivalent of the data definition language of a traditional database system. It describes the schema of the database. An *object database schema* can be defined as follows: a set of classes, their structure and their methods, the method signatures, the class hierarchy, the composition structure and the names if the naming model requires them. The schema however does not include the method or the application code.

The object definition language is used to declare classes: it defines their internal structure and their methods. It does not however include the programming language, thus the method bodies are not specified in this language, only the method signature. It only describes the schema the way the user and the developer can see it and not the way it is implemented. It uses the data model, a part of the behavior model (the method signature) and the naming model. This respects the encapsulation principle in the database way[4].

The object definition language can have its own syntax or use the same syntax as the programming language. It can also be a proprietary language or use a standard language (see Section 5).

4 Object Query Language

The query language in an object database system fulfills the same functions as in a relational system:

- it is used interactively to query the database on line,
- it is used embedded in the programming language to access data in the database.

Some persistent programming language proponents have proposed that the query language be subsumed by the programming language. This violates the simplicity requirement (see below) and the habit database users have to interact naturally with a database system.

Some of the early object database system designers have limited the query language to the simple function of associative access within the programming language: the query language simply performs the filter function on collection objects (*i.e.*, the relational

---

[4]It is customary in the database approach to consider that the specification of the object includes the internal structure and the method signature, and that the implementation of the object only include the method implementation. This is to be opposed to the programming language approach where the internal structure of the object is part of the implementation.

select operator). This violates the completeness and the orthogonality requirements (see below) and does not allow the usage of the query language interactively.

Finally, experience has proven that object database users expect to find in their query language the same level of service they find in a relational query language, *i.e.*, the ability to fully query the database structure. Thus the consensus is now evolving towards complete query languages. Of course, the query language fits the data model, and as such it supports:

Complex objects: It allows the users to navigate through objects, to build new complex objects[5] from existing ones.

Object identity: It allows to test for equality and identity of objects.

Encapsulation: It allows to send messages to objects. It has a mode to violate encapsulation and directly access the state of an object. This mode is in general restricted to the interactive access to the database without any update.

Naming: It allows to access the database from all the global names.

The query language satisfies a number of properties:

- It is *orthogonal to classes*, *i.e.*, it treats every object constructor with equal importance, it does not give an excessive weight to the set construct for instance and it allows the free composition of the constructors.

- It is *orthogonal to persistence*, *i.e.*, one queries the same way persistent and transient data.

- It is *simple*, *i.e.*, simple questions have a simple expression in this language

- It is *complete*. Even though more complex problems have been addressed in the literature, [Abiteboul and Kanellakis 89], there is (to my knowledge) no formal definition of completeness for a complex object query language, but it should not be very hard to do that[6]. The idea would be that every possible object can be extracted from the database (up to a permutation of the objects within a set) and that every possible complex object state can be constructed from these objects. Of course, in case of restriction to the special case of relational systems, the definition should match that of completeness for relational query languages. The object query language is of course not Turing complete (*i.e.*, allow every possible computation) because this would violate the simplicity condition.

- It is *optimizable:* complex queries can be reordered by the query optimizer to generate equivalent and more efficient queries. Access paths are used by the query optimizer for faster access to objects within a collection.

- It matches the *programming language*, *i.e.*, the embedding of the query language in the programming language is natural and does not cause yet another mismatch.

---
[5] or at least their *value* or their state.
[6] and I'm sure most people in the PODS community can generate such a formal definition easily.

5 Programming Language

In most (if not all) systems, a single programming language is used to write the methods associated with the objects and to write the applications that use and manage these objects. This programming language satisfies the following properties:

- It matches the object database model, *i.e.*, its class system is that of the data model. It has the same behavior model. It accesses data in the database according to the naming model and it respects the persistence model.

- It integrates the notion of transaction. Transactions are properly positioned with respect to methods and application programs.

- It supports embedded queries.

There are two forms of programming languages: *internal*, where the development and the run time environment are part of the database system and *external*, where the development and the run time environment are outside of the database system.

In terms of syntax and semantics, the language can be standard or proprietary:

- Proprietary languages are in most cases existing standard languages (C, C++ or Smalltalk) with some extension to deal with various database or object aspects.

- The standard language of choice is in general C++.

In most cases, internal languages are proprietary and external languages are standard. Of course, nothing keeps the system designer from having a standard internal language, nor from having external proprietary languages (but this would force the producer to implement and support a complete environment for this language and to keep this environment outside of the database system). Finally, it should be noted that some systems offer both internal and external languages, thus giving the choice to their users.

5.1 Internal Language

In this approach, everything is managed within the database system: the system is self sufficient and can be used to develop and to run the application.

The development environment allows class creation and modification, methods and application programs creation, update, compilation and linking. The schema manager contains and manages class definitions, method code and application programs. Tools to edit and browse the schema and the applications are available. These tools can be alphanumeric or graphical.

The run time system runs methods and application programs using the database engine and the schema manager.

Internal languages, because they are semi-proprietary (extensions of existing languages) offer a good mapping between the database data model and the programming language syntax and a good integration between the programming language, the query language and the object definition language.

In such a system, code versions (source and object) are stored and managed by the system, dependencies are maintained by the system, code is protected in case of crashes, code sharing among developers is handled by the system, commit and abort facilities on schema modifications are available. Thus, all the benefits of using a database system are given to the developer.

This results in increased user comfort, due to the existence of a single environment and a single set of commands.

5.2 External Language

In this approach, the function of the database system is limited to the specific task of data manipulation. Other tasks are performed outside of the database system by complementary third party tools: the development of the application is done outside of the database, and only a part of the schema design is done within the database system. The application is run in the runtime environment of the language.

In most systems, the external language is C++, so I will use C++ in this description. Two problems have to be solved: the object database model has to be mapped onto the language (without modifying or extending that language) and the language and the database environments have to be integrated.

Mapping the data model

- To map the data model, one has to map all the object constructs on the C++ constructs: the "struct" is used to represent the tuple construct; a library of C++ classes is used to represent the other object constructors: sets, unique sets, arrays, lists or insertable arrays. Relationships are implemented through a simple field name.

- Mapping the behavior model is the easiest part: methods and their signatures are associated to classes.

- Mapping the naming model is in general performed through a function taking as parameter a target object and a string representing the name of the object. Because a standard compiler is being used, there is no way of knowing the class of the named object and the programmer has to perform an explicit cast to handle the class of the object.

- To embed the query language, a function taking as parameter a string representing the query, an object to store the result and the parameters (if any) is used.

- To map the persistence model, the approach depends on the persistence model. One of the most common approach is that of persistent pointers. The developer first declares the persistent classes, these are the classes whose objects are potentially persistent. This is done by making them subclasses of a special persistent class.

  For each persistent database class, the system defines an associated persistent pointer class, thus for instance if "employee" is a persistent database class, the system automatically creates the class "p_employee" of persistent pointers to the database class. Persistent objects are then exclusively referenced through persistent pointers.

Integrating the environments

Application programs, class definitions and method definitions are all written in C++, they are stored in files and managed by some external environment. In some cases, class definitions can be written using a proprietary object definition language and a translator generates equivalent C++ code, but the end result is the same. These files (containing the schema and the application) are processed by a database utility which generates some new files. All these have to be linked with a library of functions that represent the extensions of C++ to support the data model (library classes for sets, lists, etc.) and run in some external environment.

This external environment is not provided by the database vendor, but by some third party, and the developer is free of the choice of his/her system. Thus, this environment is in charge of compiling, editing, maintaining dependencies, doing makes, and running the object code. One directly updates the source files, one has exactly the level of service to be expected from the programming language environment.

The benefit[7] of using a standard language are the use of a familiar language and the ability to choose one's favorite C++ environment and runtime.

6 Example

This architectural description can be used as a framework to describe object database systems. For instance, the O_2 object database system can be described as follows:

1. The O_2 *data and behavior models* support complex objects and the classical associated features including multiple inheritance in a complete and standard way. The *naming model* uses the named objects approach. The *persistence model* is fully dynamic and supports persistence by reachability.

2. The *database engine*, O_2Engine, is available to the programmer through its O_2API programming interface. It supports all the features of the object database model, including behavior (it stores, manages and executes methods), named objects and persistence by reachability.

3. A complete *Object Definition Language* is available.

4. The *query language*, O_2SQL, allows interactive and embedded access to the database. O_2SQL has an associated optimizer and can be used both from C++ and from O_2C.

5. Two language interfaces are offered:

    - an *external language* through a standard C++ interface that uses persistent pointer technology and that can be used through third party C++ environments
    - an *internal language*, the O_2C fourth generation language which is an extension of C. O_2C has its own development environment O_2Tools, that offers among other features incremental compilation.

---

[7] Despite some claims or beliefs, standard languages do not guarantee portability, because the mapping of the language on the data model bindings is still proprietary. Portability will only be guaranteed by the standardization of these bindings. This standardization is under way within the ODMG group (see conclusion).

This framework does not address GUI tools such as O_2Look.

Conclusion

Object databases properly integrate programming and data management. Thus, they address, besides the classical issue of data management, those of programming, persistence and naming. As such, they are more complete than traditional data managers and require a more elaborate description. This is not to say that object database systems introduce more complexity: they are indeed simpler and more user friendly than the heterogeneous coupling of traditional databases and programming environments.

After several years of evolution, a global architecture is emerging for operational object database systems. At the same time, the vendors are now in the process of standardizing the corresponding interfaces. The ODMG group consisting of O_2, Object Design, Objectivity, Ontos and Versant have produced a first design of the Object Definition Language and the Object Query Language. They have also addressed the issue of external language and defined bindings for C++ and SmallTalk. These standard interfaces are a strong signal of the maturity of the field and will greatly contribute to the development of the market. Further standardization could address the API interface and would allow vendors or third parties to develop and market multiplatform tools. The vendor community and the user community by transitivity would greatly benefit from this further standardization step.

Acknowledgements

I wish to thank Claude Delobel, Guy Ferran, Shojiro Nishio and Fernando Velez for their comments on earlier drafts of this paper.

References

[Abiteboul and Kanellakis 89] S. Abiteboul and P. Kanellakis, "Object Identity as a Query Language Primitive", *Proceedings of the 1989 ACM SIGMOD Conference*, Portland, June 1989.

[Atkinson et al. 89] M. Atkinson, F. Bancilhon, D. DeWitt, K. Dittrich, D. Maier and S. Zdonik, "The Object-Oriented Database System Manifesto", *Proceedings of the DOOD 89*, Kyoto, December 1989.

[Bancilhon 88] F. Bancilhon, "Object-oriented database systems", *Proceedings of the 1988 PODS Conference*, Austin, Texas, March 1988.

[Bancilhon et al. 92] F. Bancilhon, C. Delobel and P. Kanellakis eds, "Building an OODBMS, the story of O_2", Morgan Kaufman, 1992.

[Carey et al. 88] M. Carey, D. DeWitt and S. Vandenberg, "A Data Model and Query Language for EXODUS", *Proceedings of the 1988 ACM SIGMOD Conference*, Chicago, June 1988.

[Copeland et Maier 84] G. Copeland and D. Maier, "Making Smalltalk a Database System", *Proceedings of the 1984 ACM SIGMOD Conference*, Boston, June 1984.

[Deux *et al*] O. O. Deux et al, "The Story of O_2", *IEEE Transactions on Knowledge and Data Engineering*, Vol. 2, No. 1, March 1990.

[Deux *et al.* 91] O. Deux *et al.*, "The O_2 System", *Communications of the ACM*, Vol. 34, No. 10, October 1991.

[Dittrich 1986] K.R. Dittrich, "Object-Oriented Database System : The Notions and the issues", in : *Dittrich, K.R. and Dayal, U. (eds): Proceedings of the 1986 International Workshop on Object-Oriented Database Systems*, IEEE Computer Society Press, Washington, September 1986.

[Fishman *et al.* 87] D. Fishman et al, "Iris: an object-oriented database management system", *ACM TOIS 5:1, pp.48-69,* January 1987.

[Kim 88] W. Kim, "A foundation for object-oriented databases", *MCC Technical Report*, 1988.

[Maier, *et al.* 86] D. Maier, J. Stein, A. Otis, A. Purdy, "Development of an object-oriented DBMS" *Report CS/E-86-005*, Oregon Graduate Center, April 1986.

[Skarra *et al.* 86] A. Skarra, S. Zdonik and S. Reiss, "An object server for an object oriented database system," *Dittrich, K.R. and Dayal, U. (eds): Proceedings of the 1986 International Workshop on Object-Oriented Database Systems*, IEEE Computer Society Press, pp.196-204, Washington, September 1986.

Maintaining Behavioral Consistency during Schema Evolution

Paul L. Bergstein and Walter L. Hürsch*
College of Computer Science, Northeastern University
360 Huntington Avenue #CN237, Boston MA 02115
{ pberg | huersch }@ccs.neu.edu

Abstract

We examine the problem of how to ensure behavioral consistency of an object-oriented system after its schema has been updated. The problem is viewed from the perspective of both the strongly typed and the untyped language model. Solutions are compared in both models using C++ and CLOS as examples.

1 Introduction

Schema evolution and transformations have recently received increasing attention in the literature in both the area of object-oriented languages and especially in the area of object-oriented database systems: [Opd92, Ber92, Ber91, Cas91, CPLZ91, DZ91, Bar91, LH90, AH88, BKKK87, PS87, SZ86]. Most of this work has been done from the object-oriented database point of view where the focus is naturally on the structural, rather than behavioral, aspects of the evolving schema. Systems such as ORION [BKKK87], GemStone [PS87], and OTGen [LH90] guarantee the correctness of the performed schema changes and reflect the impact on the persistent instances in the database (structural consistency). However, none of them considers the impact of schema updates on existing programs (behavioral consistency).

In this paper we consider the problem of behavioral consistency for an important subset of possible schema transformations. The transformations in this subset are the schema extensions defined in [LHX93, Ber91]. We chose these transformations for three reasons. First, they have the desirable property that the transformed schema's consistency with the old objects either is maintained or can be easily restored. For object-oriented database design, this means that the database does

---

*Walter Hürsch's research has been generously supported by Mettler-Toledo AG

not need to be repopulated, or that the repopulation can be easily accomplished. In either case, no information from the old database is lost. Second, the extension transformations reflect a significant set of transformations that commonly occur in practice. Third, they can be decomposed into a sequence of primitive transformations.

The strategy we employ to solve the behavioral consistency problem relies heavily on the third property. Our approach is to divide a given extension into a sequence of primitives and then solve the problem for each of the primitives in turn. Behavioral consistency is investigated for two very different language models: strongly typed and untyped languages. We compare solutions in the two models using C++ and CLOS as examples. As one might expect, the problem is much more difficult for the strongly typed model.

The paper is organized as follows. Section 2 provides a brief description of the employed data and language models. The third section reviews the extension relation and its associated primitive transformations. In section 4 we propose a solution for untyped languages. We also present a partial solution for strongly typed languages and discuss some of the remaining problems. The last two sections present related work and conclusions.

2 The Demeter data model

2.1 Data Model

The data model used in this paper is the Demeter Kernel model which is formally defined in [LBSL91]. The Demeter Kernel model uses two kinds of classes: construction and alternation classes, and two kinds of relationships between classes: kind-of and part-of relationships.

Only the construction classes are instantiable, so every object must be an instance of some construction class. The alternation classes are used to model the union of object sets defined by the construction classes. This is often natural when modeling an application domain. For example (see Figure 1–Original, page 7), in an object-oriented drawing program the tool used to select and draw shapes on a canvas might be either a selection tool, a tool for drawing rectangles, or a tool for drawing ovals. So the objects that can be stored in the **tool** part of a **Canvas** object are either **OvalTool**, **RectTool**, or **SelectTool** objects. Alternation classes are used to define such unions. Each class which is an element of the union is called an alternative of the alternation class. One can think of an alternation class as an abstract superclass in a typical class-based object-oriented programming language, with the alternatives as immediate subclasses.

Any class may have various attributes represented by part classes. These "parts" may be thought of as an abstraction of instance variables in a typical object-oriented programming language. Each alternation class must have at least one alternative or "kind". The "kinds" of an alternation class are represented by its subclasses.

If an alternation class has parts, they are implemented by inheritance in the subclasses. For example, each tool in our drawing application has a mouse interface. This common part is expressed as a single part in the alternation class which is shared (inherited) by all of its alternatives (subclasses). Thus, a kind-of relation in the Demeter Kernel model also implies an inheritance relation. Since alternation classes are not instantiable, it is only possible to inherit from abstract classes.

The classes and their relations are defined by a class dictionary graph. Construction classes are represented by rectangles and alternation classes are represented by hexagons in a class dictionary graph.

Part-of relations are expressed as directed edges called construction edges from a class to each of its part classes. The construction edges are drawn as thin arrows. Each part must have a name, and the construction edges are labeled with the part names in a class dictionary graph. In Figure 1–Original, for example, a **DrawWindow** is a construction class with two parts: a **ShapeList** called **shapes**, and a **Screen** called **canvas** where the shapes are to be displayed.

Kind-of/inheritance relations are expressed by directed edges called alternation edges from an alternation class to each of its alternatives. The alternation edges are drawn with thick arrows.

Legal class dictionary graphs must satisfy two independent conditions: (1) No class may inherit from itself; that is, there must not be any cyclic path consisting only of alternation edges. (2) There must not be any class which has two or more parts (including inherited parts) with the same name. The first condition implies that a class definition may not depend upon itself in a circular fashion. The second condition disallows "overriding" or "shadowing" of instance variables. It guarantees that the part names in each class are unambiguous.

A class dictionary graph may be used to easily generate a set of class definitions (minus method declarations) in any class-based object-oriented programming language. This may be done either by hand or automatically by using a tool like the **Demeter System**^{TM}. In the latter case, the declaration and implementation of many commonly useful "generic" methods may also be automatically generated.

2.2 Language Model

In this paper we consider (informally) two language models: untyped and strongly typed. As representative examples we consider CLOS (Common Lisp Object System) and C++, respectively. For simplicity, we consider the class definitions and the methods of a class separately, although some languages might require forward declarations of methods in the class definitions.

A class dictionary graph is essentially a language-independent set of class definitions, and the translation to a particular programming language is a straightforward process. The kind-of relations defined by the class dictionary graph are implemented by declaring a corresponding inheritance relation in the class definitions. In most languages, this means that if there is an alternation edge from A to B, then class B is declared to inherit from class A in the definition of class B. Part-of relations are implemented by instance variables. For each part of a class, an instance variable is declared whose name is the same as the part name. In the case of a typed language, the part's type is declared to be the corresponding class. For example, the class definition for **ShapeList** from the class dictionary graph in Figure 1–Original would be written in C++ or CLOS as:

```
    C++ Version                          CLOS Version
class ShapeList : public List {    (defclass ShapeList (List)
protected:                             (firstShape restShapes))
  Shape* firstShape;
  List* restShapes;
};
```

Our two language models share several common features:

- The parts of an object are implemented as *references*.

- Any object can send another object any message for which the receiving object has a corresponding method. In C++ terminology, all methods are "public".

- Each method is attached to exactly one class. In CLOS terminology, each method has exactly one "specialized parameter", i.e. there are no "multi-methods".

- Any method available to an alternation class is also available to each of its alternatives through inheritance.

- Inherited methods may be overriden (specialized) in a subclass. In C++ terminology all methods are "virtual".

- Every object has access (through its methods) to all of its own parts, and to the parts of other objects of the same class. This level of encapsulation is equivalent to "protected" instance variables in C++.

3 Schema Extension Transformations

This section informally introduces two important kinds of schema transformations. One kind consists of the object-extending class transformations, presented formally in [LHX93]. The other kind consists of the object-preserving transformations, presented formally in [Ber91]. The latter kind is a special case of the former in that any object-preserving transformation can be regarded as an object-extending transformation. Thus, both kinds can be called schema extension tranformations. Schema extensions are defined as a relation on class dictionary graphs. This relation can be decomposed into a set of eight primitive relations that was shown to be correct, minimal and complete [Ber91, LHX93]. The completeness guarantees that for any two schemas in an object-extending relation there exists a sequence of primitive transformations that transforms the original into the extended schema. Since the completeness proofs are constructive, there also exists an algorithm to find the sequence. The primitive schema transformations will be used in the subsequent section to determine their impact on the behavioral consistency of a program.

3.1 The extension relation

For the following discussion it is important to remember that all alternation classes are abstract and only instances of construction classes can be assigned to a part. Thus, even if a construction edge points to an alternation class A, the only objects that can be assigned to the part are instances of construction classes that are subclasses of A.

Informally, two class dictionary graphs G_1 and G_2 are in an **object-equivalence relation** if they both define the same set of objects. Consequently, G_1 and G_2 must satisfy these conditions: (1) G_1 and G_2 have the same set of construction classes. (2) A construction class A of G_1 has a (inherited or direct) part b if and only if its corresponding class in G_2 has a (inherited or direct) part b . (3) An instance can be assigned to part b of class A in G_1 if and only if the instance can also be assigned to part b of class A in G_2.

As an example of two class dictionary graphs in an object-equivalence relation, consider Figures 1–Original and 1–Object-equivalent. Note that both class dictionary graphs contain the same construction classes. Furthermore, each construction class has the same parts and to each part one can assign the same instances. In particular, in both class dictionary graphs, instances of classes RectTool, OvalTool, and SelectTool can be assigned to part inputTool attached to class Screen.

Two class dictionary graphs G_1 and G_2 are in an **extension relation**, such that G_2 extends G_1, if they satisfy these conditions: (1) The set of construction classes of G_2 is a superset of the set of construction classes of G_1. (2) If a construction class A of G_1 has a (inherited or direct) part b, then its corresponding class in G_2 has a (inherited or direct) part b . (3) If an instance can be assigned to part b of class A in G_1, then the instance can also be assigned to part b of class A in G_2. An example of two class dictionary graphs in an extension relation is given in Figures 1–Object-equivalent and 1–Extended.

As a consequence of the above definitions the following relationship holds between extension and object-equivalence. Class dictionary graph G_1 is object-equivalent to class dictionary graph G_2 if and only if G_1 is extended by G_2 and G_2 is extended by G_1.

The object-preserving transformation is composed of the five primitive operations: (1) Deletion of useless alternation, (2) Addition of useless alternation, (3) Abstraction of common parts, (4) Distribution of common parts, and (5) Part replacement [Ber91]. The extension relation is composed of the above five primitives and, in addition, the three primitives: (6) Part generalization, (7) Part addition, and (8) Class addition [LHX93].

We briefly summarize the semantics of the above primitives.

Deletion of useless alternation (DUA) An alternation class is "useless" if it has no incoming edges and no outgoing construction edges. In other words, an alternation class is useless if it is not a part of any class, and defines no parts for any class to inherit. If an alternation class is useless it may be deleted by the DUA primitive. An example of a DUA operation is the deletion of the alternation class Tool shown in the transition from the partially drawn class dictionary graph in Figure 2–PRP to the class dictionary graph in Figure 1–Extended.

Addition of useless alternation (AUA) This is the inverse operation of DUA. An alternation class can be added to a class dictionary graph along with outgoing alternation edges to any other classes. An example of an AUA operation is the addition of the two alternation classes DrawingTool and CanvasTool (Figure 1–Original to Figure 2–AUA).

Abstraction of common parts (ACP) If B_i $(1 \leq i \leq n)$ are all the alternatives of an alternation class A and each of them has a part c of class C, then ACP deletes all the construction edges $B_i \xrightarrow{c} C$ $(1 \leq i \leq n)$ and replaces them with a new construction edge $A \xrightarrow{c} C$. Intuitively, if all of the immediate subclasses of a class A have the same part, that part is moved up the inheritance hierarchy so that each of the subclasses will inherit it from A. An example of the ACP operation is the abstraction of the common part

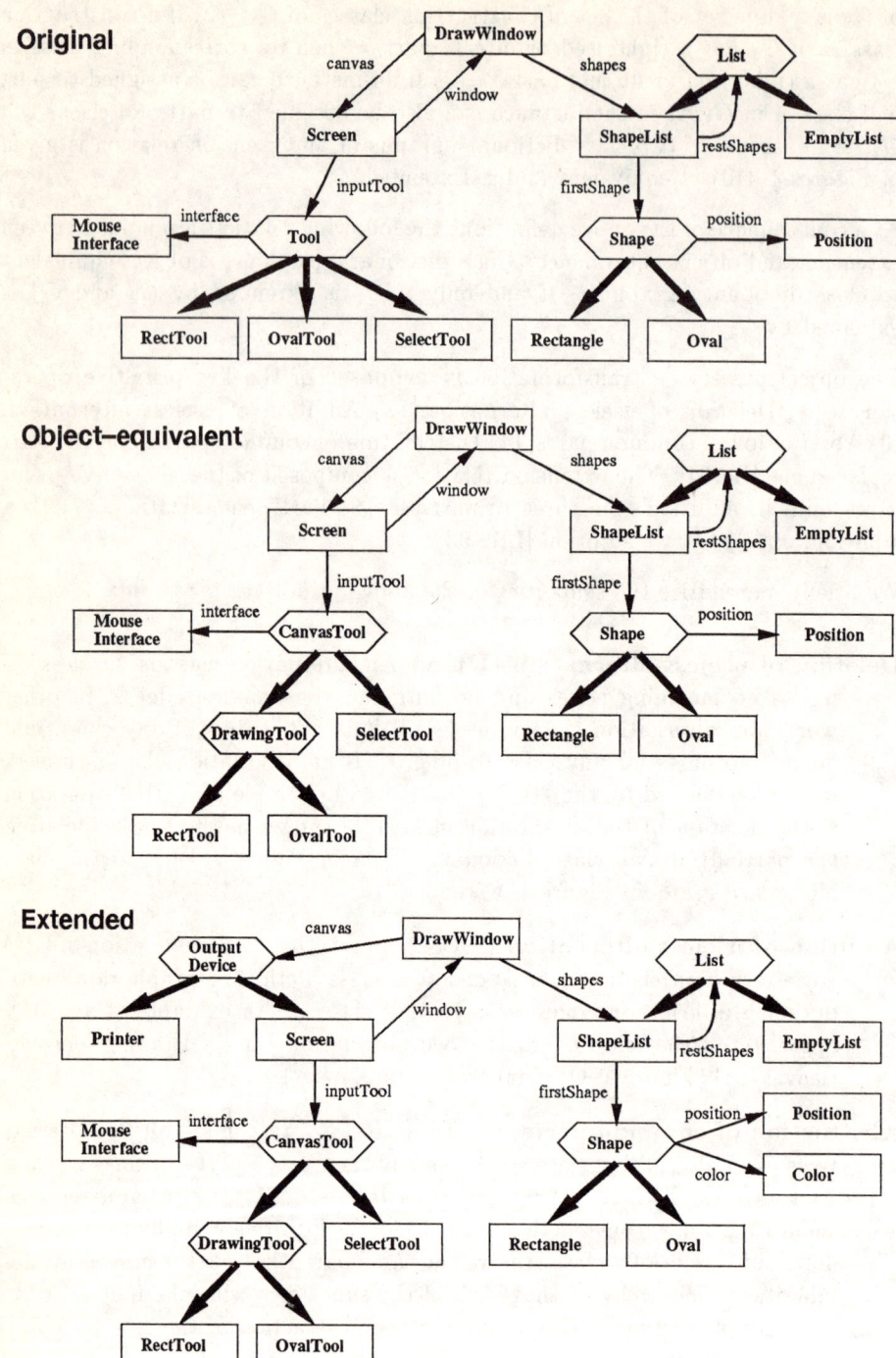

Figure 1: Extending a class dictionary graph

interface from the classes RectTool, OvalTool, SelectTool to their common superclass CanvasTool (Figure 2–DCP to Figure 2–ACP).

Distribution of common parts (DCP) This is the inverse of ACP. DCP deletes an outgoing construction edge $A \xrightarrow{c} C$ from an alternation class, A, and adds for each alternative B_i of A, a new construction edge $B_i \xrightarrow{c} C$. An example of DCP is the distribution of the part interface from class Tool to its subclasses RectTool, OvalTool, SelectTool (Figure 2–AUA to Figure 2–DCP).

Part replacement (PRP) If the set of construction classes that are subclasses of an alternation class A is the same as the set that are subclasses of another alternation class A', then PRP may delete any construction edge $X \xrightarrow{a} A$ and replace it with a new construction edge $X \xrightarrow{a} A'$. Intuitively, if two classes A and A' have the same set of instantiable (construction) subclasses then the definable objects do not change when A is replaced by A' in the definition of a part. An example of PRP is the rerouting of edge inputTool from class Tool to class CanvasTool (Figure 2–ACP to Figure 2–PRP).

Class addition (CAD) CAD adds to the existing class dictionary graph new classes and edges with the restriction that no old class may obtain new outgoing edges or new incoming alternation edges. An example of CAD is the addition of the classes Printer, OutputDevice and Color along with the outgoing alternation edges from OutputDevice (Figure 1–Object-equivalent to Figure 1–Extended).

Part addition (PAD) If the classes A and B already exist in a class dictionary graph, then PAD adds a new construction edge $A \xrightarrow{b} B$; that is, the class A obtains a new part b of class B. An example of PAD is the addition of the part color to the class Shape (Figure 1–Object-equivalent to Figure 1–Extended).

Part generalization (PGN) If a class C is a subclass of some alternation class B, then PGN reroutes a construction edge $A \xrightarrow{p} C$ to $A \xrightarrow{p} B$. In other words, PGN generalizes the domain of part p. An example of PGN is the generalization of part canvas from class Screen to the class OutputDevice (Figure 1–Object-equivalent to Figure 1–Extended).

3.2 Structural Consistency

Each of the primitive transformations, except part addition, maintains the structural consistency of the object base; that is, all the objects remain consistent with the transformed schema. When a part is added to a class A by a part addition, then structural consistency must be restored by adding an instance of that part's

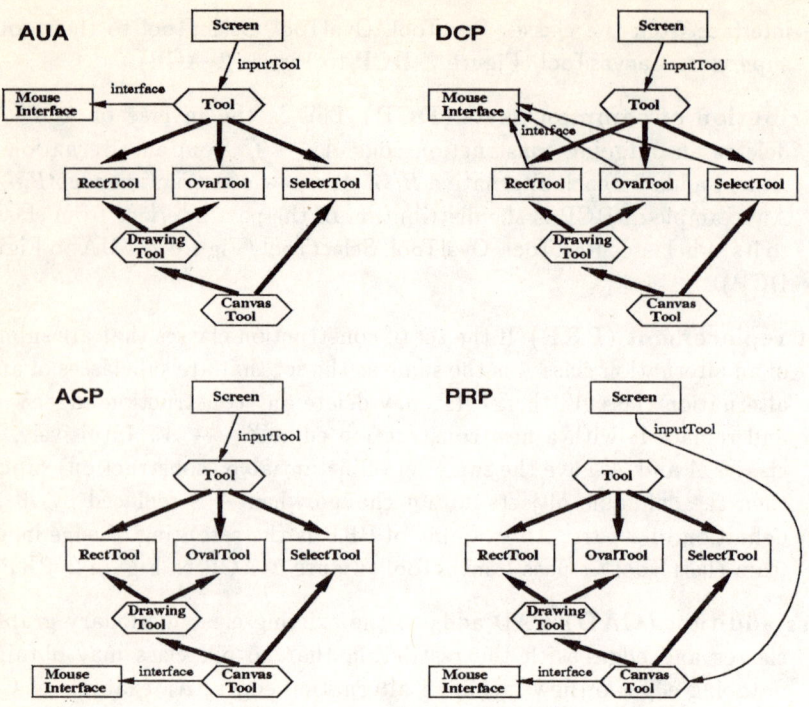

Figure 2: Steps in the object-preserving transformation

class to every instance of class A. The added object can either be some default object or specified by an object transformation function defined by the user.

4 Code Transformations

In this section we discuss how application code can be automatically updated after a class dictionary graph has been transformed or extended. The approach we take is to first reduce the transformation to a sequence of primitives. We then update the code *incrementally*, in steps that parallel the primitive transformations. Reduction to a sequence of primitives can be easily accomplished by following the constructions of the completeness proofs given in [LHX93] and [Ber91].

For each primitive transformation, we consider the rules that should be followed to update the application code so that it will meet all of the original requirements. Of course, if we wish to *extend*, rather than simply maintain the original functionality, it will be necessary to hand code some of the extension. Even so, a maintenance tool based on the primitive transformations could be used to do most of the work and generate hints for code that should be modified by hand.

4.1 Untyped Language Model

In the untyped language model the code transformations are very simple. Consider the example of the transformation of the schema in Figure 1–Original to the extended schema in Figure 1–Extended.

4.1.1 Addition of useless alternation classes

The first primitives in the sequence obtained by reducing the transformation are addition of the "useless" alternation classes DrawingTool and CanvasTool (Figure 2–AUA). The addition of these abstract classes does not require any modification of the code.

4.1.2 Distribution of common parts

In the next step (Figure 2–DCP), the interface part of the Tool class is distributed down the inheritance hierarchy to the classes RectTool, OvalTool, and SelectTool. Once again, there is no need to modify the code. Note that there may be methods attached to class Tool that refer to the interface part. In a strongly typed language such as C++, the method would no longer compile, since the part would be undefined within the scope of the method. In an untyped language such as CLOS, however, the symbol *interface* is bound at run time when the method is invoked in response to a message to a RectTool, OvalTool, or SelectTool object. Since Tool is abstract, the method can never be invoked in response to a message to a Tool object, and no run time errors occur.

4.1.3 Abstraction of common parts

When the part is moved up the new inheritance hierarchy to the CanvasTool class (Figure 2–ACP) by abstraction of common parts, there is still no need to modify the code. Every reference to interface in the RectTool, OvalTool, and SelectTool classes is still valid due to inheritance.

4.1.4 Part replacement

In the next step, the part class of Screen's inputTool is changed from Tool to CanvasTool by part replacement (Figure 2–PRP). Of course, every object that instantiates the inputTool part of a Screen must still be an instance of one of the three construction classes: RectTool, OvalTool, and SelectTool. Therefore any message that was sent to inputTool in the original code will still be understood after the class transformation and, once again, there is no need to modify existing code.

4.1.5 Deletion of useless alternations

Now that the Tool class has no incoming edges and no outgoing construction edges, it is considered "useless", and may be deleted. Note that the "useless" designation is only relevant from a data modelling point of view, since the class may have important methods attached. If the class is deleted to produce the schema in Figure 1–Object-equivalent, the functionality of the methods attached to the class must be preserved. In the simplest case, we consider only primary methods and don't allow a method to explicitly call a method defined in a superclass (i.e. **call-next-method** in CLOS). In this case each method can be copied to each of the immediate subclasses that does not override it. Now every object will respond to messages in the same way after the "useless" class is deleted.

Suppose, for example, that the **Tool** class has a method called **getPosition** which is inherited in each of its subclasses:

```
(defmethod getPosition ((self Tool))
    (getPosition (slot-value self 'interface)))
```

In this case, the **getPosition** method is copied from the **Tool** class to the **RectTool**, **OvalTool**, and **SelectTool** classes:

```
(defmethod getPosition ((self RectTool))
    (getPosition (slot-value self 'interface)))
(defmethod getPosition ((self OvalTool))
    (getPosition (slot-value self 'interface)))
(defmethod getPosition ((self SelectTool))
    (getPosition (slot-value self 'interface)))
```

If there is another alternation class that covers the same set of construction classes as the "useless" alternation, the method could just be copied to that class instead. In the example, we could just copy the **getPosition** method from the **Tool** class to the **CanvasTool** class, so that the three methods above would be replaced with:

```
(defmethod getPosition ((self CanvasTool))
    (getPosition (slot-value self 'interface)))
```

If we wish to allow "before" and "after" methods, then any before method in the "useless" class can be prepended to the before method in each subclass or the primary method if the subclass has no before method. After methods are appended to the after methods in each subclass, or the primary method if there is no after method. If we allow "call-next-method", then in each subclass, every occurrence of **call-next-method** can be removed and the "next-method" defined in the "useless" class inlined in its place.

4.1.6 Class and part addition

Extension of a class dictionary graph by class addition or part addition does not require any modification of existing code. In the current example, addition of the classes **OutputDevice**, **Printer**, and **Color** (Figure 1–Extended) does not effect the application code. When the **color** part is added to the **Shape** class, existing code will continue to provide the same functionality. In this case, however, it is likely that methods attached to the **Shape**, **Rectangle**, and **Oval** classes would be extended to make use of the new color information. For example, if there are methods attached to these classes for drawing the shapes in black and white, they will still function properly, but the additional code required to produce color renderings would have to be added by hand.

4.1.7 Part generalization

Part generalization causes a problem similar to, but more serious than, part addition. When the part class of **DrawWindow**'s **canvas** part is generalized from **Screen** to **OutputDevice** (Figure 1–Extended), the original code will continue to function properly as long as every **DrawWindow** continues to use a **Screen** as its output device. This is the case for all **DrawWindow** objects that were present in the old object store and possibly updated subsequently by an object transformation (see section 3.2) after the schema transformation. However, if new **DrawWindow** objects are introduced that use **Printer** output devices, messages to the **canvas** part will not be understood. Since it is not possible, in general, to automatically generate correct methods for the new part classes, warnings should be added to the code wherever a **DrawWindow** method accesses its **canvas** part to indicate that the part has been generalized.

4.2 Typed Language Model

For the discussion of code transformations in the typed language model, illustrated for the example of C++, we make the following simplifying assumptions on the mapping from the class dictionary graph schema to the C++ class definitions: (1) All parts are defined as protected data members. (2) In congruence with the Demeter data model, all alternation classes are mapped to abstract superclasses. (3) All member functions of alternation classes are defined as virtual member functions. (4) All data members are defined as pointers or references.

4.2.1 Addition of useless alternation classes

As for the untyped language model, the change in class definitions due to the addition of a useless alternation class requires no modification to the methods.

4.2.2 Distribution of common parts

We have seen above that, in the untyped language model, the distribution of a part from a superclass to its subclasses does not require any change in the methods. However, in the strongly typed model, the distributed part will no longer be defined within the scope of the superclass. Therefore any superclass method that accesses the part will no longer compile.

To restore behavioral consistency, every method in the superclass that accesses the part must be distributed along with the part to each of the subclasses that does not override the method. Since an object with the statically declared type of the superclass may be sent a message whose method has been distributed, we must replace the original method with a "pure virtual" method.

Constructor and destructor methods in C++ behave similarly to before and after methods in CLOS and may be treated much like the distribution of before and after methods in deletion of useless alternation classes. The body of a superclass constructor accessing a distributed part is inlined at the beginning of each subclass constructor, and replaced with an empty body.

Consider, for example, what happens when the **interface** part of the **Tool** class is distributed down the inheritance hierarchy to the classes **RectTool**, **OvalTool**, and **SelectTool** (Figure 2–DCP). Suppose that the **Tool** class defines the method:
```
Position *Tool::getPosition() { return interface -> getPosition(); }
```
Then **Tool::getPosition** is replaced by a pure virtual function, and the following new methods are added:
```
Position *RectTool::getPosition() { return interface->getPosition(); }
Position *OvalTool::getPosition() { return interface->getPosition(); }
Position *SelectTool::getPosition() { return interface->getPosition(); }
```

4.2.3 Abstraction of common parts

As in the untyped model, no change is necessary for the implementation of member functions, since data members are defined to be protected and hence member functions of any subclass that accessed an abstracted part still have access through inheritance.

4.2.4 Part replacement

In the untyped language model, part replacement does not require any modification of the code since the objects that can be assigned to the replaced part are unchanged. However, in a typed language, the part replacement implies a change in the type declaration of the part. Two problems occur in this case. First, messages sent to the part might no longer be understood since there may be no such method known to the part's new class. Second, wherever the part is involved in an assignment statement, function call (as a passed parameter), or function return (as the returned value), the part's new type will no longer be compatible.

The first problem can be solved by supplying, for each method defined in the part's old class, a corresponding pure virtual function in the part's new class. Since each construction subclass now inherits methods from both the part's new and old class, it must provide its own method to resolve the ambiguity in favor of its original (possibly inherited) method.

The second problem requires that objects be converted to the appropriate type in assignment statements, function calls, and function returns. Note that simple casting will not work in C++ under multiple inheritance.

Consider what happens when the part class of **Screen**'s **inputTool** is changed from **Tool** to **CanvasTool** by part replacement. Suppose that the following methods were originally defined:
```
void Tool::handleMouseClick(DrawWindow *win) = 0;
```

```
void Screen::handleMouseClick(DrawWindow *win)
            { inputTool -> handleMouseClick(win)}
void Screen::Screen(Tool *t) { inputTool = t; }
```

To solve the first problem, we define a pure virtual function in the CanvasTool class and a disambiguating method in each construction subclass:

```
void CanvasTool::handleMouseClick(DrawWindow *win) = 0;
void RectTool::handleMouseClick(DrawWindow *win)
            {Tool::handleMouseClick(win); }
void OvalTool::handleMouseClick(DrawWindow *win)
            {Tool::handleMouseClick(win); }
void SelectTool::handleMouseClick(DrawWindow *win)
            {Tool::handleMouseClick(win); }
```

To solve the second problem, we generate methods to transform the type of objects from Tool to CanvasTool and from CanvasTool to Tool. Wherever inputTool either occurs on the right hand side of an assignment, or is passed as a parameter to a function, or is returned from a function, it is first converted to its original type (Tool). Wherever inputTool occurs on the left hand side of an assignment statement, the expression on the right hand side is converted to its new type (CanvasTool).

```
Tool *CanvasTool::CT_to_T() = 0;
CanvasTool *Tool::T_to_CT() = 0;
Tool *RectTool::T_to_CT() { return this; }
CanvasTool *RectTool::CT_to_T()  { return this; }
Tool *OvalTool::T_to_CT() { return this; }
CanvasTool *OvalTool::CT_to_T()  { return this; }
Tool *SelectTool::T_to_CT() { return this; }
CanvasTool *SelectTool::CT_to_T()  { return this; }
void Screen::Screen(Tool *t) { inputTool = t -> T_to_CT(); }
```

4.2.5 Deletion of useless alternation classes

As in the case of the untyped language model, one problem with deleting a "useless" alternation class is that there may be methods attached to the class. There is the additional problem that the class name may be used in the static type declarations of objects.

If there are any methods attached to the useless alternation class, A, their implementations must be distributed to its immediate subclasses unless they are overridden there. If anywhere in the program an explicit call (i.e., through the scope resolution operator "::") to a method $A :: m$ is made, we create a new method with a unique name, say A_m, defined for each of A's immediate subclasses. The implementation for A_m is the same as for $A :: m$. Then, every occurrence of an explicit call to $A :: m$ is replaced with a call to A_m.

If there are any variables defined of static type A in the program, then we need to find an equivalent substitute type or else keep a class definition of A to be used only to satisfy the type system. If there is an alternation class B with the same set of derived construction classes as for A, B can serve as a substitute type for A. In this case, all the member functions which were defined for A are now declared as pure virtual functions in class B, and class A is deleted. Wherever class A appeared in a type declaration, class B is substituted. Note that in conjunction with the part replacement transformation there is always such a corresponding class B.

If there is no such corresponding class B, then A can not be deleted since it must continue to be used in type declarations. In this case, class A is preserved, but contains only pure virtual functions. We regard A as a type rather than as a class.

As an example, consider what happens when the Tool class is deleted in the transformation from Figure 2–PRP to Figure 1–Object-equivalent. Suppose the methods declared in class Tool are these:

```
virtual void handleMouseClick( DrawWindow * ) = 0;
virtual Position getPosition() = 0;
virtual CanvasTool *T_to_CT() = 0;
```

All the methods happen to be pure virtual, so there are no implementations to be distributed. Furthermore, class CanvasTool qualifies as an equivalent substitute type for class Tool. For each method declared in class Tool a pure virtual method is declared in class CanvasTool. Everywhere that class Tool is used in a type declaration it is replaced with class CanvasTool. Finally class Tool can be deleted.

4.2.6 Class and part addition

As in the untyped language case, no changes are necessary for the method implementations.

4.2.7 Part generalization

The problem that occurs with part generalization is similar to one of the problems that occurs with part replacement. If the part class C of some part is generalized to a superclass of C, say B, then we must insure that for every method in class C there is a corresponding method defined in class B. This is done by defining empty virtual functions in B wherever necessary. Moreover, as for part replacement, wherever the part is involved in an assignment statement, function call (as a passed parameter), or function return (as the returned value), the part's new type will no longer be compatible. In this case, however, a simple cast will suffice since the new class is a superclass of the original.

Note that the PGN transformation indicates that a behavior extension is in order. Our goal in this work is simply to ensure behavior preservation. The above transformation achieves this goal, but the resulting code is not desirable from a software engineering point of view. The inserted cast operations are therefore seen as a hint to the programmer as to where the behavior of the program should be extended.

4.3 Discussion

When comparing the update operations necessary in the two language models, the differences are striking. While in the untyped language model almost no updates to method implementations are necessary, the programmer working in the typed language model is faced with numerous problems. For the untyped language model, we have shown that a schema extension can always be propagated to the method implementations such that the behavior of the program is preserved. However, for the typed language model a behavior preserving update mechanism could only be outlined and is far from being satisfactory. The major reason for this is that the type system poses severe restrictions on how updates can be performed. Without semantic information on what the update's intentions are, it is not always possible to change the typing specifications in a reasonable way.

The above comparison underlines the popularity of untyped languages for prototyping purposes. Their ability to flexibly adapt themselves to different class structures gives them a major advantage over typed languages in environments where structural changes occur frequently. For typed languages, the propagation pattern approach [LXSL91, LHSLX92] achieves the same flexibility by decoupling the programs from the class structure. Consequently, any change in the class structure affects the propagation pattern only marginally.

5 Related Work

In the software refactory project at the University of Illinois, Opdyke and Johnson are investigating methods for *refactoring* object-oriented systems to support reuse [OJ90, Opd92]. Refactorings are defined as restructuring plans and are primarily used to aid the iterative design of an application framework. A feature of refactorings common to our approach is that they (1) also preserve behavior and (2) can be performed by applying a small set of basic refactorings.

Delcourt and Zicari designed a tool, called Integrity Consistency Checker (ICC), which ensures structural consistency while performing schema updates [DZ91]. The ICC guarantees that only those updates are performed that do not introduce any structural inconsistency. However, it allows behavioral inconsistencies that do not result in run-time errors. Nevertheless, the ICC is a very useful tool as a first component in the evolution process. In contrast, our tool guarantees behavioral consistency by automatically adapting programs to the new schema.

6 Conclusion

We have presented a code update mechanism for both CLOS and C++ that can be used to automate the propagation of changes from a modified schema to its affected programs. The mechanism guarantees not only that the schema and the programs stay structurally consistent, but also that the behavior of the old programs is consistently preserved after the schema update.

The ease with which CLOS programs can be adapted to extended schemas stands in striking contrast to the complexity involved in adapting C++ programs.

Acknowledgements: We would like to thank Karl Lieberherr, Ignacio Silva-Lepe and Cun Xiao for helpful discussions.

References

[AH88] Serge Abiteboul and Richard Hull. Restructuring hierarchical database objects. *Theoretical Computer Science*, 62, 1988.

[Bar91] Gilles Barbedette. Schema modifications in the $LISPO_2$ persistent object-oriented language. In Pierre America, editor, *European Conference on Object-Oriented Programming*, pages 77–96, Geneva, Switzerland, July 1991. spcs.

[Ber91] Paul Bergstein. Object-preserving class transformations. In Andreas Paepcke, editor, *Object-Oriented Programming Systems, Languages and Applications Conference*, pages 299–313, Phoenix, Arizona, October 1991. ACM Press. Special Issue of SIGPLAN Notices, Vol.26, No.11.

[Ber92] Elisa Bertino. A view mechanism for object-oriented databases. In *International Conference on Extending Database Technology*, pages 136–151, Vienna, Austria, 1992.

[BKKK87] Jay Banerjee, Won Kim, Hyong-Joo Kim, and Henry F. Korth. Semantics and implementation of schema evolution in object-oriented databases. In *Proceedings of ACM/SIGMOD Annual Conference on Management of Data*, pages 311–322. ACM Press, December 1987. SIGMOD Record, Vol.16, No.3.

[Cas91] Eduardo Casais. *Managing evolution in object-oriented environments: an algorithmic approach*. PhD thesis, University of Geneva, Geneva, Switzerland, May 1991. Thesis no. 369.

[CPLZ91] Alberto Coen-Porisini, Luigi Lavazza, and Roberto Zicari. Updating the schema of an object-oriented database. *Quarterly Bulletin of the IEEE Computer Society Technical Committee on Data Engineering*, 14(2):33–37, June 1991. Special Issue on Foundations of object-Oriented Database Systems.

[DZ91] Christine Delcourt and Roberto Zicari. The Design of an Integrity Consistency Checker (ICC) for an Object Oriented Database System. In Pierre America, editor, *European Conference on Object-Oriented Programming*, pages 97–117, Geneva, Switzerland, July 1991. Springer Verlag, Lecture Notes in Computer Science.

[LBSL91]   Karl J. Lieberherr, Paul Bergstein, and Ignacio Silva-Lepe. From objects to classes: Algorithms for object-oriented design. *Journal of Software Engineering*, 6(4):205–228, July 1991.

[LH90]   Barbara Staudt Lerner and A. Nico Habermann. Beyond schema evolution to database reorganization. In Norman Meyrowitz, editor, *Proceedings OOPSLA ECOOP '90*, pages 67–76, Ottawa, Canada, October 1990. ACM Press. Special Issue of SIGPLAN Notices, Vol.25, No.10.

[LHSLX92] Karl J. Lieberherr, Walter L. Hürsch, Ignacio Silva-Lepe, and Cun Xiao. Experience with a graph-based propagation pattern programming tool. In Gene Forte, Nazim H. Madhavji, and Hausi A. Müller, editors, *International Workshop on CASE*, pages 114–119, Montréal, Canada, July 1992. IEEE Computer Society Press.

[LHX93]   Karl J. Lieberherr, Walter L. Hürsch, and Cun Xiao. Object-extending class transformations. *Formal Aspects of Computing, the International Journal of Formal Methods*, 1993. Accepted for publication, also available as Technical Report NU-CCS-91-8, Northeastern University.

[LXSL91]   Karl J. Lieberherr, Cun Xiao, and Ignacio Silva-Lepe. Graph-based software engineering: Concise specifications of cooperative behavior. Technical Report NU-CCS-91-14, College of Computer Science, Northeastern University, Boston, MA, September 1991.

[OJ90]   William F. Opdyke and Ralph E. Johnson. Refactoring: An aid in designing application frameworks and evolving object-oriented systems. In *Proceedings of the Symposium on Object-Oriented Programming emphasizing Practical Applications (SOOPA)*, pages 145–160, Poughkeepsie, NY, September 1990. ACM.

[Opd92]   William F. Opdyke. *Refactoring: A Program Restructuring Aid in Designing object-Oriented Application Frameworks*. PhD thesis, Computer Science Department, University of Illinois, May 1992.

[PS87]   Jason D. Penney and Jacob Stein. Class modification in the GemStone object-oriented DBMS. In Norman Meyrowitz, editor, *Object-Oriented Programming Systems, Languages and Applications Conference*, pages 111–117, Orlando, Florida, December 1987. ACM Press. Special Issue of SIGPLAN Notices, Vol.22, No.12.

[SZ86]   Andrea H. Skarra and Stanley B. Zdonik. The management of changing types in an object-oriented database. In *Object-Oriented Programming Systems, Languages and Applications Conference*, pages 483–495. ACM Press, September 1986.

An Object-Centered Approach for Manipulating Hierarchically Complex Objects

Ling LIU

FB 20 - Databases & Information Systems
Johann Wolfgang Goethe-University Frankfurt
Postfach 11 19 32, Robert-Mayer-Str. 11-15
6000 Frankfurt am main 11, Germany
email: liu@informatik.uni-frankfurt.de

Abstract

We present an object-centered approach for manipulating hierarchically complex objects, which covers an extended object model and an object-centered query algebra. Extensions of the object model are mainly based on a separation of structural and semantic elements in modeling complex objects, including a general distinction between aggregation reference and association reference, an introduction of type inheritance into aggregation hierarchies and a support for combination of aggregation inheritance with subtype inheritance. Based on the extensions, we develop a query algebra as an integral part of the model. Unlike most of existing algebra-based query languages, our object algebra takes complex object collectively as a unit of high level queries and allows complex objects to be accessed at all levels of aggregation hierarchies without having resort to any kind of path expressions. Features of aggregation hierarchies, such as acyclicity and aggregation inheritance, have played important roles in such a development. We have also formally described the output type of each operator in order for dynamic classification of query results in the IsA type/class lattice. Although the design is based on the chosen object-oriented model, other object-oriented databases are possible. We feel that the proposal largely covers the query requirements for complex objects, and meanwhile provides users with an opportunity to remain within the framework of the model of complex objects while querying database. As a consequence, the flexibility and adaptability of the object-oriented model against schema changes are increased.

1 Introduction

Over past years complex objects and object-orientation have been two main research directions for improving database technology. The achievements in nested relational models[1] and in semantic data models[21] have both theoretical and practical influence on the development of complex object systems. A lot of research has been carried out along with these two directions. However there are still several aspects that deserve further investigation.

On the one hand, most of the object-oriented models proposed in the literature only provide two constructs to model relationships between complex objects. They are subtyping and reference. The reference used to model composition (aggregation) of objects and the reference used to model arbitrary association between objects are not clearly distinguished both in semantics and in syntax. Such models do not capture real "is-part-of" relationship between objects, as an object can only reference, but does not own, other objects. This way of modeling gives rise to a semantic ambiguity between composition of objects and arbitrary association of objects, and also results in a missing of structural and behavioural interaction between complex objects and their constituent (component) objects. Furthermore it provides no opportunity to support the use of complex objects collectively as a unit of high level query.

On the other hand, most of existing query languages for object-oriented models are simply an adaptation of nested relational query languages. Comparing with classical NF^2 algebra [cf.43] (where objects being queried upon have to be flattened explicitly by a sequence of unnests until the attributes of interest are at the outmost level), these query languages have indeed made improvement in one way or the other. Moreover some of them have pointed out several interesting aspects that are nice to have in a query algebra for object-oriented models. For example, Kim [25] made a first investigation about how a IsA type lattice interacts with queries and where the query results can be properly placed in such a lattice. Shaw and Zdonik [40] have realized the concept of object equality [23] in their query algebra. Scholl and Schek [38,39] emphasize a distinction between object preserving operations and object generating operations, and suggest that object preserving operators are suitable to serve for defining updatable object views. Straube and Ozsu [42] develop an algorithm for translating object calculus formula to object algebra expressions. Vandenberg and DeWitt propose an algebraic treatment for different type constructors [44]. However, in many query language proposals for object-oriented databases, complex object may not be taken collectively as a basic unit of high level query. When queries involving names that are defined in constituent types of the input objects, most of these query languages require either to use a special operator as a navigator or to associate each name of interest with a path expression explicitly to provide navigational ability for the operators, even in representing simple unary queries, like selection and projection. As a consequence, users have no opportunity to remain within the framework of the model of complex objects when querying database. Besides, it is almost out of the question in some languages to preserve the structure of complex objects while accessing them. For example, the structure of projecting attributes may change after the execution. When a join involving attributes that are nested deep inside of either of the two input objects, it becomes rather difficult, sometimes even impossible, to optimize queries because some well-known optimization principles, like performing selection and projection before join, are not applicable at all.

To circumvent these inconvenience and inefficiency and meanwhile to cover fundamental semantics of the object-oriented model, such as object identity, type inheritance, specialization and aggregation abstraction, we feel that it is indeed necessary to further extend existing query languages rather than simply adapt nested relational languages to object-oriented models. In this paper we present an extended object-oriented model and a recursive object algebra. Extensions of the object model are mainly based on a separation of structural and semantic elements in complex object modeling, including a general distinction between aggregation and association, an introduction of type inheritance into aggregation hierarchies, and a support for combination of aggregation inheritance with subtype inheritance. The most important contribution in this paper is the development of a recursive object algebra based on aggregation abstraction. Unlike most of existing algebra-based query languages, our object algebra takes complex object collectively as a unit of high level queries, and allows complex objects to be accessed at all levels of aggregation hierarchies without having resort to any kind of path expressions. Features of aggregation hierarchies, such as acyclicity and aggregation inheritance, have played important roles in such a development. We also formally describe the output type of each operator in order for dynamic classification of query results in the IsA type/class lattice. Besides, it is possible to preserve the structure of projecting attributes after projection. As a result, our framework not only provides users with an opportunity to remain within the framework of the model of complex objects when querying database, but also helps to enhance the extensibility of the object-oriented model, because the flexibility and adaptability of the object-oriented model against schema changes are highly increased.

Comparing with our previous result on aggregation semantics reported in [27], we have made several extensive investigations. In [27] we only formalize the aggregation semantics from conceptual modeling point of view. Some aspects of aggregation semantics are not clearly identified. No formal semantics are developed on how the characteristics of object-oriented model, especially the aggregation semantics, may influence the design of an object-oriented query formalism. While in the present paper we classify aggregation relationships into two types: acyclic aggregation and cyclic aggregation, and identify that in case of acyclic aggregation, the concept of aggregation inheritance can be fully explored. We also analyse the similarity and the subtle difference between aggregation and association, as well as between aggregation and specialization. More interestingly, we present a well-defined recursive object algebra as an integral part of the object model, and demonstrate the roles of aggregation inheritance and acyclicity of aggregation hierarchies in such a development.

The rest of the paper proceeds as follows: we overview the essential concepts of the extended object-oriented model, specially the notions relative to the design of the recursive object algebra in Section 2. The relational data model and the nested relational model are the special cases of this object model. In Section 3 we present a formal description of the operators provided in the object algebra and their inherent semantics. Due to the space limitation, we only present the definitions of five algebraic operators and informally discuss properties of this algebra. Readers who are interested in the rest of the operators and a formal evaluation of this algebra may refer to [28, 29]. We discuss issues that are relevant in the design of a declarative object-oriented query languages based on the present object algebra in Section 4 and compare our proposal with the related research in Section 5.

2 The Object Model

The object model supports most of the commonly accepted object-oriented concepts, such as object identity and methods, abstraction data type and encapsulation, type and class separation, as well as subtype hierarchies and subtype inheritance. The main extensions to the existing object-oriented models include the general distinction of aggregation references (used for modeling object composition semantics) from arbitrary association references both at instance level and at type level; the introduction of aggregation inheritance concept into the aggregation type hierarchies; and the combination of aggregation inheritance with subtype inheritance for supporting universal polymorphism and ad-hoc polymorphism within a unified framework.

2.1 Basic Concepts

Objects are instances of abstract data types(ADTs) each with unique identity. Objects are only accessible through the interface (a list of methods) defined on their types. A *method* is described by its signature (its name, the types of its input and output) and its body (the implementation). In this paper we restrict our attention to functional methods with no side effects. We also support methods which are built through functional composition. Suppose we have the following three methods m_1, m_2, and m_3 that are defined on types T_1, T_2, and T_3 respectively. $m_1:T_1 \rightarrow T_2$, $m_2:T_2 \rightarrow T_3$, $m_3:T_3 \rightarrow A$. The domains of T_i are the set of all possible instances of type T_i for $i=1,2,3$. The domain of A is a set of atomic values. By means of functional composition (denoted by o), we obtain a derived method $m_4 =_{def} (m_1 o m_2) o m_3$, i.e., $m_4:((T_1 \rightarrow T_2) \rightarrow T_3) \rightarrow A$. The input type of m_4 may be considered as T_1, and the output type of m_4 is A. In contrast to the methods that are locally defined in type T_1, we refer to the method like m_4 as *composite function* or *abstract function* of T_1.

Types in our object model are all abstract data types (ADTs). The definition of a type includes a type name and a list of function descriptions each with this type name as the leading input argument. We provide base type, tuple type, set type, list type and reference type. We also support *subtype hierarchies* and *subtype inheritance* (single and multiple inheritance) [cf.12]. *Class* are considered as a different concept from type [cf.32]. A class is a named collection of objects of a type, and is used to refer to a named set of objects of a type which currently exist in the database. It is possible to have more than one class of a type. Appendix A provides some illustrative examples.

2.2 Aggregation Versus Association

Although aggregation can be considered as a special case of association, it is conceptually different from association. We say two individual objects having aggregation relationship if they are tightly bound by "is-part-of" relationship. When two objects are considered as conceptually independent, even if they may often be semantically connected with each other, we would say they have an association relationship.

To capture the semantic difference between aggregation and association, it is important to make a general distinction between object composition and arbitrary object association, both at instance level and at type level. In the present object model, we explicitly distinguish *aggregation reference* and *association reference* between object types. The former is used to model object composition relationship, which carries on the "is-part-of" semantics between individual objects. It is a tightly coupled form of association with some extra semantics such as transitivity and antisymmetric character. The latter is used to model arbitrary associations of objects, where the transitivity and antisymmetric feature do not hold in general.

Concerning the syntax extension, we use set type, tuple type, and plus "**constituent-of**" construct to define aggregation reference between types, and adapt reference type "**ref**" to define arbitrary associations between types (the concept of reference type is not original, of course, see[14]). Fig2-1 gives an example application. DOCUMENT objects are composed of several CHAPTER objects. CHAPTER objects are again composed by PARAGRAPH and FIGURE objects. DOCUMENT objects also have associations with PROJECT objects and PERSON objects. The textual specification of type DOCUMENT is provided in Appendix A.

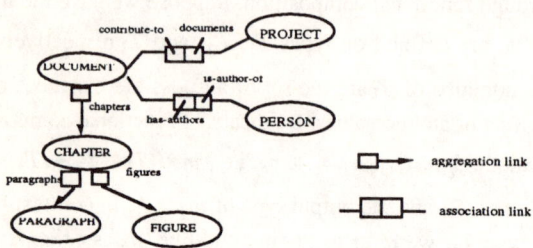

Fig2-1 An example application of DOCUMENT objects

Whenever objects of type T are composed of objects of type S, an aggregation link will be built between type T and type S (Fig2-2). Note that semantics of the aggregation link in Fig2-2 is actually overloaded. It at least implies two different meanings: (i)objects of type T are composed by objects of type S; (ii)the definition of S-component in type T is exactly same as the definition of type S (type sharing) (Fig2-3).

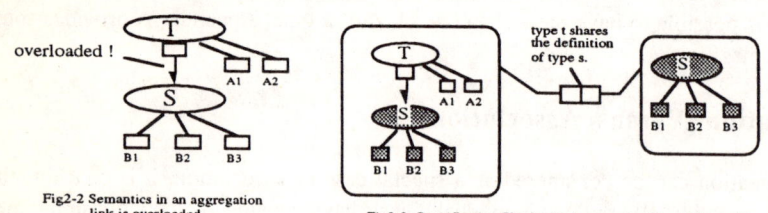

Fig2-2 Semantics in an aggregation link is overloaded

Fig2-3 Specification Sharing in Aggregation Type Hierarchies

While quite differently, if there is an association link between two types T and S, it only means that instances of type T have some semantic connection with the instances of type S. But there is neither structural nor behavioural dependencies between these two types.

2.3 Aggregation Inheritance

Due to the type sharing implied in aggregation link, we may introduce the concept of *aggregation inheritance*. It means that if type T has aggregation reference to type S, then by means of functional composition, all functions, which are applicable to the interface of type S, are also applicable to type T. For example, suppose "*fig-caption*" is locally defined in type FIGURE which is a constituent type of DOCUMENT. In terms of aggregation inheritance, "*fig-caption*" can be treated as an applicable function of type DOCUMENT when accessing database (Fig2-4).

As a matter of fact, aggregation inheritance can be easily combined with subtype inheritance in terms of specification code sharing. Consider Fig2-4, DOCUMENT objects may inherit properties (e.g., *user-name, dso#, creation-date*) from its supertypes, such as DOC_SPACE_OBJ, through the subtype link, and meanwhile "inherit" properties such as *fig-caption* from its constituent types (for instance type FIGURE) along with the aggregation hierarchy of type DOCUMENT. The major benefits of aggregation inheritance are the following.

(i) By combination of aggregation inheritance with subtype inheritance, reusability of the schema specification and database programs will be highly increased.
(ii) Queries over aggregation hierarchies does not necessarily require providing the operators with navigational ability explicitly.
(iii) Thus complex object can be considered collectively as a basic unit of high level object queries. This way of design provides users with an opportunity to remain within the object-oriented model when querying database.
(iv) Changing the schema of complex objects, especially the nested aggregation structure, may have no impact on existing database programs.

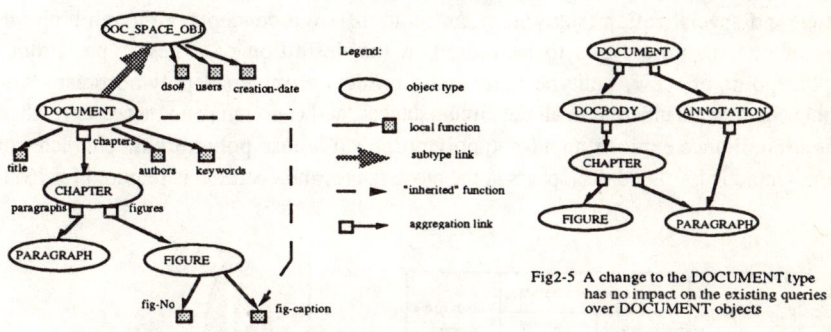

Fig2-4 An example for illustration of aggregation inheritance

Fig2-5 A change to the DOCUMENT type has no impact on the existing queries over DOCUMENT objects

To illustrate these benefits, consider the example in Fig2-4. Assume we have a query Q: "*find all documents having figure of the caption 'NIAM diagram'?*". With the support for aggregation inheritance, this query can simply be expressed as:

$$\{ x \mid x \in \text{DOCUMENTS}, x.\textit{fig-caption} = \text{"NIAM diagram"} \} \qquad (q1).$$

There is no need to resort any aggregation path expression with each name of interest in the query. However, if without the support of aggregation inheritance, we have to express the query by associating each name of interest with an aggregation path, i.e., the query Q has to be expressed as

$\{ x \mid x \in \text{DOCUMENTS}, x.chapters.figures.fig\text{-}caption = \text{"}NIAM\ diagram\text{"} \}$ (q2).

One obvious disadvantage of associating aggregation path expression with each name of interest in the query operators, is the limitation of extensibility of the object schema against changes. Suppose the DOCUMENT schema in Fig2-4 is required to add new layers in between DOCUMENT and CHAPTER, and between DOCUMENT and PARAGRAPH (see Fig2-5). With aggregation inheritance, the query Q expressed in (q1) will remain the same. It means that the addition of new layers into the aggregation hierarchy of type DOCUMENT (either at bottom and top or in between) does not require any corresponding change to the existing database query programs. A higher degree of extensibility of the object schema against changes is achieved. However without aggregation inheritance, the query Q has to be expressed in the form of (q2). The schema change in Fig2-5 requires this query formula to be rewritten by using the new aggregation path of *fig-caption* to replace the existing one in the query, i.e., the query in form of (q2) has to be reformulated as

$\{ x \mid x \in \text{DOCUMENTS}, x.doc\_body.chapters.figures.fig\text{-}caption = \text{"}NIAM\ diagram\text{"} \}$ (q3)

although the fact that *fig-caption* is a local property of FIGURE objects, and FIGURE objects are part of the DOCUMENT objects, does not change.

2.4 Aggregation Versus Specialization

Aggregation and specialization (subtyping) are quite different concepts, although both allow properties of one or more types to be reused in the definition of a new type. From the polymorphic point of view, subtype inheritance reflects a universal polymorphism whose polymorphic character is inherent in all the circumstances, and coercion is not necessary; whereas aggregation inheritance exhibits an ad-hoc polymorphism whose polymorphic character only exists at the syntactic level and disappears at the close range, and coercion is required [cf.13] (see Fig2-6a).

features inheritance	Polymorphism	polymorphic character		coercion (required)
		syntatical level	semantically inherent	
subtype inheritance	universal / true polymorphism	Yes	Yes	No
aggregation inheritance	ad-hoc / apparent polymorphism	Yes	No	Yes

(a) Different polymorphic characters

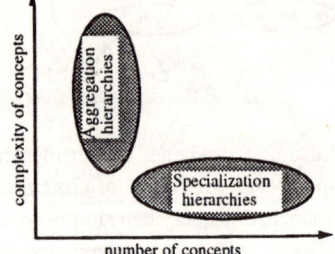

(a) Different points of view in type composition

Fig2-6 Specialization and aggregation both are mechanisms for incremental definition of concepts

Besides, aggregation and specialization can be both used as mechanisms for incremental definition of concepts, but the purpose of using them are also different (see Fig2-6b). Specialization is used to refine some existing concepts. As a result, the number of concepts is increased. While aggregation is used to define complex concepts in terms of simpler concepts. As a result, the complexity of the concepts is increased.

2.5 Acyclic Aggregation and Exceptional Case

To capture the specification sharing as well as the antisymmetric and transitive characters of aggregation relationship, we distinguish acyclic aggregation and exceptional case. When the "is-part-of" relationship holds at both instance level and type level, we call the aggregation as *acyclic aggregation* and model it by means of aggregation (reference) link, such as the aggregation between DOCUMENT objects and CHAPTER objects. If the "is-part-of" relationship holds only at instance level but not at type level, we consider it as an *exceptional case* and model it by means of association (reference) link. A typical example is the application about "bill of material". Suppose PART objects are described by *part-name, price,* and may contain other PART objects as *sub-parts*. All *sub-parts* are also objects of type PART. In this case, the *sub-part* relationship between PART objects exhibits the object composition semantics only at the instance level, but not at the type level. Cyclic aggregation is actually the extreme case of ordinary aggregation. In order to capture acyclicity of aggregation hierarchies, and to employ aggregation inheritance for avoiding duplicate specification, implementation and maintenance, we suggest to model all exceptional cases of aggregation regarding acyclicity by means of association. Thus the *subpart* relationship can be modeled by simply adding a cyclic association reference in the type definition of PART, i.e., type PART=(*part-name*:string, *price*:real, *subparts*: **ref** PART).

Note that we allow a type being a constituent type of more than one type. It is then quite possible that functions defined in some constituent type may have the same names as the functions defined in the other constituent types or in their aggregate types, although these functions are in fact semantically different concepts. To support aggregation inheritance, we have to resolve such name conflict occurring in aggregation hierarchies. One mechanism is to impose a restriction that each function "inherited" from a constituent type has to associate with the type name as a prefix. Assume type CAR has a weight function and its constituent type ENGINE also has a weight function. We will use *engine-weight* for accessing the weight of the engine of a car, and *weight* for the weight of the whole car. It is reasonable and preferable to use different names to refer to different concepts.

3 The Object Algebra

The object algebra presented in this section is a strongly typed query algebra. It provides type-specific operations on collections of objects, and allows static type checking [11]. This is ensured by restricting each class to be associated with a type in order to check if operations on objects of a class are legal. For instance, we can not access function *salary* from class PERSON because it would result in a type checking error. Besides, to preserve the closure of the object algebra under the object-oriented model, we also formally describe the output type of each operator and analyse how the output objects are related with the input objects through the IsA type/class lattice. As the input and the output of each operator are all defined to be sets of objects, all the operators can actually be applied to either classes, or set-valued functions, or query results. Before presenting the definitions of these operators, we introduce some basic notions that are used in our query model.

3.1 Basic Notions of the Query Model

3.1.1 Zero-order and High-order Functions

As every type-specific function has a well-defined range (output domain), in the sequel we call a function, locally defined in type R, which returns a single atomic value for each input, *zero-order function* of R; when a local function returns a structured value or a set of (atomic or structured) values for each input, we call it *high-order function* of R. Of course this is mainly a matter of convenience and taste.

Let $\mathcal{N}$ be a countable set of symbols which can be used as names. In terms of the object model, a complex scheme type R is of the form $R(A_1, A_2, ..., A_n)$, $R \in \mathcal{N}$ and each $A_i \in \mathcal{N}$ ($i=1,...,n;\ n \geq 1$). The list $(A_1, A_2, ..., A_n)$ includes names of all (zero-order and high-order) functions locally defined in type R or in supertypes of R. We call them *inherent functions* of type R. If A_i is a high-order function whose output type is of the form $R_i(A_{i1}, A_{i2},..., A_{im})$, then R_i is a constituent type of R. In the sequel, for a scheme type $R(A_1, A_2,..., A_n)$, we use $Lfn(R)$ to denote the set of (zero-order and high-order) function names of R. So $Lfn(R)=\{A_1, A_2,..., A_n\}$. We use $Zfn(R)$ to refer to the set of all zero-order function names in the list $(A_1, A_2, ..., A_n)$, and $Hfn(R)$ the set of all high-order function names in it. Also we refer to a scheme type $R(A_1, A_2, ..., A_n)$ simply by its name R when no ambiguity occurs. Let t be a variable range over a class of type R, for any function (say A) applicable to R, we have $t[A]=A(t)$. Suppose $X=(A_1,...,A_m)$ and $1 \leq m \leq n$, then $t[X] = (t[A_1], t[A_2],...,t[A_m])$.

Example: Consider type EMPLOYEE in Appendix A. As functions defined in supertypes of EMPLOYEE are also included in the set Lfn(EMPLOYEE), we have
Zfn(EMPLOYEE)={*pname, birthday, hiredate, salary*}.
Hfn(EMPLOYEE) = {*home-address, children, affiliates, work-for*}.
Lfn(EMPLOYEE) = {*pname, birthday, home-address, children, hiredate, salary, affiliates, work-for*}.

3.1.2 Function Space

Definition (Function space)
A *function space* of a given type R, denoted by $Fspace(R)$, is defined recursively as follows:

- if R is one of the base types (e.g., integer, real, string, date), then $Fspace(R)=\emptyset$.
- if R is a set type, say $\{T\}$, then when T is one of the base types, $Fspace(R)=\emptyset$; Otherwise, $Fspace(R)=Fspace(T)$.
- if R is a reference type, say **ref** T or **ref** $\{T\}$, then $Fspace(R)=\emptyset$.
- if R is a tuple type of the form $R(A_1,..., A_n)$, $A_1,..., A_n$ are all the inherent function names of R, i.e., $Lfn(R)=\{A_1,..., A_n\}$, $n \geq 1$, then $Fspace(R)=(\cup_{X \in Lfn(R)} Fspace(X)) \cup Lfn(R)$. □

Example: type DOCUMENT described in Appendix A has zero-order functions *docno*, and *title*, and high-order functions *authors, keywords, chapters,* and *contribute-to*. We have

$Fspace$(DOCUMENT) = $Fspace$(CHAPTER) ∪ Lfn(DOCUMENT),
Lfn(DOCUMENT) = {*docno, title, authors, keywords, chapters, contribute-to*};
$Fspace$(CHAPTER) = $Fspace$(PARAGRAPH)∪$Fspace$(FIGURE)∪Lfn(CHAPTER),
Lfn(CHAPTER) = {*chapterno, chaptertitle, text-content, figure*};
$Fspace$(PARAGRAPH) = Lfn(PARAGRAPH) = {*para-no, textbody*};
$Fspace$(FIGURE) = Lfn(FIGURE) = {*fig-position, fig-caption, bitmap-no*}. □

3.1.3 Selection Condition

A condition for selecting a collection of objects from a database, denoted by F, is a boolean expression involving comparisons between functions, and between functions and constants. The set of operators $\{==, =, \neq, <, <=, >, >=\}$ are used for comparisons between functions returning atomic values. $\{\in, ==, =, \subset, \subseteq, \supset, \supseteq\}$ are used for comparisons between functions returning set values. "==" stands for the object equality operator in contrast to the value equality operator "=" [cf.23].

Definition (*Applicability of a condition*)
Let $\mathcal{R}=(R,r)$ be a complex object scheme, r a class of objects of type R and $Fspace(R)$ the function space of R. A condition F is *applicable* to R if all functions occurring in F are in $Fspace(R)$. □

Example: Consider the database specified in Appendix A. Let d and p be variables ranged over a class of type DOCUMENT and a class of type PROJECT respectively. According to the above definition, the condition *fig-caption(d)*='NIAM diagram' is applicable to type DOCUMENT, although *fig-caption* is defined in type FIGURE. Because in terms of the **constituent-of** relationship between FIGURE and CHAPTER, and between CHAPTER and DOCUMENT, *fig-caption* is in $Fspace$(DOCUMENT). Therefore we can simply use *fig-caption(d)*='NIAM diagram' instead of *fig-caption (figures(chapters(d)))*='NIAM diagram'.

However the condition *proj-name(d)*='SPRITE' is not applicable to DOCUMENT, as *proj-name* is not included in $Fspace$(DOCUMENT). Let "self" denote a function mapping from an object to its own identity. We may correct it by *proj-name(contribute-to(d))*= 'SPRITE' or *proj-name(p)*='SPRITE'∧*p.self=contribute-to(d)*. □

3.2 Unary Selection

Unary selection operator allows selection conditions to be specified both on the functions specified at the outmost level of the input type and on those that are defined at deeper levels of the nesting, without having resort to any path expression. We identify two types of unary selections: object selection and data selection. The former *preserves* input objects during selection, while the latter allows to *extract* the subobjects of interest from each input object, and generate a collection of newly identified objects as the output of selection.

3.2.1 Object Selection

Object selection is a unary operator on a collection of database objects. When applied to a class, it returns those input objects which satisfy the selection condition. The output type is the same as the input type. So we may place the output of an object selection as a subclass of the input in the IsA class lattice.

Definition (object selection operator σ)

Let $\mathcal{R} =(R,r)$ be a complex object scheme, r be a class of objects of scheme type R, and F be any condition applicable to R. The object selection over $\mathcal{R} =(R,r)$, written as $\sigma(F, r)$, is a subset of r having the same scheme type R. The result consists of those instances of r satisfying the condition F.

$$\sigma(F, r) =_{def} \{ t \mid (t \in r \wedge F(t)=true \}.$$

Suppose F is of the form $F_0 \wedge F_1 .... \wedge F_n$, F_0 is the condition on $Zfn(R)$ and F_i is the condition applicable to R_i for $R_i \in Hfn(R)$, $i=1,...,n$ ($n>=0$). Then the selection $\sigma(F, r)$ can be fully described as:

$$\sigma(F, r) =_{def} \{ t \mid (t \in r \wedge ((F_0(t)=true)$$
$$\wedge(\sigma(F_1, t[R_1]) \neq \emptyset) \wedge (\sigma(F_2, t[R_2]) \neq \emptyset) \wedge ... \wedge (\sigma(F_n, t[R_n]) \neq \emptyset))) \}. \quad \square$$

Remarks: (i) If F is of the form $F_0 \vee F_1 \vee ... \vee F_n$, where F_0 is the condition on $Zfn(R)$ and F_i is the condition applicable to R_i for $R_i \in Hfn(R)$ ($i=1,...,n$; $n>=0$), we may simply use $(\sigma(F_1, t[R_1]) \neq \emptyset) \vee ... \vee (\sigma(F_n, t[R_n]) \neq \emptyset))$ instead of $(\sigma(F_1, t[R_1]) \neq \emptyset) \wedge ... \wedge (\sigma(F_n, t[R_n]) \neq \emptyset))$ in the definition. (ii) The recursive definition of our object selection preserves the input objects during selection. The result of a selection over the input class r is always a subset of r. A main advantage of preserving the resulting objects being identical with the input objects is to enable such queries as the arguments of subsequent update operations so that the update on these resulting objects can be propagated to the stored objects [cf.37].

Example: Consider the database described in Appendix A. Let variable LA-EMP be of the type EMPLOYEE. Then we may express the query "*find all employees who live in Los Angeles city*" by

LA-EMP:= σ(*city-name*="Los Angeles", EMPLOYEES).

The result LA-EMP is clearly a subclass of the input class EMPLOYEES (see Fig3-1).

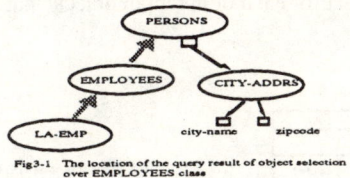

Fig3-1 The location of the query result of object selection over EMPLOYEES class

3.2.2 Data Selection

The definition of object selection is grounded on the object-preserving basis. In some cases, however, it might be more convenient if both object-preserving selection and object-creating selection are provided. Consider the sample class of CLIENT (Fig3-2) where some of the data are borrowed from [16]. We assume that CLIENT only have zero-order functions *name* and *birthday* for brevity. Now suppose we have two queries:

Q1: *find all the clients and their investments, who purchase shares on 02/10/83?*
Q2: *find the clients who purchase shares on 02/10/83, the corresponding companies and their shares?*

Note that query Q1 slightly differs from query Q2 in semantics. The preferable answers to Q1 and Q2 are given in Fig3-3a and Fig3-3b respectively. Obviously, Q1 is an object-preserving selection returning those input objects satisfying the selection condition. Q2 is an object-creating selection, which extract only the information of interest from those input objects satisfying the selection condition. The formal definition for object-creating selection, denoted by σ^e(F,r) is given below. We call σ^e(F,r) data selection for short.

Definition (data selection operator σ^e)

Let $\mathcal{R} = (R,r)$ be a complex object scheme, and F be a condition applicable to R. Assume F is of the form $F_0 \wedge F_1 .... \wedge F_n$, F_0 is the condition on $Zfn(R)$ and F_i is the condition applicable to R_i for $R_i \in Hfn(R)$, $i=1,...,n$ and $n \geq 0$). The data selection over $\mathcal{R} = (R,r)$, written as σ^e(F, r), is a collection of new objects of the same type R, which are derived from the instances of r satisfying the condition F.

$$\sigma^e(F, r) =_{\text{def}} \{ t \mid (\exists t_r \in r \wedge F_0(t) = \text{true} \wedge t[Zfn(R)] = t_r[Zfn(R)]$$
$$\wedge t[Hfn(R) - \{R_1, R_2, ..., R_n\}] = t_r[Hfn(R) - \{R_1, R_2, ..., R_n\}]$$
$$\wedge (t[R_1] = \sigma^e(F_1, t_r[R_1]) \neq \emptyset) ... \wedge (t[R_n] = \sigma^e(F_n, t_r[R_n]) \neq \emptyset)) \}. \quad \square$$

This definition states that the output type of $\sigma^e(F, r)$ is the same as the input type, but the execution of $\sigma^e(F, r)$ returns a new object for each of the input objects that satisfy the condition

CLIENTS

pname	birthday	INVESTMENTS			
		company-name	SHARES		
			purchase price	date	number
John Smith	13/05/53	XEROX	64.50	02/10/83	100
			92.50	08/10/87	500
		IBM	89.75	06/20/83	200
			96.50	11/10/84	100
Jill Brody	28/11/41	EXXON	35.00	01/30/81	100
			64.50	01/30/82	500
			59.50	02/10/83	200
		FORD	35.50	02/10/83	200
		SEARS	35.75	12/25/87	100
Frans Lee	08/06/58	FORD	35.50	02/10/84	200
			48.00	08/10/87	300

Fig3-2 A sample example of class CLIENTS

$\pi(X, \sigma(\text{company-name}='\text{FORD}', \text{CLIENTS}))$
where $X = (\text{pname, company-name, purchase-price, number})$

pname	INVESTMENTS		
	company name	SHARES	
		purchase price	number
Jill Brody	EXXON	35.00	100
		64.50	500
		59.50	200
	FORD	35.50	200
	SEARS	35.75	100
Frans Lee	FORD	35.50	200
		48.00	300

Fig3-4 An example of object projection

$\sigma_{date='02/10/83'}(\text{CLIENTS})$

pname	birthday	INVESTMENTS			
		company-name	SHARES		
			purchase price	date	number
John Smith	13/05/53	XEROX	64.50	02/10/83	100
			92.50	08/10/87	500
		IBM	89.75	06/20/83	200
			96.50	11/10/84	100
Jill Brody	28/11/41	EXXON	35.00	01/30/81	100
			64.50	01/30/82	500
			59.50	02/10/83	200
		FORD	35.50	02/10/83	200
		SEARS	35.75	12/25/87	100

(a) object selection

$\sigma^e(date='02/10/83', \text{CLIENTS})$

pname	birthday	INVESTMENTS			
		company-name	SHARES		
			purchase price	date	number
John Smith	13/05/53	XEROX	64.50	02/10/83	100
Jill Brody	28/11/41	EXXON	59.50	02/10/83	200
		FORD	35.50	02/10/83	200

(b) data selection

Fig3-3 Examples of object-sensitive selection and data-sensitive selection

F. These output objects consists of only those subobjects of the corresponding input objects which are of interest in the selection condition F. Thus the output class of $\sigma^e(F, r)$ is in general not a subclass of the input class, but an immediate subclass of the most general class (denoted as C_{top}) of type OBJECT.

3.3 Multiple-operand selection

Definition (*multiple-operand select* σ^+)
Let $R, S_1,..., S_k$ be types of the classes $r, s_1, ..., s_k$ respectively ($k \geq 1$). Assume $B_1, B_2, ..., B_k$ be reference fields of $R, S_1,..., S_{k-1}$ respectively. Each B_i is of the type **ref** S_i or **ref** $\{S_i\}$ ($i=1,...,k$). B_1 specifies an object reference from R to S_1, B_j represents an object reference from S_{j-1} to S_j ($j=2,...,k$). The *multiple-operand select*, denoted by $\sigma^+F(r,<s_1,...,s_k>)$, is defined over $R \times S_1 \times ... \times S_k$. It returns those objects of set r in each vector $<\mu_r, t_1,..., t_k> \in R \times S_1 \times ... \times S_k$, which satisfies the condition $F(\mu_r, t_1,..., t_k)$. $F(\mu_r, t_1,..., t_k)$ is the multiple-select condition of the form $(F_0(\mu_r) \wedge F_1(t_1) \wedge ... \wedge F_k(t_k) \wedge P(B_1(\mu_r), t_1) \wedge P(B_2(t_1), t_2) \wedge ... \wedge P(B_k(t_{k-1}), t_k))$, $F_0(\mu_r)$ is the condition applicable to R, and $F_i(t_i)$ is the condition applicable to S_i ($i=1,...,k$). If $B_1(\mu_r)$ returns an atomic value for each μ_r, then the predicate $P(B_1(\mu_r), t_1)$ denotes "$(\exists t_1 \in s_1) t_1.\text{self}=B_1(\mu_r)$". If $B_1(\mu_r)$ returns a set value for each μ_r, then $P(B_1(\mu_r), t_1)$ denotes "$(\theta x \in B_1(\mu_r) \exists t_1 \in s_1) t_1.\text{self}=x$", $\theta \in \{\forall, \exists\}$. A formal definition of *multiple-operand select* is as follows:

$$\sigma^+F(r,<s_1,...,s_k>) =_{def} \{ \mu_r \mid \exists t_1 ... \exists t_k (\mu_r \in r \wedge t_1 \in s_1 \wedge ... \wedge t_k \in s_k$$
$$\wedge \sigma(F_0(\mu_r), r) \neq \emptyset \wedge \sigma(F_1(t_1), s_1) \neq \emptyset \wedge ... \wedge \sigma(F_k(t_k), s_k) \neq \emptyset$$
$$\wedge P(B_1(\mu_r), t_1) \wedge P(B_2(t_1), t_2) \wedge ... \wedge P(B_k(t_{k-1}), t_k)) \}. \quad \Box$$

Remarks: Obviously the outcome of $\sigma^+F(r,<s_1...s_k>)$ is a subset of the first input argument set r. Let T denote $type(\sigma^+F(r,<s_1,...,s_k>))$. We have $Lfn(T)=Lfn(R)$. Thus, the result of $\sigma^+F(r,<s_1,...,s_k>)$ is an immediate subclass of the first input argument r. We may consider the operator $\sigma^+F(r,<s_1,...,s_k>)$ as a generic method that has class r as the input domain, classes $s_1,...,s_k$ as the parameters, and the set of objects of type R that satisfy the condition $F(\mu_r, t_1,..., t_k)$ as the output. It operates over the classes $r, s_1,...,s_k$, and selects the objects from the leading input argument class by verifying the condition $F(\mu_r, t_1,..., t_k)$ over the set $\{<\mu_r, t_1,..., t_k> \in R \times S_1 \times ... \times S_k\}$. Note that the definition is essentially applicable when $B_1, ..., B_k$ are reference fields of $S_1,..., S_k$ respectively. It means that each B_i may be of type **ref** S_{i-1} or **ref** $\{S_{i-1}\}$ ($i=1,...,k$), and B_1 specifies an object reference from S_1 to R, B_j represents an object reference from S_j to S_{j-1} ($j=2,...,k$).

Example: Consider COMPANY-MANAGEMENT database defined in Appendix A.
(i) Suppose we have a query "*find all the employees who are also the president of a company*". Let variable e range over EMPLOYEES, c over COMPANIES. Then this query can be expressed by

$$\sigma^+_{e.self=president(c)}(\text{EMPLOYEES}, <\text{COMPANIES}>).$$

The result of this query is a subset of class EMPLOYEES — a set of president employees. The output type is the same as type EMPLOYEE, so the output class is a subclass of class EMPLOYEES. □

(ii) Suppose now we add to type PERSON an additional function "*activity*: PERSON→*String*". Let variables p, q range over class PERSONS, and x over the set children(p) for p in PERSONS. A query "*Give me the persons having all children playing tennis*" can be expressed as $\sigma^+_{F(p,q)}$ (PERSONS, <PERSONS>), where $F(p,q) =_{def}$ $\forall x \in$ children(p) $\exists q$PERSONS(q) (q.self=x ∧ activity(q)="*playing tennis*"). □

3.4 Object Projection

The projection operator is also a type-specific unary operator on a collection of complex objects. As the projection over a given scheme $\mathcal{R}=(R,r)$ may involve constituent types of R, it would be unsatisfactory if one could only take a high-order function as a whole or nothing by projection. It would be also inconvenient if one would have to specify each projecting function by associating the complete aggregation path expression with it. We thus extend the definition of projection operator, in comparison with the one provided in the NF² algebras or in the conventional object algebras, in order to enable the object projection to be performed at all levels of an aggregation hierarchy uniformly.

Definition (*O-project* π)

Let $\mathcal{R}=(R,r)$ be a complex object scheme, and X be a projection list over the aggregation hierarchy of R, which is a nonempty subset of $Fspace(R)$. Assume $X=(A_1, A_2, ..., A_n)$ for convenience, each A_i ($i=1,...,n$) is an applicable function of R. The projection of $\mathcal{R}=(R,r)$ onto X, written as $\pi(X,r)$, is a collection of objects consisting of the X-value of each instance in r. I.e.,

$$\pi(X,r) =_{def} \{ t \mid (\exists t_r \in r \wedge t=[A_1:f_1(t_r), ..., A_n:f_n(t_r)]) \},$$

where if $A_i \in Lfn(R)$ then $f_i(t_r)=t_r[A_i]$, and if $A_i \in (Fspace(R)-Lfn(R))$

then $\exists R' \in Hfn(R)$, $A_i \in Fspace(R')$ and $f_i(t_r) = \pi(A_i, t_r[R'])$.

The output type T of the projection, denoted as $T=type(\pi(X,r))$, is recursively defined as follows:

For each A_i in X where $i=1,...,n$ and $n>=1$,

(i) if $A_i \in Lfn(R)$, then $A_i \in Lfn(T)$;

(ii) if $A_i \notin Lfn(R)$ but $\exists R' \in Hfn(R)$ and $A_i \in Fspace(R')$, then $R' \in Lfn(T)$ and $Lfn(R')=Lfn(T')$

where $T'=type(\pi(A_i, t_r[R]))$ and $t_r \in r$. □

Remarks: In the projection definition, the operator can recursively apply itself to traverse different aggregation levels, and each recursive call corresponds to descending one level of abstractions in the aggregation type hierarchy of R. The names of interest can be directly specified in the projection list of the operator without resorting to any aggregation path. Besides for each input object in the collection being queried, object projection returns one output object. Some output objects may contain the same value but with different identities. So duplication elimination is not necessary for object projection.

Example: Consider CLIENT of a stock-brokerage firm in Appendix A. Suppose $X=(pname, company, purchase-price, number)$ is a project list over the aggregation hierarchy of type CLIENT, and the condition *company*='FORD' is applicable to CLIENT. Then query *"list client's names and investments who purchase FORD's shares"* can be expressed by $\pi(X, \sigma(company=$'FORD',CLIENTS)). The result is given in Fig3-4. □

Note that using our algebra, it is allowable to express projection over aggregation without associating each name of interest with a path expression. However, in most of existing query algebras, any projection over aggregation has to be expressed by resorting each name of interest with an aggregation path for providing operator with navigational ability. Thus the example projection has to be specified as follows

Project((*pname, investment.company, investment.share.purchase-price*),

Select(*investment.company*="FORD", CLIENT)).

Note that we use Project and Select to stand for conventional projection and selection in contrast to our projection π and selection σ operators.

As the projection list includes a sublist of functions applicable to the input type, and the definition of our projection $\pi(X,r)$ does not change the hierarchical structure of the function names involved in the projection list X, the output type of projection is clearly a supertype of the input type (an example see Fig3-4). But the output type may not be a subtype of the immediate supertypes of the input type, unless the projection list contains all the functions defined on these immediate supertypes. Therefore the output class may not always be a superclass of the input class.

Example: Take the COMPANY-MANAGEMENT database in Appendix A. Suppose we have two projections:

Q1: π((pname, birthday, salary), EMPLOYEES).

Q2: π((pname, birthday, home-address, children), σ(salary<30.000, EMPLOYEES)).

Consider Q1, let X'=(pname, birthday, salary). It is obvious that all EMPLOYEE objects are contained in the output class of projection Q1. But the output class is not a subclass of EMPLOYEES's immediate superclass PERSONS (Fig3-5a), because the projection list X' includes *pname, birthday,* and *salary*, but does not contain all functions defined on type PERSON. Thus new objects are created in order to keep the IsA type/class lattice conceptually consistent. While consider Q2, let LOW_SAL_EMP=σ(salary<30.000, EMPLOYEES) and X=(pname, birthday, home-address, children). The query result is a superclass of the input class LOW_SAL_EMP and an immediate subclass of PERSONS. However the outcome of projection Q2 can not be a subclass of EMPLOYEES, although EMPLOYEES is an immediate superclass of class LOW_SAL_EMP (Fig3-5b), because *salary* is not included in its projection list X. In this case, no new objects are created. □

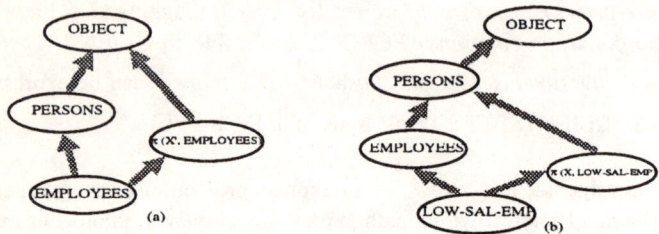

Fig3-5 The position of the output of example projections in the IsA class lattices

In what follows we define the rules for determining the position of the output type of a projection in the IsA type/class lattice. Let $sup(R)$ denote the set of all (direct and indirect) supertypes of R excluding type OBJECT. The output type of the projection $\pi(X,r)$ is

(1) a supertype of the input type R, and a subtype of some supertypes (say $T_1,...,T_k$ $\in sup(R)$ $k \geq 1$) of R, if the projection list contains some functions of R and all the functions of these supertypes. In this case, no new objects are created.

(2) a supertype of R, and an immediate subtype of the most general type OBJECT, if the projection list contains some functions of R and does not contain all the functions of any supertype of R. In this case, new objects are created, in order to preserve the closure of projection operator under the object model.

(3) a supertype of some supertypes of R if the projection list contains no local functions of R, and

   (3.1) if $\exists T_i \in sup(R)$, $i=1,...,k$; $k \geq 1$, and the projection list contains all the functions of T_i, then the output type is an immediate subtype of such T_i. In this case, no new objects are created.

(3.2) if there exist no such $T_i \in sup(R)$ that the projection list contains all the functions of T_i, the output type of the projection is an immediate subtype of OBJECT. In this case, new objects are created.

3.5 Object Join

Unlike in conventional data models, in object-oriented models many relationships between entity objects are represented within the objects themselves, such as IsA relationships, aggregation relationships and arbitrary associations. The navigation over these object-based relationships can be expressed without needing explicit join formulation. Hence join operations are used less frequently in the object algebra than in the relational algebra. However, the existing object schema in a database may not explicitly reflect all the relationships required by queries. join operator is still needed to handle the cases when a relationship being queried upon is not defined within the object types. Such a relationship is called *value-based* relationship. For example, a query "*find all the employees who have jobs in their home city?*" requires a value-based join between two classes COMPANIES and EMPLOYEES through company's *location* and employee's *home-address*. This relationship is not explicitly modeled in the interface defined on either type COMPANY or type EMPLOYEE. We provide *O-join* operator to realize queries on the objects having value-based relationship.

The definition of *O-join* operator is formally extended in comparison with the (nested) relational join. It allows combining objects of two scheme types at all levels of nesting uniformly, and creates a new type as an immediate subtype of the most general type OBJECT, holding the result of join. The definition is also intended to preserve associativity of the operator, which we expect to be used in the object query optimization in more or less the same way as it is used in the relational query optimizer.

Definition (*O-join* $\otimes$)

Let $\mathcal{R}_1=(R_1, r_1)$ and $\mathcal{R}_2=(R_2, r_2)$ be two object schemes respectively. Assume the join condition F is of the form $t.A \vartheta t'.B$, A and B are comparable functions, $t \in r_1$, and $t' \in r_2$. If A and B are both zero-order functions, ϑ is in $\{=, ==, <, <=, >, >=\}$; otherwise ϑ is in $\{\in, ==, =, \subset, \subseteq, \supset, \supseteq\}$. The *O-join* of $\mathcal{R}_1$ and $\mathcal{R}_2$ at the instance level, denoted by $\otimes_F(r_1,r_2)$, is a collection of new objects satisfying the join condition F, i.e.,

$$\otimes_F(r_1,r_2) = \{ \mu \mid \mu=[R_1:t, R_2:t'], t \in r_1, t' \in r_2, t.A \vartheta t'.B = true \}. \quad \square$$

Remarks: If the join condition $F = \emptyset$, then $\otimes_F(r_1,r_2)$ is a Cartesian Product of r_1 and r_2. Otherwise, there are four cases need to be considered:
  (i) the join directly combines objects in r_1 and objects in r_2,
  (ii) the join actually combines subobjects of instances of r_1 and instance objects of r_2,

(iii) the join combines instance objects of r_1 and subobjects of instances of r_1;
(iv) the join combines subobjects of instances of r_1 and subobjects of instances of r_2.

We develop the constructive definition of *O-join* and the formal description of the output type of $\otimes_F(r_1,r_2)$ for each case and omit them here due to the space limitation. Readers who are interested in how the *O-join* is recursively defined and how the output type is formally constructed may refer to [29].

Example: Assume the type structures of CLIENT and STOCK-DATA are as shown in Fig3-6 and Fig3-7 respectively. The query $O\text{-}join_{company\text{-}name(ct)=company\text{-}name(cp)}$(CLIENT, STOCK-DATA) actually combines subobjects of CLIENT with objects of STOCK-DATA. Fig3-8 gives the output type structure of this *O-join*.

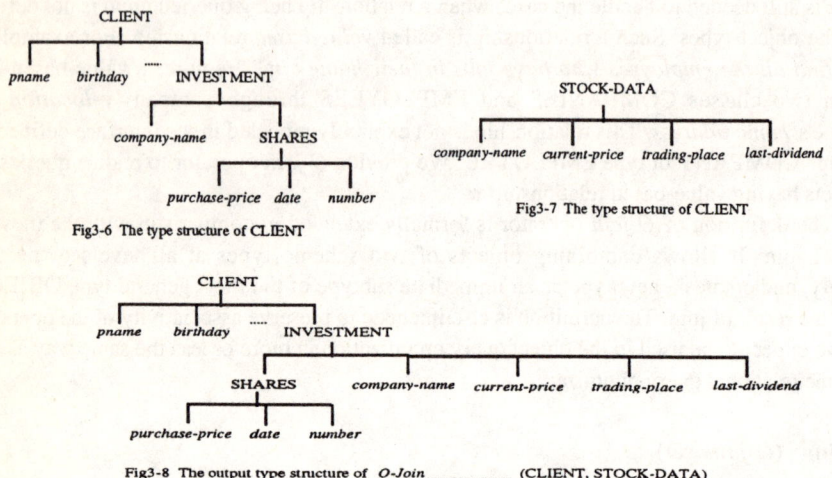

Fig3-6 The type structure of CLIENT

Fig3-7 The type structure of CLIENT

Fig3-8 The output type structure of $O\text{-}Join_{company\text{-}name}$ (CLIENT, STOCK-DATA)

3.6 General Remarks

The other operators, such as *nest*, *unnest*, *followup*, and standard set operators (*union*, *difference*, and *intersection*), are also defined recursively in our object algebra but omitted here due to the space limitation. Each definition includes the constructive description of the operator itself and the formal rules for classification of the output result of the operator in the IsA type/class lattice. The *followup* operator is special to this object-algebra. It is used to dereference the reference fields (oids) of a given scheme type by the object instances these oids refer to. Readers may refer to [28, 29] for details.

Note that the image operator introduced in [40] is not included in the minimal set of our algebraic operators, although it is useful for evaluation of function values. Let $f:R \rightarrow B$ be a function and *r* be of type *R*, then image(f,r)={$f(t)$ | t∈ r}. Obviously, image differs from the projection which has a single function in the projection list, because an image returns the set of function values, whereas a projection returns the set of objects which are identical to the input objects, but with only the function included in the projection list. But using *unnest* after $\pi(X,r)$, i.e., *unnest*(f, $\pi(X,r)$), $X=\{f\}$, we could get the same result as image(f,r).

Unlike in most of existing query languages, the recursive definition of our operators allow users to specify queries over aggregation, without resorting any path expression to the involving function names, in order to provide the operator with navigational ability. Thus complex object can be considered collectively as a basic unit of object queries. The idea is mainly motivated and guaranteed by the following facts.

(a) *The object model requires that all the accesses to objects, say having type R, be through the applicable interface of R (including the functions "inherited" from constituent types of R).*
(b) *Any aggregation hierarchy is of acyclicity.*
(c) *The aggregation hierarchy of any schema type has a finite depth, and each recursive call for evaluation of the query condition corresponds to descending one level of abstraction in the aggregation hierarchy of the input type, so the recursion ends when the leaf nodes are reached.*

The obvious advantage of this extension is twofold. First, it leads to a high level of expressiveness of query representation, because explicit specification of aggregation paths is not required. Second, it offers an opportunity for users to remain within the framework of the model of complex objects while querying database.

4 Discussion on the object-centered approach

Up to now, most of the existing query languages for object-oriented models need explicit path expressions for navigations over aggregation structures. Complex objects are not treated collectively as a basic unit of object queries in such systems. An obvious disadvantage of associating an aggregation path expression with each name of interest, when querying objects, is that it can lead to a complexity of query formulation, and also cause an incremental expense of schema evolution. This is because when an aggregation hierarchy of some existing objects is extended, for instance, adding another layer of nesting in between of the aggregation hierarchy, although the change has no influence on the identities of corresponding complex objects, query programs working on the old schema have to be explicitly modified in order to re-specify all the path expressions of the relevant names (examples may recall Section 2.3). An appeal of our recursive object algebra is that all operators defined in this algebra do not require associating the names of interest with any aggregation path expression in the parameter declaration[1]. The

---

[1] Note that whenever querying objects of complex structure, there are at least two ways to express a query. One is to formulate the query by associating each name of interest with an aggregation path expression. The other is to specify the query without having resort to any aggregation path expression. In most of existing query languages, only the first possibility is allowed, whereas in our object algebra-based query languages, both ways of query formulation are possible.

aggregation path of each name involved in queries can be automatically determined by the query processing system. This is fulfilled by employing the acyclicity and the determinism of aggregation type hierarchy, and the mechanism of aggregation inheritance during query interpretation and query reformulation. Thus using the query languages based on our object algebra, it is possible to query over aggregation without needing to resort to any aggregation path expression. Only queries over associations require explicit provision of the operators with navigational ability (one way of specifying association path is using dot notation). As a result, the formulation of queries on complex objects can be drastically simplified, and the adaptability and the data independence of the object model against changes can be highly increased. This feature seems also important in heterogeneous systems where several object schemas may be used for the same application world with different points of views.

Some reader might argue that a query algebra is usually not dedicated to the end-users, and it is more important for a query algebra to have explicit query evaluation plans generated on the basis of the operators than to be user-friendly. We in some sense agree with the argument. The reasons we develop this object algebra are the following. First, few object algebra have been formally defined so far. Some proposals introduce interesting ideas but do not provide the generality and the complete formal framework that one would expect from an object algebra. It is indeed important to make deeper investigation towards this direction. Second, we would like to demonstrate that, as far as the reference data model is object-oriented, it is interesting and also possible to take advantage of the semantic difference between aggregation references and association references to simplify queries over aggregation structures, even in the algebraic specification of queries. Of course, we may employ the notion of aggregation inheritance in the design of a high level object-oriented query interface, and develop a transformation engine to carry out the mapping from the declarative query formula to the nested relational or similar algebraic expression. Even in this case, our object algebra can be used as a sound theoretical basis in the development of such a transformation engine. Thirdly, the algebraic model of object queries provides a solid foundation for formal analysis of several query issues in object-oriented databases, because all the algebra operators have well-defined semantics so that many properties can be derived, and the formal proofs of these properties can be simplified. For instance, it is possible to formally describe the output type of each operator in terms of the definition, and thus to prove the closure of any query language based on this algebra. The equivalence-preserving rewriting rules for optimization of queries can be formally developed too.

5 Comparison and Conclusion

We have presented an extended object model and a recursive query algebra. Unlike in semantic data modeling[21] and in most of the existing object-oriented models, our object model supports a general distinction of aggregation from arbitrary association not only at instance level but also at type level. Two kinds of polymorphisms: subtype inheritance as a kind of universal polymorphism and aggregation inheritance as a kind of ad-hoc polymorphism are provided. Comparing with the previous result reported in [27], we have made some further developments.

For instance, we further classify aggregation relationships into two categories: acyclic aggregation and cyclic aggregation, and generally analyse the similarity and the essential difference between aggregation and association, as well as between aggregation and specialization. More interestingly, we have developed a sound recursive object algebra as an integral part of the model. Features of the recursive algebra are the following.

First, the definition of our algebra operators enable each operator by itself to traverse different levels of the aggregation hierarchies of querying objects. Queries over aggregation do not require resorting any path expression for providing the operator with navigational ability. This not only helps to reduce the complexity of query formulation but also provides users with an opportunity to remain within the framework of complex object model when querying database. As a result, the flexibility and adaptability of the object model against schema changes are highly increased. To our knowledge, none of the previous work offers a similar support.

Second, both object-preserving operators and object-creating operators are well defined in our object algebra. For instance, we formally define the output type of all the object-creating operators. However, many object algebra proposed so far, to our knowledge, are either ground on the object-creating basis [cf.25,40], or designed within a pure object-preserving framework [cf.42]. Very few provide both object-preserving and object-creating operators within one framework. In the proposals supporting only object-creating model, it seems not possible to capture the relationship between the input objects of a query and its output objects. Besides, it seems that no formal definitions about what is the type of newly created objects have been provided in these proposals. Whereas in the pure object-preserving query model, it seems not possible to realize the relationships that are not explicitly specified in the object-oriented model, nor to create new relationships by combining objects via the value-based relationship. Thus, the operators like our object projection and *O-join* are missing.

Although the update issue is not discussed in the current presentation, we would like to add that queries expressed by using the object-preserving operators (such as object selection, and multiple-operand select operation) can be directly taken as the arguments of subsequent update operations, because updates on the resulting objects can automatically be propagated to the stored (base) objects, and thus dynamic classification of objects during updates is possible.

Besides, in comparison with the existing object algebras [cf.15,25,38,40], we feel that definitions of *O-select, O-project, multiple-operand select, O-join,* and *followup* are original both in operational semantics and in formal description. We also support transitive closure operators for expressing recursive queries, and allow invocation of methods, which have no side effect, in the query expressions. In our view, the recursive object algebra is better suited for the object-oriented model than the other query algebras that have been proposed. It largely covers the query requirements for complex objects, meanwhile providing an interesting evolution from (nested) relational algebra to object algebra. Although the design is based on the chosen object-oriented model, we conjecture that it is possible for other object-oriented databases.

Up to now we have also investigated some other issues in the context of this recursive object algebra [cf.28]. For instance, we have developed a set of algebraic-equivalence rewriting rules for query optimization of this algebra (see [29]). We have also formally proved the expressive power of this algebra, including the transformation of the set of safe object calculus formulas [10,42] into our recursive algebra expressions.

Acknowledgement I am indebted to Robert Meersman for his encouragement and to Jan Paredaens and participants at the seminar at TUE for stimulating discussions. I would also like to thank Elisa Bertino, Marc Scholl, Hans Weigand and Roberto Zicari for helpful comments on the earlier versions of this paper.

Reference

[1] Abiteboul S., Fisher P. and Schek, H.-J (ed) Nested relations and complex objects in databases, Vol.361, Lecture Notes in Computer Science, (Springer, 1989)
[2] Abiteboul S and Kanellakis P.C. Object identity as a query language primitive. In:SIGMOD(1989) 159-173
[3] Abiteboul S. and , Objects and views, in: ACM SIGMOD (1991) 238-247
[4] Alashqur A.M., Su S.Y.W. and Lam H. OQL: A query language for manipulating object-oriented databases. in: Proc. Very Large DataBases (Amsterdam 1989) 433-442
[5] Andrews T. and Harris, C., Combining language and database advantages in an object-oriented development environment, in: Proc. 2nd Int. Conf. OOPSLA, (Orlando, Florida 1987)
[6] Bancilhon F et. al, A query language for O_2 object-oriented database system, in: Proc. 2nd Int. Workshop on Database Programming Languages (Oregon, June 1989)
[7] Banerjee J., Kim W., and Kim K.C., Queries in object-oriented databases, in: Proc. ICDE (1988) 31-38
[8] Beech D. "A foundation for evolution from relational to object databases, in: Proc.EDBT (Venice, 1988)
[9] Beeri C., Formal approach to object-oriented databases, in: Data&Knowledge Engineering 5 (1990) 353-382
[10] Bertino E. et.al, Object-oriented query languages: the notion and the issues, To appear in: IEEE Trans. on Data and Knowledge Engineering (1992)
[11] Breazu-Tannen V., Buneman P. and Ohori A., Static type checking in object-oriented databases, in: IEEE Data Engineering, Vol.12, No.3, (1989) 5-12
[12] Cardelli,L., A semantics of multiple inheritance, in: Kahn G., MacQueen D., and Plotkin G., (ed) Semantics of Data Types, 173, Lecture Notes on Computer Science (Springer Verlag, 1984) 51-67
[13] Cardelli,L. and Wegner P., On understanding types, data abstraction, and polymorphism, in: ACM Computing Surveys, Vol17, No.4 (1985) 471-522
[14] Carey M.J., DeWitt D.J. and Vandenber S.L., A data model and query language for EXODUS, in: Proc. ACM SIGMOD (1988)
[15] Cluet S., Delobel C., Lecluse C. and Richard P., RELOOP, an algebraic based query language for an object -oriented database, in: Proc. of 1st Conf. on Deductive and Object-Oriented Databases (1989) 294-313
[16] Colby L.S., A recursive algebra for nested relations, in: Info. Systems Vol.15, No.5, (1990) 567-582
[17] Dayal U., Queries and views in an object-oriented data models, in: Proc. 2nd workshop on Database Programming languages (Oregon, June 1989)
[18] Ehrich,H-D., Sernadas,A., and Sernadas,C. "From Data types to Object types" J. on Info. Processing and Cybernetics EIK, Vol.26, No.1/2, 1990, pp.33-48
[19] Gyssens, M. and Van Gucht, D., "The Powerset Algebra as a Result of Adding Programming Constructs to the Nested Relational Algebra", Proc. SIGMOD 1988, pp225-232.

[20] Gardarin,G., Cheiney,J.P., Kiernan,G., Pastre,D., and Stora,H. "Managing Complex Objects in an Extensible Relational DBMS" Proc. VLDB 1989, pp.55-56
[21] Hull R. and King R., Semantic database modeling: survey, applications, research issues, in: ACM Comput. Surveys, Vol.19, No.3 (1987) 160-172.
[22] Hull R. and Yoshikawa M., ILOG: declarative creation and manipulation of object identifiers, in: Proc. ACM SIGACT-SIGMOD Symposium on Principles of Database Systems (1991) 328-340.
[23] Khoshafian S.N. and Copeland C.P., Object identity, in: Proc. the OOPSLA (1986) 406-415
[24] Kim W. et al, Composite objects revisited, in: Proc. ACM SIGMOD (1989)
[25] Kim W., A model of queries for object-oriented databases, in: Proc. 15th VLDB (1989) 423-432.
[26] Lecluse,C. and Richard,P. "Modelling Complex structures in Object-oriented Databases" in: PODS 1989
[27] Liu L. Exploring more semantics in aggregation hierarchies for object-oriented database systems. in: Proc. 8th IEEE Data Engineering (Arizona, Feb.1992), also available as Research Report (Feb. 1991) pp1-32.
[28] Liu L., A formal approach to structure, algebra and communication behavior of complex objects. ph.D Dissertation (Dec.1992), ISBN90-9005694-7, pp1-303.
[29] Liu L., A recursive object algebra based on aggregation abstraction for manipulating complex objects. In: Journal of Data & Knowledge Engineering 8 (1993) North-Holland.
[30] Meersman R.A., Towards Models for practical reasoning about conceptual database design. In: R.Meersman and A.Sernadas (ed), Data Semantics (DS-2) (North Holland 1988)
[31] Mitschang,B. "Extending the relational algebra to capture complex objects", VLDB 1989
[32] Neuhold,E, Perl,Y., Geller,J. and Turau,V. "Separating Structural and Semantic Elements in Object-oriented Knowledge Bases" Proc. of Advanced Database System Symposium'89, Kyoto.
[33] Osborn S., "Identity, equality and query optimization, in: Dittrich K.R. (ed), Advances in Object-oriented Database Systems, 334, Lecture Notes on Computer Science (Springer Verlag, New York, 1988) 346-351
[34] Roth M.A., Korth H.F. and Batory D.S., SQL-NF: a query language for non 1NF relational databases, in: Information Systems, Vol.12, No.1 (1987) 99-114
[35] Roth M.A., Korth H.F. and Silberschatz A., Extended algebra and calculus for non-1NF relational databases, in: ACM Trans. on DataBase Systems, Vol.13, No.4 (1988) 389-417
[36] Rowe L.A. and Stonebraker M., The POSTGRES data model, in: Proc. 13th VLDB (1987)
[37] Schek H.-J. and Scholl M.H., The relational model with relation-valued attributes, in: Info. Sys. Vol.11, No.2 (1986) 137-147
[38] Scholl M.H. and Schek H.-J, A relational object model, in: Proc. Inf. Conf. Database Theory, LNCS 470, (Springer Verlag, 1990) 89-105.
[39] Scholl M.H., Laasch C. and Tresch M., Updatable views in object-oriented databases, Technical Report 150 ETH Zürich, (Dec. 1990).
[40] Shaw G. and Zdonik S.B., A query algebra for object-oriented databases, In: Proc. Inc. Conf. Data Eng., IEEE Press (1990) 154-162.
[41] Smith J.M. and Smith D.C., Database abstractions: aggregation and generalization, in: ACM Trans. on Database Systems, Vol.2, No.2 (June 1977) 105-133
[42] Straube D. and Ozsu M.T., Queries and query processing in object-oriented database systems, in: ACM Trans. on Information Systems, Vol.8, No.4 (Oct. 1990) 387-430
[43] Thomas S.J. and Fisher P.C., Nested relational structures, in: Advances in Computing Research III, The Theory of Databases (1986) 260-307.
[44] Vandenberg S.L. DeWitt D., Algebraic support for complex objects with array, identity and inheritance. in: ACM SIGMOD 1991, pp158-167.

Appendix A The Sample Database Schema

This sample database schema COMPANY-MANAGEMENT involves companies, employees working for the companies, clients of the companies, projects running by the companies, and documents of the projects. Suppose in defining type COMPANY, we need three functions: *cpname*: COMPANY→string, *location*: COMPANY→{CITY-ADDRS}, *president*: COMPANY→**ref** EMPLOYEE. We may simply use the following form instead of the above one for presentation convenience: *cpname*: string, *location*: {CITY-ADDRS}, *president*: **ref** EMPLOYEE.

```
define database schema COMPANY-MANAGEMENT:
type COMPANY = (    cpname:            string,
                    location:          {CITY-ADDRS},independent & sharable,total,
                    president:         ref EMPLOYEE,
                    staff:             ref {EMPLOYEE},total,
                    projects:          ref {PROJECT});

type PERSON   = (   pname:             string,
                    birthday:          date,
                    home-address:      CITY-ADDRS, independent & sharable, total,
                    children:          ref {PERSON});

type CITY-ADDRS = ( constituent-of:    COMPANY, PERSON,
                    cityname:          string,
                    zipcode:           string);

type EMPLOYEE = (   IsA:               PERSON,
                    hiredate:          date,
                    salary:            real,
                    affiliates:        ref COMPANY,total,
                    work-for:          ref {PROJECT});

type CLIENT = (IsA:         PERSON,
                    investments:       {INVESTMENTS},dependent & exclusive);

type INVESTMENT = ( constituent-of:    CLIENT,
                    company-name:      string,
                    shares:            {SHARES}, dependent & exclusive);

type SHARES = ( constituent-of:        INVESTMENT,
                    purchase-price:    real,
                    date:              date,
                    number:            integer);

type STOCK-DATA = ( company-name:      string,
                    current-price:     real,
                    trading-palce:     {string},
                    last-dividend:     real);
```

```
type PROJECT   =  (contract#:       integer,
                   proj-name:       string,
                   leader:          ref EMPLOYEE,
                   budget:          integer,
                   documents:       ref {DOCUMENT});

type DOCUMENT = (  docno:           integer,
                   title:           string,
                   authors:         ref {EMPLOYEE},
                   keywords:        {string},
                   chapters:        {CHAPTER}, dependent & exclusive,
                   contribute-to:   ref PROJECT );

type CHAPTER   = ( constituent-of: DOCUMENT,
                   chapterno:       integer,
                   chaptertitle:    string,
                   text-content:    {PARAGRAPH}, dependent & exclusive, total,
                   figures: {FIGURE}, independent & exclusive);

type PARAGRAPH = ( constituent-of: CHAPTER,
                   para-no:         integer,
                   textbody:        string);

type FIGURE    = ( constituent-of: CHAPTER,
                   fig-position:    integer,
                   fig-caption:     string,
                   bitmap-no:       integer);

class COMPANIES:    {COMPANY};        class PERSONS:    {PERSON};
class CITY-ADDRESS: {CITY-ADDRS};     class EMPLOYEES:  {EMPLOYEE}, subclass-of PERSONS;
class STOCK-DATA:   {STOCK-DATA};     class CLIENTS:    {CLIENT}, subclass-of PERSON;
class PROJECTS:     {PROJECT};               class DOCUMENTS:  {DOCUMENT};
class CHAPTERS:     {CHAPTER};        class PARAGRAPHS: {PARAGRAPH};
class FIGURES:      {FIGURE};

define database COMPANY-MANAGEMENT:= {COMPANIES, PERSONS, CITY-ADDRESS, EMPLOYEES,
CLIENTS, Euro-CLIENTS, STOCK-DATA, PROJECTS, DOCUMENTS, CHAPTERS, PARAGRAPHS, FIGURES}
end.
```

Towards the Unification of Views and Versions for Object Databases

Kwang June Byeon   Dennis McLeod

Computer Science Department
University of Southern California
Los Angeles, California 90089-0781
USA
E-mail: {byeon, mcleod}@pollux.usc.edu

Abstract

There have been a number of approaches to views and meta-data versioning for object databases. However, the essential similarities between the notions of views and versions have not been adequately explored. This paper introduces the concept of a virtual database to unify these two notions in the object database context. The semantics of virtual databases is presented, and a mechanism for interactively creating and deleting virtual databases and manipulating their schemas and instances is described. The application of the virtual database concept to supporting both views and versions in a unified manner is studied, and its practical utility is examined.

1 Introduction

Work on views and meta-data versions in the object database context [AB91, ASL89, Ber92, HZ90, Kim89, KC88, Run92, RB92, SLM91, SZ86, TYI88, TS93] has explored techniques to support users who may require different and often changing perspectives of an object database. Several approaches to views [AB91, ASL89, Ber92, HZ90, Kim89, Run92, RB92, SLM91, TYI88, TS93] and two major approaches to meta-data versions [KC88, SZ86] have been developed. The view approaches can be divided into two groups: *class view* and *schema view*. Similarly, the meta-data version approaches can be divided into two groups: *class version* and *schema version*. Class views (and class versions) are conceptually more limited than schema views (and schema versions); hence, we consider only the schema view and version approaches.

We can observe that schema views and versions have many structural similarities. In particular, suppose that a schema view $SVIEW_i$ has been created on top of an object database DB_i, and a schema version $SVERSION_i$ of DB_i has also been created. If we compare the schema of $SVIEW_i$ and that of $SVERSION_i$ with the schema of DB_i respectively, it is clear that both schemas are created through some schema changes from the schema of DB_i. Also, users can create, delete, change, and retrieve the instances of $SVIEW_i$ and those of $SVERSION_i$, as they do for the instances of a typical database.

These similarities motivated us to develop a new concept called a *virtual database*, which unifies the schema view and schema version concepts.

In spite of these similarities, there has been to date no approach that unifies schema views and versions, or considers both concepts in a single context. As a result, many cases that need to be supported for real-world applications have been ignored. Consider the above example of $SVIEW_i$, $SVERSION_i$, and DB_i again. First, some users may be interested in the entire $SVERSION_i$, while others may be interested in only a subset of it. Second, some may want to change the schema of $SVIEW_i$, while others may want to continue to use the current $SVIEW_i$. Third, some users may want to see only a subset of DB_i, as well as new meta-data (e.g., classes) that are neither in DB_i nor derived from the schema of DB_i. Note that what the users want in this case is a combination of a schema view and a schema version. Failure to adequately address these cases by the previous approaches is another motivation for considering schema views and versions in one context and developing a unifying concept.

Even though the above cases have not been explicitly considered by the previous approaches, they can be supported to some extent by using schema views and versions. The first case can be supported by creating a schema view on top of $SVERSION_i$, and the second case, by creating a schema version of $SVIEW_i$. Also, the third case can be supported either by creating a schema version of DB_i and then creating a schema view on top of this created schema version, or by creating a schema view on top of DB_i and then creating a schema version of this created schema view. However, the advantages of using the unifying concept (i.e., virtual databases) here are clear. The above cases can be supported by a single structure and its manipulation mechanism rather than by two different structures and their corresponding manipulation mechanisms. Also, the third case can be directly supported by creating a virtual database without creating an extra schema view or schema version.

In the remainder of this paper, we first introduce the concept of a virtual database, which unifies the schema view and schema version concepts. We define the semantics of virtual databases, and present a mechanism for interactively creating and deleting virtual databases and manipulating their schemas and instances. Second, we illustrate how virtual databases can be used as schema views or schema versions, as well as how they can support the cases that have not been adequately addressed by the previous approaches. In particular, Section 2 reviews the previous work on views and meta-data versions for object databases. Section 3 describes the semantics of virtual databases and the manipulation mechanism. Section 4 examines how virtual databases can be applied to schema views and versions. Section 5 presents the issues related to our experimental prototype implementation. Finally, Section 6 summarizes the contributions of this research.

2 Related Research

There have been several approaches for supporting views for object databases [AB91, ASL89, Ber92, HZ90, Kim89, Run92, RB92, SLM91, TYI88, TS93]. Depending on the granularity of views that they introduce, we divide these approaches into two groups: *class view* and *schema view*. In the class view group [Ber92, SLM91, TS93], a view is a single class, while in the schema view group [AB91, ASL89, HZ90, Kim89, Run92, RB92, TYI88], a view is a schema which consists of multiple classes interrelated through attributes, methods, and is-a relationships. It appears that class views are more limited than schema views, since a user often wants to see a view consisting of more than one class, and representing such view with class views is neither easy nor natural. Hence, we consider only the schema view approaches. In these approaches[1], schema views are created directly or indirectly on top of an underlying database. In fact, each schema view is created on top of one or more bases, each of which is either the underlying database or a previously created schema view. As a result, an underlying database as well as its schema views are organized into a directed acyclic graph rooted at the database. A schema view may contain classes copied (with or without schema changes) and/or classes derived (e.g., derived as subclasses/superclasses) from its bases. Conceptually, the instances of a schema view are not stored in the schema view, but are derived from the underlying database whenever needed.

There have been two major approaches to meta-data versioning in the object database context [KC88, SZ86]. [SZ86] proposes the versioning of a single class (i.e., *class version*), while [KC88] proposes the versioning of a database schema (i.e., *schema version*). It appears that class versions are more limited than schema versions, since the users of an object database often want to see the entire database after schema changes. Hence, we focus on the schema version approach [KC88]. Here, a schema version consists of a schema and instances. It represents a database (or another schema version) after some schema changes are made to the database (or the schema version). Any number of schema versions can be derived from a base, which is either a database or another schema version. As a result, an underlying database and its schema versions are organized into a hierarchy. A schema version usually contains classes copied from its base, derived classes, and/or classes that are neither copied nor derived. Conceptually, the instances of a schema version are stored in the schema version. Further, this approach uses schema versioning as well as instance versioning. Due to the adoption of instance versioning, different versions of an instance may exist in different schema versions; therefore, an instance that is deleted in one schema version may still exist in another schema version.

Relationships between views and versions have been identified, and the possibility of applying views to schema evolution has been considered [Ber92, KC88, TS93]. [Ber92] discusses how class views can be used to support some of the schema evolution cases found in [BKKK87, Mot87]; [TS93] presents a methodology for supporting schema evolution by using class views and subschemas; [KC88] discusses the possibility of schema views to support schema versions. Further, [Sci91] presents a unified approach to versioning of objects; this approach uses instance versioning (but not meta-data versioning) and class views where the former is used to store versions of objects as instances of classes, and the latter serve as means of selecting specific versions from the classes. To the best of our knowledge, however, there has been no approach that unifies schema views and versions, or attempts to consider both concepts in a single context.

3 The Concept of Virtual Databases

In this section, we introduce the concept of virtual databases. After briefly describing the object data model that we use, we discuss the semantics of virtual databases, along

---

[1]The characteristics of schema views described here are not present in all of the existing schema view approaches. They are rather the union of the characteristics that we adopt from these approaches.

with a mechanism for creating and deleting a virtual database, changing its schema, and manipulating its instances.

3.1 A Core Object Data Model

We use a simple object data model called the Core Object Data Model (CODM). This CODM provides the basic modeling constructs found in most object data models [AM89, ABD+89, BCG+87, LRV88, MSOA86]. We here describe the characteristics of the CODM that are relevant to our subsequent discussion. In this model, every real-world entity is modeled as an object, and every object has associated attributes and methods. Objects with the same attributes and methods are grouped into a class, which are termed the instances of the class. Hence, a class is represented by the attributes and methods that are applicable to its instances. An attribute is specified by its name and domain class (i.e., collection of possible values), and a method is specified by its name, input arguments, output argument, and body.

Classes are organized into a directed acyclic graph (DAG) via is-a relationships representing superclass-subclass connections; this DAG is termed a class lattice. A class inherits attributes and methods from its superclasses, and instances of a class become instances of its superclasses. We call the instances directly created for a class the direct instances of the class, and other instances (i.e., instances of its subclasses) are indirect instances. The root of the class lattice is a system-defined class called **Object**. **Object** has the system-defined classes **String**, **Integer**, and **Real** as its subclasses. Figure 1(a) represents an example database based upon this model. The classes **String**, **Integer**, and **Real** are not included for simplicity, and only direct instances of a class are associated with the class. For example, the class **RA** has the four inherited attributes *ssno*, *name*, *major*, and *empno*; it also has the single (directly-)defined attribute *advisor*; **RA** has the single defined method *has_advisor*.

3.2 The Semantics of Virtual Databases

A *virtual database* is a special database where portions of its schema and instances are copied and/or derived from the schemas and instances of its *bases*, respectively. Notice that each of its bases can be either an ordinary database or another virtual database. The schema of a virtual database may thus have three kinds of classes: *imported*, *derived*, and *local*. An imported class is a class that is copied from some bases of the virtual database, with or without schema changes and/or with renaming. Hence, each of these bases has a class corresponding to the imported class. Such class in each base is termed the *base class* of the imported class. A derived class is a class that is derived from other classes (i.e., other imported, derived, and/or local classes). A local class is a class that is newly created in the virtual database; it is neither imported nor derived. Figure 1(b) represents an example virtual database VDB_1 which is created on top of the base DB_1. Here, the classes **Person**, **TA**, **Professor**, and **Department** are imported classes, **CS_Professor** and **EE_Professor** are derived classes, and **Course** is a local class. The class definition of an imported class may be different from that of its base class, e.g., **TA** of VDB_1 vs. its base class **TA** of DB_1. **CS_Professor** and **EE_Professor** are derived from **Professor**, via the derivation predicates *professor_of.dname* = "CS" and *professor_of.dname* = "EE", respectively.

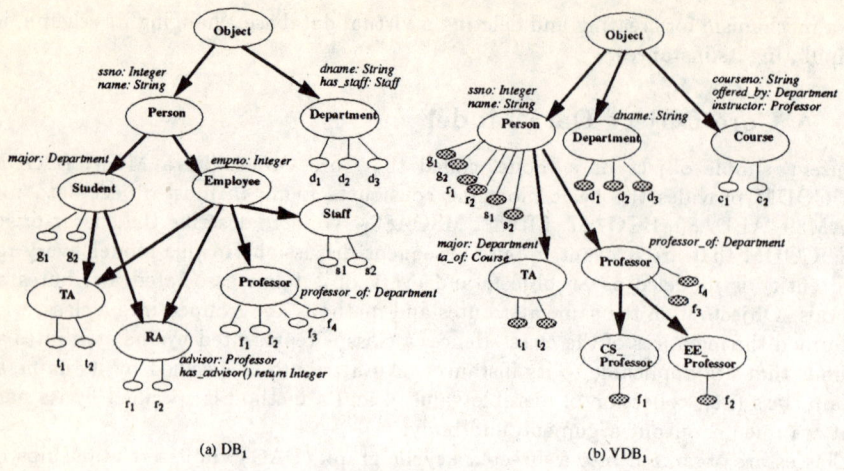

Figure 1: Database DB_1 and Virtual Database VDB_1

The instances of a virtual database are divided into two groups: *imported* and *local* instances. An imported instance is an instance that is copied from some bases of the virtual database. Each of these bases thus has an instance corresponding to the imported instance. Such instance in each base is termed a *base instance* of the imported instance. An imported instance of a virtual database serves as an image of its base instances with respect to the virtual database. Hence, if the same-named properties (i.e., attributes and/or methods) are defined for both an imported class and its base instance(s), the properties of the base instance(s) conceptually override those of the imported instance, i.e., the properties of the base instance(s) are shared by the imported instance. A local instance is an ordinary instance that is newly created in the virtual database. In VDB_1 (Figure 1(b)), imported instances are represented by "shaded" small ovals (e.g., t_1 of **TA**), while local instances are represented by "unshaded" small ovals (e.g., c_1 of **Course**). The attributes *ssno*, *name*, and *major* of the imported instance t_1 in VDB_1 are overridden by the same-named attribute of its base instance (i.e., t_1 in DB_1). Similarly, if both **TA** of DB_1 and **TA** of VDB_1 have the method *has_major*, *has_major* of the imported instance t_1 in VDB_1 is overridden by *has_major* of its base instance (see Section 3.6). However, the attribute *ta_of* of the imported instance t_1 is not overridden, since its base instance does not have this attribute (see the transforming phase in Section 3.3).

A virtual database always contains imported classes and instances, but does not necessarily contain other classes and instances. Imported instances always belong to imported classes, and may belong to derived classes that are derived from imported classes. Local instances always belong to local classes, and may belong to some imported or derived classes under certain conditions[2]. In addition, local classes and instances, as well as properties of imported classes (and instances) that their base classes (and instances)

---

[2]Details of instance manipulation will be discussed in Section 3.6.

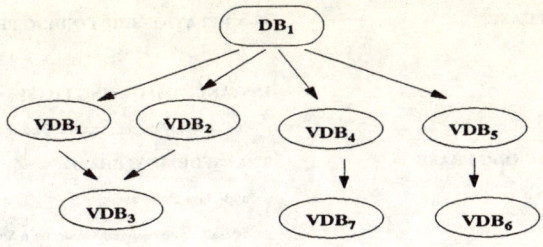

Figure 2: Virtual Database Derivation Graph of Database DB_1

do not have, allow a virtual database to contain additional information that is neither present in nor derived from the base(s) of the virtual database. In VDB_1 (Figure 1(b)), each imported class has imported instances; **CS_Professor** and **EE_Professor** also have imported instances. The local class **Course** has the local instances c_1 and c_2. This local class and its instances, as well as the attribute *ta_of* of the imported class **TA** indicate information that is neither present in or derived from the base of VDB_1. Note that the classes **CS_Professor** and **EE_Professor** are derived from the base of VDB_1.

As for an ordinary database, the classes of a virtual database VDB_i are organized into a class lattice rooted at the class **Object**. VDB_i must also contain all classes that are recursively referenced by the attributes and methods of its classes. This indicates that VDB_i must be *type-closed* [HZ90, Run92, TYI88]. The is-a relationships among the imported classes of VDB_i must be derivable from the is-a relationships in the bases of VDB_i.

Virtual databases are created directly or indirectly on top of an underlying database. In fact, each virtual database is created (directly) on top of one or more bases. Notice that when it is created on top of multiple bases, at most one base can be the underlying database. As a result, an underlying database as well as its virtual databases are organized into a directed acyclic graph (DAG) rooted at the database. We call this DAG the *(virtual database) derivation graph* for the database. Figure 2 shows a derivation graph for the database DB_1. Here, for example, VDB_1 is created on top of DB_1, while VDB_3 is created on top of VDB_1 and VDB_2.

3.3 Virtual Database Creation with a Single Base

The process of creating a new virtual database on top of a single base is divided into the following phases: *class importing, type-closure checking, is-a relationship finding, instance importing*, and *transforming*. In our approach, this is an interactive process; this requires only simple interactions with a user, except during the is-a relationship finding phase. An illustrative example is shown in Figure 3. Here, the virtual database VDB_1 (Figure 1(b)) is created on top of the base DB_1 (Figure 1(a)). The inputs provided by the user are represented in italics. We now describe each phase of the creation process by using this example.

CLASS IMPORTING PHASE:

    import-class *Person*;

    import-class *TA*;

    import-class *Professor*;

TYPE-CLOSURE CHECKING PHASE:

    Automatic checking? *no*

    Person: ssno, name
    Delete property? *no*

    TA: ssno, name, major, empno
    Delete property? *yes*
    empno

    Department: dname, has_staff
    Delete property? *yes*
    has_staff

    Professor: ssno, name, empno, professor_of
    Delete propertey? *yes*
    empno

IS-A RELATIONSHIP FINDING PHASE:

INSTANCE IMPORTING PHASE:

    Include only direct instances? *no*

TRANSFORMING PHASE:

    add-class *Course*;

    add-attribute *courseno* of domain *String* to *Course*;

    add-attribute *offered_by* of domain *Department* to *Course*;

    add-attribute *instructor* of domain *Professor* to *Course*;

    add-attribute *ta_of* of domain *Course* to *TA*;

    add-class *CS_Professor* subtype of *Professor*
    with derivation *professor_of.dname* = "*CS*";

    add-class *EE_Professor* subtype of *Professor*
    with derivation *professor_of.dname* = "*EE*";

Figure 3: Creation of Virtual Database VDB_1

Class Importing Phase

The user selects classes from DB_1. These classes are copied into the empty VDB_1, but their instances and is-a relationships are not copied. If the user selects all classes of DB_1, the is-a relationships among the classes are also copied into VDB_1; since VDB_1 is type-closed in this special case, the type-closure checking and is-a relationship finding phases are skipped.

Type-Closure Checking Phase

This phase makes VDB_1 type-closed by importing the classes of DB_1 that are recursively referenced by the attributes and methods of the classes in VDB_1 but are not yet imported. It can be done either automatically or through interaction with the user. The automatic checking is a typical approach [HZ90, Run92, TYI88], but may import classes in which the user is not interested. Hence, we provide an alternative approach, allowing the user to import only the classes that are really needed. In this approach, the user examines each class of VDB_1 and deletes its properties (i.e., attributes and/or methods) that he/she does not want to see. This deletion may substantially reduce the number of classes that are imported during this phase. In Figure 3, only **Department** is imported by the interactive checking. However, if the automatic checking is used, **Department** and **Staff** are imported even though the user is not interested in **Staff**.

Is-a Relationship Finding Phase

This phase is done without any user interaction (see Figure 3). The transitive closure of is-a relationships (TC) for DB_1 is first computed. Note that the TC for DB1 may exist if another virtual database has already been created on top of DB_1, in which case it is not recomputed. The TC for VDB_1 is then derived from the TC for DB_1. The is-a relationships that are not redundant[3] are found from this derived TC for VDB_1, and are created in VDB_1 [RB92]. Finally, the properties of the classes in VDB_1 are placed into the proper location in the class lattice. For example, class **TA** inherits the attribute *major* from class **Graduate** in DB_1. Also, since the user did not delete attribute *major* from **TA** during the type-closure checking phase, *major* is supposed to be an inherited attribute of **TA** in VDB_1. However, it is obvious that **TA** cannot inherit *major* from its only superclass **Person** in VDB_1. Hence, *major* is changed from an inherited attribute into a directly-defined attribute of **TA** in VDB_1 as shown in Figure 1(b).

Instance Importing Phase

For each class C_i of VDB_1, the direct instances of its base class (of DB_1) are copied into C_i. The user is then asked to decide whether he/she is interested in both direct and indirect instances or only direct instances of DB_1. If only direct instances are of interest, nothing is further done. Otherwise (which is the case in our example), for each class C_i of VDB_1, the indirect instances of its base class, that are not the indirect instances of C_i, are copied into C_i.

Transforming Phase

The user changes the schema of VDB_1, to modify VDB_1 into the desired form. *Schema manipulation operations* are used for doing this, which are based upon the schema evolution operations from ORION [BKKK87]; this includes operations for adding, hiding, and renaming of classes, attributes, or methods, as well as adding and hiding is-a relationships. However, the operations for adding classes (and attributes) are extended, so that classes (and attributes) can be derived from other classes (and attributes) based on derivation predicates. We adopt the method of specifying predicate-based derived classes and attributes from SDM [HM81].

The schema manipulation operations also associate imported instances with new attributes and/or methods that their base instances do not have. For example, in Figure 1(b), the imported instances of **TA** of VDB_1 have the attribute *ta_of* and may have values for this attribute. However, their base instances in DB_1 (Figure 1(a)) do not have this attribute. Note that after the transforming phase, VDB_1 becomes Figure 1(b), except for the local instances of **Course**. These local instances are created later (see Section 3.6).

3.4 Virtual Database Creation with Multiple Bases

The process of creating a new virtual database with multiple bases is divided into the following phases: *class importing, type-closure checking, is-a relationship finding, additional importing and integrating*, and *transforming*. Like the single-base case, it requires only simple interactions with a user in each phase, except during the is-a relationship finding phase. However, before it begins, the user is asked to select one base among the bases, from which the new virtual database will import the most classes. This selected base is termed the *primary base*. An example creation process is shown in Figure 4(c). Here, the virtual database VDB_3, shown in Figure 4(b), is created on top of the virtual databases VDB_1 and VDB_2, shown in Figure 1(b) and Figure 4(a), respectively.

---
[3] The transitivity of is-a relationship produces redundant is-a relationships in the TCs.

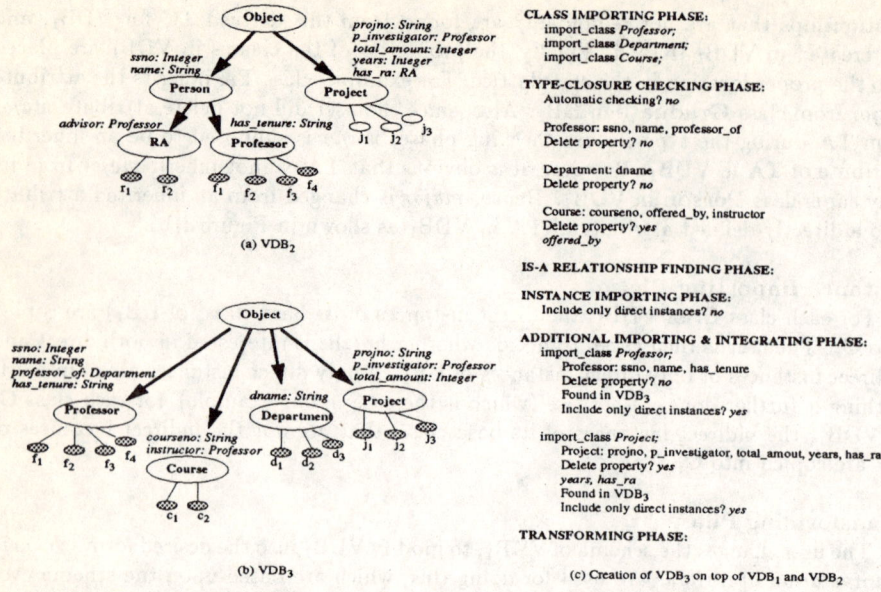

Figure 4: Creation of Virtual Database VDB_3

Suppose that the user wants to import {**Professor, Department, Course**} from VDB_1 and {**Professor, Project**} from VDB_2. Since more classes are to be imported from VDB_1, the user selects VDB_1 as the primary base. After this selection, the creation process begins.

Class Importing - Instance Importing Phases

The class importing, type-closure checking, is-a relationship finding, and instance importing phases are similar to the corresponding phases of the single-base creation process. In Figure 4(c), the classes **Professor, Department**, and **Course** are imported from VDB_1, and the attribute *offered_by* is deleted from **Course**. The direct and indirect instances of these classes are also imported from VDB_1. After these four phases, VDB_3 becomes a virtual database created on top of VDB_1.

Additional Importing and Integrating Phase

This phase imports classes and their instances from VDB_2, and integrates them into VDB_3. This phase operates similarly to the previous four phases; it consists of the following steps: class importing, type-closure checking, integrating, and instance importing. Suppose that the user selects a class C_i from VDB_2. The class importing and type-closure checking steps are similar to the corresponding phases of the single-base creation process. In the integrating step, the classes imported during the type-closure checking step as well as C_i need to be integrated into VDB_3. Hence, for each of these classes, say C_j, the following is done. If C_j is in VDB_3, its properties are merged into C_j of VDB_3.

If C_j is not in VDB_3 but is the same as the class C_j' with a different name in VDB_3, its properties are merged into C_j'. Otherwise, the user finds the direct superclass(es) and subclass(es) of C_j from VDB_3, by comparing their properties and instances with those of C_j. After this, C_j is integrated into VDB_3. The instance importing step is similar to the instance importing phase of the single-base creation process, except that an imported instance may be merged with an instance of VDB_3 if both instances indicate the same instance. This concludes the additional importing and integrating phase.

In Figure 4(c), the user first imports the class **Professor** from VDB_2, and deletes no properties from this class. Since all classes referenced by the properties of **Professor** are already in VDB_3, they need not be imported. Then, the properties and instances of **Professor** are merged into those of **Professor** of VDB_3. **Professor** of VDB_3 now has two base classes: **Professor** of VDB_1 and **Professor** of VDB_2. Similarly, each of its instances has two base instances; for example, f_1 has f_1 of VDB_1 and f_1 of VDB_2. Next, the user imports the class **Project** from VDB_2, and it is integrated into VDB_3 similar to **Professor**.

Transforming Phase

This phase is identical to the corresponding phase of the single-base creation process.

3.5 Schema Change and Deletion

The schema of a virtual database VDB_i can be changed in two different ways: simply changing the schema, and importing classes from the underlying database and/or other virtual databases including the bases of VDB_i. In the former case, schema change can be allowed if VDB_i is not a base of another virtual database. The schema manipulation operations used for the transforming phase of the creation process are also used for accomplishing this change. Otherwise, a new virtual database that includes the desired schema changes is created on top of VDB_i (i.e., like a schema version).

In the latter case, importing is allowed if VDB_i is not a base of another virtual database, and no cycle appears in the virtual database derivation graph as a result. The additional importing and integrating phase of the multiple-base creation process is used for accomplishing this importing. Otherwise, a new virtual database is created on top of VDB_i and those virtual databases from which the importing is expected.

Finally, a user may want to delete a virtual database VDB_i which is no longer needed. VDB_i can be deleted only if it is not a base of another virtual database.

3.6 Instance Manipulation

Users can manipulate the instances of a virtual database in a way similar to how they manipulate the instances of a typical database. *Instance manipulation operations* are used for doing this: operations for creating and deleting an instance, changing and retrieving the value of an attribute of an instance, and executing a method on an instance. The semantics of the operation for creating a new instance for an imported class depends upon whether a virtual database is specified (by the definer) as *strongly dependent* or *weakly dependent* on its bases.

We first explain how creating an instance for an imported class C_i is handled in a virtual database VDB_i. If VDB_i is defined as strongly dependent, this operation first chooses one base class (e.g., C_j) of C_i, and simply invokes the same operation for C_j in the base to which C_j belongs. On the other hand, if VDB_i is defined as weakly dependent, this operation first creates a local instance for C_i in VDB_i. This local instance is then imported into each virtual database that directly or indirectly imports other instances of C_i from VDB_i. This case indicates that an imported class (e.g., C_i) may have imported instances as well as local instances in a weakly dependent virtual database. For example, suppose that VDB_1 (Figure 1(b)) is the only virtual database created on top of the database DB_1 (Figure 1(a)). Consider the operation of creating an instance for the imported class **TA** of VDB_1. If VDB_1 is defined as strongly dependent on DB_1, this operation first finds the base class of **TA** (i.e., **TA** of DB_1), creates a local instance (e.g., t_3) for **TA** of DB_1, and imports t_3 from DB_1 into **TA** of VDB_1. On the other hand, if VDB_1 is weakly dependent, the operation simply creates a local instance (e.g., t_3) for **TA** of VDB_1.

We now consider the other instance manipulation operations. First, creating an instance for a derived class is prohibited. We do not allow derived classes and attributes to be updated because of the ambiguities that may arise in the course of updating [CM89]. Creating an instance for a local class is handled in the same fashion as for an imported class in a weakly dependent virtual database. In Figure 1(b), creating instances for the derived classes **CS_Professor** and **EE_Professor** are prohibited; creating instances for the local class **Course** is done by simply creating local instances (e.g., c_1, c_2) for the class.

Deleting an instance t_i is not allowed if t_i is a direct instance of a derived class. If t_i is a local instance, this operation simply deletes t_i from VDB_i,[4] and each virtual database that directly or indirectly imports t_i from VDB_i. If t_i is an imported instance, the operation chooses one base instance of t_i, and simply deletes t_i in the base (of VDB_i) to which this base instance belongs. In Figure 1(b), deleting the local instance c_1 is done by deleting it from VDB_1; deleting the imported instance t_1 is done by deleting t_1 from both DB_1 and VDB_1. However, deleting the imported instance f_1 is not allowed since f_1 is a direct instance of the derived class **CS_Professor**.

If t_i is a direct instance of a derived class, or a_i is a derived attribute, then changing the value of a_i of t_i is not allowed. Otherwise, we check whether t_i has a value for a_i. If so, the operation simply changes the value. Otherwise, it changes the value of a_i of t_i in the bases of VDB_i, each of which has t_i as an instance. In Figure 1(b), consider the (imported) instance t_1 of the class **TA**. Changing the value of the attribute ta_of of t_1 is done by simply changing the value into a new value in VDB_1; however, changing the values of the attributes $ssno$, $name$, and $major$ of t_1 is done by changing the values of these attributes for the base instance of t_1 (i.e., t_1 of DB_1). Also, changing the associated attribute values of the (local) instance c_1 of the class **Course** is done by simply changing the values in VDB_1.

Now, consider retrieving the value of an attribute a_i for an instance t_i. If t_i has the value for a_i, this operation simply returns the value. Otherwise, it checks whether a_i is a derived attribute. If so, the operation retrieves the values of the attributes (from which a_i is derived) of t_i, applies the derivation predicate of a_i to these retrieved values, and returns the result[5]. Otherwise, it retrieves the value of a_i of t_i in the bases of VDB_i, each

---

[4] Deleting an instance from a class but not from a virtual database can be achieved by repeatedly creating and deleting an instance, as well as changing the value of an attribute of an instance.

[5] This indicates that the values of derived attributes are not stored, but are computed on demand.

of which has t_i as an instance. In Figure 1(b), retrieving the value of an attribute ta_of of the instance t_1 is done by simply retrieving the value in VDB_1; however, retrieving the values of the attributes *ssno*, *name*, and *major* of t_1 is done by retrieving the values of these attributes for the base instance of t_1 (i.e., t_1 of DB_1).

Finally, consider executing a method m_i on an instance t_i. If t_i is a local instance, or m_i was newly created in (i.e., not imported into) VDB_i, this operation simply executes this method in VDB_i. Otherwise, it executes m_i on t_i in the bases of VDB_i, each of which has t_i as an instance. In Figure 1(b), suppose that a method has_major was originally created for **TA** of DB_1, and becomes a method of **TA** of VDB_1 during the process of creating VDB_1. Then, executing has_major on the instance t_1 of VDB_1 is done by executing it on the base instance of t_1 (i.e., t_1 of DB_1).

4 Applications of Virtual Databases to Views and Versions

A virtual database VDB_i can clearly be used as a schema view. Here, VDB_i is created on top of one or more bases, and typically imports some (but not all) classes from its bases. Each class of VDB_i must be either an imported class or a derived class computed from imported classes. VDB_i must also have only imported instances. Thus, it must be defined as strongly dependent on its bases, so that it has no local instances. The equivalent of schema views created on top of other schema views can be achieved in our approach by creating virtual databases on top of other virtual databases. However, by contrast with other schema view approaches, virtual databases contain imported instances. The virtual database VDB_4 shown in Figure 5(a) represents a schema view created on top of the database DB_1, which includes only information about employees[6].

A virtual database VDB_i can also be used as a schema version. In this case, since a schema version represents a database evolution [BKKK87, LBM90], VDB_i must be created on top of only one base and typically imports all classes therefrom. VDB_i can contain imported, derived, or local classes. Adding local instances to imported classes is allowed in VDB_i. This indicates that VDB_i must be defined as weakly dependent on its base. Clearly, the equivalent of schema versions of a schema version can be achieved by creating virtual databases on top of a virtual database. Compared with the schema version approach proposed in [KC88], our approach is somewhat limited, in the sense that instance versioning is not used. However, this limitation actually allows us to avoid the problems of complicated instance manipulation of [KC88]. The virtual database VDB_5 shown in Figure 5(b) represents a schema version of DB_1; it is created by adding a local class **School** to DB_1.

We have observed that a virtual database can be used as a schema view or a schema version. Since a virtual database can be created on top of one or more virtual databases, it follows that a schema view can be created on top of one or more schema versions, and a schema version of a schema view can also be created. Note that a schema version can have only one base. The virtual database VDB_6 in Figure 5(d) represents a schema view on top of the schema version VDB_5, which includes only information about professors, departments, and schools. Also, the virtual database VDB_7 in Figure 5(c)

---

[6] Note that Figure 5 omits instances for simplicity.

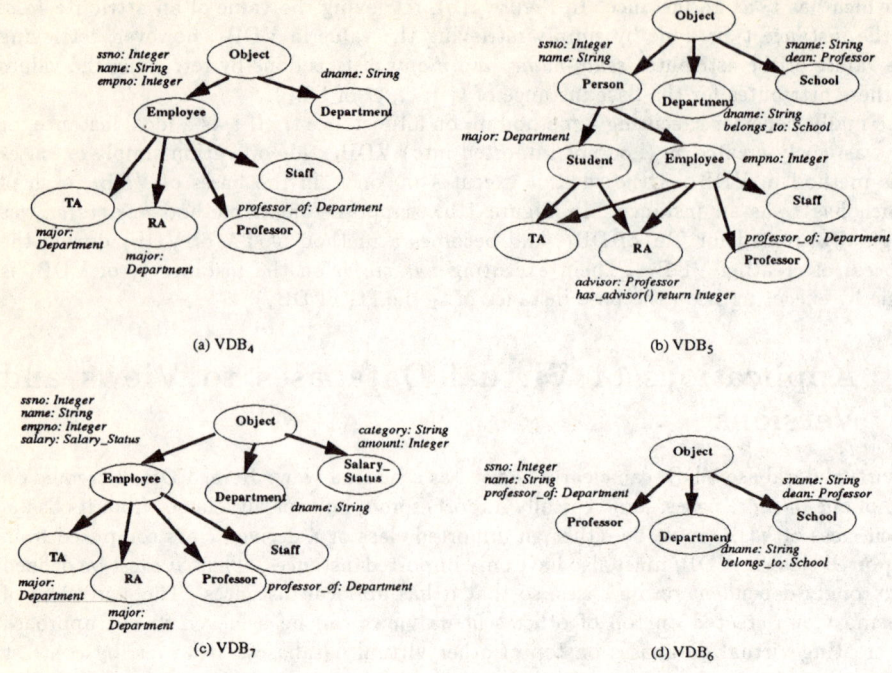

Figure 5: Example Usages of Virtual Databases

represents a schema version of the schema view VDB_4; it is created by adding a local class **Salary_Status** to VDB_4.

The creation processes described in Sections 3.3 and 3.4 indicate that a virtual database VDB_i can be created by importing some (but not all) classes from its base(s), and adding local classes. This VDB_i represents a combination of a schema view and a schema version, which is neither of them alone. Regardless of whether VDB_i is defined as strongly or weakly dependent, it is different from a schema view, in the sense that it contains local classes (and instances) that are neither imported nor derived. Further, VDB_i is not a schema version. If it has multiple bases, or it is defined as strongly dependent, it is obviously different from a schema version. If it has only one base and is defined as weakly dependent, VDB_i may look like a schema version, but is still different. In particular, VDB_i is created by importing only some classes of its base and transforming them, while a schema version is created by importing all classes of a base and transforming them. One may argue that VDB_i can be created by importing all classes of its base and transforming them. However, this could be very expensive since a virtual database often imports only a small number of classes from its base. Further, VDB_i can be created on top of other virtual databases, and vice versa. This indicates that it can be created on top of schema views and/or schema versions, and vice versa. The virtual databases VDB_1 and VDB_2 shown in Figure 1(b) and Figure 4(a) represent this kind of

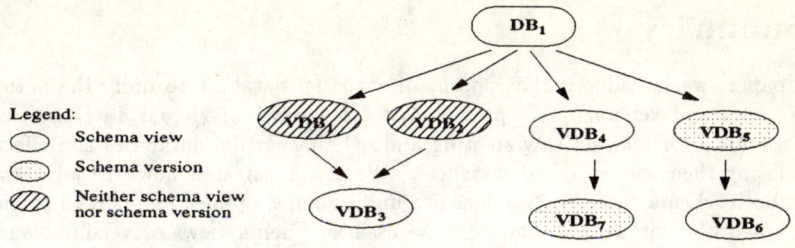

Figure 6: Virtual Database Derivation Graph of DB_1

virtual database. Also, the virtual database VDB_3 in Figure 4(b) represents a schema view on top of VDB_1 and VDB_2.

Finally, since a virtual database can be created on top of other virtual databases, schema views, schema versions, and the combination of schema views and schema versions (for a single underlying database) can be organized into a directed acyclic graph (DAG) rooted at the underlying database. This DAG is actually the virtual database derivation graph for the database. Figure 6 shows the derivation graph of the database DB_1, which includes all examples considered in this section.

5 An Experimental Prototype Implementation

An initial experimental prototype implementation of the virtual database mechanism described in this paper has been developed. In order to allow this proof-of-concept system to be rapidly produced, we chose to build it using another existing research system available to us. In particular, the Remote-Exchange experimental system developed at USC supports the sharing and exchange of information among a federation of database components [FGMS93]. Here, a core object data model, similar to that used in this paper, is employed as the basis for class, instance, and method sharing among database systems.

In our prototype virtual database mechanism, a component in the federation is used for each virtual database. The Remote-Exchange class, object, and method importation techniques are employed to simulate the connections between virtual databases. As the Remote-Exchange prototype supports actual Iris [FBC+87] and Omega [Gea91] databases, this has allowed us to experiment with the virtual database approach. The initial user interface to the virtual database mechanism is limited and menu-based; we are presently developing a graphical interface that provides additional prescriptive guidance to users for defining and managing virtual databases.

Conceptually, since all virtual databases are derived from an underlying database, the Remote-Exchange approach is more general than is necessary, viz., it supports sharing among autonomous database systems. However, using Remote-Exchange has allowed us to explore interesting relationships between the notion of virtual databases on the one hand, and the notion of sharing among existing database systems on the other.

6 Summary

In this paper, we introduced the concept of a virtual database to unify the notions of schema views and versions. We presented the semantics of virtual databases as well as a mechanism for interactively creating and deleting virtual databases and effectively manipulating their schemas and instances. We also illustrated how virtual databases support both schema views and versions in a unified and simplified manner. In particular, we examined how virtual databases can be used as schema views or versions, and how they can support the cases that have not been adequately addressed by the previous schema view and schema version approaches. Finally, we briefly discussed the issues related to an experimental prototype implementation.

References

[AB91] S. Abiteboul and A. Bonner. Objects and views. In *Proceedings of the ACM SIGMOD International Conference on Management of Data*. ACM SIGMOD, May 1991.

[ABD+89] M. Atkinson, F. Bancilhon, D. DeWitt, K. Dittrich, D. Maier, and S. Zdonik. The object-oriented database system manifesto. In *Proceedings of the 1st International Conference on Deductive and Object-Oriented Databases*, December 1989.

[AM89] H. Afsarmanesh and D. McLeod. The 3DIS: An extensible, object-oriented information management environment. *ACM Transactions on Information Systems*, 7(3):339–377, October 1989.

[ASL89] A. M. Alashqur, S. Y. W. Su, and H. Lam. OQL: A query language for manipulating object-oriented databases. In *Proceedings of the International Conference on Very Large Databases*. VLDB Endowment, August 1989.

[BCG+87] J. Banerjee, H. Chou, J. Garza, W. Kim, D. Woelk, N. Ballou, and H. Kim. Data model issues for object-oriented applications. *ACM Transactions on Office Information Systems*, 5(1):3–26, January 1987.

[Ber92] E. Bertino. A view mechanism for object-oriented databases. In *Proceedings of the International Conference on Extending Database Technology*, 1992.

[BKKK87] J. Banerjee, W. Kim, H.-J. Kim, and H. F. Korth. Semantics and implementation of schema evolution in object-oriented databases. In *Proceedings of the ACM SIGMOD International Conference on Management of Data*. ACM SIGMOD, May 1987.

[CM89] I. A. Chen and D. McLeod. Derived data update in semantic databases. In *Proceedings of the International Conference on Very Large Databases*. VLDB Endowment, August 1989.

[FBC+87] D. Fishman, D. Beech, H. Cate, E. Chow, T. Connors, T. Davis, N. Derrett, C. Hoch, W. Kent, P. Lyngbaek, B. Mahbod, M. Neimat, T. Ryan, and

M. Shan. Iris: An object-oriented database management system. *ACM Transactions on Office Information Systems*, 5(1):48–69, January 1987.

[FGMS93] D. Fang, S. Ghandeharizadeh, D. McLeod, and A. Si. Implementation and evaluation of an object-based sharing mechanism for federated database systems. In *Proceedings of the International Conference on Data Engineering*. IEEE, April 1993.

[Gea91] S. Ghandeharizadeh et al. Design and implementation of OMEGA object-based system. Technical Report USC-CS, Computer Science Department, University of Southern California, Los Angeles, CA 90089-0781, September 1991.

[HM81] M. Hammer and D. McLeod. Database description with SDM: A semantic database model. *ACM Transactions on Database Systems*, 6(3):351–386, September 1981.

[HZ90] S. Heiler and S. Zdonik. Object views: Extending the vision. In *Proceedings of the International Conference on Data Engineering*. IEEE, 1990.

[KC88] W. Kim and H. Chou. Versions of schema for object-oriented databases. In *Proceedings of the International Conference on Very Large Databases*. VLDB Endowment, September 1988.

[Kim89] W. Kim. A model of queries for object-oriented databases. In *Proceedings of the International Conference on Very Large Databases*. VLDB Endowment, August 1989.

[LBM90] Q. Li, K. J. Byeon, and D. McLeod. An experimental system for conceptual evolution in object databases. In B. Srinivasan and J. Zeleznikow, editors, *Proceedings of the Australian Database Research Conference*, February 1990.

[LRV88] C. Lecluse, P. Richard, and F. Velez. O_2, an object-oriented data model. In *Proceedings of the ACM SIGMOD International Conference on Management of Data*. ACM SIGMOD, June 1988.

[Mot87] A. Motro. Superviews: Virtual integration of multiple databases. *IEEE Transactions on Software Engineering*, SE-13(7), 1987.

[MSOA86] D. Maier, J. Stein, A. Otis, and Purdy A. Development of an object-oriented DBMS. In *Proceedings of the Conference on Object-Oriented Programming Systems, Languages, and Applications*. ACM, September 1986.

[RB92] E. A. Rundensteiner and L. Bic. Automatic view schemata generation in object-oriented databases. Technical Report 92-15, University of California, Irvine, January 1992.

[Run92] E. A. Rundensteiner. MultiView: A methodology for supporting multiple views in object-oriented databases. In *Proceedings of the International Conference on Very Large Databases*. VLDB Endowment, 1992.

[Sci91]   E. Sciore. Multidimensional versioning for object-oriented databases. In *Proceedings of the 2nd International Conference on Deductive and Object-Oriented Databases*, December 1991.

[SLM91] M. H. Scholl, C. Laasch, and Tresch M. Updatable views in object-oriented databases. In *Proceedings of the 2nd International Conference on Deductive and Object-Oriented Databases*, December 1991.

[SZ86]   A. H. Skarra and S. B. Zdonik. The management of changing types in an object-oriented database. In *Proceedings of the Conference on Object-Oriented Programming Systems, Languages, and Applications*, 1986.

[TS93]   M. Tresch and M. H. Scholl. Schema transformation without database reorganization. *ACM SIGMOD Record*, 22(1), March 1993.

[TYI88]   K. Tanaka, M. Yoshikawa, and K. Ishihara. Schema virtualization in object-oriented databases. In *Proceedings of the International Conference on Data Engineering*. IEEE, January 1988.

Abstract View Objects for Multiple OODB Integration

Qiming Chen and Ming-Chien Shan
Database Technology Department
HP Laboratories
Palo Alto, California 94034
qchen@hpl.hp.com, shan@hpl.hp.com

Abstract

The notion of **Abstract View Object** (AVO) is introduced to support abstract representations of foreign or integrated objects in a multidatabase environment. This approach allows OODBs to be cooperated without physical integration, underlies a consistent universal object identification mechanism, and provides an intuitive set-theoretic foundation for linking object identification, object integration and function inheritance semantically over multidatabases.

1 Introduction

In a multiple Object-Oriented Database (OODB) environment, conceptually related objects are often physically distributed in multiple autonomous sources. Interoperating such databases requires the handling of *foreign objects* and multi-sourced *integrated objects*. A foreign object is used in a database but managed by another. An *integrated object* unifies the *underlying objects* stored in different databases but representing the same entity in reality [6] [10] [11]. Integrating an area's geographic and transportation information, which are stored in different databases but overlapping each other, is an example.

Since the management autonomy and media versatility of different databases, a foreign object or a multi-sourced integrated object required by a database is only *registered* in that database, the actual data values are *imported* at run-time if necessary [14] [13], very often, a function applied to a foreign object, or a foreign part of an integrated object, is pushed down to its home database.

We propose using **Abstract View Object** (AVO) to provide an abstract representation of a foreign or integrated object. This approach allows OODBs to be cooperated without physical integration, allows objects to be globally referred consistently, and provides an intuitive set-theoretic foundation for object integration and function inheritance over multidatabases.

We shall first extend an object identifier (OID) from a single-term to an *oid-set*. The *oid-set* for a native object, i.e., an object which is not an integration of any object other than itself, is a singleton, and the *oid-set* for an integrated object is the union of *oid-sets* of its underlying objects. An AVO describes an object in terms of its *oid-set*. In a multiple homogeneous OODBs environment, or in a multiple heterogeneous OODBs environment with an appropriate data exchange standard, an AVO can be created in any participating OODB, used in any application, and exported to any OODB with a unique identifier. Such a simple treatment offers the following significant features:

- An AVO representing the same (one or more) underlying objects is identified uniquely and consistently over multidatabases, regardless of *when* and *where* it is created.

- AVOs express intrinsic links of objects stored in different databases, and serve as logical indices to the actual data, regardless of their heterogeneity (e.g. text, image, ...etc).

- The relationships between AVOs generated for different application domains but with overlapping underlying objects, are globally tractable.

- Generating AVOs has no *intrusiveness* [5] to the existing objects of any database.

- Cross-database AVO type hierarchy and function inheritance can be easily supported.

Different from *value-based views*, AVOs are primarily used as logic indices to the objects which are conceptually related but physically distributed. This feature provides a flexible way for dealing with *multimedia objects* managed by autonomous databases. Moreover, the use of *oid-sets* leads to a set-theoretic semantics of cross-database object integration and function inheritance. Like value-based views, AVOs are defined by deductive rules. Unlike value-based views, AVO derivations only result in *oid-sets*. Functions may be inherited by AVOs from underlying databases, or defined on AVOs for dealing with cross-database applications.

AVO manipulations are *oid-set* based and in connection with object integrations. Although our this focus differs from some existing efforts on object calculus such as [16] [15] [17] [7] [2] [4] [8], we share the similar view to incorporating OIDs into the semantics of object calculus for providing abstract object representations.

2 Oid-Set based Universal Object Identification

Handling AVOs requires identifying objects universally and consistently, in the presence of object importation and integration.

The current object identification approaches commonly follow a basic principle, the OID atomicity principle, that is, an OID is a single term which is either a literal or a concatenation of several literals (such as the concatenation of database, type and instance identifiers) but *not a set*. Under this principle, the typical approach for identifying an imported or integrated object in a database is to *generate* a new, single-term OID for it. This new OID either replaces or maps to the OIDs of underlying objects in the same database. However, changing the OID of an underlying object O requires maintaining all the relationships involving O (e.g. instance OIDs of any type possessed by O, stored functions, i.e. data records, involving O or its supertype and subtype objects), and therefore causes update propagations. The use of OID mappings brings the above maintenance difficulty from an one-time object integration to every run-time object manipulation. Cross-database OID mappings are even more difficult to maintain.

Furthermore, such a mechanism obviously does not guarantee the imported or integrated objects with the same underlying objects to be identified uniquely and consistently in different databases or database operation sessions.

An intuitive solution to the above problem is to *relax the OID atomicity principle* by extending an OID from a single term to an **oid-set**. Every object is then uniquely identified by an *oid-set* where the *oid-set* for a native object is just a singleton, and the *oid-set* for an integrated object *contains* those of its underlying objects. To ensure the right part of an *oid-set* to be used at the right place, the notion of **effective oid-set** is also introduced. This idea is very close to reality, as for example, a person may have a set of identifiers such as ATM-CARD#, MASTER-CARD#, DRIVERS-LICENSE#, each associated with different (possibly overlapping) information and used in different situations.

Oid-Set and Home-Tag-Set

The *oid-set* of object O, denoted by μO, is expressed as

$$\mu O = \{d_0.s_0, d_1.s_1, ..., d_n.s_n\}$$

where $d_i.s_i$ is an *element-oid*, the prefix d_i is a database identifier called *home-tag* and the suffix s_i is a surrogate in that database.

The *home-tag-set* of O is denoted by ηO and defined as

$$\eta O = \{d | d.s \in \{d_0.s_0, d_1.s_1, ..., d_n.s_n\}\}$$

For example, the native object with *oid-set* $\{d_0.s_0\}$ has *home-tag-set* $\{d_0\}$; the integrated object with *oid-set* $\{d_0.s_0, d_1.s_1, d_1.s_2\}$ has *home-tag-set* $\{d_0, d_1\}$.

The notion of object *home-tag-set* can be extended to the notion of type *home-tag-set* easily. For a type T with its underlying types defined in the set of distinct databases identified by $d_0, d_1, ..., d_n$, its *home-tag-set* is denoted by ηT and defined as

$$\eta T = \{d_0, d_1, ..., d_n\}$$

The *home-tag-set* of a native type defined on database d is simply the singleton $\{d\}$. The *home-tag-set* of an integrated type is the union of the ones of its underlying types. A type can be the underlying type of itself.

To associate *oid-sets* with types for supporting type related inheritance, the notion of *effective oid-set* is introduced. The *effective oid-set of an object wrt a type* is the subset of its *oid-set* with such a *home-tag-set* that is the intersection of the *home-tag-sets* of the object and the type.

Effective Oid-Set of an Object wrt a Type

Let O be an object with *oid-set* μO and *home-tag-set* ηO, T be a type with *home-tag-set* ηT. The *effective oid-set* of O wrt T, denoted by $\mu_T O$, is defined as

$$\mu_T O = \{d.s | d.s \in \mu O \land d \in \eta O \bigcap \eta T\}$$

It is clear that
$$\mu_T O \subseteq \mu O$$
and
$$\eta \mu_T O = \eta O \bigcap \eta T$$

For example, given integrated object O with *oid-set* $\{d_0.s_0, d_1.s_1\}$ and type T with *home-tag-set* $\{d_1\}$, $\mu_T O = \{d_1.s_1\}$.

The use of *oid-sets*, together with a proper OID exchange standard, offers a simple solution to the development of universal OIDs, which supports not only OID *uniqueness* but also OID *spatial stability* and *temporal stability*, namely, a foreign or integrated object with the same set of underlying objects can be uniquely identified in any database and in any import/export session. The *oid-set* of a foreign or integrated object is never "assimilated" (re-assigned) by any local database. Object integration has no "intrusiveness" to the existing *oid-sets* of any database. The *oid-sets* union of all AVOs over multidatabases always remains the same as the *oid-sets* union of the native objects in those databases.

Oid-sets can be implemented on the basis of variable length OIDs [12] [9]. In an environment involving multiple OODB of the same type, such as multiple OpenODB systems [6], an *oid-set* can also be represented by the combination of several fixed length *element-oid* fields with a header indicating the number of them. It is this fact that the *oid-set* cardinality of an integrated object is limited to, and often smaller than the number of interoperating databases. The *home-tags* of native objects and types can be ignored by default to reduce the memory cost.

The proposed AVO approach aims at providing abstract representations of foreign and integrated objects in a way independent of physical object importation and integration. The concept of *oid-set* provides a basis for achieving this goal. AVO instances are identified by *oid-sets*, and *oid-sets* are setwise manipulatable, that provides an intuitive set-theoretic foundation for developing an AVO based semantics for linking object identification, object integration and function inheritance over multidatabases. In fact, unable to provide such semantic links, is the fundamental drawback of single-term OID based approaches.

Since this work is primarily concerned with the interoperability of multidatabases, we can simplify our discussion by assuming that a native object is unique in its home database, which is referred to as *Unique Native Object Assumption*. This consideration constitutes a reason for not introducing "type tag" to express an *element-oid* as *db.type.surrogate*; other reasons for that are: one object may have multiple types, and there already exist function resolution mechanisms in a single database without using OID "type tag". An "effective *oid-set*" based function resolution mechanism is to be introduced latter, which aims at turning multidatabase oriented function resolution to a single database oriented function resolution, without overriding the function resolution mechanism supported by autonomous local databases.

In reality, applying a function to an object is usually performed by applying the function to the OID of that object. Therefore, throughout this paper *the uses of an object and its oid-set are exchangeable*. It is also assumed that functions are referred by distinct identifiers (overloading functions have different identifiers).

3 Abstract View Objects

Under our approach, AVOs, as usual objects, are identified by *oid-sets*. AVOs are classified into AVO types. The minimal specification of an AVO type includes the following:

- name;

- functions describing its attributes and operations;

– deduction rules for generating its instances.

Similar to the relational view mechanism where every relation can be considered as a view of itself, every type in an OODB can be considered as an AVO type derived from itself. However, AVOs and AVO generations have the following special features.

- AVO instances are *oid-set* based rather than *value based*.

- AVOs inherit functions defined on its underlying objects. An AVO representing an integrated object, called an *integrated AVO*, inherits functions from each underlying object. An integrated AVO type "upward inherits" functions defined on the underlying types from different databases. Upward inheritance is partial inheritance between types which is essentially based on the inheritance between objects. Functions can be defined on an AVO type for describing attributes and operations, in addition to the inherited ones.

- AVOs are derived from objects (or AVOs) of *underlying types* by deduction rules. An AVO type has instances which represent either integrated objects or single objects, from underlying types. Therefore, an AVO type generation is carried out by the following three steps:

    a) Derive integrated AVOs based on specified conditions.

    b) Create an AVO from each object of underlying types.

    c) Union the above two, and then **reduce** the resulted set to ensure that none of AVOs has such a *oid-set* that is a subset of another. This step filters any AVO that already participates in an integrated AVO.

AVO generation rules form a subset of what we developed for dealing with cross-database complex objects [3]. These rules focus to the construction of AVOs and have *oid-sets* as the only domain of atomic values. Constructs of rules include *types*, *terms*, *logical connectives* and *comparison operators*. A term is either an *element-oid*, a variable, a function, a constant, or a typed *oid-sets*. Syntactically, if $\forall i \in \{1,..,n\}$ t_i is an *element-oid* then $T{:}\{t_1,..,t_n\}$ is a typed set-term of T. An AVO instance is represented by such a typed set-term. A ground term is one that is free of variables. The special notation $T{:}x$, where x is a variable or a term containing variables, denotes a typed set-term of arbitrary cardinality.

A top-level typed term, or a comparison operator (including $\in$ and $\subseteq$) with arguments, is a formula; the conjunction of formulas is a formula. A rule is specified as **head** ← **body**, where **body** is a formula and **head** is a positive atom; a fact is a ground rule without a body.

A special unification rule for (and only for) *oid-sets*, called *oid-set intersection-union unification rule*, is introduced. Under this rule, two *oid-sets* match each other if they have non-empty intersection, and their *union* can be derived for representing an integrated object. Functions on *oid-sets*, such as *union* and *intersection*, are pre-defined.

The example given in Figure 1 shows how AVOs provide abstract views to multi-sourced objects and link object identification, object integration and function inheritance over multidatabases semantically. This example is based on the following information.

- **env** is an AVO type representing the integration of underlying types **area_trans_info** and **geo_info**, where **area_trans_info** is native to database d_0, and **geo_info** is imported to d_0 from database d_1. An AVO instance of **env** represents either an *integrated object*, or a *native object*, from these underlying types.

- O and O'_0 are instances of **env**. O is formed by O_0 of type **area_trans_info** and O_1 of type **geo_info**. O'_0 is directly mapped from itself under type **area_trans_info**. The *oid-set* of O_1 is $\{d_1.s_1\}$. The *oid-sets* of O_0 and O'_0 are $\{d_0.s_0\}$ and $\{d_0.s'_0\}$ respectively.

- Stored function *geo_code* is defined on type **geo_info**, and

    $geo\_code(\{d_1.s_1\}) = \text{'W4-01-02'}$,

    stored function *area_name* is defined on type **area_trans_info**, and

    $area\_name(\{d_0.s_0\}) = \text{'Santa Clara'}$,
    $area\_name(\{d_0.s'_0\}) = \text{'Tracy'}$.

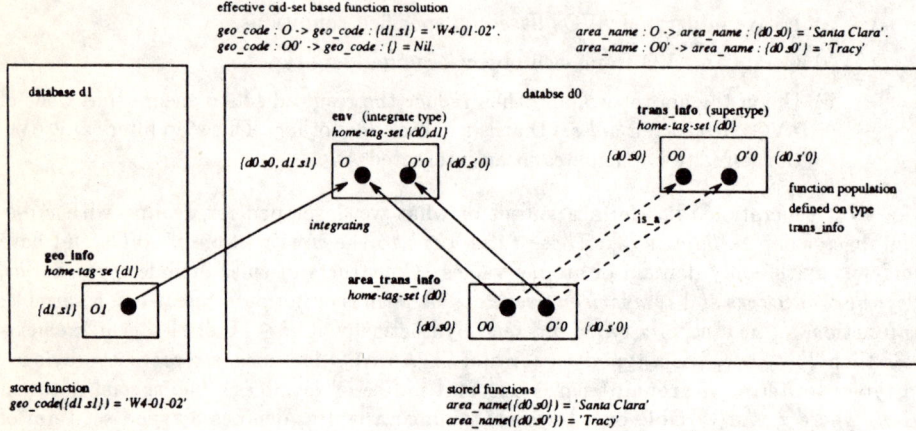

Figure 1: Multidatabase based Abstract View Objects

The notion of **object integration** is directly linked with oid-set union. For instance, the *oid-set* of O_0 and O_1 is $\{d_0.s_0\}$ and $\{d_1.s_1\}$ respectively, AVO O is the integrated view of O_0 and O_1, and therefore its *oid-set*, $\{d_0.s_0, d_1.s_1\}$, is the union of them. AVO O'_0 represents the integration of itself so that its *oid-set* remains the same.

AVO generation in this example can be expressed by rules and facts. For instance, the following facts represent a set of *geo_info* objects stored in database d_1, and a set of *area_trans_info* objects stored in database d_0:

$geo\_info:\{d_1.s_1\}$,
$area\_trans\_info:\{d_0.s_0\}$,
$area\_trans\_info:\{d_0.s'_0\}$.

Let geo_id be a function defined on type $area\_trans\_info$ and

$geo\_id(\{d_0.s_0\}) = geo\_code(\{d_1.s_1\})$.

Assume that the geo_info object and $area\_trans\_info$ object with the equal geo_code and geo_id can be integrated. Such an integration is represented by the following rule, where x, y stand for oid-$sets$:

$env{:}x \cup y \leftarrow geo\_info{:}x \;\&\; area\_trans\_info{:}y \;\&\; geo\_code(x) = geo\_id(y)$.

With the above rule and facts, the following AVO can be derived:

$env{:}\{d_0.s_0, d_1.s_1\}$,

Note that besides the above multi-sourced integrated objects, an integrated AVO type also has instances that directly represent underlying objects. The rules used to derive all instance of AVO type env should be

$env{:}x \cup y \leftarrow geo\_info{:}x \;\&\; area\_trans\_info{:}y \;\&\; geo\_code(x) = geo\_id(y)$.
$env{:}z \leftarrow geo\_info{:}z$.
$env{:}z \leftarrow area\_trans\_info{:}z$.

However, the resulted set of AVOs must be *reduced* as described above. Then the derived set of AVOs are represented by the following:

$env{:}\{d_0.s_0, d_1.s_1\}$.
$env{:}\{d_0.s_0'\}$.

The proposed approach tolerates the existing mechanisms for resolving function name conflicts and domain mismatches although discussing a wide spectrum of heterogeneity is not the focus of this paper.

4 Cross-Database AVO Type Hierarchy

We have shown an *oid-set union view to object integration*, which can be formally described by the following, where an object can be an AVO, and a type can be an AVO type.

Object Integration
Integrating objects $O_0, O_1, ..., O_n$ of types $T_0, T_1, ..., T_n$ defined in different databases results in an AVO O, such that the *oid-set* of O is the union of the *oid-sets* of $O_0, O_1,..., O_n$, as

$$\mu O = \bigcup_{i=0}^{n} \mu O_i$$

and it is said that $O_0, O_1,... O_n$ underlie O.

Type integration is the generalization of object integration, which forms an AVO type with instances representing either integrated or native objects from underlying types. A type can be viewed as the integration of itself, and the transitivity of *oid-set* containment provides the basis of *cross-database type hierarchy*. Such a hierarchy is significant for *determining inheritance paths in a multidatabase environment*. The foundation of cross-database object integration hierarchy is the lattice property of the following underlying relationship between AVOs, or in general, between objects.

Underlying Relationship
   Object O_1 underlies object O_2, denoted as $O_1 \sqsubseteq O_2$ iff $\mu O_1 \subseteq \mu O_2$

Theorem 4.1

Lattice Property of Underlying Relationship
The set of objects over multidatabases, including AVOs, form a lattice under the underlying relationship.

> **Proof Skeleton**: Since $O_1 \sqsubseteq O_2$ means $\mu O_1 \subseteq \mu O_2$, $\sqsubseteq$ is reflexive, transitive and antisymmetric. Then the set of cross database objects form a partial order, with a unique *lub* and a unique *glb* for any subset of them.

As usual, we view a class of objects as a set of identifiers of them. From this point of view, generalization is subsumption based [1], namely, the set of OIDs of the supertype objects subsumes that of the subtype objects. *Oid-set* based AVO mechanism provides a natural link between *oid-set union* based integration and *subsumption based* generalization. From a set-theoretic point of view, *generalization is just a special case of integration*. They can be formally compared as follows, where an object may actually mean an AVO.

Integration vs. Generalization

- If O_1 is the underlying object of O_2, then $\mu O_1 \subseteq \mu O_2$.
   If O_1 is the subtype object of O_2, then $\mu O_1 = \mu O_2$.
- If T_1 is the underlying type of T_2, then $\forall O_1 \in C_{T_1} \exists! O_2 \in C_{T_2}(\mu O_1 \subseteq \mu O_2)$
   ($\exists!$ stands for "exist unique")
   If T_1 is the subtype of T_2, then $\forall O_1 \in C_{T_1} \exists! O_2 \in C_{T_2}(\mu O_1 = \mu O_2)$
- If O is the integrated object formed by $O_0, O_1, .., O_n$, then $\eta O = \bigcup_{i=0}^{n} \eta O_i$
   If O is the supertype object of O_0, then $\eta O = \eta O_0$
- If T is the integrated type of $T_0, T_1, .., T_n$, then $\eta T = \bigcup_{i=0}^{n} \eta T_i$
   If T is the supertype of $T_0, T_1, .., T_n$, then $\eta T = \bigcup_{i=0}^{n} \eta T_i$

A cross database generalization relationship example is shown in Figure 2. This example involves six types defined in four databases where trans_info1 is the supertype of bus_trans_info1 in database d_1; trans_info2 is the supertype of bus_trans_info2 in database d_2; bus_trans_info is the integrated AVO type of bus_trans_info1 and bus_trans_info2 generated in database d_3; and trans_info is the integrated AVO type of trans_info1 and trans_info2 generated in database d_4. Referring to the information given in Figure 2, O'_1 is the supertype object of O_1 with the same *oid-set* $\{d_1.s_1\}$; O'_2 is the supertype object of O_2 with the same *oid-set* $\{d_2.s_2\}$. Based on the *oid-set* union semantics of object integration, O representing the integration of O_1 and O_2, and O' representing the integration of O'_1 and O'_2, have the same *oid-set* $\{d_1.s_1, d_2.s_2\}$. More generally, the instances of trans_info *subsume* the instances of bus_trans_info, which allows us to view trans_info in database d_4 as the supertype of bus_trans_info in database d_3, and further, specify a cross-database type generalization hierarchy in the presence of object integration.

Most importantly, the link between integration and generalization allows us to develop a generalized inheritance mechanism.

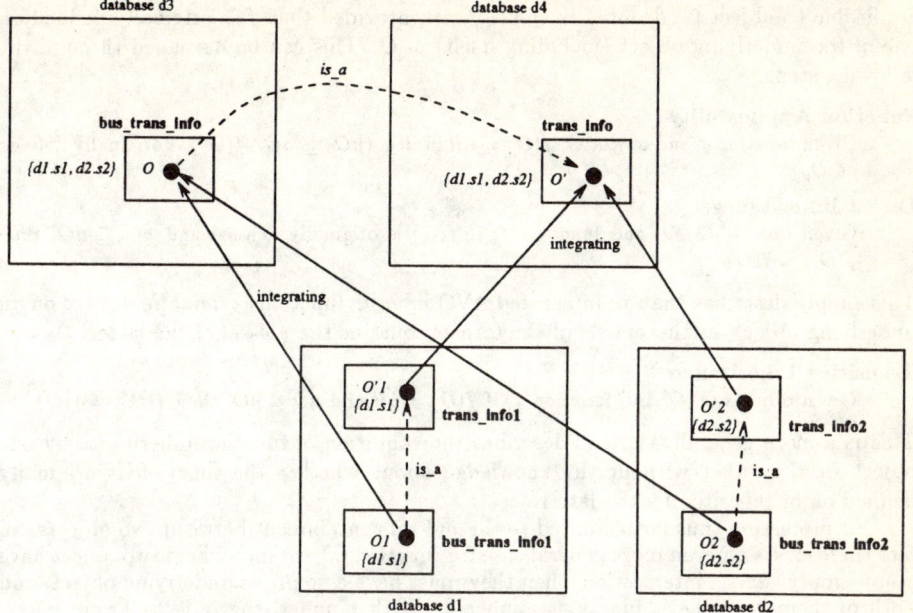

Figure 2: Cross Database Generalization Relationship

5 Cross-Database Inheritance

5.1 Oid-Set Containment based Function Inheritance

Inheritance between AVOs is essentially based on their oid-set containment. In the example shown in Figure 1, integrated AVO O is able to inherit functions defined on its underlying object O_1 since the *oid-set* of O, $\{d_0.s_0, d_1.s_1\}$, contains the *oid-set* of O_1, $\{d_1.s_1\}$; object O'_0 is unable to inherit functions defined on object O_1 since the *oid-set* of O'_0, $\{d_0.s'_0\}$, does not contain the *oid-set* of O_1, $\{d_1.s_1\}$.

Further, we can extend the above example by adding a supertype of area_trans_info called trans_info. Let us assume that *population* is a function defined on type trans_info. It can be fully inherited by the subtype area_trans_info, and partially inherited by the integrated AVO type env. This, somehow, indicates the indirect partial inheritance path between types env and trans_info via type area_trans_info. For example, function *population* defined on O_0 can be inherited by AVO O since the *oid-set* of O, $\{d_0.s_0, d_1.s_1\}$, contains that of O_0, $\{d_0.s_0\}$.

Traditionally function inheritance between a pair of subtype and supertype is based on the *OID equality* relationship, namely, object O_1 of type T_1 can inherit functions defined on object O_2 of type T_2 provided that O_1 has the same OID as O_2. With *oid-set* based AVOs, we can extend such *OID equality* relationship to *oid-set containment* relationship to develop a more generalized function inheritance semantics for multidatabase systems. Such a semantics covers both generalization and integration.

Oid-set containment based semantics of inheritance consists in that function f is applicable to object O, denoted by $f(O) \neq nil$, provided that f is originally defined on one of the underlying object (including itself) of O. This can be discussed through the following steps.

Function Applicability

Given function f and object O, $f(O) \neq nil$ iff $\exists O_0 \ (\mu O_0 \subseteq \mu O \wedge f(O_0)$ is originally defined on $O_0)$.

Direct Inheritance

Given objects O, O' and function f, if $f(O)$ is originally defined and $\mu O \subseteq \mu O'$ then $f(O') = f(O)$.

This simply describes that an integrated AVO inherits functions *originally defined* on an underlying object, as the *oid-set* of the former contains the *oid-set* of the latter.

Transitive Inheritance

Given objects O, O' and function f, if $f(O) \neq nil$ and $\mu O \subseteq \mu O'$ then $f(O') = f(O)$.

This is a more general case that describes the condition of function inheritance by one object from another without the knowledge about whether the function is originally defined on or inherited by the latter.

Our discussion thus far is limited to the *oid-set* containment between two objects. In fact there exists an even more general case for function inheritance where two object have a non-empty *oid-set* intersection, then they must have a common underlying object, and both of them can inherit functions applicable to that underlying object. From *oid-set* overlapping point of view, object O' can inherit function f applicable to object O if

– O and O' are identical with the same *oid-set*, or more generally,

– the *oid-set* of object O' *contains* the *oid-set* of object O, or more generally,

– $\mu O \cap \mu O' \neq \emptyset$, and f is *applicable* to the object identified by $\mu O \cap \mu O'$.

The last case is the most general one which covers the first two. In a multidatabase environment, a real world object may be recorded in multiple data sources as different database objects (e.g. personal, academic, driving, financial, health records of a single person), and it is may not be necessary for an integrated AVO to cover all of them (e.g. one integrated AVO covers personal and academic records, another covers personal and financial records). It is often important to figure out the relationship between those *partially integrated AVOs* over multidatabases. Single-term OIDs cannot be used to compare partially integrated AVOs with overlapping underlying objects, since they are distinct atomic values without any inclusion relationship.

When we say that two integrated AVOs O_1 and O_2 represent some aspects of the same real world object, we are implying certain overlapping relationship between O_1 and O_2. Based on the notion of *oid-set*, such a relationship can be described formally.

ω-meet

The $\omega-meet$ of AVOs O_1 and O_2 is defined as

$$\omega(O_1, O_2) = \mu O_1 \cap \mu O_2$$

O_1 and O_2 are $\omega-meet$ iff

$$\mu O_1 \cap \mu O_2 \neq \emptyset$$

It can be seen that an integrated AVO $\omega-meet$ its underlying objects, and partially integrated AVOs with overlapping underlying objects $\omega-meet$, and thus can be easily associated.

However, $\omega(O, O')$ may not be a defined integrated AVO. For example, assuming that object O is the integration of O_0, O_1, O_2 and O' is the integration of O_0, O_1, O_3, and O_0, O_1, O_2, O_3 are identified by *oid-sets* $\{d_0.s_0\}, \{d_1.s_1\}, \{d_2.s_2\}, \{d_3.s_3\}$ respectively, then O and O' have *oid-sets*

$$\mu O = \{d_0.s_0, d_1.s_1, d_2.s_2\}$$
$$\mu O' = \{d_0.s_0, d_1.s_1, d_3.s_3\}$$

The ω−*meet* of O, O' should be identified by

$$\{d_0.s_0, d_1.s_1\}$$

If incidentally there is no such an integrated AVO actually defined, we can introduce a **virtual oid-set**, as a subset of the *oid-set* of a defined AVO. Under our notion of object integration, a *virtual oid-set* can be simply considered as the *oid-set* for a possible "intermediate" integrated AVO. With this notion the *semantics of oid-set containment based inheritance* can be recursively described by the following theorem, where the ω−*meet* of two AVOs can be identified by a *virtual oid-set*.

Theorem 5.1
ω-meet based Inheritance
Let O, O' be AVOs (in general, objects), and f be a function, and $f(O) \neq nil$. $f(O') = f(O)$ iff O' ω−meet O and $f(\omega(O, O')) = f(O)$.

> **Proof Skeleton:** (if) $f(\omega(O, O')) \neq nil$ implies that $\exists O_0(\mu O_0 \subseteq \mu\omega(O, O') \wedge f(O_0) \neq nil)$. As $\mu O_0 \subseteq \mu\omega(O, O'))$ implies $\mu O_0 \subseteq \mu O$ and $\mu O_0 \subseteq \mu O'$, we have, $f(O') = f(O) = f(O_0)$. (only if) $(f(O') = f(O)) \neq nil$ and the nonexistence of the above O_0 (as a result of $\omega(O, O') = \emptyset$ or $f(\omega(O, O')) = nil$), eventually (through iteration) conflict with the notion of function applicability.

It is clear that the above notions cover both upward and downward inheritances, and underlie both object integration and generalization. Furthermore, they can be easily extended to handle functions with hybrid argument type signatures, as

- Given $f(O_1, ..., O_n) \neq nil$. If $\forall i \in \{1, ..., n\}$ $\mu O_i \subseteq \mu O_i'$, then $f(O_1', ..., O_n') = f(O_1, ..., O_n)$.
- Given $f(O_1, ..., O_n) \neq nil$. $f(O_1', ..., O_n') = f(O_1, ..., O_n)$ iff $\forall i \in \{1, ..., n\}$ O_i' ω−meet O_i and $f(\omega(O_1, O_1'), ..., \omega(O_n, O_n')) = f(O_1, ..., O_n)$

Obviously the *oid-set containment based function inheritance* is compatible with the subsumption based sub/super type relationship, as subsumption is just a special case of containment.

5.2 Effective Oid-Set based Mechanism for Function Resolution

While underlying the semantics of inheritance, *oid-set containment* is not directly used for function resolution, as practically inheritance paths are concerned with types rather than objects.

The **effective oid-set based function resolution** is a mechanism for implementing the *oid-set containment based function inheritance*. It shifts the focus from "inheriting functions from an object" to "inheriting functions from a type". Under this mechanism, applying a function, that is defined on or partially inherited by a type, to an object, implies applying the function to the *effective oid-set* of the object wrt that type, if that *effective oid-set* is $\emptyset$, the function returns *nil*. Iteratively applying this mechanism eventually pushes a function resolution down to a single database. How to handle the function resolution in that single database depends on its own autonomous facility.

By referring the example show in Figure 1 we can see how function inheritance in object integration is dealt with by using *effective oid-sets*.

- Since function *area_name* is defined on type **area_trans_info**, applying *area_name* to object O implies applying it to the *effective oid-set* of O wrt type **area_trans_info**. As the *oid-set* of O is $\{d_0.s_0, d_1.s_1\}$, the *home-tag-set* of object O is $\{d_0, d_1\}$, the *home-tag-set* of type **area_trans_info** is $\{d_0\}$, and their intersection is $\{d_0\}$, the *effective oid-set* of O wrt type **area_trans_info** is $\{d_0.s_0\}$. Thus *area_name*(O) is performed by

  $$area\_name(\{d_0.s_0, d_1.s_1\}) = area\_name(\{d_0.s_0\}) = \text{'Santa Clara'}.$$

- Applying *area_name* to O'_0 implies applying *area_name* to the *effective oid-set* of O'_0 wrt type **area_trans_info** that is the same as the *oid-set* of O'_0, $\{d_0.s'_0\}$, thus *area_name*(O'_0) is performed by

  $$area\_name(\{d_0.s'_0\}) = area\_name(\{d_0.s'_0\}) = \text{'Tracy'}.$$

- Since function *geo_code* is defined on type **geo_info**, applying *geo_code* to O implies applying *geo_code* to the *effective oid-set* of O wrt type **geo_info**, thus *geo_code*(O) is performed by

  $$geo\_code(\{d_0.s_0, d_1.s_1\}) = geo\_code(\{d_1.s_1\}) = \text{'W4-01-02'}.$$

- However, since the *effective oid-set* of O'_0 wrt type **geo_info** is $\emptyset$, function *geo_code* is not applicable to O'_0, thus *geo_code*(O'_0) yields *nil*, as

  $$geo\_code(\{d_0.s'_0\}) = geo\_code(\emptyset) = nil.$$

This mechanism is formally described as follows (note again that expressions $f(O)$ and $f(\mu O)$ are exchangeable, thus $f(O)$ actually means $f(\mu O)$).

Effective Oid-Set Mechanism for Function Resolution

Let O be an object and f be a function defined on or inherited by type T. if $f(\mu_T O) \neq nil$ then $f(O) = f(\mu_T O)$.

Note that the above mechanism does not ensure the applicability of f to O. If $f(\mu_T O) = nil$ then $f(O) = nil$. For example, if $\mu_T O = \emptyset$, then $f(\mu_T O) = nil$, and therefore $f(O) = nil$.

As computing the *effective oid-set* from a given *oid-set* yields a subset of the latter, we refer to it as oid-set reduction. Iteratively applying *oid-set* reduction eventually simplifies a multidatabase oriented function resolution to a single database oriented function resolution, and the latter can be handled locally in terms of functions *type* and *class* as usual.

In the presence of multilevel integrations, *oid-set* reduction can be iteratively applied down to the appropriate type where a function is originally defined. For example, consider a type integration hierarchy $T_1, T_2, ..., T_{n-1}, T_n$ where T_1 underlies T_2, ..., T_{n-1} underlies T_n. Given an object of type T_n, resolving function overloading (by name, not function identifier) often requires checking the applicability of functions defined types at different integration levels, in the order of $T_n, T_{n-1}, ..., T_2, T_1$.

The above mechanism can also be extended to the following for handling functions with hybrid argument type signatures.

Let $T_0, T_1, ..., T_n$ be the argument type signatures of function f, and $O_1, ..., O_n$ be objects. If $\forall i \in \{1, ..., n\}$ $\mu_{T_i} O_i \neq \emptyset$ and $f(\mu_{T_1} O_1, ..., \mu_{T_n} O_n) \neq nil$ then $f(O_1, ..., O_n) = f(\mu_{T_1} O_1, ..., \mu_{T_n} O_n)$

It is worth noting that the effective *oid-set* based function resolution mechanism does not replace or override that provided by a local database. Its value consists in turning a multidatabase oriented function resolution to a single database oriented function resolution. Although the effective *oid-sets* of an AVO wrt all the types (including AVO types) defined in the same database, are identical, it does not mean any function defined on any of those types is applicable to the object with that effective *oid-set*. Resolving such applicability locally is a basic functionality provided by every OODB.

6 Conclusions

The notion of **abstract view object** is introduced to support multidatabase integration at an abstract level. This approach supports abstract object representations, and such representations are temporally and spatially stable. Furthermore, it links the semantics of object identification, integration and inheritance in a multidatabase environment.

AVOs are useful in managing multimedia data by extracting their structural relationships and suppressing their media dependent details. A rule-based **abstract view object** calculus has been developed for reconstructing abstract representations of multi-sourced and multimedia data.

References

[1] H. Ait-Kaci. Type subsumption as a model of computation. In *Expert Database Systems, Kersburg ed.*, 1986.

[2] Q. Chen and G. Gardarin. An implementation model for reasoning with complex objects. In *Proc. ACM-SIGMOD'88, SIGMOD Rec. Vol.17, No.3*, 1988.

[3] Q. Chen and Y. Kambayashi. Nested relation based database knowledge representation. In *Proc. ACM-SIGMOD'91, SIGMOD Rec. Vol.20, No.2*, 1991.

[4] W. Chen and D. Warren. C-logic of complex objects. In *Proc. PODS'89*, 1989.

[5] Madnick et. al. Cisl: Composing answers from disparate information systems. In *1989 Workshop on Heterogeneous Database, NSF, Northwest Univ. and IEEE*, 1989.

[6] R. Ahmed et al. The pegasus heterogeneous multidatabase system. *IEEE-Computer, Vol.24, No.12*, 1992.

[7] S. Khoshafian and G. Copeland. Object identity. In *Proc. OOPSLA*, 1986.

[8] M. Kifer and G. Lausen. F-logic - a higher order language for reasoning about objects, inheritance and schema. In *Proc. ACM-SIGMOD'89*, 1989.

[9] W. Kim, N. Ballou, J. Garza, and D. Woelk. A distributed object-oriented database system supporting shared and private databases. *ACM Trans. on Information System, Vol.9, No.1*, 1991.

[10] R. Krishnamurthy, W. Litwin, and W. Kent. Language features for interoperability of database with schmatic discrepancies. In *ACM-SIGMOD'91, SIGMOD Rec. Vol.20, No.2*, 1991.

[11] W. Litwin, L. Mark, and N. Roussopoulos. Interoperability of multiple databases. *Computer Survey*, 1990.

[12] F. Manola and S. Zdonik. Dfugue: A model for engineering information system and other baroque applications. In *Proc. Int. Conf. on Knowledge and Databases*, 1988.

[13] V. Markowitz. An architecture for identifying objects in multidatabases. In *1st Int. Workshop on Interoperability in Multidatabase Systems*, 1991.

[14] E. Neuhold, W. Kent, and M-C. Shan. Object identification in interoperable systems. In *1st Int. Workshop on Interoperability in Multidatabase Systems*, 1991.

[15] A. Ohori. Representing object identity in a pure functional language. Technical report, 1991.

[16] G. Shaw and S. Zdonik. A query algebra for object-oriented databases. Technical Report CS89-19, Brown University, 1989.

[17] S. Vandenberg and D. DeWitt. Algebraic support for complex objects with arrays,identity, and inheritance. In *ACM-SIGMOD'91, SIGMOD Rec. Vol.20, No.2*, 1991.

An Object-Oriented Query Model Supporting Views

Suk I. Yoo   Hai Jin Chang

Department of Computer Science
Seoul National University
Shilim-dong, Kwanak-ku, Seoul, 151-742
Korea
email: sukinyoo@krsnucc1.bitnet

Abstract

This paper suggests an object-oriented query model. The model is algebraically-closed and supports a view mechanism. In the view mechanism, a view is simply defined as a named query expression, and queries issued against views can be translated into equivalent queries against databases by means of the query modification technique as used in relational database systems, and a view makes it possible for its user to see a subset of its base objects, a subset of the methods of its base objects, or new relationships created by combining two or more sets of its base objects.

1 Introduction

In response to the requirement for more complete modeling of complex data in new data-intensive applications such as CAD/CAM, software engineering, office information systems and multimedia systems, much attention has centered on OODB (Object-Oriented Database) systems.

The ANSI SPARC three-schema architecture [Date90] has application programs (or users) which access the database through views. Traditional database systems have included view definition facilities. OODB systems also need view mechanisms [Kim90].

In RDB (Relational Database) systems, view mechanisms are supported by relational query models. Every relational query operator is closed on relations, and a query expression can be used to define a subset of columns of a base table, a subset of rows of a base table, or a new table created by combining two or more base tables. So, in RDB systems, column subset views, row subset views, or join views can be defined by named queries [Date90], and queries issued against views can be translated into equivalent queries against base relations by query modification. Query modification is a well-known and flexible technique. By query modification, a query expression Q against a view is translated into a more deeply nested query expression Q' (than Q) against databases, and more alternate orders of the query operators in Q' can be considered before an optimal order of the query operators is determined and executed.

This paper suggests a query model which can be the basis for a view mechanism as well as an ad hoc query language for OODB systems. The query model not only takes into account fundamental object-oriented concepts such as object identifier, encapsulation, class hierarchy and inheritance, but also provides a set of algebraically closed query operators which supports a view mechanism satisfying the following conditions.

(c1) Views are simply defined by named query expressions. View definitions do not require the creation of new classes or introduction of additional mechanisms to specify the methods and attributes of the objects in the views.

(c2) Queries issued against a view can be translated into equivalent queries against base objects by means of the query modification technique, as used in RDB systems.

(c3) A view, called a *select-view* in this paper, allows the user to see a subset of its base objects.

(c4) A view, called a *project-view* in this paper, allows the user to see a subset of methods of its base objects.

(c5) A view, called a *combine-view* in this paper, allows the user to see new relationships created by combining 2 or more sets of its base objects.

The next section will discuss related works on query models and view mechanisms for OODB systems. Section 3 will specify a reference data model. In section 4, our query model will be defined on the basis of the reference model. Section 5 shows the view mechanism supported by our query model. Section 6 comprises the conclusion.

2 Related Work

In some related works [Ta88, Abi91], views are defined not on the basis of queries, but on the basis of some special mechanisms only for views. In reference [Ta88], a view is defined as a set of *virtual classes* and IS-A edges between the virtual classes. This system does not support project-views and combine-views. Reference [Abi91] suggests a view mechanism based on the O_2 data model. In this system, select-views, project-views, and combine-views can be defined. However, views are regarded as databases, and are not defined on the basis of a query model. Queries can only be used as a way to populate the virtual classes.

At this point, the terms "project-view" and "combine-view" should be clarified and examined.

project-views: Compared with other data models, an object-oriented data model has a unique feature that the behavior (i.e., methods) as well as the structure (i.e., attributes) of data (i.e., objects) can be defined in a database schema. Objects are manipulated by their methods. Thus, views in OODB systems should be able to hide or expose an arbitrary subset of the methods of their base objects. For example, it may be necessary to hide some methods of base objects having side-effects (e.g., database updates) from some users. To define project-views on the basis of queries, a query operator which can project an arbitrary subset of methods of its input objects on its output is required.

combine-views: Many OODB systems (e.g., an early version of ORION) only support the selection of objects already existing in their databases. But the requirement for combining objects into new relationships does exist - either for output purposes and for further processing. The simple selection of objects already existing in databases is not sufficient to explicitly reflect all of the relationships requested by users [Sha90, Str90].

In order to define combine-views on the basis of queries, a query operator which can combine the pairs of its input objects into new objects is needed.

The query operators for project-views or combine-views may create new objects as their outputs. However, since every object should generally have a class (or a type depending on data models) which specifies its structure and behavior, query operators that create new objects for their outputs may raise a number of issues: namely, what are the classes of the new objects and what methods do they support [Str90], especially when the creation of new classes is required in order to specify the attributes and methods of the new objects. The dynamic creation of a new class (or type) during the evaluation of a query operator not only imposes some performance penalties since they may be rather expensive [Ber91] but also requires careful consideration of some difficult theoretical problems related to class hierarchy and inheritance.

Therefore, some query models do not provide query operators that create new objects for their results, while other models impose restrictions on such object-creating query operators to avoid the dynamic creation of new classes (or types) [Ber91]. But, in such models, project-views and combine-views cannot be freely defined only on the basis of queries.

In other related works [Sha90, Hei90, Kimu91], views are defined not only on the basis of queries but also additional mechanisms specifying the structures and/or methods of the objects in the views. Reference [Sha90] defines a query algebra. A set of new tuple objects can be created by a query, where they are created by combining the return values of properties or object identifiers of the query input objects. On the basis of the algebra, reference [Hei90] shows an attempt to transfer concepts of relational views into OODB systems. However, in this system, project-views and combine-views are not defined only by query expressions. A view is defined by a derived type as well as by a set of objects which may be specified by a query expression. The derived type defines the functions (i.e., methods) that can be applied to the objects in the view.

Reference [Kimu91] suggests a view mechanism called view classes. In this system, select-views, project-views, and combine-views can be defined. However, view classes are created by additional methods as well as query primitives.

Reference [Sch91] suggests a view mechanism which supports updatable views. The view mechanism is based on the query algebra where object-preserving semantics is given to all query operators. Select-views, project-views, and combine-views can be defined by query operators. However, in this system, the query operators for project-views and combine-views dynamically create new types specifying the methods of their output objects.

3 Reference Data Model

Our reference data model supports a number of fundamental object-oriented concepts. In addition, it provides a special system-defined class named REF in order to represent the results of the query operators which can be used to define project-views and combine-views without the creation of new classes and without introducing additional mechanisms for specifying the methods of objects in the views.

3.1 Basic Concepts

In this reference model, we assume that the following sets, and special symbols **Err** and **Unknown** are given.

- A countably infinite set *OID*.

- A countably infinite set *NAME*.

- The set of all integers *INTEGER*, the set of all real numbers *FLOAT*, the set of all strings *STRING*, and the set of all Boolean symbols *BOOL* (i.e., {**True**, **False**}), where the sets *INTEGER*, *FLOAT*, *STRING*, *BOOL*, *OID*, *NAME*, {**Err**}, and {**Unknown**} should not have common elements in pairs.

(1) Object, Object Identifier

Let us now define the notion of *value*. The notion is defined in a recursive manner as follows.

Definition 1. Value
1) If v is an element of the set $INTEGER \cup FLOAT \cup STRING \cup BOOL \cup NAME \cup OID \cup \{\textbf{Err}\} \cup \{\textbf{Unknown}\}$, then v is a *value*.
2) If v_i is a *value* which is not **Err** for every integer i satisfying $n \geq i \geq 1$, then the list $\langle v_1, \ldots, v_n \rangle$ is a *value*, called a list-value. The empty list $\langle \rangle$ is a *value*, also called a list-value.
3) If v_i is a *value* which is not **Err**, and $v_i \neq v_j$ if $i \neq j$, for all integers i and j satisfying $n \geq i, j \geq 1$, then the set $\{v_1, \ldots, v_n\}$ is a *value*, called a set-value. The empty set $\{\}$ is a *value*, also called a set-value.
4) If v_i is a *value* which is not **Err** for every integer i satisfying $n \geq i \geq 1$, and $p_1, \ldots, p_n$ are distinct elements of set *NAME*, then the tuple $[p_1: v_1, \ldots, p_n: v_n]$ is a *value*. The empty tuple $[]$ is a *value*, also called a tuple-value. □

Err and **Unknown** are special values. For example, **Err** results from operations with type mismatching arguments. If v be a tuple-value $[p_1: v_1, \ldots, p_n: v_n]$, then $p_1, \ldots, p_n$ denote the *tuple-attribute* names of v, and v_i denotes the value of a *tuple-attribute* p_i of v.

Definition 2. Object
If $id \in OID$ and v is a tuple-value, then the pair (id, v) is an object. □

The value of an object is always a tuple-value. However, the value of the tuple-attribute p_i of a tuple-value $[p_1: v_1, \ldots, p_n: v_n]$ can be a set-value or a list-value. So, we can represent objects for sets or lists. In our reference model, set *OID* means the set of all possible *object identifiers*. Every object has a unique identifier. For two arbitrary objects (id, v) and (id', v'), if $id = id'$ then $v = v'$. However, the converse is not true. The object identifiers of objects cannot be modified by applications.

(2) Class

Every object should belong to a class. That is, every object should have a class which defines its attributes and methods. Each class has a unique name which distinguishes it from other classes. An attribute is defined by its name and domain (i.e., the set of all values which can be stored in the attribute). A method is defined by its *signature* and *body*. A signature is an expression $m: D_1 \times D_2 \times \ldots \times D_n \to D$. The signature specifies a method name m, and the domains ($D_1, \ldots, D_n$, and D) and the number of the input parameters of the method. A method body provides the implementations of the method and consists of a sequence of statements written in some programming language. The names of all attributes and methods of a class should be distinct from one another. Every name is an element of *NAME*. It is assumed that every method has a return value.

Let $(id, [p_1 : v_1, \ldots, p_n : v_n])$ be an object o belonging to a class C, and let m be a method of class C, and let $a_1, \ldots, a_n$ be values. Then, $\text{obj}(id)$, $id.p_i$, and $id.m\,(a_1, \ldots, a_n)$ denote, respectively, the object o, the value of the attribute p_i of the object o, and the return value of the method-call $m(a_1, \ldots, a_n)$ to receiver o. If a method is called with input arguments whose number and domains do not correspond to its signature, then it is assumed that its return value is **Err**.

(3) Class Hierarchy, Inheritance

Classes are organized into a class hierarchy. The class hierarchy models the semantic IS-A relationships among classes. A subclass inherits attributes and methods from its super class, and in addition, may have specific attributes and methods. There exists a special system-defined class, called OBJECT, which is the root of the class hierarchy. Suppose that a class hierarchy and a database are given. The database is the set of all the objects belonging to the classes in the class hierarchy rooted at OBJECT. Given a class C, notation **Inst**(C) denotes the set {x $\in$ *OID* | obj(x) belongs to a class C', and C' is a class in the class hierarchy rooted at C}. For example, **Inst**(OBJECT) is the set of the identifiers of all the objects existing in the database.

Table 1 shows an example of definitions of classes STUDENT, RECORD and SCHOOL. (In Table 1, method bodies are omitted, but assume that methods PutName, PutAge, PutSex, PutRec, PutCity, PutMusic and PutMath may update objects)

```
class STUDENT [
    super OBJECT
    attributes
        Name: STRING
        Age: INTEGER
        Sex: STRING
        Rec: RECORD
        City: STRING
    methods
        GetName: STUDENT → STRING
        GetAge: STUDENT → INTEGER
        GetSex: STUDENT → STRING
        GetRec: STUDENT → RECORD
        GetCity: STUDENT → STRING
```

                PutName: STUDENT × *STRING* → *STRING* /* Put a new name */
                PutAge: STUDENT × *INTEGER* → *INTEGER* /* Put a new age */
                PutSex: STUDENT × *STRING* → *STRING*
                PutRec: STUDENT × RECORD → RECORD
                PutCity: STUDENT × *STRING* → *STRING*]

    class RECORD [
        super OBJECT
        attributes
            Music: *INTEGER*
            Math: *INTEGER*
        methods
            GetSum: RECORD → *INTEGER* /* Music + Math */
            PutMusic: RECORD × *INTEGER* → *INTEGER*
            PutMath: RECORD × *INTEGER* → *INTEGER*]

    class SCHOOL [
        super OBJECT
        attributes
            Name: *STRING*
            City: *STRING*
        methods
            GetName: SCHOOL → *STRING* /* get the name of a school */
            GetCity: SCHOOL → *STRING*
            PutName: SCHOOL × *STRING* → *STRING* /* Put a new name */
            PutCity: SCHOOL × *STRING* → *STRING*]

Table 1. An Example of Classes

(4) Encapsulation

Every object satisfies *procedural encapsulation* [Catt91]. Every object can be manipulated only by its methods.

3.2 REF class

REF is a system-defined class which represents the results of the queries used to define project-views and combine-views. Suppose the following.

1) REF class is a direct subclass of OBJECT.
2) REF class defines an attribute **Refval** and a method **GetVM** (abbreviation of Get-Virtual-Method-value).
3) REF class has no method definitions for updating its objects (i.e., to update the values stored in attribute **Refval** of the object).
4) Every object belonging to the REF class is created only in the course of processing some query operators, which will be defined in the next section.

Definition 3. Virtual Method Value

If obj(i) be an object which belongs to a class not named REF, and p be a method name of the object, then the list-value $\langle i, p \rangle$ is a *virtual method value*. □

Every object is uniquely identified by its object identifier. Therefore, an object identifier can be used as a logical pointer to the object. Similarly, a virtual method value can be used as the logical pointer to a method of an object, since all method names of an object are distinct from one another.

Let VM be the set of all virtual method values. The domain of the attribute **Refval** is the set $\{[p_1 : v_1, \ldots, p_n : v_n] \mid$ for every integer i satisfying $n \geq i \geq 1$, $p_i \in NAME$, and $v_i \in VM \cup \{\textbf{Unknown}\}\}$. That is, if $id \in \textbf{Inst}(\text{REF})$, and $id.\textbf{Refval} = [p_1 : v_1, \ldots, p_n : v_n]$, then the value v_i of the tuple-attribute p_i is a virtual method value or **Unknown** for every integer i satisfying $n \geq i \geq 1$. Every object belonging to REF class is represented in the form of $(i, [\textbf{Refval}: [p_1 : v_1, \ldots, p_n : v_n]])$. Note that a virtual method value pointing to another virtual method value is not permitted. This paper do not use virtual attribute values, but our query model can be extended to use them.

Definition 4. GetVM

Let REF be **Inst**(REF), and let VM be the set of all virtual method values. Then **GetVM**: $REF \times NAME \to VM \cup \{\textbf{Unknown}\} \cup \{\textbf{Err}\}$ is defined as

$\textbf{GetVM}(r, p) = v$

for any $(r, p) \in REF \times NAME$, where

1) if p is a tuple-attribute name of $r.\textbf{Refval}$, then v is the value of the tuple-attribute p of $r.\textbf{Refval}$.

2) otherwise, $v = \textbf{Err}$. □

Example 1. Let i be the object identifier of an object belonging to class STUDENT in Table 1, and let $(j, [\textbf{Refval}: [\text{xGetName}: \langle i, \text{GetName}\rangle, \text{xPutName}: \langle i, \text{PutName}\rangle]])$ be an object of REF class. Then $j.\textbf{GetVM}(\text{xGetName}) = \langle i, \text{GetName}\rangle$, and $j.\textbf{GetVM}(\text{xPutName}) = \langle i, \text{PutName}\rangle$.

4 Query Model

4.1 Access to Object

By encapsulation, every object can only be accessed or updated by its methods. **RunMethod** is the operator which executes the methods of objects.

Definition 5. RunMethod

Let V be the set of all possible values, and let LST be the all possible list-values. Then, **RunMethod**: $OID \times NAME \times LST \to V$ is defined as

$\textbf{RunMethod}(id, m, \langle a_1, \ldots, a_n \rangle) = v$

for any $(id, m, \langle a_1, \ldots, a_n\rangle) \in OID \times NAME \times LST$, where

1) if $id \in \{x \mid x \in \textbf{Inst}(\text{OBJECT}) \text{ and } x \notin \textbf{Inst}(\text{REF})\}$, and m is a method of the obj(id), then $v = id.m(a_1, \ldots, a_n)$.

2) if $id \in \textbf{Inst}(\text{REF})$, and m is a tuple-attribute name of $id.\textbf{Refval}$, then

- if $id.\mathbf{GetVM}(m) = \mathbf{Unknown}$, then $v = \mathbf{Err}$
- otherwise, if $id.\mathbf{GetVM}(m)$ is a virtual method value (let the value be $\langle x, y \rangle$), then $v = x.y(a_1, \ldots, a_n)$

3) otherwise, $v = \mathbf{Err}$. □

By **RunMethod**, we can now treat an object $(id, [\mathbf{Refval}: [p_1 : v_1, \ldots, p_n : v_n]])$ of the REF class as an object which has real methods $p_1, \ldots, p_n$. That is, if $id.\mathbf{GetVM}(p_i)$ is a virtual method value $\langle x, y \rangle$, then p_i can be treated as the name of the method whose signature and body are the same as the signature and body of the method y of the obj(x). For example, in **Example 1** of Section 3.2, **RunMethod**(j, xPutName, $\langle$ "John" $\rangle$) and **RunMethod**(i, PutName, $\langle$"John"$\rangle$) always have the same return value and side-effects.

4.2 Query Operators

Our query model defines query operators **Restrict**, **V-Project**, **V-Combine**, **Union**, and **Difference**. They are algebraically closed on sets of object identifiers and **Err**. Note that queries are meaningful only if applied to sets of objects, and that sets as the targets of queries can always simulate classes as the targets of queries, but in general the opposite is not true [Yu91].

This paper uses lambda notation to represent predicates with/without parameters. For example, $\lambda(x)$ $(x \geq 1)$ is a predicate with a parameter which can be bound to integers. The predicate is **True** if $x = 2$, and is **False** if $x = 0$. Notation card(x) means the cardinality of x, and notation power(x) means the power set of x, if x is a set.

Given a predicate p and a subset S of **Inst**(OBJECT), **Restrict** returns a subset of S whose elements satisfy the predicate p.

Definition 6. Restrict

Let $OSET$ be power(**Inst**(OBJECT)) ∪ {**Err**}, and let P be the set of all predicate with a parameter which can be bound to object identifiers. Then **Restrict**: $OSET \times P \to OSET$ is defined as

Restrict(S, p) = R

for any (S, p) ∈ $OSET \times P$, where
1) if S = **Err**, then R = **Err**
2) otherwise, R = $\{s \in S \mid \lambda(s)\ p(s) = \mathbf{True}\}$. □

Example 2. A query "Retrieve all STUDENTs whose age is greater than or equal to 30" can be represented as **Restrict**(**Inst**(STUDENT), $\lambda(x)$ (**RunMethod**(x, GetAge, $\langle\rangle$) $\geq$ 30))). Operator **Restrict** supports *reference join* [Catt91]. For example, **Restrict** (**Inst** (STUDENT), $\lambda(x)$ (**RunMethod** (**RunMethod** (x, GetRec, $\langle\rangle$), GetSum, $\langle\ \rangle$) $\geq$ 180)) is an example of reference join.

Given two sets S_1 and S_2 of object identifiers, **Union** returns the set of object identifiers that are in S_1 or S_2 or both.

Definition 7. Union

Let $OSET$ be power(**Inst**(OBJECT)) $\cup$ {**Err**}. Then **Union**: $OSET \times OSET \to OSET$ is defined as

$\textbf{Union}(S_1, S_2) = R$

for any $(S_1, S_2) \in OSET \times OSET$, where
1) if $S_1 = \textbf{Err}$, or $S_2 = \textbf{Err}$, then $R = \textbf{Err}$
2) otherwise, $R = \{x \mid x \in S_1 \text{ or } x \in S_2\}$. $\square$

Definition 8. Difference

Let $OSET$ be power(**Inst**(OBJECT)) $\cup$ {**Err**}. Then **Difference**: $OSET \times OSET \to OSET$ is defined as

$\textbf{Difference}(S_1, S_2) = R$

for any $(S_1, S_2) \in OSET \times OSET$, where
1) if $S_1 = \textbf{Err}$, or $S_2 = \textbf{Err}$, then $R = \textbf{Err}$
2) otherwise, $R = \{x \mid x \in S_1 \text{ and } x \notin S_2\}$. $\square$

Note that the query operators **Restrict**, **Union**, **Difference** do not create new objects.

Definition 9. V-Project

Let $OSET$ be power(**Inst**(OBJECT)) $\cup$ {**Err**}, and let NN be the set $\{x \mid x \text{ is a non-empty finite element of power}(\{\langle A, B\rangle \mid A \in NAME, B \in NAME\})\}$. Then, **V-Project**: $OSET \times NN \to \text{power}(OID)$ is defined as

$\textbf{V-Project}(S, \{\langle A_1, B_1\rangle, \ldots, \langle A_n, B_n\rangle\}) = R$

for any $(S, \{\langle A_1, B_1\rangle, \ldots, \langle A_n, B_n\rangle\}) \in OSET \times NN$ ($n \geq 1$), where
1) if $A_1, \ldots, A_n$ are distinct elements of set $NAME$, then R is the set $\{r_s \in OID \mid s \in S\}$ which satisfies the following conditions:
   - card(R) = card(S)
   - for each $s \in S$, $(r_s, [\textbf{Refval}: [A_1 : v_1, \ldots, A_n : v_n]])$ is a new object of REF class, where, for every integer i satisfying $1 \leq i \leq n$,
     - if $s \in \textbf{Inst}(REF)$, then $v_i = s.\textbf{GetVM}(B_i)$
     - if $s \in \textbf{Inst}(OBJECT)$ and $s \notin \textbf{Inst}(REF)$, and B_i is a method of obj(s), then $v_i = \langle s, B_i\rangle$
     - otherwise, $v_i = \textbf{Unknown}$
2) otherwise, $R = \textbf{Err}$. $\square$

Example 3. Let obj(s_1) and obj(s_2) be objects belonging to STUDENT class in Table 1. Then **V-Project**($\{s_1, s_2\}, \{\langle \text{xGetName}, \text{GetName}\rangle\}) = \{x_1, x_2\}$, where ($x_1$, [**Refval**: [xGetName: $\langle s_1, \text{GetName}\rangle$]]) and ($x_2$, [**Refval**: [xGetName: $\langle s_2, \text{GetName}\rangle$]]) are new objects of REF class.

Given a set of object identifiers, **V-Project** creates a set of new objects belonging to the REF class, and returns the set of their object identifiers. The objects contain virtual method values corresponding to the selected subset of the methods of the input objects. **V-Project** can be used to define project-views.

Definition 10. V-Combine

Let $OSET$ be power(**Inst**(OBJECT)) $\cup$ {**Err**}, and let NN be the set {x | x is a non-empty finite element of power({$\langle A, B \rangle$ | A $\in NAME$, B $\in NAME$})}. Then **V-Combine**: $OSET \times NN \times OSET \times NN \to$ power(OID) is defined as

V-Combine(S, {$\langle A_1, B_1 \rangle, \ldots, \langle A_t, B_t \rangle$}, Q, {$\langle A_{t+1}, B_{t+1} \rangle, \ldots, \langle A_n, B_n \rangle$}) = R

for any (S, {$\langle A_1, B_1 \rangle, \ldots, \langle A_t, B_t \rangle$}, Q, {$\langle A_{t+1}, B_{t+1} \rangle, \ldots, \langle A_n, B_n \rangle$}) $\in OSET \times NN \times OSET \times NN$ (n > t $\geq$ 1), where

1) if $A_1, \ldots, A_n$ are distinct elements of $NAME$, then R = { $r_{sq} \in OID$ | $s \in$ S, $q \in$ Q} which satisfies the following conditions:
- card(R) = card(S) * card(Q)
- for every $(s, q) \in S \times Q$, $(r_{sq}$, [**Refval**: $[A_1 : v_1, \ldots, A_t : v_t, A_{t+1} : v_{t+1}, \ldots, A_n : v_n]$]) is a new object of REF class, where
  - for every integer i satisfying $1 \leq i \leq t$,
    - if $s \in$ **Inst**(REF), then $v_i = s.\textbf{GetVM}(B_i)$
    - if $s \in$ **Inst**(OBJECT), $s \notin$ **Inst**(REF), and B_i is a method of obj(s), then $v_i = \langle s, B_i \rangle$
    - otherwise, $v_i =$ **Unknown**
  - for every integer i satisfying $t+1 \leq i \leq n$,
    - if $q \in$ **Inst**(REF), then $v_i = q.\textbf{GetVM}(B_i)$
    - if $q \in$ **Inst**(OBJECT), $q \notin$ **Inst**(REF), and B_i is a method of obj(q), then $v_i = \langle q, B_i \rangle$
    - otherwise, $v_i =$ **Unknown**

2) otherwise, R = **Err**. □

Example 4. Assume that obj(s_1) and obj(s_2) belong to STUDENT class, and obj(r) belongs to RECORD class in Table 1. Then **V-Combine**({s_1, s_2}, {$\langle$xGetAge, GetAge$\rangle$}, {r}, { $\langle$xGetSum, GetSum$\rangle$}) = {y_1, y_2}, where (y_1, [**Refval**: [xGetAge: $\langle s_1$, GetAge$\rangle$, xGetSum: $\langle$r, GetSum$\rangle$]]) and (y_2, [**Refval**: [xGetAge: $\langle s_2$, GetAge$\rangle$, xGetSum: $\langle$r, GetSum $\rangle$]]) are new objects of REF class.

Given two sets of object identifiers, **V-Combine** creates a set of new objects belonging to REF class, and returns the set of their object identifiers. **V-Combine** is similar to **V-Project**. But V-Combine creates a set of new objects from two input sets of object identifiers. **V-Combine** makes it possible for users to get a set of new objects created by combining two or more sets of base objects. By nesting **V-Combine** operations twice or more, three or more sets of base objects can be combined into a set of new objects. A query expression which is a composition of **Restrict** and **V-Combine** can be used to make new relationships which do not exist in the base objects (Table 2 in Section 5.1 shows an example of the composition).

5 View Support

5.1 View Definition

In this paper, a view is defined as a name-query pair (n, q), where n is an element of $NAME$, and q is a query expression. We assume that a set $\{(n_1, q_1), \ldots, (n_i, q_i)\}$ of view definitions is given to a user (where $n_1, \ldots, n_i$ should be distinct from one another), and every query from the user is issued against the set of views. If (n, q) is a view definition, notation **vInst**(n) means the set of object identifiers resulting from q. Table 2 shows a set of views (i.e., YOUNG-STUDENT, BOY, GIRL, SAME-CITY-STUDENT-SCHOOL, and NAME-AGE). A view can be defined in terms of other views.

> **view YOUNG-STUDENT is** /* a view defined in terms of class STUDENT */
> **Restrict(Inst** (STUDENT), $\lambda(x)($**RunMethod**$(x, GetAge, \langle\rangle) \leq 30))$
>
> **view BOY is** /* a view defined in terms of another view YOUNG-STUDENT */
> **Restrict(vInst** (YOUNG-STUDENT),
> $\lambda(x)($**RunMethod**$(x, GetSex, \langle\rangle) = $ "M"))
>
> **view GIRL is**
> **Restrict** (**vInst** (YOUNG-STUDENT),
> $\lambda(x)($**RunMethod**$(x, GetSex, \langle\rangle) = $ "F"))
>
> **view NAME-AGE is**
> **V-Project(Inst**(STUDENT),
> $\{\langle Name, GetName\rangle, \langle Age, GetAge\rangle, \langle PutAge, PutAge\rangle\})$
>
> **view SAME-CITY-STUDENT-SCHOOL is**
> **Restrict (V-Combine(**
>   **Inst**(STUDENT), $\{\langle pCity, GetCity\rangle, \langle pName, GetName\rangle\}$,
>   **Inst**(SCHOOL), $\{\langle sCity, GetCity\rangle, \langle sName, GetName\rangle\}$,
> $\lambda(x)($**RunMethod**$(x, pCity, \langle\rangle) = $ **RunMethod**$(x, sCity, \langle\rangle))$)

Table 2. An Example Set of Views

Our view mechanism supports select-views, project-views, and combine-views. In Table 2, YOUNG-STUDENT, BOY and GIRL are examples of select-views, NAME-AGE is an example of a project-view, and SAME-CITY-STUDENT-SCHOOL is an example of a combine-view. The view SAME-CITY-STUDENT-SCHOOL shows new relationships which are created by combining the methods GetCity and GetName of STUDENTs and the methods GetCity and GetName of SCHOOLs into the set of new objects (having methods pCity, pName, sCity, and sName), where pCity = sCity.

5.2 Processing Queries and Database Operations Against Views

In RDB systems, query expressions against views are modified into query expressions against base tables by means of the query modification, before their execution. Similarly, in our view mechanism, if (n, q) is a view, then **vInst**(n) existing in the queries against the view n is substituted with the query expression q.

Example 6. Let YOUNG-STUDENT be the view in Table 2. Now, the query **Restrict(** **vInst** (YOUNG-STUDENT), $\lambda(y)$ (**RunMethod**$(x, GetAge, \langle\rangle) \geq 20$) against the view YOUNG-STUDENT can be translated into the equivalent query **Restrict (Restrict (Inst**(STUDENT), $\lambda(x)$ (**RunMethod**$(x, GetAge, \langle\rangle) \leq 30$)), $\lambda(y)$ (**RunMethod** $(x, GetAge, \langle\rangle) \geq 20$)) against the base objects.

Our query model provides a basis for updatable views. In our query model, all methods are explicitly defined in classes, and updates against views must be accomplished only by means of method calls. Every method-call from queries may only be accomplished by **RunMethod**$(i, m, \langle a_1, \ldots, a_n \rangle)$ operator defined in **Definition 5**. So, the effects of all update operations (i.e., methods having side-effects) against views can be propagated to base objects. Let i be an object identifier contained in the result of a query which is used to define a view V. Then,

1) if $i \in$ **Inst**(OBJECT), $i \notin$ **Inst**(REF), and m is a method of obj(i), then every update request **RunMethod**$(i, m, \langle a_1, \ldots, a_n \rangle)$ against V makes a method call $i.m(a_1, \ldots, a_n)$ without ambiguity.

2) otherwise, obj(i) must be an object belonging to class REF. In this case, if **GetVM**(i, m) is a virtual method value (let it be $\langle x, y \rangle$), then every update request **RunMethod**$(i, m, \langle a_1, \ldots, a_n \rangle)$ against V makes a method call x.y$(a_1, \ldots, a_n)$ without ambiguity.

6 Conclusion

This paper defines an object-oriented query model which can be the basis for a view mechanism as well as an ad hoc query language for OODB systems. The model not only accommodates the fundamental object-oriented concepts such as object identifier, encapsulation, class hierarchy and inheritance, but also provides a set of algebraically closed query operators (based on the notion of *virtual method value* and REF class defined in Section 3) which can be used to define select-views, project-views, and combine-views. The views are simply defined by named queries without the dynamic creation of new classes (or types) or the introduction of additional mechanisms to specify the methods of the objects in views. In our system, queries against views can be processed by the query modification technique. Furthermore, the query model provides a basis for updatable views.

References

[Abi91] Serge Abiteboul, Anthony Boonner, "Objects and Views," *Proceedings of the 1991 ACM SIGMOD Conference on Management of Data*, pp. 238-247, 1991.

[Ber91] Elisa Bertino, Lorenzo Martino, "Object-Oriented Database Management Systems: Concepts and Issues," *IEEE Computer*, pp33-47, April 1991.

[Catt91] R.G.G. Cattell, Object Data Management, Addison Wesley, 1991.

[Date90] C. J. Date, An Introduction to Database Systems Vol. 1, Addison Wesley, 1990.

[Hei90] Sandra Heiler, Stanley Zdonik, "Object Views: Extending the Vision," *Proceedings of the 6th International Conference on Data Engineering*, pp. 86-93, 1990.

[Kim90] Won Kim, Introduction to Object-Oriented Databases, The MIT Press, 1990.

[Kimu91] Yutaka Kimura, Kunitoshi Tsuruoka, "A View Class Mechanism for Object-Oriented Database Systems," *Proceedings of the 2nd International Symposium on Database Systems for Advanced Applications*, pp. 269-273, 1991.

[Sch91] Marc H. Scholl et al, "Updatable Views in Object-Oriented Databases," *Proceedings of the 2nd International Conference DOOD'91*, pp. 189-207, 1991.

[Sha90] Gail M. Shaw and Stanley B. Zdonik, "A Query Algebra for Object-Oriented Databases," *Proceedings of 6th International Conference on Data Engineering*, pp. 154-162, 1990.

[Str90] Dave D. Straube and M. Tamer Özsu, "Queries and Query Processing in Object-Oriented Database Systems," *ACM Transactions on Information Systems*, Vol. 8, No. 4, pp. 387-430, Oct. 1990.

[Ta88] Katsumi Tanaka, Masatoshi Yoshikawa, Kozo Ishihara, "Schema Virtualization in Object-Oriented databases," *Proceedings of the 4th International Conference on Data Engineering*, pp. 23-30, 1988.

[Yu91] Li Yu and Sylvia L. Osborn, "An Evaluation Framework for Algebraic Object-Oriented Query Models," *Proceedings of the 7th International Conference on Data Engineering*, pp. 670-677, 1991.

(Invited Paper)

Refactoring and Aggregation

Ralph E. Johnson
Department of Computer Science
University of Illinois at Urbana-Champaign
Urbana, Illinois 61801
johnson@cs.uiuc.edu

William F. Opdyke
AT&T Bell Laboratories
Naperville, Illinois 60566
opdyke@iexist.att.com

Abstract

Object-oriented programs evolve by means other than just the addition of new classes. The changes to object-oriented programs that have been most studied are those based on inheritance, on reorganizing a class hierarchy. However, aggregation is a relationship between classes that is just as important as inheritance, and many changes to an object-oriented design involve the aggregate/component relationship. This paper describes some common refactorings based on aggregation, including how to convert from inheritance to an aggregation, and how to reorganize an aggregate/component hierarchy just as one might reorganize a class inheritance hierarchy.

1 Introduction

Object-oriented programming is advertised as leading to more extensible programs than conventional programming [Mey88]. Modifications to a system that would require many changes in conventional programming often can be carried out in an object-oriented program by simply adding new classes. Nevertheless, there are many times that even object-oriented programs must be changed.

Object-oriented programs must sometimes be changed to reuse them. Consider the problem of integrating two independently developed class libraries [Hol93]. The libraries are likely to have gratuitous differences, such as different definitions for basic classes like list or rectangle, or different names for operations that they have in common, or one library requiring the objects that it manipulates to be subclasses of X, and the other requiring the objects it manipulates to be subclasses of Y, where X and Y are orthogonal. These inconsistencies can be eliminated by changing one library to use the basic classes of the other, or the operation names of the other, or declaring that classes X and Y are different views of the same class. The inconsistencies can be hard to eliminate without changing either library. The usual strategy, to use wrappers to try to make objects from one library act like objects from the other library, has many disadvantages[Hol93].

Changes to requirements often require changes to a design. Consider adding a new formatting algorithm to a text editor, or a new interest calculation algorithm to a bank's accounting system. If the original system had only one choice of algorithm then it was probably made the responsibility of the central objects of the application, such as the text editor or an account. But if there are many alternative algorithms then an algorithm will probably be represented as a separate component. A text editor will have a "current formatting mode", and a bank account will have an "interest rate rule". If the original designer of the class didn't forsee this variability then it will be necessary to refactor the class by creating a new component and reassigning some of the class's responsibilities to it.

Even the simplest refactorings can be hard to implement. Changing the name of a variable is not just performing a search-and-replace on the source file; variable scopes can be nested and determining the scope of a variable requires parsing its program. Changing the name of a procedure requires determining the set of procedures that can be invoked by a procedure call, which requires type checking in a object-oriented program. Although these refactorings are non-trivial to implement, they pose no new theoretical problem.

High-level refactorings are not only hard to implement, they are hard to define. Consider the problem of finding a common superclass for two classes. It is not hard to move identically implemented operations and variables to the new superclass. In fact, it is possible to find a set of superclasses that minimize code duplication [Ber91, Cas91, Cas92, GM93]. These algorithms assume that operations will not change their name or be rewritten in any way, so the problem is one of deciding on a class hierarchy and where operations and variables are placed in it. If operations have to be renamed, split into pieces, or rewritten, then the problem becomes much harder[OJ93], and that is what happens when abstract superclasses are discovered in practice.

This paper describes high-level refactorings based on aggregations. These include how to reorganize an aggregate/component hierarchy just as one might reorganize a class inheritance hierarchy and how to convert from inheritance to an aggregation. One of the main conclusions is that the aggregate/component relationship is not well supported by our current programming languages.

2 A Software Refactory

This work is driven by our goal of a *software refactory*, an environment for refactoring programs. A refactoring is a program transformation that reorganizes a program without changing its behavior. We have noticed that programs are often refactored to make them more reusable and easier to maintain [JF88, OJ90]. Not all program changes are refactorings, but refactorings are often used to make other program changes easier. For example, in the case of adding an algorithm to a text editor, the refactoring that converts the algorithm into an object will be followed by a program change that adds the new algorithm. Thus, we believe that the ability to refactor a program easily will make programs more reusable and extensible.

A software refactory will be similar to a high-level editor, except that many of the changes it would make would require understanding the semantics of the programming language. For example, changing the name of a function, or moving a function from one class to another, would change all the places that the function was called. The refactory would support high-level refactorings such as reorganizing the class hierarchy, converting reuse by inheritance into reuse by composition, and breaking an object into smaller objects. It would check for conditions in which a refactoring cannot be applied, and would be able to undo refactorings so that users could experiment and see which design alternative was best.

A refactory will always be language dependent, because it must understand the language of the programs that it is manipulating. First, we examined refactorings with the goal of making a refactory for C++, but we could not find any tools for manipulating C++ programs. We developed one of our own, but, due to the complexity of C++, we were not able to make it handle all of C++ in the time that we had. Nevertheless, it was sufficient for prototyping some of the refactoring algorithms [Opd92].

Currently we are developing a refactory for Smalltalk-80 that we hope will be a useful tool. Smalltalk-80 makes it easy to manipulate programs, and has classes for representing classes, methods, and parse trees. The major problem with refactoring Smalltalk-80 programs is its lack of a type system. We have dealt with this problem by using conservative analysis algorithms, by depending on user guidance, and by introducing type information in various ways to guide the refactory. If we were able to use an existing system for manipulating C++ programs then it would probably be easier to make a refactory for C++ than for Smalltalk.

Our experience is that refactoring is commonly practiced by both C++ and Smalltalk programmers, and we believe that it is a fundamental part of the object-oriented development process. Moreover, the kind of refactorings and they way that they are carried out are similar in these two languages. The differences between these languages result in some difference in how refactorings are carried out, and we will describe these differences in this paper.

The desire to automate refactorings leads to a desire to be able to ensure that a given refactoring is correct. "Correct" cannot mean that it actually makes the design easier to reuse, since this depends on the intent of the designer. Thus, "correct" means only that the refactoring does not change the behavior of the program, that it does not introduce any faults into the program. This has an impact on what we consider a refactoring.

3 Aggregation

Inheritance models the *is-a* relation, while aggregation models the *has-a* relation. However, these relations are less distinct than might be thought at first. Is a window a rectangle with extra behavior [CH86, Kay84], or does a window have a shape, which is a rectangle? Is a pixel a point, or does a pixel have a location, which is a point [Ros92]? Different people give different answers to these questions, and it is common for a person's answer to change over time. On the one hand, both points of view can lead to working programs. On the other hand, they differ in how the resulting designs will be reused and the kind of changes that can easily be made to them. It is important to be able to change software so it reflects the current point of view.

It is usually easy to distinguish between these relations when we are modeling physical objects. For example, a car *is a* vehicle, but it *has* an engine, and it is unlikely that anyone would decide otherwise. However, assigning responsibilities to objects can still be arbitrary. For example, it is easy to imagine cases where the fuel efficiency of a car would be modeled as an attribute of an engine, though in general it is an attribute of the car that depends on the car's weight and chassis, as well as the engine. When assigning responsibility to objects is arbitrary, it will be common for designers to change their minds about how it should be assigned, and it is important to be able to change software so that responsibility is shifted from one object (like the engine) to another (like the car).

Previous work on refactorings for object-oriented programs focused on reorganizing inheritance hierarchies and moving variables and functions within inheritance hierarchies [Ber91, Cas91, Cas92, OJ93]. But it is possible to move variables and functions between aggregates and components just like they can be moved between subclasses and superclasses. This paper not only describes refactorings that refine aggregations by moving variables and functions between aggregate and component classes, it describes refactorings that replace inheritance with aggregation.

3.1 An Example

Consider a class Drawing that consists of a collection of GraphicalObjects. Initially, the Drawing was responsible for keeping track of the location of each GraphicalObject; hence, the location of each GraphicalObject was stored in the Drawing class. This approach was reasonable for handling operations such as moving GraphicalObjects around the screen and selecting them. However, as the program matured, features were added that modeled constraints between GraphicalObjects, so that (for example) when a GraphicalObject was moved, other GraphicalObjects would automatically reposition or resize themselves. To implement these features, it was more natural to store the location of a GraphicalObject within the GraphicalObject itself; when a GraphicalObject was moved, other GraphicalObjects were notified of the change. They could then access the locations of the objects that they depended on and could automatically reshape or reposition themselves based on their (locally stored) position.

3.2 Exclusive Components

One might think that it is easy to move a variable from an aggregate class to the class of one of its components: add accessing functions to the component for reading and writing the variable and change each access of the variable in the aggregate to a call on one of these accessing functions of the component. But this works only if there is a one-to-one mapping between the old variable (in the aggregate class) and its replacement variable (in the component class).

For example, if a Drawing associates a list of GraphicalObjects with a list of locations, the locations can be moved to the GraphicalObject only if each GraphicalObject is unique. If a GraphicalObject can be inserted into a Drawing several times, each with its own location, then locations cannot be moved on GraphicalObject.

There are many ways to model aggregation in current programming languages. In C++, for example, there are three ways; having the class of the component as a "private" superclass [ES90], having a member variable of the class of the component, and having a member variable that points to the class of the component. The first two are essentially the same, allocating space for the component along with the aggregate, ensuring that a component can belong to only one aggregate, and specifying the class of the component at compile-time. The third technique is more powerful, since it makes it possible to use components of varying classes and for an aggregate to dynamically vary its components, but is dangerous. Possible problems include:

- it is possible to omit the initialization of the variable that points to the component
- it is possible for an object to be referenced by many other objects
- when an aggregate gets a new component dynamically, it may lose values previously stored in the old component.

Smalltalk has only the third technique.

None of these techniques exactly matches what is needed to express the aggregate/component relationship. What is needed is something like the *exclusive composite* references of ORION [BK87, Kim90]. A one-for-one mapping also implies that each instance of the aggregate class contains a unique component; that is, that a component object is exclusive to one aggregate object. What we need is to make sure that a component object can only be assigned to one aggregate object at a time. Put another way, an instance (object) assigned to one component member variable must not simultaneously be assigned to another component member variable. For example, in an **Automobile** object the same **Tire** object cannot be assigned as both the *leftFrontTire* and *rightFrontTire*; similarly, it cannot be assigned to two **Automobiles** at the same time. But we need the freedom to swap tires, or to replace tires of one class with tires of another class.

Programmers that carry out refactorings by hand have to analyze the program first to tell whether a variable is a exclusive component. Thus, this is important design information that should be captured by either the programming language or by the programming environment. An automated tool to support refactoring will also need information about which variables hold exclusive components. Because current languages lack support, the programming environment must keep track of exclusive components.

3.3 Refactoring

One of the main issues in moving functions from an aggregate class to the class of one of its components is whether these functions reference variables and functions remaining in the aggregate class. This gives rise to two different refactoring approaches for handling such references: storing in the component a pointer to the aggregate object (as in section 4.2.1) or passing a pointer to the aggregate object as an argument in calls to all functions that reference variables and functions remaining in the aggregate class (as in section 4.2.2).

A useful refactoring is to add to each component a pointer to the aggregate of which it is a part. First, the component class must be given a variable **aggregate**. Whenever the aggregate inserts a component, it must initialize the component's **aggregate** variable. As long as the component is an exclusive component, all of an aggregate's components will have a pointer to their aggregate.

There are some conservative dataflow algorithms that can detect the most common situations in which a variable holds an exclusive component and that will detect the most common situations. However, it is not hard to invent programs that these algorithms cannot handle [Opd92]. It is probably better to check that a component is an exclusive component dynamically, by setting a component's **aggregate** variable to nil when the component is removed from an aggregate, and checking that a component has no aggregate when it is inserted into an aggregate. Statically checking that a variable holds an exclusive component would ensure that the transformation was only carried out if it were behavior preserving, *i.e.*, if it were a refactoring. Using dynamic checks will create programs that produce run-time errors if the variable does not in fact hold an exclusive component. However, these errors will be easily detected and can be accurately reported, so the extra power of the dynamic checking might be preferred to the safety of the static checks. A refactory could perform both static and dynamic checks, warning of transformations that it cannot guarantee to be correct. As long as refactorings are easy to reverse, this might be a satisfactory solution.

3.4 Moving Variables to Components

A variable can be moved from an aggregate class to a component class only if the component is an exclusive component, *i.e.*, the component is a part of no more than one aggregate at a time. Moreover, the variable can be moved only if it is currently updated every time the component is replaced. In many cases components are never replaced, so this precondition is easy to check. Otherwise, each place in the program where the component is changed has to be examined to find whether the value of the variable is changed, too.

If these preconditions are met, the refactoring is easy to carry out. First, the variable access should be abstracted, *i.e.*, the aggregate should be given functions to read and and write the variable, and all accesses of the variable should be replaced by function calls. A C++ program might also need a function that returns the address of a variable. Then the variable should be moved and the accessing functions should be changed to access the component instead of the aggregate. Since C++ allows direct access to public variables in other objects, it isn't strictly necessary to create accessing functions, but it is generally considered good style. Accessing functions are always required in Smalltalk.

Other changes are usually needed to clean up after the refactoring. For example, if the component was accessing the variable that was moved from the aggregate then it is possible for the component class to use expressions of the form aggregate−>getVar() where getVar is of the form return component−>getVar(). In other words, the component is going through the aggregate to get a value stored in the component. These cases should be changed to access the variable directly.

3.5 Moving Functions to Components

The refactoring described in this section moves a single function F from an aggregate class A to a component class C. In practice, a set of functions and variables will be moved all at once, but it is easier to think about a single function at a time.

Moving F does not require that C be an exclusive component of A, but it does require being able to find a reference to C whenever F is called. Moreover, it is likely that F must still be able to refer to an instance of A even after it has been moved from A. Suppose that F calls a function G defined in A. After F is moved, it must still be able to refer to an instance of A so that it can call the same definition of G that it called before it was moved. This reference could be one of the arguments to F, which probably means that an extra argument must be added to F, or it could be stored in one of the variables of the component. Passing a reference as an argument to F results in delegation, which is a general technique for replacing inheritance with aggregation [Lie86, JZ91]. If an extra argument is added to F then the interface to F will change when it is moved. All accesses to variables in A by F should be abstracted before F is moved. Thus, we only have to consider the problem of having F call functions in A, not accessing variables.

Moving a function means that the name of the aggregate and component inside the function will change. Before the move, the aggregate was self (in Smalltalk) or this (in C++), but afterwards the component will be self or this. Thus, every use of the aggregate should be changed to the **aggregate** variable. If each component has a variable that points to its aggregate (*i.e.*, if it has declared aggregate as a variable) then that variable can be used. Otherwise, the aggregate must be an argument to the function, which implies that the signature of the function will change when it is moved. Similarly, uses of the component should be replaced with uses of self or this. Of course, if F does not use any variables or functions of A or use a reference to the aggregate in any way then there is no problem in simply moving it to C.

F can be replaced with a forwarding function in A, or every original call to F by clients of A can be converted into an operation on C. For example, anA− >f() might be converted to anA− >component− >f(). It is probably better to use accessing functions unless the client already has a reference to the component, but either transformation preserves the behavior of the program. Since the signature of F in C might be different from its signature when it was in A, forwarding functions in A can hide this change from clients.

When a set of variables and functions is moved it will be common for all the references to some of those variables and functions to be from C. Thus, some of the forwarding functions left behind will have no calls on them, and they should be removed.

C++ requires that F only reference public members of A, since functions in C will not be able to reference "protected" members of A. Thus, it might be necessary to make members of A public before moving F. Another possible solution is to use the "friend" feature of C++. This concern will occur with any statically-typed language that supports multiple interfaces to a single class, but will not effect dynamically typed languages such as Smalltalk.

During refactoring, the new variables and functions of the component class are added before the old variables and functions are deleted from the aggregate class. Sometimes a component class will be a superclass (or subclass) of an aggregate class. For example, in the original Smalltalk-80 Model/View/Controller framework the class View was both the superclass of all windowing classes, but also had a set of subviews that were its components. In this case, naming conflicts might occur when the variables and functions are added to the component class. When potential naming conflicts are detected, the variables and functions being added to the component class should be automatically renamed. After the refactoring is finished, the user can restore the original names of the variables and functions that have moved.

3.6 Moving Members into Aggregate(s)

Just as variables and functions are sometimes moved from aggregate to component classes, the inverse operation (from component to aggregate class) is sometimes useful. This refactoring adds variables and functions to an aggregate class, replacing variables and functions in one of its components.

This refactoring is similar to the previous one. Variables can be moved only if the component is an exclusive component. If an aggregate has more than one instance of a component then moving a variable will require adding a variable for each instance.

Moving a function might require changing its signature. The aggregate almost always has a reference to its component, so often this reference can be used and the functions do not need an extra argument. However, if the aggregate has many components of the same class then the extra argument will be needed to distinguish between the various components.

4 Replacing Inheritance with Aggregation

Not only can the aggregate/component graph be refactored just like the class inheritance graph, but the two graphs are duals of each other, and one relationship can be replaced with the other for the purposes of code sharing. This has been shown by work on delegation [Lie86]. The refactoring described in this section usually, but not always, results in delegation, and can be seen as an algorithm for transforming a program to use delegation in a language that does not support it directly.

Although it is possible to convert aggregation to inheritance, converting inheritance to aggregation seems to be more common. Perhaps this is because inheritance seems more stylish, or perhaps people overuse inheritance because it is a new technique. Another possibility is that inheritance is used more because object-oriented languages tend to support it better. Classes must explicitly delegate operations to their components, but they transparently inherit operations from superclasses.

Whatever the reason, it is well known that programs are often made more reusable by replacing a use of inheritance with aggregation. Many design patterns, such as Wrapper and Strategy, are essentially ways of using aggregation instead of inheritance[GHJV93]. Components can be changed dynamically, so using components instead of inheritance often makes it easier for a user to customize a system at run-time. On the other hand, systems with many small components are hard to understand and it is easier to see the inheritance relationships in a program than the relationships between aggregates and components.

The next two examples illustrate how inheritance can be replaced with aggregation. The first was created to be an example. Although we believe it is realistic, its main virtue is its simplicity. The second example occurred during the development of a large system written in C++. Although it is not as easy to understand, it is very realistic.

4.1 Matrix Example

Consider the case where the class TwoDimensionalArray contains the variable *elements* to store the array values, and the functions *get* and *put* to access and update array elements.

A new class Matrix is added, as a subclass of TwoDimensionalArray. The Matrix class inherits the array representation and operations *get* and *put* from its superclass, and adds the functions *matrixMultiply, rotate* and *matrixInverse*, which are defined in terms of the functions inherited from TwoDimensionalArray. For example, the function *matrixMultiply* can be defined as:

```
Matrix matrixMultiply (Matrix anotherMatrix)
  { ... j=get(x,y);
    ... put(k,x,y); ...};
```

It seems reasonable at first to model this relationship using inheritance. A Matrix could in some sense be thought of as a subtype of TwoDimensionalArray. Also, the higher level matrix operations call the lower level functions inherited from the superclass.

There are problems with this design, however. For applications where (for example) matrices are sparse, a representation other than a two dimensional array would be more efficient. More fundamentally, a matrix is a mathematical abstraction that can be represented in different ways. A matrix *has* a representation, as opposed to being a kind of representation. Operations on the abstraction should be separated from operations on its representation.

One way to realize this separation is to include an instance of TwoDimensionalArray as a component of the (aggregate) Matrix class. This could be done by:

1. adding an instance of the class TwoDimensionalArray as a variable in class Matrix (here called *matrixRepr*).

2. replacing all calls to the functions *get* and *put* in class Matrix with calls to the corresponding functions in the component.

Now (for example) the function *matrixMultiply* in class Matrix can be defined as:

```
Matrix matrixMultiply (Matrix anotherMatrix)
  { ... j=matrixRepr->get(x,y);
    ... matrixRepr->put(k,x,y); ...};
```

The *get* and *put* functions are now referenced through the new component.

The inheritance link can now be removed between the classes Matrix and TwoDimensionalArray without affecting the behavior of the program.

These refactorings allow the program to be expanded later to support multiple representations for multiple uses. For example, a sparse matrix could be implemented using a different type (class) of *matrixRepr*.

4.2 MemoryObjectContainer Example

The *Choices* file system framework [Mad92, MCRL89] is one of several interlocking frameworks that are part of the *Choices* object-oriented operating system project at the University of Illinois. A *Choices* file system has MemoryObjects, which are objects like files and disks that support read and write operations, and InodeSystems, which create and provide access to MemoryObjects. One of the subclasses of MemoryObject is MemoryObjectView, which treats a piece of another MemoryObject as a separate MemoryObject. InodeSystems manage tables stored on the disk, so an early version of the file system framework (see Figure 1) defined InodeSystem as a subclass of MemoryObjectView, hence MemoryObject. This allowed InodeSystem to inherit low level operations such as read and write from MemoryObjectView. However, InodeSystem really represents a different abstraction from a MemoryObject. The design of the framework was refined as follows:

1. component variables, which were instances of MemoryObject, were added to InodeSystem to represent the table that it used.

2. The high level operations defined in InodeSystem were changed to invoke behavior in the new components.

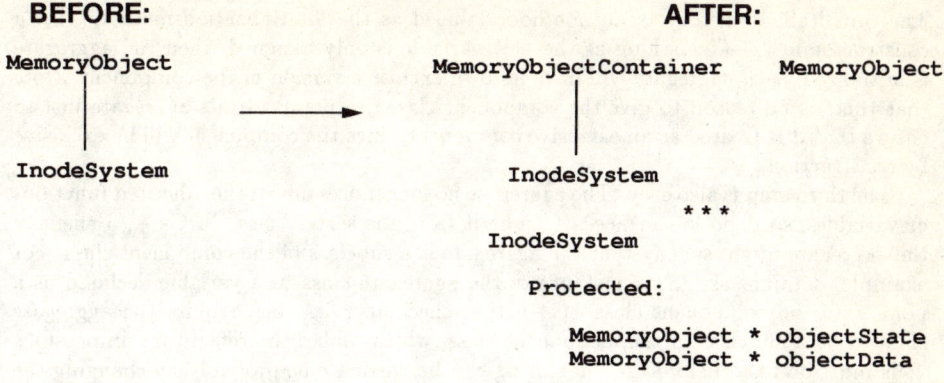

Figure 1: Superclass Converted to Component

Later the class MemoryObjectContainer was added, and InodeSystem was made a subclass of it. A MemoryObjectContainer kept track of partitioning a large MemoryObject into a set of smaller MemoryObjects (i.e. a disk into a set of files). An InodeSystem was a specialization of MemoryObjectContainer. This shows how one refactoring often leads into another.

Both before and after the refactorings were applied, the MemoryObject (server) class provided operations to the InodeSystem (client) class.[1] Before the refactoring, the services were inherited by the InodeSystem class; later, they were provided by instances of the MemoryObject class that were stored as components of InodeSystem.

4.3 How to Convert Inheritance to Aggregation

Suppose that A is a subclass of C. A can reuse behavior of C by aggregation instead of inheritance by:

1. adding an instance of C as a component variable of A.

2. replacing references to variables and functions inherited from C with references to the component

3. removing the inheritance link between A and C.

Simply adding a new variable without referencing it is trivial. However, the variable needs to be properly initialized with an instance of C. This is not hard to do in C++, because there is a single point (the constructor) at which the aggregate is created and where the component variable must be initialized. It is harder in Smalltalk, because initialization of new objects is done by convention rather than being a part of the language.

---

[1] Looking at classes from the client/server point of view is described, for example, in [Sny86, WBWW90]. A superclass is a server to its (client) subclasses, as is a component a server to its (client) aggregate classes.

The Smalltalk Refactory treats methods labeled as the "initialization method" like a constructor in C++. As long as the new variable is only assigned when the aggregate is initialized, each aggregate will have its own exclusive version of the component. Note that there is no reason to give the component class C a pointer to its aggregate just to ensure that it is treated as an exclusive component, since the component will be exclusive by construction.

The third step is also easy. The aggregate no longer uses any of the inherited functions or variables, so it no longer needs to inherit from the server class. In C++, a client of the aggregate might specify that the aggregate is a subclass of the component class. For example, it might assign an instance of the aggregate class to a variable declared as a pointer to the component class. C++ type-checking rules then require the aggregate class to be a subclass of the component class, which makes the refactoring impossible. This must be fixed before the refactoring can be carried out, probably by changing the type of the variable to a common superclass of the aggregate and component. It is not a problem in Smalltalk, because Smalltalk relies on run-time type-checking.

The second step is the hard one. References to inherited variables and functions must be replaced, not only in A, but also in its clients. The easiest way to ensure this is to move each function inherited by A to its component C, to abstract all uses of inherited variables that remain, (i.e. to convert uses of them in the A or its clients to calls on functions in A), and then to change the accessing functions to use the component function.

Note that C is both the source and the destination of the functions being moved. Functions have to be changed to ensure that they have a reference to the aggregate and so can call functions defined for it. If C is given a pointer to its aggregate then the new versions of the function will use that. Otherwise, each function will be given a pointer to the aggregate as an argument. If clients of A call any of the functions that it inherited from C then A should be given forwarding functions that have the same signature as the original inherited functions, but that are implemented by calling the moved function on the component.

Converting inheritance to aggregation may thus require changing the server class (superclass) as well as the client class (subclass). Regardless of whether pointers are set up statically or are passed in at each call on the client, these changes are error-prone and so programmers tend to postpone making them if their only tool is a text editor. Performing these changes automatically eliminates the possibility of introducing errors and should encourage programmers to refactor programs more often.

5 Discussion

5.1 Related Research in Object-Oriented Databases

This work is related to research in schema evolution in object-oriented databases (OODBs). Schema evolution has been studied for several OODB systems[PS87, WP91, DZ91] in addition to the work on ORION cited above, which is the work that influenced us the most. Casais [Cas91] compares schema evolution features of these object-oriented database systems. ORION represents aggregations as *complex objects*. A *composite link* represents a relationship between a composite object and its component. A *composite link* can carry special semantics, such as that the component is exclusive to one composite object. We used this concept to define our notion of exclusive components.

OODB schema changes need to not only change the variable definitions but also change any existing *live* instances. Since our research originally focused on refactoring C++ programs, we were not concerned with *live* instances, since we assumed that after refactoring the program would be recompiled and started up without any preexisting objects. Instead, we focused on changes to both functions and data. OODB schema evolution research has placed less emphasis upon member functions, only ensuring that functions are recompiled when their class is changed, but not ensuring that they behave the same. One way to say this is that they ensure structural consistency, but not behavioral consistency, which is our goal[DZ91].

A Smalltalk refactory must deal with live instances. Current Smalltalk systems already support adding and removing functions, so it is only moving variables that is a problem. The refactorings described in this paper require a one-to-one relationship between old and new variables, so it should be possible to implement them by replacing old instances with new using the **become**: operations, but we haven't implemented this yet.

5.2 Conclusion

A designer does not always choose the correct mechanism for modeling a particular relationship. A modeling mechanism should be chosen that minimizes the effort required to develop a program and, more importantly, to evolve it over time. A program should be structured such that the encapsulation boundaries - the boundaries between easily substitutable piece-parts - correspond to the most probable scenarios for requirements evolution. Moving from inheritance to aggregation or moving variables and functions between aggregate and component classes draws new encapsulation boundaries, which will make future modifications easier if the new requirements fall along those boundaries. Aggregation provides a cleaner separation between parts of a program than inheritance, which is appropriate if in the future one of these parts may be replaced while the other part(s) are not. Since it is impossible to know in advance what future requirements will be, encapsulation boundaries sometimes need to be refined later.

This paper has described a transformation between two modeling mechanisms: inheritance and the aggregate/component relationship. It has also described how to refine aggregations by moving variables and functions between aggregate and component classes, in a manner analogous to moving variables and functions within inheritance hierarchies.

An important focus of our research has been on automatically supporting refactorings in a way that preserves the behavior of a program. This is important since otherwise programmers avoid carrying out refactorings because of the well-founded fear of creating errors, and so the design of the program diverges from the way the programmers think about it.

Most of the refactorings are easy to implement (given the appropriate program representation) and it is almost trivial to show that they are behavior preserving. However, some of the refactorings are much more complicated, and this paper has focused on some of them. In addition to the refactorings involving aggregations, we have investigated refactorings for refining object-oriented programs by generalizing or specializing a class [Opd92, OJ93] and for eliminating case analysis [Opd92].

Although this paper has focused on refactoring programs, refactoring designs or other object-oriented models would be essentially the same.

Current programming languages provide poor support for aggregations. Delegation based languages and some database languages emphasize aggregations more than conventional languages, and there have been a few other examinations of aggregation [BC87, WP91], but we feel that aggregation is not appreciated as much as it should be. As object-oriented technology is maturing and as aggregations are being recognized as an important modeling mechanism, we expect to see better support for making aggregations explicit.

6 Acknowledgments

Larry Mayka, Ed Rak and Larry Zurawski reviewed drafts of this paper. Brian Foote proposed the matrix example, and has provided helpful comments. Peter Madany was the main author of the *Choices* file system framework and helped us understand its evolution. Dan Walkowski has been the main implementor of the Smalltalk Refactory, and Don Roberts has also helped implement it.

AT&T Bell Laboratories supported William F. Opdyke's research at the University of Illinois under the full-time doctoral support program. The work on the Smalltalk Refactory was supported in part by a grant from the Union Bank of Switzerland.

References

[BC87] E. Blake and S. Cook. On including part hierarchies in object-oriented languages, with an implementation in smalltalk. In *Proceedings of ECOOP '87, Special Issue of BIGRE*, pages 45–54, June 1987.

[Ber91] Paul L. Bergstein. Object-preserving class transformations. In *Proceedings of OOPSLA '91*, 1991.

[BK87] Jay Banerjee and Won Kim. Semantics and implementation of schema evolution in object-oriented databases. In *Proceedings of the ACM SIGMOD Conference*, 1987.

[Cas91] Eduardo Casais. *Managing Evolution in Object Oriented Environments: An Algorithmic Approach*. PhD thesis, University of Geneva, 1991.

[Cas92] Eduardo Casais. An incremental class reorganization approach. In *Proceedings of ECOOP '92: European Conference on Object-Oriented Programming*, pages 114–132, June 1992.

[CH86] Brad Cox and Bill Hunt. Objects, icons, and software-ICs. *Byte*, pages 161–176, August 1986.

[DZ91] Christing Delcourt and Roberto Zicari. The design of an integrity consistency checker for an object oriented database system. In *Proceedings of ECOOP '91: European Conference on Object-Oriented Programming*, pages 97–117, July 1991.

[ES90] Margaret A. Ellis and Bjarne Stroustrup. *The Annotated C++ Reference Manual*. Addison-Wesley Publishing Co., Reading, MA, 1990.

[GHJV93] Erich Gamma, Richard Helm, Ralph E. Johnson, and John Vlissides. Design patterns: Abstraction and reuse of object-oriented design. In *Proceedings of ECOOP '93, European Conference on Object-Oriented Programming*, pages 406–431, July 1993.

[GM93] Robert Godin and Hafedh Mili. Building and maintaining analysis-level class hierarchies using galois lattices. In *Proceedings of OOPSLA '93*, September 1993. to be presented.

[Hol93] Urs Holzle. Integrating indepently-developed components in object-oriented languages. In *Proceedings of ECOOP '93, European Conference on Object-Oriented Programming*, pages 36–56, July 1993.

[JF88] Ralph E. Johnson and Brian Foote. Designing reusable classes. *Journal of Object-Oriented Programming*, 1(2):22–35, 1988.

[JZ91] Ralph E. Johnson and Jonathon Zweig. Delegation in C++. *Journal of Object-Oriented Programming*, 4(7):31–34, November/December 1991.

[Kay84] Alan Kay. Computer software. *Scientific American*, 251(3):53–59, September 1984.

[Kim90] Won Kim. *Introduction to Object-Oriented Databases*. MIT Press, 1990.

[Lie86] Henry Lieberman. Using prototypical objects to implement shared behavior in object-oriented systems. In *Proceedings of OOPSLA '86*, pages 214–223, November 1986. printed as SIGPLAN Notices, 21(11).

[Mad92] Peter W. Madany. *An Object-Oriented Framework for Filesystems*. PhD thesis, University of Illinois at Urbana-Champaign, 1992. Also Technical Report No. UIUCDCS–R–92–1751, Department of Computer Science, University of Illinois at Urbana-Champaign.

[MCRL89] Peter W. Madany, Roy H. Campbell, Vincent F. Russo, and Doublas E. Leyens. A class hierarchy for building stream-oriented file systems. In *Proceedings of ECOOP '89: European Conference on Object-Oriented Programming*, pages 311–328, July 1989.

[Mey88] Bertrand Meyer. *Object-oriented Software Construction*. Prentice Hall, 1988.

[OJ90] William F. Opdyke and Ralph E. Johnson. Refactoring: An aid in designing application frameworks and evolving object-oriented systems. In *Proceedings of Symposium on Object-Oriented Programming Emphasizing Practical Applications (SOOPPA)*, September 1990.

[OJ93] William F. Opdyke and Ralph E. Johnson. Creating abstract superclasses by refactoring. In *Proceedings of CSC '93: The ACM 1993 Computer Science Conference*, February 1993.

[Opd92] William F. Opdyke. *Refactoring Object-Oriented Frameworks*. PhD thesis, University of Illinois at Urbana-Champaign, 1992. Also Technical Report No. UIUCDCS-R-92-1759, Department of Computer Science, University of Illinois at Urbana-Champaign.

[PS87] D. Jason Penney and Jacob Stein. Class modification in the GemStone object-oriented dbms. In *Proceedings of OOPSLA '87*, 1987.

[Ros92] J. P. Rosen. What orientation should Ada objects take? *Communications of the ACM*, 35(11):71–76, November 1992.

[Sny86] Alan Snyder. Encapsulation and inheritance in object-oriented programming languages. In *Proceedings of OOPSLA '86*, pages 38–45, November 1986. printed as SIGPLAN Notices, 21(11).

[WBWW90] Rebecca Wirfs-Brock, Brian Wilkerson, and Lauren Wiener. *Designing Object-Oriented Software*. Prentice-Hall, 1990.

[WP91] Francis Wolinski and Jean-Francois Perrot. Representation of complex objects: Multiple facets with part-whole hierarchies. In *Proceedings of ECOOP '91: European Conference on Object-Oriented Programming*, pages 288–306, July 1991.

Transverse Activities:
Abstractions in Object–Oriented Programming *

Bent Bruun Kristensen

Aalborg University
Institute for Electronic Systems
Fredrik Bajers Vej 7, DK-9220 Aalborg Ø, Denmark
e-mail: bbkristensen@iesd.auc.dk

Abstract

A *transverse activity* is an activity executed by several objects in some combination. The activity is described as a single unit, separately from the descriptions of the participating objects. A transverse activity is described and executed by using the usual object–centric actions, i.e. the methods of the objects, and is seen as a natural supplement to the description of the cooperation of active objects.

Transverse activities support the modeling of our conceptual understanding of combined activities. Our conceptual understanding not only includes the recognition of usual components but also the recognition of activities combined from the individual actions of such components. We are used to recognize components as phenomena, but transverse activities are phenomena also and these activities may be classified, specialized, and aggregated, i.e. abstraction in this sense is possible also for such activities.

The description of a transverse activity must at least include a listing of the components participating in the activity and a listing of the sequence of actions making up the combined directive of the activity. In the specialization or aggregation of activities by means of other activities both the participants and the directive can be included in these forms of abstraction to support the underlying intention of transverse activities.

Usual language mechanisms such as class, object etc. in various forms are used to model phenomena and concepts. A ongoing revision and extension of such usual object–oriented language mechanisms is necessary to be able to model, directly and naturally, additional differentiating elements of conceptual understanding, such as e.g. transverse activities.

Transverse activities are illustrated and motivated by means of several minor fragments of a complex example and an conceptual understanding of transverse activities is outlined. Language mechanisms supporting the classification, specialization, and aggregation of transverse activities is defined by means of special activity–classes and –objects. Various possibilities for adding new and powerful features as part of such mechanisms are discussed. The meaning of the execution of activity–objects in relation to the execution of the components involved in the activity is defined in terms of interleaved execution.

1 Introduction

Object–Oriented Modeling In the "Scandinavian school of object–orientation" the view of programming is modeling, cf. the (simulation) models in SIMULA 67 [Dahl et al. 84]. An example of the consequences of the modeling view is that inheritance (or subclassing) is seen as the specialization of concepts, cf. e.g. the BETA language [Madsen et al. 93].

---

*This research was supported in part by the Danish Natural Science Research Council, No. 11-0061.

A more explicit interpretation of the modeling view is that language mechanisms support conceptual understanding in general. I.e. according to our knowledge of conceptual understanding we may introduce language mechanisms reflecting this knowledge, cf. [Kristensen & Østerbye 91]. In addition to concepts and phenomena as such this includes among others the intention and extension of concepts, the notion of properties, and elements of abstraction in the form of classification, specialization, and aggregation. Furthermore several views are possible on the characterization of the phenomena in the extension of a concept, such as the Aristotelian view or the prototypical view.

The approach is to get a better understanding of conceptual modeling and from this understanding to design (object–oriented) programming language mechanisms to support the understanding. In this way object–oriented programming is also object–oriented modeling.

As an illustrating example we shall use the "Conference Organizing Problem", [Olle et al. 82]. As discussed by Wasserman [1] concepts such as conference, technical-program, program-committee, PC-chairman, PC-member, and paper are introduced in the model. The concept paper may be refined to a hierarchy with accepted-paper and rejected-paper as specialized concepts of submitted-paper (corresponding to paper). The technical-program may be aggregated form paper-session, panel-session, and plenary-session.

Active Objects and Method Activations The modeling view on object–orientation implies that objects may be active. I.e. a description of an object may include an action part modeling the life cycle of the phenomenon. An active object may have its own thread and be executing concurrently with other objects. The abstraction mechanisms supporting e.g. specialization and aggregation must also handle such active objects, especially the action parts of the objects. An example of an active object is the system object in BETA.

In our example the objects created according to e.g. PC-chairman and PC-member may be seen as active objects. The "Conference Organizing Problem" is also discussed by Rumbaugh [2] where the life cycles of the concepts conference, submission, review, and registration are shown using state diagrams. Objects created according to these concepts may be seen as active objects which change state depending upon external (or internal) events.

Methods describe actions and actions are phenomena also. Such actions may be classified and the corresponding methods aggregated, cf. the attributes and (local) patterns in BETA. Methods are descriptions of object–centric actions only. But such actions may be specialized also, giving specialization hierarchies for actions, cf. the general use of patterns for describing methods in BETA.

In our example methods are introduced to model actions for the available components, e.g. PC-chairman will have the method register-paper and PC-member will have the method assign-paper.

Non Object–Centric Actions In the example it is natural to think of combined activities such as e.g. the total reviewing process and the reviewing activity for a single, given paper. Such activities may be identified as phenomena and be classified by concepts, e.g. review-activity. The activities are clearly different from the component–type phenomena usually identified in the modeling process. The reviewing activity is very important for our understanding and modeling of the conference organization and we may want to describe this activity in addition to, but separately from the usual components (and other similar activities). Such an activity can not exist without components and the components take part in the activity. The activity has an action sequence composed of method activations of the components and possible other transverse activities. Thus the activity is described transversely to the components and appears

---

[1] "From Object–Oriented Analysis to Design" and "Behavior and Scenarios in Object–Oriented Development", JOOP–92.
[2] "An Object or not an Object ?" and "Onward to OOPSLA", JOOP–92.

as a non object–centric action sequence. A motivation for transverse activities is also given in [Kristensen 93]. Figure 1 shows a snapshot of an activity aa with the components o1, o2, o3, and o4 taking part in the activity; currently the action sequence of the activity is activating a method of o4.

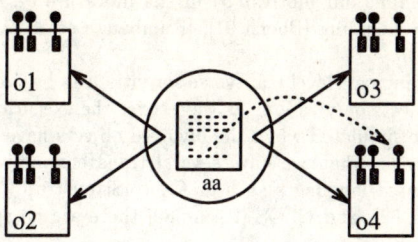

Figure 1: Transverse activity

In Wasserman's example components such as the PC-chairman, a number of PC-member's and the author take part in the reviewing activity. In Rumbaugh's example conference is described as an active object with three states Preconference, During-Conference, and Postconference in the state diagram. Thus conference may be seen as a transverse activity where author's, reviewer's, attendee's etc. take part and each of the three states itself is some activity. Also submission and review, where a submission generates many review's to be performed concurrently, may naturally be seen as transverse activities. However Rumbaugh's actual description of the life cycles of these concepts is some usual (possibly active) objects with a number of available methods to be executed in the usual object–centric way. Figure 2 shows a snapshot of a usual sequence of method activations among the associated components o1, o2, o3, and o4; a method of o1 is activated from outside and currently a method of o2 is executing.

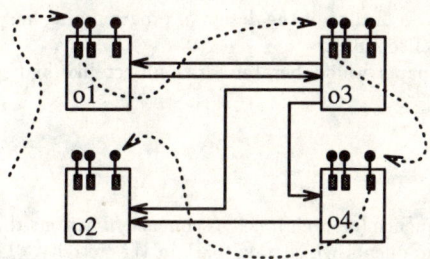

Figure 2: Object–centric method invocations

Analysis, Design, and Implementation Transverse activities are non object–centric actions involving several usual (component) objects. Such activities are not part of the existing methodologies for object-oriented analysis, design, and implementation; but such activities may to some extent be simulated by the existing mechanisms for classes and objects.

The motivations and benefits listed in [Coad & Yourdon 91a] and [Coad & Yourdon 91b] for the use of object-oriented analysis and design are promising; but this is not enough: The OOA and OOD methods presented are based on problem–domain constructs modeling components only. Problem–domain constructs modeling activities are equally important. Our thesis is that transverse activities may be as stable as the usual components in the model. Our claim is, that in order to better understand and carry out the modeling process we need transverse activities; and thus to distinguish between activities and components. Furthermore our claim is, that this distinction is not found (and motivated) in the literature on object–oriented modeling, analysis, and design, also including [Booch 91], [Rumbaugh et al. 91], [Wasserman et al. 90], and [Wirfs–Brock et al. 90].

At the programming language level transverse activities can be simulated by the usual mechanisms for classes and objects only as long as we restrict the execution to sequential execution. Such activities can not be simulated when the involved objects have their own action part and are executed concurrently or when we have several transverse activities to be executed concurrently. In object–oriented languages such as C++ [Stroustrup 91], Smalltalk [Goldberg & Robson 83], Eiffel [Meyer 92], and CLOS [Keene 89] there are no special mechanisms for the support of transverse activities.

Paper Organization In section 2 we discuss transverse activities from the modeling point of view. We see such activities as a powerful means of abstraction and we illustrate what the meaning of classification, specialization, and aggregation may be for activities. The presentation is given in terms of small examples. These are all related to the "Conference Organizing Problem" but they are not intended to form one complete model. The objective of this section is to give an intuitive understanding of the usefulness and expressiveness of transverse activities as abstractions in the modeling process. Section 2 is an illustration of additional conceptual understanding.

In section 3 we outline proposals for programming language mechanisms supporting transverse activities. The proposals are closely related to existing class and object mechanisms. We present basic mechanisms supporting a minimal version of activities and we discuss various possibilities for the design of more powerful mechanisms. Small examples from the "Conference Organizing Problem" are used to illustrate the proposals. The objective is partly to show that it is straightforward to introduce programming language mechanisms for transverse activities and partly to illustrate various possibilities for adding new and powerful features as part of such mechanisms. Section 3 is an outline of the design of programming language mechanisms derived from the understanding of section 2.

In the figures of the paper we deliberately draw object–like figures and use class names for these, and visa versa.

2 Modeling

An activity has a life sequence (or cycle), i.e. a sequence of actions to be executed. The actions involve a number of components which take part in the activity. Therefore a mechanism for modeling a transverse activity must have at least two parts, namely: The activity participants – describing the participants in the activity, and an activity directive – describing the combined action sequence for the participants. Participants are components taking part in the activity. The action sequence includes among others activations of the methods of the participating objects in some combination.

In our model for the "Conference Organizing Problem" we focus especially on the reviewing activity for papers. We may identify additional concepts such as author and reviewer and various actions (described as methods) performed by such components. In a traditional description without the use of transverse activities the reviewing activity as such is only implicitly described, distributed among the components involved in this activity: A collection of methods for the components and how these methods activate other components. Thus the review activity is described from the individual components view only.

Concepts and Phenomena Actual activities may be classified by some concept; the concept has some name, say activity. The description of activity includes the participants and the directive. The exemplification an-activity of activity is then classified as activity. Figure 3 is an illustration of the activity.

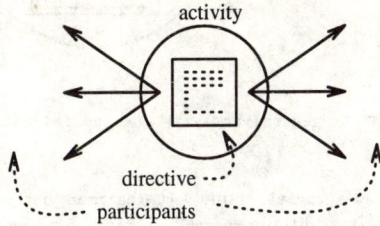

Figure 3: activity with directive and participants

To introduce transverse activities in the model we identify phenomena such as the reviewing activities and we classify such phenomena by concepts. The review-activity is a *concept* modeling the reviewing activity for a single paper. For the review-activity the *activity participants* are PC-chairman, author, and paper. The *activity directive* for the review-activity may be outlined as follows:

```
pre-review
notify PC-chairman about paper
paper-evaluation
notify author about evaluation
post-review
```

The directive is composed of other transverse activities and actions of the participating components. The directive is general for the various different kinds of reviewing activities; there may be some pre-review activity, e.g. involving some feedback on an extended abstract submitted by the author; and there may be a post-review activity at least involving the delivery of the final manuscript from the author. Thus pre-review, post-review, and paper-evaluation are seen as (exemplifications of) concepts too.

The actions notify PC-chairman about paper and notify author about evaluation are examples of actions of the transverse activity executed on behalf of the participating components, in this case the PC-chairman and the author.

Specialization Some special-activity may be described as a specialization of some other general-activity. The special-activity then has all the properties, i.e. general-participants and general-directive, of general-activity as well as the properties added in the description of the special-activity. In this way activities may form a specialization hierarchy. Figure 4 is an illustration of some general-activity and how the elements of this are intergated in the elements of the special-activity.

The review-activity is a concept being part of a specialization hierarchy of activities: review-activity is the most general concept and conference-review, workshop-review, and periodical-review are specializations of this. Also e.g. conference-review may itself be further specialized according to e.g. standard or non-standard conference review.

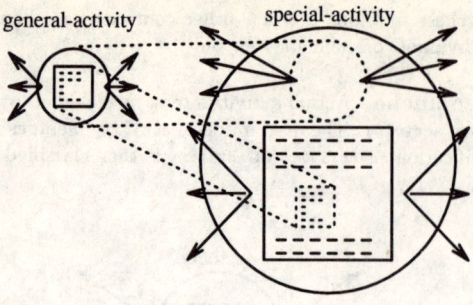

Figure 4: general-activity and special-activity

The participants of review-activity, namely PC-chairman, author, and paper are also participants of conference-review. In addition program-committee may be a participant in conference-review. Alternatively we may see program-committee as a participant only in the paper-evaluation activity appearing in the directive of review-activity and by the specialization also in the directive of conference-review.

An activity such as paper-evaluation may itself be part of a specialization hierarchy: In the workshop-review the chairman probably makes the decision alone, in the conference-review a fixed program committee may be available and in the periodical-review a collection of referees are usually available. Also this activity may possibly involve e.g. an iterative acceptance activity in situations where a paper may be conditionally accepted.

Let us consider a specialization of paper-evaluation as part of the conference-review. Assume that the participants of paper-evaluation are the PC-chairman, the reviewers, and the paper, where the PC-chairman and paper are available from the review-activity. In the conference-paper-evaluation the reviewers are a program-committee, which may be seen as a specialization of the reviewers in paper-evaluation. The specialization of the directive of paper-evaluation may be the following:

```
PC-chairman selects reviewers
the reviewers evaluate the paper
PC-chairman makes a decision
```

These are all examples of actions of the activity executed on behalf of the participating components, namely method activations of the reviewer's and the PC-chairman.

Aggregation Some whole-activity may be described as an aggregation of – among others – some part-activity. The properties, i.e. part-participants and part-directive, of the part-activity are used in various ways to form the corresponding properties of the whole-activity. In this way activities may form an aggregation hierarchy. Figure 5 is an illustration of some part-activity and how an exemplification of this is built-in as a part in (the directive of) a whole-activity.

We see the review-activity as an aggregation hierarchy of activities: The concepts pre-review, paper-evaluation, and post-review are used in the aggregation of (the directive of) review-activity.

```
pre-review    ...    paper-evaluation    ...    post-review
```

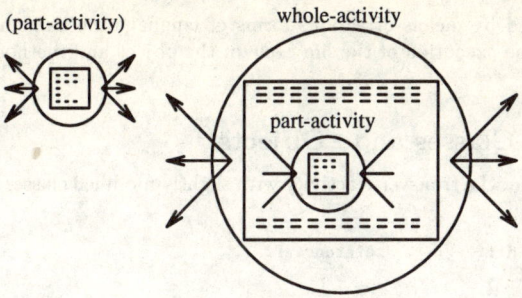

Figure 5: part-activity and whole-activity

Each of these subactivities may involve the activation of some remind-activity to keep the author and others aware of deadlines. The remind-activity may be described in general, i.e. outside the context of the review-activity and may as such have participants in a more general form, e.g. as sender, receiver, subject and a directive describing the possible iterative interaction between the sender and the receiver about the subject.

As part of the aggregation of paper-evaluation the sender, receiver, and subject must in the context of review-activity context denote respectively PC-chairman, author, and paper.

3 Language Mechanisms

We need programming language mechanisms to describe transverse activities including abstraction. Our goal is not to introduce an additional set of mechanisms to support transverse activities. Rather the intention is that slightly modified classes and objects, i.e. with references, methods, and an individual action sequence, can be used. In most object-oriented programming languages an object may have references to other objects and in some object-oriented languages objects may be active, executing concurrently. Our approach is to model (i.e. implement) a transverse activity with an active object with references, such that the activity participants are modeled by a list of references to the participating objects and the activity directive is modeled by the action part.

The following is a schematical illustration the language mechanisms of some general object-oriented language: The reference R in class C illustrates that the object oC (of class C) has a reference R to some other object of some class CC (not described). The action(...) clause illustrates that objects like object oC may have an individual action part and thus be inherently active. The action part describes the life cycle of the object and the object initiates its execution of this part when it is created. Also methods, M and M", are illustrated in class C.

```
C: (class
      ... method M:(...) ... method M":(...) ... reference R: CC
      ... action(... M" ... R.MM ...)
   class)

oC: object C
```

The description of the action part may involve the activation of methods in class C and methods for other objects than oC. Because the objects are active the interaction between objects is usually coordinated by means of various forms of language mechanisms [3] available for the synchronization of the execution of the life cycle of the object and method activation requests from other objects.

3.1 Activity–Classes and –Objects

Our approach is to model a transverse activity with slightly modified classes and objects, namely:

```
A: (a-class
      ... method M':(...) ... reference P: ...
      ... action( ... )
    a-class)

oA: a-object A
```

A is a special kind of class, an activity–class, and oA an activity–object of this class. A participant, modeled by a reference, and the directive, modeled by the action part, is similar, but not identical, to respective a reference and the action part of a usual class. Methods, such as M', may have a special meaning in activity–objects, but are not discussed further.

PC-chairman, author, and paper are activity participants of review-activity. The activity directive is composed of other transverse activities, namely pre-review, post-review, and paper-evaluation and actions of the participating components, namely notify-paper and notify-result (methods of PC-chairman and author):

```
review-activity:                          action
  (a-class                                ( pre-review
     reference The-chair: PC-chairman       The-chair>>notify-paper
     reference The-author: author           paper-evaluation
     reference The-paper: paper             The-author>>notify-result
                                            post-review )
                                          a-class)
```

In the following we discuss language mechanisms supporting abstraction (in terms of specialization and aggregation) for transverse activities and as a part of this the concurrent execution such activities.

Thesis: *An activity–object has participanting objects and a directive; the directive may include other activity–objects and method–activations of the participants*

3.2 Execution of Activity–Objects

In the action part of an object (modeling some transverse activity) we want to be able to describe the interactions of the activity. We see the transverse activity as an additional description of the life cycle of the object in accordance with the intention of transverse activities. I.e. the life cycle of an active (component) object is described both in its own action part and in various transverse activities in which it is participating.

In [Kristensen 93] is given a preliminary proposal for additional language mechanisms for describing the interactions of a transverse activity in terms of method activations. The intention is to avoid to introduce additional synchronization due to this kind of method activations. It is proposed to define the meaning in terms of interleaved execution of a participating objects own action part and methods of the object being activated as part of (one or more) transverse activities.

The following schematical example illustrates the mechanisms introduced:

---

[3] According to [Chin & Chanson 91] we have an *active object model*; the model is *static* with exactly one thread per object; the thread is controlled by the description in the action part.

```
A:(a-class ... reference rC: C ... action( ... rC>>M ... ) a-class)

oA: a-object A
```

The class A models a transverse activity and the object oA an activity–object of class A. The object rC is a participating object of class C; we assume that rC denotes the object oC. The construct rC>>M, appearing in the activity–object, has the meaning that the object rC is requested to execute its method M, cf. figure 6. The meaning of this construct is as if the object rC itself requested the execution of M. [4] This corresponds to the object rC activating one of its own methods, only is the description given outside oC. The object oC may at the same time be executing its action part, including the execution of e.g. M". The method M and the action part of the object are executed interleaved, i.e. at language–defined points the object will switch between the execution of M and its action part. [5]

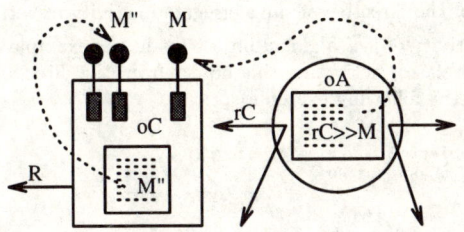

Figure 6: Execution of rC>>M

In the review-activity example we may have that both the PC-chairman and the author are actively doing other activities, such as respective research or teaching and writing activities, besides taking part in the review-activity. Such other activities may naturally be described in the life cycles (action parts) of these objects. Furthermore the PC-chairman and the author may participate of other (concurrent) transverse activities, either other kinds of activities e.g. selection committees or similar review activities, – and possibly in different roles.

```
PC-chairman:
(a-class
   ... method notify-paper: ...            review-activity:
   action                                  (a-class
   ( ... teaching-activity                    reference The-chair: PC-chairman
     ... research-activity ... )              reference The-author: author
a-class)                                      ...
                                              action
author:                                       ( ... The-chair>>notify-paper
(a-class                                         ... The-author>>notify-result ... )
   ... method notify-result: ...           a-class)
   action( ... writing-activity ... )
a-class)
```

Thesis: *A method–activation of a participant is executed interleaved with the action part of the participant*

---

[4] If action(... rC.M ...) instead appears as the action part of some usual active object, the execution of rC.M may imply a synchronization with the object rC and hence possibly require an explicit accept from the object rC of the communication before the activation of the method M can take place.

[5] The construct rC>>M (where we use >> instead of the usual remote .) is only one example of the mechanisms we may allow to be used in transverse activities on behalf of the participating objects; another example is rC'>>rC.M where the intention is that the participating object rC' is executing rC.M, i.e. rC' is requesting rC to execute its method M, possibly involving some synchronization between rC and rC'.

3.3 Aggregation Mechanisms

Activity–objects may be aggregated [6] by other activity–objects:

```
P: (a-class                        W: (a-class
      ... reference pP: ...              ... reference pW: ...
      ... action( ... )                  ... action( ... oP ... )
    a-class)                           a-class)

    oP: a-object P                     oW: a-object W
```

The activity–object oP of activity–class P is used in the aggregation of the activity–object oW of activity–class W. The aggregation has implications for the participants and the directive of oW.

Aggregation: The Activity Directive The directive of an activity–object of P (only shown as ...) – including some sequence of activations of the methods of its participating objects – may be part of the directive of the aggregated activity in various ways:

- by making the activity object a global object (as in the example above) or a local object and then (in both cases) activating this object from the directive (as illustrated by the local object oP in the following example)

```
W: (a-class
      ... oP: a-object P   ... reference pW: ...
      ... action(... oP ... oP ...)
    a-class)
```

The object oP can be activated several places in the directive.

- by inserting the activity object directly in the directive (as illustrated by oP' in the following example where the name oP' may possibly be omitted in order to make it anonymous)

```
W: (a-class
      ... reference pW: ...
      ... action(... oP': a-object P ...)
    a-class)
```

When the execution of the directive of oW reaches oP (or oP': a-object P) then the directive of oP (or oP is executed. When this directive has been executed the execution of the directive of oW is continued. [7]

Aggregation: The Activity Participants Correspondingly the participants, e.g. pP – i.e. the list of references to the participating objects – may be part of the participants of an aggregated activity:

- if the object is declared as a (global or local) object: Its participants are accessible by means of usual remote access (e.g. oP.pP using the dot–notation)
- if the activity object is inserted (in the example oP', but possibly anonymously) directly in the directive: The participants of the activity are only implicitly accessible from the directive of the aggregated activity, – and then consequently only when it (the inserted object) is executed

---

[6] We understand *aggregation* as a special case of *association* between classes (and objects) in general. For activity–classes (and –objects) we only discuss aggregation as an important and powerful special case to get a better understanding before possibly generalizing to associations.
  Actually we prefer to use *association* for the relation between the activity–objects oP and oW in the situation illustrated because the instantiations of oP and oW are at the same level; and then use *aggregation* where the oP is instantiated local to oW as it is the case for the examples in the following.

[7] Here we assume the usual sequential execution of the various elements in the directive of oW. However a language may also include sequencing mechanisms for expressing concurrent or interleaved execution of aggregated activity–objects, of say oP and some other similar activity–object oP":
```
action( ...  concurrent(oP, oP") ... )
```

Binding and Change of Participants In addition various other possibilities exist for the participants of an aggregated activity–class, namely:

- Change between the various groups of participants of the aggregated activities; the participants of an aggregated activity are available when it is executing.
- Binding the aggregated participants to the participants of the aggregated activity (statically for locally declared activity objects and dynamically for inserted activity objects).

In the above schematical example the dynamic change implies that the participant pP of oP' may be available only when oP' is executing. The binding can be illustrated by binding pP of oP to pW from W (using the notation ==), i.e. making pP the same object as pW in W–objects.

```
W: (a-class ... oP: a-object P (pP==pW) ... a-class)
```

"Conference Organizing Problem" The classes modeling pre-review, paper-evaluation, and post-review are used in the aggregation of review-activity. The class remind-activity is used in the aggregation of (among others) paper-evaluation. A remind-activity–object, Remind, is declared locally in paper-evaluation and activated in several places.

```
review-activity:                paper-evaluation:
(a-class                        (a-class
   action                          reference The-chair: PC-chairman
   ( a-object pre-review           reference The-reviewers: reviewers
     ... a-object paper-evaluation reference The-paper: paper
     ... a-object post-review )   Remind: a-object remind-activity
a-class)                          action(... Remind ... Remind ...)
                                a-class)
```

The participants of the remind-activity namely Sender, Receiver, Subject are accessible from paper-evaluation (and bound to The-chair, The-author, and The-paper, respectively) and the directive of Remind (some interaction between Sender and Receiver is executed as part of paper-evaluation:

```
paper-evaluation:
(a-class ...                    remind-activity:
   Remind: a-object remind-activity (a-class
      ( Sender==The-chair          reference Sender: ...
        Receiver==The-author       reference Receiver: ...
        Subject==The-paper )       reference Subject: ...
   action( ... Remind ... )        action( ... )
a-class)                        a-class)
```

As mentioned the conference may be seen as a transverse activity and as such be described as an active object aggregated from three activity objects described by the activity classes Preconference, During-Conference, and Postconference. The participants of these part–activities may be different but possibly overlapping. Therefore the participants of the conference may be changing according to the execution of its directive: In the Preconference some of the participants may be author's and reviewer's, whereas in the During-Conference some of the participants may be speaker's and attendee's, as illustrated below. The same participant may play several roles in these part-activities and may also play different roles in different part-activities: A reviewer may also be an author in Preconference and an author in Preconference may change to a speaker (and attendee) in During-Conference.

```
conference:
(a-class ...
    action
    ( a-object Preconference
      a-object During-Conference
      a-object Postconference )
a-class)

Preconference:
(a-class
    reference An-author: author
    reference A-reviewer: reviewer
    ... action( ... )
a-class)
```
```
During-Conference:
(a-class
    reference A-speaker: ...
    reference An-attendee: ...
    ... action( ... )
a-class)

Postconference:
(a-class ... a-class)
```

Thesis: The directive may be aggregated from other activity objects by activating these from the directive and by inserting these directly in the directive

Thesis: The participants may be aggregated from other activity objects by explicit remote access and by implicit access when the aggregated activity is executed

Thesis: Aggregation of activities supports dynamic change of the availability among the participants of the aggregated activities – and dynamic or static binding of the participants of the aggregated activities

3.4 Specialization Mechanisms

Activities–classes may be specialized form other activity–classes:

```
G: (a-class ... reference pG:...          S: G (a-class ... reference pS:...
    ... action( ... )                         ... action( ... )
    a-class)                                  a-class)

                              oS: a-object S
```

The activity–class S is specialized from the activity–class G (here using the prefixing notation S: G ...). The specialization has implications for the participants and the directive of the activity–object oS.

Specialization: The Activity Participants The activity participants may be refined in several ways:

- by adding more participants (such as e.g. pS is added in the description of S in the above example)
- by refining the description of existing participants (by rebinding e.g. pG of class C from G to the subclass C' of C in the description of S, using the notation :< for the preliminary binding and ::< for the rebinding (but without renaming) of an object to a subclass of its class):

```
G: (a-class ... reference pG:< C          S: G (a-class ... reference pG::< C'
    ... a-class)                              ... a-class)
```

"Conference Organizing Problem" In the following example the program committee, PC, is added as a participant in conference-review:

```
review-activity:                      conference-review: review-activity
(a-class                              (a-class
   reference The-chair: PC-chairman      reference PC: program-committee
   reference The-author: author          action( ... )
   reference The-paper: paper         a-class)
   action( ... )
a-class)
```

Alternatively The-reviewers may be participant(s) only in the paper-evaluation activity (appearing in the directive of review-activity and by means of the specialization of this also in the directive of conference-review):

```
paper-evaluation:                     review-activity:
(a-class                              (a-class ...
   reference The-reviewers:< reviewers   action
   action( ... )                         (... a-object paper-evaluation ...)
a-class)                              a-class)
```

The program-committee may be a specialization of reviewers; the participant The-reviewers of paper-evaluation is then being further bound to program-committee in the description of conference-paper-evaluation:

```
program-committee: reviewers          reference The-reviewers ::< program-committee
(a-class ... a-class)                 action
                                      ( The-chair>>select-reviewers
conference-paper-evaluation:            The-reviewers>>evaluate-paper
paper-evaluation                        The-chair>>make-decision )
(a-class                              a-class
```

Thesis: The participants may be specialized by adding more participants and by refining the existing participants

Specialization: The Activity Directive

The activity directive may also be refined:

- by refining the (transverse) activities already part of the action sequence, i.e. by refining oA in the example below, possibly be specializing the activity–class A (to say A') as a part of the description of the activity–class S. oA appears in the description (of the directive) of G and is therefore also part of the directive of S but will – like A' objects declared in oS – be adjusted according to its specialization (here A') in the description of S

```
A: (a-class ... a-class)              S: G (a-class ... oA::< A'
A': A (a-class ... a-class)               ... action( ... )
                                      a-class)
G: (a-class ... oA:< a-object A
       ... action( ... oA ... )       oS: a-object S
   a-class)
```

- by extending the action sequence of the directive e.g. by introducing a *multiple inner mechanism* [8] to support a combined execution of the directive of G and the addition to this in S; basically the form is interleaved execution [9] of these two parts, supplied with synchronization in a simple way. This is illustrated below, where ...g,i... and ...s,i... denote fragments of the directives for respective G and S; the name-i:< inner Ai construct in the directive of G declares an activity object of class Ai with synchronization effect; the object is refined by the corresponding construct in the directive S: name-i::<

---

[8] In objects like oS the usual inner mechanism in G: (a-class ... action(... inner ...) a-class) is substituted by the directive given in the description of S.

[9] Interleaved execution in relation to the specialization of action parts of objects in general is discussed in [Thomsen 86], where the action part added in the description of a class and the action parts of its *multiple* super classes etc. all are executed interleaved.

For simplicity reasons we choose interleaved execution; concurrent execution is another possibility not discussed further here.

inner `Ai'` refines `name-i` to be of activity class `Ai'`, which is some specialization of `Ai`; (as special cases the `Ai` may be omitted and `Ai'` may then be either any class, or some a class description (a-class ... a-class), including the empty class (denoted ()). The meaning of the multiple inner mechanism is that for any i from 1 to n the `Ai'` object is executed *after* the (interleaved) execution of ...g,i-1... and ...s,i-1..., and *before* the (interleaved) execution of ...g,i... and ...s,i...: [10]

```
G: (a-class ...                    S: G (a-class ...
      action                              action
        ( ...g,0...                         ( ...s,0...
          name-1:< inner A1                   name-1::< inner A1'
          ...g,1...                           ...s,1...
          ...                                 ...
          name-i:< inner Ai                   name-i::< inner Ai'
          ...g,i...                           ...s,i...
          ...                                 ...
          name-n:< inner An                   name-n::< inner An'
          ...g,n... )                         ...s,n... )
   a-class)                           a-class)
```

"Conference Organizing Problem" In the example the class `workshop-review` is a specialization of `review-activity`. In `workshop-review` the participants of `review-activity`, namely `The-chair`, `The-author`, and `The-paper`, may be specialized appropriately, e.g. `paper` may be restricted to `extended-abstract` or `position-paper`. We may specialize the class `paper-evaluation` accordingly in the workshop case to `ws-paper-evaluation`, without actually renaming it and just including the additional description.

```
review-activity:                   workshop-review: review-activity.
(a-class ...                       (a-class ...
  paper-E:< a-object paper-evaluation  paper-E::< ws-paper-evaluation
  action( ... paper-E ... )          ... a-class)
a-class)
                                   ws-paper-evaluation: paper-evaluation
                                   (a-class ... a-class)
```

The ws-paper-evaluation activity is a specialization of `paper-evaluation` where the special characteristics of the evaluation activity in the workshop case is added, i.e. actions the ensure, e.g. that a number of well-reputed researchers are accepted to join the workshop without actually writing a `position-paper` as such. For a `workshop-review` activity object the `paper-E` appearing in the directive of `review-activity` now implies the execution of an `ws-paper-evaluation` activity object.

Alternatively we may use the inner mechanism by replacing `paper-evaluation` in the directive for the `review-activity` by `eval:< inner ...` and specify this to be of activity class `paper-evaluation`; and then refine this in `workshop-review` by binding `eval` to class `ws-paper-evaluation`:

---

[10] The understanding behind this definition is that in the description of a specialization of a directive two related requirements are present: the one is to describe sequences of actions, which are seen as simple additions, i.e. things which must be done along with, but which are not directly related to the existing general description; the other is to refine some of the parts of the existing description and to ensure that the existing part and the additions to this are executed together as a unit. These two kinds of additions may typically appear in some mixed sequence.

```
review-activity:
  (a-class ...                          workshop-review: review-activity
    action                                (a-class
      ( pre-review                         action
        The-chair>>notify-paper              ( pre-ws-review
        eval:< inner paper-evaluation        eval::< ws-paper-evaluation
        The-author>>notify-result            post-ws-review )
        post-review )                    a-class)
  a-class)
```

In pre-ws-review and post-ws-review the special characteristics of pre-review and post-review in the workshop case is added, e.g. to encourage well–reputed researchers to participate and possibly arrange that such researchers also give introductory or concluding presentations. For a workshop-review activity object the pre-ws-review and pre-review activities is executed interleaved; and this is also the case for post-ws-review and post-review; the eval enforces a synchronization of the directive of review-activity and the addition to this in workshop-review in the execution of the ws-paper-evaluation activity object.

Alternatively multiple inner constructs may be introduced, in the form of here-1 and here-2 in review-activity such that execution of the otherwise unrelated directive of review-activity and the addition in workshop-review is synchronized at these two (empty) activities:

```
review-activity:
  (a-class ...                          workshop-review: review-activity
    action                                (a-class
      ( pre-review                         action
        here-1:< inner                       ( pre-ws-review
        The-chair>>notify-paper              here-1::< inner ()
        paper-evaluation                     paper-ws-evaluation
        The-author>>notify-result            here-2::< inner ()
        here-2:< inner                       post-ws-review )
        post-review )                    a-class)
  a-class)
```

Again in pre-ws-review, post-ws-review, and paper-ws-evaluation we add the special characteristics of pre-review, post-review and paper-evaluation in the workshop case, (notice that in this case paper-ws-evaluation is not a specialization of paper-evaluation). For a workshop-review activity object the pre-ws-review and pre-review activities are executed interleaved; this is also the case for paper-ws-evaluation and paper-evaluation and for post-ws-review and post-review; here-1 and here-2 enforce synchronization of the directive of review-activity and the addition to this in workshop-review to ensure that both "pre"–activities are concluded before the "evaluation"–activities are initiated; and in turn that both these "evaluation"–activities are concluded before the "post"–activities are initiated.

Thesis: *The directive may be specialized by extending the action sequence by a multiple inner (synchronization) mechanism and by refining the activities already part of the action sequence*

4 Conclusion

Comparisons Our claim is, that there is no support for transverse activities in the existing methodologies for object–oriented analysis and design, including those of Booch, Rumbaugh (OMT), Wirfs–Brock, and Wassermann (OOSD). Booch's description of *things intellectually apprehendable, and things toward which thought or action may be directed* clearly includes transverse activities. But it is not clear whether these are excluded by the definition stating that an object has state, behavior, and identity. OMT combines three views of systems: the object –, the dynamic –, and the functional model. The dynamic model is a collection of state diagrams interacting via shared events. A state diagram is describing the life cycle of a class of objects from a local perspective only. State diagrams have an organization independently from the object model but are also related to the object structure; as such these are similar to the directives discussed here. The aggregation of objects implies the aggregation of the state diagrams of these objects, resulting in composite states. The specialization of classes implies that a subclass inherits the state diagram of its superclass and together with the state diagram added it works as a composite of concurrent state diagrams; this is similar to the specialization of directives discussed here. Events in OMT may form a hierarchical structure; but an event has no duration and is a one-way transmission of information between objects only.

Contracts in [Helm et al. 90] are specifications of behavioral dependencies amongst cooperating objects. Contracts are object-external abstractions and include invariants to be maintained by the cooperating objects. The focus is on inter-object dependencies to make this explicit by means of supporting language mechanisms. The result is, that the actions, i.e. the reactions of an object, now are removed from the object and described explicitly, centralized in the contracts only. It seems, that objects are turned into reactive objects, where the reaction-patterns for an object in its various relations with other objects are described in the corresponding contracts. The intention is not modeling, i.e. to reflect in the model and in the supporting language mechanisms our conceptual understanding of real world phenomena and their inter-dependencies; rather the intention is to have a mathematical, centralized description, such that provable properties may be obtained. The description is mathematically rigorous, especially for the invariant and the preconditions. The descriptions seem to be complex and compressed and it is not obvious how these may be implemented. The instantiations of contracts are not some specialized kind of objects and can not have methods etc.

Our claim is that there is no support for (concurrently executing) transverse activities in the existing object-oriented programming languages, including C++, Smalltalk, Eiffel, and CLOS. The *generic* function and the *method combination* mechanisms of CLOS support the distribution of the implementation of an operation among several of its arguments (like the participants of a transverse activity); but the result of a call of a generic function is a function call only (i.e. not an active object) and its arguments are fixed during its execution; furthermore the hierarchies of generic functions are possible in terms of specialization of (methods for) its arguments only (i.e. there are no specialization (and aggregation) hierarchies for generic functions independent of the hierarchies of their arguments). This also holds for the multi-methods of Cecil [Chambers 92]. Multi-methods are introduced to combine the multiple dispatching with the dataabstraction-oriented programming style. This is achieved by defining that a multi-method is "inside" of the all the dispatch-objects so that it is granted access to the private information of all these objects (whereas transverse activities are not intended to get access to private information of the participating objects). A *mixin* class of CLOS may be used to describe (separate from the participant description) a participants role in some transverse activity. The role is merged with other similar mixin roles to form the transverse activity. This kind of simulation of transverse activities is indirectly and not complete; and the meaning of the *mixing* of action parts needs to be defined. Also in BETA there is no special support for transverse activities; BETA has active objects in the form described here but no mechanisms for supporting the combined execution of the directive of an activity-object and the life cycles of its participants. The various facilities presented here for the aggregation and specialization mechanisms can with a few exceptions be seen as adaptations of corresponding mechanisms of the BETA language to transverse activities.

Frameworks, as discussed in [Johnson & Foote 88], are abstract programs, – usually application specific. Frameworks describe not only the components but also cooperation structure between these. Transverse activities are general language mechanisms; the mechanisms support abstraction and may appear to be powerful for the support of the explicit description of the interaction structures among the components in object-oriented frameworks.

Summary The following extensions in relation to activity-classes and -objects with usual methods – and the meaning of these – have not been discussed:

```
A: (a-class ... method M':(...) ... a-class)
```

An A-object is an activity-object; and the methods, such as M', may have a their usual meaning without problems; but various alternatives exist:

- Given that transverse activities may have methods we may also allow these methods to include method activations of the participating objects with the same meaning as when these appear in the directive. This implies that also such *transverse methods* of the transverse activity somehow must be executed in some combination with the objects life cycles.
  ```
  A: (a-class ... reference rC: C ... method M':( ... rC>>M ... )
      ... action( ... rC>>M ... )
    a-class)
  ```
  It is possible to have a transverse activity without the directive, i.e. more likely a *transverse component*. Such a transverse component is different from the usual components only if it has transverse methods.

- It is possible to make the methods of an aggregated activity available only when the activity-object is executing; i.e. the method mQ is available only when oQ is executing and similarly for mQ' and oQ':

  ```
  Q: (a-class ... method mQ:(...)        A: (a-class ...
      ... a-class)                           a-object oQ: Q
                                             a-object oQ': Q'
  Q': (a-class ... method mQ':(...)          action( ... oQ ... oQ' ... )
      ... a-class)                         a-class)
  ```

- General associations between transverse activities – and not only aggregation as discussed in this paper as a special case – is another extension. A transverse activity can then dynamically involve the execution of the transverse activities associated with it. Also a transverse activity can activate methods of the transverse activities associated with it. The actual possibilities and the consequences of these extensions are not obvious.

The underlying thesis is, that not only components, but also transverse activities are natural and indispensable constructs in the modeling process and software system life cycle. The derived main theses may be summarized as follows:

- In the modeling view on object-orientation, especially when based on conceptual understanding, activities are phenomena also. Therefore we have proposed that activities may be modeled by objects, including abstraction in the form of classification, specialization, and aggregation.

- Activities may be object-centric actions, described as as part of the object, or activities may involve several objects in some combination, and be described separately as transverse activities. The transverse activity is offering an additional perspective on object-oriented programming. Therefore we have proposed class- and object-like language mechanisms to support transverse activities.

- Objects may be active. Therefore we have proposed language mechanisms to support the execution of transverse activities, either several such activities executed concurrently or executed in combination with active objects.

- Transverse activities may be aggregated and specialized. Therefore we have proposed mechanisms to support this for both the participants and the directive of an activity. The mechanisms offer synchronized interleaved execution of the directives of specialized activities; also the mechanisms offer the possibility for dynamic change of the availability of – as well as dynamic or static binding of – the participants of aggregated activities.

Based on these theses we have outlined proposals for new and powerful object–oriented programming language mechanisms to support the modeling of transverse activities.

References

[Booch 91] G.Booch: Object Oriented Design with Applications. Benjamin/Cummings 1991.

[Chambers 92] C.Chambers: Object–Oriented Multi–Methods in Cecil. Proceedings of the European Conference on Object–Oriented Programming, 1992.

[Chin & Chanson 91] R.S.Chin, S.T.Chanson: Distributed Object–Based Programming Systems. ACM Computing Surveys, Vol. 23, No. 1, 1991.

[Coad & Yourdon 91a] P.Coad, E.Yourdon: Object–Oriented Analysis. 2/E, Prentice–Hall, 1991.

[Coad & Yourdon 91b] P.Coad, E.Yourdon: Object–Oriented Design. Prentice–Hall, 1991.

[Dahl et al. 84] O.J.Dahl, B.Myhrhaug, K.Nygaard: SIMULA 67 Common Base Language. Norwegian Computing Center, edition February 1984.

[Goldberg & Robson 83] A.Goldberg, D.Robson: SMALLTALK 80: The Language and its Implementation. Addison Wesley 1983.

[Helm et al. 90] R.Helm, I.M.Holland, D.Gangopadhyay: Contracts: Specifying Behavioral Compositions in Object–oriented Systems. Proceedings of the European Conference on Object–Oriented Programming / Object-Oriented Systems, Languages and Applications Conference, 1990.

[Johnson & Foote 88] R.E.Johnson, B.Foote: Designing Reusable Classes. Journal of Object–Oriented Programming, 1988.

[Keene 89] S.E.Keene: Object–Oriented Programming in Common Lisp. Addison Wesley, 1989.

[Kristensen 93] B.B.Kristensen: Transverse Classes & Objects in Object–Oriented Analysis, Design, and Implementation. Journal of Object–Oriented Programming, 1993.

[Kristensen & Østerbye 91] B.B.Kristensen, K.Østerbye: Conceptual Modeling and Programming. R 91-42, Department of Mathematics and Computer Science, Aalborg University, 1991.

[Madsen et al. 93] O.L.Madsen, B.Møller-Pedersen, K.Nygaard: Object Oriented Programming in the Beta Programming Language. Addison Wesley 1993.

[Meyer 92] B.Meyer: Eiffel, The Language. Prentice Hall, 1992.

[Olle et al. 82] T.W.Olle, A.A.Verrijn–Stuart, H.G.Sol, Eds.: Information System Design Methodologies: A Comparative Review. North-Holland, 1982.

[Rumbaugh et al. 91] J.Rumbaugh, M.Blaha, W.Premerlani, F.Eddy, W.Lorensen: Object–Oriented Modeling and Design. Prentice–Hall 1991.

[Stroustrup 91] B.Stroustrup: The C++ Programming Language. 2/E, Addison–Wesley 1991.

[Thomsen 86] K.S.Thomsen: Multiple Inheritance, a Structuring Mechanism for Data, Processes and Procedures. DAIMI PB–209, Department of Computer Science, Aarhus University, 1986.

[Wasserman et al. 90] A.I.Wasserman, P.A.Pircher, R.J.Muller: The Object–Oriented Structured Design Notation for Software Design Representation. IEEE Computer, 23(3), 1990.

[Wirfs–Brock et al. 90] R.Wirfs–Brock, B.Wilkerson, L.Wiener: Designing Object–Oriented Software. Prentice Hall, 1990.

Dynamic Extensibility in a Statically-compiled Object-oriented Language[*]

Jawahar Malhotra

Computer Science Department, Aarhus University
Ny Munkegade 116, DK-8000 Aarhus C Denmark
e-mail: jmalhotra@daimi.aau.dk
tel: (+45) 8942 3271
fax: (+45) 8613 5725

Abstract

Statically-typed object-oriented compiled languages, like Simula, Beta, Eiffel, are desirable because of the safety and efficiency of the resulting code. Dynamically-typed, interpreted languages, like Smalltalk, are useful as they provide the possibility of dynamically extending a program. In this paper, we reconcile the safety and efficiency goals of compiled languages with the benefits of interpreted languages by presenting an embeddable interpreter for a compiled language, namely Beta. The interpreter is designed to be embedded into any compiled Beta application, thus enabling it to accept dynamic extensions. This paper examines the Application Programmer's Interface to the interpreter and illustrate some aspects of our implementation.

1 Introduction

Statically-typed object-oriented compiled languages — e.g. Simula [BDMN73], Beta [MMPN93], Eiffel [Mey88] — are desirable because of the safety, efficiency, and readability of the resulting code. Dynamically-typed, interpreted languages — e.g. Smalltalk [GR83] — are useful as they provide, among other things, the possibility of dynamically extending a program. In other words, it's possible to incorporate new code into an already compiled, and possibly executing, application without recompiling the application.

Our goal is to allow type-safe dynamic extensibility in a compiled language, namely Beta, without sacrificing the efficiency of the already compiled parts. We want to be able to write Beta applications that can extend themselves dynamically. One technique for supporting dynamic extensibility is to build an incremental compiler as has been done for Simula in the Mjølner Orm system [Mag93]. Another is to build an interpreter which can interface with the compiled parts of the application. We have taken the interpreter approach for Beta; we have built an interpreter which can be embedded into a compiled Beta application i.e. it can be invoked from a compiled Beta application to dynamically interpret programs in the context of the application. The interpreter is provided as a

---

[*]Research supported by the Danish Research Programme for Informatics, grant number 5.26.18.19

library with an Application Programmer's Interface (API) and must be linked into the compiled application.

Our motivation for introducing dynamic extensibility in Beta is our need for building dynamically tailorable applications. We envisage, developing in Beta, a class of applications similar in terms of customizability and extensibility to GNU Emacs [Sta84]. It is an established fact that object-oriented techniques are well suited for writing extensible software: classes may be extended by defining subclasses. Our goal is to exploit these techniques in a dynamic setting.

As an example of such an application, consider an extensible spreadsheet application which allows end-users to define new types of cells. The application has a command named **Define New Cell**. The user defines a new cell type by executing this command and providing the Beta code for the class declaration of the new cell type e.g. a VideoCell. Upon completion of this command, the application extends its **Create** command to include VideoCell as one of the possibilities. Selecting VideoCell creates a video cell (or converts an existing cell into a video cell) using the user-supplied declaration.

Given such functionality, users will be able to customize the spreadsheet application according to their own needs, or extend it with functionality they find lacking. The use of object-oriented techniques, such as specialization and virtuals, will allow them to reuse parts of the original application, thus minimizing the effort required to write the extensions. While such extensions may be installed by recompiling the entire application with the extensions, the ability to install the extensions dynamically is far more appealing to end-users.

The interpreter is a means of processing these extensions dynamically. The spreadsheet application is compiled with the interpreter embedded within it. The **Define New Cell** command uses the interpreter to process the user-supplied Beta code.

We use the word *extension* rather than *modification*. An interpreter supporting dynamic modifications would allow for the possibility of dynamically replacing compiled code with interpreted code, thus allowing a self-modifying program to be written. This is not our goal, although it would be a useful side-effect for a certain class of applications such as development environments and debuggers. We touch upon this issue again later.

This work shows that it is possible to write a dynamically extensible application in a compiled, statically-typed, block-structured, object-oriented language; an application which allows the extension language to be the same as that in which the original application was written. This is accomplished without sacrificing any of the good properties of the language e.g. typing and block-structure. Furthermore, it shows that this can be accomplished, without much overhead, by embedding an interpreter into the extensible application. It presents a small, yet very general, API for the interpreter. To the best of our knowledge, such an embeddable interpreter is not available for any of the other well known compiled object-oriented languages.

1.1 Background

The interpreter is part of the Mjølner Beta System (MBS) [MI92b]. All programs in the MBS are stored in Abstract Syntax Tree form (AST).[1] The static-semantics checker

---

[1] The reader may safely think of ASTs as source code text except in places where we talk of semantically decorated ASTs. In that case it is equivalent to the source code plus the symbol table.

works on ASTs too; it is responsible for type-checking as well as generating a symbol-table. In the MBS, this symbol-table is not a separate entity; it is encoded directly into the AST. The code generator emits assembly code in the appropriate assembly language e.g. MC68000 assembly on the HP Series 400 machines. To produce an executable, the MBS relies on tools from the environment in which it is running. For example, under UNIX, it uses the standard assembler, linker, and loader to assemble, link and execute programs. Both compiled Beta modules and executable Beta programs conform to the a.out file format (under UNIX).

1.2 Overview

Dynamic Extensibility using an embeddable interpreter is illustrated further in Section 2. The interpreter API, and the implementation of the supporting interpreter core, are presented in Section 3. The example presented here illustrates the use of the interpreter in a dynamically extensible system. The interpreter may also be used to build an interactive development environment or to enhance the functionality of a debugger. These applications are shown in Section 4. The applicability of these concepts to other languages is also discussed (Section 5).

In order to be comfortable with the examples presented, it is recommended that the reader glance at the very brief Beta primer (Appendix A).

2 Achieving Dynamic Extensibility — the general idea

Figure 1 presents an overview of the interpreter and its environment in the context of the spreadsheet example. This view is abstract; it is incomplete with respect to many details. Its purpose is to present an idea of how the interpreter fits into the traditional model of an application. It does this by showing the relevant parts and their interactions (invocations and information access). The interpreter is shown embedded within the Spreadsheet application (*host-application*). The large box labeled SPREADSHEET APPLICATION is the executable produced by the Beta compiler from the AST labeled SPREADSHEET APPL. (this is the source code for the spreadsheet application). The interpreter comprises of the Application Programmer's Interface (API) via which the host-application invokes the interpreter to install new definitions, and the core which is the part responsible for actual interpretation. The interpreter is designed to work directly on semantically decorated Abstract Syntax Trees (ASTs); no intermediate code is generated. The ASTs labeled VideoCell and AudioCell are user-supplied dynamic extensions to the spreadsheet application; they contain declarations for the corresponding classes.

Within the application, the Define New Cell command implementation invokes the interpreter, via its API, providing it with the code to be interpreted and some context information i.e. the context (within the host-application's source code) in which interpretation should take place (arrow 1; Figure 1). Let's assume this code is the AST VideoCell. The interpreter pre-processes the AST VideoCell, producing some run-time "entities" which allow compiled parts of the application to view VideoCell as if it were also compiled. The box labeled VideoCell represents such an "entity" produced by the interpreter. With this, we can say that the application has been extended by VideoCell.

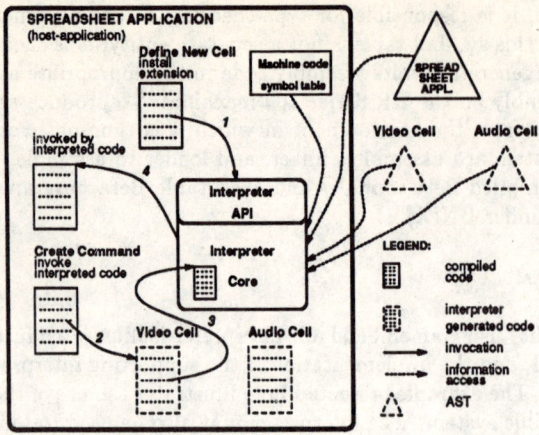

Figure 1: The interpreter and its environment

A reference to this run-time "entity" is returned to the caller (arrow 1, backwards). One may think of this return value as a closure denoting the class (similar to function-closures in functional languages). We also assume that Define New Cell extends the Create command with an option for video cells which uses the returned reference to create them.

When the user attempts to create a video cell, the implementation of the create command invokes VideoCell via the returned reference (arrow 2). Control is transferred by VideoCell to the interpreter core (arrow 3) which accesses the AST for VideoCell and interprets it. During interpretation, it may come across references to compiled parts of the host-application. It resolves these into addresses by accessing the host-application AST and the machine-code symbol table. It then accesses the compiled code (arrow 4).

3 The Interpreter API

The Application Programmer's Interface (API) to the interpreter defines the necessary functions (known as patterns in Beta) for applications to interface with the interpreter. It has been designed to allow the following operations on the host-application: *Add* new pattern (class) definitions to any context (block) and *Execute* a new pattern (class) in any context (block). Intuitively, a context denotes a block in the source program; it is a static property of the program; it is *not* an object. The API comprises of the following patterns (functions):[2]

```
AddDecl             : (context * declText) -> ()
MakeDeclExecutable  : (context * originObject * declText) -> executablePattern
getCurrentContext   : () -> context
getEnclContext      : context -> context
getCurrentObject    : () -> object
getOrigin           : object -> object
```

---

[2]The signatures presented here are informal and are only intended to convey the functionality of the pattern. They are *not* in Beta syntax.

AddDecl can be used by an application to add a new pattern declaration to itself; this declaration then becomes available to subsequent declarations within its scope; it is not directly executable by the caller of **AddDecl**. **MakeDeclExecutable**, in addition to adding the pattern declaration (like **AddDecl**), also returns, to its caller, a reference to the pattern; this reference may be used to execute (instantiate/invoke) the pattern. The other functions in the API are support functions used to compute context and object arguments for **AddDecl** and **MakeDeclExecutable**.

Returning to our spreadsheet example, one may define VideoCell and AudioCell by first defining an abstract super-pattern called MultiMediaCell as a specialization of Cell (assume that **Cell** is declared by the spreadsheet application), and then defining VideoCell and AudioCell as specializations of MultiMediaCell. In this case, **AddDecl** should be used to process MultiMediaCell while **MakeDeclExecutable** should be used to process VideoCell and AudioCell. The reason: the spreadsheet application never needs to execute MultiMediaCell directly, while it does need to execute VideoCell and AudioCell. We will assume that the spreadsheet application has a command called Define Abstract Pattern which may be used to define an abstract super-pattern like MultiMediaCell. This is in addition to the Define New Cell command discussed earlier.

3.1 AddDecl

This function is used by an application to add one or more new pattern declarations to a given context. The **declText** argument is the text of the new pattern declaration. The function **getCurrentContext** should be used to obtain a context. The following example and the accompanying explanation illustrate the idea. Here **Spreadsheet** is the pattern (class) describing the spreadsheet application.

```
Spreadsheet :
(#
    Cell : (# ... #);              (* Cell is an abstract superclass *)
    TextCell : Cell (# ... #);     (* TextCell is a subclass of Cell *)

    (* loads an abstract pattern declaration *)
    DefineAbstractPattern :
    (#
        c : @context;
        decl : @text;
     DO
        getCurrentContext -> getEnclContext -> c;
        loadPatternDecl -> decl;
        (c, decl) -> AddDecl;                   (* declare decl in context c *)
    #) (* DefineAbstractPattern *)
#) (* Spreadsheet *)
```

The functionality of the Define Abstract Pattern command is captured by the pattern **DefineAbstractPattern** shown above. As an example, the following declaration could be loaded using Define Abstract Pattern.

```
MultiMediaCell : Cell (# ... #)
```

The effect of calling **DefineAbstractPattern** in this scenario is shown in Figure 2(a); here the extended version of the spreadsheet application's source code is shown. Another

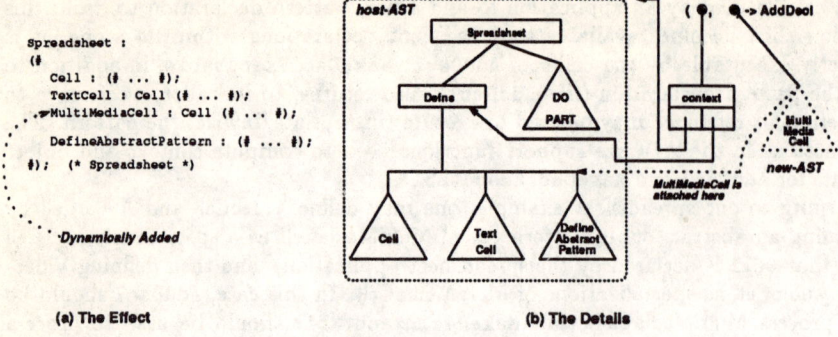

Figure 2: Illustrating `AddDecl`

way to think about this is as follows: the spreadsheet application, after dynamically adding `MultiMediaCell`, is equivalent to an application obtained by compiling the contents of Figure 2(a).

3.1.1 AddDecl details

The execution of `DefineAbstractPattern` proceeds as follows:

1. `getCurrentContext` yields the current context. context is static information about the program itself. Intuitively, it denotes a block in the source program. In our case, as all Beta programs are stored and manipulated as ASTs, a context refers to a node (descriptor-node) within an AST.

    `getEnclContext`, given a context, returns the enclosing context i.e. in our example, the block corresponding to the body of `Spreadsheet`.

    `loadPatternDecl` inputs, as text, a Beta pattern declaration such as the `MultiMediaCell`. It could get this text from the user, a file, another process, etc.

2. `AddDecl` then installs the declaration into the body of `Spreadsheet` and then preprocesses it. In order to do this, it (see Figure 2(b)): (a) parses the new declaration, into a bare (without symbol-table info) AST (*new-AST*); (b) uses the context information to load the AST of the spreadsheet application (*host-AST*) and locate the `Spreadsheet`-body block node within it; (c) installs new-AST into host-AST within that block; (d) type checks new-AST as if it appears in that block. If the new AST is type correct, it is updated with symbol-table information; (e) generates the runtime object corresponding to the new pattern declaration.[3]

3.1.2 Extensions not Modifications

It is important to note that `AddDecl` doesn't replace an existing compiled declaration of the same name. In other words, loading a new declaration for `TextCell` in the above

---

[3]this is called a prototype in Beta terminology; other common terms are template (Simula) or class descriptor (Eiffel).

example would not have the effect of replacing the old compiled `TextCell` declaration. If we were to load a new declaration for `TextCell` using `AddDecl`, it would override the old declaration only for subsequent declarations made within its scope. Old users of `TextCell` will continue to use the old version. This semantics is in conformance with static binding semantics.

3.2 MakeDeclExecutable

This function allows the host-application to execute (instantiate/invoke) patterns in addition to declaring them. Presented below is the spreadsheet application with the implementation of the command Define New Cell; it illustrates the use of `MakeDeclExecutable`. Also shown is `CreateDynamicCell` which illustrates how one uses the return value of `MakeDeclExecutable`. The Create command would do something similar to allow users to create video cells. We assume that the application has been extended with the declaration of `MultiMediaCell`.

```
Spreadsheet :
(#
   Cell : (# ... #);
   TextCell : Cell (# ... #);

   DefineAbstractPattern : (# ... #);

   DynamicCell : ##Cell;                          (* pattern variable *)

   DefineNewCell :
   (#
      spreadSheetBody : @context;
      spreadSheetObj : ^Object;
      decl : @text;
   DO
      getCurrentContext -> getEnclContext -> spreadSheetBody;
      getCurrentObject -> getOrigin -> spreadSheetObj[];
      loadNewCellTypeDecl -> decl;
      (spreadSheetBody, spreadSheetObj[], decl)      (* assign to *)
            -> MakeDeclExecutale -> DynamicCell##;  (* pattern variable *)
   #);   (* DefineNewCell *)

   CreateDynamicCell :
   (#
      DO ... DynamicCell ...                      (* execute a pattern variable *)
   #)   (* CreateDynamicCell *)
#)   (* Spreadsheet *)
```

An example of a declaration that can be processed in this way is:

```
VideoCell : MultiMediaCell (# ... #)
```

The pattern `DefineNewCell` encapsulates the functionality of the Define New Cell command. It differs from `DefineAbstractPattern` in that it calls `MakeDeclExecutable` which takes an object as an argument; this is in addition to the context and declaration arguments, both of which have the same purpose and interpretation as in the case of **AddDecl**. The object argument is an instance of the block denoted by the context. Its need becomes evident once we examine the return value of **MakeDeclExecutable**.

The value returned by **MakeDeclExecutable** can be thought of as a pattern-closure i.e. a value which denotes a pattern, may be passed as a parameter, returned as a result, stored in a variable, or used to execute the pattern. In a procedural language, its counterpart would be a procedure pointer, while in a functional language its counterpart would be a function-closure.

For a pattern P, its closure must have an environment link; this is true of closures in functional languages. This environment link is used, at run-time, to resolve names not local to P. In the Beta implementation, such an environment link is simply a reference to an instance of the block with lexically encloses P. The object argument to **MakeDeclExecutable** is used as an environment link while building the pattern-closure. The context argument specifies the block in which P should be processed; thus, this block lexically encloses P. Hence, the object argument should be an instance of this block.

In Beta terminology such a pattern-closure is called a *structure value*. It may be instantiated and executed like a pattern and used almost any place a pattern may be used. In the Beta implementation, a pattern's structure value comprises of a reference to the pattern's prototype and the environment link. Structure values are stored in variables known as *pattern variables*. These concepts are illustrated in Section A.1 in a setting independent of the interpreter. The reader unfamiliar with these concepts in Beta is advised to take a cursory glance at that very brief section.

Returning to the example, observe the pattern variable called **DynamicCell**. The return value of **MakeDeclExecutable** is stored in this pattern variable. **DynamicCell** may then be used to execute the pattern denoted by the structure value within it. In the example, **CreateDynamicCell** uses **DynamicCell** to create an instance of the dynamically defined pattern **VideoCell**.

As Beta patterns are the unifying construct for classes, procedures, types, etc., a structure value is capable of denoting all of these. By allowing **MakeDeclExecutable** to return structure values, we get a *simple* but *general* mechanism for embedding new declarations into compiled programs; *simple* because the **MakeDeclExecutable** always returns a structure value denoting a pattern, *general* because everything in Beta can be encapsulated in a pattern.

3.3 Implementation Issues

3.3.1 Plugging the type-checking loophole

Type checking occurrences of **AddDecl** is simple; no special treatment is required. But **MakeDeclExecutable** is a little more interesting. We have declared it to return a structure value of the most general type:

```
MakeDeclExecutable : (context * originObject * declText) -> ##Object
```

Given this type, it will be possible, for example, to assign a **VideoCell** structure value to a pattern variable of type **Text**. This problem necessitates the use of a runtime type-check. The runtime check should ensure that the pattern of the structure value returned by **MakeDeclExecutable** is a subclass of the pattern variable to which it is assigned.

3.3.2 Access to compiled machine code

If the interpreter comes across a pattern application where the corresponding declaration is compiled, it resolves the application by locating the compiled machine code rather than interpreting the declaration. In a Beta executable, every compiled pattern has a prototype. In addition, each of these prototypes has an assembly-level name. It is possible to determine this assembly-level name from the AST node which declares the pattern. So, to locate the prototype of a compiled pattern declaration, the interpreter accesses the declaration node in the AST, gets the corresponding assembly level symbol-name, and reads the corresponding memory address from the linker-generated symbol-table stored within the executable.

The prototype of a pattern is all that's needed to create an instance of a pattern or to execute it. Hence, by getting access to the prototype, the interpreter is able to support creation and execution of compiled patterns. To transfer parameters into a pattern instance before executing it, and to get results out it, the interpreter also needs the signature of the pattern. For this it uses the pattern declaration node in the AST.

Our method for determining the addresses of compiled prototypes works because prototypes are non-relocatable. Should they be relocatable, one would have to do some additional bookkeeping to keep the executable's symbol-table consistent.

3.3.3 Interpreter-generated prototypes

We stated earlier that interpreter-generated prototypes are identical in structure and interface to compiler generated ones. This property enables us to return interpreter-generated prototypes to compiled code without any problems. These prototypes are illustrated by the following abstract example:

```
COMPILED:                              INTERPRETED:
P : (#                                 Q : P (#
    V :< (# DO ... INNER; ... #);          V ::< (# DO ... #);
    DO                                     DO
    ...                                    ...
    V;                                     #);
    ...
    INNER;
    #);
```

The pattern P is declared with a virtual pattern V. In P's body, V is executed; then INNER is called to transfer control to the specialization of P. The virtual V also calls INNER to transfer control to its specialization.

Q is declared as a specialization (subclass) of P. It binds the virtual V further.[4] For the sake of this discussion, we will refer to V declared in P and Q as Vp and Vq respectively. Now, suppose the compiled code also does the following:

```
(Defn of Q, Q's context) -> MakeDeclExecutable -> X##;   (* load defn *)
X;                                                       (* execute Q *)
```

Figure 3 illustrates the scenario after an instance of Q has been created via X. This instance is created by compiled code using the structure value returned by MakeDeclExecutable.

---
[4] The further binding is a subclass of V declared in P.

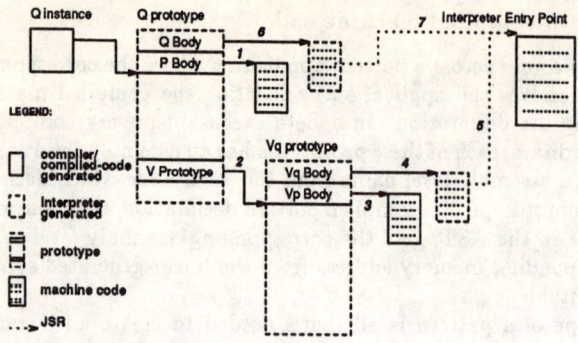

Figure 3: Interpreter-generated prototypes

The Q instance has a reference to its prototype. This prototype is interpreter generated. It has a table with references to Q's body and P's body; the bodies are machine code. Q's body is interpreter generated and is really some "glue" which transfers control to the interpreter core (arrow 7). There is also a virtual-table with an entry for each virtual in Q. This points to the prototype for Vq. This prototype is also interpreter generated. It is similar in structure to Q's prototype except that it doesn't have any virtuals.

1. Q is executed (via X) by transferring control to the body of P (arrow 1).[5]

    (a) When P executes V, V's prototype is accessed from the current object's (Q) prototype's (Q) virtual-table (arrow 2). This is used to create an instance of Vq and control is transferred to the body of Vp(arrow 3).

    (b) When the INNER is encountered, control flows to the body of Vq (arrow 4). This is interpreter-generated machine code; it transfers control to the interpreter (arrow 5). The interpreter is provided with the current object (Vq instance; not shown in figure) and a reference to the AST to be interpreted (i.e. Vq's AST).

2. Control first returns to the body of Vp and then to the body of P (from where V was executed).

3. When the INNER is encountered, control flows to Q's body (arrow 6) which again transfers control to the interpreter (arrow 7), this time with the Q instance and a reference to Q's AST.

For more information about the Beta run-time system and compilation techniques see [Mad93].

4 Other Applications of the Embeddable Interpreter

In addition to dynamically extensible systems, there are other applications of such an embeddable interpreter. One obvious application is an interactive development envi-

---

[5]In Beta, execution begins in the top of the superclass chain and travels down to specializations via INNER statements.

ronment for Beta programs. We have built a simple "listener" loop (similar to a lisp read-eval-print loop) for Beta. Using such a loop, users can start a session in which all the pervasive Beta definitions are available; users can interactively define new Beta patterns as well as execute them. The loop supports the definition of patterns by calling **AddDecl** with a context which contains all the pervasive definitions; as a result, the pattern is processed and installed into this context. Execution of patterns is supported by calling **MakeDeclExecutable**.

Another interesting application is in a source-level debugger for Beta programs. The interpreter can be used to support the execution of arbitrary Beta code at a break point. In a debugger, at a break point, we can determine the context (i.e. the block in which we are stopped) and the current object (i.e. the object in which control is stopped). Using this information, we can call **MakeDeclExecutable** providing it the user-supplied source code.

We have also explored the role of the embeddable interpreter, in making incremental a rapid prototyping tool called the Application Builder (*ApplBuilder*) [GHT91]. The ApplBuilder, among other things, allows users to create user-interfaces by direct manipulation techniques. It generates Beta code which must be compiled before the interface can be tested. Should the interface need editing, the generated code may be reloaded into ApplBuilder and edited. We have devised a scheme which allows the edited version to be executed without regenerating or recompiling a new executable. This is accomplished by interpreting the changes in the context of the original compiled application. The details of this are too lengthy to report here.

5 Applicability to Other Languages

The interpreter API and its supporting interpreter core, dictate a set of requirements on the language and implementation. The previous sections have indirectly touched upon these requirements in the context of Beta. In order to make these ideas more widely applicable, we list these requirements in a language independent manner. We also explore the possibilities of having such an embeddable interpreter for Simula [BDMN73], Eiffel [Mey88], and C++ [ES90]. These languages belong to the family of compiled, statically- and strongly-typed languages, and hence stand to benefit from having such an embeddable interpreter.

The requirements include the following:

- *Classes as Values.* For the API to include a function like **MakeDeclExecutable**, the language must support the notion of *class-values* (structure values in Beta). It is *not* necessary to have classes be full-fledged objects whose behavior can be specified in the metaclass as is the case in Smalltalk [GR83]. Class-values should be just "black-box" values (like closures, their internals should be of no interest at the language level); it should be possible to pass them as parameters and store them in variables, in addition to using them just as we would use a statically declared class i.e. for creating instances. In Beta, structure values are surprisingly simple objects.

  As an alternative to returning class-values, the function **MakeDeclExecutable** could simply execute the class and return the result of the execution as its result. Although this approach accomplishes our goal, it isn't as elegant as the one using class-values. With the class-value approach, we get an almost seamless boundary between compiled and interpreted code. Once an interpreted pattern declaration has been processed into a structure value, the compiled code doesn't need to be aware of the creator of the structure value; it may use it just as it would a compiler-generated structure value.

- *Classes at Runtime.* Our implementation relies on the fact that there exists at run-time, for each class, a data structure providing information about the class. These data structures are called prototypes in Beta, templates in Simula, and class descriptors in Eiffel. Note that these are not the same as class-values; this is a run-time data structure, while a class-value is a language level notion.

- *Context Specification.* We rely on being able to uniquely address any block in the source program (even if it's in multiple files). In addition, it must be possible to get such address information about a program from within that program. The functions `getCurrentContext` and `getEnclContext` provide such information in our implementation. This is not much of an issue in languages without block structure.

- *Object Specification.* If we can compute the address of a block, then we should also be able to get a handle on its corresponding instance. `getCurrentObject` and `getOrigin` are the counterparts of the context specification functions in our implementation. In a language without block structure, the origin, if maintained, would be a fixed (root) object.

- *Symbol Table.* It is imperative that the interpreter be able to map source level names of compiled classes into run-time memory addresses of the corresponding prototypes (templates/class descriptors).

- *Type Checking.* It must be possible to determine the type of a structure value at run-time. This is the basis for the dynamic type-check.

Beta resembles Simula in many ways; those relevant to this discussion include block-structure, and typing. The primary difference (for this discussion) is that Simula doesn't have the notion of class-values. This can be overcome by either introducing such a concept or by using the alternative approach which doesn't require class-values. Simula also doesn't have patterns as the unifying concept for classes, types, functions, procedures, etc. As a result, if we want dynamic interpretation of syntactic constructs of granularity finer than class, we will have to support it explicitly. In other words, if we want to be able to dynamically interpret procedures (to add it to a class, for example), we have to have an API function for procedures as well as one for classes. In the Lund Software system for standard Simula [Lun92], it is possible to map a source-level class name into the address of its corresponding prototype [LM84, Hed93].

It should be possible to build an embeddable interpreter for Eiffel, without sacrificing the safety of programs that use it. Class-values are not present in Eiffel; hence, the alternative approach as described for Simula can be used. According to the implementation description in [Mey88], class descriptors, the data structures representing classes, are present at run-time. It is not clear if one can map a class name into the address of its class descriptor, but one would expect this to be possible. Context and object specification is much simpler as there are no nested classes. Like Simula, class, procedure, and function declarations are not unified into a single abstraction. With respect to our concerns here, C++ [ES90] falls into the same category as Eiffel.

6 Related Work

To the best of our knowledge, statically-compiled object-oriented languages like Eiffel [Mey88] and C++ [ES90] don't have such embeddable interpreters. To obtain dynamic extensibility in an application written in these languages, developers have to resort to designing an interpreted extensibility language with a predefined set of functions which access the underlying application's functionality. Another approach used in [ZC92] is to embed an interpreter for an interpreted language like Scheme [Bet89] into the application. The authors of [ZC92] state "The Scheme interpreter is used mainly to invoke C++ functions and this might seem to be an overkill." Using Scheme, or another such language, to extend an object-oriented application cannot possibly allow very general extensions to be written. Extending Beta applications, using Beta, one can utilize the application's object-oriented model to the maximum in writing the extensions.

Embeddable interpreters are most common in the Lisp world. GNU Emacs has a lisp interpreter embedded within it [Sta85]. The interpreter is available to emacs lisp programs as the function `eval`. Our interpreter has all the flexibility of such an `eval`, but in the context of a block-structured, statically-scoped, statically-bound, statically-typed, object-oriented language. Block-structure and static-scoping force us to introduce interpretation-contexts. To overcome static-binding we introduce pattern variables and the related structure values. These concepts also help solving the problem of what should be returned by the interpreter. In Beta, programs are not data; this problem is solved by using ASTs. Strong typing is enforced by a run-time type check. For an interesting discussion on strong typing in object-oriented languages, see [MMMP90]. The idea of pattern variables in Beta was originally introduced in [AFO89]. In [AF89], Agesen and Frølund present a mechanism for building extensible systems using dynamic linking and loading.

CLOS [Kee89] also provides access to its interpreter (`eval`) its compiler (`compile`) and binding environment (`boundp` and `makunbound`). From our point of view, this is similar to the Emacs lisp capabilities, except that, here we are in an object-oriented setting.

Due to the dynamic nature of Smalltalk [GR83], dynamically extensible applications can easily be implemented in it. Smalltalk makes this possible by providing its compiler as just another object to which "eval" messages may be sent. The source code to be evaluated is provided as a string, while the context is provided in the form of dictionaries. The returned value, an instance of `CompiledMethod` can then be manipulated by the user program; it can, for example, be stored in some dictionary where it would influence the behavior of the rest of the program. This flexibility in Smalltalk comes, however, at the expense of safety, efficiency, and readability. One only discovers a problem with the extension when the extension gets executed. Also, Beta's table-driven method lookup provides constant time access for methods (even for interpreted ones). This is in contrast with Smalltalk's dynamic method lookup technique which depends on the length of the superclass chain (caching techniques help a little here).

It is also possible to have an embeddable incremental compiler. There is no conceptual problem in replacing the interpreter core with an incremental compiler. The API should remain the same. In fact, the interpreter is already generating machine code "glue" which branches to the interpreter core. Instead of this, it could just as well generate all the machine code. The Mjølner Orm system [Mag93] has an incremental compiler for Simula. Fine discussions of incremental compilation problems are presented in [Hed92, HM87, HM86].

A number of commercial systems use dynamic linking and loading as a basis for extensibility. They are generally able to load an extension and thus enhance/modify their functionality; they generally don't support the definition of the extension. In such systems, extensions are generally not meant to be user defined, and in cases where they are, they are very rarely meant to be defined interactively. Our approach, in addition to supporting the loading and linking of extensions, also supports their dynamic and interactive definition. Our approach allows for the development of applications in which the distinction between extending and using is blurred.

Another approach to supporting extensibility is to have a meta-level architecture as in the metaobject protocol for CLOS [KdRB91]. Given such a metaobject protocol for Beta, we would be able to create new classes and methods dynamically by creating the appropriate metaobjects. But, in order to construct the "raw materials" (e.g. the machine code of a method body) needed to create the metaobjects, from the source code provided by the user, we would need a processor (interpreter) like the one we have described here. So, adding a metaobject layer doesn't preclude the need for an embeddable interpreter like the one we have described. A metaobject layer would complement the ideas we have presented here; the interpreter could, for example, be used to modify metaobjects of existing classes. Furthermore, introspection and analysis could prove very useful in a user-tailorable system. In our approach, structure values returned by the interpreter, can be thought of as metavalues; API functions like `AddDecl`, `getCurrentContext`, etc. are reflective in that they allow us to operate on the program itself.

Extensibility in C++ with a meta-level architecture is presented in [CM93]. They present a language called OpenC++ in which classes and methods may be declared reflective. Reflective classes have metaobjects; these can be used to extend or change the semantics of method calls. These facilities, while potentially providing the necessary infrastructure in C++, for building an embeddable interpreter like the one we have described, don't preclude the need for an embeddable interpreter.

7 Current Status, Performance Issues, Future Work

The interpreter has been developed on an HP-UX series 400 machine. There are plans to make it available on other HP architectures, SUN, and Macintosh; an intermediate version during development was able to run on a Macintosh. As the majority of the system is written in Beta, we don't anticipate many porting problems.

We have successfully embedded the interpreter into a simple listener loop (Section 4) to create an interactive development environment. On a standard Beta demonstration program which creates a simple database, populates it with entries, and displays the entries under various categories, the interpreter performed as follows (all times in seconds):

Interpreted			Compiled
Definition	Execution	Total	Execution
0.62	5.22	5.84	0.20

The demonstration program comprises of 284 lines of Beta code. Of the 5.84 secs taken by the interpreter, 0.10 secs (1.7% of total) are spent on loading ASTs (of the development environment and the demonstration program). These measurements are for the first *unoptimized* version of the interpreter.

A potential area of concern, from a performance standpoint, is the loading of the assembly-level symbols from the executable. This happens *only once* for every instance of the interpreter, when the interpreter is initialized; it takes 8.34 secs for the listener loop application which has 9295 symbols. Note that the number of symbols depends on the application into which the interpreter is embedded; an application with more classes linked in will have more symbols.

We are also experimenting with embedding the interpreter into Beta applications with graphical user-interfaces, our goal being the development of a framework for extensible user-interfaces. At present we have embedded the interpreter into an X-windows based text editor. To get an idea of the size overhead of the interpreter, we measured the size of the editor without the interpreter (2.07MB) and with the interpreter (3.42MB), an increase of 1.35MB or 65%. In the case of the editor, the number of symbols is 18088.

We plan next to embed the interpreter into an X-windows based drawing tool written in Beta. The interpreter will be used to make extensible various components of the application e.g. we will allow users to define new types of graphical objects.

On another course, we plan to embed the interpreter into *sif* (the syntax-directed editor) [MI93]. We envision users being able to interpret parts of the program they are editing by specifying (interactively) the context in which to execute it. Integration of the interpreter with *valhalla* [MI92a], the Beta source-level debugger is also forthcoming.

8 Acknowledgements

I would like to thank Prof. Ole Lehrmann Madsen for the numerous discussions on the material presented here and for countless personal consultations on the secrets of the Beta implementation. I thank Görel Hedin and Charles Lakos for their valuable comments on earlier versions of this paper. Thanks to the anonymous referees; their comments helped improve the paper. Randall Trigg and Kaj Grønbæk stimulated me with the problem of making the ApplBuilder incremental; I thank them. Furthermore, I appreciate the help of Elmer Sandvad, Jørgen Nørgaard, Jørgen Lindskov Knudsen, Søren Christensen, Niels Damgaard Hansen, and the folks at Mjølner Informatics. I thank Kurt Jensen for helping me come to Aarhus. And last, but not least, thanks to all the folks working hard at keeping the DeVise project going and the sources that fund the DeVise project.

A A brief Beta primer

This very brief primer provides a very superficial introduction to Beta. For more detailed treatment, please consult the Beta book [MMPN93].

A Beta program execution is a collection of objects.[6] An object is statically or dynamically created as an instance of a so-called *pattern*. The pattern is an abstraction mechanism that unifies type, function, procedure and class. A pattern PP is written as:

---
[6]Some ideas for this brief introduction borrowed from [NS90]

```
PP:  P
    (#  Decl1; Decl2; ...; Decln              (* attribute-part *)
       enter Inputs                            (* enter-part *)
       do Imperatives                          (* do-part *)
       exit Outputs                            (* exit-part *)
    #)
```

where P is the super-pattern. The declarations Decli can be of the following forms. (1) A : @Q where Q is a pattern; this means that an instance of Q is part of every instance of PP. (2) A : ^Q; this means that a reference to an instance of Q is part of every instance of PP. (3) QQ : Q (# ... #); this is a declaration of a new pattern QQ nested within pattern PP.

The enter-part Inputs describes the input parameters (formal parameters), Imperatives describes the actions to be performed (body), and Out describes the output parameters (return value). The Beta syntax unifies assignments and procedure calls; the symbol -> denotes both of these operations. For this paper, one should understand E1 -> E2 as E2 := E1 if E2 is an l-value. Otherwise, it means E2(E1)

A special variant of a pattern is called a *virtual pattern*. A virtual pattern allows one to defer the specification of some of its details until later. It is declared and specialized as follows:

```
P : (# V :< (# ... #) ... V ... #)
Q : P (# V ::< (# ... #) ... #)
```

In P, V is declared as a virtual; there is also a reference to V within the body of P. In Q, the inherited virtual V is further bound. Hence, in an instance of P, the V-reference refers to the V declared in P, while in an instance of Q, the same V-reference (inherited from P) refers to the further binding of V in Q.

A.1 Structure Values, and Pattern Variables

In the following program, the pattern variable X is declared and initialized first with the structure value denoting the pattern P2, and then with the structure value denoting P3.[7] The first call to new(X) will create a P2 instance and the second a P3 instance.

```
P : (#
       P1 : (# ... #);
       P2 : P1 (# ... #);
       P3 : P1 (# ... #);
       X : ##P1;                        (* pattern variable declaration *)
    DO
       P2## -> X##;                     (* structure value for P2 stored in X *)
       new(X);                          (* use X like a pattern *)
       P3## -> X##;                     (* structure value for P3 stored in X *)
       new(X);
    #)
```

---

[7] The syntax ##P1 implies *reference to pattern* as opposed to *reference to instance of pattern*. In the declaration, CurrentCellType is restricted to refer to Cell or its sub-patterns.
The syntax P2## implies *get the structure value of the pattern* as opposed to *execute the pattern*.
The syntax X## implies *store a structure value in the variable* as opposed to *execute the pattern denoted by the variable*.

The structure value for P2 created by P2## encapsulates the prototype for P2 along with the instance of P.

References

[AF89]   O. Agesen and S. Frølund. Dynamic Link and Load as a Basis for Implementing Extensibility. Technical report, Aarhus University, December 1989.

[AFO89] O. Agesen, S. Frølund, and M. H. Olsen. Persistent and Shared Objects in BETA. Technical Report DAIMI IR-89, Computer Science Department, Aarhus University, Denmark, April 1989. Master's thesis.

[BDMN73] G. Birwistle, O. Dahl, B. Myrhaug, and K. Nygaard. *Simula Begin*. Auerbach Publishers (New York), 1973.

[Bet89] D. M. Betz. XScheme: An Object-Oriented Scheme. Technical report, P.O. Box 144, Peterborough, NH, 1989.

[CM93]   S. Chiba and T. Masuda. Designing an Extensible Distributed Language with a Meta-Level Architecture. In *Proceedings of the European Conference on Object-Oriented Programming (ECOOP)*, Kaiserslautern, Germany, July 1993.

[ES90]   M. A. Ellis and B. Stroustrup. *C++ Reference Manual*. Addison-Wesley Publishing Company, 1990.

[GHT91] K. Grønbæk, A. Hviid, and R. H. Trigg. ApplBuilder — an Object-Oriented Application Generator Supporting Rapid Prototyping. In *Proceedings of the Fourth International Conference on Software Engineering and its Applications, Toulouse*, December 1991.

[GR83]   A. Goldberg and D. Robson. *Smalltalk-80. The Language and its Implementation*. Addison-Wesley Publishing Company, 1983.

[Hed92] G. Hedin. *Incremental Semantic Analysis*. PhD thesis, Department of Computer Science, Lund University, March 1992.

[Hed93] G. Hedin. *Personal Communication*, March 1993.

[HM86]   G. Hedin and B. Magnusson. Incremental Execution in a Programming Environment based on Compilation. In *Proceedings of the 19th Hawaii International Conference on System Sciences*, January 1986.

[HM87]   G. Hedin and B. Magnusson. Supporting Exploratory Programming in Simula. In *Proceedings of the Fifteenth SIMULA Conference, Jersey*, pages 73–88, September 1987.

[KdRB91] G. Kiczales, J. des Rivières, and D. G. Bobrow. *The Art of the Metaobject Protocol*. MIT Press, Cambridge, MA, 1991.

[Kee89] S. E. Keene. *Object-Oriented Programming in Common Lisp: A Programmer's Guide to CLOS*. Addison-Wesley Publishing Company, 1989.

[LM84] M. Løfgren and B. Magnusson. An Execution Environment for Simula on a Small Computer. Technical Report LUTFD2/(TFCS-3006)/1-96/1984, Department of Computer Science, Lund University, Sweden, March 1984.

[Lun92] Lund Software House AB, Box 7056, S-220 07 Lund, Sweden. *SIMULA User's Guide*, 1992.

[Mad93] O. L. Madsen. The Implementation of BETA. In *Object-Oriented Software Development Environments: The Mjølner Approach*. Prentice Hall International, 1993. To be published.

[Mag93] B. Magnusson. The Mjølner Orm system. In *Object-Oriented Software Development Environments*. Prentice Hall International, 1993. To be published.

[Mey88] B. Meyer. *Object-oriented Software Construction*. Prentice Hall International, 1988. Series in Computer Science. ISBN 0-13-629031-0.

[MI92a] Mjølner Informatics. *The Mjølner BETA System — The BETA Source-level Debugger — User's Guide*, 1992. MIA 92-12.

[MI92b] Mjølner Informatics. *The Mjølner BETA System, Reference Manual*, 1992. MIA 90-04(1.0).

[MI93] Mjølner Informatics. *Sif, A Hyper Structure Editor, User's Guide*, 1993. MIA 91-11(1.0).

[MMMP90] O. L. Madsen, B. Magnusson, and B. Møller-Pedersen. Strong Typing of Object-Oriented Languages Revisited. In *Proceedings of OOPSLA/ECOOP '90*, pages 140–149, October 1990. SIGPLAN Notices, Volume 25, Number 10.

[MMPN93] O. L. Madsen, B. Møller-Pedersen, and K. Nygaard. *Object Oriented Programming in the BETA Programming Language*. Addison-Wesley Publishing Company, 1993.

[NS90] C. Nørgaard and E. Sandvad. Reusability and Tailorability in the Mjølner BETA System. Technical Report DAIMI PB-300, Aarhus University, January 1990.

[Sta84] R. M. Stallman. Emacs: The extensible, customizable, self-documenting display editor. In *Interactive Programming Environments*. McGraw-Hill, 1984.

[Sta85] R. Stallman. *GNU Emacs Manual*. Free Software Foundation, 1985.

[ZC92] C. L. Zarmer and C. Chew. Frameworks for Interactive, Extensible, Information-Intensive Applications. In *Proceedings of UIST'92*, pages 33–41, November 1992.

(Invited Paper)

Managing Change in Persistent Object Systems

Atkinson, M.P.[*]   Sjøberg, D.I.K.[*]   Morrison, R.[†]

Abstract

Persistent object systems are highly-valued technology because they offer an effective foundation for building very long-lived *persistent application systems* (PAS). The technology becomes more effective as it offers a more consistently integrated computational context.

For it to be feasible to design and construct a PAS it must be possible to incrementally add program and data to the existing collection. For a PAS to endure it must offer flexibility: a capacity to evolve and change. This paper examines the capacity of persistent object systems to accommodate incremental construction and change.

Established store based technologies can support incremental construction but methodologies are needed to deploy them effectively. Evolving data description is one motivation for inheritance but inheritance alone is not enough to support change management.

The case for supporting incremental change is very persuasive. The challenge is to provide technologies that will facilitate it and methodologies that will organise it.

This paper identifies change absorbers as a means of describing how changes should propagate. It is argued that if we systematically develop an adequate repertoire of change absorbers then they will facilitate much better quality change management.

1 Introduction

The primary interest in object technology arises from its capacity to be an essential material from which large and long-lived application systems are built. Such long-lived applications are called *Persistent Application Systems* (PAS). Examples of such systems are CAD systems, geographic information systems, urban planning systems, health-care management systems, etc. They are characterised by becoming large, often being distributed with a wide variety of users and being concerned with the *long-term* support of cooperative activity. Large investments are involved in their construction and operation. People and organisations depend on them.

As PAS attain central importance to an organisation (for example, a hospital trusts all its medical histories, accounting information and staff records to a health-care management system) the continuance of the organisation and the adaptability and continuity of the PAS become strongly interrelated. If the PAS fails the organisation may also fail.

---

[*]Department of Computing Science, University of Glasgow, Glasgow, G12 8QQ, Scotland
[†]Department of Computational Science, University of St Andrews, St Andrews, KY16 9SX, Scotland

Equally, if the PAS cannot be adapted to the changing environment and needs of the organisation sufficiently quickly and economically it will inhibit the organisation from adapting. Such rigidity may lead to the demise of the organisation. This paper assumes that PAS will be built using object technologies and enquires about the adequacy of their provisions for change.

Persistent object storage enables a wide range of program and data forms to be built and to endure for as long as the storage technology which holds them and the execution technology which interprets them continue to exist. The stability of references based on identity allows long-term representation of constructional relationships. The binding mechanisms allow incremental growth of the total body of program and other data. The mechanisms of inclusion polymorphism (loosely, inheritance and subtyping) allow certain kinds of change to be accommodated and localised. Hence, at first sight, we might be complacent and regard existing persistent object systems as adequate. This paper attempts to assess precisely where that complacency is well founded and where advances are necessary before organisations may safely become dependent on persistent object technology, or more precisely on PAS built using persistent object technology.

The paper is divided into two parts. In the first part (Sections 2 and 3) the progress towards achieving a consistent platform on which to build PAS is examined. This is very much a sample of actual progress, focusing on orthogonal persistence and the relationship between data models and type systems. Two recent developments in type systems are examined: the provision of parametric type constructors (3.3.1) allows modelling and descriptive capacity to be extended, and the provision of infinite unions (3.3.2) permits certain forms of change absorber to be defined.

The second part of the paper deals with various aspects of change management. Section 4 restates why change management is essential and proposes that improved methods will emphasise incremental change. Section 5 identifies what might be expected from change management tools, how they may be improved with persistent object technology and why they will remain deficient until better structural description is available. Section 6 presents change absorbers as a means of providing this description. Three categories are proposed: automatic transformers (6.1), partial transmitters (6.2) and active responders based on enquiry mechanisms (6.3).

Current practice for managing program change is reformulated in terms of change absorbers in Section 7. It is postulated that the necessary primitives, e.g. dynamic binding and incremental linking may already exist, but regular patterns for their use need to be better characterised. Section 8 shows that coping with type/schema change is a good deal more problematic. The infinite union types that currently exist and type subsumption provide only a partial solution. This leads to a conclusion that identifies research challenges.

2 Progress towards Uniformity

Persistence is provision for values to remain computationally available for an arbitrary length of time; as long as they are required for computation. This period may be very brief or the full life-time of a PAS. Note that, for the PAS envisaged, these maximum life-times may be tens or even hundreds of years.

Orthogonal persistence is the provision of persistence equitably to all values [Atkinson et al., 1982]. It is important as it ensures that PAS designers and programmers may choose data structures freely from all those available. If persistence isn't orthogonal, they will need to choose representations suitable for processing and other representations for storage. This additional modelling complexity and the inevitable translations between representations that result from a failure to make persistence orthogonal are needless impediments to the construction and maintenance of PAS.

It should be noted that the choice of the type system is a separate issue. It might be based entirely on relations, be appropriate only to formatted text processing or be based on the type system of an object oriented programming language. That choice will be made to provide appropriate modelling capabilities for the application area.

A further principle that guides the provision of persistence is that of *persistence independence*. This means that code should not need to be different for data of different age or longevity. A consequence of this principle is that programmers should not be required to explicitly move data from long-term storage to processing storage. Transfers must be automated.

Avoiding the need for translation and explicit transfer reduces the volume of code in a typical PAS by about one third. A more important gain from orthogonal persistence is the reduction of cognitive load on designers and programmers. In a typical system (shown in Figure 1) they are trying to envisage, implement and manage three mappings. They have the particularly tricky task of keeping any pair of the mappings consistent with the other one.

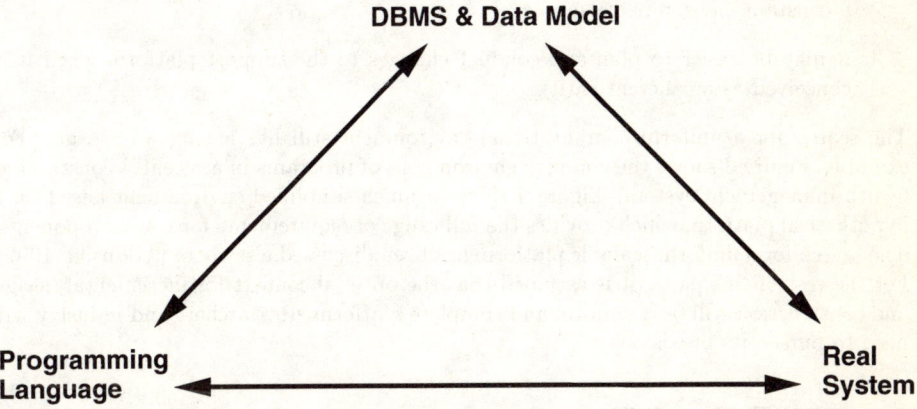

Figure 1: Many PAS are constructed using two models: one in the database and one in the programs

This complexity and the need for programmers to maintain this consistency are both avoided with orthogonal persistence as only one model is used and one mapping maintained (see Figure 2).

Those object-oriented systems that use different notations to describe schemata from those they use to describe data in their operations (methods), fail to deliver this orthogonality. Such object-oriented systems re-introduce the complexity piecemeal as fragmented triple mappings for each operation.

The successful persistent object systems are therefore likely to be those that take some programming language and provide it with orthogonal persistence [Atkinson *et al.*,

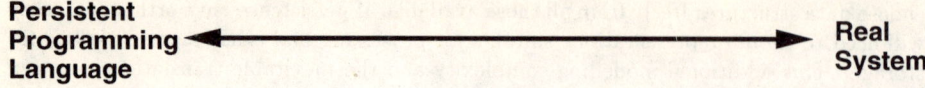

Figure 2: New PAS may be constructed using only one model in a PPL

1983] or those that are designed explicitly to provide orthogonal persistence [Morrison et al., 1989]. The most popular versions of persistent systems at present are derived from C++ [Richardson and Carey, 1987; Bancilhon et al., 1992; Object Design Inc., 1991; Ontologic Inc., 1991].

Provision of orthogonal persistence may be viewed as a step in the process of providing a more uniform computational environment. If the environment in which PAS computation takes place is made uniform several advantages may be expected:

1. programming will be simpler (and hence more economic and less error prone) as programmers have less detailed rules to comprehend;

2. programs will have a more easily specified environment (and therefore it is more reasonable to assume that it can be perpetuated unchanged);

3. incremental construction is simplified as the successive components all interact with a constant environment; and

4. it may be easier to plan and conduct changes to the support platform when it is conceived as a coherent entity.

The search for a uniform computational environment still has a long way to go. For example, Figure 3 shows the complex environment of programs in a recently constructed health management system. Figure 4 shows a much simplified environment based on a hypothetical platform which provides the full range of requirements for PAS components. The search for a uniform scalable platform has been discussed elsewhere [Atkinson, 1992]. For the rest of this paper it is assumed that the optimal context for incremental design and construction will be a uniform and complete platform. Researchers and industry will need to pursue its provision.

3 The Rôle of Types

Throughout the last two decades database researchers have made considerable progress with data models while programming language researchers have made significant progress with type systems. It is helpful to review aspects of that progress to recognise the common goals. This is important if we espouse uniformity of computational environment, as to achieve it requires that *only one* of these is part of that environment.

Type systems will be examined first and then their relationship with data models will be reviewed. A type system services four interrelated tasks:

1. description of the data;

2. restriction of programs to reduce errors;

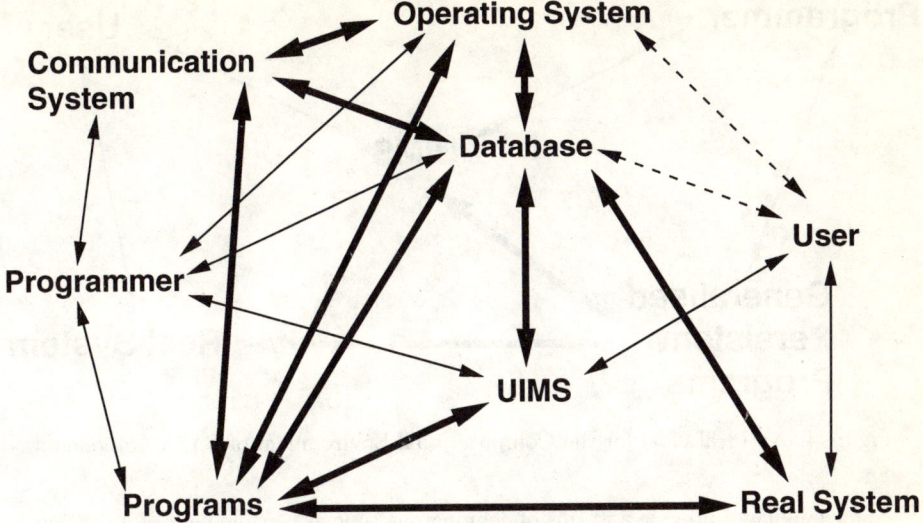

Figure 3: A Recent PAS shows the Complex Environment of its Programs

3. protection of critical structures; and

4. provision of information to implementations.

3.1 Description of Data

A type system provides a means of describing the forms values may take. Typically this may involve a (possibly recursive) combination of the following:

1. choice of some predefined forms, called *base types* (e.g. integer, boolean, real, string, date, etc.);

2. composition of types using *type constructors* to register relationships between values (e.g. aggregations in records, alternatives in unions or tagged sums, collections in sets, mappings in maps and arrays, etc.);

3. *reference*, usually defined via *recursive types*, which implies instances and identity;

4. declaration and naming of new (usually parametric) type constructors;

5. abstract data types, that provide encapsulation; and

6. combination of data structures with program (e.g. operations or procedures) that will manipulate the data in those structures.

Many programming languages provide particular forms and additional forms of the mechanisms listed above; the **env** and **any** types used later (see Sections 3.3.2 and 8) are examples.

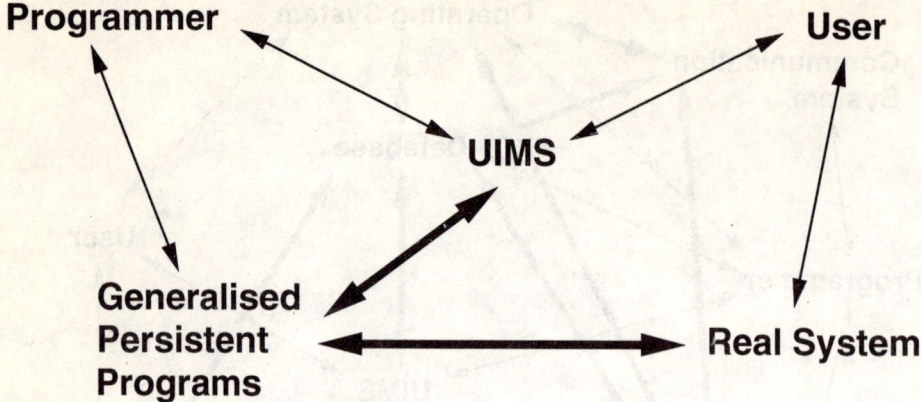

Figure 4: An Ideal Goal for the Computational Environment of PAS Components

Some languages provide a means of defining one type as a refinement of a previously defined type, e.g. Simula [Birtwistle et al., 1973], SmallTalk [Goldberg and Robson, 1983], C++ [Ellis and Stroustrup, 1990], Galileo [Albano et al., 1985], Oberon [Reiser, 1991], Fibonacci [Albano et al., 1993], etc. This facility will be called "type inheritance" in this paper, though some call it "explicit subtyping". These languages, and some others e.g. Machiavelli [Ohori et al., 1989], Quest [Cardelli, 1990], Tycoon [Matthes, 1992], etc., permit values of one type to be used where values with less properties are required. This property of types will be called "subtyping" in this paper, though it is more properly called "inclusion polymorphism". Where it isn't combined with type inheritance it may be referred to as "implicit subtyping" [Connor et al., 1990a].

A number of languages (e.g. SETL2 [Schwartz et al., 1986], Pascal/R [Schmidt, 1977], Modula/R [Koch et al., 1983], DBPL [Matthes et al., 1992], P-Pascal [Berman, 1991], RAPP [Hughes and Connolly, 1990], etc.) provide a variety of bulk type constructors, e.g. set, relation, sequence, map, etc. as a means of constructing collections.

This exploration of descriptive components out of which a model can be built is reminiscent of the contemporaneous exploration of data models, e.g. SDM [Hammer and McLeod, 1981], Daplex [Shipman, 1981], RM/T [Codd, 1979], IFO [Abiteboul and Hull, 1987], etc.

The crucial common goal is to impose a structure on the data by mapping it to a composition of standard but flexible, appropriate and suggestive building blocks. The results are useful for several reasons:

- they enable parts or features of the *structure* to be named, thus allowing people and programs to refer to them;

- they give access to operations that are associated with the component structures, for instance, iteration over the elements of some collection and tests on the current form of variants; and

- they facilitate communication among a system's designers, builders and users via related textual and diagrammatic representations.

The programming languages have supported a model of reference and identity and seen it as an important modelling tool for many years [Hoare, 1975; Atkinson, 1978]. They have had a concern for specifying the relationship between code and data, for example, in Fortran subprograms and in modules in many languages. Higher-order languages[1], languages with modules and languages with abstract data types all provide a means of describing a static relationship between program and data. (More flexible relationships will be considered later in the paper — see Section 3.3.2.)

In recent years Object-Oriented Databases (OODBs) have attempted to support similar modelling structures [Atkinson *et al.*, 1989].

3.2 Equivalences between Data Models and Type Systems

The preceding discussion shows that similar activities and common goals can be recognised in data model research and in type system research. Approximate equivalences are summarised in the following table:

Database Vocabulary	Programming Language Vocabulary
data models	type systems
schema	type expression
database	variable
database extent	value

Although detailed comparison shows that in both cases features[2] are tagged onto the concepts that invalidate these equivalences, they hold well at a conceptual level. Therefore it is feasible that one of type systems or data models will fulfill the common rôle. Of importance here is current type system research into methods of describing bulk types [Atkinson *et al.*, 1993]. These allow regular structures to be described and provide operators that abstract over iteration.

3.3 Extensible and Universal Type Constructs

Three areas of innovation now increase the power of type systems:

1. regular and powerful polymorphisms [Cardelli and Wegner, 1985];

2. mechanisms for handling parametric type definitions [Cardelli, 1989]; and

3. models of infinite union types which support incremental evolution and binding [Morrison, 1979].

The latter two of these are now illustrated in a little more detail. It is assumed that the reader is already familiar with parametric and inclusion polymorphism. For a fuller discussion of type system research applicable to persistent application systems the reader is referred to [Connor, 1991; Connor, 1993].

---

[1] Those that have procedures in their value space, so that procedures may be the arguments to, and results of, other procedures; may be elements of data structures and values of variables.

[2] Typically those concerned with efficiency, such as placement or representation annotations.

3.3.1 Defining New Type Constructors

A type constructor is a programming language or data model construct which when supplied with suitable parameters generates a new type. Readers will be familiar with built-in type constructors, such as **array** and **record** in Pascal-like languages, **table** in SQL and **set** and **sequence** in semantic data models and OODBs. The set of built in constructors is inevitably a compromise between complexity and completeness. A compromise may be unsatisfactory for everyone: the suppliers of the system find it overly complex to build, the users find it overly complex to understand but still lacking in constructs they would like to use in their particular application.

Parametric type definitions allow a programmer to define new constructors in terms of already provided and user-defined constructors. These can be equivalent to those that have already proved their utility in data model research or can be new constructors appropriate to particular application domains.

Where type constructors require parameters these may be supplied with: a base type, another constructed type or with another type constructor. In the last case a new type constructor is defined, in the other cases a type is the result. This will be illustrated by developing an example that describes a database of a teaching department.

> **type** Student **is** record[MatricNo: **integer**; Name: **string**]
> **type** Students **is** Set[Student]
> **type** Course **is** record[Cname: **string**; Max_enrolment: **integer**]
> **type** Courses **is** Set[Course]
> **type** Prerequisites **is** DAG[Course]
> **type** Enrolment **is** record[course: Course; start: Date; enrolled: Students]
> **type** YearsWork **is** Set[Enrolment]
> **type** History **is** Sequence[YearsWork]
> **type** TreadMill **is** Ring[Courses]

Four different constructors have been used: *Set*, with its usual mathematical meaning but probably an implicit order; *DAG*, a directed acyclic graph; *Sequence*, again with its standard meaning and *Ring*, with the obvious meaning. The composition is well illustrated by the type *History* which is itself a *Sequence* of *Sets*, each element of these *Sets* contains a *Set* of students.

Of course, such composition can be a property of any data model that provides *orthogonality* and *data type completeness*; that is, types constructed with any constructor may be parameters to any other constructor. The additional important feature is that these constructors may themselves be defined (out of other constructors). So, while *Set* and *Sequence* might be provided, it is scarcely credible that *DAG* and *Ring* would already be provided. The importance of the current work on types is that they can be defined and then re-used elsewhere. For example, the *DAG* constructor might be used to model descendants in a genetics experiment and *Ring* might be used to model the phases in the life cycle of species in a palaeo-zoological data collection.

The new constructors can be defined by composing those already defined as is illustrated in this example:

> **type** Chain[E] **is** Sequence[Ring [E]]
> **type** Forest[T] **is** Set[DAG[T]]

type Pairs[A, B] **is** Sequence[**record**[first: A; second: B]]

The identifier E denotes a type parameter which is supplied when a type is constructed. Thus an expression like:

type Citations **is** Forest[**string**]

occurring at any subsequent point will be equivalent to:

type Citations **is** Set[DAG [**string**]]

The ability to establish new constructors is used later in the paper.

3.3.2 Infinite Unions and Extensibility

Some type systems provide types that denote an infinite union of types, that is a value that is described by one of these types has an infinite number of possible types from which it was injected into the infinite union. In this context, the type information must be associated with the value to ensure that when it is eventually projected out of the union it is treated in a way compatible with the original type; otherwise, type safety is compromised. A typical name for this type is **any**.

Such types are important as they allow type-safe program to be written that will perform operations on values whose types have not even been defined or thought of at the time of writing. A typical example is a browser [Dearle and Brown, 1988]. Other examples would be form generators or other standard interfaces. The reader should note that this is fundamentally different from the code which can be written using parametric polymorphism alone.

These infinite union types permit a new kind of incremental program development that will be motivated and discussed below. Essentially, a type-check is postponed until projection out of the infinite union occurs. This means that for any code that does not need to unpack the value, type checking is satisfied without enquiry into the type of the injected value. When projection occurs, the system has to examine the type and ensure that the code which will be applied to the projected value only carries out operations compatible with that value. Hence the type checking (correctness validation) has been partitioned into parts:

1. the code prior to the projection which can be checked completely statically;

2. the code after the projection which can be checked completely statically on the assumption that the projection performs satisfactorily; and

3. the projection itself, which is checked dynamically at the time when the projection is performed.

This will be made concrete with another infinite union construct, **env**, in the programming language Napier88 [Dearle, 1989; Morrison *et al.*, 1989] which will be used for illustrative purposes below.

The type **env** denotes any set of bindings. Each binding is a quadruple: a unique identifier, a type, a value, and a constancy. The value must conform to the type. Values of type **env** are therefore a set of such bindings and have all the rights of any value in the language. Operations exist to construct new instances of this type, to add bindings to an **env** value, to remove them, to extract the value, to assign a new value, and to scan all the bindings.

The projection operation takes the form:

>**use** e **with** x:int; p: **proc**(int) **in**
>   **begin**
>   p(x)
>   ...
>   **end**

where the code between the **begin**, **end** pair is statically type checked as is the code outside the **use** statement. However, when the expression e is evaluated (it is statically determined that it must produce an **env**) there is a dynamic check to establish that the particular environment produced actually contains (at least) the bindings specified in the signature after **with** which have been assumed in the compilation of the clause after **in**.

This mechanism is an example of developing support for incremental program development. Such mechanisms allow programs providing definitions, services or values to be developed and replaced independently of the programs which will use those components.

Before discussing other incremental mechanisms, it is important to review (in Section 4) why incremental approaches to large scale system design and maintenance are becoming important.

3.4 Summary of the Provision of Uniform Technology

The case for providing a uniform technology is that it simplifies the processes of PAS design, construction and maintenance. It will also facilitate incremental methods for building and maintaining PAS. The relationship between type systems and data models provides an example of technology which could be made to converge to provide a more uniform computational platform for PAS. For the purposes of this paper, type systems will be used as the putative limit of that convergence. They are chosen as they already have notations for regular extensibility (Section 3.3.1) and incremental binding (Section 3.3.2).

4 Incremental Design and Construction

Incremental construction is one of the traditional reasons for using databases. The database is a central repository and the suites of application programs attached to it are added or replaced incrementally. Schema editors have also provided a mechanism for incrementally extending and changing the definition of the total body of data.

Incremental design is the primary motivation for object orientation. Initial, quite general object specifications (classes) are refined to provide specialisations or to capture increments in the understanding of the modelled system.

These may be seen as examples of a more general principle:

> To be effective all technologies and methodologies for PAS construction must support incremental design, incremental construction and incremental change.

Any PAS will have been developed to support human activity in an organisation. Since human behaviour is sophisticated and in organisations particularly complex, the requirements for a PAS are inevitably sophisticated and complex. It is infeasible to expect that they can be comprehended and converted into a design in a single effort. Early database methodology, in contrast, expected to fully understand an organisation and develop a schema that "represented the enterprise". Experience has shown that for modern requirements it is necessary to understand and design the PAS incrementally. A portion of the enterprise is understood, the corresponding design is developed and the construction is often undertaken before other parts of the enterprise are tackled. This is also a common strategy for organising other large engineering endeavours, e.g. chemical plant design and construction.

It usually transpires that the initial understanding of requirements, even for these parts is inadequate and further revision of the design is undertaken even before the relevant subsystem is complete. Again, it is partly the limitation of implementors' conceptual capacities that engenders this incrementalism. It is almost impossible to fully understand even a part of the activity to be supported and an iterative approach results. System development methodologies normally recognise this, insisting, for example, on dialogue with representatives of all those who will eventually use the PAS, to detect and correct such misunderstandings.

This dialogue and the introduction of parts of the system, is however, a further stimulus to change. It is therefore normal to find that the user community immediately perceives ways in which their operations and the system might now be improved.

However carefully this design process is undertaken, the system continues to require change. Existing operational practices are revised and elaborated and new activities are added. This is a manifestation of a strength of cooperating humans, they continually review and revise their working practices in order to improve their performance or product. This has long been understood.

For example, it was traditional to arrange workers in craft-villages. In Burma, as you travel west from Mandalay to Sagaing, you pass through a village of woodcarvers, a village of people making alabaster casts, a village of bronze casters and a village of gold leaf makers. Clustering the people resulted in more rapid improvement of their technology as they copied each other's improvements and further developed them. A process of incremental change.

As Persistent Application Systems are built it is important that they do not inhibit this process of incremental improvement. Indeed, modern systems make possible the mutual stimulus towards improvement between cooperating workers that are geographically distributed — a "distributed craft-village". To respond, it is necessary that the PAS be able to be incrementally changed both rapidly and economically. There is a danger that massive databases and software will stultify change by embedding the organisation in a mass of "digital concrete". To combat this danger the PAS technologies and methodologies must be developed to support incremental change as a matter of course.

There are other more mundane reasons for espousing incrementalism as a matter of course. Organising design and construction becomes more manageable. The work can be split into separate, relatively small components that match the capacities of small teams. Teams with different expertise, such as requirements, design, implementation and testing, can move ahead of one another preparing the ground for the next team while it is working on another increment.

As PAS and the organisations they support become both more extensive and more intertwined so the feasibility of making radical changes is reduced. It becomes progressively harder to turn off an old system and transfer work to a new one. It becomes impracticable to stop a system for hours or even days while schemata are re-organised and software is replaced.

There is, therefore, an unassailable case for founding the technology and methodology that supports PAS on the observation that change is normal throughout the PAS's lifetime of design, construction, maintenance and operation. Incremental change is easier to manage and probably easier to sustain than cataclysmic change. The challenge is to develop methodologies and technologies that support incremental change well in the context of the very large and very long-lived systems which we aspire to achieve. The following sections assess our current levels of success and identify the challenge more precisely.

5 Change Management Requirements

Change management is concerned with the organisation of change. If the change is to be incremental and if the system is to go on functioning correctly for its users there are two requirements to be met:

1. all the consequences of a change must be properly propagated; and

2. no unnecessary changes should be made.

These requirements will be illustrated with an example from a health care system. It has previously been the practice to record a patient's next-of-kin. It is now noted that for many elderly patients the next-of-kin is unable to perform some required actions as they too are elderly. A new fact about a patient is therefore to be recorded, the responsible-person (perhaps a care-worker, the organiser of a home in which the patient resides, etc.).

The schema is changed to accommodate the extra information. All extant records will not have that extra information and it will not be collected unless or until the patient re-presents. Therefore, it is probably desirable not to change the existing records until the new information becomes available (this also avoids an initial value problem).

Similarly, most programs will not be concerned with handling the new information and should operate unchanged in the future. However, certain programs must be changed, in particular, those that enter a new patient into the system, those concerned with checking the continued correctness of patient details and those that generate letters that should now go to the responsible-person.

These program changes will also require that certain screen designs need to be changed, certainly those used for inputting and checking patient details and at least some of those for displaying patient details in other circumstances. But screen re-design may overload a screen so that the information must be re-organised and split between two screens. This results in a change to the sequence of screen operations. Similarly pro forma, report formats and letter templates may have to be changed.

Some of these changes will affect users. For example, staff admitting patients now have to ask extra questions and enter extra data. The relevant existing staff will need re-training, user documentation will need to be revised, training manuals and documentation of hospital procedures will also need revision. Design and maintenance documentation will also need to be revised.

We may enquire how common such changes are, how much of the system is affected by each change, etc. Recently Sjøberg [Sjøberg, 1993a] has measured such parameters for 18 months in the development of a health care system. There are not many similar studies, so it is impossible to be sure how generally applicable are his observations. However, his study detected very high rates of change and extensive consequential changes. Hopefully, similar studies will soon be available to allow relevant norms to be included in the estimation of development and operational costs.

Sjøberg's data supports anecdotal evidence that it is worthwhile investing in technology that supports the change management process and in methods that make implementing the changes less error prone and costly. There are at present two levels of support:

1. informative systems that provide PAS developers and maintainers with data about the existing system, its present representation and perhaps some of its dependencies; and

2. automatic systems that directly implement some of the steps necessary to deal with the consequences of change.

Examples of the former are data dictionaries, repositories and build management tools. Examples of the latter are automatic forms interfaces that, at the cost of not having a tailored screen design, automatically generate a user interface and automatic re-structuring tools that propagate change to the existing data.

Sjøberg has also implemented a prototype change management system that utilises the reliable references available in persistent systems. As a result of this reliability, his system is able to discover and record dependency information automatically and provide reliable information about the consequences of changes [Sjøberg *et al.*, 1993]. He is also investigating the automation of some aspects of change propagation based on the more reliable information [Sjøberg, 1993b]. However, automation is limited by the lack of information about which changes should be propagated and which absorbed. It is here suggested that this additional information may be provided by a combination of two techniques:

1. the division of the system into cells which communicate through well defined interfaces; and

2. the use of *change absorbers* to specify more precisely the system architect's intent about when and how change should propagate.

A methodology is then needed to ensure that there is disciplined and sufficient provision of the propagation specification information. Given this additional information, it should be possible to use techniques such as those developed by Sjøberg to provide much more helpful information for those considering a change and to automate more of the change processes.

6 Change Absorbers

An important adjunct of change management tools are *change absorbers*. Without them the extent to which change would propagate would be intolerable. Most users want the illusion that the system is unchanging except on the (what they consider rare) occasions when they want a change or they wish to exploit a new feature.

Typical examples of change absorbers are:

1. database views, which protect programs using the view from changes in the schema[3];

2. type subsumption in object oriented systems which allows procedures to continue to operate with refinements of the data types originally expected; and

3. infinite union types which protect part of a type or schema definition from "seeing" changes beyond the infinite union.

A comprehensive repertoire of change absorbers will be needed to permit fluent incremental change. The important property of a change absorber is that it transmits the changes that are important across a boundary and suppresses propagation of all other changes.

The system can then be visualised as a composition of cells. Each cell would be protected by a semi-permeable membrane constructed from change absorbers that transmitted change important to the cell and kept out extraneous change. Such a structure would be recursive, compositions of cells behaving as a cell. The cellular analogy is intended to suggest a total system in which its smallest components are undergoing almost continuous change or replacement.

System architects would then need a methodology to decide on the appropriate boundaries for the cells and to choose the correct change absorbers. System constructors and maintainers would then need tools that report on the cell structure and how it would react to particular changes.

This differs from much modular construction in that the cellular boundaries are not as rigid. In most modular systems, the modules are statically bound together and it is not possible to replace modules, or add modules without massive reconstruction.

It is expected that architects will deliberately build in significant change absorption capacity so as to avoid rigidity. This requires investment during design and construction, but it should be more than repaid during the system's life-time of change. Some computational costs are inevitably incurred as information and control passes across cell boundaries. The designer can trade these change costs by adjusting the size of cells and the units of work and information transmitted between them.

The repertoire of change absorption techniques can be categorised as:

1. automatic transformers;

2. partial transmitters; and

3. enquiry mechanisms.

---

[3]Not necessarily automatically, someone may have to redefine the view to maintain the old image.

6.1 Automatic Transformers

These attempt to absorb change entirely and to continue to transmit the same information. Typical examples are communication protocols, for example RPC mechanisms on top of TCP/IP or the database interfaces on PCs such as ODBC [MICROSOFT, 1993]. Another example is the object transmission mechanism of CORBA [Schaffert, 1992]. In such cases, the intermediate machinery will perform transformations to recover from representational changes across the interface.

An early example in the database context was the System/R access mechanism. Access code was compiled to deliver results for a query under the assumption that the database had a certain structure. If, when the query was eventually applied, it transpired that that structure had changed, the access code would be regenerated automatically to achieve the *same* result.

When considered from the viewpoint of absorbing change within a system we might expect significant developments in these standard interfaces. They effectively give guarantees to cells that they can rely on certain invariants. It is likely to become a major architectural issue, identifying precisely what invariants a cell can assume. For example, there may be some global invariants and others that are provided or promised more locally. Without such invariants it is almost impossible to construct a system. There is a challenge finding sufficient invariants without seriously inhibiting change.

It is probable that reflection [Stemple *et al.*, 1992] will be an important technology for building automatic change handlers. Just as type enquiry, program generation and reflection can be combined to give type dependent behaviour [Stemple *et al.*, 1990; Sheard, 1991] so it can use delivery and target descriptions to automatically generate transformers.

6.2 Partial Transmitters

The example already given of database views illustrates this kind of mechanism. It hides from the programs/users connected to the view: schema changes, changes to data values outside the view and some operations. It transmits all data changes that are within the view.

Another example is the use of subsumption at interfaces, such as in ADT signatures and as procedure parameters. This hides change which introduces additional properties and behaviours in excess of those specified. It transmits changes that reduce or change the properties of the expected type. It also transmits changes to the accessible values.

As was exhibited in the health care example, additions should not always be hidden. It should be possible to specify that at some interfaces any deviation from an exact match is unacceptable and requires change propagation.

However, it is possible to admit interfaces that propagate increases but perhaps hide certain removals from the object's properties. The increases might always be passed on to the target because its job was to present or preserve full information. However, established formats might be important so that omitted data should be replaced by a default (typically a null value) so that the code, etc. in the target does not have to be altered.

Combinations of subsumption and substitution would permit an interface to apparently present a constant type, absorbing all type changes with automatic transformations. Clearly the transformation functions would soon become complex and would need to be structured systematically. They would inevitably lose information and this is potentially dangerous. The change management tools that reported on the propagation structure would need to make it easy to obtain notification of their dangers.

It seems likely that an extensive repertoire of these partial transmitters will evolve as typical change propagation patterns are recognised.

6.3 Enquiry Mechanisms

The two previous mechanisms essentially consider the cells as passive objects. It is possible to make them active in the change process and to introduce special classes of cells that mediate in the change propagation process.

An important form of active change handling is that of *environment enquiry*. Here the cell changes its behaviour of its own volition on the basis of what it finds in its environment. Good examples appear on personal machines: word processors offer fonts based on the fonts they find on the system, and they offer printers after enquiring which are available. Similarly, program building aids and spreadsheets, enquire what libraries are mounted before presenting the user with the available options. In all cases it is expected that changes will occur, and that these will result in changed component behaviour.

Dynamic linking mechanisms and command interpreters find and load program based on information they find when they search for a module or command.

Such enquiries have been systematised in distributed file servers as name servers and in the ISA architecture for distributed object systems as object trading [ANSA, ; ISO,].

A common feature of these enquiry mechanisms is that a cell or cells (in our vocabulary) is introduced to hold some information that is expected to change. Programs causing such changes then record the information in these inquiry servers. Cells that wish to be sensitive to these changes then precede operations that use the affected facility by enquiries to the relevant enquiry server.

This use of enquiry mechanisms is important as it permits anticipated changes to be propagated completely automatically. In persistent object systems it is of course trivially easy to arrange that the data against which the enquiry is made is made persistent and changed transactionally. Thus, a cell having made an enquiry may trust the result of the enquiry until it has been used.

It is expected that such enquiry mechanisms will be used systematically to avoid having to explicitly propagate change.

7 Managing Program Change

Several authors have recently looked at the possibilities of managing program change in persistent object stores [Connor, 1991; Kirby, 1993; Cutts, 1993; Kirby *et al.*, 1992; Farkas *et al.*, 1992]. All three aspects of the above categorisation may be observed:

1. A standard structure in the persistent object store holds information about the available programs — thus the store acts as an enquiry server.

2. the program parts are held in variables which are themselves reached via bindings in **env** instances — which act as partial transmitters. Consequently, changes such as the insertion and removal of other program parts are hidden (see Section 3.3.2).

3. Changes to program parts that do not change their type are transmitted automatically whereas changes that do alter the part's type are detected and require programmers to manually accommodate the change.

The handling of some kinds of change to the types of program components might be automated with the caveats given above. This could be done by automatically introducing a "correcting procedure" that accepted the old call and called the new form, or vice-versa.

It has already been shown that in these systems it is easy to specify and control the propagation of changes to program components. For example, it is possible to statically bind to a value (using higher-order procedures as values and persistent identities in the source — hyper-references) immutably, so that whatever happens the value chosen at construction will be used. At the other extreme, programs can find other program parts they require every time they use them. As this all takes place in a transactional store, it is "safe" as programs using other code will behave like readers on that code.

It is expected that this structure of program parts will be regularised into various patterns of binding that allow the builders and architects to choose the corresponding patterns of change propagation. It is suspected that the necessary primitive types describing various forms of binding have already been developed in experimental systems. The patterns still need formal identification and capture in the form of defined type constructors.

8 Managing Type Change

Type change (or schema change) is perhaps the most difficult class of changes to manage in a PAS. There are several problem areas.

1. It is desirable to preserve as much of the type graph as possible unperturbed. Types refer to other types when they are defined, e.g. the parameters given to a constructor are referred to by the generated type. When type T1 is changed it is undesirable that every type that refers to T1 should appear to have changed — it would often produce a substantial cascade of changes. On the other hand, it is difficult to avoid this as for any model of type equivalence those types have changed.

2. Existing instances of the types must be changed. This can be done either in an immediate but expensive sweep of the store or incrementally whenever the objects whose type has been changed are next used.

3. The graph of instance references must be preserved but the preceding process may involve making new copies or changing addresses. Indirection mechanisms are one solution commonly employed in databases but they lose any performance potential of references.

4. The programs that handle the data either have to operate with the new data unchanged or respond to the changes.

Several partial solutions to this class of problem have already been discussed above. They are also well known in the literature [Skarra and Zdonik, 1987; Wegner and Zdonik, 1988;

Connor *et al.*, 1990b]. Solutions to all these problems can be arranged if the costs of anticipating change are tolerable. For example, objects that may change could be defined using the following constructor.

type ChangeProtected[InvariantPart] **is record**[fixed: InvariantPart; extra: **any**]

Any object is now declared with a type such as that in the following example.

type Patient **is** ChangeProtected[**record**[name: **string**; ...; next_of_kin: **string**]]

This works because, both at the type level and at the instance level the outer record structure is invariant and so type references, instance references and program interfaces are unperturbed by changes that are localised to the *extra* field. Initially all instances of this field would hold a null value.

When the previously described change occurs, a new structure for responsible-person information is introduced.

type ExtraPatient1 **is record**[responsible_person: **string**]

All subsequent and upgraded *Patient* objects now have a value of type *ExtraPatient1* injected into their *extra* field. This can be accessed via a projection by programs that need to use this data. All other programs are unchanged. The population of instances can be changed incrementally.

But there are some drawbacks to this method. An extra field access has been introduced and code has become more complex to write and execute. Optimisations and automatic code generation might overcome these problems. However, there is a more serious problem. The quality of the types as a description of the data has been seriously impaired. It is only in running text and in similarities of identifiers that the relationship between *Patient* and *ExtraPatient1* is established. The operational system and future programmers would not know that the field *extra* of *Patient* was only meant to have values of type *Extrapatient1* injected into it and no other.

Such notations will suffice for experiments that allow classes of change absorber to be investigated. Subsequently, more precise notations that actually limit the allowed changes to intended patterns, will be required. It is suspected that new primitives in the type system defining other classes of infinite union will be needed and/or defining other type matching rules. These will then be combined into standard patterns using defined type constructors.

9 Conclusions

The challenge of building Persistent Application Systems that will satisfy expectations is very great and of economic importance. They should enhance human cooperative behaviour. The work of the last decade on the development of persistence and object oriented systems has been much concerned to facilitate this design and construction process. The fundamentally important aspect of that research is to develop uniform computational environments so that unnecessary complexity in the Persistent Application System is avoided. There is still opportunity for further improvement.

It is apparent that a successful PAS will be expected to service its user community for a very long time, tens or hundreds of years. As the sophistication of PASs increases these required lifetimes will extend. In consequence an even greater challenge is to facilitate the maintenance and evolution of PASs. If that challenge is not met and the PASs become rigidly resistant to change or even just uneconomic to change then they will seriously harm the performance of their user communities. They will do this by inhibiting the normal processes of improvement that go on among a group of interacting people.

To achieve the required uniformity careful attention has been paid to orthogonality. For example, the rights to persistence are equal for values of all types and the parameters for type constructors are any type. Uniformity is also achieved by removing unnecessary duplication of concepts. The example given in the paper is the convergence of data model and type system.

An important issue, not covered in this paper, is how to maintain and evolve this uniform platform with adequate stability over the long lifetimes of PASs [Atkinson, 1992]. PASs built on technology for which that problem hasn't been solved — most persistent and object-oriented systems perhaps — will fail their user communities as they will not be able to capitalise on improved technology.

Type constructors enable the definition of new modelling constructs. This will allow the development of constructs appropriate to classes of PASs or even to parts of a PAS. Infinite union types are important in permitting code to be written which accommodates change. They have the property that new types can be injected into them and manipulated within them that were not defined when that manipulation code was written. Subsequently the injected type can be recovered by projection.

The preferred basis for accommodating change is an incremental approach to maintenance operations. This would extend throughout the life cycle. It is argued that only such an approach will ensure the capacity for change. It requires that from requirements capture, through design, construction and maintenance, the PAS is considered in terms of small units which are able to change with varying degrees of independence.

Although the above approach makes change possible it still leaves many technical problems to be solved. The maintainers still need accurate and relevant information to guide them as they plan and perform changes. Some work is reported which exploits the stable reference properties of persistent object systems to collect and maintain that information [Sjøberg, 1993b].

However, the various modes of change propagation between components have not yet been fully described. Consequently, the change management tools that can be built at present are of limited utility. In practice, PAS builders will use various techniques for limiting the propagation of change, but with present practices these are not identified and to tools are indistinguishable from other code.

It is proposed that forms of change propagation be identified. Here the interface components that permit various aspects of change to be absorbed or transmitted through a boundary have been called "change absorbers". The research community could therefore study the existing change propagation arrangements and requirements in order to properly identify an adequate repertoire of change absorbers. If these are then defined, named and provided by the technology they will enhance the capacity of PAS to change and permit the construction of tools that are more helpful when managing and implementing change.

The focus on describing the behaviour of the system under change will be the most important outcome of such a line of research. As indicated in the paper, many *ad hoc* developments to accommodate change and actively respond to it can be found in current research and current technology. The challenge is to systematise these into regular structures so that they can be more easily and extensively used by PAS architects, builders and maintainers. If this is done it will enhance the quality as well as the durability of a typical Persistent Application System.

Acknowledgements

Discussions with Tim King, Ray Welland, Richard Connor and Rich Cooper were important in formulating the ideas. In particular, Professor Morrison's team — including Richard Connor, Quintin Cutts and Graham Kirby — at St Andrews University, Scotland provided the language Napier88 that engenders thought about these ideas and allows them to be explored. We were much helped by Paul Philbrow in the preparation of this paper and some of the reported work was supported by a European Community ESPRIT Basic Research Action, FIDE$_2$, number 6309. Dag Sjøberg was also supported by the Research Council of Norway, Division NAVF.

References

[Abiteboul and Hull, 1987] S. Abiteboul and R. Hull. IFO: A formal semantic database model. *ACM Transactions on Database Systems*, 12(4):525–565, December 1987.

[Albano et al., 1985] A. Albano, L. Cardelli, and R. Orsini. Galileo: A strongly typed, interactive conceptual language. *ACM Transactions on Database Systems*, 10(2):230–260, June 1985.

[Albano et al., 1993] A. Albano, R. Bergamini, G. Ghelli, and R. Orsini. An introduction to the database programming language Fibonacci. Technical Report FIDE/93/64, ESPRIT Basic Research Action, Project Number 6309—FIDE$_2$, 1993. 30pp.

[ANSA,] The ANSA Model for Trading and Federation, AR.005, APM.

[Atkinson et al., 1982] M.P. Atkinson, K.J. Chisholm, and W.P. Cockshott. PS-algol: An algol with a persistent heap. *ACM SIGPLAN Notices*, 17(7):24–31, July 1982.

[Atkinson et al., 1983] M.P. Atkinson, P.J. Bailey, K.J. Chisholm, W.P. Cockshott, and R. Morrison. An approach to persistent programming. *The Computer Journal*, 26(4):360–365, November 1983.

[Atkinson et al., 1989] M.P. Atkinson, F. Bancilhon, D. DeWitt, K. Dittrich, D. Maier, and S. Zdonik. The object-oriented database system manifesto. In *Deductive and Object-Oriented Databases. Proceedings of the First International Conference on Deductive and Object-Oriented Databases (Kyoto, Japan, 4th–6th December 1989)*. Elsevier Science Publisher B.V., 1989.

[Atkinson et al., 1993] M.P. Atkinson, F. Matthes, and J.W. Schmidt. Progress with bulk types, 1993. Report in preparation, ESPRIT Basic Research Action, Project Number 6309—FIDE$_2$.

[Atkinson, 1978] M.P. Atkinson. Programming languages and databases. In S.B. Yao, editor, *The Fourth International Conference on Very Large Data Bases (Berlin, West Germany, September 1978)*, pages 408–419, September 1978.

[Atkinson, 1992] M.P. Atkinson. Persistent foundations for scalable multi-paradigmal systems. Invited paper. In M.T. Özsu, U. Dayal, and P. Valduriez, editors, *Pre-Proceedings of the International Workshop on Distributed Object Management (Edmonton, Canada, 18th-21st August 1992)*, 1992. The final proceedings will be published as: M.T. Özsu, U. Dayal and P. Valduriez (eds.), *Distributed Object Management*, Morgan Kaufmann, 1992.

[Bancilhon et al., 1992] F. Bancilhon, C. Delobel, and P. Kanellakis, editors. *Building an Object-Oriented Database System: The Story of O_2*. Morgan Kaufmann Publishers, 1992.

[Berman, 1991] S. Berman. *P-Pascal: A Data-Oriented Persistent Programming Language*. PhD thesis, University of Cape Town, Department of Computer Science, August 1991.

[Birtwistle et al., 1973] G.M. Birtwistle, O.J. Dahl, B. Myrhaug, and K. Nygaard. *Simula BEGIN*. Auerbach Press, Philadelphia, 1973.

[Cardelli and Wegner, 1985] L. Cardelli and P. Wegner. On understanding types, data abstraction and polymorphism. *ACM Computing Surveys*, 17(4):471–523, December 1985.

[Cardelli, 1989] L. Cardelli. Typeful programming. Technical Report Digital Systems Research Center Report 45, Digital Eqipment Corp., Systems Research Centre, 130 Lytton Avenue, Palo Alto, Calif., USA, May 1989.

[Cardelli, 1990] L. Cardelli. The Quest language and system (tracking draft). Technical report, Digital Equipment Corporation, Systems Research Center, 130 Lytton Avenue, Palo Alto, CA 94301, June 1990.

[Codd, 1979] E.F. Codd. Extending the relational model of data to capture more meaning. *ACM Transactions on Database Systems*, 4(4):397–434, December 1979.

[Connor et al., 1990a] R.C.H. Connor, A.L. Brown, Q. Cutts, A. Dearle, R. Morrison, and J. Rosenberg. Type equivalence checking in persistent object systems. In A. Dearle, G.M. Shaw, and S.B. Zdonik, editors, *Implementing Persistent Object Bases, Principles and Practice. Proceedings of the Fourth International Workshop on Persistent Object Systems, Their Design, Implementation and Use (Martha's Vineyard, USA, September 1990)*, pages 154–167. San Mateo, CA: Morgan Kaufmann Publishers, 1990.

[Connor et al., 1990b] R.C.H. Connor, A. Dearle, R. Morrison, and A.L. Brown. Existentially quantified types as a database viewing mechanism. In F. Bancilhon, C. Thanos, and D. Tsichritzis, editors, *Proceedings of the Second International Conference on Extending Database Technology (Venice, Italy, March 1990)*, number 416 in Lecture Notes in Computer Science, pages 301–315. Springer-Verlag, 1990.

[Connor, 1991] R.C.H. Connor. *Types and Polymorphism in Persistent Programming Systems*. PhD thesis, Department of Computational Science, University of St Andrews, 1991.

[Connor, 1993] R.C.H. Connor, 1993. In preparation: a survey paper on persistent type systems. Department of Computational Science, University of St Andrews.

[Cutts, 1993] Q.I. Cutts. *Delivering the Benefits of Persistence to System Construction and Execution*. PhD thesis, Department of Computational Science, University of St Andrews, 1993.

[Dearle and Brown, 1988] A. Dearle and A.L. Brown. Safe browsing in a strongly typed persistent environment. *The Computer Journal*, 31(3), 1988.

[Dearle, 1989] A. Dearle. Environments: A flexible binding mechanism to support system evolution. In B.H. Shriver, editor, *Proceedings of the Twenty-Second Annual Hawaii International Conference on System Sciences, Volume II Software Track (January 1989)*, pages 46–45, 1989.

[Ellis and Stroustrup, 1990] M.A. Ellis and B. Stroustrup. *The Annotated C++ Reference Manual*. Addison-Wesley, 1990.

[Farkas et al., 1992] A. Farkas, A. Dearle, G.N.C. Kirby, Q.I. Cutts, R. Morrison, and R. Connor. Persistent program construction - a new paradigm. In A. Albano and R. Morrison, editors, *Fifth International Workshop on Persistent Object Systems. Design, Implementation and Use (San Miniato, Italy, 1st-4th September 1992)*, Workshops in Computing. Springer-Verlag in collaboration with the British Computer Society, 1992.

[Goldberg and Robson, 1983] A. Goldberg and D. Robson. *Smalltalk80: The Language and its Implementation*. Addison Wesley, 1983.

[Hammer and McLeod, 1981] M. Hammer and D. McLeod. Database description with sdm: A semantic database model. *ACM Transactions on Database Systems*, 6(3):351–386, September 1981.

[Hoare, 1975] C.A.R. Hoare. Recursive Data Structures. *International Journal of Computer and Information Science*, 4(2):105–132, 1975.

[Hughes and Connolly, 1990] J.G. Hughes and M. Connolly. Data abstraction and transaction processing in the database programming language RAPP. In F. Bancilhon and O.P. Buneman, editors, *Advances in Database Programming Languages. Based on Proceedings of the Workshop on Database Programming Languages (Roscoff, Brittanny, France, September 1987)*, ACM Press, Frontier Series, chapter 11, pages 177–186. Addison-Wesley Publishing Company and ACM Press, 1990.

[ISO,] Draft Recommendation X.903: Basic Reference Model of Open Distributed Processing - Part 3: Prescriptive Model, ISO/IEC JTC1/SC21/WG7, ISO.

[Kirby et al., 1992] G. Kirby, R. Connor, Q. Cutts, A. Dearle, A. Farkas, and R. Morrison. Persistent hyper-programs. In A. Albano and R. Morrison, editors, *Fifth International Workshop on Persistent Object Systems. Design, Implementation and Use (San*

Miniato, Italy, 1st-4th September 1992), Workshops in Computing. Springer-Verlag in collaboration with the British Computer Society, 1992.

[Kirby, 1993] G.N.C. Kirby. *Reflection and Hyper-Programming in Persistent Programming Systems*. PhD thesis, Department of Computational Science, University of St Andrews, 1993.

[Koch et al., 1983] J. Koch, M. Mall, P. Putfarken, M. Reimer, J.W. Schmidt, and C.A. Zehnder. Modula/R report, Lilith version. Technical report, Institute fur Informatik, Eidgenossische Technische Hochschule Zürich, February 1983.

[Matthes et al., 1992] F. Matthes, A. Rudloff, J.W. Schmidt, and K. Subieta. The database programming language DBPL user and system manual. Technical Report FIDE/92/47, ESPRIT Basic Research Action, Project Number 3070—FIDE, 1992.

[Matthes, 1992] F. Matthes. *Generic Database Programming: A Linguistic and Architectural Framework*. PhD thesis, Fachbereich Informatik, Universität Hamburg, Germany, September 1992. (In German).

[MICROSOFT, 1993] Microsoft ODBC programmer's reference, June 1993. 01.03.0005.

[Morrison et al., 1989] R. Morrison, A.L. Brown, R.C.H. Connor, and A. Dearle. The Napier88 reference manual. Technical Report PPRR-77-89, Universities of Glasgow and St Andrews, 1989.

[Morrison, 1979] R. Morrison. *On the development of algol*. PhD thesis, Department of Computational Science, University of St Andrews, 1979.

[Object Design Inc., 1991] Object Design Inc. *The ObjectStore Technical Overview*. Product Marketing, One New England Executive Park, Burlington, Mass, MA 01803, USA, May 1991.

[Ohori et al., 1989] A. Ohori, O.P. Buneman, and V. Breazu-Tannen. Database programming in Machiavelli – a polymorphic language with static type inference. In *Proceedings of the ACM SIGMOD 1989 Conference on the Management of Data (Portland, Oregon, May-June), SIGMOD Record 18, 8, June 1989*, pages 46–57, 1989.

[Ontologic Inc., 1991] Ontologic Inc. *The ONTOS Developer's Guide*. Three Burlington Woods, Burlington, Mass, MA 01803, USA, 1991.

[Reiser, 1991] M. Reiser. *The Oberon System — User Guide and Programmer's Manual*. Addison-Wesley Publishing Company, Wokingham, 1991.

[Richardson and Carey, 1987] J.E. Richardson and M.J. Carey. Programming constructs for database system implementation in EXODUS. In *Proceedings of the ACM SIGMOD 1987 Conference on the Management of Data (San Francisco, CA, 27th-29th May)*, pages 208–219, 1987.

[Schaffert, 1992] C. Schaffert. CORBA: OMG's object request broker. In M.T. Özsu, U. Dayal, and P. Valduriez, editors, *Pre-Proceedings of the International Workshop on Distributed Object Management (Edmonton, Canada, 18th-21st August 1992)*, 1992. The final proceedings will be published as: M.T. Özsu, U. Dayal and P. Valduriez (eds.), *Distributed Object Management*, Morgan Kaufmann, 1992.

[Schmidt, 1977] J.W. Schmidt. Some high level language constructs for data of type relation. *ACM Transactions on Database Systems*, 2(3):247–261, September 1977.

[Schwartz et al., 1986] J.T. Schwartz, R.B.K. Dewar, E. Dubinski, and E. Schonberg. *Programming with Sets: An Introduction to SETL*. Texts and Monographs in Computer Science. Springer-Verlag, 1986.

[Sheard, 1991] T. Sheard. Automatic generation and use of abstract structure operators. *ACM Transactions on Programming Languages and Systems*, 13(4):531–557, 1991.

[Shipman, 1981] D.W. Shipman. The functional data model and the data language DAPLEX. *ACM Transactions on Database Systems*, 6(1):140–173, March 1981.

[Sjøberg et al., 1993] D. Sjøberg, M.P. Atkinson, J. Lopes, and P.W. Trinder. Building an integrated persistent application — a multi-author, multilevel, Napier88 project. In *Proceedings of the Fourth International Workshop on Database Programming Languages (Manhattan, USA, 30th August–1st September 1993)*. Springer-Verlag, 1993. To appear.

[Sjøberg, 1993a] D. Sjøberg. Quantifying schema evolution. *Information and Software Technology*, 35(1):35–44, January 1993.

[Sjøberg, 1993b] D. Sjøberg. *Thesaurus-Based Methodologies and Tools for Maintaining Persistent Application Systems*. PhD thesis, Submitted to University of Glasgow, July 1993.

[Skarra and Zdonik, 1987] A.H. Skarra and S.B. Zdonik. Type evolution in an object-oriented database. In B.S. Shriver and P. Wegner, editors, *Research Directions in Object Oriented Programming*, Computer Systems, pages 393–415. MIT Press, Cambridge, MA, 1987.

[Stemple et al., 1990] D. Stemple, L. Fegaras, T. Sheard, and A. Socorro. Exceeding the limits of polymorphism in database programming languages. In F. Bancilhon, C. Thanos, and D. Tsichritzis, editors, *Proceedings of the Second International Conference on Extending Database Technology (Venice, Italy, March 1990)*, number 416 in Lecture Notes in Computer Science, pages 269–285. Springer-Verlag, 1990.

[Stemple et al., 1992] D. Stemple, R.B. Stanton, T. Sheard, P.C. Philbrow, R. Morrison, G.N.C. Kirby, L. Fegaras, R.L. Cooper, R.C.H. Connor, M.P. Atkinson, and S. Alagic. Type-safe linguistic reflection: A generator technology. Technical Report FIDE/92/49, ESPRIT Basic Research Action, Project Number 3070—FIDE, 1992. 29pp.

[Wegner and Zdonik, 1988] P. Wegner and S.B. Zdonik. Inheritance as an incremental modification mechanism or what like is and isn't like. In S. Gjessing and K. Nygaard, editors, *Proceedings of the European Conference on Object-oriented Programming (Oslo, August 15-17, 1988)*, Lecture Notes in Computer Science 322, pages 55–77. Springer-Verlag, 1988.

An Object-Oriented Pattern Matching Language

Marc Gemis   Jan Paredaens

Department of Mathematics and Computer Science,
University of Antwerp (UIA),
Universiteitsplein 1, B-2610 Antwerp
Belgium
Email:{makke,pareda}@wins.uia.ac.be

Abstract

A graphical model for describing schemes and instances of object-databases and a graphical data manipulation language based on pattern matching, called *PaMaL*, are introduced. The operations of PaMaL (addition and deletion of nodes and edges) use patterns to indicate the parts of the instance that are affected by the operation. We give the syntax and semantics of the operations and the programming constructs (loop, procedure and program) of PaMaL. We add a reduce-operation to work with a special group of instances, the *reduced instances*.

1 Introduction

One of the first *visual* or *graphical* interfaces for databases was QBE [Zlo77]. It introduced a new way of user-database interaction, by providing the user some tools to interact directly with the database and its structure. Since then, the research of visual interfaces has evolved in two directions. One group develops specialized interfaces for geographical or pictorial information (some relevant information can be found in [vl, Coo93]). This class of interfaces generally provides the user methods to navigate and manipulate data of unconventional type and structure.

The second group studies general purpose graphical interfaces (see [sig90, BCCL91] for a reference list). In this class the main objectives are to provide tools to simplify the task of formulating *associative, set-oriented queries* and to represent in a convenient way the result of these queries on a computer screen. The systems in this class are window-based programs that guide the user during the construction of a query. Another common characteristic is that the user can construct simple *select-project-join* queries from a scheme representation. This representation could be a table as in [CRR88], an extension of the *entity-relationship* model [ADD+91, ACS90, CER89], a special-developed diagrammatic representation [GPVG90, KKS88] or even icon-based as in [THTI90]. In some cases the constructed query is a textual one, while in other systems the query is represented in the same graphical formalism as the scheme. We believe that a graphical representation of the query is easier to understand and therefore cheaper to maintain.

However, it takes a lot of time to construct such graphical queries on a screen without appropriate tools. Therefore special-purpose graph-editors were developed which allow the user to construct queries by means of mouse-driven copy and paste operations and invoking commands from pop-down menus and buttons.

Still, most of these graphical systems have some major drawbacks. First, not all systems provide a manipulation or query language (e.g. IFO [AH87]). Second, the computational power of the graphical query languages is rather limited, e.g. GraphLog [CM90] has the expressive power of linear stratified datalog. Only a few graphical systems have a computationally complete graphical query language, e.g. GOOD [GPVG90]. Providing a textual extension for the graphical query language to increase the expressive power, leads to a problem similar to the *impedance mismatch* for relational query languages and is therefore not desirable.

Third, the systems are mostly based on relational databases, in which it can be problematic to represent information that does not fit (easily) in tables, such as sets, lists and other structured data. It is well known [KA91, LR89, ABD+89] that object-oriented data-models are better suited to model the real world. Besides, object-oriented modeling has other advantages such as modularity, re-usability and natural support for information hiding. In this paper we focus on object-identity, as we are still investigating inheritance and encapsulation.

A possible danger of graphical languages is that they overwhelm the user with different symbols, each with a very specific meaning (as e.g. in [HGPN93]). This is wishful for database application designers, who need to be able to specify all details of the database, such as the arity of relations and the difference between several kinds of inheritance. We believe however that the naive or occasional user does not want to know all these details for query construction.

For this group of users we developed the *Pattern Matching Language* (PaMaL), which is a graphical query language with an object-oriented data-model that we also discuss here. We also consider the actual instance of a database to be graphically represented, as was observed in [AK89, Bee90, GPVG90, LRV88].

The notion of instance graph leads naturally to the use of *graph-pattern-matching* as a simple and elegant object manipulation primitive [AGP+92]. Patterns offer the user a methodology to specify the desired information in quite a direct way, preserving at the same time the "set-oriented" nature of database queries. With the appropriate tools, the construction of a pattern is just a matter of copy and paste.

The purpose of this paper is to present a language that can serve as a framework for pattern matching languages. We will not discuss details of a possible interface of an application developing environment for PaMaL.

PaMaL is the result of the continuing research done on GOOD. In PaMaL we explicitly represent tuples and sets, and propose a different set of operations, which we believe, has simpler semantics and is therefore user-friendlier.

In Section 2 we introduce the PaMaL data model. It is an object-oriented model with a graphical representation for both the scheme and the instances. However, the instance graph is only meant for the conceptual modeling. In Section 3 we present PaMaL, a graphical data manipulation language. We give a detailed description of the syntax of all operations and formally define their semantics.

2 The Data Model

In this section we present the graphical representation of the data model. The scheme is represented by means of a directed, labeled graph. The example scheme (Figure 1) models a small part of the interface of a window application. The classes of the scheme

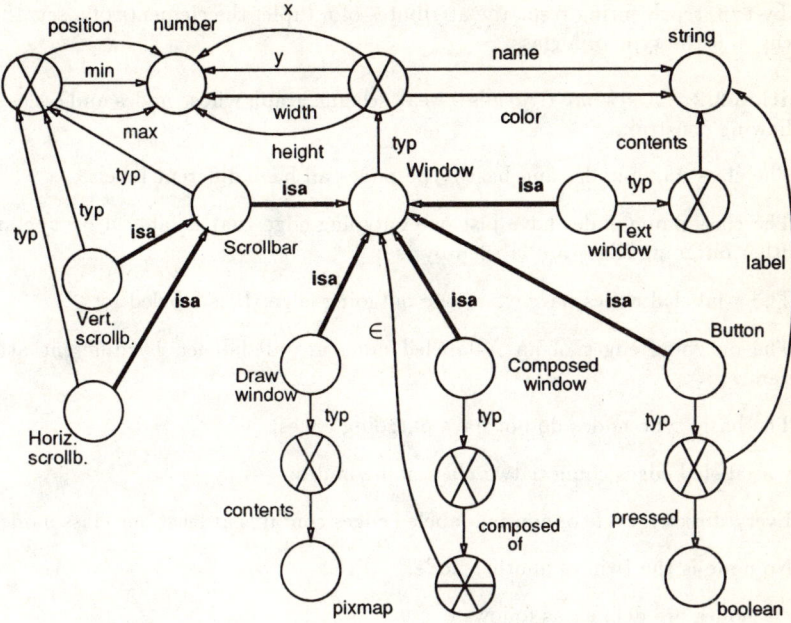

Figure 1: Part of a window interface scheme.

are represented by circles labeled with the class name. For example, the class of all windows is represented by the node with label **Window**. The basic types are represented in the same way as the classes. However, as a convention the labels of class-nodes begin with a capital, while the labels of the basic type-nodes begin with a lower-case letter. For example, the node **string** stands for the type of character strings. Unconventional types such as pixmaps and long character strings can also be modeled. The visual representation of such types is part of the implementation aspects and is therefore not discussed here. The tuples are represented by circles containing an X, sets are represented by circles containing an $*$. This gives us four kinds of nodes: the class name-nodes, the basic type-nodes, the tuple-nodes and the set-nodes.

There are also four kinds of edges. The first kind indicates the types of the attributes of the tuples and are labeled by the name of that attribute. The second kind indicates the type of the elements in a set. They are labeled with $\in$ and start in set-nodes. The third kind indicates the type of the classes. They are labeled with **typ**. The last kind are the **isa**-labeled edges, which indicate the hierarchical relationships between the classes.

For example the class `Text window` inherits all attributes of the class `Window`.

Definition 2.1 Given a finite set of basic types T_b, a finite set of class names C and a finite set of attribute names U. A *weak scheme graph* over (T_b, C, U) is a directed labeled graph with four kinds of nodes. They are labeled by an element of T_b (basic type-nodes), by an element of C (class name-nodes), by X (tuple-nodes) or by $*$ (set-nodes). The graph also contains four kinds of edges. They are labeled by an element of U, by $\in$, by **isa** or by **typ**, representing resp. the attributes of a tuple, the elements of a set, the class hierarchy and the type of a class. □

Definition 2.2 A *scheme Graph* is a weak scheme graph whose nodes and edges satisfy the following constraints:

- The class name-nodes and basic type-nodes all have different labels;
- The class name-nodes have just one outgoing edge that is labeled by **typ** and the other outgoing edges are labeled by **isa**;
- The $*$-labeled nodes have exact one outgoing edge. It is labeled by $\in$;
- The outgoing edges of an X-labeled node are all labeled by different attribute names;
- The basic type-nodes do not have outgoing edges;
- **isa**-labeled edges connect two class name-nodes;
- Every directed cycle of non-**isa**-labeled edges contains at least one class name-node;
- No node is the twin of another node. □

Twin nodes are defined as follows:

Definition 2.3 Twin is the smallest reflexive relation on the nodes of the weak scheme graph such that two nodes n_1 and n_2 are twins iff

- $label(n_1) = label(n_2)$[1];
- The number of outgoing edges from n_1 equals the number of outgoing edges from n_2;
- For every outgoing edge of n_1 there is an outgoing edge of n_2 with the same label and ending in a twin node, and vice versa. □

The graph in Figure 2 is not a scheme graph, since the nodes n_1 and n_2 represent the same tuple and therefore the nodes n_3, n_4 and n_5 represent the same set. Hence, the twin relation is $\{\{string\}, \{integer\}, \{n_1, n_2\}, \{n_6\}, \{n_3, n_4, n_5\}, \{A\}, \{B\}, \{C\}\}$ and is showed in Figure 3.

We defined the graphical database model so that there is exact one node for each class, and it is uniquely identified by its label. A class has a unique type and can inherit by the **isa**-relation from several other classes. Classes are types themselves.

---
[1] The function *label* gives the label of a node or edge.

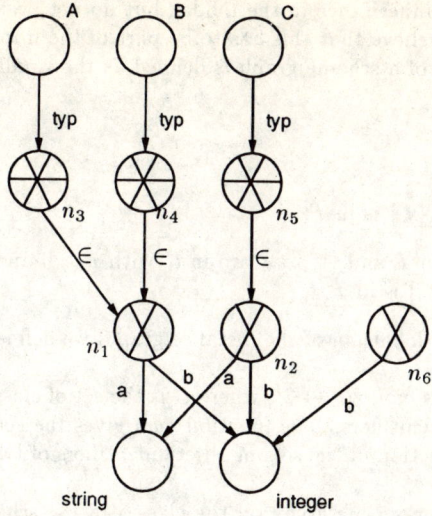

Figure 2: An example of a graph which contains nodes that are not twin.

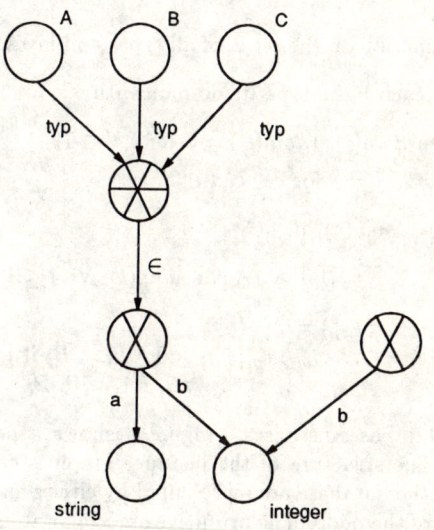

Figure 3: The twin relation.

We allow multiple inheritance in the model, but do not provide a conflict resolution mechanism, since we believe that this has to be part of the implementation.

The set of types T of a scheme graph is defined as the smallest set with:

- T_b is a subset of T;

- C is a subset of T;

- if t is in T, then $\{t\}$ is in T;

- if $t_1, \ldots, t_n$ are in T and $A_1, \ldots_n$ are in U with $n \geq 0$ and $A_i \neq A_j$ for $i \neq j$ then $[A_1 : t_1, \ldots A_n : t_n]$ is in T.

Before we give the definition of the instance graph, we define some functions, we will need later on.

The first function is $own : C \to 2^I$, where C is the set of class names and I a possibly infinite set of object identifiers. The function own gives the set of object identifiers for each class. The intersection of the sets of object identifiers of two different classes has to be empty.

The **isa**-edges define an hierarchy on the classes in the scheme graph S. We define **isa*** as the transitive closure of the **isa**-relation. This means that **isa*** is the smallest relation on the classes of S such that:

$$\forall c_1, c_2 \in C : c_1 \text{ \textbf{isa}}^* c_2 \Leftrightarrow (c_1 = c_2 \vee \exists_{c_3 \in C} : c_1 \text{ \textbf{isa} } c_3 \wedge c_3 \text{ \textbf{isa}}^* c_2)$$

The functions N en E give respectively the set of nodes in a graph and the set of edges.

Finally, dom is a function on the set T of all types and gives for each type its domain.

- $dom|_{T_b}$ gives for each basic type its domain with:
  - if $t \neq t'$ then $dom(t) \cap dom(t') = \phi$ for $t, t' \in T_b$
  - $own(c) \cap dom(t) = \phi$ for $c \in C, t \in T_b$

- $dom(d) = \bigcup_{c \text{ \textbf{isa}}^* d} own(c), d \in C$

- $dom(\{t\}) = \{\{v_1, \ldots, v_n\} \mid n \geq 0 \wedge v_i \in dom(t), \forall i, 1 \leq i \leq n\}$

- $dom([A_1 : t_1, \ldots, A_n : t_n]) =$
  $\{[B_1 : v_1, \ldots, B_m : v_m] \mid m \geq 0 \wedge B_i \neq B_j \text{ if } i \neq j \wedge$
  $\forall B_i \exists A_{j_i} \text{with } B_i = A_{j_i} \wedge v_i \in dom(t_{j_i})\}$

We now discuss database instances. Figure 4 shows a possible instance over the scheme in Figure 1. The structure of the instance graph is determined by the scheme graph. The objects of the database are represented by circles and their object identifier is indicated by the label of the node. The primitive objects or atomic values are represented by circles too. In this case the labels indicate values from the domain of the basic type. The instance contains a composed window `C7654` with name `Editor`, which has 2 red buttons `B4376` and `B1232` labeled `Quit` and `Clear` respectively; and a text window `T1345` as subwindows. The set and tuple-objects are represented by circles with a $*$ and a X respectively.

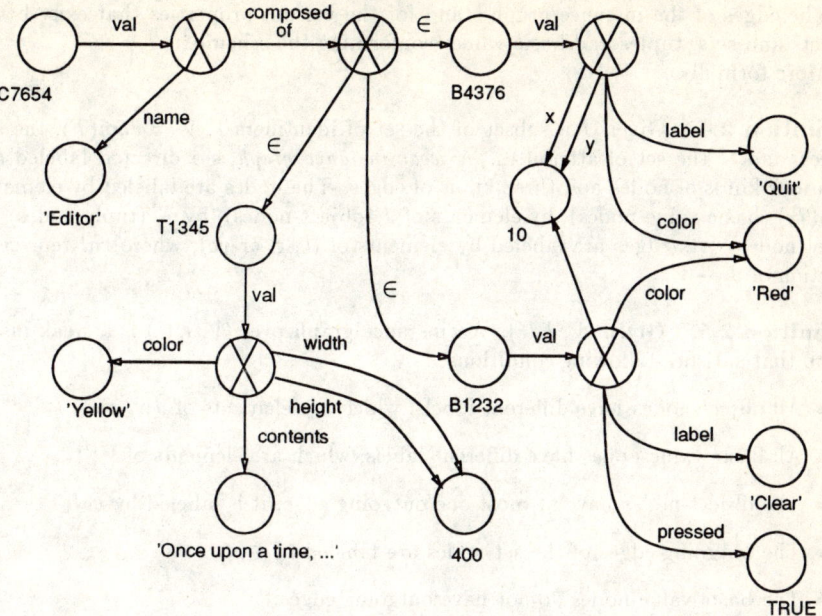

Figure 4: An example graph instance.

The edges of the instance graph stand for the various properties that exist between objects and sets, tuples and basic values conforming the scheme.

More formally,

Definition 2.4 Given J a subset of the set of identifiers I, $V = dom(T)$, the set of values, and U the set of attributes. A *weak instance graph* is a directed labeled graph with four kinds of nodes and three kinds of edges. The nodes are labeled by elements of $dom(T_b)$ (basic value-nodes), by elements of J (object-nodes), by X (tuple-nodes) or by $*$ (set-nodes). Its edges are labeled by elements of U, $\in$ or val, where val represents a function of $J \to V$. □

Definition 2.5 Given (V, J, U). An *instance graph* over (V, J, U) is a weak instance graph that satisfies following conditions:

- All object-nodes have different labels, which are elements of J;
- All basic value-nodes have different labels, which are elements of V;
- The object-nodes have at most one outgoing edge, it is labeled by val;
- The outgoing edges of the set-nodes are labeled by $\in$;
- The basic value-nodes do not have outgoing edges;
- The outgoing edges of an tuple-node are all labeled by different attribute names;
- Every directed cycle contains at least one object-node. □

By convention we do not draw the basic value-nodes with no incoming edge in an instance graph.

A special kind of instance graphs are those where there are no twin-nodes. Such instance graphs are called *reduced instance graphs*. Thus in a reduced instance graph there are no two nodes that represent the same set or tuple.

3 The Data Manipulation Language

In this section we define the syntax of the instructions of the data manipulation language, PaMaL.

PaMaL is a two-dimensional graph-oriented language based on pattern matching. A pattern is a directed labeled graph which describes those parts of the database on which the operation will be executed. The pattern in Figure 5 indicates the composed windows with a red button whose x-coordinate is 10. It has two embeddings in the instance graph of Figure 4.

We now formally define a pattern and an embedding of a pattern to an instance graph:

Definition 3.1 A *pattern* P over a scheme graph S is a directed labeled graph which contains six kinds of nodes. They are labeled by an element of $dom(T_b)$, by an element of T_b, by an element of $own(C)$, by an element of C, by X or by $*$. It contains also three kinds of edges, labeled by elements of U, by $\in$ or by val. □

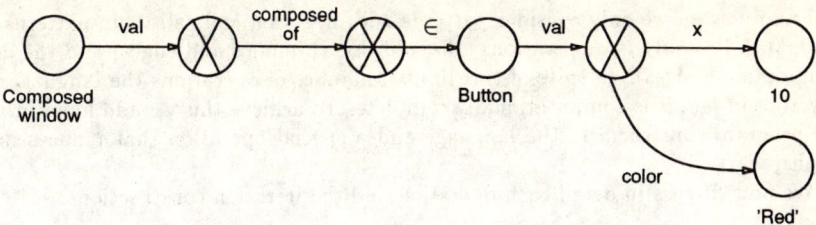

Figure 5: An example of a PaMaL-pattern.

The difference between an instance graph and a pattern, is that in a pattern we allow nodes to be labeled by class names or by basic types. The reason for this will become clear after the definition of an embedding.

Definition 3.2 Given a pattern P over a scheme graph S. An *embedding* of P to an instance graph over S is a function E: {nodes of pattern} $\rightarrow$ {nodes of instance graph} with:

- $label(E(n)) = label(n)$ if $label(n) \in dom(T_b)$
    $= label(n)$ if $label(n) \in own(C)$
    $= label(n)$ if $label(n) = X$
    $= label(n)$ if $label(n) = *$
    $\in dom(label(n))$ if $label(n) \in T_b$
    $\in dom(label(n))$ if $label(n) \in C$

- if there is an edge from m to n in P then there is an edge with the same label from $E(m)$ to $E(n)$. □

The basic value-nodes, object-nodes, set- and tuple-nodes in the pattern are only mapped to nodes with an identical label in the instance. Nodes labeled by class names or basic types are mapped on nodes with respectively an object identifier belonging to that class or a value belonging to that basic type. In this way we can specify all objects of a class, resp. of a type.

Definition 3.3 A *pattern with negation* P over a scheme graph S is a pattern where some of nodes and/or edges have a label that is preceded by ¬, they are called *negated* nodes and edges. The other nodes and edges are called *positive*. The positive nodes and edges have to form a pattern, called the *positive* pattern P^+. □

Definition 3.4 The *embedding* of a pattern with negation P over a scheme graph S to an instance graph I over S is a function E_{neg}: {nodes of positive pattern P^+} $\rightarrow$ {nodes of instance graph} with:

- E_{neg} is an embedding;

- There exists no extension of E_{neg} to the nodes of P that is an embedding to I. □

From now on we only consider patterns with negation and call them patterns.

PaMaL has only two operations: the addition (of nodes and edges) and the deletion (of nodes and edges). In spite of this limited number of operations the language is very powerful, in fact it is computationally complete. To achieve this we add loop, procedure and program constructs to the language and a special operation that reduces instance graphs.

We now discuss in detail each operation and the iteration constructions.

3.1 Addition

An addition over a scheme graph S is a pattern A over S with some bold edges and/or nodes. The non-bold part $A_{\text{non-bold}}$ is a sub-pattern. No node labeled by an element of T_b nor $dom(T_b)$ is bold. No bold node nor edge is negated.

An example of an addition is showed in Figure 6. Here, a button labeled 'Quit' at point (10, 10) is added to every composed window that has not color 'Yellow'. More

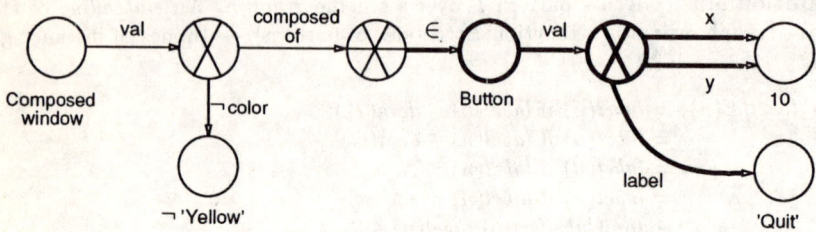

Figure 6: A PaMaL addition.

formally, the effect $Eff_A(G)$ of an addition A on an instance graph G is a new instance graph that is obtained by:

1. let $Eff_A(G)$ be equal to G;

2. for each embedding of $A_{\text{non-bold}}$ in G extend $Eff_A(G)$ in parallel with new nodes and edges such that the embedding of $A_{\text{non-bold}}$ in G can be extended to an embedding of A in $Eff_A(G)$. The new nodes that correspond to nodes labeled by a class name c are all labeled by new and different elements of $own(c)$.

3. if $Eff_A(G)$ is not an instance graph, $Eff_A(G)$ becomes undefined.

The addition specifies a graph transformation between two instance graphs. The transformation adds new nodes and edges at the places where the pattern can be embedded. In general, it can only be checked at run-time whether or not the effect of an addition is a valid instance graph, although the results of the additions of Figure 7 are always undefined.

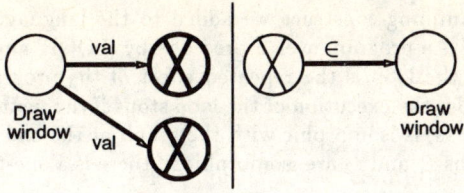

Figure 7: Additions with undefined results.

3.2 Deletion

A deletion over a scheme graph S is a pattern D over S with some dashed edges and/or nodes. The dashed part is called D_{dashed}. None of the edges and nodes of D_{dashed} is negated, nor is labeled by an element of T_b or $dom(T_b)$. The effect of the deletion D on an instance graph G is again an instance graph $Eff_D(G)$, which is obtained by:

1. let $Eff_D(G)$ be equal to G;

2. for each embedding of D in G remove from $Eff_D(G)$ in parallel all the nodes and edges that are in the embedding of D_{dashed}.

The example deletion in Figure 8 deletes all direct subwindows of the windows called 'Root'. The children of any composed subwindow are not deleted. The latter cannot be achieved with just the two basic operations. We need some additional programming constructs to express this data manipulation.

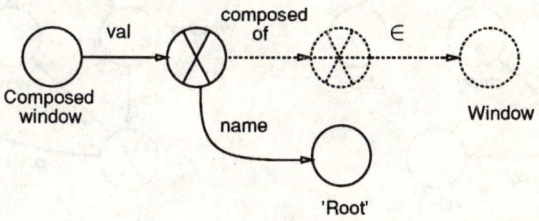

Figure 8: A PaMaL deletion.

3.3 Programs and Loop Constructs

The first and most simple programming mechanism is sequencing. We define a program over a scheme graph S as a sequence of operations over S, separated by ';'. The possible operations are addition, deletion, reduction, program, loop and procedure.

The separator symbol is only used to make a clear distinction between the graphs of two successive operations.

The second programming construct we added to the language is the loop. A loop over a scheme graph S is a program over S preceded by 'LOOP' and succeeded by 'END-LOOP'. The effect of the loop is the repeated effect of the program until a fixpoint is reached. In other words: the execution of the loop stops if the instance graph with which a cycle of the loop starts, is isomorphic with the graph at the end of the cycle.

Two instance graphs I_1 and I_2 are isomorphic, if there is a one-to-one function h such that:

- $\forall n \in N(I_1) : label(h(n)) = label(n);$
- $\forall (n, \alpha, m) \in E(I_1) : (h(n), \alpha, h(m)) \in E(I_2).$

3.4 Procedures

To express the query "Delete all subwindows of the composed window called Root" in an elegant way, we provide a recursive iteration methodology. called *procedures*. We first give the syntax of a procedure definition.

A procedure definition P with parameters $a_1, \ldots, a_n$ is a program with its additions, deletions and procedures augmented by a diamond-shaped node labeled P, with n outgoing edges labeled respectively $a_1, \ldots, a_n$.

An example of a procedure definition can be found in Figure 9. The purpose of this procedure is to change the color of the windows with a given name into a given color. In

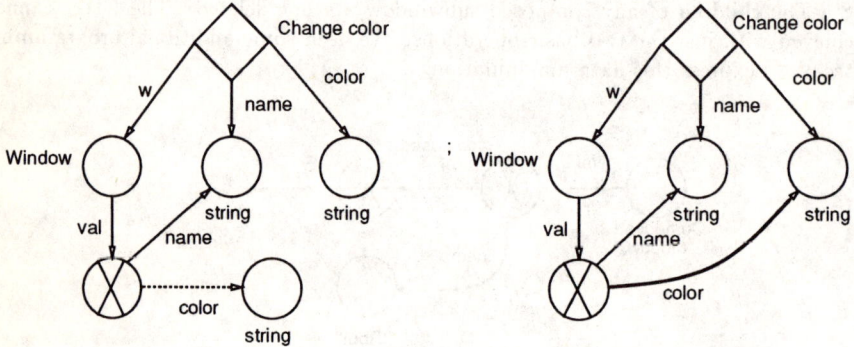

Figure 9: The definition of the procedure Change Color.

the first step of the procedure the old color is deleted. In the second step the new color is assigned. The parameter binding is done by the outgoing edges of the diamond-shaped node. The actual values of the color and name will be determined when the procedure is called.

A procedure call P with parameters $a_1, \ldots, a_n$ is a pattern augmented by a diamond-shaped bold node labeled P, with n outgoing edges labeled respectively $a_1, \ldots, a_n$. The effect of procedure call P is that the definition of P is executed for each embedding of the pattern of the call. An example procedure call for the previous defined procedure is showed in Figure 10.

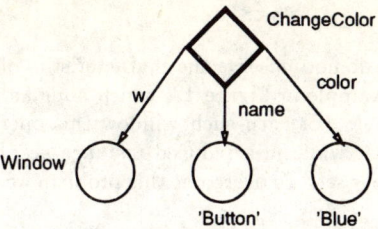

Figure 10: Call the procedure `Change Color` for all windows called `Button` and color them `Blue`.

Since we allow recursive procedures, we can easily write a procedure that deletes all the subwindows of a given window (see Figure 11). In the first step of this procedure, we recursively call the `Delete subwindow`-procedure to delete all the subwindow's subwindows. If that is done, the subwindow is removed in the second step.

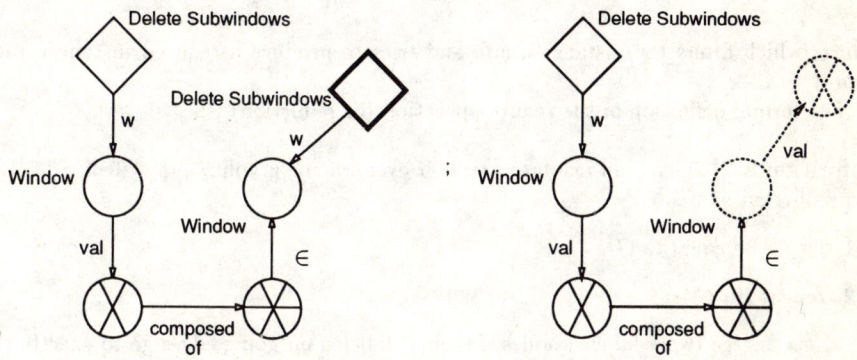

Figure 11: An example of a recursive procedure that removes all subwindows of a given window.

Note that in general, one cannot decide whether or not a recursive procedure ends.

It may seem strange that PaMaL has procedures and not methods as is usual for data manipulation languages for OODB's. We believe however that their is little or no difference between procedures and methods in the context of this paper. The main difference is that a method has an implicit parameter, namely the receiver of the method. One can easily call one of the parameters `receiver` and obtain so a more object-oriented like approach. We do not provide an encapsulation mechanism, but this can easily be incorporated in a programming environment for PaMaL.

3.5 Reduce-operation

The addition and deletion do not preserve the characteristics of a reduced instance graph. This is shown with the example in Figure 12, which adds an new composed window in the windows called 'Frame'. For each such window this operation creates a new node representing the empty set, while in a reduced instance graph there is only one such a representation for the empty set. To overcome this problem we introduce a new operation

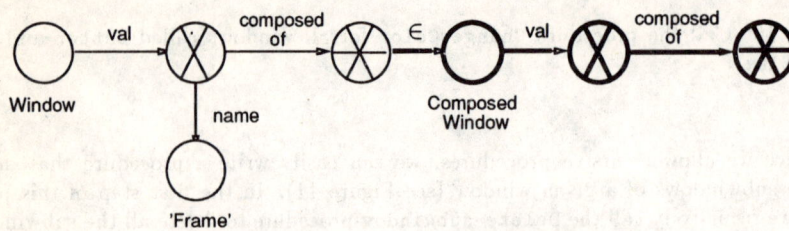

Figure 12: A set creating operation, which does not always result in an instance graph.

reduce, which filters the instance graph and tries to produce a reduced instance graph from it.

The formal definition of the reduce-operation (or reduction) is:

Definition 3.5 Given an instance graph G over scheme graph S, the effect $Eff_R(G)$ of a reduction is:

1. let G' be equal to G

2. repeat (in G')

    - merge two $*$-labeled nodes if their $\in$-labeled outgoing edges go to exactly the same set of nodes;
    - merge two X-labeled nodes if they have the same set of U-labeled outgoing edges, if all such edges with the same label point to the same node;

    until nothing is changed.

We could have incorporated the reduce-operation in the definitions of addition and deletion. However, with a separated reduce-operation there is no automatic reduction, but the programmer has the possibility to work with non-reduced instances, if he or she wants so. A limited number of reductions can be desirable for efficiency reasons.

Theorem 3.1 PaMaL is computationally complete.

Proof We can simulate GOOD, which is proved to be computationally complete [GPVdBVG92, VdBVGAG92]. The technical details are omitted here. □

4 Conclusion

In this paper we presented a graphical object-oriented database model and a graph-based manipulation language. We formally explained the syntax of scheme graphs. Then we defined the syntax of instance graphs and reduced instance graphs. Reduced instance graphs have the benefit that there are no two nodes representing the same set or tuple. Thereafter we introduced the graphical data manipulation language PaMaL. PaMaL is a pattern-based graphical language with only a few operations. Patterns are used to specify the parts of the instance on which the operation has to be executed. We explained the semantics of the operations and defined the iteration mechanisms loop, program and procedure. The reduce-operation allows the users to decide when to use reduced instance graphs.

References

[ABD+89] M. Atkinson, F. Bancilhon, D. DeWitt, K. Dittrich, D. Maier, and S. Zdonik. The object-oriented database system manifesto. In W. Kim, J.-M. Nicolas, and S. Nishio, editors, *Proceedings 1st International Conference on Deductive and Object-Oriented Databases*, pages 40–57. Elsevier Science Publishers, 1989.

[ACM90] *Proceedings of the Ninth ACM Symposium on Principles of Database Systems*. ACM Press, 1990.

[ACS90] M. Angelaccio, T. Catarci, and G. Santucci. QBD*: A graphical query language with recursion. *IEEE Transactions on Software Engineering*, 16(10):1150–1163, 1990.

[ADD+91] A. Auddino, Y. Dennebouy, Y. Dupont, E. Fontana, S. Spaccapietra, and Z. Tari. SUPER: A comprehensive approach to database visual interfaces. In *IFIP 2nd Working Conference on Visual Database Systems*, pages 359–374, 1991.

[AGP+92] M. Andries, M. Gemis, J. Paredaens, I. Thyssens, and J. Van den Bussche. Concepts for graph-oriented object manipulation. In A. Pirotte, C. Delobel, and G. Gottlob, editors, *Advances in Database Technology— EDBT'92*, volume 580 of *Lecture Notes in Computer Science*, pages 21–38. Springer-Verlag, 1992.

[AH87] S. Abiteboul and Richard Hull. IFO: A formal semantic database model. *ACM Transactions on Database Systems*, 12(4):525–565, 1987.

[AK89] S. Abiteboul and P. Kanellakis. Object identity as a query language primitive. In J. Clifford, B. Lindsay, and D. Maier, editors, *Proceedings of the 1989 ACM SIGMOD International Conference on the Management of Data*, number 18:2 in SIGMOD Record, pages 159–173. ACM Press, 1989.

[BCCL91] C. Batini, T. Catarci, M.F. Costabile, and S. Levialdi. Visual query systems. Technical Report 04.91, University of Roma, "La Sapienza", Italy, 1991.

[Bee90] C. Beeri. A formal approach to object-oriented databases. *Data & Knowledge Engineering*, 5(4):353–382, 1990.

[CER89] B. Czejdo, D. Embley, and V. Reddy. A visual query language for an ER data model. In *Proceedings of the IEEE Workshop on Visual Languages*, pages 165–170, 1989.

[CM90] M.P. Consens and A.O. Mendelzon. Graphlog: a visual formalism for real life recursion. In ACM [ACM90], pages 404–416.

[Coo93] R. Cooper, editor. *Interfaces to Database Systems*, Workshops in Computing. Springer-Verlag, 1993.

[CRR88] B. Czejdo, V. Reddy, and M. Rusinkiewicz. Design and implementation of an interactive graphical query interface for a relational database management system. In *Proceedings of the IEEE Workshop on Visual Languages*, pages 14–20, 1988.

[GPVdBVG92] M. Gyssens, J. Paredaens, J. Van den Bussche, and D. Van Gucht. A graph-oriented object database model. Technical Report 92-35, University of Antwerp (UIA), 1992. Revised version of Technical Report no. 327, Computer Science Department, Indiana University, and of UIA Technical Report 91-27.

[GPVG90] M. Gyssens, J. Paredaens, and D. Van Gucht. A graph-oriented object database model. In ACM [ACM90], pages 417–424.

[HGPN93] M. Halper, J. Geller, Y Perl, and E.J. Neuhold. A graphical schema representation for object-oriented databases. In Cooper [Coo93], pages 282–307.

[KA91] Henry F. Korth and Silberschatz Abraham. *Database System Concepts*. Computer Science Series. McGraw-Hill International Editions, 2nd edition, 1991.

[KKS88] H.J. Kim, H.F. Korth, and A Silberschatz. PICASSO: A graphical query language. *Software Practice and Experience*, 18(3):169–203, 1988.

[LR89] C. Lécluse and P. Richard. The O_2 data model. Technical Report 39-89, Altaïr, 1989.

[LRV88] C. Lécluse, P. Richard, and F. Velez. O_2, an object-oriented data model. In H. Boral and P.A. Larson, editors, *1988 Proceedings SIGMOD International Conference on Management of Data*, pages 424–433. ACM Press, 1988.

[sig90] SIGMOD. session on user interfaces. In H. Garcia-Molina and H.V. Jagadish, editors, *Proceedings 1990 SIGMOD*. ACM Press, 1990.

[THTI90] K. Tsuda, M. Hirakawa, M. Tanaka, and T. Ichikawa. Iconic browser: An iconic retrieval system for object-oriented databases. *Journal of Visual Languages and Computing*, 1(1):59–76, 1990.

[VdBVGAG92] J. Van den Bussche, D. Van Gucht, M. Andries, and M. Gyssens. On the completeness of object-creating query languages. In *Proceedings 33nd Symposium on Foundation of Computer Science*, pages 372–379. IEEE Computer Society Press, 1992.

[vl] *Proceedings IEEE Workshop on Visual Languages*. IEEE Computer Society Press.

[Zlo77] M. Zloof. Query-by-example: a data base language. *IBM Systems Journal*, 16(4):324–343, 1977.

CLOG : A Class-Based Logic Language For Object-Oriented Databases

Siu Cheung Hui   Angela Goh   Jose K. Raphel

Division of Computer Technology
School of Applied Science
Nanyang Technological University
Singapore
E-mail: asschui@ntuvax.ntu.ac.sg

Abstract

In this paper a class-based logic language for object-oriented databases which is called CLOG is described. CLOG is based on many sorted horn clauses with concept of classes, objects, object identity, multiple class membership of objects and non-monotonic inheritance. The database view of a class is maintained as a collection of objects and a type. Class is a collection of many sorted horn clauses and functions which define the structural and behavioral aspects of an object. Generic classes give parametrized types. Queries are class-based. Support for view and derived classes are inherent.

1 Introduction

There has been considerable interest in combining logic with object-oriented concepts. The integration is very reasonable [5] as each world provides useful concepts to the other. It is argued that the weaknesses of logic are the strengths of object-oriented and the vice-versa. The advantages provided by logic include declarativeness and uniformity in the treatment of queries, updates, views and constraints. Two important approaches to extend logic towards object concepts are extensions of Datalog [2,16] and Prolog [1,7,9,10,11,14]. There are certain limitations with Datalog which make Prolog more suitable for object-oriented extensions to logic. In object-oriented terminology, class is a collection of objects of similar type providing a structural and behavioral template for the objects it subsumes. To justify this view, parametrized class is a necessary feature. Datalog does not support this feature [14]. A comparative study of the logical and object-oriented formalisms is presented in [5].

We have developed a class-based logic language for object-oriented databases which is called Class-oriented LOGic (CLOG). We call our logic class-based [6] as opposed to object-based [7,11,12,14] since all the operations take a class and result in a class. Messages are sent to the class rather than to the object because of obvious reasons [3]. A class-based database language has important effects on the performance. The availability of factored methods, default data, clustering of objects on the class basis and the possibility of indexing the properties (attributes) in the class level are some of the advantages. CLOG may be treated as a Prolog extension for object-oriented database operations.

In this paper, we discuss the syntax and semantics of CLOG. The remainder of this paper is organized as follows. In section 2, the related work is surveyed. Sections 3 and 4 describe the CLOG syntax and semantics. In section 3, the syntax is formally introduced. Section 4 describes the rationale behind the labeling to introduce the inheritance, complex structures, object identity etc. CLOG is discussed with the help of examples in section 5. A note on implementation is presented in section 6 followed by the conclusions in section 7. Appendix A summarizes the inference rules.

2 Related Work

Two Prolog extensions, LLO [14] and ODDS [11], have similarities with our work. Similar to LLO, the alphabet in CLOG is also typed. The type of an object in CLOG is its inheritance-composition path. Typing is expressed by labels associated with a term and is called a labelled term. Labels may be variables or constants in CLOG. Since multiple inheritance and cyclic composition hierarchy is permitted in CLOG, an object may have more than one type. LLO can primarily be treated as an attempt to support method inheritance which was not present in its predecessors. Even though ODDS permits sets, a class is never treated as a set. Moreover, classes in ODDS are not generic. Many of the other object-oriented extensions to logic do not address important database issues such as views, queries as definition of views and queries resulting in a class of objects instead of a set of tuples. In this paper we extend the principles found in many object-oriented logic systems and introduce the following:

- An inferencing system based on class labels to support both method and data inheritance. We express the composition and inheritance hierarchy associated with objects, classes and methods (attributes) through labels.

- Supporting named and unnamed value collections. The unnamed value collections are not limited to weak entities where the object identity is insignificant, but also to collection of values.

- Disambiguation using type labels: inheritance of an attribute present in multiple superclasses of a class. When multiple parent classes have the same attribute, which one of them is to be used is specified through the class labels.

- Support for parametric and inheritance polymorphism providing generic classes along with method inheritance and abstract types [4].

- Facility to define abstract query objects (eg. transitive closure, reflexive closure and transitive- reflexive closure).

F-Logic [8] also uses the concept of labels, but it is different from our treatment. Our treatment of labels is similar to that of path expressions[9,14]. While path expressions describe the paths along the composition hierarchy, CLOG labels describe inheritance path too. The labels in F-Logic can be considered as methods.

3 CLOG Syntax

In this section, the CLOG syntax is formally introduced. We follow the notations used in [12]. The typed alphabet consists of parentheses, colon, double colon, $<=, <<$, usual logical connectives and the following mutually disjoint (with an exception in query class) set of symbols:

1. Labelled constants and variables

2. Labelled function symbols

3. Labelled predicate symbols

Variables start with uppercase letters. The constant may be a class name or an object represented by its identity.

Definition Labelled Terms.

1. A constant is a labelled term with its type(s) or class names as the label.

    e.g. integer :: age :: 30.
    person :: john.

2. A variable is a labelled term with its associated type labels or class labels.

    e.g. integer :: age :: Age.
    Age.

3. If $(t_1, t_2, ..., t_n)$ are labelled terms and f is a function symbol, then $f(t_1, t_2, ..., t_n)$ is also a labelled term.

    e.g. grand_father(person :: john).

Definition Ground Labelled Term.

A Labelled term is ground if it does not have any variables occurring in it.

Definition Atom.

1. All labelled terms are atoms

2. If $t_1, t_2, ..., t_n$ are atoms and p is a predicate symbol of class c, then $c{:}p(t_1, t_2, ..., t_n)$ is an atom. This is called the class term.

    e.g. person : age(integer :: 30).

Definition Literal.

If $c{:}p(t_1, t_2, ...t_n)$ is an atom called positive literal, then $\neg\ c{:}p(t_1, t_2, ..., t_n)$ is a negated atom known as the negative literal. The set of literals contains both positive and negative literals.

Definition Clause.

A clause is a disjunction of literals with at most one positive literal. This restricts the clauses to be horn. It is of the form $L \leftarrow L_1, L_2, ..., L_n$ where L is a positive literal and $L_1, ..., L_n$ are Literals. L is called the head of the clause.

Definition Class.

A class is a collection of clauses having a common label prefix. The common label prefix is the label of the class enclosing the clauses.

Definition Object.

If c is a class name and $t_1, .., t_n$ are ground labelled terms, the $c(t_1, .., t_n)$ is an object. Note that this definition only guarantees the syntactic correctness of the object. An object is semantically correct, if $t_1, ..., t_n$ are of correct type with respect to class c.

e.g. *person(name :: "John", color :: white)*.

Definition Class Rule.

If t_1 and t_2 are class terms, then

1. $t_1 <= t_2$ is a class rule (Monotonic Inheritance).
2. $t_1 << t_2$ is a class rule (Non-monotonic Inheritance).

Definition Constructor Clause.

A clause is a constructor clause, if the predicate symbol at the head of the clause is of the same name as that of the class name.

Definition Query.

A query is a class with one constructor clause and zero or more other clauses.

Definition Program.

Program is a finite set of classes, objects and class rules.

4 CLOG Semantics

This section informally describes the semantics. The formal treatment can be found in appendix A.

4.1 Inheritance Label

Inheritance label (::) describes the inheritance path of the class or the object to which the label is attached. The existence of *age* belonging to the domain of *integer* as in (i) *integer :: age* and (ii) *age :: 20*, where the existence of an object *20* belonging to *age* can be described as follows:

$$\text{integer :: age} \leftrightarrow \exists \text{ age} \in \text{integer} \qquad (1)$$
$$\text{age :: 20} \leftrightarrow \exists \text{ 20} \in \text{age} \qquad (2)$$

Consider the predicate *age(20)*. It is an assertion on the existence of object 20 belonging to *age*. This means

$$\text{age(20)} \leftrightarrow \exists \text{ 20} \in \text{age} \qquad (3)$$

From (1), (2) and (3)

$$\text{age :: 20} \leftrightarrow \text{age(20)} \qquad (4)$$

From the equivalence of membership and inheritance label, it is simple to observe that inheritance labeling is transitive. Hence, from (1) and (4) we get *integer :: age(20)*. This is a labelled predicate. A labelled predicate is used for describing a property associated with an object. To avoid ambiguity in the label interpretation, we use *age(integer :: 20)* instead of *integer :: age(20)*. It is easy to observe that this method directly allows to label predicates of multiple arity. For example, *birth_date(day :: 20, month :: july, year :: 1992)* is simpler than *method (day, month, year) :: birth_date(20, july, 1992)* to interpret.

4.2 Composition Label

Composition label (:) is used to indicate the component properties. For example, *john's age* is a component property of john. It is represented by *john : age*. We have seen in the previous sub-section that a property can be represented by a labelled predicate. Hence using composition and inheritance labels, properties associated with an object can be represented. For example:

> *john : name(string :: "John").*
> *john : color(colors :: white).*
> *john : father(person :: jacob).*

4.3 Object and Class

The components of an object or class has identical label prefix which can be factored. The labels associated with john can be factored as follows. We use '{' and '}' for factoring the common labels.

john : {
    name(string :: "John").
    color(colors :: white).
    father(person :: jacob).
}

A class is a collection of truth assertions which are valid in the instances it encompasses. It collects a set of clauses and functions to represent the properties of objects of similar kind. Class construct is used to impose structure over the clauses by collecting properties (clauses) related to an object. So we can generalize *john* and similar objects to a class *person*.

person (N, C, F) : {
    name(string :: N).
    color(colors ::C).
    father(person::F).
}

An object of a class is specified through instantiation. For example, consider the definition of the object *john*.

john = person("John", white, jacob).

This generates labelled terms such as *person :: john : name(string :: "John")*. Some of the classes are just enumeration of a set of property values or a range restriction over a domain. For example, *colors* is an unnamed value collection through enumeration.

colors : {
    symbol :: (blue, black, white).
}

This generates labelled terms such as *colors : symbol :: blue.*

Sometimes it is easier to use a shorter method to enumerate ordinals when it belongs to a range. For example,

day : {
    integer :: (1..31).
}

5 CLOG Features

CLOG supports both data and method inheritance. A unified view of queries, derived classes and database views are some of the features of CLOG. This section presents the features through examples.

5.1 Method and Data Inheritance

$person(N,D::B,C,F)$:{
    $name(string :: N)$.
    $birth\_date(D :: B)$.
    $color(colors :: C)$.
    $father(person :: F)$.
    $grand\_father(set(person) :: Y)$.
    $grand\_father(Y)$:- $self : father(X)$,
                  $X : father(Y)$;
                  $X : grand\_father(Y)$.
}
$student(E,D,I)$: {
    $enrolled\_in(set(course) :: E)$.
    $degree(string :: D)$.
    $reqd\_credit(integer :: X)$.
    $id(integer :: I)$.
    $reqd\_credit(140)$:- $degree("ba")$.
    $reqd\_credit(30)$:- $degree("ms")$.
    $reqd\_credit(40)$:- $degree("phd")$.
    $instructors(set(faculty) :: I)$.
    $instructor(I)$:- $E:taught\_by(I)$.
}
$course(T,P)$: {
    $taught\_by(faculty :: T)$.
    $prerequisites(set(course) :: P)$.
}
$employee(M,S,I)$: {
    $manager(employee :: M)$.
    $salary(integer :: S)$.
    $id(integer :: I)$.
}
$faculty$: {
    $offering\_courses(set(course) :: C)$.
    $offering\_courses(C)$:-
    $course :: C : taught\_by(self)$.
}
$research\_asst$: {
    $salary(employee :: real :: S)$.
    $obtain\_concession$:- $student : id(I)$, ...
    pay_tax :- $employee : id(I)$, ...
}
$employee, student <= person$.
$faculty <= employee$. $research\_asst <= student, employee$.

Figure 1. An Example Schema

A class can inherit from its superclasses either completely or partially. When the properties have both local and inherited definitions, the class either can inherit the properties monotonically or its local properties override the inherited. In monotonic inheritance, both inherited and local definitions of a property coexist. The type of inheritance is specified by class rules. The operator ($<=$) is used to indicate non-overriding inheritance and the operator ($<<$) denotes overriding [7]. When properties override, local properties override the inherited one's.

An example schema is shown in Figure 1. The class *employee* inherits not only the labelled facts, but also the methods from *person*. So one can ask for the *employee's color* or *grand_father of an employee*. So it is valid to use *employee:grand_father(X)*. It is also legal to define

$$jacob = employee(name::"jacob", salary::1660).$$

When a class inherits properties from more than one superclasses, some of the properties may be having more than one inheritance path. This is shown in class *research_asst*. The *id* attribute is present in both *student* as well as in *employee*. Which *id* to use is indicated by prefixing the property with the class label. In addition, the attribute *salary* of the *research_asst* is obtained from the class *employee* and is applicable to all the methods, whereas the *id* attribute can be obtained from *student* or *employee* depending on the requirement.

```
figurative_date(D,M,Y) : {           words_date(D,M,Y) : {
    day(day :: D).                       day(day :: D).
    month(integer(1..12)::M).            month(string :: M).
    year(integer::Y).                    year(integer::Y).
}                                    }
```

figurative_date::(24,5,60).   *words_date::(24,"May",1960).*

5.2 Polymorphism

Polymorphism allows the same class to encompass a larger set of types and methods to act on data types defined by its subclasses irrespective of their structural mismatches. This is made possible through parametric and inheritance polymorphism.

5.2.1 Parametric Polymorphism

A class is parametrized on its attribute values to represent countably infinite instances it can subsume or on the labels to represent its variable type association. The class *person* is parametrized on type as well as attribute value as shown in Figure 1. The attribute *birth_date* might be from different representations of *date* as shown above:

5.2.2 Inheritance Polymorphism

Subclasses inherit the methods of the superclass. For example, consider the two classes *person* and *employee*. Any method defined in the class *person* is automatically inherited by the class *employee*. So it is correct to associate inherited attributes with the object of any subclass, e.g. *employee* with *name*. In this example, the object *jacob* belongs to the class *employee* by definition of instance. But through the inheritance rule, it also belongs to the class *person*. So a method defined in the class *employee* is also applicable to its subclasses unless it is overridden.

5.3 Derived Classes

From any given class, new classes can be derived. Derived classes do not have their own instances. It is shared with other classes from which it is derived. Consider the class *graduate* which is derived from the class *student* by validating a constraint.

$$graduate: \{$$
$$\quad string :: degree(X) :- X = "ms";$$
$$\quad\quad\quad\quad\quad\quad\quad\quad X = "phd".$$
$$\}$$
$$graduate <= student.$$

In this, the *graduate* is a *student* studying for "ms" or "phd". In a more generalized way, derived classes can be parametrized. For example, assume a class *company* having one of its attribute as *location*. Then a new derived class *localCompany* can be defined as follows.

$$localCompany(City) :\{$$
$$\quad location(string:: City) :-$$
$$\quad\quad\quad company:location(City).$$
$$\}$$

The above class states that *"localCompany of a city is the collection of companies having location same as the city"*. Note that the attribute *location* is derived since it is defined by a rule.

5.4 CLOG Queries

Queries operate on the class to produce a new class. We will introduce the operations through examples. Consider the classes defined in Figure 1. The class rules express the generalization hierarchy. The composition hierarchy is inferred by the class properties. In CLOG, the same variable can be used for the label as well as for object. The context determines the usage. A method with the same name as the class name is a constructor. It is used in query classes to define the instances it subsumes. In schema classes, this function is done by the methods. The following queries explain different features of the language. Consider the query involving a classical projection *"Find the father of john"*, it can be expressed as follows:

$$query : \{$$
$$\quad query(F) :-$$
$$\quad\quad\quad person::john:father(F).$$
$$\}$$

Consider a more complex query *"Find all the black persons named john whose father is black colored":*

$$\begin{aligned}
&query : \{ \\
&\quad query(P) :- \\
&\quad\quad set(person)::P, \\
&\quad\quad P:(name("john"), color(black)), \\
&\quad\quad P:father:color(black). \\
&\}
\end{aligned}$$

The label *set(person)* qualifies the variable *P* to be of type set. This ensures that set valued attributes are not mixed with non-sets. A generalization of this query will result in *"Find all persons with a given name and color and whose father also have the same color as they are"* as follows:

$$\begin{aligned}
&myquery\ (Name,\ Color): \{ \\
&\quad myquery(P) :- \\
&\quad\quad set(person)::P, \\
&\quad\quad P:(name(Name), color(Color)), \\
&\quad\quad P:father:color(Color). \\
&\}
\end{aligned}$$

The previous query can now be written as *myquery("john", black)*. In these queries, we use the fact that the labels are distributed into *name* and *color* in the labelled term *P:(name(Name), color(Color))*.

Labels in CLOG are used to navigate through the generalization hierarchy as well as the composition hierarchy. Consider the following queries which navigate through the cyclic relationships among objects.

A cycle is present in the class *person* through the attribute *father*. The query, *"Find all persons having the same color as his father"*, navigates through this cycle:

$$\begin{aligned}
&query : \{ \\
&\quad query(P) :- \\
&\quad\quad set(person)::P, \\
&\quad\quad P:color(C), \\
&\quad\quad P:father::color(C). \\
&\}
\end{aligned}$$

There is another cycle in the schema shown in Figure 1 between classes *course* and *faculty* and the following queries use this cycle. For example, consider *"List all the courses taught by the instructors of student john"*:

$$\begin{aligned}
&query : \{ \\
&\quad query(\ C\ ) :- \\
&\quad\quad student::john:enrolled\_in(E), \\
&\quad\quad E:taught\_by(T), \\
&\quad\quad T:offering\_courses(C). \}
\end{aligned}$$

Note that we have not specified the *set type* for the *course*. In this case, it is inferred. In the following query, the same cycle is used along with another class. Consider the query, *"List all instructors teaching the prerequisites of all courses they teach"*. Here, *in* is a built-in predicate for set membership test.

$$query : \{$$
$$query(I):\text{-}$$
$$faculty::I,$$
$$I:offering\_courses(C),$$
$$C:prerequisites(P),$$
$$in(P,C).$$
$$\}$$

A query can be formulated in a more abstract form than the above queries. For example, consider the query, *"Find the transitive closure of an attribute of a given object in a given class"*:

$$transitive\_closure(Class, Attribute, Object) : \{$$
$$transitive\_closure(Class, Attribute, Object, V):\text{-}$$
$$Class::Object:Attribute(V);$$
$$Class::Object:Attribute(S),$$
$$transitive\_closure(Class, Attribute, S, V).$$
$$\}$$

In this query, the recursive call in the clause body is to the constructor and not the class label. The constructor is defined. Such queries could be added as built-in features. A query may also optionally contain a disjunction. The disjunction operator (;) is used to represent this. Disjunction is left associative and have a higher precedence than conjunction to avoid the parenthesis. The query *"Retrieve all students who are black or brown"* demonstrates the usage of disjunction as shown below:

$$query : \{$$
$$query(S):\text{-}$$
$$student::S:color(black);$$
$$student::S:color(brown).$$
$$\}$$

6 Current Status of the Work

The implementation of CLOG is through an abstract machine which is based on **WAM** [17]. The design is influenced by a recent work on compiling Object-oriented extensions to prolog, the S-WAM [18]. Some of the deviations from the WAM philosophy are type checking, parameter passing, indexing on attributes rather than on attribute types and viewing object as data terms. Two contexts, the class context and object context, represent the executing environment. The implementation of the abstract machine is currently in progress at Nanyang Technological University.

7 Conclusions

In this paper we have discussed the syntax and semantics of CLOG which is a logic language used for object-oriented and deductive database operations. CLOG is typed and has object-oriented features such as object identity, methods and method inheritance. It has a class-based message mechanism and queries are closed under class operations. Inheritance (both data and method) comes through the label propagation. Non-monotonic inheritance allows specialization. Every value (object) in a class has a set of labels generated as per the inference rules. An object may have several roles. Its different labels reflect the composition-generalization hierarchy. Generic classes and abstract queries are powerful mechanisms for prototyping data definition and manipulation respectively. Derived classes promote object sharing and formulation of views.

References

[1] H. Ait-Kaci and R. Nasr, *"LOGIN: A logic programming language with built-in inheritance"*, J. logic Programming, Oct. 1986, pp. 185-215.

[2] A.S. Greco, N. Leone and P. Rullo, *"Complex - An Object-Oriented Logic Programming System"*. IEEE Trans. On Knowledge and Data Engineering, Aug.1992. pp. 344-359.

[3] J. Banerjee et. al, *"Data model issues in object-oriented databases"*, ACM OIS, 1987, pp. 3-26.

[4] L. Cardelli and P. Wegner, *"On understanding Types, Data Abstraction and Polymorphism"*, ACM Comp. Surveys, Dec. 1985, pp. 471-522.

[5] S. Ceri, F. Cacace and L. Tanca, *"Object orientation and logic programming for databases: a season's flirt or long-term marriage?"*, Int. Nat. Conf. Next Generation Information system Technology, 1990, pp. 124-143.

[6] S. Danforth and C. Tomlinson, *"Type theories and Object Oriented Programming"*, ACM Comp. Surveys, March 1988, pp. 29-72.

[7] F. McCabe, *"Logic and Objects"*, Prentice Hall, 1992.

[8] M. Kifer and G. Lausen, *"F-Logic: A Higher order Language for Reasoning about Objects, Inheritance and Scheme"*, Proc. 1989 ACM SIGMOD, pp. 134-136.

[9] M. Kifer, W.Kim, Y.Sagiv, *"Querying Object-Oriented Databases"*, Proc. 1992 ACM SIGMOD, pp. 393-402.

[10] M. Kifer, G. Lausen, J. Wu, *"Logical Foundations of Object-Oriented and Frame-Based Languages"*, TR#90/14, Dept. of Comp. Science, SUNY at stony Brook, Aug. 1990.

[11] K. Lee and S. Lee, *"An Object-Oriented Approach to Data/Knowledge Modeling Based on Logic"*, Proc. IEEE Conf. on Data Engineering, 1990, pp.289-294.

[12] E. Laenens, D. Vermeir and B. Verdonk, *"LOCO, a logic based language for Complex Objects"*, ESPRIT, 1989, pp. 604-616.

[13] J.W. Lloyd, *"Foundations of Logic Programming"*, Springer-Verlag, 1984.

[14] Y. Lou and Z.M. Ozsoyoglu, *"LLO: An object-oriented deductive language with methods and method inheritance"*, Proc. ACM SIGMOD, 1991, pp. 198-207.

[15] W. Kim, *"Introduction to Object-oriented Databases"*, The MIT Press, 1990.

[16] S.A. Naqvi and S. Tsur, *"A Logic Language for Data and Knowledegebases"*, Computer Science Press, Rockville, 1988.

[17] D.H.D.Warren, *"An Abstract Prolog Instruction Set"*, SRI Technical Note 309, SRI International, Menlo Park, California, Oct. 1983.

[18] E. Lamma, P. Mello and A. Natali, *"An Extended Warren Abstract Machine for the Execution of Structured Logic Programs"*, Journal of Logic Programming, Vol.14, No.2, pp. 187-222.

Appendix A Rules of Inference
I1 : Label propagation to the instances

$$\vdash \frac{L :: A \to O}{L :: A :: O}$$

I2 : Label decomposition

$$\vdash \frac{c : L :: A}{\begin{array}{c} c : A \\ L :: A \end{array}}$$

I3 : Label distribution through classes

(i) $\quad \vdash \dfrac{c : \{ L :: A. \}}{c : L :: A}$

(ii) $\quad \vdash \dfrac{c : \{ L1 :: A1. \ L2 :: A2. \}}{\begin{array}{c} c : L1 :: A1 \\ c : L2 :: A2 \end{array}}$

I4 : Label distribution in composition

$$\vdash \frac{\begin{array}{l} c1 : \{ \ c2 :: A1. \ \} \\ c2 : \{ \ L1 ::A2. \ \} \end{array}}{\begin{array}{l} c1 : c2 :: A1 \\ c1 : c2 : A1 :: L1 :: A2 \end{array}}$$

I5 : Subtyping and Inheritance

$$\vdash \frac{\begin{array}{l} c1 : \{ \ L1::A1. \ \} \\ c2 : \{ \ L2::A2. \ \} \end{array}}{\begin{array}{l} c1 : L1 :: A1 \\ c2 : L1 :: A1 \\ c2 : L2 :: A2 \end{array}}$$

I6 : Non-monotonic Inheritance with Overriding

$$\vdash \frac{\begin{array}{l} c1 : \{ \ L1::A1. \ \} \\ c2 : \{ \ L2::A1. \ \} \\ c2 <\!<c1 \end{array}}{\begin{array}{l} c1 : L1 :: A1 \\ c2 : L2 :: A1 \end{array}}$$

I7 : Selective Inheritance with overriding

$$\vdash \frac{\begin{array}{l} c1 : \{ \ L1 :: A1. \\ \quad\quad L2 :: A2. \ \} \\ c2 : \{ \ L3 :: A3.\} \\ c2 <\!< c1 : \{A1.\} \end{array}}{\begin{array}{l} c1 : L1 :: A1 \\ c1 : L2 :: A2 \\ c2 : L2 :: A2 \\ c2 : L3 :: A3 \end{array}}$$

I8 : Nesting Labelled Terms

$$\vdash \frac{l :: v}{l(v)}$$

I9 : Repeated Nesting

$$\vdash \frac{l :: m :: v}{\dfrac{l :: m(v)}{l(m(v))}}$$

I10: Unnesting Predicates

$$\vdash \frac{p(v)}{p :: v}$$

I11: Repeated Unnesting

$$\vdash \frac{p(q(v))}{p :: q(v)}$$
$$\vdash \frac{}{p :: q :: v}$$

I12: Unnesting Multi-arity Predicates

$$\vdash \frac{l :: m\ (v1,\ v2,\ v3)}{l :: m ::\ (v1,\ v2,\ v3)}$$

(Invited Paper)

Name Management and Object Technology for Advanced Software [*]

Alan Kaplan   Jack C. Wileden

Computer Science Department
University of Massachusetts
Amherst, Massachusetts 01003 USA
e-mail: kaplan@cs.umass.edu, wileden@cs.umass.edu

Abstract

Name management is so fundamental to every aspect of computing that it is frequently overlooked or taken for granted. Our research is aimed at developing both *models* to improve understanding and *mechanisms* to improve practical application of name management approaches in various computing domains. One domain that seems to have particularly strong connections to name management is object technology for advanced software. Object technology has already proven very useful in our investigation of name management models and mechanisms. We also see great potential for beneficial application of improved name management mechanisms to object technology for advanced software. In this paper, we first outline our overall approach to research on name management and discuss some specific name management concerns arising in object technology for advanced software. We then illustrate the application of object technology in our efforts to construct name management models and mechanisms. Finally we give an example of how enhanced name management mechanisms might be incorporated into a representative instance of object technology for advanced software.

1 Introduction

Name management is so fundamental to every aspect of computing that it is frequently overlooked or taken for granted. By *name management*, we mean how a computing system allows names to be established for objects, permits objects to be accessed using names, and controls the availability and meaning of names at any point in time.

Names are used, and hence name management mechanisms are needed, for many purposes in all kinds of computing systems. Traditional programming languages rely on names for structuring programs as well as for managing data flow and control flow. Different languages use different scoping rules, and occasionally

---

[*]This material is based upon work sponsored by the Defense Advanced Research Projects Agency under grant MDA972-91-J-1009. The content does not necessarily reflect the position or policy of the U.S. Government and no official endorsement should be inferred.

other mechanisms, to manage names and where and how they are used within a program. In operating systems, names are employed by users and processes to access commands and files. Again, various mechanisms, such as the environment variables, search paths and hierarchical directory structure found in Unix,[1] are used to manage the availability and meaning of names. Networks and distributed systems rely on names to support sharing and communication of information and resources among users and processes. Name servers are one mechanism used in managing the availability and meaning of names in these systems. Even in relational database management systems, where associative retrieval is the primary means of access, names are used to identify and organize databases, relations and attributes.

Despite, or perhaps because of, its ubiquitous role in computing, name management has received relatively little attention from computing researchers. We believe, however, that as systems become larger and more complex, underlying name management mechanisms will increasingly become focal points with respect to the ability to develop, maintain, integrate and port systems. Moreover, as domains such as programming languages, operating systems and database management systems continue to converge in coming years (a trend particularly notable in, and probably accelerated by, object technology), the incompatibility of their respective approaches to name management will become increasingly apparent and problematic. We are, therefore, actively pursuing a broad-based investigation of name management. Our research is aimed at developing both *models* to improve understanding and *mechanisms* to improve practical application of name management approaches in various computing domains.

One domain that seems to have particularly strong connections to name management is object technology for advanced software. In fact, we first encountered many of the issues and problems that have motivated our investigation of name management while working on, or with, object-oriented programming languages, object-oriented databases and software object bases. At the same time, object technology has already proven very useful in our investigation of name management models and mechanisms. In addition, we see great potential for beneficial application of improved name management mechanisms to object technology for advanced software.

In this paper we examine these various connections between name management and object technology for advanced software. We lay the groundwork, in Section 2, by briefly outlining our overall approach to research on name management and describing some preliminary models that we have developed. Then, in Section 3, we discuss some specific name management concerns arising in object technology for advanced software. In Section 4 we illustrate the application of object technology in our efforts to construct name management models and mechanisms. Finally, in Section 5, we give an example of how enhanced name management mechanisms might be incorporated into a representative instance of object technology for advanced software. We conclude with a summary and an indication of ongoing and future directions for our investigation of name management and object technology for advanced software.

---

[1] Unix is a registered trademark of Unix System Laboratories, Inc.

2 Name Management Basics

Our research on name management has two primary facets. One facet is the development of *models* that can serve as a basis for enumerating, explicating or evaluating various approaches to various aspects of name management. The long-range goal of this facet is to provide a foundation for fundamental understanding of name management and its role in all domains of computing. The other facet of our research is the definition and implementation of, and experimentation with, prototype *mechanisms* for particular aspects of name management. Here the long-term goal is to provide a comprehensive set of powerful, flexible, uniform and broadly applicable mechanisms that will ease the construction and maintenance of (especially large and complicated) computing systems. These two facets are closely interrelated, as we will demonstrate in Section 4, since modeling both guides and is influenced by experimentation with mechanisms. The initial steps in our investigation of name management were directed toward modeling, however. In the remainder of this section we describe some models that have served as a starting point for ongoing iterative development of both models and mechanisms, and in particular have influenced our subsequent work on name management and object technology.

A first step in modeling is to establish basic terminology. We consider the following to be primitive, fundamental concepts related to name management:

object: An item of interest in a given setting. In a computer program, for instance, variables, functions, procedures, statements, etc. could all be examples of objects.

name: An identifier used to reference, access or manipulate an object.

binding: In its simplest, most basic form a (name,object) pair. Given the availability of binding (A, B), it is possible to use name A to reference, access or manipulate object B.

binding space: A collection of bindings.

context: A collection of bindings that is currently available for use in referencing, accessing or manipulating objects. A context may consist of, or be formed from, one or more binding spaces, or parts of binding spaces.

resolution: An operation that, given a name and a context, returns the object(s) bound to the name.

Given this basic terminology, we would like to have a means of characterizing and differentiating distinct approaches to name management. Informally, a particular approach can be described in terms of a particular set of choices regarding such things as: what kinds of objects can be named, the form of names, how bindings may be established, how binding spaces may be created and manipulated, and how contexts may be formed and manipulated. In an effort to formalize this view, we are developing a reference model, or classification framework, for name management that we call the NamingSpace reference model. In its current form, the NamingSpace reference model characterizes the universe of approaches to name management as a five dimensional space. Here we outline this classification framework by listing and briefly describing the five dimensions. For each of the five dimensions, we indicate some of the questions addressed in that dimension and identify a few representative points corresponding to one or more of the questions.

The Object Dimension: A primary question in this dimension is: What kinds of objects can be named? Representative points in the object dimension that might correspond to answers to this question include:

Transient, persistent or both: A typical programming language would only allow naming of transient objects, while an operating system might only allow naming of persistent objects (such as files) and an object-oriented database or a database programming language (e.g., Napier [DCBM89]) might allow both.

Names, bindings, binding spaces, contexts: Different choices are made in different name management approaches. For example, traditional programming languages allow none of these to be named, while in Unix names, binding spaces and contexts can all be named, but bindings cannot.

The Name Dimension: Among the questions in this dimension are: Are names first-class? What form can names take? Representative of points corresponding to the latter question is:

Simple identifier ↔ Hierarchical ↔ Multi-level hierarchical: Simple variable names in a typical programming language generally take the form of simple identifiers. Qualified variable names (e.g., record fields or object methods) in a programming language often take a hierarchical form. Internet path names, with their multiple different separators, are an example of multi-level hierarchical names.

The Binding Dimension: Among the questions in this dimension are: Are bindings first-class? How are bindings established? When are bindings established? What information is included in bindings? Representative points corresponding to the latter question include:

Simple (name, object) pairs: The most common answer – typical in most programming languages, operating systems, etc.

Support for typed objects/overloading/polymorphism: In effect, bindings are (name, type, object) triples [LB88]. Applies, for example, to certain classes of objects in Ada.

Support for type and mutability differentiation: The Napier language, for instance, views bindings as quadruples of the form (name, type, mutability, object) [MABD90].

Arbitrary subsets of object properties: In the limit, this supports associative access (e.g., [Bow90]).

The Binding Space Dimension: Among the questions in this dimension are: How are binding spaces created and manipulated? How are binding spaces related to one another? Representative of points corresponding to the latter question is:

Flat space ↔ Hierarchy/tree ↔ Directed graph: Examples of all of these can be found in Unix.

The Context Dimension: Some of the basic questions in this dimension are: How can contexts be formed? How can contexts be manipulated? What determines which context(s) will be used in interpreting a given name? Representative answers to the first of these questions include:

A single binding space: A Unix working directory, for example, can be a context.

Nested scope: Many programming languages, as well as the combination of directories represented by a Unix search path, provide examples of context formation based on nesting.

Arbitrary combination of (subsets of) binding spaces: Two examples of this approach to context formation are PIC/Ada [WCW85, WCW89] and Napier environments [Dea89].

The NamingSpace reference model is still evolving as we seek to capture the range of name management options more completely and accurately. Nevertheless, the model has already served as a basis for some experimentation with a variety of name management mechanisms. That experimentation, in turn, is leading to further insights about the range of options and hence will contribute to the evolution of the NamingSpace reference model. We illustrate this interplay between model and mechanism in Section 4.

Another class of useful models provides rigorous foundations for defining the semantics of approaches to, or components of, name management. Along these lines, we have been exploring some models based on set theory, using sets of bindings to model binding spaces and various set theoretic operations as basic context formation operators. Detailed treatment of these models is beyond the scope of the current paper, though their influence will be seen in some of the mechanisms described in Section 4.

A few other researchers have proposed models that are related, to some extent, to our name management modeling work. In the earliest such effort that we are aware of, Fraser developed a formalism, based on a simple extension of Church's λ notation [Chu41], that can be used to describe context and manipulations on context [Fra71]. The model includes methods for concatenating and composing contexts, and the implication of the formalism is that it could provide a rigorous semantics for the naming aspects of programming languages and file systems. In [CP89], Comer and Peterson present a formal model of name resolution in distributed systems. This model is very specific to distributed systems and, like the Fraser model, is directed primarily toward providing a formal semantics for certain aspects of name management. Not only are both of these models focused on specific domains, but, in terms of the NamingSpace reference model, both address only a subset of the dimensions, and even so they only cover a subset of the points that can be identified in those dimensions. The classification model presented by Morrison, Atkinson, Brown and Dearle in [MABD90] is more broadly focused, having been developed to categorize the various binding mechanisms found in languages, including database programming languages, and operating systems. Their model is still somewhat more narrowly focused than the NamingSpace reference model, however, presenting only four dimensions (two of which are in fact subsumed by the binding dimension of the NamingSpace model) and identifying only two points on each dimension.

3 Name Management and Object Technology

As we noted earlier, name management and object technology for advanced software seem to have a particularly strong connection. On reflection this is not too surprising, since in object-oriented computation the identification of objects and operations by their names is at the heart of almost every computational step. As a result of their strong connection, however, we find some specific name management concerns arising in object technology for advanced software. Thus, in object-oriented programming languages the importance of names in identifying classes, object instances, and operations is immediately apparent, while the various proposed approaches to resolving name clashes in (especially multiple) inheritance mechanisms (see, e.g., [Knu88]) exemplify name management concerns that are specific to object-oriented computing. The addition of persistence, yielding object-oriented databases or database programming languages, places an even higher premium on name management, since more names, with longer durations, become relevant to a program, which leads to a higher probability of name clashes and an increased need for name management. Software object bases, which for our purposes here have much in common with object-oriented databases, place similarly heavy demands on name management.

Another indication of the strong connection is the fact that we first encountered many of the issues and problems that have motivated our investigation of name management while working on, or with, object technology for advanced software. In the remainder of this section we briefly survey some examples of name management issues that arise in object-oriented programming languages, object-oriented databases and software object bases, highlighting those that have arisen in our own experience. This brief survey elaborates on the nature of the connection between name management and object technology for advanced software, indicates some of the problems that we and others have encountered in existing approaches to name management, provides a starting point for populating the NamingSpace classification framework with example instances of particular choices in particular dimensions, and motivates our ongoing research in this area, which is discussed in subsequent sections.

3.1 Object-Oriented Programming Languages

Names are used in many ways in traditional programming languages. The name management mechanisms employed, however, have tended to cover a rather limited set of points along the various dimensions of the NamingSpace classification framework. Languages have always had their own idiosyncratic syntactic restrictions on how names may be formed. Bindings are usually defined via declarations of some kind, while binding spaces typically correspond to program units, such as procedures, functions or blocks. In the many languages that use static, nested scoping to control visibility, context is defined by iteratively considering the most deeply nested to the least deeply nested binding space, starting from the current program counter location, and augmenting the context with all bindings whose name components are not found in any of the bindings already included in the context. The name resolution function simply returns the object with the given name relative to this context.[2] We, and many others, have often encountered problems resulting from the limits that this approach to context formation imposes on the ability to manage control flow and data flow in programs [CWW80]. Some recent languages, such as Ada and Modula, have provided additional mechanisms for defining binding spaces (e.g., the Ada package) and for forming contexts (e.g., the Ada with and use constructs). Even these provide relatively limited flexibility, though, so various proposals have been advanced to support yet additional control over context formation (e.g., [WCW89]).

Most object-oriented programming languages are based on one or more of the traditional languages, and hence inherit some or all of (the shortcomings associated with) their name management approaches. Object-oriented programming languages introduce some additional name management issues, however. One issue is the impact of inheritance, especially multiple inheritance, on binding space and context definition. It is worth noting that the standard approach to name resolution in a single inheritance structure is essentially the same as the nested scope mechanism found in traditional languages, with successive subclass definitions corresponding to successively nested blocks (binding spaces) and context formation defined by iterative consideration of successive superclasses. In a multiple inheritance mechanism, though, some additional semantics for handling name conflicts is typically added. In C++, for instance, a class is permitted to inherit more than one binding (member) with the same name from other binding spaces as long as that name is never actually referenced. Eiffel, on the other hand, does not allow a class to inherit multiple bindings with the same name.[3] Finally, CLOS relies on the specification order of inherited binding spaces to resolve name conflicts.

Another issue concerns the use of names, bindings, binding spaces and context in the construction of programs. While object-oriented programming languages clearly facilitate the description and construction of complex entities in programs, sophisticated capabilities are still lacking for the description and construction of complex programs. Shortcomings in current approaches to name management are one aspect of the overall problem. We have repeatedly found name management shortcomings to be the cause of problems in building large systems, most recently while attempting to install a large C++ system imported from another laboratory.

In C++, programs are typically built by compiling separate modules and linking the modules together to form a single main program. To facilitate separate compilation, header files (whose names, by convention, end with .h) containing class definitions are included into source files using the #include directive. One prob-

---
[2] Some languages allow names to be overloaded by type.
[3] To remove a name clash, the rename clause can be used in the heir class.

```
#include <foo.h>
#include <bar.h>
main () {
  Foo f;
  Bar b;
  ...}
```

Figure 1: C++ Code Fragment

lem with this approach is that it is difficult to flexibly and arbitrarily specify context for header files. In particular, most systems typically provide a single context formation operation that we call *UnionOverride* (which Meyer calls "overriding union" in [Mey88]). The *UnionOverride* operation forms a new context given two directories (or binding spaces) in exactly the same way that nested scope forms a context from two nested blocks.[4] That is, the resulting context consists of all the bindings in the first directory and all the bindings in the second directory whose name components do not exist in any of the bindings in the first directory. In general, therefore, the order of the given directories is significant.

As a (very simplified) example of the problems that we have encountered, consider the C++ source code fragment in Figure 1, which includes class definitions contained in foo.h and bar.h. Suppose that there are two directories named DIR1 and DIR2, each containing files named foo.h and bar.h. Now suppose a software developer wants to form a context that uses the file foo.h contained in directory DIR1 and the file bar.h contained in directory DIR2. The *UnionOverride* operation clearly does not allow the desired context to be formed. In the C++ compilation command:

```
CC -IDIR1 -IDIR2 main.C
```

the -IDIR1 -IDIR2 specification results in the foo.h and bar.h from DIR1. Switching DIR1 and DIR2 results, of course, in the foo.h and bar.h from DIR2. To create the desired context, the software developer is faced with two alternatives. The first choice involves changing the references in the source code (for example, changing #include <foo.h> to #include <DIR1/foo.h>). The second choice involves changing the file and directory structure to form the required context. Clearly neither of these solutions is desirable since modifying source code or modifying the file and directory structure, especially in large systems, is an error-prone, tedious and expensive process.

3.2 Object-Oriented Databases and Software Object Bases

From the perspective of name management issues, object-oriented databases and software object bases have a great deal in common. Indeed, vendors of object-oriented databases often cite software object bases as one of their intended applications, and some software object bases (e.g., Triton [Hei92]) have been implemented

---
[4]In other words, iterative application of the *UnionOverride* operation directly corresponds to the standard notion of nested scope in programming languages.

by customizing an object-oriented database. We therefore address name management issues related to object-oriented databases and software object bases jointly here.

In conventional object-oriented programming languages, the name management mechanisms for transient and persistent objects are quite separate. For transient objects (e.g., classes, objects), name management is dictated by the syntax and semantics of the language. Persistent objects are typically implemented using files; therefore, name management for persistent objects is provided by the underlying file system. Because distinct name management mechanisms are provided depending on the persistence property of an object, programmers are forced to use different, often conflicting, name management mechanisms. Such a separation is confusing and prone to cause errors in the development of advanced software.

Recent developments in object-oriented databases have attempted to make persistence an orthogonal property of types, thus obviating the need for files. While this approach addresses the impedance mismatch problem by providing a single, unified type model, there is little evidence of powerful, flexible and uniform approaches to name management in such systems. For example, many commercially available systems, such as GemStone [BOS91], ONTOS [ONT93], ObjectStore [LLOW91] and O_2 [Deu91], provide C++-based type models for both transient and persistent objects; however, these systems tend to provide rather limited support for name management. For instance, in GemStone and ONTOS, binding spaces may be organized hierarchically, but context formation is restricted to *UnionOverride* semantics. In ObjectStore, there are two kinds of names — names for databases (binding spaces) and names for objects. Database names are external to the system and are managed by the underlying file system, while object names are handled by a separate name management mechanism. Moreover, because database names cannot be bound in other databases, ObjectStore is restricted to a single level hierarchy of binding spaces.

The major alternative to basing a software object base on an object-oriented database is to build it as an extension to a (possibly not object-oriented) programming language. Generally such an extension involves adding persistence to the programming language. Software object bases of this kind, by integrating programming language and database (and/or operating system) capabilities, give rise to interesting name management problems that are essentially similar, however, to those arising in object-oriented databases. In fact, our interest in the general topic of name management grew out of earlier work on PGraphite [WWFT88, TWW89] and R&R [TWC90], two complementary prototype systems that together implemented (potentially) persistent relation, relationship and directed graph types as extensions to Ada. The goal of this work was to provide a software object base for use in Arcadia software environments [Kad92]. Experimental use of these systems highlighted a number of name management problems, arising primarily from the need to simultaneously manage naming of both transient and persistent objects. Among these, the two most fundamental were related to:

1. the lack of integration between names for transient (programming language-internal) and persistent (programming language-external) data objects, and

2. the incommensurate, and inadequate, mechanisms for controlling exactly

which names (of both transient and persistent objects) were available for use (at any given point) within a program.

Having noted these problems while experimenting with PGraphite and R&R, we soon discovered that similar problems existed in most other software object bases as well as in most object-oriented databases.[5]

Although these problems are prevalent in present generation systems, the desirability of improved approaches to name management in both object-oriented databases and software object bases seems to be widely recognized. For instance, various proposals for architectures for object-oriented database systems acknowledge the need for name management services, though only a few details are provided [OMG92],[WBT92]. Similarly, emerging standards for interfaces to software object bases [Tho89] and reference architectures for software engineering environments [ECM91] also allude to name management services as necessary components while offering few specifics. Thus the prospects for future developments in the area of name management and object technology for advanced software seem quite promising.

4 Object Technology Applied to Name Management

Object technology has proven very useful in our investigation of name management models and mechanisms. We have found the concepts of object orientation to be quite natural for formulating models of specific approaches to name management. In particular, they have helped us to create concrete descriptions of various components of an approach and how those components are interrelated. In addition, the fact that an object-oriented description, and especially the interrelationships among its components, can be so easily altered has facilitated our exploration of related alternative approaches. This has been particularly valuable for our efforts at exploring and evolving the NamingSpace classification framework. At the same time, because an object-oriented description can be so straightforwardly transformed into code, then combined with an experimental harness and executed, we have been able to easily experiment with running instances of the various approaches. Such experimentation with prototype mechanisms provides feedback and suggests additional approaches, which can in turn be described and then, almost as soon as the description is completed, experimentally evaluated. Thus object technology is contributing to our definition, evaluation and evolution of both models and mechanisms, while facilitating the crucial interplay between model building and mechanism development.

In this section we present some examples of our use of object technology in investigating name management models and mechanisms. These examples serve to illustrate some interesting aspects of some alternative name management approaches, or points in the NamingSpace, as well as the value of object technology when applied to name management.

---

[5]Others have made similar observations. For instance, in their list of requirements for database programming languages [AB87], Atkinson and Buneman appear to refer to both of these problems (requirements (4) and (9)).

4.1 Modeling and Implementing a Basic Name Management Approach

We begin by considering a basic approach to name management, corresponding to some of the most straightforward and elementary choices that can be made in the various dimensions of the NamingSpace. As a first step in studying this approach, we produce a simple graphical depiction of it, as shown in the diagram of Figure 2. The

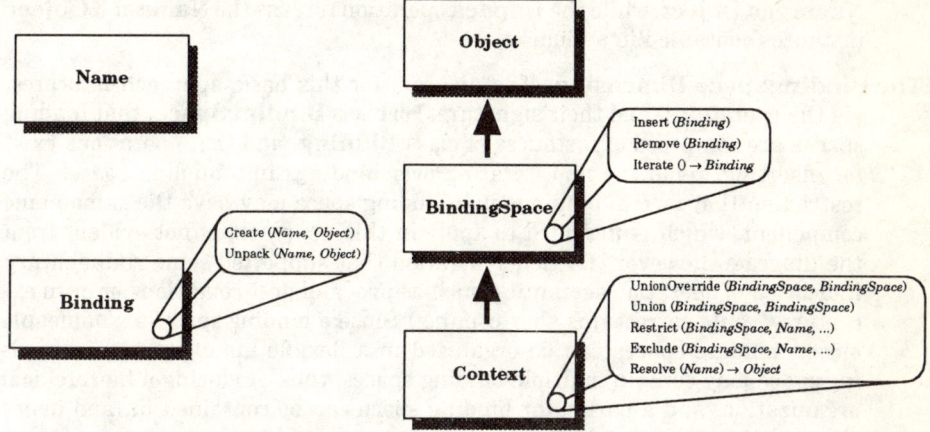

Figure 2: Model of a Basic Name Management Approach

graphical notation that we employ is an informal representation of an object-oriented structure, in which classes are represented as labeled rectangles, their associated operations are given as lists of operation signatures, and subclass relationships are represented by directed arcs from subclass to superclass. Some of the details of this notation, notably the way that operations are described, are influenced by the fact that we eventually implement our models in C++. Some ramifications of this will become apparent shortly.

The graphical depiction expresses many of the properties of this particular approach relatively clearly. Some other properties are not so evident from the diagram, however. Following the organization of the NamingSpace classification framework, the properties of the basic approach, and how (and how well) they are depicted in the diagram, are as follows:

The Object Dimension: The basic approach depicted in Figure 2 does not distinguish persistent and transient objects, so this approach does not restrict naming based on persistence. The diagram does, however, indicate that binding spaces and contexts can be named, while names and bindings cannot. This information is derived from the signature of the **Create** operation of the **Binding** class and the presence (or absence) of subtype arcs leading to class **Object**.

The Name Dimension: The diagram for this basic approach gives no information about the **Name** class beyond the fact that it exists. Thus, at the current level of abstraction, this approach takes no position about any questions in this dimension.

The Binding Dimension: The basic approach depicted in Figure 2 uses simple (name,object) pairs as bindings, as indicated by the signatures of the operations of class **Binding**. The **Create** operation creates a binding given instances of **Name** and **Object**, while the **Unpack** operation returns the **Name** and **Object** instances contained in a binding.

The BindingSpace Dimension: The diagram for this basic approach indicates, via the operations (and their signatures) of class **BindingSpace**, that binding spaces are composed of instances of class **Binding**, and that operations exist for inserting, removing and iterating over bindings in a binding space. The restriction that no two bindings in a binding space may have the same name component, which is intended to apply in this approach, is not evident from the diagram, however. (A richer notation that supported some rudimentary indication of operation semantics, such as pre- and post-conditions or even exceptions, could correct this shortcoming.) Since a binding space is a nameable object, binding spaces can be organized in a flexible manner – e.g., a binding space may contain multiple binding spaces, thus producing a hierarchical organization, and a particular binding space can be contained in (and hence shared by) multiple binding spaces.

The Context Dimension: In the basic approach depicted in Figure 2, contexts are formed from binding spaces or, given that **Context** is a subclass of **BindingSpace**, other contexts. Name resolution is an operation specific to contexts in this basic approach, so the context to be used in resolving a given name will be explicitly indicated. The context formation and manipulation operations are:

UnionOverride: Forms a new context given two binding spaces. The resulting context consists of all the bindings in the first binding space and all the bindings in the second binding space whose name components do not exist in any of the bindings in the first binding space.

Union: Used to combine two binding spaces. Since binding spaces must be unique with respect to the name components in the bindings, the operation fails when the binding spaces contain bindings whose name components are the same, but whose objects are not identical.

Restrict: Forms a new context by extracting from a given binding space the bindings whose name components match a specified set of names. The resulting context is a subset of the original binding space.

Exclude: Forms a new context by excluding from a given binding space the bindings whose name components match a specified set of names. The resulting context is a subset of the original binding space.

Of course, the diagram does not indicate any of the semantic details of these operations, although the names and signatures of the operations may suggest the intended interpretations in most cases. (Again, a richer notation that supported some rudimentary indication of operation semantics could correct this shortcoming.)

Our choice of the particular set of context formation operations included in this basic name management approach is, in part, a response to problems of the kind illustrated by the example corresponding to Figure 1. To assess how successfully this set of operations overcomes those problems, which arise in name management approaches where *UnionOverride* is the only context formation operation, we could consider some possible ways in which they might be used to form a desired context for header files in C++, as discussed in the earlier example. A set of possible context specifications to be used in the C++ compilation command, in place of the options discussed earlier, appears in Figure 3. In the figure, subscripted lower

(1) $c_1.UnionOverride(DIR1, DIR2)$

(2) $c_1.UnionOverride(DIR2, DIR1)$

(3) $c_3.UnionOverride(c_1.Restrict(DIR1, foo), c_2.Restrict(DIR2, bar))$

(4) $c_3.Union(c_1.Restrict(DIR1, foo), c_2.Restrict(DIR2, bar))$

(5) $c_2.UnionOverride(c_1.Restrict(DIR1, foo), DIR2)$

(6) $c_2.UnionOverride(c_1.Restrict(DIR2, bar), DIR1)$

(7) $c_2.UnionOverride(c_1.Exclude(DIR2, foo), DIR1)$

(8) $c_2.UnionOverride(c_1.Exclude(DIR1, bar), DIR2)$

(9) $c_1.Union(DIR1, DIR2)$

Figure 3: Some Possible Context Specifications

case letters denote instances of **Context**, uppercase identifiers denote instances of **BindingSpace**, lowercase identifiers denote instances of **Name**, binding spaces $DIR1$ and $DIR2$ represent the directories DIR1 and DIR2 and names foo and bar represent the files foo.h and bar.h. Thus, for instance, possibility (1) of Figure 3 corresponds exactly to the context specification contained in the C++ compilation command:

```
CC -IDIR1 -IDIR2 main.C
```

Of course, since they employ only *UnionOverride*, the contexts represented by possibilities (1) and (2) of Figure 3 both fail to satisfy the software developer's requirements as discussed in the earlier example. The remaining possibilities all accomplish the desired result, however, with the choice among them depending upon some further assumptions about the situation. For instance, suppose that the software developer wishes to form a context containing *only* the foo from $DIR1$ and the bar from $DIR2$. Using the *Restrict* operation in addition to *UnionOverride*, this can be accomplished using possibility (3). Alternatively, the same result can be achieved using *Restrict* and *Union*, as in possibility (4). Suppose, however, that in addition to having the preferred bindings for *foo* and *bar*, the software developer wants (or is willing) to have a context containing all of the other bindings in *one* of the directories. Then, depending upon *which* of the other directories is wanted, either possibility (5) or (6) will also produce an acceptable context. If instead the software developer wants (or is willing) to have a context containing *all* of the other (non-conflicting) bindings in *both* of the directories, along with the preferred bindings for *foo* and *bar*, using the *Exclude* operation as in possibilities (7) or (8) will accomplish the goal. Finally, suppose that the software developer does not know precisely what bindings are in $DIR1$ and $DIR2$,[6] but believes that the desired context should contain all the bindings in both[7] and wants to know if the resulting context is ambiguous. The *UnionOverride* operation is not sufficient, since the bindings in one binding space may override the bindings in the other binding space, but a context specification using the *Union* operation, like possibility (9), will suffice. Of course, given the hypotheses of our example, possibility (9) would raise an exception, since $DIR1$ and $DIR2$ each contain different bindings with the same name. This is precisely what the software developer wants, however, since it provides a notification that there is an ambiguity in the context specification.

4.2 Experimentation: Implementation and Variations

As the preceding discussion demonstrates, the graphical depiction of this basic approach to name management provides a significant amount of information and permits us to begin assessing its properties, and thereby positioning it in the NamingSpace. In order to study it further, we can quite straightforwardly translate from the graphical representation into an implementation in an object-oriented programming language. As noted earlier, we have been using C++ as our implementation language. The C++ implementation is, in fact, a more detailed representation of the approach than was the depiction in our simple graphical notation. It can, in particular, capture the semantic details of the operations associated with the various classes, which can only be inferred from the names and signatures appearing in the listings of operations in the graphical depiction. Of course, in the C++ implementation these details are buried in the coding of the specific methods. While this still does not facilitate reasoning about properties of a modeled approach as much as a more declarative representation might, it is certainly better than not capturing the information at all.

Naturally, the most important thing about being able to easily translate from model to implementation is that it permits us to experiment quite directly with any approach that we might choose to model. Initially we have carried out this experimentation by combining the C++ class definitions derived from a model of a name management approach with a simple testing harness, also implemented in C++, and then executing some simple scenarios that exercise the name management capabilities. In Section 5 we discuss steps directed toward providing a larger and more realistic testbed in which to experiment with implementations of various name management approaches. Even the simple experimentation using the testing

---

[6] In a realistic case, this might occur because the binding spaces are very large or change frequently.
[7] Or possibly more realistically all but some specified subset, which could be described using *Exclude*.

harness can yield some useful insights and information, however. It allows us, for instance, to empirically investigate the use of context formation operations by actually running experiments corresponding to possibilities like those enumerated in Figure 3.

Experimenting with the implementation of the basic approach described above reveals some interesting characteristics and suggests several possible variations. One striking characteristic of this approach is the central role that the **Binding** plays; naming is accomplished by explicitly creating a binding and then explicitly inserting that binding into a binding space, for example. Another characteristic, which may be considered more serious, concerns the name resolution function. Since the **Resolve** function returns any possible nameable object, the function's return type is **Object**. In using the C++ implementation, we found that this means the programmer must cast the result of the **Resolve** function into the appropriate type. Figure 4 illustrates the resolution of an instance of **Person** in some context. Based on these

```
Name n;
Person *p;
Context some_context;
...
p = (Person *) some_context.Resolve (n);
```

Figure 4: Casting the Result of the Resolve Function

two observed characteristics, we might designate the basic approach described in Figure 2 as a *type-weak, binding-centered* approach to name management.

A possible alternative worthy of some consideration might be called a *type-preserving, nameable-object-centered* approach. A modification to the model of Figure 2 that yields such an approach is shown in Figure 5, where the small box within the rectangle representing a class stands for a generic parameter and the dashed arrows mean "is an instantiation of".

The modification centers around the definition of a new class, i.e., **NameableObject** and the removal of the **Binding** class. **NameableObject** is a generic (or parameterized) class that inherits from the **Object** class. A C++ definition of such a generic class is shown in Figure 6. This class defines three operations:

AssignName: Assigns a name to an (instance of) **NameableObject** in a binding space.

RemoveName: Removes a name from an (instance of) **NameableObject** in a binding space.

Resolve: Returns an object of the parameterized type with the given name in the given context.

To use this class, an entity's class definition inherits from a **NameableObject** class parameterized by the entity class itself. Figure 7 shows an example of such a class definition in the C++ implementation of this model.

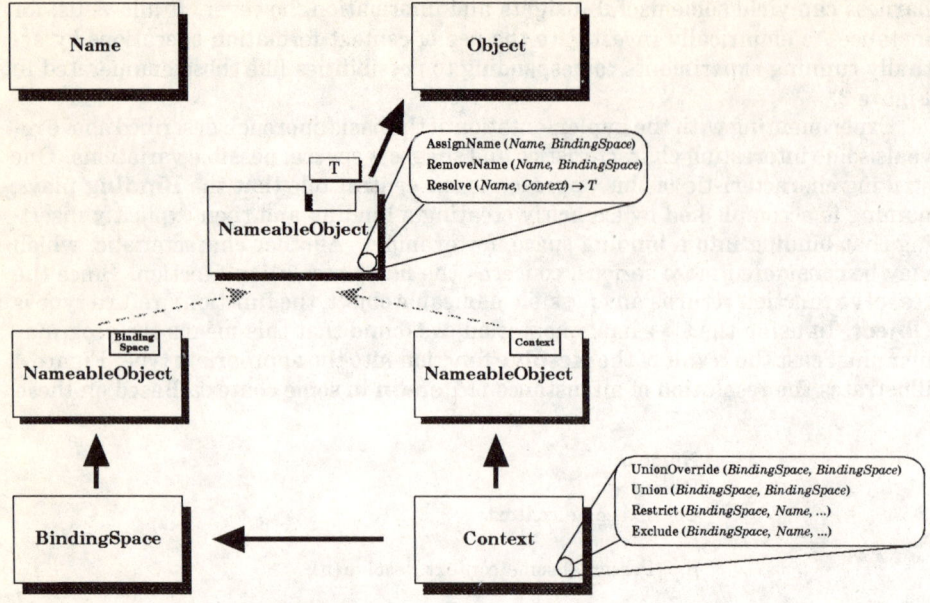

Figure 5: Model of a Type-Preserving, Nameable-Object-Centered Approach

The use of parameterized classes and inheritance in this model leads to every subclass of **NameableObject** having the appropriate name assignment, name removal and name resolution operations associated with it. As before, we can use both the model and the corresponding C++ implementation to assess properties of this approach and to position it in the NamingSpace. The major benefit of the approach is that the name resolution function returns the proper type and precludes the need for type casting. Another notable characteristic, of course, is that bindings are not explicitly manipulated in this approach; instead naming is accomplished using the **AssignName** operation associated with every nameable object. On the other hand, having the **Resolve** operation associated with the object, instead of with the context, may seem somewhat unnatural.

Any number of other alternative approaches, based on major or minor modifica-

```
template <class T> class NameableObject : public Object {
public:
    int AssignName (Name& n, BindingSpace& b);
    int RemoveName (Name& n, BindingSpace& b);
    static T* Resolve (Name& n, Context& c);
};
```

Figure 6: NameableObject Class

class Person : **public** NameableObject<Person> {...}

Figure 7: Using the NameableObject Class

tions to the models, and corresponding C++ implementations, described here could be envisioned. One might, for example, want to consider how and whether names or bindings, or both, might be made nameable objects, what alternative context formation operations might be useful, or how name management approaches and persistence should interact. We have, in fact, already begun to investigate some of these questions. Based on our successful experience with it to date, we believe that the use of object technology, as illustrated in this section, will continue to prove valuable in exploring these and a wide variety of other issues related to name management.

5 Name Management Applied to Object Technology

Although most of our work in the area of name management and object technology for advanced software has focused on using object technology to study name management, we have also begun exploring the potential for beneficial application of improved name management mechanisms to object-oriented programming languages, object-oriented databases and software object bases. In this section, we give a brief outline of our experience incorporating an enhanced name management mechanism, implemented in C++, into a representative instance of object technology for advanced software, namely Open OODB, an open, extensible object-oriented database management system [WBT92]. Open OODB is designed to be easily tailored for a wide variety of advanced software applications such as software development environments, computer-aided design and manufacturing, and hypermedia systems. One goal of Open OODB is to allow researchers to experiment with, improve upon and refine various approaches to a broad range of object services such as persistence, name management, transaction, indexing and data dictionary services. Thus, Open OODB provides an excellent testbed in which to experiment with implementations of various name management approaches. We have currently installed an Alpha release of Open OODB on a SUN SPARCstation 10 running Unix 4.1.3. The release uses the EXODUS Storage Manager 2.2 [CDS89] as its underlying object store.

The persistence service in Open OODB provides an interface that allows applications to make instances of arbitrarily complex C++ classes persist. The present persistence mechanism used in our particular instantiation of Open OODB is based on a reachability model of persistence. When an object is made to persist, all objects reachable from the persistent object are also made to persist. The use of this mechanism, along with the object-oriented capabilities provided by C++, facilitates integration of, and hence experimentation with, our prototype name management mechanisms and Open OODB.

The first step towards integrating a particular name management mechanism with Open OODB involves the use of the Open OODB persistence extending tools, which are used to extend C1+ classes with the necessary persistence capabilities.

The tools are initially applied to the constituent classes of the name management mechanism. Next, a root binding space must be created and made persistent. A function that returns this binding space is made available to all applications that are using the prototype name management mechanism. Applications must then modify class definitions accordingly so that instances of a class may be nameable. For example, to use the mechanism described in Section 4.1 classes are required to inherit from the **Object** class, while the mechanism described in Section 4.2 requires classes to inherit from the **NamedObject<T>** class (where **T** represents the name of the heir class). Finally, the Open OODB persistence extending tools must be applied once again, this time to the modified class.

The integration of our name management mechanism into Open OODB results in a name-based persistence mechanism (i.e., an alternative persistence model based on name assignment and manipulation). Instances of any class may use the name management mechanism to assign names to objects, access objects using names, organize named objects (or, more precisely, (name,object) bindings) into binding spaces, and construct contexts in flexible and arbitrary ways. Since persistence is based on reachability, assigning a name to an object in a binding space that is (directly or indirectly) reachable from the persistent root binding space results in the binding, the name and the object being made persistent.

The results of this experiment have highlighted the advantages both of an object-oriented database architecture like that of Open OODB and also of our object technology implementations of advanced naming capabilities. Open OODB's capabilities for extending C++ classes with persistence, combined with our C++ implementations, facilitates the integration of a variety of name management mechanisms in a richer and more realistic testbed for experimentation. It is relatively straightforward to change the name management mechanism in this system, simply by substituting one of our C++-implemented approaches for another. Therefore, we will now be able to experiment with how improved name management capabilities affect an object-oriented database and also conduct much more realistic and extensive evaluations of alternative name management approaches than could be performed using only the simple testing harness employed in our initial experimentation.

Although this first attempt at integrating our name management work with a realistic instance of object technology for advanced software has been remarkably successful and worthwhile, there are several improvements and further steps that we would like to pursue. First, we would like to unify the name management capabilities provided by our mechanism with those in the C++ language that provides the application programming interface to Open OODB. While the name management mechanism that we have integrated into the system can be used to name both transient and persistent objects, it is still quite separate from the name management mechanism (applicable to transient objects only, of course) provided in C++. Another useful enhancement would be to support type checking in conjunction with the name management services that our mechanism provides. The data dictionary service in Open OODB provides information about types, but our current prototype does not utilize that information. We plan to rectify this in future versions. Further experimentation with the present and future versions of this prototype integration of our name management mechanisms and Open OODB promise to yield additional insights and suggest other aspects to address.

6 Conclusions and Future Directions

Name management is fundamental to every aspect of computing, and it seems to have especially strong connections to object technology for advanced software. In particular, object technology has been instrumental in the two complementary facets of our research on name management, and it also appears that improved name management mechanisms could greatly benefit object-oriented programming languages, object-oriented databases and software object bases.

In this paper we have outlined our overall approach to research on name management, described some preliminary models that we have developed as a starting point for that research, discussed some specific name management issues arising in object technology for advanced software and given examples both of contributions that object technology has made to name management research and of the benefits that enhanced name management capabilities can make to object technology for advanced software. In the former category we have illustrated contributions to both facets of our research agenda – the use of object-oriented *modeling* in investigating various alternative approaches to name management as well as the value of object-oriented programming in implementing prototype *mechanisms* that can be used for empirically assessing modeled alternatives. In the latter category we have described how our extended name management mechanisms can be integrated into a particular object-oriented database system, resulting in a novel persistence control method as well as richer and more powerful name management features.

We believe that the work described in this paper provides a foundation for increased understanding and improved practical utilization of name management, especially as it relates to object technology for advanced software. Our models and our exploration strategy, based on object technology, offer a basis for enumerating, explicating and evaluating various approaches to various aspects of name management. Building on these, it will be possible to select or develop better and more appropriate name management approaches for use in current and future systems, especially object-oriented programming languages, object-oriented databases and software object bases. Our own future directions include expanding the scope of our investigation of name management, to encompass such things as its role in interoperability (e.g.,[WWRT91]), while continuing to develop and enhance both models and mechanisms for name management. With more and better models, coupled with more and better implementations, we hope to contribute to further progress in name management and object technology for advanced software.

Acknowledgements

The authors wish to thank Dr. Philip Johnson for his comments on an earlier draft of this paper.

References

[AB87] Malcolm P. Atkinson and O. Peter Buneman. Types and persistence in database programming languages. *ACM Computing Surveys*, 19(2):105–190, June 1987.

[BOS91] Paul Butterworth, Allen Otis, and Jacob Stein. The GemStone object database management system. *Communications of the ACM*, 34(10):64–77, October 1991.

[Bow90] C. Mic Bowman. *Univers: The Construction of an Internet-Wide Descriptive Naming System*. PhD thesis, The University of Arizona, Tucson, Arizona, August 1990.

[CDS89] M. Carey, D. DeWitt, and E. Shekita. Storage management for objects in EXODUS. In W. Kim and F. Lochovsky, editors, *Object-Oriented Concepts, Databases, and Applications*. Addison-Wesley, 1989.

[Chu41] Alonzo Church. *The Calculi of the Lambda-Conversion*. Princeton University Press, Princeton, 1941.

[CP89] Douglas E. Comer and Larry L. Peterson. Understanding naming in distributed systems. *Distributed Computing*, 3(2):51–60, May 1989.

[CWW80] Lori Clarke, Jack C. Wileden, and Alexander L. Wolf. Nesting in Ada programs is for the birds. In *Proceedings of an ACM-SIGPLAN Symposium on the Ada Programming Language*, pages 139–145, 1980. Appeared as *SIGPLAN Notices* 15(11).

[DCBM89] Alan Dearle, Richard Connor, Fred Brown, and Ron Morrison. Napier88–A database programming language? In *Second International Workshop on Database Programming Languages*, pages 213–229, June 1989.

[Dea89] Alan Dearle. Environments: A flexible binding mechanism to support system evolution. In *22nd Hawaii International Conference on System Sciences*, pages 46–55, Hawaii, U.S.A., January 1989.

[Deu91] O. Deux, et al. The O_2 system. *Communications of the ACM*, 34(10):34–49, October 1991.

[ECM91] ECMA. Reference model for frameworks of software engineering environments. Technical Report ECMA TR/55, 2nd Edition, ECMA/NIST, December 1991. (NIST Special Publication 500-201).

[Fra71] A.G. Fraser. On the meaning of names in programming systems. *Communications of the ACM*, 14(6):409–416, June 1971.

[Hei92] Dennis Heimbigner. Experiences with an object-manager for a process-centered environment. In *Proceedings of the Eighteenth International Conference on Very Large Data Bases*, Vancouver, B.C., August 1992.

[Kad92] R. Kadia. Issues encountered in building a flexible software development environment: Lessons from the Arcadia project. In *Proceedings of the Fifth ACM SIGSOFT Symposium on Software Development Environments*, pages 169–180, Tyson's Corner, VA, Dec 1992.

[Knu88] Jorgen Lindskov Knudsen. Name collision in multiple classification hierarchies. In *Proceedings of the European Conference on Object Oriented Computing (Lecture Notes In Computer Science 322)*, pages 93–109, Oslo, Norway, August 1988.

[LB88] B. Lampson and R. Burstall. Pebble, a kernel language for modules and abstract data types. *Information and Computation*, 76(2/3):278–346, Feb/Mar 1988.

[LLOW91] Charles Lamb, Gordon Landis, Jack Orenstein, and Dan Weinreb. The ObjectStore database system. *Communications of the ACM*, 34(10):50–63, October 1991.

[MABD90] R. Morrison, M.P. Atkinson, A.L. Brown, and A. Dearle. On the classification of binding mechanisms. *Information Processing Letters*, 34(1):51–55, February 1990.

[Mey88] Bertrand Meyer. *Introduction to the Theory of Programming Languages*. Prentice Hall, 1988.

[OMG92] OMG. Object services architecture, revision 6.0. OMG Document 92.8.4, Object Management Group, Framingham, MA, August 1992.

[ONT93] ONTOS, Inc. Technical overview. Burlington, MA, May 1993.

[Tho89] Ian Thomas. PCTE interfaces: Supporting tools in software-engineering environments. *IEEE Software*, 6:15–23, November 1989.

[TWC90] Peri L. Tarr, Jack C. Wileden, and Lori A. Clarke. Extending and limiting PGRAPHITE-style persistence. In *Implementing Persistent Object Bases : Principles and Practice / The Fourth International Workshop on Persistent Object Systems*, pages 74–86, Aug 1990.

[TWW89] Peri L. Tarr, Jack C. Wileden, and Alexander L. Wolf. A different tack to providing persistence in a language. In *Second International Workshop on Database Programming Languages*, pages 41–60, June 1989.

[WBT92] David L. Wells, Jose A. Blakely, and Craig W. Thompson. Architecture of an open object-oriented management system. *Computer*, 25(10):74–82, October 1992.

[WCW85] Alexander L. Wolf, Lori A. Clarke, and Jack C. Wileden. Ada-based support for programming-in-the-large. *IEEE Software*, 2(2):58–71, March 1985.

[WCW89]   Alexander L. Wolf, Lori A. Clarke, and Jack C. Wileden. The AdaPIC tool set: Supporting interface control and analysis throughout the software development process. *IEEE Transactions on Software Engineering*, 15(3):250–263, March 1989.

[WWFT88] Jack C. Wileden, Alexander L. Wolf, Charles D. Fisher, and Peri L. Tarr. PGRAPHITE: An experiment in persistent typed object management. In *Proceedings of SIGSOFT '88: Third Symposium of Software Development Environments*, pages 130–142, September 1988.

[WWRT91] Jack C. Wileden, Alexander L. Wolf, William R. Rosenblatt, and Peri L. Tarr. Specification level interoperability. *Communications of the ACM*, 34(5):73–87, May 1991.

Constraints in Object-Oriented Analysis

Stefan Van Baelen[*], Johan Lewi, Eric Steegmans and Bart Swennen

Katholieke Universiteit Leuven, Department of Computer Science
Celestijnenlaan 200A, B-3001 Leuven (Heverlee) - BELGIUM
Tel: +32 16-20.10.15 x 3596 - Fax: +32 16-20.53.08
E-mail: Stefan.VanBaelen@cs.kuleuven.ac.be

[*] Research Assistant of the Belgian National Fund for Scientific Research

Abstract

Object-oriented analysis methods can incorporate the concept of constraints to express rules of the problem domain in the specification model, restricting the possible instances of the model. As such, constraints describe properties that must be true at each moment in time for the entire system, without determining how they are to be preserved. The ways in which these constraints are introduced in the model differ from method to method, and even between distinct constraint types in a single method. Different ways in which constraints can be described, are illustrated and compared.

Specifying constraints as informal annotations or by operational restrictions is too informal and low level for analysis. According to the properties, importance and influence of the constraint types on the object model, they ought to be described differently. Some constraints, such as connectivity constraints, should best be integrated in existing model concepts to focus on the constraint during the concept definition and as a reminder for these kind of constraints Others, such as attribute value constraints, are best introduced as independent items part of a separate concept grafted on a general model to get a consistent, unambiguous, symmetrical and general applicable constraint description. Yet others, such as relational and existential dependency constraints, should be expressed implicitly by a hierarchical model structure. This approach enriches the object model in such a way that it highlights the logical structure of the problem domain to its right extent.

Keywords
Object-Oriented Analysis, Constraints, Object Model Structure

1. Introduction

Many object-oriented analysis methods have incorporated the concept of constraints to reflect rules of the external world in the specification model. Constraints are a means to express general properties of objects of a class. Constraints must hold during the entire life time of all objects of a class. As such, the number of possible valid instances of the specified model is diminished because the information present in the system must obey the constraint rules. By means of constraints, intrinsic properties of the system to be modeled can be described in a very elegant way. Indeed, in formulating constraints at the analysis level, only the aspect of *'what properties must be satisfied by objects of the class'* is covered, thereby abstracting from how these properties can be and when these properties must be controlled. These aspects are deferred to the design phase of the software life cycle.

The ways in which these constraints are introduced in the model differ from method to method. Constraint rules can be incorporated in the structure of the model, they can be introduced as a distinct concept next to the more classical ones, they can be integrated in the specification of the existing concepts, they can be described in an operational way or they can be considered as a mostly informal addendum to the model specification. The existing object-oriented analysis methods use a mixture of different specification techniques for distinct constraint types. However, some ways not always reflect the importance of certain constraint types, while some others are improper notations that cannot be applied consistently to related cases. The different ways in which constraints can be described will be examined and compared.

2. Constraints in O-O Analysis

Constraints play an important role in most object-oriented analysis methods. Their importance in the method is mostly reflected in the specification notation, which can vary from an informal textual part of the description to integrated or separate description parts. The description of constraints is almost totally neglected in some analysis methods, while other methods use them as glue to compose the whole model together properly. None of these extremes are desirable. We will discuss the different ways for constraints, highlight their advantages and disadvantages and suggest the domains in which they can be used.

2.1 Constraints as Informal Text

Almost all current object-oriented analysis methods have only informal support for general constraints on the model structure. However, some special constraint types are supported more formally. The degree in support for constraints varies from method to method. Some object-oriented analysis methods, such as OOA [Coad & Yourdon 91], Responsibility-Driven Design [Wirfs-Brock *et al.* 90] and OOSA [Shlaer & Mellor 88], neglect almost totally the importance of constraints. Properties of the external world cannot be expressed explicitly, but only as an additional part of the OOA documentation set. Instead of incorporating them as a major part in the analysis phase, they are considered to be a minor point of interest of the model. This leads to a neglect of the important role of constraint in the external world and in the analysis model of this external world. Although constraints are generally of utmost importance, whether they express rules of logic, physics or human-defined law and regulations, they would never get the same impact on the developed software models.

This is part of one of the current controversies in object-oriented analysis, namely formal versus informal specifications. One of the main reasons stated for informal specifications is to stimulate the creative process of analysis by not imposing strict rules on this analysis process. As a consequence, a strict formal description is also rejected. We think that, although the analysis process must keep its creativity, its outcomes must be formal. Indeed, if the design phase must start with an informal analysis description, errors will almost certainly be inevitable. An informal specification is exposed to human interpretation. This will not often correspond with the intention of whoever formulated it. Too much is left to the interpretation of the designer. If a formal analysis description with clear, well-defined semantics is produced, the following phases of the software life cycle have a solid base to go on with the development of the software system. In addition, formal verification techniques can be used to verify the obtained analysis model before going into design. This will prevent logical development errors from the analysis phase on. Also, although the outcomes of the analysis process must not be executable, it will be a good thing to make them interpretable. Then, efficient checking, testing and prototyping can be done at the analysis level, and maybe even a straightforward implementation can be produced semi-automatically. Therefore, we try to provide next to a formal description of the effect of the actions, a formal definition of the constraints for the problem domain.

We will try to illustrate this with a simple example which we will use throughout the text. Consider a Banking system in which banks grant car loans to their clients. A person can only get a car loan if she/he is client at the bank (she/he owns an account), if she/he has reached the legally defined adult age and if she/he is of course using the money to buy a car (it will be considered as the mortgage for the loan). A possible model for such system is presented in Fig 1.

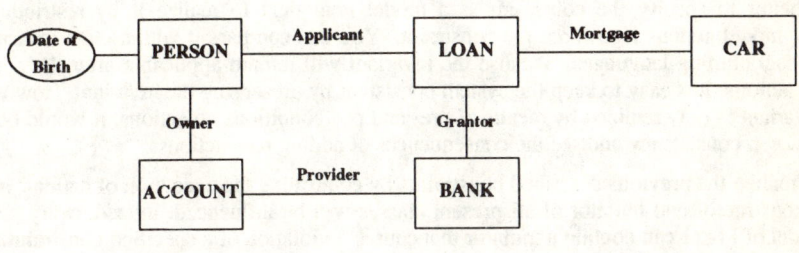

Fig. 1

The informal constraints that have to be added to this model are the following :
A. An account can only exist if a person and bank are related with it.
B. A loan can only exist if a person, a bank and a car are related with it.
C. The person related with the loan must be of adult age.
D. The person related with the loan must have an account at the same bank that granted the loan.

These informal specified constraints will never get the same important impact on the analysis outcomes as the original constraints have on the external world. More formal specification techniques are more fitted to express the importance of these constraints. Constraints are, just like classes, attributes, relations and actions, important items of an object-oriented analysis model. Therefore, the analysis model must contain a more formal definition of constraints instead of the informal textual constraint definitions. Different ways in which this can be done are presented in the next sections.

2.2 Constraints as Operational Restrictions

One possibility to incorporate constraints in the actual model is by controlling the execution of actions. This is supported by almost all current object-oriented analysis methods. By means of state transition diagrams, control flow diagrams or pre- and postconditions on actions, violations of the real world properties can be avoided. Such approach causes several problems.

A first problem is the gap that is introduced between the problem space and the obtained analysis model. Instead of describing what rules apply in the real world, the analysis model describes how they are realized. This must certainly be specified during the development, but at the design level rather than at the analysis level. The analysis phase must be centered around the reflection of the external world into the developed model, a direct mapping from the problem domain to the system model. Specifying constraints by means of action control introduces a gap between the problem domain and the system model. The final goal of a workable software development method is not only a smooth transition from analysis through design to implementation, but also from the problem space to the analysis model. It is actually this transition that gets disturbed when constraints are not an important concept of the analysis method, but realized by artificial, not well-suited means.

Another problem of specifying the constraint realization instead of the constraint itself concerns future revisions and modifications. When a constraint is specified as an independent item, it will remain present as such in revised and modified systems. However, when the constraint is realized in an operational way, it would be hard to see the consequences of new additions or changes to the model on the constraint realization. The revisor must perform a sort of reverse engineering by extracting the constraint from its realization. Therefore, it is much better to specify the constraint as a model item than to realize it by restricting the existing model actions to enforce the constraint. You can compare it with a class invariant in some programming languages. Because the invariant will remain applicable after the addition of new actions, it is easy to keep the system consistent by preserving the invariant. However, if this invariant is only realized by means of pre- and postconditions on actions, it would be very hard to keep consistency and see the consequences of adding new actions.

To realize the previous described constraints by controlling the execution of actions, almost every constructor and mutator of all present classes will be influenced. Indeed, every class in the model of Fig. 1 can contain a mutator that causes a violation of a specified constraint. This is because every class has the right to change the instances of the relations in which it takes part. The possible (semi-) control flow diagrams for constraints A, B, and D are represented in Fig. 2. It only expresses the order of construction and destruction of the objects. The interpretation, for instance of the diagram for constraint A, is as follows : A creation of an object of *ACCOUNT* is only possible after the creation of objects of both *PERSON* and *BANK* which are not yet destroyed. Hereafter the destruction of that account object must precede the destruction of either the person or the bank object. So it is possible to create a new account immediately after the destruction of an account with the same participant objects.

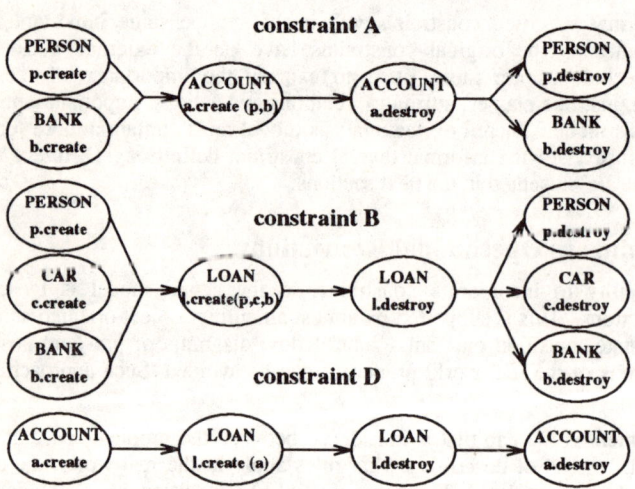

Fig. 2

If there are actions that can change the relations directly, such as moving an account from one person to another or changing the mortgage to another car, the state diagrams have to be extended. After an addition of a new action of any class, one is obliged to review the entire state diagram to keep its correctness. Indeed, because it is already a realization of the constraints, this realization has to be corrected after the slightest change of the model. Therefore, it is very hard to keep the constraint correct during the whole software life cycle, which contains many revisions, modifications and adaptations.

The constraint C can be expressed by means of a precondition on the creation of the objects of *LOAN*, for instance as follows:

class LOAN **is**
  constructors
    create (p : PERSON, ...)
      require : p.age[1] $\geq$ adult_age
  ...
end LOAN

However, if new actions are added to manipulate the relation *Applicant*, these actions have also to be placed under control. Thus, every addition of an action causes a possible violation of the constraint. When the constraint was formulated directly, this would not be the case. Future additions will then not give rise to revisions of existing constraints.

The analysis phase is centered around the problem space, describing what must be done. Therefore, constraints must be specified as such, and not already be realized by means of operational constructs such as preconditions and control flow and state transition diagrams. The constraint specification must be formal and explicit to get the greatest benefit during the whole software life cycle.

2.3 Constraints Integrated in Existing Model Concepts

Most Object-Oriented Analysis Methods that try to incorporate constraints in their software model in a formal and explicit way, integrate them with other concepts of the method, mostly restricted to one model item of one concept. Constraints about relations and attributes are integrated in the definition of the relation and attribute, constraints about objects of a class are specified as part of the class description and so on. This can be very useful and adequate for certain groups of constraints. Other constraint groups however are defined for one of the existing concepts or model items, although they can spread out over several of them[2].

The definition of connectivity (multiplicity) constraints on relations is almost always integrated in the relation definition. Obviously, such constraint is a basic part of a relation. Separating the connectivity from the relation definition will introduce the possible danger of

---

1. Actually, we can get the age of a person by comparing the current time with the date of birth. This can be expressed as 'now - p.Date of Birth'. Because the age of a person is a semantic real world property of a person, we will define it as a query *age* for the class *PERSON*, returning the age at the actual moment in time.

2. There is a slight difference between constraints that spread out over more than one concept and constraints that spread out over more than one item of the same concept. An example of the first type is constraint C, that includes both an attribute and a relation, whereas constraint A, B and D only deal with relations between classes, but more than one at the same time.

overlooking this important aspect of relations during the development of the analysis model. Another example of a useful integration is the multiplicity of attributes (one or many possible attribute values for an object) and the mutability properties of an attribute. It is useful to specify if certain attributes may only be defined at creation time of the object or can change during the life cycle of the object. For instance, the date of birth of a person may only be defined at the birth of a person and it may not more be changed during the life of that person. Also the name of a person[3], the agreement date of an account and the approval date of a loan are examples of immutable attributes. On the other hand, the address of a person, his length and weight are examples of attributes of which the actual value will vary during the life cycle of a person. The absence of a mutator for the attribute is not enough because these mutator can always be added later without any control. So the property of immutability has to be defined as such. These constraints that can be integrated easily, only bear upon a single item of one concept of the analysis method, which is in the previous cases one relation or one attribute definition.

However, if a constraint can spread out over more items of the same concept or several concepts, it is not possible to integrate constraints with a particular concept in a decent manner. Constraints over several relations cannot be placed with one particular relation definition. A method may decide to place rules between attributes of the relation participants in the relation definition, e.g., as in OMT [Rumbaugh *et al.* 91]. But, for instance, rules between attributes of objects connected by one or more consecutive relations, or join and anti-join constraints in a relation ring (if an object *a* of class A is connected through successive relations with *a'*, also of class A, then a = a', respectively a ≠ a') cannot be adjudged to a particular dedicated relation or class. Such constraints spread out over the whole model instead of some instances of just one concept. When such constraints are placed in a single class or with a single relation, arbitrariness will have a huge impact on the model. Indeed, we could have chosen an alternative viewpoint for placing and specifying the same constraint. In some cases, it would be even hard to see that two constraints are actually identical. Also, the information distribution in the obtained model will be very asymmetrical. Useful information for classes is hidden in the definition of other classes, relations or attributes. Another possibility, next to placing constraints in one particular class, is to place a constraint in every class that is influenced by it. This will give rise to an enormous amount of information duplication and overloading. Bad placement of constraints in the model will also lead to the diminishing of reuse. It will be very hard to get a proper insight in the existing structure, which will give rise to start all over again. A separate notation mechanism for constraints influencing more than one specific element of the model is therefore advisable.

The example of the previous section can be extended with connectivity constraints, as presented in Fig. 3. An account and a loan can be related with at most one person, one bank and one car. Persons and banks can be related with many accounts and loans. However, a car can be related with at most one loan, because it serves as the mortgage for the loan. The multiplicity of the attributes will also cause no problems for the model. It is obvious that a person can only have one date of birth at each moment in time.

The only problem that arises is the allocation of the four constraints of our example to the best fitted model items already present. Constraint A can be placed with the class *ACCOUNT*, but also with the two relations *Owner* and *Provider* (This is often done by means of the notion of a mandatory participant in a relation). Constraint B is of the same kind as constraint A. Constraint C can be placed with the classes *PERSON* or *LOAN*, with the relation *Applicant* or with the attribute *Date of Birth*. The choice between these alternatives will always remain

---

3. Neglecting the legal possibilities to change one's name

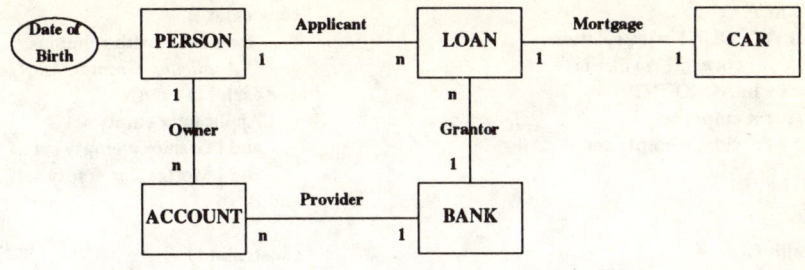

Fig. 3

rather arbitrary. Constraint D is an example of a join constraint in a relation ring. There are four classes and four relations involved. Which criteria can we use to select one of them instead of the others? No matter which one we choose, it will always introduce arbitrariness and asymmetry in the model.

To conclude, we can say that some constraint types are indeed strong related to existing concepts. An example of them is the connectivity (multiplicity) restriction for a relation. It would be obvious to integrate them with the concepts they belong to. However, most constraints spread out over a number of elements of the model and can therefore not be placed properly with only one of them. Therefore, we would like a mechanism to specify constraints formally and explicitly, but next to the classical model concepts that are present in the existing analysis methods.

2.4 Constraints as a Separate Concept

To overcome the difficulties of placing constraints with the existing concepts of the analysis model and to get a workable specification mechanism for all constraint types, a separate notation mechanism for constraints is developed as part of the ER⊚S project[4] [Lewi et al. 90, Van Baelen et al. 92, Lewi et al. 93]. Such constraint specifications contain the actual specification of the constraint itself in first-order logic, a name as a mnemonic for it, and the part of the model on which it is applied. This affected model part is automatically derived from the actual specification of the constraint and is especially useful for design purposes (see further). The specification of the involved classes can include the constraint name to highlight the restriction on their instances. However, the constraint definition will be a separate information item of the model, not integrated in other model elements. Otherwise, some of the problems of the previous case would appear again. The notation of constraints as a separate concept leads to a consistent, unambiguous and symmetrical constraint specification and placement.

We will illustrate this with a specification of some of the previous mentioned constraints in Fig. 4. We will use the same names for the constraints as given earlier.[5]

---

4. ER⊚S is an object-oriented development method that supports the full software life cycle, from analysis (ER⊚S-A), through design (ER⊚S-D) and implementation (ER⊚S-I), to the maintenance and running (evolution) phase. A full description of the ER⊚S method falls beyond the scope of this paper.

5. The operation 'a.Relation Name' stands for the set of objects to which the object a is related by the relation 'Relation Name'. The required adult age is modeled as a predefined value of the domain *DURATION*, which is an abstract data type for indicating a period in time.

```
constraint A                                constraint B
--   for ACCOUNT with relations            --   for LOAN with relations
--        Owner, Provider is               --        Applicant, Grantor, Mortgage is
for each a in ACCOUNT :                    for each l in LOAN :
   a.Owner ≠ empty set                        l.Applicant ≠ empty set
   and a.Provider ≠ empty set                 and l.Grantor ≠ empty set
end A                                         and l.Mortgage ≠ empty set
                                           end B


constraint C                                constraint D
--   for LOAN with relations Applicant     --   for LOAN with relations
--        to PERSON with attributes Date of Birth is   --   ( Applicant to PERSON
for each l in LOAN :                       --        with relations Owner,
   l.Applicant.age                         --        Grantor to BANK
        ≥ DURATION'adult_age               --        with relations Provider ) is
end C                                      for each l in LOAN :
                                              l.Applicant.Owner intersection
                                              l.Grantor.Provider ≠ empty set
                                           end D
```

Fig. 4

The only asymmetry that is still present arises from the fact that the affected model part and the constraint specification is described starting from one of the involved classes. However, this affects only the specification of the constraint itself, not the position of the constraint in the whole model. In the next section, we will abolish this asymmetry totally by introducing a hierarchy between classes and relations. We can then specify every constraint starting from the highest class(es) of the hierarchy.

The constraint specification can be extended with the specification of a trigger, a sort of exception handling mechanism for the constraint. The trigger describes a number of actions that must be performed when a violation of the constraint occur. In this case, the trigger actions are executed and hereafter the constraint must become valid again. The rule that a constraint is always satisfied is still valid. Only the actions that are used to keep the constraint valid are stated precisely. This trigger constraint is especially useful for the specification of constraints involving time, when certain actions must be performed after the exceeding of a predefined moment in time. The action that causes the violation of the constraint, the evolution of time, cannot be prevented.

The cases that are not well supported by this constraint specification technique are twofold. In the first place, classes that are actually materializations of relations, such as *ACCOUNT* (relation between *PERSON* and *BANK*) and *LOAN* (relation between *PERSON*, *BANK* and *CAR*), always imply an additional constraint on the presence of an object of the participant classes. Examples of them are constraint A and B. They emerge due to the fact that a relationship cannot exist without the knowledge of the participants it relates. As such, an account cannot exist without the person and the bank that are part of the account relationship. When the relation *ACCOUNT* is transformed into a class, the old characteristics must be enforced by means of a constraint.

The second inconvenience appears when one object is dependent of the existence of another object. Such dependency is expressed by constraint D, stating that a loan can only exist if a person has an account at the same bank. As such, there exist an existential dependency between each loan object and a corresponding account object. Such constraints are like glue, holding the model instances consistent w.r.t. the problem space. When a flat model is developed, many structure dependent constraints have to be enforced explicitly. This approach is not favorable, neither of the viewpoint of the model developer nor of that of the model reviewer and re-user.

This is because the logic structure dependencies are only specified by means of additional constraints, not by the model structure elements themselves. The modeler has to make an explicit transition between the logic structure of the problem space information and the model equivalent, a combination of model structure elements and structure related constraints. The reviewer of a loose model with many structure constraints will have to put the pieces of the puzzle together before she/he gets insight in the model. Instead of highlighting the basic structure of the model, one of the important things of an analysis description, this structure is neglected and shifted to the specified constraints. Moreover, it is possible to end up with a certain model without having thought of the implied structure constraints that are present in the problem space. A good model should capture many constraints through its structure. This is however not the case in a flat relation structure.

To conclude, we can say that the notation of constraints as a separate concept leads to a consistent, unambiguous and symmetrical constraint specification and placement for all constraint types. But important structure dependencies are hidden in these constraint specifications, instead of being part of the basic model structure. Therefore, we will extend our basic model structure elements to reflect the logic structure dependencies directly in the model structure. Then, the model will capture the current structure and relation dependency constraints implicitly.

2.5 Constraints Implied by the Model Structure

To diminish the gap between the logical structure and the model structure by enriching the expressive power of the model structure elements, a hierarchical relation structure can be used. A hierarchical relation structure will treat relations as classes themselves.[6] As such, the choice to model a certain relational thing, e.g., accounts, as a relation or a class will disappear. It will be modeled as both class and relation. Such class will be called a refined class (or a class refined by a relation), because the relation refines the objects of the class as relationships between objects of other classes.[7] Such approach has two major benefits concerning constraints : It captures implicitly the structure constraints and the constraints about the relationship objects. By defining the class *ACCOUNT* as a class refined by a relation between *PERSON* and *BANK*, it is stated that account objects also represent a relationship between a person and a bank. Therefore, such objects cannot exist without being related to a person and a

---

6. OMT [Rumbaugh *et al.* 91] and OSA [Embley *et al.* 92] also provides the possibility to model an association as a class. But it is not really a class of objects with their own identity, but merely a class of associations of two objects, which identities are defined as a combination of the identities of the objects part of the association. Duplicates, for instance, are not possible. Furthermore, you have to make a choice already at the analysis level whether a problem space relation is going to be modeled as a straight relation, a relation as a class (actually an exceptional case in OMT, rarely used), or just a class with two additional relations for the two participants. In ER◎S-A, every relation is encapsulated in a class. It is only in the design phase that we have to decide if a relation will be implemented by means of a class or an ordinary association.

7. The definition of an attribute for a class is called a decoration of that class. One can see a class as a naked body, that can be dressed with all kind of information : refined by a certain relation, decorated by several attributes and so on.

bank. This property is generally referred to as existential dependency. Constraint A has thus become superfluous.

Existential dependencies among objects may seem too restrictive for the ultimate system. A great deal of run-time flexibility, for instance in populating the model with instances, would be lost. However, object-oriented analysis is basically concerned with building an abstraction of the external world. Therefore, focusing on the external world in its *normal* appearance should have priority over the run-time issues. Refining accounts thus means that, under normal circumstances, each account must have an owner and a provider.

Before treating the dependencies for *LOAN*, the structure constraint D will be examined. This constraint can be reformulated as follows : When a person wants to get a loan from a bank, she/he has to own an account at that bank. So a loan can only exist if an account is associated with it. Therefore we refine the class *LOAN* by a relation between *CAR* and *ACCOUNT*. The account part of a loan captures the applicant and the grantor of the loan, together with the account that must exist before the loan can exist. The account serves as the contract base for the negotiated loan. Finally, this relation for *LOAN* also captures the dependency constraint B. So the only constraint that needs to be formulated explicitly is constraint C. The final model is presented in Fig. 5.

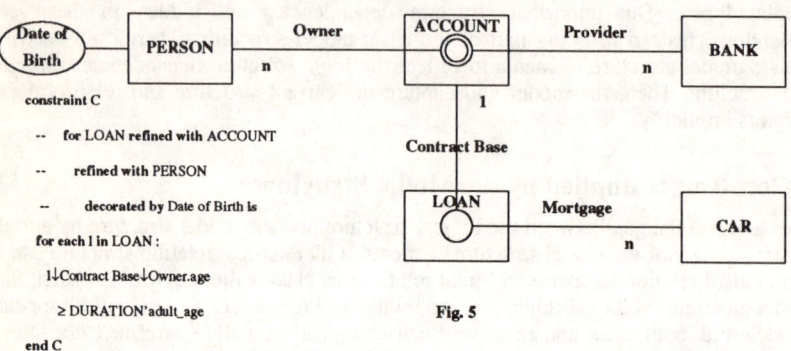

Fig. 5

The query 'a↓Role Name' (e.g., 1↓Contract Base) in the constraint specification stands for the object of the Role Name class that is a basic part of the relationship object a. The inverse query 'b↑CLASS NAME' stands for the set of objects of the CLASS NAME class in which b participates. If $a \approx (b,c)$[8] then a↓Role B = b, a↓Role C = c, $a \in$ b↑A and $a \in$ c↑A. This notation supports the view of zooming into the elements that are part of an object (projection ↓), and zooming out to the items that contains the object (election ↑). The circle for *LOAN* represents the relation (between *ACCOUNT* and *CAR*) that is encapsulated in the class *LOAN*. The double circle for *ACCOUNT* indicates that duplicates are allowed for the encapsulated relation. So a person can have more than one account at the same bank. Duplicates are indeed possible when relationships are considered as objects. Indeed, the object identity will always present, even if two objects have the same participants.

---

8. a is not really equal to (b,c), but it contains (b,c). In addition, it has its own object identity, which allows also that another object of class A, say a' ≈ (b,c).

When a class is existential dependent of only one other class, this can be expressed as in Fig. 6. In this case, the class is refined by a unary relation of the participant class. It is also possible to define a connectivity value for unary relation to express the fact if a participant object can participate in one or many refined objects.

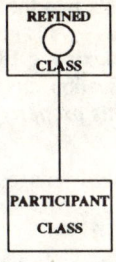

Fig. 6

Notice that we can now avoid arbitrary asymmetry in the constraint specifications. The description of the affected model part and the constraint itself will be seen from the highest classes in the relation hierarchy. As such, it is always definite how a certain constraint must be formulated. This mechanism is incorporated in EROOS-A,. Connectivity and attribute multiplicity constraints are integrated with existing concepts, structure and relationship constraints are implied by the model structure whereas the remaining constraints are described as independent model items.

We can try to go even further and capture the remaining constraint also in our model structure by providing a special construct for it. For instance, by introducing subgroups within classes, we can define the group of adult accounts by defining the group of adults for class *PERSON*. This construction will capture also constraint C in its model structure, as presented in Fig. 7. The oblique line in the left corner is an indication of a subgroup of a class.

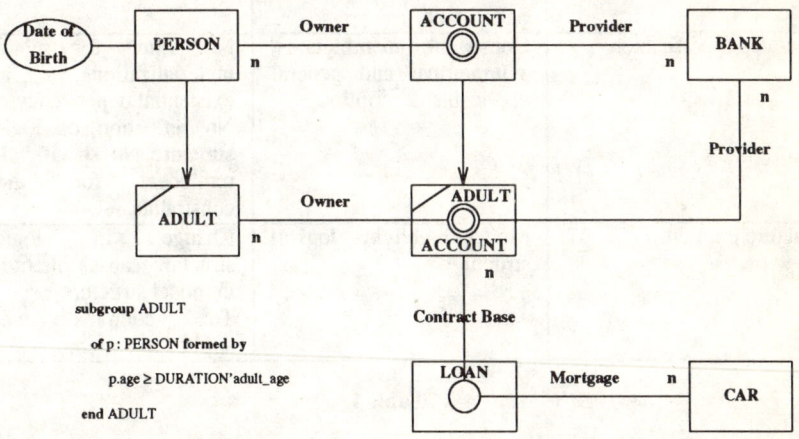

Fig. 7

However, a trade-off is necessary between model complexity and model simplicity and understandability. The step from a flat relation structure to a hierarchical relation structure has shown its use in practice. It provides a solid base for mapping the problem space into an analysis model. Whether or not more constraints have to be supported explicitly in the model structure, is not clear yet. But we are planning to experiment in the future with new structure mechanisms for capturing more constraints into the model structure. After evaluation of each proposal on criteria like *'model complexity versus model simplicity and understandability'*, the accepted concepts will be added to the existing ER①S-A modeling concepts. We are also planning to extend our constraint specification mechanism with temporal logic to be able to express temporal constraints, such as *'this property until that happens'* or *'this property will become valid in the future'*.

A summary of the advantages and disadvantages of the discussed specification techniques is presented in Table 1.

Constraint specification	Advantages	Disadvantages
Informal text	Expressivity of English language	Neglection of constraints Imprecise description No verification possible
Operational restrictions	Classical technique	Operational description Gap between analysis and problem domain Revision problems
Integrated in other concepts	Logical description Focus on constraint in concept definition Specification reminder for this kind of constraints Useful for relation connectivity, Attribute multiplicity and mutability of attribute and relation participant	Arbitrariness and improper description when used over several items
Separated specification	Consistent, unambiguous, symmetrical and general applicable description	Not fitted for relation materializations and existential dependency No reflection of logical structure No specification reminder for these constraints
Structure implied	Model highlights logical structure	Change in logical structure causes alteration in model structure Too complex when applied in extreme

Table 1

3. Realization of Constraints during O-O Design

The analysis of a software system must be focused on the problem space. The final outcomes of the analysis phase contains, amongst others, a complete description of the entire system on a high level of abstraction. Aspects of the solution domain are not incorporated in the analysis model. Therefore, constraints are introduced as a high level specification mechanism of rules and regulations of the problem space, without incorporating the decision of how and when they are going to be checked and realized. The design phase will introduce more details about the actual realization of the specified model. This is the right place and time to take the decisions regarding to the realization of the specified constraints. This section will present some design issues regarding constraints.

The design approach presented here is aimed at classical object-oriented languages, such as Smalltalk, C++ and Eiffel. Further research about design issues that arise when constraint-based object-oriented languages are used as a target language is planned in the near future.

3.1 Design Issues for Separate Constraints

Constraints that are specified as a separate concept item, as described in a previous section, still have to be realized in the lower levels of the system development life cycle. At the design phase, several topics arise during the constraint realization. The main issues are concerned with the place and time the system must be checked for possible constraint violations, and the actions that must be performed when a violation is going to occur or has occurred. Two distinct approaches can be applied :

- The first approach consists of preventing the occurrence of a constraint violation. First of all, the set of actions that can be the source of a constraint violations are derived. For each action, a require condition can be determined that must be fulfilled before the action can be executed. These require conditions will prevent the system of going into a wrong state. The execution of certain actions cannot be tolerated for certain system states. This approach causes a loss of efficiency due to a high number of tests, but keeps the system in a highly consistent state at each moment in time.

- Another approach consists of detecting fault system states, whereupon the system itself will perform either a sort of rollback to an older valid state, or the invocation of an error recovery procedure that tries to fix the system. This results in an important gain of efficiency, but leaves the system in an inconsistent state during a certain time.

The choice between these two approaches is often situation specific. A trade-off has to be made between efficiency and consistency, depending on which criteria are of utmost importance for the required system.

A tunable constraint realization approach by preventing constraint violations is already developed as part of the ER(0)S project. The amount of decisions that have to be made is ordered in several successive levels, for a separation of concern. We will locate where and when each constraint can be violated. This will reduce the moments and the objects to be checked. Reduction is done in four steps :

- Firstly, the classes that are involved in each constraint will be determined. The constraint has to be checked on each object of such class after the invocation of each of its actions. Other classes cannot be of any influence on the realization of the constraint. This will decrease the moments on which a constraint has to be checked.

- Then, the set of objects of the involved classes that have to be verified after an action on an object of the class will be determined. Mostly, it will not be necessary to check each object of the class, after execution of an action on a certain object of that class; checking the involved object will be sufficient. Such situations will give rise to a decrease of the objects on which a constraint has to be checked.

- Thirdly, the actions that can cause a constraint violation must be determined. Actions concerning certain characteristics of an object, whether they are attributes or participants, will mostly not violate constraints about other characteristics. The moments on which the constraint has to be checked will hereby decrease.

- Finally, the require conditions that have to be tested before each action can be invoked, are derived. Mostly, these require conditions can be made simple and efficient, compared to the actual constraint expression. These transformations from the original constraint specification into a rather straightforward tests will increase efficiency quite a lot.

3.2 Design Issues for Implied Constraints

A hierarchical structuring of relations may result in more classes and a more complicated structure to implement. Therefore it is often advisable to transform the introduced structures to a simpler structure, a flat one for example. It is rather straightforward to transform the developed hierarchical model into a bipartite, flat model, consisting of classes on the one hand and flat relations on the other. Flat relations are preferred at the design level for reasons of simplicity and implementation ease. There is no identity or functionality associated with a flat relation. A flat relation corresponds with the relation concept of entity-relationship modeling and many object-oriented methods. It is also possible to change a refined class together with its relation into a flat relation, with the consequence that the functionality of the class must be shifted to neighboring classes. In this way, the number of classes of the analysis level can be diminished at the design level. This design level is the right place to decide which classes have to be optimized and which ones have to be kept as such. The main concern here is to find a good balance between the information amount and the procedural amount of the design.

4. Conclusion

After comparison of the different ways to specify for constraints, our conclusion for integration in the ER(O)S Method is the following :

- Specifying constraints as informal text is too informal as an outcome of the analysis phase. This will give rise to the introduction of human interpretation errors during later stages of the development.

- Specifying constraints explicitly by operational restrictions is too low level during analysis. Such approaches are not advisable because they cause a gap between the problem space and the analysis model. Instead of describing what rules apply in the real world, the analysis model describes how they are realized. In addition, they have always to be converted from their conceptual meaning to their implementation and vice versa.

- Certain constraints, such as connectivity and attribute multiplicity constraints, and mutability constraints of attributes and relation participants can easily be integrated in existing model concepts. When constraints can spread out over several concepts, it is not advisable to define them for just one of them. This leads to asymmetry and arbitrariness in the constraint specification.

- Constraints can be considered as independent items part of a separate concept. It highlights the importance of constraints to its right extent. However, constraints about the relationship objects and structure constraints have to be enforced explicitly. Instead of highlighting the basic structure of the model, one of the important things of an analysis description, this structure is neglected and shifted to the specified constraints.
- A hierarchical relation structure will capture such constraints implicitly by the model structure. This will reduce the relationship and structure constraints, often present in flat models, and avoid arbitrary asymmetry in the constraint placement. It will highlight the logical structure of the model to its right extent.

No other special constructs are included yet in EROOS, as trade-off between model complexity and model simplicity and understandability. But we are planning to experiment in the future with new structure mechanisms for capturing more constraints into structure. Such structure mechanisms can be introduced in EROOS-A after a positive evaluation.

References

[Coad & Yourdon 91] Coad, P., and Yourdon, E., *Object-Oriented Analysis Second Edition*, Yourdon Press, Englewood Cliffs (New Jersey), 1991.

[Embley *et al.* 92] Embley, D.W., Kurtz, B.D., and Woodfield, S.N.,, *Object-Oriented Systems Analysis*, Yourdon Press, Englewood Cliffs (New Jersey), 1992.

[Lewi *et al.* 90] Lewi, J., Steegmans, E., and Van Baelen, S., EROOS : Entity-Relationship Object-Oriented Specifications, Department of Computer Science, K.U.Leuven, CW Report 111, 1990.

[Lewi *et al.* 93] Lewi, J., Steegmans, E., Dockx, J., Swennen, B., Van Baelen, S., and Van Riel, H., *Object-Oriented Software Development with EROOS: The Analysis Phase*, Department of Computer Science, K.U.Leuven, CW Report 169, 1993.

[Rumbaugh *et al.* 91] Rumbaugh, J., Blaha, M., Premerlani, W., Eddy, F., and Lorenson, W., *Object-Oriented Modeling and Design*, Prentice Hall, Englewood Cliffs (New Jersey), 1991.

[Shlaer & Mellor 88] Shlaer, S., and Mellor, S. J., *Object-Oriented Systems Analysis : Modeling the World in Data*, Yourdon Press, Englewood Cliffs (New Jersey), 1988.

[Van Baelen *et al.* 92] Van Baelen, S, Lewi, J., Steegmans, E., and Van Riel, H., EROOS : An Entity-Relationship based Object-Oriented Specification Method, *Technology of Object-Oriented Languages and Systems TOOLS 7*, Heeg, G., Magnusson, B., and Meyer, B. (ed.), Prentice Hall, Hertsfordshire, UK, pp. 103-117.

[Wirfs-Brock *et al.* 90] Wirfs-Brock, R., Wilkerson, B., and Wiener, L., *Designing Object-Oriented Software*, Prentice Hall, Englewood Cliffs (New Jersey), 1990.

Integration of the Tool (AWB) Supporting the O* Method in the PCTE-Based Software Engineering Environment

Sai Peck LEE   Colette ROLLAND

Centre de Recherche en Informatique
Université de Paris 1 - La Sorbonne
17, Rue de Tolbiac
75013 Paris, FRANCE
e-mail : {saipeck, rolland}@masi.ibp.fr

Abstract
Most existing object-oriented analysis and design tools supporting various methods are stand-alone and are not agreed on a common standard. This results in the issues of tool integration in software engineering environments. Our main aim in this paper is to illustrate the integration of the analysis tool named Analyst WorkBench (AWB) supporting the O* object-oriented method in the PCTE[1] Emeraude-based software engineering environment. The integration is achieved through data sharing and the reuse of types. The O* method and the AWB have been developed within the framework of the ESPRIT II project named Business Class.[2]
Keywords : *tool integration, software engineering environment, object-oriented analysis, information systems development, data sharing, reuse of types.*

1 Introduction

Towards the end of 1990s, there has been a significant proliferation of object-oriented analysis and design methods [Coad90, Essink91, Prakash91, Rumbaugh91] to cater for the acquisition of information requirements. Perhaps, this can be considered as a great step forward in software development at the early phases of object-oriented information systems development life-cycle [Booch86, Cauvet89, Rolland91, Shlaer88, Sutcliffe91]. However, more often than not, the development tools supporting the various methods are stand-alone in the sense that they do not share data and are not agreed on a common standard. As such, this gives rise to the issues of tool integration with the aim of bridging the gap between tools supporting different phases of the development life-cycle.

---

[1] Portable Common Tools Environment (PCTE) was developed by GIE Emeraude (France).

[2] This project is supported by the European Commission under the contract 5311 of the second European Strategic Program for Research and Development in Information Technology (ESPRIT). The main partners include Télésystèmes (France), Société des Outils du Logiciel (France), Applied Logic (United Kingdom), Eritel (Spain) and Datamont (Italy). Université de Paris 1 as the sub-contractor of Télésystèmes, was involved in the development of the O* method and the integration of AWB in the PCTE-based software engineering environment.

Our main aim is to illustrate the integration of the analysis tool named *Analyst WorkBench (AWB)* [Télésystèmes92] supporting the *O* object-oriented analysis method* [Brunet91, Lee92] in the *PCTE Emeraude-based software engineering environment* [Boudier88, Emeraude92]. This environment is constituted of a set of integrated tools, and the norm named PCTE as the main contributor in binding the tools together to form a cohesive and uniform tool set.

The main objective of the integration of AWB into the environment is to promote *shareability*, that is to say, to allow the cooperation of AWB with other tools via public persistent data sharing. Other than the shareability aspect, the *reuse of types* will also be recommended so as to allow the cooperation of AWB with other higher-level tools supporting some generic models via the reuse of types, and as a result, implying also the persistent data reuse.

In section 2, we shall present some background on some Software Engineering Environments (SEEs) and the O* method. This is followed by the explanation of how the integration objective can be met in section 3. The details of the setting up of the PCTE Schema Definition Sets (SDSs) for accomplishing this objective will be given in section 4. A SDS contains the meta-model of a part of a tool's information. This section illustrates on the one hand, how the shareability objective can be achieved by introducing a design tool, and on the other hand, how the reuse of types by AWB from the types declared in the SDS of a higher-level tool supporting a generic model can be done. Finally, some concluding remarks will be given in the last section.

2 Background

In this section, we intend to describe some state-of-the-art SEEs with somewhat presentation of the PCTE Emeraude-based SEE. The overview of the O* method and its model will also be given in this section.

2.1 Software Engineering Environments

A *Software Engineering Environment (SEE)* [Legait88, Thomas89] is actually a framework that provides an integrated support for a set of related but multi-vendor tools to coexist together through a set of common services. The services for integration are offered through its built-in integration technology. It cannot be denied that this technology is actually wholly supported by an underlying Database Management System (DBMS) integrated into the environment.

In the SEE context, tool integration means the cooperation of different tools supplied by multiple sources by sharing a logically consistent database. For instance, the *AD information model* together with a set of *Repository services* has been built into the *IBM AD/Cycle* [Mercurio90] as a support mechanism for the integration of IBM tools and vendor-supplied tools. In the *REuse Based on Object-Oriented Techniques (REBOOT)* environment, various facilities are offered to facilitate tool integration as well as to enhance productivity and quality in software development by promoting reuse [Faget92].

PCTE has been accepted as a norm (standard) whose principal role is to provide an infrastructure solution for integrating together a set of different but related tools from multiple sources. In the PCTE Emeraude-based environment, the integration technology is provided by an underlying Object-oriented DBMS (ODBMS) named *Object Management System (OMS)* [Gallo87, Minot88]. The data model of OMS is based on the *Entity-Relationship model* [Chen76] with the extension of some object-oriented concepts such as *inheritance*. The OMS acts as a support mechanism for its environment as well as for achieving data integration for multi-vendor tools. Thus, the tools that are being plugged into its environment use the data model of the OMS to achieve data integration. Sometimes, the OMS database is also called the *object base* or *repository* of the PCTE.

2.1.1 PCTE Emeraude-based Services

In this section, we shall give a brief explanation on the PCTE common services, tools and object base. Figure 1 illustrates the layered architecture of these components.

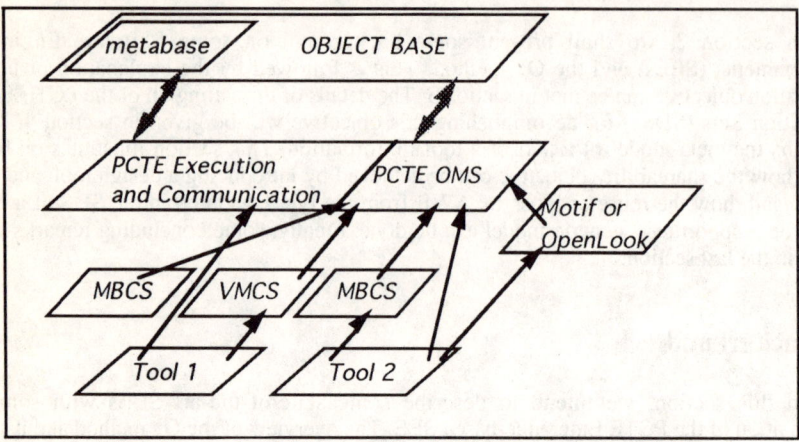

Fig. 1 Layered architecture of the PCTE Emeraude-based SEE

Emeraude PCTE is catered for environment designers, tool developers and integrators in the creation of a SEE. It can be accessed via Motif or OpenLook.

The *PCTE object base* is stored as objects, links and attributes. As a whole, they form the persistent storage information in the object base. A part of the object base called *metabase*, holds objects representing all the object, link and attribute type definitions, as well as the SDSs that present in the environment in a consistent manner. A SDS is a group of inter-related type definitions.

The three main Emeraude common services built on top of the PCTE OMS are as follows :
- the *Metabase Common Services (MBCS)* which can be used to store or retrieve information about the OMS type definitions;
- the *Version Management Common Services (VMCS)* for the management of versions of objects;
- the *Data Query and Manipulation Common Services (DQMCS)* for data query manipulation on the object base.

2.2 Overview of the O* Method

The *O* object-oriented analysis method* is composed of the O* model and a set of methodological guidelines. The background of the O* method and its model will be presented in the following sub-sections. For reasons of space limitation, the methodological guidelines are not presented in this paper.

2.2.1 Background

The O* method [Brunet91, Lee92] is defined within the framework of the ESPRIT II project named *Business Class*. The AWB allows the analyst to define a conceptual schema representing the description of a real-world system with the aid of the O* methodological guidelines [Télésystèmes92]. Moreover, a set of interactive and defered controls corresponding to the O* verification of the conceptual schema has been built into the tool. The conceptual schema is divided into two main parts, namely, the static schema representing the structural aspects of an information system, and the dynamic schema representing the behavioral aspects of the information system, through the hypothesis that the behavioral aspects are responsible for causing state changes to the structural aspects of the information system.

2.2.2 The O* Model

The three main concepts of the O* model, which are used to formalize real-world phenomena together with their underlying relationships as well as the abstraction mechanisms are shown in figure 2.

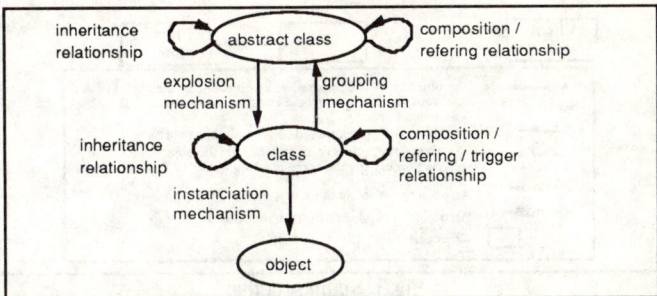

Fig. 2 The main concepts of the O* model

The two basic concepts of the *O* model*, namely, *object* and *class*, are adopted from the object-oriented paradigm. The main aim of the model is to adopt the concept of objects from the analysis phase right through the implementation phase. Moreover, the model also takes into account the *life cycles* of objects for the determination of *static links* between classes, besides the inheritance links of the object-oriented paradigm. Two types of static links are distinguished : *refering link* and *composition link*, where each link can be defined between two classes after identifying the dependency between the life cycles of objects in these classes. A refering/composition link can be simple or multiple : a simple refering link connecting two classes indicates that a refering object refers to one and only one refered object. On the other hand, a multiple refering link indicates that a refering object can refer to 1 - N refered objects.

Other than the structural aspects, the model has considered the concepts of *event* and *operation* to take into account the behavioral aspects of information systems at the conceptual level. Two groups of events are distinguished : *external events and internal events*. External events correspond to the events occuring in the environment outside an information system. Internal events correspond to the internal state changes or rather the system responses of the information system, and temporal internal events correspond to the events whose occurrences depend on the description of time. A particular group of external events interacts with the information system via an actor to which they are attached. Hence, it is presumed that the actors are agents interacting with the information system, and thus, they are situated outside the system. Regarding the operations, they are divided into *external operations* that are defined in actors, and *internal operations* that are defined in classes. An external operation represents an action triggered by a system response, that will then be intercepted by an agent corresponding to the actor in which this external operation is defined. On the other hand, an internal operation represents an action that can be performed on an object of a class, thus, causing a state change to that object.

We shall represent the formalization of the various aspects of the O* model through an example showing two main functions of a business firm, namely, order processing and inventory management. Having studied the requirement and the behavior of these functions of the organization, the structural aspects and behavioral aspects of the business conforming to the O* model are established respectively in the *static schema* and *dynamic schema* as shown in figure 3 and figure 4, with the aid of the O* methodological guidelines.

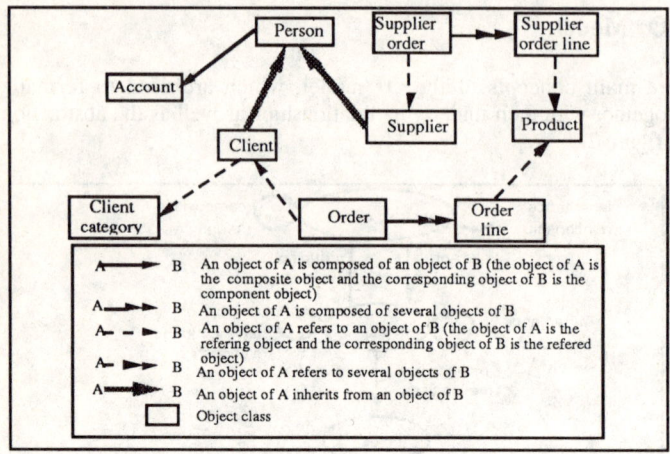

Fig.3 Static schema

The static schema has been set up with a set of object classes storing the persistent information of the organization. These classes are interrelated among themselves through static links. A composition link between a composite class and a component class expresses a strong coupling of behavior between a composite object and its component object. It is derived semantically in such a way that the life cycle of the component object is totally included in the life cycle of its composite object. In other words, the existence of the component object depends on the existence of its composite object. Moreover, a component object belongs to one and only one composite object and their life spans are approximately the same. In contrast, a refering link defined between a refering class and a refered class expresses a weak coupling of behavior between a refering object and a refered object. The life cycle of the refering object is totally included in the life cycle of its refered object. Moreover, a refered object may be shared by several refering objects.

The representation of the behavior of the business activities has been summarized as shown in figure 4. Its interpretation can be explained through an example. For instance, the arrival of an order via a sales personnel is represented by an external event named *arrival of order*. The sales personnel is modeled by using the concept of actor. Therefore, when this event happens, an object corresponding to the order and an object corresponding to the client who made the request for the order might be created depending on the triggering conditions defined on the triggers of the event. For instance, the condition *not c2* specifies the non-existence of an object of this client in the class *Client*. Note that the component classes are not represented in the dynamic schema as they have been encapsulated into the composite classes. The details of the abstraction mechanisms can be refered from [Lee92].

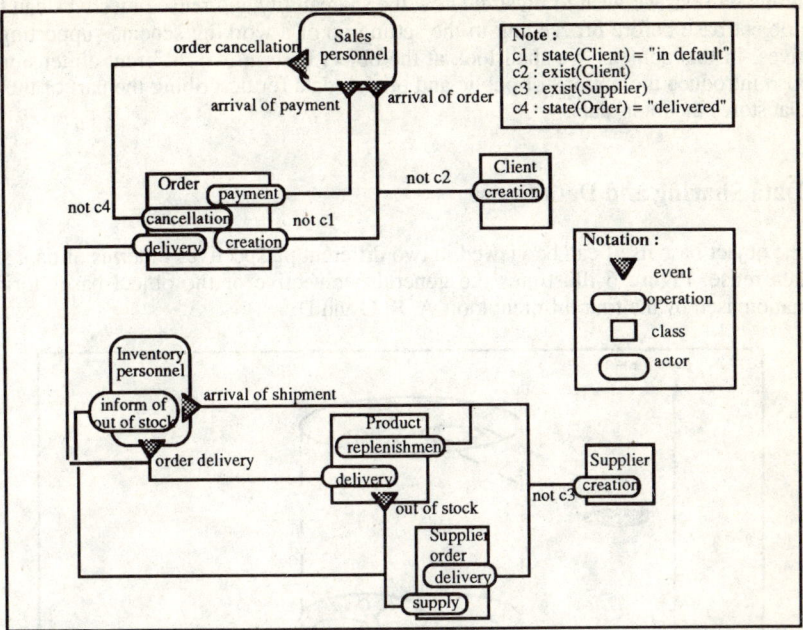

Fig. 4 Dynamic schema

Other than the dynamic schema, a *state transition graph* can be attached to a class for describing the local behavior of its objects. It defines a set of distinct object states. An object persists in one of these states during a certain period of its life cycle. State changes of an object are specified by a set of state transitions described in the form of a triplet (*initial state, operation, final state*). This describes how an object undergoes state change at a certain point in time. The pair *initial state, internal operation* describes the object pre-condition, whereas *final state* describes its post-condition. An example of a state transition graph is given in figure 5.

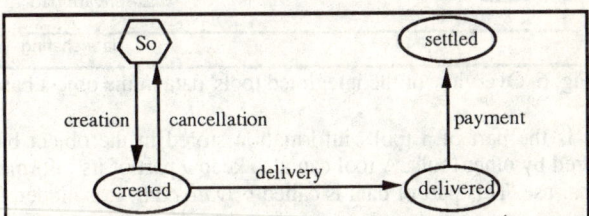

Fig. 5 State transition graph of the class *Order*

The state *So* specifies the non-existence of object and it is compulsory to define it in each graph. The state transition (*created, delivery, delivered*) stipulates that the operation *delivery* can be executed only if the object initial state is *created*, and as a result of this condition, the object will be in only a possible final state, *delivered*.

3 How to Meet the Shareability and Reuse Objectives

In this section, we wish to illustrate how the shareability and reuse objectives can be met in the object base before proceeding to the setting up of a working schema supporting these objectives. In this context, we shall look at the object base in two different dimensions. We shall also introduce the notions of public and private data for describing the part of the object base that stores the tools' data.

3.1 Data Sharing and Data Reuse

The object base itself can be viewed in two different perspectives in terms of data sharing and data reuse. Figure 6 illustrates the general perspective of the object base storing the information used by the four different tools A, B, C and D.

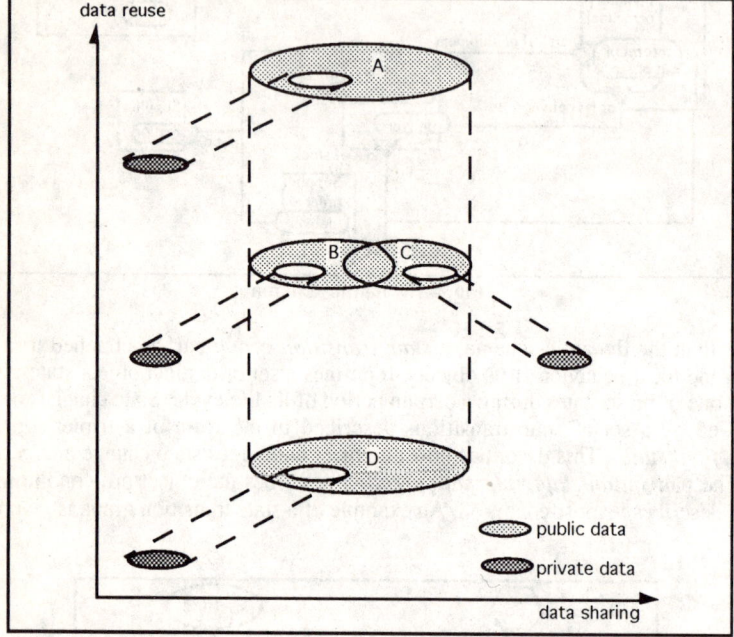

Fig. 6 Overview of the integrated tools' data in the object base

Public data is the part of a tool's information stored in the object base that has been defined to be shared by other tools. A tool can also keep a part of its information in the object base for its internal use. This part of data is called *private data*. It is hidden from the views of other tools.

The degree of data sharing can be judged from the number of intersections of the integrated tools' data located horizontally across the same level of the object base. For a tool whose data is located in the inner-most intersection, the degree of data sharing increases as the number of intersections increases. For instance, C shares part of B's public data besides having its own private data. The part of B's data shared by C are the semantically equivalent data of both tools.

Another perspective of the object base can be viewed in terms of data reuse. The higher a tool's data is located in the object base, the greater degree the data is being reused. In other words, the tool actually derives part of its data from those located at the underlying levels. For instance, the public data of the tool A is derived from the public data of B and C. As such, this enables the data of the integrated tools to be organized vertically into views at different levels in the object base.

Therefore, in this case, A can be a higher-level tool supporting a generic model that provides some generic concepts for the concepts used by both B and C. As an illustration for the rest of the sections, B will be the AWB and C will be a designer tool named *Designer WorkBench (DWB)* supporting the *BON methodology* [Nerson92] that needs to access AWB's data. The DWB is developed by *Société des Outils du Logiciel (France)*. A will be a browser tool named *SCalable Browser (SCB)* which requires to browse AWB's data and DWB's data in a uniform way. The SCB is developed by *Datamont (Italy)*.

4 Integration Support

All data stored in the object base are supported by the OMS public type definitions. As mentioned earlier, tool integration can be achieved either through the reuse of type definitions or through data sharing by using the same type definitions.

These type definitions support the sharing and exchange of data between tools. They are classified into three main types : object types, link types and attribute types. Each of these type definitions respectively represents objects, links and attributes that are stored in the object base.

An object type defines a set of objects having common characteristics. The characteristics of an object can be modeled by using link type and/or attribute type.

4.1 Integration via Reuse of Types

Data types used by a tool can be reused and extended for use by other tools. Reuse of types is achieved through the OMS schema type importation mechanism.

In order to demonstrate an efficient reuse of types by a set of integrated tools, generalization and characterization of the common and abstract features of the tools need to have been supported by a *higher-level tool*, which we shall also refer to as a *generic tool*. A generic tool is usually supported by a *generic model* [Lee91, Li90]. A generic model formalizes a set of abstract or generic concepts. These concepts provide an abstract view or overall perspective of the information used by other tools, which we shall refer to as *lower-level tools*. Therefore, it is possible to organize a hierarchy of generic types used by a set of tools. Each level in the hierarchy provides an appropriate perspective of the data used by the lower-level tools.

To allow the reuse of types of a generic tool by some lower-level tools, the common and abstract features of the generic tool can be modeled by the OMS type definitions and identified into a SDS. For instance, the SCB that is supported by a generic model, possesses some generic concepts that can be reused by the AWB and the DWB. In its generic model, there is an abstract concept called *feature* that is a generalization of its lower-level concepts such as *assertion*, *event*, *attribute* and *routine*. In addition, it has also the concept of *class*. These concepts can be organized into an inheritance hierarchy as shown in figure 7.

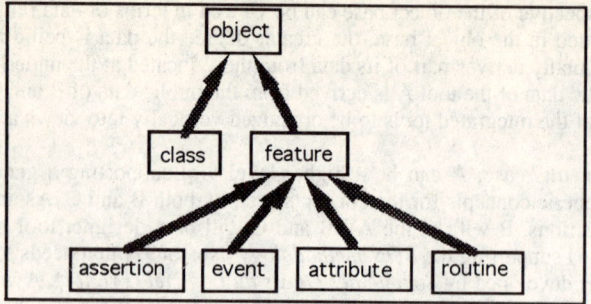

Fig. 7 The hierarchy of some generic concepts

The type definition *object* is the common ancestor type of all object types and is actually the most general pre-defined concept of the OMS. The concept of *class* is used to model components. Components are the basic units of information handled by the browser. Therefore, they are the instances of *class*. The components include documents, source code, object code, binary code and test data. Each component has a number of named attributes whose values belong to the associated data types, a number of assertions used to describe the constraints in it, a number of events for characterizing its behavior and a number of routines representing the actions that can perform on it.

There are two other generic concepts of SCB called *inheritance* and *client-supplier* that can be modeled by the OMS relationships. The concept of *inheritance* is used to model the inheritance of the properties of one component by another, whereas the concept of *client-supplier* is used to model the transfer of messages from one component to another.

Each relationship is composed of two link type definitions. Other relationships between the concepts are also modeled by using the OMS relationships. Figure 8 shows the SDS of SCB containing the various type definitions for the concepts and their relationships. It is actually the meta-model of SCB.

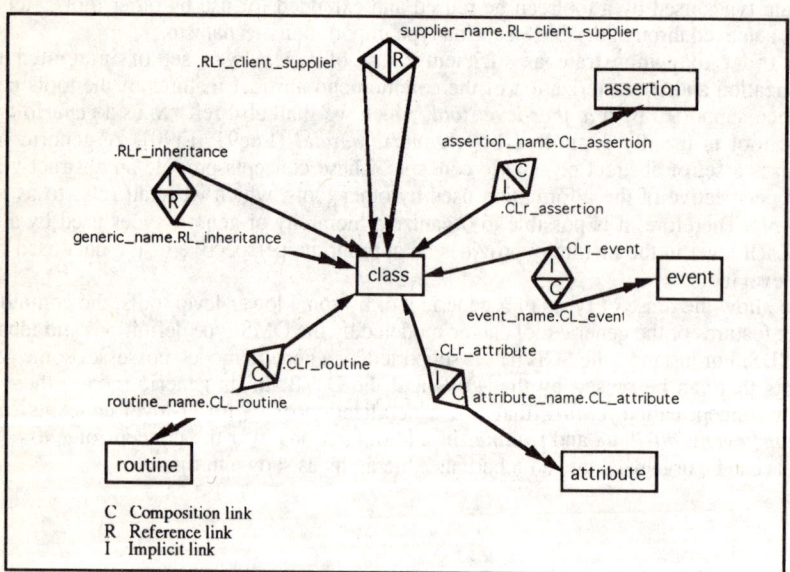

Fig. 8 The SDS of SCB

Notice that there are three categories of links : composition links, reference links and implicit links. Notice also that the inheritance and client-supplier relationships are modeled through the reference and implicit link types. This signifies respectively that an object of *class* inherits from another object of *class* and an object of *class* provides a client-supplier service to another object of *class*.

Other relationships are modeled using the composition and implicit link types. A composition link type has a stronger semantic in the sense that a component object cannot exist without a composition link leading to it from an object. The figure illustrates that an object of *class* possesses some objects of *assertion*, some objects of *event*, some objects of *attribute* and some objects of *routine*. For instance, an object of *event* can only be created by an object of *class* through a composition link called *CL_event* leading to it from the object of *class*, and in this case, the event name can be given to qualify the link. However, a reference link can be created as long as there are any two objects exist. For instance, an object of *class* called *person* and another object of *class* called *client* can be related to each other through the reference link *RL_inheritance* of the inheritance relationship, signifying that *client* inherits from *person* as shown in figure 9 at the instance level. In this case, *generic_name* will be instancated as *person*.

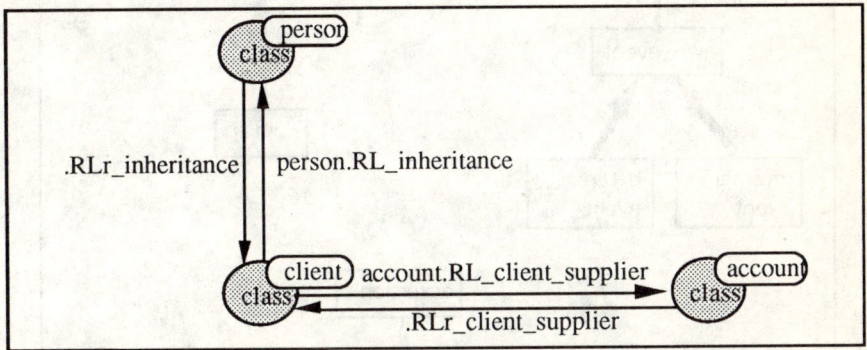

Fig. 9 Instanciation of the inheritance and client-supplier relationships

The same case arises in the client-supplier relationship. For instance, an object of *class* called *client* and another object of *class* called *account* are related to each other through the relationship that is composed of the reference link type *RL_client_supplier* and the implicit link type *RLr_client_supplier*. These two relationships can be deleted without affecting the instances of *class*.

An implicit link serves only as a purpose of navigation. For instance, it is possible to navigate from the object *person* to all its specializations.

4.1.1 Reuse of the Existing Types by the AWB

Certain concepts used by AWB can be treated as specializations of the concepts used by the generic model of SCB. This can be done by importing the object types declared in the SDS of SCB that represent SCB's various concepts into the SDS of AWB by the OMS type importation mechanism. An object type representing a certain AWB's concept can then be related to the appropriate imported object type through a specialization link. Figure 10 illustrates the reuse of the type definitions of SCB by the AWB. The O* concepts of AWB are represented by the shaded object types.

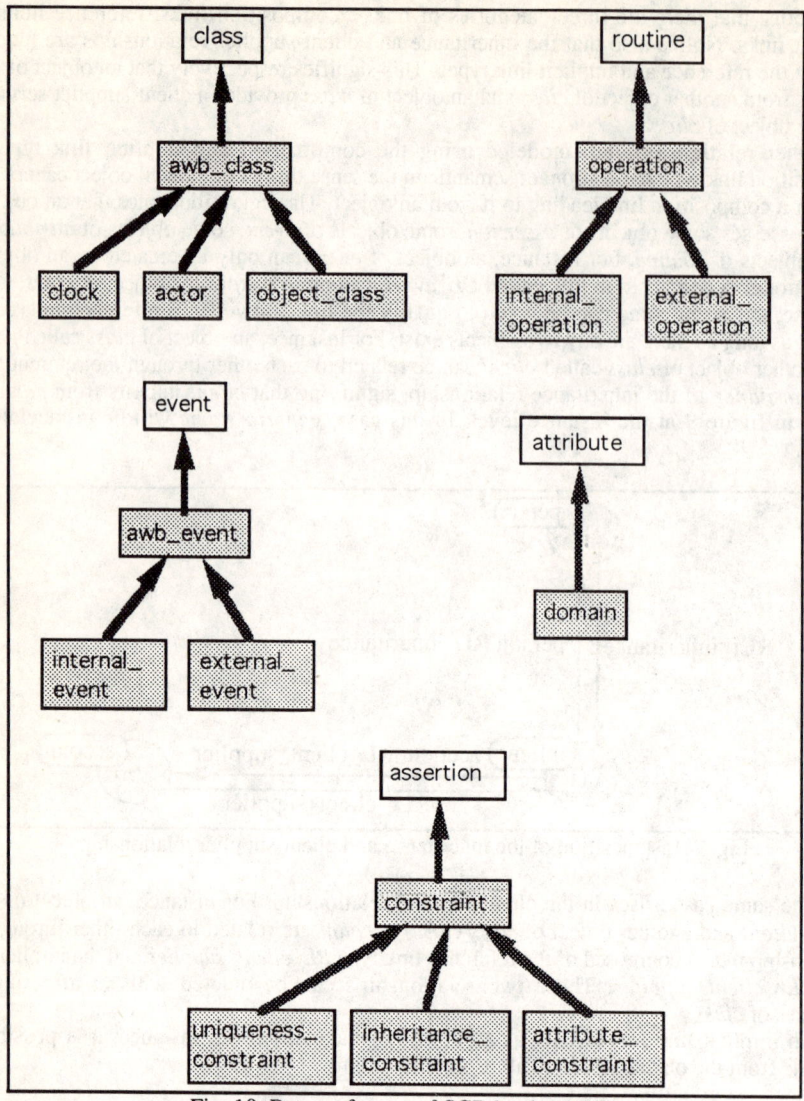

Fig. 10 Reuse of types of SCB by the AWB

Other than the concepts of operation and event, an object of an AWB class also possesses some domain properties and various types of constraints as illustrated in the figure. As a result of the importation and specializations, all relationships of the object type *class* declared in figure 8 will be inherited by the object type *awb_class*, which in turn, by the object types *clock*, *actor* and *object_class*. Each of these latter types has its appropriate features. These features are of no interest to SCB, but are used internally by the AWB. They will be dealt with in the next section.

As for the DWB, it is also possible to reuse certain type definitions of SCB. For instance, the concept *designer_class* can also be a specialization of *class*. The details of the concepts used by the model supporting the DWB will not be presented here.

As a result, it is possible for the SCB to access all objects of AWB and DWB without having to know their underlying features. This means that the SDS of SCB is the only SDS which is needed to be included in the SCB's working schema. A working schema contains a list of SDSs describing a tool's environment. The working schema of SCB will then serve as an inherited working schema for both the AWB and the DWB.

4.2 Integration via Data Sharing

A tool can have several SDSs describing about the information used by it. Therefore, it is possible to have a SDS describing its private data and another SDS describing its public data, where the latter is meant to be shared by other tools. Such case arises in AWB where part of its data is to be shared by DWB to allow any changes to the data to be made in the design phase. The changes can later be restored from the loading of the PCTE specifications into the AWB environment.

4.2.1 Public Working Schema

The SDS describing the public data of AWB possesses the type definitions for objects, links and attributes that are common to DWB. This implies that their semantics must be common to both tools too. It is through this SDS that the cooperation of AWB and DWB can be achieved. Semantically equivalent data of both tools are therefore modeled by using the same public type definitions of the OMS.

The public working schema of AWB contains all object type definitions as declared in figure 10 besides having a relationship that is composed of the reference link type *RL_operation_trigger* and the implicit link type *RLr_operation_trigger* as shown in figure 11. This relationship describes how an event triggers operations.

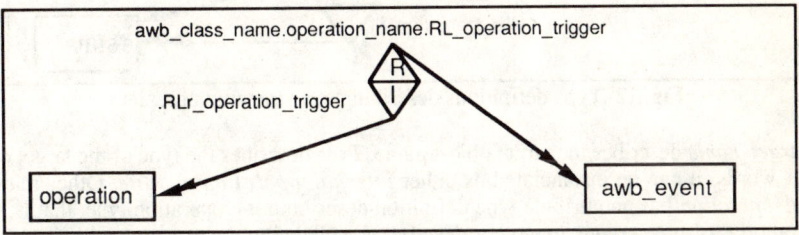

Fig. 11 Relationship describing an AWB event triggers AWB operations

In addition, the inheritance and client-supplier relationships declared in the browser's SDS have also been imported into the SDS of AWB so that these relationships can be extended to represent the concepts of AWB inheritance, composition and refering. The features that have been extended are the two attribute definitions called *client_supplier_category* and *client_supplier_type* which are attached to *RL_client_supplier. Client_supplier_category* describes the link categories of O* model, that is, whether a link is of type composition or refering, whereas *client_supplier_type* describes whether a link is of simple type or multiple type. The following describes the attribute type definitions that have been attached to each object type definition of AWB.

Object type definition	Attribute type definitions attached
1. *domain*	*domain_type* (contains all pre-defined types)
	domain_class (either simple or multiple)
2. *operation*	*text_operation*
3. *internal_operation*	*inherited* (either true or false)
4. *RL_operation_trigger*	*trigger_condition*
	trigger_factor
5. *awb_event*	*comment*
6. *constraint*	*constraint_text*
7. *internal_event*	*internal_event_predicat*
8. *external_event*	*external_event_message*
9. *awb_class*	*comment*

In order to share AWB's data, the working schema of DWB has to include the SDS of SCB besides the SDS of AWB describing the public data.

4.2.2 Private Working Schema

The AWB possesses a SDS describing the private data for its internal use. For instance, the definitions for state transition graphs and abstract classes of AWB are not meant to be shared by other tools. Therefore, they are included in the SDS constituting the private working schema. The state transition graphs are described by the type definitions as shown in figure 12.

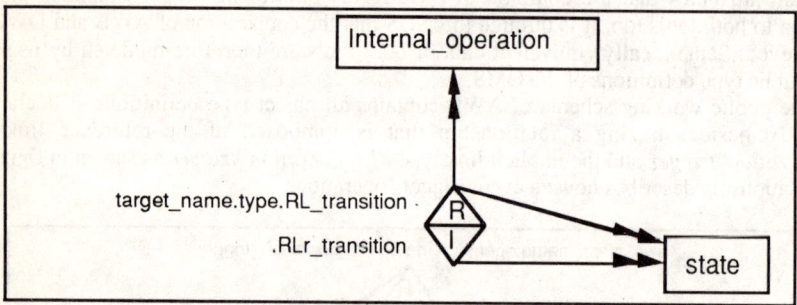

Fig. 12 Type definitions describing state transition graphs

Target_name describes the target object name. *Type* describes the type of the target object, in other words, it can be instanciated as either *internal_operation* or *state*. Other than this, *internal_operation* has an attribute type definition describing the operation type, that is, either an operation is of type *create*, *update* or *delete*. It is included in the private working schema so that there is no way for the DWB to modify the type of an operation once it has been created in the analysis environment. There are also two attribute type definitions called *state_description* and *initial_state* that have been attached to *state*, indicating respectively the state description and whether the state is an initial state. Other type definitions of the SDS providing information for describing AWB's static schema and abstract classes can be summarized as in figure 13.

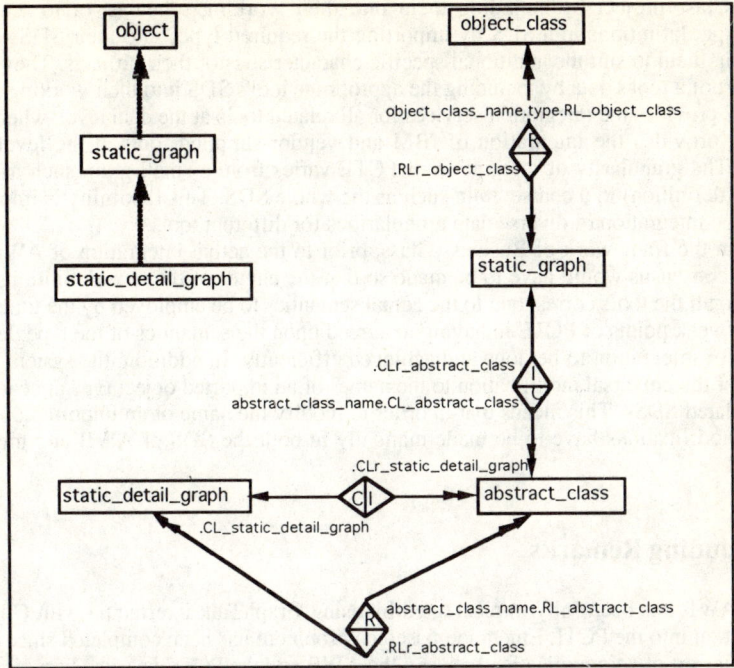

Fig. 13 Description for AWB's static schema and abstract classes

The static graph that indicates AWB's static schema references the set of all AWB object classes and is also composed of some abstract classes. These are described respectively in the relationship containing the reference link type *RL_object_class* and the relationship containing the composition link type *CL_abstract_class*. Every abstract class possesses a static detail graph that describes its underlying classes and the relationships between these classes. The fact that an abstract class includes AWB classes (object classes and abstract classes) is described in the inheritance hierarchy comprising the object type *static_graph* as the generic object type and the object type *static_detail_graph* as the specialized object type. In this case, the object type *static_detail_graph* inherits the relationship type containing the reference link type *RL_object_class* from *static_graph*. Moreover, the possibility for an abstract class to refer to some other abstract classes is described in the relationship containing the reference link type *RL_abstract_class*. It indicates that a static detail graph can refer to some other abstract classes.

5 Comparisons with Related Work

The main reason of using PCTE as an integration medium for our development work is due to its open architecture that caters for all kinds of software tools, unlike the IBM AD/Cycle that only caters for IBM tools and vendor-supplied tools. In terms of type reuse and data sharing, it is possible for other developers to reuse the ideas of an existing project such as the Business Class and to share the information of its tools if they find that their projects possess some similar characteristics in terms of type definitions. For instance, they might discover that it is possible to reuse all existing type definitions in one of the SDSs used in the

Business Class project by including them into their working schemas, or to reuse some existing type definitions in a SDS by importing the required types into their SDSs and then specializing them to suit the additional specific characteristics of their projects. They can also share a part of a tool's data by including the appropriate tool's SDS into their working schemas.

PCTE provides the integration services for all related tools at the data level, whereas IBM AD/Cycle provides the integration of IBM and vendor-supplied tools at the level of user interface. The granularity of integration of PCTE varies from a small grain such as a single data type (definition) to a coarse grain such as the whole SDS. This flexibility is important as it allows the integration of diverse data granularities for different tools.

Within the framework of Business Class, prior to the actual integration of AWB, DWB and SCB, consensus would have to be made so that the names of the type definitions that are common to all the tools correspond to the actual semantics to be employed by the tools. This is one of the weak points of PCTE in having to agreed upon the semantics of the type definitions precisely for integration to be done and achieved efficiently. In addition, the system does not take care of the universal modification to the names of an imported object type appeared in the various related SDSs. This means that in order to modify the name of an imported object type of SCB, modifications have to be made manually in both the SDS of AWB and the SDS of DWB.

6 Concluding Remarks

The AWB has been fully implemented by using GraphTalk interfacing with C language. Its integration into the PCTE Emeraude-based environment has been completed since February 1993. Some sort of communication between the AWB and the PCTE has also been done, as for instance, it is possible to generate the PCTE specifications of a given information system modeled by the O* model from the AWB and vice-versa. The results of cross evaluations of AWB in terms of completeness, correctness, robustness, user friendliness and the quality of documentation carried out by the various partners are satisfactory. The integration aspect will be evaluated soon in accordance with these criteria.

The integration of AWB in the PCTE Emeraude-based SEE via data sharing and reuse of types from a generic tool has been presented. It is through these two aspects that two tools are able to communicate with each other by imposing a common standard on their data definitions. With this, there is no question of allowing two tools to be developed independently and simultaneously, such as the case of AWB and DWB that have been developed in two different phases of the development life-cycle. It is through such integration that allows a larger tool to be composed of other lower-level tools.

Acknowledgments : We are grateful to Jean-Luc Barbe of Télésystèmes for his valuable ideas and the useful discussions during the development work. We thank the anonymous referees for their helpful remarks and useful suggestions.

References

[Booch86] Grady Booch, "Object-Oriented Development", IEEE Transactions on Knowledge and Data Engineering, Vol. SE-2, No. 2, February 1986.

[Boudier88] G. Boudier, F. Gallo, R. Minot, I. Thomas, "An Overview of PCTE and PCTE+", Proceedings of 3rd ACM Symposium on Software Environments, Nov., 1988.

[Brunet91] Jöel Brunet, "Modeling the World with Semantics Objects", <u>Conference on Object Oriented Approach in Information Systems</u>, Quebec, 1991.

[Cauvet89] Corine Cauvet, Colette Rolland, Christophe Proix, "A Design Methodology for Object-Oriented Database", <u>International Conference on Management of Data</u>, Hyderabad, 1989.

[Chen76] P. P. Chen, "The Entity-Relationship Model : Towards a Unified View of Data", <u>ACM Transactions on Database Systems</u>, Vol. 1, No. 1, March, 1976.

[Coad90] P. Coad, E. Yourdon, "Object-Oriented Analysis", <u>Prentice-Hall</u>, Englewood Cliffs, N. J., 1990.

[Emeraude92] GIE Emeraude, "Version Management, Integration & Development", <u>Syntagma Systems Literature</u>, UK, 1992.

[Essink91] L. J. B. Essink, "Object Modeling and System Dynamics in the Conceptualization Stages of Information Systems Development", <u>Conference on Object Oriented Approach in Information Systems</u>, Quebec, 1991.

[Faget92] ESPRIT P5327 REBOOT : "REBOOT Reference Book", edited by Faget, BULL, April 1992.

[Gallo87] F. Gallo, R. Minot, I. Thomas, "The Object Management System of PCTE as a Software Engineering Database Management System", <u>Proceedings of 2nd. ACM Symposium on Software Development Environment</u>, Jan., 1987.

[Legait88] A. Legait, F. Oquendo, "An advanced Software Engineering Environment Framework", <u>Second International Workshop on CASE</u>, Cambridge, July 12 - 15, 1988.

[Minot88] R. Minot, I. Thomas, "The Object Management System of PCTE and PCTE+", <u>Proceedings of IEEE Colloquium on Standard Interfaces for Software Tools</u> Sep., 1988.

[Li90] Q Li, "Extending semantic object model : towards more unified view of information objects", <u>Information and Software Technology</u>, Vol. 33, No. 2, 1990.

[Mercurio90] V.J. Mercurio, B. F. Meyers, A. M. Nisbet, G. Radin, "AD/Cycle Strategy and Architecture", <u>IBM Systems Journal</u>, Vol. 29, No. 2., 1990.

[Nerson92] Jean-Marc Nerson, "Applying Object-Oriented Analysis and Design", <u>Communications of the ACM</u>, Vol. 35, No. 9., 1992.

Prakash91] Naveen Prakash, "Specifying Operational Characteristics of Information Systems in OOD", <u>Conference on Object Oriented Approach in Information Systems</u>, Quebec, 1991.

[Lee91] Sai Peck Lee, "Mapping d'un réseau sémantique normalisé (modèle O*) en schéma O2 via un modèle Pivot", <u>Research report of DEA of Information Systems</u>, June, 1992.

[Lee92] Sai Peck Lee, Jöel Brunet, Colette Rolland, "Abstraction in the O* Object-Oriented Method", <u>Proceedings Indo-French Workshop on Object-Oriented Systems</u>, Goa, India, Nov. 2 - 6, 1992.

[Rolland91] Colette Rolland, O. Foucaut, G. Benci, "Conception des Systèmes d'Information", <u>EYROLLES</u>, 1991.

[Rumbaugh91] J. Rumbaugh, M. Blaha, W. Premerlani, F. Eddy, W. Lorensen, "Object-Oriented Modeling and Design", <u>Prentice Hall</u>, 1991.

[Shlaer88] S. Shlaer, S. J. Mellor, "Object Oriented Systems Analysis", <u>Yourdon Press</u>, 1988.

[Sutcliffe91] A. G. Sutcliffe, "Object Oriented Systems Analysis : The Abstract Question", <u>Conference on Object Oriented Approach in Information Systems</u>, Quebec, 1991.

[Télésystèmes92] Télésystèmes, "Analyst Workbench Tutorial", <u>Esprit II project 5311 (Business Class)</u>, prepared by Jöel Brunet, Sai Peck Lee and Jean-Luc Barbe, Feb. 1992.

[Thomas89] I. Thomas, "Software Environments : PCTE and related Projects", <u>IFIP World Computer Congress</u>, Aug., 1989.

Minimizing Dependency on Class Structures with Adaptive Programs [*]

Karl J. Lieberherr   Cun Xiao

Northeastern University, College of Computer Science
Cullinane Hall, Boston MA 02115
lieber@CCS.neu.EDU   cunxiao@CCS.neu.EDU

Abstract

Adaptive software is a new kind of generic software which attempts to minimize and localize dependency on the context in which the software will be used. An adaptive program is written in terms of constraints on the customizing context in which the program may be used. The constraints are written so that they only encode necessary dependencies and at the same time they localize information on groups of collaborating classes.

Adaptive software is usually written for a given context in mind and therefore it is important that the adaptive program does not use too much information from the current context. Therefore, we introduce in this paper a dependency metric which measures context dependency between an adaptive program and a customizer. The paper also discusses how constraints on customizing contexts can be written so that information loss is eliminated.

1   Introduction

A key feature of object-oriented programming is that methods are attached to classes (C++, Smalltalk, Eiffel, Beta) or to a group of classes (CLOS). An object-oriented program is usually written in such a way that details of the class structure are encoded into methods repeatedly. This leads to programs which are hard to evolve and maintain. Therefore, today's object-oriented programs often contain a lot of redundant application specific information which limits their reusability.

This paper goes beyond object-oriented programming, yet it builds on all the advantages of the object-oriented paradigm. Figure 1 summarizes how we generalize object-oriented programming by binding methods to classes beyond program-writing time. Component C contains a list of propagation patterns[LHSLX92, Lie92, LX93, LSLX93, Lie94] which keep the assignment of methods to classes flexible. Each propagation pattern defines a family of procedures or functions involving a group of collaborating classes. A member of the family is selected by a class structure. As soon as a class structure is selected, the methods defined by a propagation pattern are assigned to specific classes.

---

[*]Supported by the National Science Foundation under grant numbers CCR-9102578 (Software Engineering) and CDA-9015692 (Research Instrumentation).

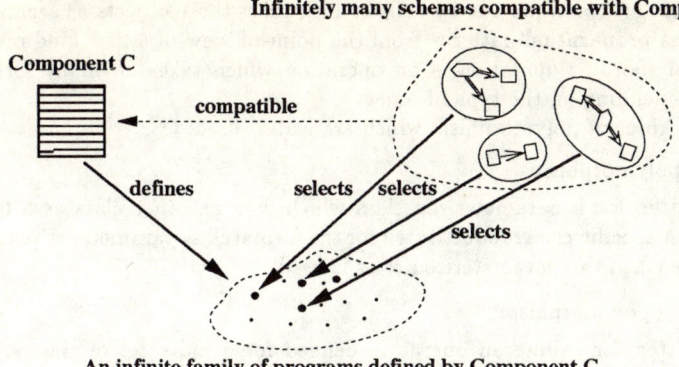

Figure 1: Select programs from a family

A propagation pattern is written in a succinct notation at a higher level of abstraction than an object-oriented language such as C++ or Smalltalk. The consequence is that a propagation pattern describes a family of programs. We can select a member of the family by providing a specific class structure which satisfies the assumptions made in the adaptive program.

We use the following analogy between SQL and propagation patterns to explain propagation patterns [Ada93]. An SQL query selects data records from a database while a propagation pattern selects a family of object-oriented programs from the set of all object-oriented programs. An SQL query is written at a logical level, abstracting from the implementation details in the database. By analogy, a propagation pattern is written at a logical level, abstracting from the details of a class structure.

At WOOD '93 (Workshop on Object-Oriented Design) in Snowbird, Utah, the style rule "keep your programs minimally dependent on the class structure" was considered as a useful guideline. Propagation patterns allow to follow this rule since a propagation pattern is written in terms of a partial class structure and it can be used with any complete class structure which is compatible with the partial class structure. A partial class structure is written in terms of "path expressions" in a generalized entity-relationship diagram, known as a class dictionary graph.

Another topic discussed at WOOD '93 was the overspecification present in object-oriented software. Propagation patterns make an important contribution to avoid overspecification, by allowing the user to follow the Pareto-principle which also applies here: for a given task, 80% of the work is done by 20% of the "interesting" classes. Propagation patterns allow to focus on those interesting classes.

A propagation pattern is similar to a genre [Ada93]. According to the Random House Dictionary a genre is a category of artistic endeavour having a particular form, content or technique. A collection of propagation patterns describes a category of object-oriented programs all having a particular form, but the details of the programs is left open. Even the input objects to the programs are left flexible. The artistic metaphor of a genre carries further: a propagation pattern describes how to "bring the actors on the stage" without hardcoding the class structure. Bringing the actors on the stage means to assemble the right objects so that an operation can be called which takes those objects as arguments.

Next we discuss propagation patterns from the point of view of a new kind of polymorphism. A polymorphic operation is an operation which takes on many forms of implementation depending on the type of object.

There are two kinds of polymorphism which are widely used:

- parametric polymorphism

    Code is written for a parameterized class which uses an other class as a formal parameter. A specific class is substituted for the formal class parameter at program-writing time when the parameterized class is used.

- operation-call polymorphism

    Code is written for calling an operation defined for a finite set of classes. The decision which operation to call is made at run-time.

Propagation patterns use a new kind of polymorphism, called adaptive polymorphism. Code is written for a group of collaborating classes which satisfy a partial class structure. A specific class structure compatible with the partial class structure is substituted when the code is used. Adaptive polymorphism relies both on parametric and operation-call polymorphism.

How does a propagation pattern program compare to an object-oriented program? In an object-oriented program, one codes object behavior as operations attached to specific classes. If one desires to call a behavior at the bottom of a composite object, many objects in that hierarchy must have a behavior which "passes the call" down one level. This sequence of behaviors is absolutely dependent on the existing class structure, and any changes to the class structure require that this sequence be examined, and possibly modified. If propagation patterns are used, all the "pass the call" behaviors are generated *automatically* for all classes for which they are required, and the code for the desired behavior is inserted in the bottom class and/or in important classes in between. The important result is that object behaviors coded as propagation patterns are *not* specifically attached, at coding time, to any class. Since the "pass the call" behaviors are generated automatically, they are somewhat insensitive to changes in the class structure. Propagation pattern programs are data-structure-shy programs which repel data-structure details even in the implementation. Object behaviors coded as propagation patterns can also be re-used, without modification, in a different context (i.e., for a different application with different classes and a different class structure). Therefore, propagation patterns are adaptive programs.

In the following we use the Demeter model, because of its simplicity, for explaining propagation patterns. However, propagation patterns can also be integrated into other object-oriented models, such as Rumbaugh and Booch (see section 5). Consider the following example of a propagation pattern which adds the cost of Thing-objects in a Container-object.

```
operation  int cost() init (@ 0 @)
    traverse
        from Container via Thing to Cost
    wrapper Cost
    prefix
    begin  return_val += val;  end
```

The partial class structure defined by this propagation pattern says that there must be a class `Container` which is related to a class `Thing` which itself is related to a class `Cost`. The relations are any kind of binary relations, such as knows-about, part-of or has-a, and is-a or kind-of. The `Cost` class is required to be in a relation, called `val`, with a class for which addition of an integer is defined.

Two class structures which satisfy the rules of the partial class structure are given in Figs. 2 and 3. They lead to two possible customizations of the program. The class structures are drawn like entity-relationship diagrams and are described in more detail later.

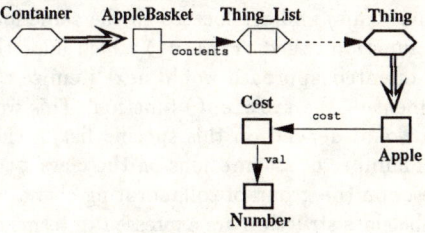

Figure 2: AppleBasket

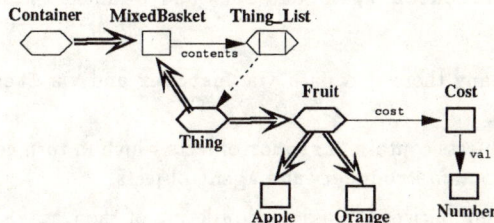

Figure 3: MixedBasket

An important goal when writing adaptive software is to minimize assumptions on class structure since this will make the software more flexible. Therefore, we introduce a dependency metric to analyze adaptive programs. The dependency metric indicates for a given a class structure how dependent the adaptive program is on the class structure. Therefore programmers can develop their adaptive programs for concrete class structures and measure how many unnecessary assumptions they have built into their adaptive programs.

Also, before testing an adaptive program, a compatible class structure has to be chosen. Again, the dependency metric serves as a useful guide to choose a test-case which exercises all aspects of the partial class structure in the adaptive program.

The rest of the paper is organized as follows: Section 2 gives examples of adaptive and extensible software. Section 3 discusses information loss and how to control it. Section 4 shows how to measure the dependency of an adaptive program on a class structure. Section 5 briefly discusses the applicability to other models. The conclusions are in Section 6.

2 Adaptiveness and Extensibility Example

We use an example to show how to design and write an adaptive and extensible object-oriented program.

2.1 Program Families

Suppose we have a company which works with producers who manufacture product items which are sold by sales agents to customers. We would like to find all the triples of customers, producers and sales agents such that they do business together (i.e. they buy, produce and sell the same items) and are located in the same location. In other words, we need to implement a function called `triples()` which finds the desired entities.

The standard object-oriented approach would next itemize a group of collaborating classes needed for implementing the `triples()` function. This would have the disadvantage that the algorithm would depend on this specific list of classes. Instead, we only want to make a minimal number of assumptions on the class structure and we then use those assumptions to describe the group of collaborating classes we need.

Assumptions about the class structure are expressed in terms of *class-valued variables* and *relation-valued variables*. The class-valued variables will be mapped to real classes later when we select a specific program from the infinite set of programs we are going to describe. We assume about the class structure that we have class-valued variables `Company`, `Customer`, `Producer`, `Agent` and `Item` and we make the following additional assumptions:

Company: From `Company` there is a path via `Customer` and via `Item` to `Producer` and `Agent`.

> I.e., `Company`-objects contain `Customer`-objects which in turn contain `Item`-objects which in turn contain `Producer`- and `Agent`-objects.
>
> The following summarizes the assumed ordering of the classes:
>
> ```
>         Company
>         Customer
>         Item
> Producer  Agent
> ```

Customer: We assume that a customer has a name and a location.

Item: The relations between `Item` and `Producer` and between `Item` and `Agent` are 1-1 relations.

Producer: We assume that a producer has a name and a location.

Agent: We assume that an agent has a name and a location.

With those assumptions we can now formulate a program which will work with any class structure which satisfies those assumptions. Therefore, we have now set up the right structure to write an infinite family of programs. We can later select specific programs from this family by applying the program to a class structure which satisfies the assumptions. To write the program, we first describe the group of collaborating classes which are needed to implement the `triples()` function. Since the details of the class structure are not known, a generic specification of the collaboration group is given, instead of an itemized list of collaborators. The generic specification is expressed (in our notation which allows us to describe object-oriented programs) as:

$$\underline{\text{from}}\ \texttt{Company}\ \underline{\text{via}}\ \texttt{Customer}\ \underline{\text{via}}\ \texttt{Item}\ \underline{\text{to}}\ \texttt{Producer Agent}. \qquad (1)$$

Expression (1), called *a propagation directive*, specifies a group of collaborating classes, namely all the classes on the paths from `Company` via `Customer` and `Item` to `Producer` and `Agent`. For a formal definition of reachability we refer the reader to [LX93]. The *propagation directive* not only specifies a group of collaborating classes but also traversal code, which will find all the `Producer`- and `Agent`-objects which are reachable via `Customer`- and `Item`-objects from a given `Company`-object. This traversal function does good work for us, but it does not solve yet the problem. Therefore, we need an annotation mechanism which allows us to adjust the traversal code. The annotations are needed to allow code modifications to be expressed at the level of abstraction of adaptive software; the annotations are specified independently of the traversal code specifications which makes the software more flexible. We allow two different kinds of annotations:

1. Code enhancement

   When a propagation directive such as (1), is applied to a specific class structure, we get a set of paths which describe the traversal defined by the propagation directive. Generating methods for the classes belonging to the set of paths implements the traversal (see Fig. 8 for an example). The generated traversal code can be enhanced by adding code fragments to various classes which participate in the traversal.

   We can add more code before and/or after the generated methods of some classes. We call the additional code *wrapper code fragments*.

2. Transportation directives

   With transportation directives, we can flexibly control the transportation of objects as we traverse objects.

The annotations needed for our example, are given and commented in Figs. 4 and 5. Fig. 7 shows how objects are transported to an `Item`-object where the bulk of the computation is done.

Component `triples` defines a family of programs which provide the `triples()` function implemented by the propagation pattern in Fig. 5.

Two class dictionary graphs will be given to customize the adaptive program and to select two different C++ programs from the family. The two class dictionary graphs have different structures and define different objects. We will explain the customization process in detail by using the class structure in Fig. 6. The customization interprets component `triples` in the context of a class dictionary graph.

2.2 Selecting Members from a Family of Programs

In Fig. 6 is the first customizer, called `Company1`. It is a class structure in graphical form which satisfies the assumptions listed in Figs. 4 and 5. We call such a graph structure

Component description: If customer C orders an item made by producer P through agent A and they are all located in the same place, then print out their names.	
Component specification	Comments

<u>component</u> triples
 	
  <u>class dictionary graph examples</u> Company1
  <u>meta</u>
    <u>class-valued variables</u>
      Company, Customer, Item, Producer, Agent
      Producer, Agent
    <u>relation-valued variables</u>
      location, name
    <u>directives</u>
      $C\_PA =$ <u>from</u> Company
              <u>via</u> Customer
              <u>via</u> Item
              <u>to</u> Producer Agent;
      $C\_I =$ <u>from</u> Customer <u>to</u> Item;
      $I\_P =$ <u>from</u> Item <u>to</u> Producer;
      $I\_A =$ <u>from</u> Item <u>to</u> Agent;
  <u>end</u>
  <u>provides</u>
    <u>public</u>
      <u>operation</u> triples()
        <u>access</u> Company
<u>end</u> triples
	Component triples can be applied to class dictionary graph Company1.
	
	C_PA, C_I, I_P and I_A are graph-valued variables defining collaboration graphs and transportation graphs.
	
	Operation triples() is public to the outside of the component. It can only be accessed through class Company.

Figure 4: Component triples

which is like a generalized entity-relationship diagram, a *class dictionary graph*[LBSL91, LX93]. There are two kinds of relations in the class structure, kind-of relations (drawn as $\Longrightarrow$) and part-of relations (drawn as $\longrightarrow$). In the class dictionary graph, we call kind-of relations *alternation edges*, part-of relations *construction edges*. Each construction edge has a label which is the name of the relation the edge represents. There are two kinds of classes in the class structure, abstract classes (drawn as $\bigcirc$) and concrete classes (drawn as $\square$). In the class dictionary graph, abstract classes are called *alternation vertices*, and concrete classes are called *construction vertices*.

Propagation pattern	Comments

operation triples()
   access Company
   traverse C_PA
   carry c_name,c_location: in Ident
        along C_I
   at Customer
     c_name = this→get_name();
     c_location = this→get_location();
   carry p_name,p_location: out Ident
        along I_P
   at Producer
     p_name = this→get_name();
     p_location = this→get_location();
   carry a_name,a_location: out Ident
        along I_A
   at Agent
     a_name = this→get_name();
     a_location = this→get_location();
   wrapper Item
     suffix
     begin
       if (c_location→g_equal(a_location)
       && p_location→g_equal(a_location))
       {
         c_name→g_print();
         p_name→g_print();
         a_name→g_print();
       }
     end
 end triples
	The functionality provided by the propagation pattern can only be used through class Company with signature operation triples().
	
	 The traversal is defined by C_PA and the object transportation is expressed with 3 transportation directives.
	
	 Two Ident-objects which are the name and location of the customer are transported from the Customer-object to the Item-object contained by the Customer-object.
	
	 Four Ident-objects which are the names and locations of the Producer- and Agent-objects are transported back to the Item-object which contains them. Argument mode out means call-by-reference. Argument mode in means call-by-value.
	
	 See Fig. 7.
	 At each Item-object, locations are compared and names are printed if required. g_equal and g_print are generic functions for comparison and printing.

Figure 5: Propagation pattern **operation triples()**

We explain the class dictionary graph in English. Construction class Company has a part-of relation called customers with alternation class Customer_List. In other words, a Company-object has a list of Customer-objects called customers which are the customers of the company. In part customers can be either an object of construction class Customer_Empty or of construction class Customer_NonemptyList. Alternation class Customer_List represents a list of zero or more Customer-objects. Construction class `Customer_Empty` represents an empty list of `Customer`-objects. Construction class `Customer_NonemptyList` represents a list of at least one `Customer`-object and it has two part-of relations with `Customer` and `Customer_List`. The first relation, called `first`, represents the first `Customer`-object in the list. The second relation, called `rest`, represents the rest of the `Customer`-objects in the list. Construction class `Customer` has three part-of relations. Part-of relations `name` and `location` are with construction class `Ident`. Part-of relation `orders` is with alternation class `Item_List`. In terms of objects, a `Customer`-object has three part-objects. The `Ident`-object referred by `name` is the name of the customer. The `Ident`-object referred by `location` is the location where the customer lives. The `Item_List`-object referred by `orders` is the list of `Item`-objects the customer has ordered.

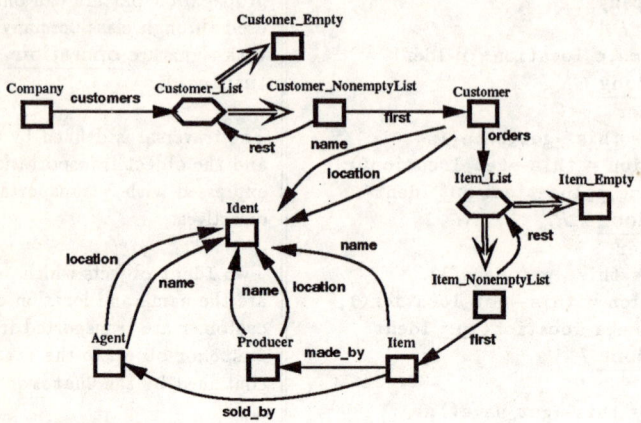

Figure 6: Customizer 1: Class dictionary graph `Company1`

Propagation directive (1) defines a set of paths from `Company` to `Producer` and `Agent`. Three examples are:

1. $\text{Company} \xrightarrow{customers} \text{Customer\_List} \Longrightarrow \text{Customer\_NonemptyList} \xrightarrow{first} \text{Customer} \xrightarrow{orders}$
   $\text{Item\_List} \Longrightarrow$
   $\text{Item\_NonemptyList} \xrightarrow{first} \text{Item} \xrightarrow{sold\_by} \text{Agent}$

2. $\text{Company} \xrightarrow{customers} \text{Customer\_List} \Longrightarrow \text{Customer\_NonemptyList} \xrightarrow{first} \text{Customer} \xrightarrow{orders}$
   $\text{Item\_List} \Longrightarrow$
   $\text{Item\_NonemptyList} \xrightarrow{first} \text{Item} \xrightarrow{made\_by} \text{Producer}$

3. $\text{Company} \xrightarrow{customers} \text{Customer\_List} \Longrightarrow \text{Customer\_NonemptyList} \xrightarrow{first} \text{Customer} \xrightarrow{orders}$
   $\text{Item\_List} \Longrightarrow$
   $\text{Item\_NonemptyList} \xrightarrow{rest} \text{Item\_List} \Longrightarrow \text{Item\_NonemptyList} \xrightarrow{first} \text{Item} \xrightarrow{sold\_by} \text{Agent}$

According to the first path, we locate the first `Customer`-object in a list of `Customer`-objects which belongs to a `Company`-object, then we follow part-of relation `orders` to locate its part-object, an `Item_List`-object, then we locate the first `Item`-object in the `Item_List`-object. The `Item`-object is the first item ordered by the customer. Finally we reach the `Agent`-object which is the part-object of the first `Item`-object.

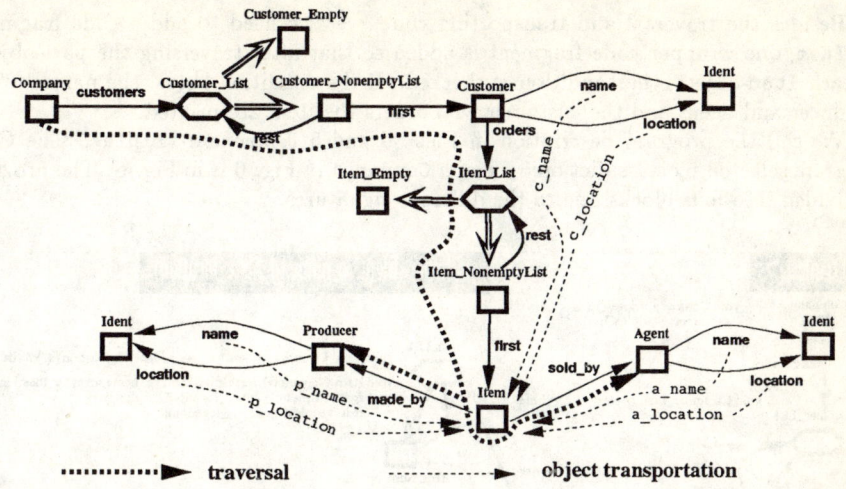

Figure 7: Bringing the actors on stage

The second path describes the same traversal as the first one except that finally we reach a `Producer`-object instead of an `Agent`-object.

The third path also describes the same traversal as the first one except that we choose the second `Item`-object from an `Item_List`-object instead of the first `Item`-object.

We call all such paths *knowledge paths*, since they follow the knowledge links between objects [LX93].

In order to solve the problem we posed, we need to transport objects during traversing from each `Customer`-object to the `Producer`- and `Agent`-objects (see Fig. 7). We want to transport two `Ident`-objects which are the name and location of a `Customer`-object to each `Item`-object ordered by the customer. For each `Item`-object, we also want to transport the four `Ident`-objects which are the names and locations of its producer and agent to the `Item`-object. Then, at each `Item`-object conditions can be checked and desired actions are taken. In other words, at an item object we need six "actors", all identifier objects, to "play" the next "scene". Recall that **&&** is the *and* operator of C++.

The object transportation is specified by transportation directives which are implemented by adding arguments to the signatures of those classes which participate in the transportation. This implementation process is called *signature extension*. A transportation directive consists of an argument declaration part, a transportation part (after the keyword **along**) and an initialization part (after the keyword **at**). The arguments name the variables which will be transported, the transportation part specifies the transportation scope and the initialization part defines initialization of the arguments. Similar to the argument modes in Ada, argument mode **in** is provided. It is used to pass down `Ident`-objects from each `Customer`-object to each `Item`-object contained by the `Customer`-object. Argument mode **out** is also provided. By using mode **out**, for example, after traversing each `Item`-object the four `Ident`-objects which are the names and locations of the `Item`-object's producer and agent can be brought back. The signature syntax we use conforms with the CORBA and IDL notation which OMG uses.

Besides the traversal and transporting code, we also need to add a code fragment. At `Item`, one wrapper code fragment is added so that after traversing the part-objects of each `Item`-object, the condition is checked. If the condition holds, the names of the producer and agent and the customer who orders the item are printed.

We call the program description in Figs. 4 and 5 *component* `triples`. The C++ program selected by class dictionary graph `Company1` in Fig. 6 is in Fig. 8. The program is divided into four blocks due to the different signatures.

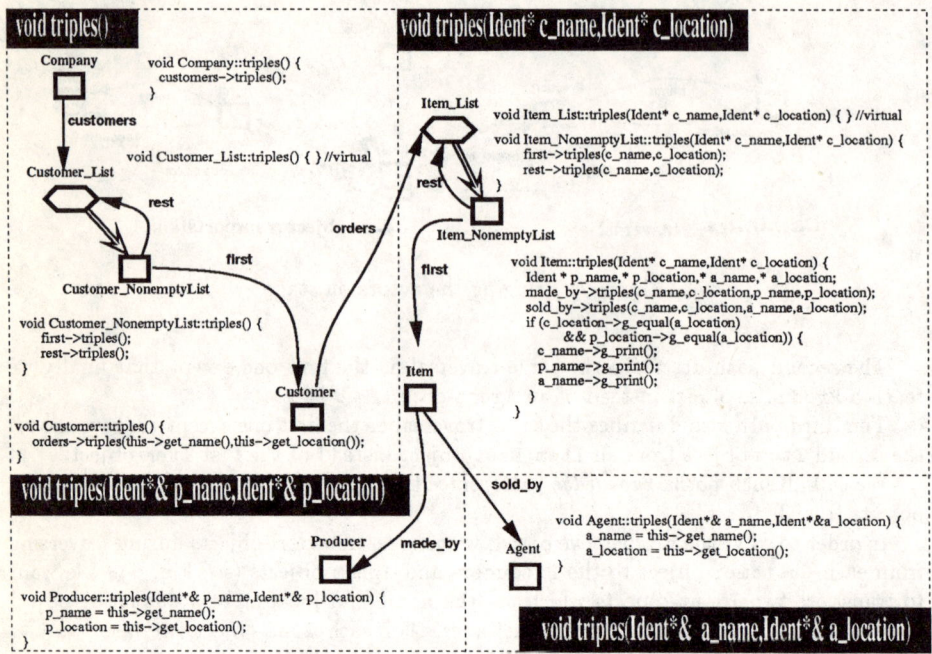

Figure 8: After customization of `triples` with class dictionary graph `Company1`

2.3 Adaptiveness of Components

Component `triples` is adaptive since it works for many different class structures. In Fig. 9 a second customizer is shown which uses two repetition vertices (drawn as ⬲) `Customers` and `Items` and a construction class `Warehouse` are introduced. The two repetition vertices are used to replace two alternation vertices and four construction vertices which are `Customer_List`, `Customer_Empty`, `Customer_NonemptyList`, `Item_List`, `Item_Empty` and `Item_NonemptyList`. Repetition vertices stand for collection classes. Repetition class `Customer_List` has a repeated part-of relation with `Customer` and it represents a list of zero or more `Customer`-objects, and the same for repetition class `Item_List`. Despite of these changes, component `triples` can still be used on class dictionary graph `Company2`, because the component does not depend on how list structures are specified, and what exactly the relation is between `Item` and `Producer`.

When we use class dictionary graph Company2 to select a C++ program from the family of programs defined by component triples, we will get a program different from the one in Fig. 8 because of the different class structure.

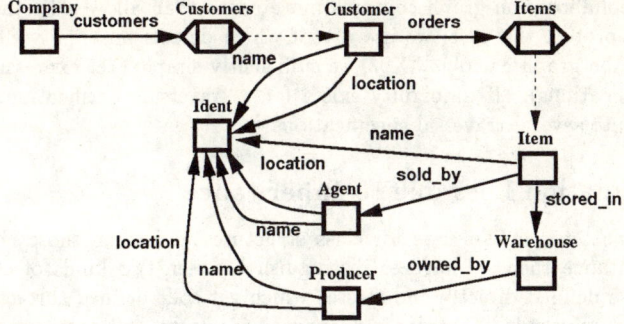

Figure 9: Customizer 2: Class dictionary graph Company2 with repetition vertices

Propagation patterns are much more flexible software artifacts than traditional object-oriented programs. We have shown how a program adapts itself to different class structures. When there is a large change to a class structure, it is much easier to adjust the propagation pattern rather than the corresponding object-oriented program. Propagation directive updates can be expressed by a propagation directive expression in the propagation directive calculus[LX93].

3 Avoiding Information Loss

Next we turn to two issues which are important for the practical use and implementation of propagation patterns.

3.1 Information Loss due to Path Union

When a propagation pattern is applied to a class dictionary graph, the collaboration graph is determined by the union of the knowledge paths. The reason for this encapsulation of a set of knowledge paths into a graph is that the collaboration graphs can be easily composed using a graph calculus. To manipulate sets of knowledge paths would be much harder. Unfortunately, the union of the paths into a graph can lose information: The union of paths might create new paths which are not among the original paths.

Let's consider the information loss problem with the class dictionary graph in Fig. 3. The propagation directive

  from MixedBasket
    through $\implies$ Thing, MixedBasket
  to Apple

says that the collaboration graph is determined by the union of all paths from MixedBasket to Apple which pass through the alternation edge from Thing to MixedBasket. However, the collaboration graph also includes the path which does not go through the alternation edge from `Thing` to `MixedBasket`. Therefore we have lost information by taking the union.

We say that a propagation directive is ambiguous with respect to a class dictionary graph if the collaboration graph contains more paths than allowed by the propagation directive. To protect the user, we use a tool which detects ambiguity efficiently. This requires that the graph calculus[LX93] be sufficiently simple (yet expressive enough for practical applications). If ambiguity exists for a traversal specification, it has to be decomposed into several traversal specifications.

3.2 Information Loss due to Inheritance

Propagation patterns define code for class structures and when those class structures contain inheritance then we have to distinguish between two kinds of classes: classes which get code defined directly and classes which get code defined through inheritance. This can cause unintended behavior in propagation patterns unless we limit the influence of the inheritance relations. Consider the class dictionary graph in Fig. 3 and the following propagation pattern:

```
operation int sumApples() init (@ 0 @)
   traverse
      from MixedBasket via Apple to Cost
   wrapper Cost
      prefix
      begin return_val += val; end
```

The intention of this propagation pattern is to sum the cost of all apples into the predefined variable `return_val`. This only works, if class `Orange` does not inherit the code from class `Fruit`. Otherwise, the above propagation pattern has the same effect as:

```
operation int sumApples() init (@ 0 @)
   traverse
      from MixedBasket to Cost
   wrapper Cost
      prefix
      begin return_val += val; end
```

This would be undesirable since we lost the information that the path is forced through `Apple`. Therefore the following rule is used:

> For every alternation class C (except target classes) in a collaboration graph all the subclasses of class C which are contained in the original graph but not in the collaboration graph, get an empty operation generated.
>
> A target class is a class used in the __to__ clause in a propagation directive.

In the above example, class `Orange` will get an empty method generated.

4 Analysis and Testing of Adaptive Programs

When developing an adaptive program, we can either start with writing a class dictionary graph or with writing propagation patterns. In either case, we would like to keep the two as independent as possible. Suppose we start with writing propagation patterns. How can we test them once they are written? This question reduces to how we can test a propagation directive.

Given a propagation directive p, we assume that it is robust and will properly define a set of collaborating classes for a given task. We select a smallest class dictionary graph S compatible with p. Class dictionary graph S is the simplest case to test propagation directive p. Consider the propagation directive below.

$$\underline{\text{from}} \text{ Company } \underline{\text{through}} \longrightarrow \text{*, customers, * } \underline{\text{to}} \text{ Producer Agent} \qquad (2)$$

The above propagation directive combines all the paths from Company through some relation called customers to Producer and Agent. The stars mean "any class" and $\longrightarrow$ denotes a construction edge which is defined by a triple. The class dictionary graph in Fig. 10 is the minimal class dictionary graph which can be used to test the propagation directive. Class dictionary graphs in Figs. 6 and 9 are compatible with the propagation directive, but they are not of minimal size.

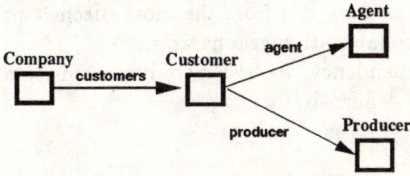

Figure 10: The smallest class dictionary graph

Now suppose that we already have a class dictionary graph S and that we know the evolution history of S in the form of a set of class dictionary graphs which describe the expected later versions of S. We want to write propagation patterns for S and the other class dictionary graphs. There are usually many ways of writing the propagation patterns and the designer needs guidance. The problem reduces to the following question: Given a group of class dictionary graphs and their corresponding desired collaboration graphs, how can we write a good propagation directive which selects the desired collaboration graphs for each of them?

A propagation directive for a class dictionary graph S has to satisfy two conflicting requirements: On one hand it should succinctly describe the paths which currently exist in S in order to make the propagation directive more adaptive, on the other hand it should make minimal assumptions on the paths which currently do not exist in S. The first requirement says that a propagation directive should use class dictionary graph information (vertices and labels) minimally, the other one says that to plan for future growth we use more than what is needed. An example explains this tradeoff. Consider the following two propagation directives.

$$\underline{\text{from}} \text{ Company } \underline{\text{to}} \text{ Number} \qquad (3)$$

$$\text{\underline{from} Company \underline{through} } \longrightarrow \text{*, salary, * \underline{to} Number} \qquad (4)$$

For a Company-object, we could use propagation directive (3) to find all the numbers which represent salary information if we have a class dictionary graph where Number is only used to represent salary information. However, to plan for future growth of the class dictionary graph, it is better to use propagation directive (4).

To succinctly express the existing paths, we need to write a propagation directive in such a way that it properly computes the collaboration graph for each class dictionary graph in a set which illustrates possible changes in class structure. To minimize the assumptions on the existing paths, we want to find a propagation directive p_{min} such that p_{min} and the set of class dictionary graphs are minimally dependent, which means that we cannot find a "smaller" propagation directive p' such that p' and p_{min} define the same collaboration graph for each class dictionary graph in the set.

To formalize the dependency concept used above, we introduce a function $Dep(p, \Upsilon)$ for a propagation directive d and a set of class dictionary graphs Υ. $Dep(p, \Upsilon)$ expresses the succinctness of a propagation directive p with respect to class dictionary graphs in Υ. A propagation directive is most succinct if it references a minimal number of class-valued variables and/or relation-valued variables.

If a propagation directive does not have minimal dependency w.r.t. a set of class dictionary graphs Υ, then the propagation directive must be motivated by robustness under expected class dictionary graph changes to the class dictionary graphs in Υ.

$Dep(p, \Upsilon)$ says how far away p is from the most succinct propagation directive p_{min} which defines the same collaboration graphs as p.

To formally define dependency, we first introduce a function $metaSize(p)$ for a propagation directive p. It is defined by:

$$metaSize(p) = \text{the number of distinct class-valued variables in } p\ +$$
$$\text{the number of distinct relation-valued variables in } p.$$

For example, the meta size of propagation directive (3) is 2, and of (4) is 3 and of (1) is 5.

In addition, we need an algorithm which solves the following minimization problem: Given a propagation directive p and a set of class dictionary graphs Υ, find a propagation directive p_{min} such that (**apply** p S) = (**apply** p_{min} S) for each class dictionary graph S in Υ and so that p_{min} has the minimal meta size. (**apply** means to compute the collaboration graph defined by a propagation directive and a class dictionary graph.) We call the algorithm $PDmin(p, \Upsilon)$ and it returns a propagation directive which makes minimal assumptions on the existing paths in Υ. For example, $PDmin$(propagation directive (1), {Company1}) returns the directive:

$$\text{\underline{from} Company \underline{to} Producer Agent} \qquad (5)$$

which has meta size 3.

We define the *dependency* for a propagation directive p and a set of class dictionary graphs Υ to be:

$$Dep(p, \Upsilon) = 1 - metaSize(PDmin(p, \Upsilon))/metaSize(p).$$

For example, Dep(propagation directive (1), { Company1 }) is 2/5. Nevertheless, propagation directive (1) is a good propagation directive since it is more robust under changing class structures.

We have $0 \leq Dep(p, \Upsilon) < 1$. The closer to zero the dependency is, the more succinct the propagation directive.

In object-oriented programs, all the classes and their attributes involved are explicitly mentioned. Instead of being written succinctly as with propagation patterns, each class involved will get a method which tells how the class participates. Therefore object-oriented programs have a dependency which is far away from 0. The consequence is that they are not adaptive and easy to evolve.

We can also use the dependency function to find better class dictionary graphs for testing a propagation directive p. Instead of only choosing a minimal, compatible class dictionary graph Φ, we choose one for which $Dep(p, \{\Phi\}) = 1$ and among all those we choose one with minimal size. This will result in a class dictionary graph which is minimally complex to justify all the aspects of the propagation directive.

This section has introduced a metric for propagation directives and class dictionary graphs which is useful for designing and testing propagation patterns. Given a propagation directive, the metric helps to find a good class dictionary graph for testing the directive and given a class dictionary graph, the metric helps to properly formulate a propagation directive.

When developing software with propagation patterns, we recommend that class dictionary graphs are used so that the dependency between all propagation directives and the corresponding class dictionary graphs is 0 unless the exception is motivated by robustness.

5 Applications to Other Models

We have presented propagation patterns in the context of the Demeter model which uses class dictionary graphs. Class dictionary graphs are a "minimal" object model which can be mapped easily into other object models. As an example, we show here how to map class dictionary graphs into Rumbaugh's OMT object model and how to use the propagation pattern technique with OMT.

The following mapping only covers a subset of OMT but it is sufficient to show that propagation patterns can be applied to OMT.

$Demeter$	OMT
construction class	class without subclasses
alternation class	class with subclasses
construction edge	attribute, or binary association or binary aggregation association
alternation edge	class/subclass link
path	derived association
optional construction edge	multiplicity of zero or one (open dot)
repetition edge	multiplicity of many (black dot)

In the OMT object model, associations are bidirectional, while in the Demeter object model parts are unidirectional. If needed, bidirectional associations can always be modeled with unidirectional parts.

6 Related Work

Ivar Jacobson writes in [Jac92]: "Use cases are a way to make complex systems understandable without, as a first step, trying to structure the system into ... objects ... Such structuring creates very technical descriptions which tend to shift the focus from the problem of understanding the requirement to dealing with implementation-like descriptions." We use Jacobson's vision when we work with propagation patterns: they can describe specific uses or views of an object system without, as a first step, defining the detailed structure of objects. A collaboration has started to integrate use cases and the Demeter Method.

Schema evolution is an important topic for object-oriented data bases [DZ91]. Propagation patterns facilitate evolution of the dynamic part of a schema.

Markku Sakkinen writes in [Sak88]: "The methods of a class should not depend in any way on the structure of any class, except the immediate top-level structure of their own class." With propagation patterns we can now go further and require that in addition to Sakkinen's view of the Law of Demeter, methods only depend on the really interesting classes.

7 Conclusion

Propagation patterns [Lie92, LHSLX92, LSLX93] and adaptive software are a useful addition to the concepts of object-oriented technology. The object-oriented programs which are written today can be significantly improved by lifting them to the higher level of abstraction of propagation patterns. The benefits are:

- Early pay-off. Propagation pattern programs contain as a special case ordinary object-oriented programs. The worst-style propagation patterns are programs written in one of today's object-oriented programming languages. Therefore, propagation patterns should be used in any project where an object-oriented programming language is used. Propagation patterns do not compromise execution efficiency; they are easy to learn and will pay off in the first project.

- Adaptiveness. For interesting changes to the structure of input, intermediate and output objects, propagation patterns adapt without modification.

- Extensibility. Propagation patterns can be easily modified to better meet particular needs.

- Reduced size of software. Propagation patterns are often significantly shorter than their object-oriented program counterparts. The reason is that a propagation pattern is description of an object-oriented programming and is therefore at a higher level of abstraction.

The key contributions of this paper are techniques to avoid information loss when designing propagation patterns and an analysis metric for propagation directives which helps to design and test adaptive software.

Acknowledgements

This work is also supported in part by IBM, Mettler-Toledo and Citibank. We would like to thank Doug Guptill, Walter Hürsch, Linda Keszenheimer, Cristina Lopes, Ignacio Silva-Lepe and Greg Sullivan for their feedback.

References

[Ada93] Sam Adams. Private communication. WOOD (Workshop on Object-Oriented Design, Snowbird, Utah, March 8-10), March 1993.

[DZ91] Christine Delcourt and Roberto Zicari. The design of an integrity consistency checker (ICC) for an object-oriented database system. In *European Conference on Object-Oriented Programming*, pages 377–396, Geneva, Switzerland, 1991. Springer Verlag.

[Jac92] Ivar Jacobson. The use case construct in object-oriented software engineering. Technical report, Objective Systems, 1992.

[LBSL91] Karl J. Lieberherr, Paul Bergstein, and Ignacio Silva-Lepe. From objects to classes: Algorithms for object-oriented design. *Journal of Software Engineering*, 6(4):205–228, July 1991.

[LHSLX92] Karl J. Lieberherr, Walter Hürsch, Ignacio Silva-Lepe, and Cun Xiao. Experience with a graph-based propagation pattern programming tool. In *International Workshop on CASE*, pages 114–119, Montréal, Canada, 1992. IEEE Computer Society.

[Lie92] Karl J. Lieberherr. Component enhancement: An adaptive reusability mechanism for groups of collaborating classes. In J. van Leeuwen, editor, *Information Processing '92, 12th World Computer Congress*, pages 179–185, Madrid, Spain, 1992. Elsevier.

[Lie94] Karl J. Lieberherr. *The Art of Growing Adaptive Object-Oriented Software*. PWS-Kent Publishing Company, 1994.

[LSLX93] Karl J. Lieberherr, Ignacio Silva-Lepe, and Cun Xiao. Adaptive object-oriented programming using graph-based customization. *Communications of the ACM*, 1993. Accepted for publication.

[LX93] Karl Lieberherr and Cun Xiao. Object-Oriented Software Evolution. *IEEE Transactions on Software Engineering*, 1993. in print.

[Sak88] Markku Sakkinen. Comments on "the Law of Demeter" and C++. *SIGPLAN Notices*, 23(12):38–44, December 1988.

First Class Messages as First Class Continuations*

Ken Wakita

Tokyo Institute of Technology
Department of Information Science
2-12-1, Ookayama, Meguro-ku
Tokyo 152 Japan
e-mail: wakita@is.titech.ac.jp

Key Words: Object-oriented concurrent programming, first class message, first class continuation, extensibility, communication, synchronization

Abstract

First class messages, which we call message continuations, provide object-oriented concurrent programming languages with extensibility in modeling and programming communication schemes such as asynchronous communication, multicasting, sophisticated synchronization constraints, inter-object synchronization, concurrency control, resource management, and so on. In spite of its powerful extensibility, the framework is sound in that the framework guarantees that no program can destroy the semantics of the built-in communication primitives. This good property was obtained by categorization of message continuations and careful design of the primitive operations on message continuations.

1 Introduction

Object-oriented programming languages provide powerful mechanisms for data abstraction and code reuse through encapsulation, inheritance, delegation, polymorphic type substitution, etc. However most object-oriented programming languages have very limited support of modeling and describing control structures (or communication structures). Due to this lack of extensibility in the dimension of *control abstraction*, the programmer often suffers from contaminating method definitions with fractions of code that implement protocols of control/communication structures. For instance, when asynchronous communication is required, the programmer has to modify the code of both the sender and the receiver to add asynchronous protocol. A flaw here is that the code that implements communication protocol is scattered over all the participants of asynchronous communication, leading to degradation of modularity and poor maintainability of the program. Another and still more serious problem is that addition of asynchronous protocol makes the reuse of classes more difficult because the method code includes part of the protocol, which is not part of the specification of the original class. Needless to say, concurrent programming languages should support such a simple communication primitive as asynchronous communication.[1] However, the

---

*The research was conducted during the author's six months visit to TRESE project, the University of Twente, the Netherlands.

[1]In practice, many communication primitives, including asynchronous message passing, have been proposed and incorporated in concurrent languages.

point is that even the most sophisticated set of communication protocols can not deal with all different kinds of communication schemes required by wide variety of applications. When a new communication scheme is required, lack of extensibility will exhibit the similar problems as adding asynchronous communication will take place. The goal of our research is not to propose yet another communication primitive, but to give powerful extensibility to concurrent languages, whereby almost any kind of communication scheme is programmable.

Lack of extensibility in modeling communication becomes a serious problem in distributed programming, because each application program requires different forms of communication and different synchronization schemes. Existing object-oriented concurrent programming languages have various synchronous/asynchronous communication primitives [YT86, Yon90, Ame87, Nie87, IT87, BHJL86] and some languages have built-in concurrency control features [BK91, WY90a]. However, these powerful but non-extensible communication primitives are not sufficient for modeling and describing more advanced communication/synchronization schemes, such as flexible concurrency control [BK91, WY90a], notification [EG89], intelligent negotiation platform [dJ91], etc.

The article introduces the concept of *first class continuation* into concurrent computation models. A *continuation* of a expression is the *rest of the computation* relative to the evaluation of the expression. Continuations can be defined for sequential execution of any program. The notion of continuations was introduced in describing denotational semantics of control structures such as **goto** statement and **while** loop [Sto77]. To the author's knowledge, Scheme [RC86], a dialect of Lisp, is the first programming language that incorporated first class continuations as a built-in language feature. Scheme provides a primitive function which captures the current continuation as a form of a function. First class continuations, thus obtained, can be bound to a variables and stored in data structures. A first class continuation is represented as a function, sometimes called an *escape function*. Invocation of an escape function results in giving the control back to the time when the continuation was obtained. Though Scheme has very small number of built-in control structures, it is known that more complicated control structures such as *catch-and-throw* and *unwind-protect* can be implemented using first class continuations. Furthermore, continuations allow us to express more advanced features such as non-local jumps, exception handling, backtracking, and co-routines [HF87, Wan80].

We introduce the notion of first class continuations into object-based concurrent computation. Computation in object-based concurrent computation models has two dimensions of computation, namely *internal computation* (execution of methods) and *external computation* (communication between objects via messages). Because of this duality in object-based computation, we can define two independent classes of continuations, namely **method continuation** and **message continuation**. A *method continuation* is "the rest of the computation" with respect to execution of a method. From similarity between method execution and function evaluation, method continuations can be considered as an object-based version of ordinary continuations. A *message continuation* is a message itself. A message determines the rest of the computation in that it determines which method to invoke at which object (the *target*), to which object to send the reply (the *reply destination*), etc. Thus a message is a good device for expressing a continuation with respect to external computation. We have designed an object-based concurrent language, called HARMONY/2, which integrates both dimensions of continuations with object-based computation models. The article focuses on the message continuation features[2]. First class message continuations allow us to describe various communication schemes such as synchronization schemes, message scheduling policies, emulation of multi-processor environment, concurrency control,

---

[2] Uniform integration of method continuations and message continuations will be reported in the forth-coming article.

system monitoring, notification mechanism, distributed constraint resolving, and so on.

Particular emphasis is on **soundness** of the framework. One of the problem with highly extensible systems is that programmer's customization may destroy the semantics of the built-in primitives of the system, thus making it impossible to reason about the behavior of the system. To protect the system from dangerous customization, most extensible systems impose certain disciplined programming style on the programmer. The system guarantees system's correct behavior as far as the programmer do not violate the discipline.

In designing the message continuation framework, we took more conservative and safer approach. The system, rather than the programmer, is responsible for protecting system's semantics. Thus the framework imposes no discipline but still the semantics of the built-in primitives never changes, whatever code is executed. We claim that our framework is *sound* with respect to this safer property compared with most extensible systems. Soundness was obtained by careful design of primitive operations on message continuations. To achieve soundness, we introduced two categories of message continuations, namely **asynchronous message continuations** and **synchronous message continuations**.

In the rest of the article, the object-based computation model is introduced in Section 2, the message continuation framework and its soundness is explained in Section 3, and Section 4 shows several programming examples with message continuations. Section 5 compares the framework with related work and Section 6 concludes the article.

2 Computation Model

Message continuation framework presented in the article can be tailored to various message-based distributed computation models. However, to clarify the discussion, we use the syntax and semantics of a subset of HARMONY/2. HARMONY/2 is an object-based concurrent language which is designed and being implemented at Tokyo Institute of Technology. Its syntax is Standard ML [MTH89] with extensions of object-oriented features. Inter-object communication is based on RPC-like message passing. The computation model is a multi-threaded model; an object may have more than one methods execute concurrently.

```
Class BinPlus
    var x = 0;   var y = 0;         ①
    initialize (a, b) = (x:=a;  y:=b)   ②
    mth result() = ↑(x+y)           ③
EndClass
```

The above is an example of class definition. It defines a class named BinPlus, which implements a binary addition operator. The class declares two instance variables (x and y; ①) and defines the initialization method (②) and a method that returns the sum of the instance variables (result; ③). The instance variable declaration using **var** has similar syntax as **val** declaration of Standard ML. The value assigned to an instance variable is referred to by its name. Unlike values of Standard ML, an instance variable may be reassigned to another value by using assignment operator (:=). An **initialize** declaration defines an instance initialization method. When an instance is created, the initialization method is invoked. A **mth** declaration defines a method. The syntax is similar to **fun** declaration of Standard ML. The body of a method body may contain arbitrary expressions of Standard ML. Additionally, following three special forms are allowed to appear in the method body:

Instance Creation Form:	Class ← New($a_1, a_2, \ldots$)
Message Passing Form:	object ← method_name($a_1, a_2, \ldots$)
Reply Form:	↑*value*

Special Forms of HARMONY/2

Execution of an *instance creation form* creates an instance of the specified class. In the example below, an instance of BinPlus class is created and the instance is bound to an instance variable named p. The parameters given to an instance creation form (e.g., (3, 5)) are passed to the initialization method (**initialize**) of the class. The second line of the example is message passing to the object referred to by p. Conceptually, a message is created and sent to the object which is referenced by p (the *target* of the message). The identifier following ← is called the *method selector*. When the message is delivered to the target the message invokes the method whose name is the same as the method selector of the message.

```
let var p = BinPlus ← New(3, 5)
in   p ← result()
end
```

The computation model is based on RPC-like synchronous message passing; the sender of the message waits for the receiver to send reply back. Though, HARMONY/2 supports both synchronous and asynchronous message passing, we did not add asynchronous one in the presented model as a built-in feature, trying to make the model simpler and to avoid readers' confusion between the built-in asynchronous primitive and asynchronous communication protocols implemented by message continuations.

The model is a multi-threaded model. Whether or not a message is being processed in an object, a delivered message is immediately accepted and corresponding method starts execution. Consequently, multiple methods may execute in an object. In other words, an object has internal concurrency. The programmer can use method guards to control internal concurrency.

As the model does not have asynchronous message passing nor multicasting protocol, the reader might think there is no source of concurrency in the model. Two sources of concurrency are early reply mechanism and instance creation. A method may send reply before it completes the execution. After sending reply, methods of the sender and the receiver may execute concurrently. Instance creation also increases the number of concurrency. Execution of an instance creation form produces a new instance, immediately sends the object identifier back to the creator as the reply of instance creation, and then invokes the initialization method on the new instance. Consequently, the rest of method execution at the sender side and execution of initialization at the new instance may execute concurrently.

3 Message Continuations

This section presents the message continuation framework. A message continuation is a first class message obtained through **message conversion**. Three primitive operations are defined for message continuations. Subsection 3.1 gives an overview of the message continuation framework. Subsection 3.2 exemplifies the use of message continuations. Subsection 3.3 goes into further detail of the semantics of the primitive operations and explains **soundness** property of the framework.

3.1 Message Conversion

The principle idea of message conversion is to convert a message into a first class object so that the message becomes accessible in the method code. We call this process *message conversion* and the result of conversion, namely the first class message, a *message continuation*.

HARMONY/2 represents a message continuation as an instance of MsgCont class, which is one of the built-in classes of HARMONY/2. Conceptually, a message continuation contains all the information that the original message carried, such as the sender, the target, the method selector, the arguments (real parameters given to the message sending expression), the reply destination (where to send reply to the message), etc. In this sense, a message continuation can be regarded as a *representation* of the original message. Message continuation framework allows the programmer to reason about the information carried by a message, to store the representation of a message in data structures, and to reproduce a message using the information contained in a message continuation.

Another task of message conversion is to create a new message that carries the message continuation as its argument and delivers to some specified target. We call this new message the **message continuation carrier** of the message continuation. The method selector of a message continuation carrier is always Cont. Thus, when a message continuation carrier is accepted by the specified target, it invokes a method named Cont[3]. Because a message continuation carrier contains a message continuation as its real argument, the message continuation is passed to the Cont method on its invocation.

Like other objects, the information kept by a message continuation is encapsulated and the programmer does not have direct access to the implementation of a message continuation. The programmer can manipulate a message continuation indirectly through three primitive operations which are defined as methods of MsgCont class, namely fire, copy, and reply:

Reactivation — "$k \leftarrow \text{fire}()$"

> *Reactivation* operation produces a message which carries the same information as is represented by the message continuation, k.

Copy — "$k \leftarrow \text{copy}(target)$"

> *Copy* operation creates a copy of the message continuation, k. The argument to this operation (*target*) specifies the target for the copy. Multicasting (Subsection 4.2) is realized using this feature. If Nil is given for the argument, the target of the copy is the same as the original message continuation (k).

Forced Reply — "$k \leftarrow \text{reply}(result)$"

> *Forced reply* operation on a message continuation sends reply to the reply destination contained in the message continuation, k. It is possible to send reply in advance of reactivation of the message continuation. In this case, forced reply releases the blocked sender before the message continuation invokes the method with the future reactivation, thus allowing the original sender and the receiver to execute concurrently. This asynchrony is used in the implementation of asynchronous communication in Subsection 4.1.

---

[3] HARMONY/2 has more sophisticated naming mechanism and pattern matching features but we will only give an outline in this article.

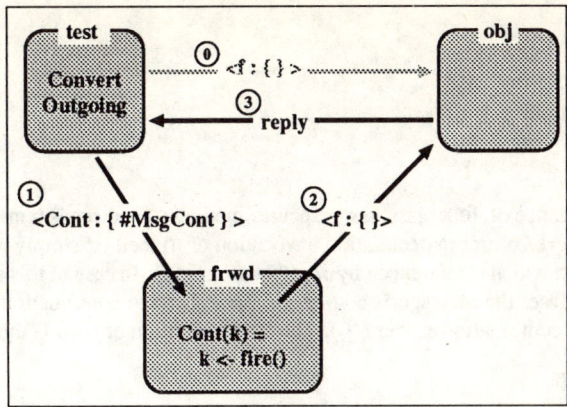

Figure 1: Example 1

Programming with message continuations consists of two parts: specification of message conversion and definition of Cont method.

Message conversion is specified in per-class basis using two special forms **Convert Incoming** form and/or **Convert Outgoing** form. "Convert Incoming $\langle pattern \rangle \Rightarrow target$", specifies message conversion to take place for every incoming message that matches the pattern ($\langle pattern \rangle \Rightarrow target$). The pattern can be either a method name, which matches a message having the same name for the method selector, or unspecified ('*'), which matches any message. If a message delivered to the instance of the class matches the pattern, the message is converted and the message continuation is delivered to the specified target (*target*), by a message continuation carrier. Another special form, "**Convert Outgoing** $\langle pattern \rangle \Rightarrow target$" has the same effect except that it applies to the messages that are sent out of the instance by message passing.

A Cont method is defined just like an ordinary method using **mth** method definition form. The programmer can manipulate the message continuation by the three primitive operations. Also, like an ordinary object, the message continuation can be saved in an instance variable or be sent to another object.

3.2 Examples

This subsection shows two very simple examples of the use of message continuations. Though, they are not practically very interesting, they capture essence of programming with message continuations. With slight modification to these examples, we can implement asynchronous communication, multicasting, object aggregate, message monitoring systems, and so on.

Example 1

This example explains *message conversion* and *reactivation operation* of a message continuation (Figure 1). The class definition below declares a class named Test. It declares two instance variables, *frwd* and *obj*, and one method, m. **Convert Outgoing** declaration specifies every message which has f as its method selector to be converted into a message continuation, and carried to the object referenced by *frwd*.

```
Class Test
    var frwd : Forward;
    var obj  : SomeClass;
    Convert Outgoing f ⇒ frwd;
    mth m() = obj ← f()
EndClass
```

Suppose an instance of Test class, *test*, executes method m and sends a message to *obj*. If it were not for **Convert Outgoing** declaration, invocation of m method simply results in message passing to the object which is referenced by *obj* (⓪ in Figure 1). In case of this example, message conversion takes place; the message is converted into a message continuation, and delivered to *frwd* by a message continuation carrier (①). The class definition of *frwd* is the following:

```
Class Forward
    mth Cont(k : MsgCont) = k ← fire();
EndClass
```

The message continuation carrier invokes Cont method, passing the message continuation as the real argument (k). (In the subsequent programming examples, k and k' denote message continuations). Cont method simply reactivates the message continuation by fire method and produces an identical message with the message produced by the message passing in the body of method m (②). The message is delivered to the original target (*obj*) and invokes method f as if the message had originated from *test* and were directly passed to *obj* (②). The reply from *obj* is sent back to the original sender (③) instead of the reactivator (i.e., *frwd*). In this example, Cont method does nothing but to reactivate the message continuation. Its behavior is analogous to invocation of Scheme's continuation immediately after calling *call/cc*.

Example 2

This example explains *copy operation* and *forced reply operation*. The implementation scheme is illustrated in Figure 2. The definition of Test class remains the same. Forward class is redefined as below. This version of Cont method makes a copy of the message continuation (k'), reactivates the copy (②), and then replies back to the original sender by forced reply operation (reply) on k (③). As will be explained in detail in the next subsection, behavior of reactivation operation and treatment of *obj*'s reply differ from those given in Example 1. When a copy of a message continuation is reactivated, as in this example, the reply is not sent to the original sender (*test*) but to the object that reactivated the message continuation (*frwd*).

```
Class Forward
    mth Cont(k : MsgCont) =
        let val k' = k ← copy();
            val res = k' ← fire()
        in  k ← reply(res)
        end
EndClass
```

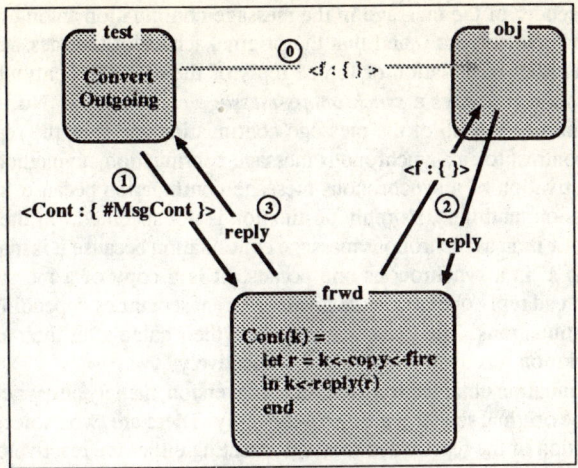

Figure 2: Example 2

3.3 Soundness

The message continuation framework provides concurrent languages with powerful extensibility in describing communication protocols and synchronization schemes. However it is not desirable to make the framework so powerful that it could change the semantics of built-in primitives and crash the system. To make our framework safe, we would like to minimize the effect of extensibility features upon semantics of built-in communication primitives. To achieve this goal, we categorized message continuations into two different kinds, namely **asynchronous message continuations** and **synchronous message continuations**, and gave them different semantics. The most interesting result obtained from this categorization is that the framework does not change the following three essential properties of synchronous communication:

Ⓐ *The sender of a message receives at most one reply.*

In normal synchronous message passing, method execution sends reply at most once. If multiple replies are sent, the sender receives the first one and the rest are never received because the sender continues execution of the method code.

Ⓑ *Every message has its reply destination.*

In normal synchronous message passing, the sender waits until the receiver completes method execution and sends reply back. If reply destination is not specified for a message, the receiver (or the method execution) cannot reply.

Ⓒ *Every message has exactly one method execution waiting for the reply of the message.*

In normal synchronous message passing, the sender waits until it receives reply. This property avoid a situation where the method execution specified by the reply destination does not wait for the reply and thus the receiver of the message cannot send reply.

In our message continuation framework, each message continuation is either an asynchronous message continuation or a synchronous message continuation. An *asynchronous message continuation* is the one which is created by message conversion. Note that message conversion stores the original sender of the message in the message continuation among other information (e.g., target, method selector, etc.) and that the original sender of the message waits from the reply coming from either reactivation or forced reply of the message continuation. A copy of a message continuation is always a *synchronous message continuation*. No method execution waits for reply from reactivation of the message continuation and thus the reply destination is not specified[4]. In contrast to an asynchronous message continuation, no method execution waits for reply from reactivation of a synchronous message continuation because it was not created by message conversion, and thus, its reply destination is not specified. In the examples of the previous subsection, k is an asynchronous message continuation because it is made from message conversion whereas k' is a synchronous one because it is a copy of a message continuation. Reactivation and forced reply operations are given different semantics depending on the category of the message continuations. The two categories took their name after their asynchronous and synchronous behavior on reactivation operation, respectively.

A message continuation obtained from message conversion, namely an asynchronous message continuation, has the original sender waiting for the reply. There are two choices in the treatment of the reply destination of the reactivated message: treating either the reactivator of the message continuation (e.g., *frwd* in Figure 1) or the original sender (e.g., *test*) to be the reply destination. With the former design the reactivator waits for the reply and the reactivator is responsible for sending the reply back to the original sender by forced reply operation. With the latter design the reactivator does not wait for the reply because the reply is sent directly back to the original sender. Reactivation of an asynchronous message *immediately* results in **Nil** and the method that performed reactivation continues the rest of the method execution. Thus method execution of the reactivator and the processing of the reactivated message execute concurrently. We chose the latter design to take advantage of increased concurrency. This asynchronous behavior is the origin of the name of the '*asynchronous* message continuation'.

To guarantee the *at most one reply* property (property Ⓐ), the semantics of the message continuation should change after the first reactivation. Otherwise, more than one reply may be sent by repeated forced reply and/or reactivation the same message continuation. In the framework, reactivation operation (fire method) has side effect. It changes an asynchronous message continuation into synchronous one which does not send reply to the original sender upon subsequent reactivation or forced reply. From an implementation point of view, the side effect simply nullifies the reply destination kept in the asynchronous message continuation. It ensures property Ⓐ for repeated reactivation of the same asynchronous message continuation. From the same reason, reply method also leaves similar side effect.

The reply destination of a synchronous message continuation is nullified. If reactivation of a synchronous message continuation simply produces a message using the information kept in the message continuation, the reactivated message will have no reply destination. This is against property Ⓑ. For this reason, in the framework, reactivation assigns the reactivator (*frwd* in Figure 2) to be the reply destination of the reactivated message. Consequently, the reply of processing the reactivated message goes to the reactivator. Reactivation of a synchronous message continuation blocks and waits for the reply. This synchronous behavior of reactivation of a synchronous message continuation and treatment of the reply for it is depicted in Figure 2. Forced reply operation on a synchronous message continuation is meaningless because no reply destination is nullified. It does nothing and simply results in **Nil**.

By careful design of the semantics of primitive operations on message continuations the framework guarantees the three properties of synchronous message communication (properties

---

[4]Note: This is not against property Ⓑ. Ⓑ applies to messages but not to message continuations

Ⓐ, Ⓑ, and Ⓒ). The following is a rough sketch of the proof of soundness:

Ⓐ In normal message passing, a sender receives at most one reply from the target of the message.[5] A sender never receives reply from reactivation or forced reply of a synchronous message continuation because the reply destination of a synchronous message continuation is always nullified. A synchronous message continuation may send at most one reply to the sender because it changes to an asynchronous message continuation after the first reactivation or forced reply.

Ⓑ In case of normal message produced from message passing, the reply destination is the sender. Reply destination of a reactivated message is either the original sender, in case of an asynchronous one, or the reactivator, in case of a synchronous one. So in both cases, a reactivated message has reply destination.

Ⓒ For normal message and a reactivated message produced from an asynchronous message continuation, the (original) sender waits for the reply. For a reactivated message produced from a synchronous message continuation, the reactivator waits for the reply.

In the previous design of message continuation framework, we did not consider soundness. One of the flaws with the earlier design were that an object may receive multiple replies for single message passing because of repeated forced replies and/or reactivation of the same message continuation. In the correct framework, this never happens because an asynchronous message continuation becomes synchronous after the first reactivation or forced reply operation.

The reader might think that the three properties are too restrictive, and would spoil extensibility. However, the properties only restrict the use of messages, and they don't constrain the use of message continuations. For instance, multicasting can be implemented by multiple reactivation of a message continuation; in this case what the message continuation framework guarantees is that "the original sender of the multicasted message receives at most one reply". As we will see in Subsection 4.2, the sender receives the reply for the first reactivation operation and replies for the subsequent reactivation operations are sent to the object that implements the multicasting protocol.

4 Practical Examples

This section presents how message continuations can be used to implement various communication protocols.

4.1 Asynchronous Message Passing

In RPC-like synchronous communication, the sender blocks and waits for a reply while the receiver processes the message. Three major roles of synchronous communication are sending information (message sending), receiving information (receiving reply), and synchronization with message processing (blocking). In some cases, not all these functionalities are necessary. Asynchronous message sending is a form of communication where only sending information takes place. In asynchronous communication, the receiver processes the message while the sender

---

[5]It may be the case that the sender never receives the reply due to synchronization or an infinite loop in the method definition at the target side, though.

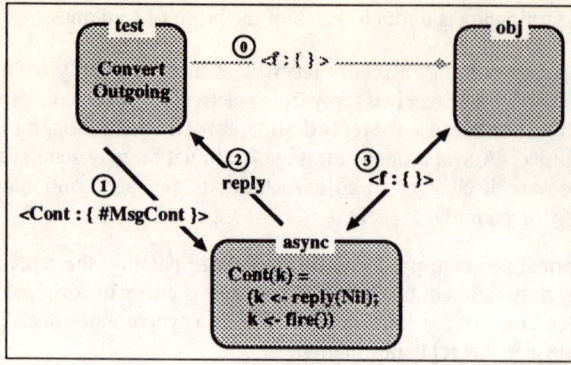

Figure 3: Asynchronous Message Passing

executes subsequent method code. There is no synchronization nor reply. Many object-based concurrent languages, including HARMONY/2, have built-in support of asynchronous communication [YT86, Yon90, IT87, BHJL86, WY90a].

In this subsection, we implement asynchronous communication using a synchronous message passing primitives and message continuations. The implementation scheme is depicted in Figure 3. We add **Convert outgoing** declaration in the class definition of the sender. Message conversion takes place and a message whose method selector is f is sent out of *test* object and converted into a message continuation. A message continuation carrier is also created and delivers the message continuation to an object named *async*, which is an instance of Asynchronous class (①).

    Class Test
        var *async* : Asynchronous
        var *obj* : SomeClass
        Convert Outgoing f $\Rightarrow$ *async*
        mth m() = *obj* $\leftarrow$ f()
    EndClass

Asynchronous class implements asynchronous communication. Cont method first performs forced reply to release the blocking sender, and let it execute subsequent method code (②). Then it reactivates the message continuation (③). As k becomes a synchronous message continuation by the forced reply operation, the reply for the reactivated message is sent to *async* (③).

    Class Asynchronous
        mth Cont(*k* : MsgCont) =
            (*k* $\leftarrow$ reply (Nil)
            k $\leftarrow$ fire ())
    EndClass

It is well-known that asynchronous communication can be implemented by buffered synchronous communication. However, to achieve asynchrony, we need to modify the method definitions of all the classes that participate in asynchronous communication by adding some code which implements asynchronous protocol on both the sender side and the receiver side.

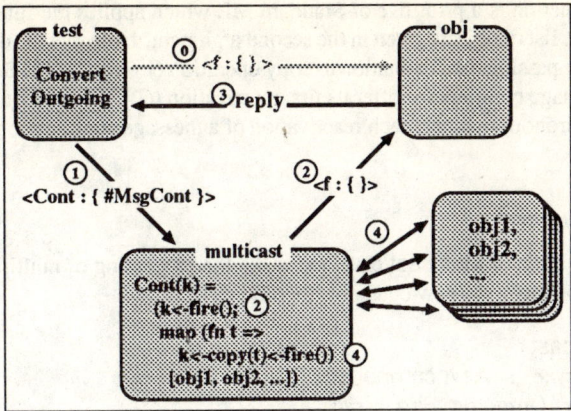

Figure 4: Serial Multicasting

In contrast, by using message continuation framework, the required modification is merely an addition of conversion specification at the sender side. Because we also have **Convert Incoming** declaration, we can also add conversion specification at the receiver side, instead of adding **Convert Outgoing** declaration at the sender.

4.2 Multicasting

Multicasting is a form of communication, where copies of a message are delivered to multiple destinations. There are many variations of protocols which differ in targets specification, treatment of replies, semantics of synchronization, etc. Here we present two implementations of multicasting. First one, which we call *serial multicasting*, sends messages to multiple targets one after another. Each message is sent only after the processing of the former message completes. Second one, which we call *concurrent multicasting*, sends messages concurrently. Messages do not synchronize with each other.

Serial Multicasting

    Class Multicast
        mth Cont(k : MsgCont) =
            ($k \leftarrow$ fire() ;
            map (**fn** t => $k \leftarrow$ copy(t) $\leftarrow$ fire())
            [obj_1, obj_2, ...])
    EndClass

A message continuation obtained by message conversion (① in Figure 4) is reactivated and the reactivated message is delivered to the original target, *obj* (②). Reply for the message goes to the original sender (③) because the message had originated from an asynchronous message continuation. The behavior, so far, is the same as Example 1 of Subsection 3.2. Because, up to the moment of the first reactivation, k is an asynchronous message continuation, Cont method proceeds its methods execution while *obj* processes the reactivated message. The expression, "*map* ... [obj_1, obj_2, ...]", implements sequential multicasting of a list of objects, "[obj_1, obj_2,

...]". The *map* function is a primitive of Standard ML which applies the function given as the first argument to the list of objects given in the second argument. Note that the destination of each copy is specified by passing the destination to copy operation ($k \leftarrow \text{copy}(t)$). Because k becomes a synchronous message continuation after its first reactivation (②), the subsequent reactivation is performed in synchronous manner; each reactivation of a message continuation blocks and waits for reply.

Concurrent Multicasting

We can modify the code of Multicast class and make the processing of multiple copies to work concurrently. Following is the new code of Multicast class.

```
Class Multicast
    var async : Asynchronous
    Convert Outgoing Fire ⇒ self
    mth Cont (k : MsgCont) =
        (k ← fire () ;
         map (fn t => self ← Fire (k ← copy (t) ) )
             [obj₁, obj₂, ...])
    mth Fire (k' : MsgCont) =
        k' ← fire ()
EndClass
```

In this version, reactivation of copies is not performed in the body of Cont method named Fire. Cont repeatedly creates the copies and pass them to Fire by message passing to *self*. Because of **Convert Outgoing** declaration, the message passing is performed asynchronously by an instance of Asynchronous class (see Subsection 4.1). Consequently, reactivation of copies in Fire method is performed concurrently.

4.3 Emulation of Multi-processor Environment

When we write parallel programs, we think of arbitrary number of concurrent activities and in fact we implement them as arbitrary number of logically concurrent objects. However, in reality, the amount of computing resource is bounded by the number of the processor elements and thus assignment of logically concurrent objects to physical processor elements (*processor assignment*) is one of the key issues in developing efficient concurrent systems. This subsection presents that message continuations can be used to control the number of concurrent activities and thus eases processor assignment. What we try here is to limit the number of concurrent activities by the number of processors of a parallel computer. [MWY91] presents a solution to this problem based on reflection. The solution implements metalevel object scheduler which schedules all the threads of control running inside objects.

We present another solution using message continuations. Instead of scheduling objects, we schedule messages by a message queue. All the messages in the system are collected in the form of message continuations and stored in the message queue. The message scheduler is represented by a multi-threaded object (*sched*). Figure 5 illustrates the implementation scheme. The message scheduler collects all the messages in the system. For this purpose, when a message is sent out, it is converted and sent to the scheduler object (①), whose Cont method puts the message continuation in the message queue (②).

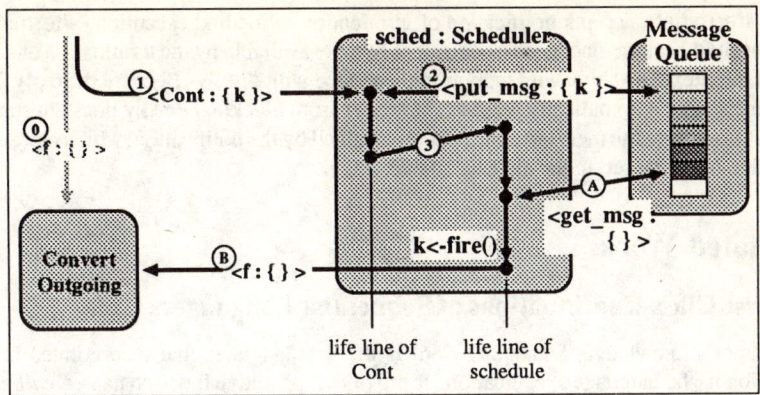

Figure 5: Emulation of Multi-processor Environment

The code below implements the Scheduler class. A method execution running at schedule method of *sched* object corresponds to process execution at some processor element. Initially, *sched* object invokes *proc_num* of schedule methods. Note that with **Convert Outgoing** declaration, those methods execute work concurrently. Schedule sends get_message message to the message queue to retrieve the next message continuation to process (Ⓐ). The message queue may implement a simple FIFO queue or some sophisticated scheduling policy. We don't go into further details of the implementation of the message queue. Then, schedule reactivate the obtained message continuation (Ⓑ). Because the reactivated message starts a method execution at the original target, reactivation of the message continuation implements process creation.

```
Class  Scheduler
    Convert Incoming  schedule ⇒ async
    fun  schedule () = message_queue ← get_message () ← fire ()
    initialize (proc_num) =
        if (proc_num = 0)
        then Nil
        else ( self ← schedule () ;
               self ← initialize (proc_num − 1 ) )
    fun Cont (k : MsgCont) =
        ( message_queue ← put_message (k) ;  self ← schedule () ;  )
    fun #terminate () = self ← schedule ()
fun #reply (k : MsgCont) =
    message_queue ← put_message (k)
    EndClass
```

In this implementation, context switching is performed in three places: message sending, replying, and method termination. When a message is sent the Cont method stores the message continuation in the message queue. This corresponds to giving up the thread of control. Then Cont invokes schedule to give the thread of control to another process (or message continuation kept in the message queue). Method termination can be detected by extended feature of HARMONY/2, which represent events, such as replying and termination, as notification messages.

Methods #terminate accepts notification of termination of method execution. #terminate invokes schedule because one processor element became available by the termination of a method execution. Context switching with reply is implemented with #reply. Because the reply from the target to the sender automatically releases the sender from blocking, #reply does not start a new process. It just stores the message continuation obtained by the notification, which represents the continuation of the target, in the message queue.

5 Related Work

5.1 First Class Continuations of Sequential Languages

To the author's knowledge, Scheme [RC86] is the first language that incorporated first class continuation in the language specification. It provides a primitive function named *call/cc*[6]. The function *call/cc* packages up the current continuation as an *escape function* and passes it as an argument to the unary function given to *call/cc*. Invocation of the escape function gives the control to the packaged continuation. For example, in the following code, *call/cc* binds the current continuation to k and "(k **true**)" gives the control back to the continuation by calling the escape function.

(*call/cc* (*lambda* (*k*) ... (*k* **true**) ...))

A Standard ML compiler developed at ATT Bell laboratory, called SML/NJ, has several non-standard features which include first class continuation feature [AM91]. SML/NJ provides two functions, *callcc* and *throw*. The former is for obtaining first class continuations and the latter is for invocation of continuations. The SML/NJ's equivalent for the above Scheme code is:

callcc (**fn** *k* => ...; *throw k* **true**; ...)

In HARMONY/2, a message continuation is obtained by **Convert Incoming** or Convert Outgoing declaration and the message continuation is reactivated by fire operation. Message conversion and fire operation corresponds to call/cc and invocation of an escape function, respectively. Copy and reply operations of HARMONY/2 are peculiarities with concurrent languages. In Scheme and SML/NJ, we can give different names to a first class continuation by **let** binding. However those names simply share the same continuation but do not create copies. As we saw in the implementation of multicasting, copy operation creates multiple copies of message continuations which correspond to multiple threads of control. The copy operation is also used to control synchronization by producing a synchronous message continuation out of an asynchronous one. reply can change the order of method execution and reply sending, and thus increases concurrency.

5.2 Reflective Computation

From our experience with message continuations, the framework seems as expressive as a class of reflective computation called *Group-wide Reflection* [WY90b, MWY91]. Examples of object migration [WY90b] and multi-processor emulation [MWY91], which was solved using group-wide reflectivity, can be easily described in the framework of message continuations. On the other hand, it is not simple to describe Time Warp Simulation example that appears in [MWY91].

---

[6]In the language specification of Scheme [RC86], the function is named *call-with-current-continuation* but most implementations of Scheme provide this abbreviation.

The example requires metalevel modeling of both objects and communication, where message continuations only feature the latter. [MWY91] solves this using a concurrent reflective languages, ABCL/R2, which supports two dimensions of reflectivity, namely group-wide reflectivity and *individual reflectivity*.

The programs written by HARMONY/2 tends to be much shorter and more readable than the solutions described by reflective languages. One reason is that the abstraction level of message continuations is higher than ABCL/R2's metalevel message objects. Another reason is that in ABCL/R2, the programmer has to write additional protocols to protect the system from possible dangerous reflective code, while in HARMONY/2, such protection is hidden in the semantics of primitive operations on message continuations because the framework guarantees soundness.

Most reflective systems demand the programmer to follow a certain discipline, called *Meta Object Protocol*, to make the system work correctly. A problem with this approach is that when the programmer breaks the discipline, whether on purpose or inadvertently, the system can not guarantee the semantics of basic features, such as method execution, instance creation, message passing, etc. In contrast our framework is much safer in that the semantics of basic features are protected by the carefully designed primitive operations (i.e., fire, copy, and reply).

The message continuations and reflection are not conflicting concepts. They can co-exist in the same language by making message continuations as a member of the metalevel objects. Incorporation of message continuation framework in reflective computation will replace ad hoc treatment of messages in the existing reflective systems with well-founded, highly abstract primitives and improve understandability of reflective programs.

5.3 Meta Filter

Sina [ABV92] is an object-oriented programming language which is implemented at the University of Twente. The author's previous design of first class message framework was added as Sina's Meta filter. Description power is almost compatible with message continuation framework. Meta filter has extended features that allow the programmer to refer to or to modify information kept in the first class messages, giving more flexibility compared with message continuation framework. [AW+92] discusses integration of Meta filter with Sina's other filter mechanisms that allow the programmer to implement code reuse and synchronization.

6 Concluding Remarks

We introduced the concept of continuation in object-based concurrent computation. The framework of message continuations was designed to provide concurrent languages with extensibility in modeling and programming various communication protocols. It has been used over a year to describe wide variety of communication schemes such as asynchronous communication, multicasting, sophisticated synchronization constraints, inter-object synchronization, concurrency control, resource management, and so on. In spite of its powerful extensibility, the framework is sound in that no program can destroy the semantics of built-in communication primitives. The article explained the framework using synchronous communication model. However, the framework can be also applied to asynchronous communication model. In fact, HARMONY/2 integrates both asynchronous and synchronous message passing with message continuation framework. Another advantage of the framework is that message continuations can be implemented very efficiently. Message conversion has almost no overhead and primitive operations defined for message continuations are cheap operations. A compiler of HARMONY/2 is being developed at

Tokyo Institute of Technology. Features of HARMONY/2 that are not found in the article include asynchronous message passing, inheritance, and delegation. The languages is going to be used as a platform of distributed programming and inter-linguistic communication model.

Acknowledgements The author would like to thank Mehmet Aksit, Lodewijk Bergmans, Jan Bosch, and other members of TRESE project at the University of Twente for their continuous encouragement and discussing the framework of first class messages, Aki Yonezawa and a number of people at the University of Tokyo for joining the discussion and giving comments on the earlier design of message continuation framework and its soundness. Hidehiko Masuhara at the university of Tokyo kindly explained the specification and implementation of ABCL/R2. Shigeru Chiba, Shigekazu Inohara, Hiroyuki Matsuda, Hiroto Morizane, Satoshi Matsuoka, Nobuyuki Tomizawa read the earlier drafts and gave me fruitful comments. Comments and insights given by the referees from ISOTAS '93 have improved the paper. Finally, I would like to address my thanks to colleagues at Tokyo Institute of Technology for their kindness and support.

References

[ABV92] Mehmet Aksit, Lodewijk Bergmans, and Sinan Vural. An object-oriented langauge-database integration model: the composition-filters approach. Technical report, The university of Twente, 1992.

[AM91] A. Appel and D. MacQueen. Standard ML of New Jersey. In M. Wirsing, editor, *Third International Symposium on Programming Language Implementation and Logic Programming*, Lecture Notes in Computer Science, New York, August 1991. Springer-Verlag.

[Ame87] P. America. POOL-T: A parallel object-oriented language. In A. Yonezawa and M. Tokoro, editors, *Object-Oriented Concurrent Programming*, pages 199 – 220. MIT Press, Cambridge, Mass., 1987.

[AW+92] M. Aksit, K. Wakita, et al. Abstracting object interactions using composition filters. Project Report of TRESE group, the university of Twente, the Netherlands, 1992.

[BHJL86] A. Black, N. Hutchinson, E. Jul, and H. Levy. Object structure in the Emerald system. In *Object-Oriented Programming Systems, Languages and Applications*, volume 21(11), pages 78 – 86. SIGPLAN Notices (ACM), November 1986.

[BK91] N. S. Barghouti and G. E. Kaiser. Concurrency contorl in advanced database applications. *ACM Computing Surveys*, 23(3):269–318, September 1991.

[dJ91] Peter de Jong, editor. *Conference on Organizational Computing Systems '91*. ACM press, 1991. SIGOIS Bulletin vol. 12, number 2 (3).

[EG89] C. A. Ellis and S. J. Gibbs. Concurrency control in groupware systems. In *Proceedings of International Conference on the Management of Data, SIGMOD RECORD*, pages 399–407, Portland, Oregon, June 1989.

[HF87] C. T. Haynes and D. P. Friedman. Embedding continuations in procedural objects. *ACM Transactions on Programming Languages and Systems*, 9(4):582–598, April 1987.

[IT87]   Y. Ishikawa and M. Tokoro. Orient84/K: An object-oriented concurrent programming language for knowledge representation. In A. Yonezawa and M. Tokoro, editors, *Object-Oriented Concurrent Programming*, pages 159 – 198. MIT Press, Cambridge, Mass., 1987.

[MTH89] R. Milner, M. Tofte, and R. Harper. *The Definition of Standard ML*. MIT Press, Cambridge, MA, 1989.

[MWY91] S. Matsuoka, T. Watanabe, and A. Yonezawa. Hybrid group reflective architecture for object-oriented concurrent reflective programming. In P. America, editor, *Proceedings of European Conference on Object-Oriented Programming '91*, volume 512 of *Lecture Notes in Computer Science*, Geneva, Switzerland, July 1991. Springer-Verlag.

[Nie87] O. M. Nierstrasz. Active objects in Hybrid. In *Object-Oriented Programming Systems, Languages and Applications*, volume 22(12), pages 243 – 253. SIGPLAN Notices (ACM), December 1987.

[RC86]   J. Rees and W. Clinger. Revised^3 report on the algorithmic language Scheme. *ACM SIGPLAN Not.*, 21(12):37–79, December 1986.

[Sto77] J. Stoy. *Denotational Semantics: The Scott-Strachey Approach to Programming Language Theory*. MIT Press, Cambridge, MA, 1977.

[Wan80] M. Wand. Continuation-based multiprocessing. In *Conference Record of the 1980 Lisp Conference*, pages 19–28, 1980.

[WY90a] K. Wakita and A. Yonezawa. Linguistic supports for development of distributed organizational information systems in object-oriented concurrent computation frameworks. In *ACM Conference on Organizational Computing Systems*, pages 185–198, November 1990.

[WY90b] T. Watanabe and A. Yonezawa. An actor-based metalevel architecture for group-wide reflection. In *Proceedings of the REX School/Workshop on Foundations of Object-Oriented Languages (REX/FOOL)*, Lecture Notes in Computer Science, Noordwijkerhout, the Netherlands, May 1990. Springer-Verlag.

[Yon90] A. Yonezawa. *ABCL: An Object-Oriented Concurrent System*. MIT Press, Cambridge, Mass., 1990.

[YT86]   Y. Yokote and M. Tokoro. The design and implementation of ConcurrentSmalltalk. In *Object-Oriented Programming Systems, Languages and Applications*, volume 21(11), pages 331 – 340. SIGPLAN Notices (ACM), November 1986.

A typing system for a calculus of objects *

Vasco T. Vasconcelos
vasco@mt.cs.keio.ac.jp

Mario Tokoro[†]
mario@mt.cs.keio.ac.jp

Keio University
Department of Computer Science
3-14-1 Hiyoshi Kohoku-ku Yokohama 223
Japan

Abstract

The present paper introduces an implicitly typed object calculus intended to capture intrinsic aspects of concurrent objects communicating via asynchronous message passing, together with a typing system assigning typings to terms in the calculus. Types meant to describe the kind of messages an object may receive are assigned to the free names in a program, resulting in a scenario where a program is assigned multiple name-type pairs, constituting a typing for the process. Programs that comply to the typing discipline are shown not to suffer from runtime errors. Furthermore the calculus possesses a notion of principal typings, from which all typings that make a program well-typed can be extracted. We present an efficient algorithm to extract the principal typing of a process.

1 Introduction

Most of the attempts to introduce some type discipline into object-oriented languages start from lambda-calculus, by extending this with some kind of records. There are several limitations to this approach, mainly deriving from the fact that objects are not extensions of functions. In particular, objects do not necessarily present an input-output behavior; objects usually communicate by asynchronous message passing (instead of function application); objects do maintain a state (in contrast with the stateless nature of functions), and objects may run concurrently.

Inspired by Milner's polyadic π-calculus [4], Honda's ν-calculus [3] and Hewitt's actor model [1], we present a basic object-calculus where the notions of objects, asynchronous messages and concurrency are primitive, and introduce a type discipline along the lines of Honda [2] and Vasconcelos and Honda [7] for the (untyped) calculus, enjoying the properties that programs that verify the discipline will never run into errors of the kind "message not understood", and that there is an effectively computable notion of principal typings from which all typings that make a process well-typed can be derived.

---

*To appear in the Proceedings of the International Symposium on Object Technologies for Advanced Software (ISOTAS), Springer-Verlag, LNCS, November 1993.

[†]Also affiliated with Sony Computer Science Laboratory.

Terms of the calculus are built from names by means of a few constructors. Messages of the form $a \triangleleft l(\tilde{v})$ are directed to an (object located at) name a, select a method labelled with l and carry a sequence of names $\tilde{v}$. Terms of the form $a \triangleright [l_1(\tilde{x}_1).P_1 \& \cdots \& l_n(\tilde{x}_n).P_n]$ represent objects located at name a, and comprising a collection of methods, each of which composed of a label l_i, a sequence of formal parameters $\tilde{x}_i$ and an arbitrary process as the method body. Processes are put together by means of the usual concurrent composition. Scope restriction and replication complete the set of constructors the calculus is built from.

Following [2, 7], types are assigned to names, and not to processes, the latter being assigned multiple name-type pairs, constituting a typing for the process. Types are built from variables by means of a single constructor $[l_1:\tilde{\alpha}_1,\ldots l_n:\tilde{\alpha}_n]$, representing a name associated with an object capable of receiving messages labelled with l_i carrying a sequence of names of types $\tilde{\alpha}_i$, for $1 \leq i \leq n$. A typing assignment system assigns a type to each free name in a term, thus specifying in some sense the interface of the process. It turns out that the basic typing assignment system possesses no simple notion of principal typing. To provide for a notion of principal typings and to derive an efficient algorithm to extract the principal typing of a process, we use constraints on the substitution of type variables in the form of Ohori's kinds as well as kinded unification [5].

The outline of the paper is as follows. The next section introduces the calculus and section 3 the notion of types and the typing assignment system. Sections 4 and 5 deal with principal typings and typing inference. Section 6 compares the calculus to the polyadic π-calculus [4] and its typing system as proposed in [7]. The last section contains some concluding remarks.

2 The Calculus

This section introduces the calculus to the extent needed for typing considerations. Structural congruence caters for equivalence of terms over concrete syntax and, together with normal forms and message application, makes the formulation of the transition relation quite concise.

2.1 Syntax

Programs are build from names, by means of six basic constructors: messages, objects, concurrent composition, scope restriction, replication and inaction. The set of all terms is **P** and $P, Q, \ldots$ will denote particular terms.

Messages are directed to a single object and carry a method selector as well as the message contents itself. *Method selectors* are just labels $l, m, \ldots$ taken from a *set of labels* **L**. The contents of a message is a sequence of names; that is, messages carry nothing but names. All basic data a program often needs (including for example boolean values and natural numbers) will be coded in such a way that every piece of data is identified by a single name. Names $a, b \ldots$ or $v, x, y, \ldots$ are taken from an infinite *set of names* **N**. If $x_1, \ldots x_n$ ($n \geq 0$) are names in **N**, we write $\tilde{x}$ to mean the sequence $x_1 \cdots x_n$ in $\mathbf{N}^*$. A message targeted to an object identified by name a, selecting a method labelled with l, and carrying a sequence of names $\tilde{v}$, is written as,

$$a \triangleleft l(\tilde{v})$$

Object methods are parameterized by a sequence of names (intended to match the contents of an incoming message) followed by a method body. The body of a method is an arbitrary process. A method with a selector l, a sequence formal parameters $\tilde{x}$, and a body P is written as $l(\tilde{x}).P$. Intuitively, such a method matches a communication $l(\tilde{v})$ and behaves as P with occurrences of names in $\tilde{x}$ replaced by those in $\tilde{v}$.

Objects have a single identifier — a name again — and a collection of methods each labelled with a different label in **L**. An object with a collection of methods $l_1(\tilde{x}_1).P_1, \ldots l_n(\tilde{x}_n).P_n$ and a name a, is written as,

$$a \triangleright [l_1(\tilde{x}_1).P_1 \& \cdots \& l_n(\tilde{x}_n).P_n]$$

The remaining constructors in the language are fairly standard in process-calculi. *Concurrent composition* puts together arbitrary processes. If P and Q are two processes, then P,Q denotes the process composed of P and Q running concurrently. *Scope restriction* allows for local name creation avoiding unwanted communications with the exterior. If x is a name and P is a process, then $(\nu x)P$ denotes the restriction of x to the scope defined by P. Multiple name restrictions on a process $(\nu x_1)\cdots(\nu x_n)P$ will be written $(\nu \tilde{x})P$.

Replication accounts for unbounded computation power, and in particular for recursive definition of objects. A replicated object of the form $!\, a \triangleright [l_1(\tilde{x}_1).P_1 \& \cdots \& l_n(\tilde{x}_n).P_n]$ represents an unbounded number of copies of the object $a \triangleright [l_1(\tilde{x}_1).P_1 \& \cdots \& l_n(\tilde{x}_n).P_n]$. *Inaction* is the last constructor of the calculus. Denoted by **0**, it represents the process which does nothing, and could have been defined as $(\nu x)x \triangleright []$. The length of the sequence of names $\tilde{x}$ is denoted by $len(\tilde{x})$, and the set of names occurring in $\tilde{x}$ by $\{\tilde{x}\}$. The syntax of the calculus is summarized below.

Definition 2.1 (Syntax) Let **N** be an infinite set of *names* and $\mathbf{N}^*$ the set of (finite) sequences over **N**. Let **L** be a set of *labels*. The set of *terms* **P** is given by the following grammar.

$$P ::= a \triangleleft l(\tilde{v}) \mid a \triangleright [l_1(\tilde{x}_1).P_1 \& \cdots \& l_n(\tilde{x}_n).P_n] \mid P,Q \mid (\nu x)P \mid !\, a \triangleright [l_1(\tilde{x}_1).P_1 \& \cdots \& l_n(\tilde{x}_n).P_n] \mid \mathbf{0}$$

where $a,b,\ldots$ and $v,x,y,\ldots$ range over **N**; $\tilde{v},\tilde{x},\tilde{y},\ldots$ range over $\mathbf{N}^*$; $l,m,\ldots$ range over **L** and $P,Q,\ldots$ range over **P**. Labels $l_1,\ldots l_n$ and names in $\tilde{x}_i$, $i=1,\ldots n$, are assumed to be pairwise distinct.

For succinctness we will often write $!P$ instead of the more verbose form $!\, a \triangleright [l_1(\tilde{x}_1).P_1 \& \cdots \& l_n(\tilde{x}_n).P_n]$, but one should keep in mind that we only allow replication over objects.

2.2 Semantics

Objects and scope restriction are the binding operators of the calculus, which justifies the following definition.

Definition 2.2 (Free names) The set of *free names* in P, denoted $\mathcal{FN}(P)$, is inductively defined by:

$$\mathcal{FN}(\mathbf{0}) = \emptyset$$

$$\begin{align}
\mathcal{FN}(a \triangleleft l(\tilde{v})) &= \{a\} \cup \{\tilde{v}\} \\
\mathcal{FN}(a \triangleright [l_1(\tilde{x}_1).P_1 \& \cdots \& l_n(\tilde{x}_n).P_n]) &= \{a\} \cup \mathcal{FN}(P_1) \setminus \{\tilde{x}_1\} \cup \cdots \cup \mathcal{FN}(P_n) \setminus \{\tilde{x}_n\} \\
\mathcal{FN}(P, Q) &= \mathcal{FN}(P) \cup \mathcal{FN}(Q) \\
\mathcal{FN}((\nu x)P) &= \mathcal{FN}(P) \setminus \{x\} \\
\mathcal{FN}(!P) &= \mathcal{FN}(P)
\end{align}$$

A notion of *substitution* of free occurrences of x by z in P, denoted $P[z/x]$, is defined in the usual way, and so is α-conversion. Also, whenever $len(\tilde{z}) = len(\tilde{x})$ and the names in $\tilde{x}$ are all distinct, $P\{\tilde{z}/\tilde{x}\}$ denotes the result of the *simultaneous replacement* of free occurrences of $\tilde{x}$ by $\tilde{z}$ in P (with change of bound names where necessary, as usual.)

Definition 2.3 (Structural congruence) $\equiv$ is the smallest congruence relation over processes defined by the following rules.

i. $P \equiv Q$ whenever P is α-convertible to Q

ii. $(\mathbf{P}, `,', \mathbf{0})$ forms a commutative monoid with equality $\equiv$

iii. $a \triangleright [l(\tilde{x}).P \& m(\tilde{y}).Q] \equiv a \triangleright [m(\tilde{y}).Q \& l(\tilde{x}).P]$

iv. $(\nu x)P, Q \equiv (\nu x)(P, Q)$ whenever $x \notin \mathcal{FN}(Q)$

v. $!P \equiv P, !P$

There is a *normal form* into which every process can be transformed. Let us call *base-terms* to messages and objects, replicated or not.

Proposition 2.4 (Normal form) *For any process P in $\mathbf{P}$ there is an equivalent process P' of the form,*

$$(\nu \tilde{u})(P_1, \cdots, P_m)$$

where where $P_1, \ldots P_m$ denote base terms, for some $m \geq 1$. P' (usually not unique) is called a normal form *of P.*

Message application constitutes the basic communication mechanism of the calculus, and represents the reception of a message by an object, followed by the selection of the appropriate method, the substitution of the message contents by the method's formal parameters, and the execution of the method body.

Definition 2.5 (Message application) Let $l(\tilde{v})$ be the communication of some message, and let $[l_1(\tilde{x}_1).P_1 \& \cdots \& l_n(\tilde{x}_n).P_n]$ be a collection of methods. Message application is defined by,

$$[l_1(\tilde{x}_1).P_1 \& \cdots \& l_n(\tilde{x}_n).P_n] \bullet l(\tilde{v}) \to P_k\{\tilde{v}/\tilde{x}_k\}$$

whenever $l = l_k \in \{l_1, \ldots l_n\}$ and the lengths of $\tilde{v}$ and $\tilde{x}_k$ match.

Reduction models the computing mechanism of the calculus. By using structural congruence, normal forms and message application, it can be concisely defined.

Definition 2.6 (Reduction) *One-step reduction*, denoted by $\to$, is the smallest relation generated by the following rules.

$$\text{STRUCT} \quad \frac{P' \equiv P \quad P \to Q \quad Q \equiv Q'}{P' \to Q'}$$

$$\text{COMM} \quad \frac{M \bullet C \to P}{(\nu\tilde{x})(\partial, a \triangleleft C, a \triangleright M, \partial') \to (\nu\tilde{x})(\partial, P, \partial')}$$

where ∂ and ∂' represent concurrent composition of base-terms, C is a communication of the form $l(\tilde{v})$ and M is a collection of methods of the form $[l_1(\tilde{x}_1).P_1 \& \cdots \& l_n(\tilde{x}_n).P_n]$. The *reduction relation* $\twoheadrightarrow$ is the reflexive and transitive closure of one-step reduction.

Objects are recursive in nature, yet we have no explicit way of providing recursion. Since recursion can be eliminated in favor of replication (see, e.g. [4]), we will freely write,

$$X(\tilde{x}) \stackrel{\text{def}}{=} P \qquad (\{\tilde{x}\} = \mathcal{FN}(P))$$

and let X occur in P, to mean the process,

$$(\nu c)(c \triangleleft \mathsf{recur}(\tilde{x}), !c \triangleright \mathsf{recur}(\tilde{x}).P') \qquad (c \text{ fresh})$$

where P' is obtained from P by replacing occurrences of $X(\tilde{a})$ for $c \triangleleft \mathsf{recur}(\tilde{a})$.[1] The replicated process can be proved to behave (weakly) similarly to its recursive counterpart. In this way we have an unbounded number of copies of P', each one capable of being activated trough **recur** with a particular instance of P's "local variables".

Example 2.7 One of the simplest stateful objects is a buffer cell. Such an object has two methods, **read** and **write**, intended to read and write a value in the cell. Together with a **read** request comes a name intended to receive the **value** the buffer is holding. Here is a possible definition.

$$Cell(sv) \stackrel{\text{def}}{=} s \triangleright [\mathsf{read}(r).\, r \triangleleft \mathsf{value}(v), Cell(sv) \,\&\, \mathsf{write}(u).\, Cell(su)]$$

3 Types and Typing Assignment

This section introduces a notion of types for names and a basic typing system to assign types to the free names in terms. We then state some important properties of the typing system.

3.1 Types for Names

Types are intended to describe some property of the entity they are associated with. In our calculus names identify objects and hence types should represent a property of objects. Objects in **P** do not possess an input-output behavior and thus a function space construct makes no sense. Instead, objects receive messages, messages of a certain form, and that is the property types will describe.

---

[1] Label recur is, of course, arbitrary.

Definition 3.1 (Types) Let $\mathbf{V}$ be an infinite set of *type-variables*. The set of *types* $\mathbf{T}$ is defined by the following grammar.

$$\alpha ::= t \mid [l_1:\tilde{\alpha}_1,\ldots l_n:\tilde{\alpha}_n]$$

for $n \geq 0$, where labels $l_1,\ldots l_n \in \mathbf{L}$ are pairwise distinct; $t,t'\ldots$ range over $\mathbf{V}$; $\alpha,\beta\ldots$ over $\mathbf{T}$, and $\tilde{\alpha},\tilde{\beta}\ldots$ over $\mathbf{T}^*$.

Informally, an expression of the form $[l_1:\tilde{\alpha}_1,\ldots l_n:\tilde{\alpha}_n]$ is intended to denote some collection of names identifying objects containing n methods labelled with $l_1,\ldots l_n$ and whose arguments of method l_i belong to type $\tilde{\alpha}_i$.

3.2 Typing Assignment

Type assignment formulas are expressions $x:\alpha$, for x a name in $\mathbf{N}$ and α a type in $\mathbf{T}$, where x is called the formula's *subject* and α its *predicate*. *Typings* are sets of formulas of the form $\{x_1:\alpha_1,\ldots x_n:\alpha_n\}$, where no two formulas have the same name as subject. $\Gamma,\Delta,\ldots$ will denote typings.

Definition 3.2 (Typing compatibility) Typings Γ and Δ are compatible, denoted $\Gamma \asymp \Delta$, if and only if,

$$x:\alpha \in \Gamma \text{ and } x:\beta \in \Delta \text{ implies } \alpha = \beta$$

The following notation simplifies the treatment of the typing assignment system. Let $\tilde{x} = x_1\cdots x_n$ be a sequence of names, $\tilde{\alpha} = \alpha_1\cdots\alpha_n$ a sequence of types and Γ a typing. Then, $\{\tilde{x}:\tilde{\alpha}\}$ denotes the typing $\{x_1:\alpha_1,\ldots x_n:\alpha_n\}$; $\Gamma\cdot\tilde{x}:\tilde{\alpha}$ denotes typing $\Gamma \cup \{\tilde{x}:\tilde{\alpha}\}$, provided names in $\tilde{x}$ do not occur in Γ; and $\Gamma/\tilde{x}$ denotes the typing Γ with formulas with subjects in $\tilde{x}$ removed.

Typing assignment statements are expressions $P \succ \Gamma$ for all processes P and typings Γ. We will write $\vdash P \succ \Gamma$ if the statement $P \succ \Gamma$ is provable using the axioms and the rules of TA below. Whenever $\vdash P \succ \Gamma$ for some typing Γ, we say P is *typable*, and call Γ a *well-typing* for P.

Definition 3.3 (Typing assignment system TA) TA is defined by the following rules.

$$\text{NIL} \quad \vdash \mathbf{0} \succ \emptyset$$

$$\text{MSG} \quad \vdash a \triangleleft l(\tilde{v}) \succ \{\tilde{v}:\tilde{\alpha}, a:[l:\tilde{\alpha},\ldots]\} \quad (\{\tilde{v}:\tilde{\alpha}\} \asymp \{a:[l:\tilde{\alpha},\ldots]\})$$

$$\text{OBJ} \quad \frac{(\{a:[l_1:\tilde{\alpha}_1,\ldots l_n:\tilde{\alpha}_n]\} \asymp \Gamma_i, \Gamma_i \asymp \Gamma_j, 1 \leq i,j \leq n)}{\vdash P_i \succ \Gamma_i \cdot \tilde{x}_i:\tilde{\alpha}_i}$$
$$a \triangleright [l_1(\tilde{x}_1).P_1 \ \&\cdots\&\ l_n(\tilde{x}_n).P_n] \succ \{a:[l_1:\tilde{\alpha}_1,\ldots l_n:\tilde{\alpha}_n]\} \cup \Gamma_1 \cup \cdots \Gamma_n$$

$$\text{SCOP} \quad \frac{\vdash P \succ \Gamma}{\vdash (\nu x)P \succ \Gamma/x} \qquad \text{CONC} \quad \frac{\vdash P \succ \Gamma \quad \vdash Q \succ \Delta}{\vdash P,Q \succ \Gamma \cup \Delta} \quad (\Gamma \asymp \Delta)$$

$$\text{REPL} \quad \frac{\vdash P \succ \Gamma}{\vdash !P \succ \Gamma} \qquad \text{WEAK} \quad \frac{\vdash P \succ \Gamma}{\vdash P \succ \Gamma \cdot x:\alpha}$$

Example 3.4 Consider the buffer cell in example 2.7. Since method **write** expects a name of any type t (the type of the value the cell holds), and method **read** expects a name capable of receiving a message of type $\textsf{value}\colon t$, a typing for $Cell(sv)$ is given by,

$$\{s\colon[\textsf{read}\colon[\textsf{value}\colon t], \textsf{write}\colon t],\ v\colon t\}$$

Notice that this is not the only possible well-typing for $Cell(sv)$. In fact, apart from substitutions on variable t, we have that, e.g.

$$\{s\colon[\textsf{read}\colon[\textsf{value}\colon t, \textsf{print}\colon u], \textsf{write}\colon t],\ v\colon t\}$$

is also a well-typing for the process. However, the typing,

$$\{s\colon[\textsf{read}\colon[\textsf{value}\colon t], \textsf{write}\colon t, \textsf{think}\colon u],\ v\colon t\}$$

is not acceptable since it would allow us to compose $Cell(sv)$ with $s \triangleleft \textsf{think}(x)$, which would surely run into a type error.

3.3 Some Properties of the Typing System

Whenever a process P is typable, there exists a TA derivation which produces a typing containing only assignments on the free names of P. If Γ is a typing, let $\Gamma{\restriction}P$ be the restriction of Γ to the free names in P. We shall call typings of this form P-*typings*.

Lemma 3.5 *If* $\vdash P \succ \Gamma$, *then all free names of P occur in Γ and* $\vdash P \succ \Gamma{\restriction}P$.

The following lemma ensures that structural congruent processes have the same typings.

Lemma 3.6 *If* $\vdash P \succ \Gamma$ *and* $P \equiv Q$, *then* $\vdash Q \succ \Gamma$.

The following fundamental property of the typing assignment system TA ensures that the typing of a process does not change as it is reduced and is closely related with the lack of runtime errors.

Theorem 3.7 (Subject Reduction) *If* $\vdash P \succ \Gamma$ *and* $P \twoheadrightarrow Q$, *then* $\vdash Q \succ \Gamma$.

Notice that the converse of subject reduction does not hold, since non typable terms can be reduced to typable ones (e.g. $a \triangleleft l(a), a \triangleright l(x).\mathbf{0} \twoheadrightarrow \mathbf{0}$), and also because freenames may be lost in the course of reduction (e.g. $\vdash \mathbf{0} \succ \emptyset$ and $a \triangleleft l(v), a \triangleright l(x).\mathbf{0} \twoheadrightarrow \mathbf{0}$ but $\not\vdash a \triangleleft l(v), a \triangleright l(x).\mathbf{0} \succ \emptyset$). Also due to the loss of free names during reduction, if $\vdash P \succ \Gamma$, $P \twoheadrightarrow Q$, and $\vdash Q \succ \Delta$, then $\Delta{\restriction}Q \subseteq \Gamma{\restriction}P$.

A consequence of the subject-reduction property is that typable programs will not run into type errors during execution. We say P contains a possible *runtime error*, and write $P \in \textsc{Err}$, if there exists a term Q such that $P \twoheadrightarrow Q \equiv (\nu \tilde{u})(\partial, a \triangleleft l(\tilde{v}), a \triangleright [l_1(\tilde{x}_1).P_1 \ \&\ \cdots\ \&\ l_n(\tilde{x}_n).P_n], \partial')$ and $[l_1(\tilde{x}_1).P_1 \ \&\ \cdots\ \&\ l_n(\tilde{x}_n).P_n] \bullet l(\tilde{v})$ is not defined; that is, either $l \notin \{l_1, \ldots l_n\}$ or else $l = l_k \in \{l_1, \ldots l_n\}$ but $len(\tilde{v}) \neq len(\tilde{x}_k)$.

Corollary 3.8 *If P is typable, then $P \notin \textsc{Err}$.*

4 Principal typings

We have seen in example 3.4 that the system TA as presented in section 3 possesses no simple notion of principal typings, solely based on substitution of types for type variables, and on the number and nature of labels present in a type. In this section we introduce an alternative presentation of the system, compatible with TA, by using constraints on the substitution of type variables in the style of Ohori [5], which allows to talk about principal typings.

4.1 Kinds and Kinded Typing Assignment

Kinds describe constraints on the substitution of type variables, and are defined as follows.

Definition 4.1 (Kinds) The set of kinds **K** is given by all expressions of the form

$$\langle l_1 : \tilde{\alpha}_1, \ldots l_n : \tilde{\alpha}_n \rangle$$

where $l_1, \ldots l_n$ are distinct labels in **L** and $\tilde{\alpha}_1, \ldots \tilde{\alpha}_n$ are sequences of types in $\mathbf{T}^*$, for $n \geq 0$. $k, k', \ldots$ will range over **K**.

Intuitively, a kind of the form $\langle l_1 : \tilde{\alpha}_1, \ldots l_n : \tilde{\alpha}_n \rangle$ denotes the subset of types containing (at least) the components $l_1 : \tilde{\alpha}_1, \ldots l_n : \tilde{\alpha}_n$.

Kind assignments are expressions $t : k$, for t a type variable and k a kind. *Kindings* are acyclic sets of kind assignments[2] where no two assignments have the same type variable as subject. $K, K', \ldots$ will range over kindings. We say a type α *has a kind k under a kinding K*, denoted by $K \vdash \alpha : k$, if and only if,

$$K \vdash [l_1 : \tilde{\alpha}_1, \ldots l_n : \tilde{\alpha}_n, \ldots] : \langle l_1 : \tilde{\alpha}_1, \ldots l_n : \tilde{\alpha}_n \rangle$$
$$K \cdot t : \langle l_1 : \tilde{\alpha}_1, \ldots l_n : \tilde{\alpha}_n, \ldots \rangle \vdash t : \langle l_1 : \tilde{\alpha}_1, \ldots l_n : \tilde{\alpha}_n \rangle$$

Kinded typing assignments are expressions of the form $K \vdash P \succ \Gamma$, where all type variables in typing Γ occur in kinding K.

We will write $K \vdash_k P \succ \Gamma$ if the statement $P \succ \Gamma$ is provable from kinding K, using the rules and axioms of TA_k below.

Definition 4.2 (Kinded typing assignment system TA_k) TA_k is defined by the rules in TA with sequents of the form $\vdash P \succ \Gamma$ replaced by $K \vdash P \succ \Gamma$ and by replacing rule MSG for rule MSG_k below.

$$\text{MSG}_k \quad \frac{K \vdash \beta : \langle l : \tilde{\alpha} \rangle}{K \vdash a \triangleleft l(\tilde{v}) \succ \{\tilde{v} : \tilde{\alpha}, a : \beta\}} \quad (\{\tilde{v} : \tilde{\alpha}\} \asymp \{a : \beta\})$$

We can easily prove that TA_k is correct with respect to TA. In fact, deductions in TA are valid in TA_k if we start from a kinding assigning an arbitrary kind to every variable appearing in the deduction.

---
[2] A cycle in a set of kind assignments is a sequence of elements $t_1 : k_1, \ldots t_n : k_n$ such that t_{i+1} occurs in k_i and t_1 occurs in k_n, for $n \geq 1$.

Theorem 4.3 *If* $\vdash P \succ \Gamma$ *then* $K \vdash_k P \succ \Gamma$, *for any kinding K assigning every variable occurring in the deduction of* $\vdash P \succ \Gamma$.

Proof: By induction on the length of deductions. When the last rule is MsG, make $[l:\tilde{\alpha},\ldots] = \beta$. Then $K \vdash \beta : \langle l:\alpha \rangle$, and the result follows by rule MsG$_k$. The remaining cases are trivial. The condition that all variables appearing on the deduction of $\vdash P \succ \Gamma$ are bound in K ensures that all kinded typings in the deduction of $K \vdash_k P \succ \Gamma$ are well-formed. □

Conversely we can prove that, deductions in TA$_k$ can be mapped into deductions in TA, by replacing kinded type variables by types constrained to the kinding.

Theorem 4.4 *If* $K \vdash_k P \succ \Gamma$ *then* $\vdash P \succ \Gamma'$, *where Γ' is a typing obtained from Γ by recursively replacing type variables t for record types of the form $[l_1:\tilde{\alpha}_1, \ldots l_n:\tilde{\alpha}_n]$ whenever* $K \vdash t: \langle l_1:\tilde{\alpha}_1, \ldots l_n:\tilde{\alpha}_n \rangle$.

Proof: By induction on the length of deductions. When the last rule is MsG$_k$ and β is a type variable, since β does not occur in $\tilde{\alpha}$ by the definition of kinding, we have $\{\tilde{v}:\tilde{\alpha}\} \asymp \{a:[l:\tilde{\alpha},\ldots]\}$, and the result follows by rule MsG. The remaining cases are trivial. The fact that kindings are acyclic, ensures that the replacement of type variables for types is finite. □

4.2 Kinded Unification and Principal Kinded Typings

A *substitution on types* is a mapping $s : \mathbf{V} \to \mathbf{T}$ from type variables to types. Such a substitution can be easily extended to types, typings and kinds. A *kinded substitution* is a pair (K, s) composed of a kinding K and a substitution s. We say a kinded substitution (K', s) *respects* a kinding K if and only if,

$$K' \vdash st:sk \qquad \text{whenever} \qquad t:k \in K$$

A kinded substitution (K, s) is *more general* than (K', r) if there is a substitution u such that,

$$r = us \qquad \text{and} \qquad (K', u) \text{ respects } K$$

A *kinded set of equations* is a pair (K, E) composed of a kinding K and a set of equations of the form $\alpha = \beta$, for α and β types in $\mathbf{T}$. We say a kinded substitution (K, s) is a *unifier* of (K', E) if and only if,

$$(K, s) \text{ respects } K' \qquad \text{and} \qquad s\alpha = s\beta \text{ for all } \alpha = \beta \in E$$

Theorem 4.5 (Kinded unification [5]) *There is an algorithm $\mathcal{U}$ which, given any kinded set of equations, computes a most general unifier if it exists, and reports failure otherwise.*

A *kinded typing* is a pair (K, Γ) composed of a kinding K and a typing Γ. We say that a kinded typing (K', Δ) is *an instance* of (K, Γ) (or alternatively that (K, Γ) is *more general than* (K', Δ)) if there is a substitution s such that,

$$(K', s) \text{ respects } K \qquad \text{and} \qquad s\Gamma \subseteq \Delta$$

One important fact about instances is that every instance of a well-typing is also a well-typing.

Lemma 4.6 *If $K \vdash_k P \succ \Gamma$ and (K', Δ) is an instance of (K, Γ), then $K' \vdash_k P \succ \Delta$.*

All possible typings for a given process are instances of its *principal kinded typing*.

Definition 4.7 (Principal kinded typing) A kinded typing (K, Γ) is *principal* for a process P if and only if,

i. $K \vdash_k P \succ \Gamma$, and

ii. if $K' \vdash_k P \succ \Delta$, then (K', Δ) is an instance of (K, Γ).

It should be obvious that the principal typing of a process, when it exists, is unique up to renaming of type variables, and that it contains exactly the free names in the process.

Example 4.8 Recall the buffer cell object of example 2.7, and let t be the type of the value of the cell. By assigning a type variable u (subject to the constraint that it must be assigned a record type having at least a component value:t) to the object intended to receive the reply to a read request, the principal kinded typing of $Cell(sv)$ is given by

$$(\{t: \langle \rangle, u: \langle \text{value}: t \rangle\}, \{s: [\text{read}: u, \text{write}: t], v: t\})$$

Theorem 4.9 (Existence of principal typings) *If P is typable then there exists a principal kinded typing for P. It can be effectively computed.*

An algorithm to extract the principal kinded typing of a process is described in the next section.

5 Typing Inference

This section introduces an efficient algorithm to extract the principal kinded typing of a process, together with a proof of its correctness with respect to the typing assignment system TA_k. The algorithm is based on that of Vasconcelos and Honda [7] for the polyadic π-calculus, which in turn is based on Wand's [8].

5.1 The Algorithm

The algorithm builds from a process P_0 with all bound names renamed to be distinct, a typing and kinded set of equations to be submitted to the kinded unification procedure. Suppose the algorithm to be described produces a typing Γ_0 and a kinded set of equations (K, E), and use kinded unification on the set of equations. If (K', s) is a unifier of (K, E), then $s\Gamma_0$ is a well-typing for P_0 under kinding K'. Conversely, if P_0 is typable, then all its P-typings under kinding K' are of the form $s\Gamma_0 \upharpoonright P_0$, for (K', s) a unifier of (K, E). If Γ is a typing, we will write Γa for the type associated with name a in Γ, and $\Gamma \tilde{a}$ for the sequence of types associated with the sequence of names $\tilde{a}$ in Γ.

Input: A term P_0 with all bound names renamed to be distinct.

Initialization: Set $E = \emptyset$, $G = \{P_0\}$, Γ_0 to a typing assigning to all names in P_0 distinct type-variables, and K to a kinding assigning to all variables in Γ_0 an empty kind $\langle \rangle$.

Loop: If $G = \emptyset$, then halt and return (K, E). Otherwise choose a goal P from G, delete it from G and add to G, E and K, new goals, equations and kind assignments as specified below.

Case P is 0: Generate nothing.

Case P is $a \triangleleft l(\tilde{v})$: Generate the equation $\Gamma_0 a = t$ and the kind assignment $t : \langle l : \Gamma_0 \tilde{v} \rangle$, for t a fresh variable.

Case P is $a \triangleright [l_1(\tilde{x}_1).P_1 \& \cdots \& l_n(\tilde{x}_n).P_n]$: Generate the equation $\Gamma_0 a = [l_1 : \Gamma_0 \tilde{x}_1, \ldots l_n : \Gamma_0 \tilde{x}_n]$ and the goals $P_1, \ldots P_n$.

Case P is Q, R: Generate the goals Q and R.

Case P is $(\nu x)Q$ or $!Q$: Generate the goal Q.

To build the principal kinded typing of a term P_0, we use the above algorithm on P_0 and then the kinded unification algorithm on the resulting kinded set of equations (K, E). If (K, E) has no solutions, then P_0 is not typable. Otherwise let (K', s) be the most general unifier of (K, E). Then, $(K', s\Gamma_0 \restriction P_0)$ is the principal typing of P_0. If follows by Lemma 4.6 that every instance of $(K', s\Gamma_0 \restriction P_0)$ is a well kinded typing for P_0.

Example 5.1 To show how the algorithm behaves, let us consider the buffer cell described in Example 2.7. We first eliminate recursion by the method described at the end of Section 2, and rename bound names to obtain the process P_0 below.

$(\nu x)(x \triangleleft \mathsf{recur}(cv),$
$\quad !x \triangleright [\mathsf{recur}(c'v').\ c' \triangleright [\mathsf{read}(r).\ r \triangleleft \mathsf{value}(v'), x \triangleleft \mathsf{recur}(c'v')\ \&\ \mathsf{write}(u).\ x \triangleleft \mathsf{recur}(c'u)]])$

Let $\{x : t_x, c : t_c, v : t_v, c' : t'_c, v' : t'_v, r : t_r, u : t_u\}$ be the typing Γ_0. We trace the execution of the algorithm by means of a table. The first column of each line describes the current set of goals. We pick the left-most goal in the list, and write, in the first column of the next line the new set of goals, in the second column the generated equations, in the third column the generated kind assignments, and in the forth column a comment on the rule used. Processes in the set of goals are separated by semi-colons.

$\{P_0\}$			Initial state
$\{x \triangleleft \mathsf{recur}(cv), !x \triangleright [\cdots]\}$			Scope
$\{x \triangleleft \mathsf{recur}(cv); !x \triangleright [\cdots]\}$			Composition
$\{!x \triangleright [\mathsf{recur}(c'v').\cdots]\}$	$t_x = t_1$	$t_1 : \langle \mathsf{recur} : t_c t_v \rangle$	Message
$\{x \triangleright [\mathsf{recur}(c'v').\cdots]\}$			Replication
$\{c' \triangleright [\mathsf{read}(r).\cdots\ \&\ \mathsf{write}(u).\cdots]\}$	$t_x = [\mathsf{recur} : t'_c t'_v]$		Object
$\{r \triangleleft \mathsf{value}(v'), x \triangleleft \mathsf{recur}(c'v'); \cdots\}$	$t'_c = [\mathsf{read} : t_r, \mathsf{write} : t_u]$		Object
$\{r \triangleleft \mathsf{value}(v'); x \triangleleft \mathsf{recur}(c'v'); \cdots\}$			Composition
$\{x \triangleleft \mathsf{recur}(c'v'); x \triangleleft \mathsf{recur}(c'u)\}$	$t_r = t_2$	$t_2 : \langle \mathsf{value} : t'_v \rangle$	Message
$\{x \triangleleft \mathsf{recur}(c'u)\}$	$t_x = t_3$	$t_3 : \langle \mathsf{recur} : t'_c t'_v \rangle$	Message
$\{\}$	$t_x = t_4$	$t_4 : \langle \mathsf{recur} : t'_c t_u \rangle$	Message

Solving the resulting kinded set of equations using the unification algorithm yields the kinded substitution composed of kinding $K = \{t_v : \langle \rangle, t_r : \langle \mathsf{value} : t_v \rangle\}$ and substitution $s = \{t_x \mapsto [\mathsf{recur} : [\mathsf{read} : t_r, \mathsf{write} : t_v]t_v], t_c \mapsto t'_c \mapsto [\mathsf{read} : t_r, \mathsf{write} : t_v], t_v \mapsto t'_v \mapsto t_u\}$. The principal kinded typing $(K, s\Gamma_0 \restriction P_0)$ for the input process is the one in Example 4.8.

5.2 Correctness and Complexity of the Algorithm

Following [7, 8], we prove that the algorithm preserves a certain invariant and terminates. To simplify the statement of the invariant, we introduce some notation. Let (K', s) be a kinded substitution and (K, E) a kinded set of equations. We say (K', s) solves (K, E), denoted $(K', s) \models (K, E)$, if and only if (K', s) is a unifier of (K, E). Given a typing Γ_0, we write $(K, s) \models P$ to mean $K \vdash_k P \succ s\Gamma_0$, for some process P. If G is a set of goals, we write $(K, s) \models G$ if and only if $(K, s) \models P$ for each process P in G. Finally, we say (K', s) solves (K, E, G), denoted $(K', s) \models (K, E, G)$, if and only if $(K', s) \models (K, E)$ and $(K', s) \models G$. The invariant of the algorithm is as follows.

(Soundness) $\forall (K', s).(K', s) \models (K, E, G) \Rightarrow K' \vdash_k P_0 \succ s\Gamma_0$

(Completness) $K \vdash_k P_0 \succ \Gamma \Rightarrow \exists (K', s).(K', s) \models (K, E, G) \land \Gamma \upharpoonright P_0 = s\Gamma_0 \upharpoonright P_0$

At termination, when $G = \emptyset$, we have,

$$\forall (K', s).(K', s) \models (K, E) \Rightarrow K' \vdash_k P_0 \succ s\Gamma_0$$

$$K \vdash_k P_0 \succ \Gamma \Rightarrow \exists (K', s).(K', s) \models (K, E) \land \Gamma \upharpoonright P_0 = s\Gamma_0 \upharpoonright P_0$$

so that the algorithm only produces well kinded typings for the input process, and if the input process is typable, then its P-well-typings under kinding K' are given by $s\Gamma_0 \upharpoonright P_0$, for some unifier (K', s) of the kinded set of equations produced.

Theorem 5.2 (Termination) *The algorithm always terminates.*

Proof: Each action generates subgoals involving terms strictly smaller than the original. □

Theorem 5.3 (Correctness) *The invariants are established by the initialization step and preserved by each case in the loop.*

Proof: (Soundness) The first part is trivial; the second follows by a simple induction on the structure of deductions.
(Completeness) For the first part take s to be the substitution that assigns α to t whenever $x : t \in \Gamma_0 \upharpoonright P_0$ and $x : \alpha \in \Gamma \upharpoonright P_0$, and take K' to be K. Then (K, s) unifies $(K, \emptyset)$; and $K \vdash_k P_0 \succ s\Gamma_0$ implies $K \vdash_k P_0 \succ \Gamma \upharpoonright P_0$ by lemma 3.5, which in turn implies $K \vdash_k P_0 \succ \Gamma$ by consecutive applications of rule WEAK; and $\Gamma \upharpoonright P_0 = s\Gamma_0 \upharpoonright P_0$.
The proof of the second part follows by induction on the structure of terms. The most difficult cases are when terms are messages and objects; the remaining cases are a simple adaptation of the corresponding in [7].
Case $a \triangleleft l(\tilde{v})$. Assume $K \vdash_k a \triangleleft l(\tilde{v}) \succ \Gamma$. We need to show that

$$\exists (K', s).(K', s) \models (K \cup \{t : \langle l : \Gamma_0 \tilde{v} \rangle\}, \{\Gamma_0 a = t\}) \land \Gamma \upharpoonright P_0 = s\Gamma_0 \upharpoonright P_0$$

By the typing rules we know that $K \vdash \beta : \langle l : \tilde{\alpha} \rangle$ and $\Gamma \upharpoonright P_0 = \{a : \beta, \tilde{v} : \tilde{\alpha}\}$. Make $s = \{t \mapsto \beta, \Gamma_0 a \mapsto \beta, \Gamma_0 \tilde{v} \mapsto \tilde{\alpha}\}$ and $K' = K$. We then have $K \vdash st : \langle l : s\Gamma_0 \tilde{v} \rangle$; $s\Gamma_0 a = st$ and $\{a : \beta, \tilde{v} : \tilde{\alpha}\} = s\{a : \Gamma_0 a, \tilde{v} : \Gamma_0 \tilde{v}\}$.

Case $a \triangleright [l_1(\tilde{x}_1).P_1 \& \cdots \& l_n(\tilde{x}_n).P_n]$. Assume $K \vdash_k a \triangleright [l_1(\tilde{x}_1).P_1 \& \cdots \& l_n(\tilde{x}_n).P_n] \succ \Gamma$. By induction hypothesis we know that $\exists (K',s).(K',s) \models (K,E,G) \wedge \Gamma {\restriction} P_0 = s\Gamma_0 {\restriction} P_0$, and we need to show that,

$$\exists (K'',s').(K'',s') \models (K, E \cup \{\Gamma_0 a = [l_1:\tilde{\alpha}_1,\ldots l_n:\tilde{\alpha}_n]\}, G \cup \{P_1,\ldots p_n\}) \wedge \Gamma {\restriction} P_0 = s'\Gamma_0 {\restriction} P_0$$

By taking $(K'',s') = (K',s)$ we only have to show that $s\Gamma_0 a = s[l_1:\tilde{\alpha}_1,\ldots l_n:\tilde{\alpha}_n]$ and $K' \vdash_k P_i \succ s\Gamma_0$, for $1 \leq i \leq n$. So let $s\Gamma_0 = \Gamma' \cdot \tilde{x}_1 : \tilde{\alpha}_1 \cdots \tilde{x}_n : \tilde{\alpha}_n$, for some typing Γ' and sequences of types $\tilde{\alpha}_1,\ldots \tilde{\alpha}_n$. By the typing rules we have a derivation of $K \vdash_k P_i \succ \Gamma_i \cdot \tilde{x}_i : \tilde{\alpha}_i$ with $\Gamma_i \asymp \Gamma_j$, $\{a : [l_1:\tilde{\alpha}_1,\ldots l_n:\tilde{\alpha}_n]\} \asymp \Gamma_i$ and $\Gamma_1 \cup \cdots \Gamma_n = \Gamma'$. Use the WEAK as many times as needed to establish the result, for each i. As for the equations, the result follows from the fact that $\{a : [l_1:\tilde{\alpha}_1,\ldots l_n:\tilde{\alpha}_n]\} \asymp s\Gamma_0$ and that a occurs in Γ_0. □

As for the complexity, it is easy to see that Γ_0 and the initial kinding can be built in a time linear on P_0, and should take a space proportional to the number of different names in P_0. If types and kinds are implemented with a directed acyclic graph, each equation and kind assignment generated introduces a single node in the graph, and can be computed in a time proportional to the number of names and labels involved. Also, since no copy is needed, each subgoal may be generated in constant time. Hence, the loop executes in a time linear on the size of P_0, produces a number of equations and kind assignments proportional to the number of names in P_0, and introduces a number of new nodes in the graph no larger than the number of names in P_0.

As a corollary, the algorithm to find the principal typing of a process is linear on the size of the textual representation of the input term, provided that the kinded unification algorithm is linear on the number of nodes in the graph.

6 Comparison to the Polyadic π-Calculus

The calculus so far introduced can be easily translated into the polyadic π-calculus [4]. It seems however not be a method of encoding both terms into π-terms and types into π-types (as presented in [7]) in a satisfactory manner. In what follows, we present two candidates that fail either to transform types or terms.

The first encoding uses summation to represent the disjunctive nature of methods. An object of the form,

$$a \triangleright l(\tilde{x}).P \,\&\, m(\tilde{y}).Q \tag{1}$$

is translated into a polyadic π-process of the form,

$$a_l(\tilde{x}).P + a_m(\tilde{y}).Q$$

where a_l and a_m are distinct names. Similarly, a message of the form,

$$a \triangleleft l(\tilde{v}) \tag{2}$$

is translated into a π-process $\bar{a}_l[\tilde{x}].\mathbf{0}$. It is easy to see that terms in our calculus and their images in π-calculus behave strongly similarly. However, instead of translating types, we have to translate typings, for there is not a one-to-one correspondence between the free names in an object and those in its π image. So, for example a typing $\{a:[l:\tilde{t}, m:\tilde{u}]\}$ would have to be translated into the π-typing $\{a_l:(\tilde{\alpha}), a_m:(\tilde{\beta})\}$.

We can also translate terms in our calculus into polyadic π-terms without summation, by using a technique in [3]. The idea is to have a two step protocol, in which a message first asks the object method names, and then selects one of them. Assuming that we have a complete order in **L**, in such a way that, e.g. $l < m$, the object (1) above can be translated into,

$$(\nu lm)(a(r).\overline{r}[lm].(l(\tilde{x}).P \mid m(\tilde{y}).Q))$$

In this way, message (2) would be translated into,

$$(\nu r)(\overline{a}[r].r(lm).\overline{l}[\tilde{v}])$$

Terms in our calculus and their images in the polyadic π-calculus now behave only weakly similarly. The drawback of this encoding is that it assumes we know all the methods in the target object, and therefore it is not context independent. On the other hand types may be translated directly since we now have a one-to-one correspondence between the free names in an object and those in its image. For example, the type $[l:\tilde{t}, m:\tilde{u}]$ could be naturally translated into the π-type $(((\tilde{\alpha}),(\tilde{\beta})))$.

7 Concluding Remarks

We presented a basic calculus aiming to capture some essential notions present in systems of concurrent objects communicating via asynchronous message passing, together with a typing system for the calculus. Types are assigned to names and are intended to describe the kind of messages objects associated with the name are able to receive. Processes are not assigned types, but else a collection of name-type pairs. The typing system presented assigns a type to each free name in a process, thus specifying in some sense the interface of the process. Programs that conform to the typing discipline were shown not to run into errors. Furthermore, we presented an algorithm to extract the principal typing of a program, from which all typings that make the program well-typed can be extracted. Finally, we discussed the lack of a satisfactory encoding of the present calculus into the polyadic π-calculus.

The approach seems an interesting basis from which explore further aspects present in objects, namely the notion of inheritance (by introducing new or redefining existing methods in objects) and that of subtyping (by introducing new components in a record type) as well the relationship between these. Also, an extension of the typing system to include recursive types, indispensable to type objects denoting basic data such as natural numbers and lists, can be easily done along the lines of [7]. Another related line of investigation, in the style of [6], encompasses the introduction of variables over process accompanied by a notion of predicative polymorphism, and a ML-like let construct. Such a system would allow the declaration of an object of a polymorphic type, which could be used in a program multiple times with different types, instances of the type of the declared object.

On the pragmatic side, one should study the applicability of the calculus as a means to describe semantics and types of object-oriented concurrent programming languages such as Actor based languages, Concurrent Smalltalk, ABCL and POOL, as well as a clean incorporation of functions as a particular discipline of object definition and usage.

Acknowledgements. The authors wish to thank Kohei Honda for long and fruitful discussions on the nature of concurrency and types for concurrency.

References

[1] Carl Hewitt. Viewing control structures as patterns of passing messages. *Artificial Inteligence*, 8(3):323–364, 1977.

[2] Kohei Honda. Types for Dyadic Interaction. In *Proceedings of CONCUR'93*, Springer-Verlag, LNCS, August 1993.

[3] Kohei Honda and Mario Tokoro. An Object Calculus for Asynchronous Communication. In *1991 European Conference on Object-Oriented Computing*, pages 141–162, Springer-Verlag, 1991. LNCS 512.

[4] Robin Milner. *The Polyadic π-Calculus: a Tutorial*. ECS-LFCS 91-180, University of Edinburgh, October 1991.

[5] Atsushi Ohori. A compilation method for ML-style polymorphic record calculi. In *19th ACM Symposium on Principles of Programming Languages*, pages 154–165, 1992.

[6] Vasco T. Vasconcelos. A predicative polymorphic type system for the polyadic π-calculus. May 1993. Keio University.

[7] Vasco T. Vasconcelos and Kohei Honda. Principal typing-schemes in a polyadic π-calculus. In *Proceedings of CONCUR'93*, Springer-Verlag, LNCS, August 1993.

[8] Mitchell Wand. A simple algorithm and proof for type inference. *Fundamenta Informaticae*, X:115–122, 1987. North-Holland.

A Type Mechanism Based on Restricted CCS for Distributed Active Objects

Yasunori Harada

NTT Basic Research Laboratories
9-11 Midori-Cho 3-Chome Musashino-Shi
Tokyo 180, Japan
e-mail: hara@seraph.ntt.jp

Abstract

Ordinary object type is a one-to-one relation between caller and callee. When communication patterns are introduced into object types, they must be extended to relations among to two-or-more object. We propose a new type framework that expresses communication patterns and two-or-more object connections, and its implementation on asynchronous faulty networks using future communication property. Although our type is static and not higher order, we can construct a computational model with dynamic properties.

1 Introduction

Large-scale or open-ended distributed systems consist of many software components connected together. For safe construction of such software, it will be described using a formal description. Since there are large or infinite number of components, almost all the formal examinations of whole system are impossible. We assume that each component is connected to a small subset of all the components. Consequently, we concentrate local consistency. Components have multiple connectors by which components are connected with others.

We want to regard several connected components as one component. Then, we also want to regard several connections as one connection. For example, when three components (A, B, C) connect as (A-B, B-C, C-A) and we regard A, B as new component AB, what is the connection C-AB? Then, we extend definition of connection to involving three-or-more component.

Object-oriented techniques play an important role in constructing such software components. Those techniques facilitate encapsulation, in which data and procedures are linked together, and abstraction, which allows the definition of abstract interfaces. As distributed software components are autonomous, it is essential that they be treated as active objects[Yone90]. We define objects which have several connectors. Each connector is attached connector type, only components with matching connector types can be connected. If a connection is a parent-children relationship, the connector type is an extension of the function call. However, many connections with active components have a peer relationship[HHWM92], so the connector type is represented by the communication specification. In addition to one-to-one connections, three-or-more connector may also be connected together by a single connector.

Nierstrasz[NP90, Nier92] proposed an object type using process calculus. We are interested in a distributed object implementation with asynchronous message passing, nondeterministic arrival order, and lost messages. Honda[HT92] proposed asynchronous nondeterminism process calculus. It is difficult to directly write programs which are considered working in asynchronous faulty networks. Therefore, we use the future communication and restricted process calculus expressions for communication specifications, which is easy to write programs and implement.

Such distributed systems also have dynamic properties, which are dynamic object creation, migration and connection. Although some process calculuses[MPW89] treat there properties, we don't introduce dynamic properties into our communication type. Instead of static types, we propose a computational model with dynamic properties.

This paper describes a type mechanism for distributed active objects using communication specifications that is easy to implement in faulty networks. For type matching, a Linda[CG89]-like computational model is proposed. In section 2, we mention group connections. Section 3 describes how types suitable for distributed systems are defined and how these types can be matched. Section 4 presents a computational model that incorporates the component connectivity based on these types. Section 5 introduces a programming language that incorporates this method. Section 6 presents comparisons and discussion.

2 Group Connection

Let's consider that the connector type can be expressed by a set (a denominator) and its subset (a numerator), for example $\{1\}/\{1,2\}$, $\{c\}/\{a,b,c\}$. A connection is successful if all denominators are equal, the union of the numerators is equal to the denominator, and there are no overlapping numerators. For example, $\{1\}/\{1,2\}$ and $\{2\}/\{1,2\}$ is a successful connection, but $\{a\}/\{a,b,c\}$ and $\{c\}/\{a,b,c\}$ is not due to the absence of $\{b\}/\{a,b,c\}$. For example, in a Smalltalk-80 system, one visual component is assembled from three objects: Model, View and Controller[GB83]. We can treat the relations of these objects as three different connections ($\{M,V\}$, $\{V,C\}$ and $\{C,M\}$), so each object has two kinds of connectors for each connection (ex. for Model. $\{M\}/\{M,V\}$ and $\{M\}/\{M,C\}$). However, we can also treat these relations as one connection ($\{M,V,C\}$), so that each object has only one kind of connector(ex. for Model $\{M\}/\{M,V,C\}$). The latter is useful for understanding functions and checking errors in detail. Figure 1 shows objects, connectors and connections relations.

We can consider a composition of connectors. For example, View and Controller are connected then its type is $\{V,C\}/\{M,V,C\}$, and we can regard it as one connector.

3 Asynchronous Communication Types

Instead of using asynchronous process calculus[HT92], we use restricted synchronous process calculus as communication type. This restriction comes from a implementation on asynchronous communication system.

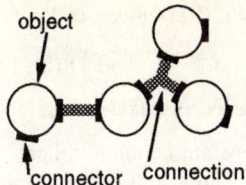

Figure 1: Objects, Connectors and Connections

3.1 Future Communication

One basic idea for an implementation of communication is future communication[Yone90, YC88] using a concurrent logic programming language. When two patterns,

$$[A, B, C] \quad [X, Y, Z],$$

are unified, there are three possible future communications between each pair of (A,X), (B,Y), and (C,Z). We can thus regard these patterns as message definitions. To simplify implementing this model with sequential languages, we add these patterns to the message order and direction of communication. For example,

$$[A, \overline{B}, C] \quad [\overline{X}, Y, \overline{Z}]$$

is the definition of the ordered message sequence:

$$A \leftarrow X$$
$$B \rightarrow Y$$
$$C \leftarrow Z.$$

Because of the future communication property, preserving the message order and detecting message transfer failures are easily implemented[KMPS91]. Thus when writing these patterns, we need not consider such characteristics of faulty networks.

Since our communication type is static, its type matching can do statically. Then, we regard the type matching as a unification of patterns. We will extend such patterns to selection, repetition and communication between three-or-more object.

3.2 Type Expression

Our asynchronous communication types are based on CCS (Calculus of Communicating Systems)[Mil92], mainly because CCS has a simple transition mechanism, and the τ action is useful for type extraction of the programs that are discussed below.

In the first place, we define a CCS process which is omitted some feature. Next, we show that some CCS expressions are not fitted in asynchronous communication. Then, we define a asynchronous communication process by restricted CCS.

Let $\mathcal{L}$ be a set of labels, $\mathcal{A} = \mathcal{L} \cup \{\overline{a} | a \in \mathcal{L}\} \cup \{\tau\}$ a set of actions, and $\mathcal{C}$ a set of processes.

DEFINITION 3.1 *processes $p \in \mathcal{C}$ are given in the following form:*

$$p = 0 \mid \alpha.p' \mid p_1 + p_2 \mid p_1|p_2 \mid \mu x.p',$$

where $\alpha \in \mathcal{A}$, $p', p_1, p_2 \in \mathcal{C}$ and x is a variable range over $\mathcal{C}$.

Action a indicate a message reception, action $\overline{a}$ indicate a message transmission, and action τ indicate a internal action. The $+$ and $\mid$ are commutative and associative operators; $\mu x.p$ is a recursive operator. They satisfy the following relations.

$$p + 0 = p$$
$$p|0 = p$$
$$\mu x.p = p[\mu x.p/x]$$

where $p[A/x]$ is substitution of free x in p to A.

DEFINITION 3.2 *Transition relation $\xrightarrow{\alpha}: \mathcal{C} \times \mathcal{C}$ is defined as follows.*

$$\alpha.p \xrightarrow{\alpha} p$$

$$\frac{p \xrightarrow{\alpha} p_1}{p + p_2 \xrightarrow{\alpha} p_1}$$

$$\frac{p \xrightarrow{\alpha} p_1}{p|p_2 \xrightarrow{\alpha} p_1|p_2}$$

$$\frac{p_1 \xrightarrow{a} p_1' \quad p_2 \xrightarrow{\overline{a}} p_2'}{p_1|p_2 \xrightarrow{\tau} p_1'|p_2'}$$

The label $* \in \mathcal{L}$ is used as a special label to indicate a send or receive value. Labels are not first-class values, so $*$ can not transfer labels. Whether $*$ has a type will be addressed later.

In asynchronous communications, objects can not send a message related to an external choice, because sending operations are always successful. On the other hand, if an object can freely change its set of acceptable messages, then cooperation with it is difficult. For example, processes $\overline{a} + \overline{b}$, $a + \overline{a}$ and $\tau.a + \tau.b$ only works on synchronous communication. Therefore, type expressions of asynchronous communications are more restricted than synchronous communication expressions.

Let $\sum_{i=1}^{k} p_i$ denote the process

$$p_1 + p_2 + \cdots + p_k,$$

and let $\bigoplus_{i=1}^{k} p_i$ denote the process

$$\tau.p_1 + \tau.p_2 + \cdots + \tau.p_k.$$

DEFINITION 3.3 *A set of asynchronous communication processes $\mathcal{S}$ is a subset of process $\mathcal{C}$. $s \in \mathcal{S}$ is given by form:*

$$s = 0 \mid \sum_{i=1}^{n} a_i.s_i \mid \bigoplus_{i=1}^{n} \overline{a}_i.s_i \mid \mu x.s,$$

where $a_i \in \mathcal{L}$ and $s_i \in \mathcal{S}$.

$\sum a_i.s_i$ is an external choice with message receptions; $\bigoplus \overline{a}_i.s_i$ is an internal choice with message transmissions. The choices are clearly divided into internal and external. The process $\bigoplus \overline{a}_i.s_i$ has a communication initiative. $\mathcal{S}$ includes no concurrent operations.

This restriction may appear to lower the descriptive power of the process, but it is not a problem in practice, as it is possible to achieve the same result by combining multiple asynchronous messages. For example, the process $\tau.\overline{whichAB}.(a.\tau.\overline{a}+b.\tau.\overline{b})$ can be implemented in the process $\overline{a}+\overline{b}$.

3.3 Successful Communication

When some asynchronous communication processes $s_i \in \mathcal{S}$ work together, we are interested in whether their communications are successful or not. It is not a p-test relation[Henn88]. p_1 satisfies a p-test if for any transition sequence of $p|p_1$, p reaches a success state. In our definition p and p_1 have the successful communication relation (SCR) if and only if for any transition sequence of $p|p_1$, both p and p_1 reach success states together. We can extend the SCR to the three-or-more process relationship, in which some processes $p_1, \cdots, p_k$ are SCR if for any transition sequence of $p_1|\cdots|p_k$, all $p_1, \cdots, p_k$ reach success states together. We define such a success state as 0.

DEFINITION 3.4 *We define a successful communication $\sigma(p)$ as*

$$\sigma(0)$$

$$\frac{p \xrightarrow{\tau} p_1 \quad \sigma(p_1)}{\sigma(p)}.$$

$\sigma(p)$ *is true if for any transition sequence p becomes 0.*

Let us regard $s \in \mathcal{S}$ as an object connector type and $\sigma(s_1|\cdots)$ as an connector type-matching. The object type is the collection of these connector types.

For any two processes $p_1, p_2 \in \mathcal{C}$, $\sigma(p_1)$ and $\sigma(p_2)$ do not imply $\sigma(p_1|p_2)$ if p_1 may communicate with p_2 (by using same labels). For example $\sigma(a.\overline{a}|\overline{a}.a)$ and $\sigma(a.\overline{b}|\overline{a}.b)$ are true, but $\sigma(a.\overline{a}|\overline{a}.a|a.\overline{b}|\overline{a}.b)$ is not true, because one of the transition sequences is

$$a.\overline{a}|\overline{a}.a|a.\overline{b}|\overline{a}.b \xrightarrow{\tau} \overline{a}|\overline{a}.a|a.\overline{b}|b \xrightarrow{\tau} 0|\overline{a}.a|\overline{b}|b \xrightarrow{\tau} \overline{a}.a\ .$$

Thus it is difficult to define a general procedure for determining $\sigma(p)$ for any p. The process $\overline{a}.a$ in $a.\overline{a}|\overline{a}.a|a.\overline{b}|\overline{a}.b$ can send the message a to the process $a.\overline{a}$ or $a.\overline{b}$. This nondeterminism is an obstacle. We define a new restriction of process, Single Receiver Communication (SRC).

DEFINITION 3.5 *Let $p = s_1|\cdots|s_k, s_i \in \mathcal{S}$ $(1 \leq i \leq k)$ and $S = \{s_i | 1 \leq i \leq k\}$,*

- *0 is SRC,*
- *p is SRC if $s_i = \mu x.s_i'$ and $s_1|\cdots|s_i'[s_i/x]|\cdots|s_k$ is SRC when assuming p is SRC.*
- *p is SRC if*

  $\forall s \in S, a \in \mathcal{L}. (s \xrightarrow{\overline{a}} s')$ *implies*
  $\exists r \in (S - \{s\}).(r \xrightarrow{a} r'), \neg(\exists r_1 \in (S - \{s,r\}).r_1 \xrightarrow{a} r_1'),$
  and $s'|r'|(S - \{s,r\})$ is SRC.

This last statement means that only one process receives a message.

3.4 Type Graph

An asynchronous communication process $s \in \mathcal{S}$ can be expressed as a directed graph (type graph). The type graph has information on which process has the initiative and what label is transferred.

Let $\mathcal{ST}$ be a set of process statuses $\mathcal{ST} = \{Active, Passive, Terminate\}$. The type graph is a quintuplet $\langle N, E, b, st, l \rangle$, where N is a set of nodes, E is a set of edges ($E \subset N^2$), b is a starting node ($b \in N$), st is a function of process statuses ($st\colon N \to \mathcal{ST}$), and l is a function of labels ($l\colon E \to \mathcal{L}$). The type graph $\langle N, E, b, st, l \rangle$ of an asynchronous process $s \in \mathcal{S}$ is defined as follows,

let $b = tg(s)$ where,

1. $tg(0) = n$ where $st(n) \stackrel{def}{=} Terminate$,
2. $tg(\sum_{i=1}^{k} a_i.s_i) = n$ where $st(n) \stackrel{def}{=} Passive$, and $l(n, tg(s_i)) \stackrel{def}{=} a_i$ $(1 \le i \le k)$
3. $tg(\bigoplus_{i=1}^{k} \overline{a}_i.s_i) = n$ where $st(n) \stackrel{def}{=} Active$, and $l(n, tg(s_i)) \stackrel{def}{=} a_i$ $(1 \le i \le k)$
4. $tg(\mu x.s') = tg(s') = n$ where $n = tg(x)$;;; $\mu x.s'$ makes a cycle.

Denote an *Active* state as a black node, a *Passive* state as a white node and a *Terminate* state as a T marked node. Figure 2 shows the case in which $P = \mu x.a.(\tau.\overline{b}.0 + \tau.\overline{c}.a.\tau.\overline{c}.x)$ and $Q = \mu x.\tau.\overline{a}.(b.0 + c.x)$.

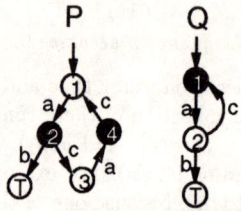

Figure 2: Communication Graph Example

3.5 Type Matching

Let $s_1, \cdots, s_k \in \mathcal{S}$ be object types. Type matching of object connectors depends on whether $\sigma(s_1|\cdots|s_k)$ is true or not. The type matching algorithm constructs a matching graph (MG) using a type graph representation.

Let k type graphs, g_i $(1 \le i \le k)$, be $\langle N_i, E_i, b_i, st_i, l_i \rangle$ and G be a set of type graph indices $\{1, \cdots, k\}$, we define MG as a quintuplet $\langle \hat{N}, \hat{E}, \hat{b}, \hat{i}, \hat{m} \rangle$, where $\hat{N}$ is a set of nodes ($\hat{N} \subset N_1 \times N_2 \times \cdots \times N_k$), $\hat{E}$ is a set of edges ($E \subset \hat{N}^2$), $\hat{b} \in \hat{N}$ is a starting node ($\hat{b} = (b_1, \cdots, b_k)$), $\hat{i}$ is an initiative function ($\hat{i}\colon \hat{N} \to 2^G$), $\hat{m}$ is a message (composed a receiver and a label) function, ($\hat{m}\colon \hat{E} \to G \times \mathcal{L}$).

The algorithm for creating a matching graph is as follows,

$match(\hat{b})$ where

$match(\hat{n}) =$ if $\forall i \in G.\ st_i(n_i) = Terminate$ then **true**

$match(\hat{n}) =$

if $\exists s \in G.st_s(n_s) = Active$;;; s means sender.
loop between 1 and 8 for all $(n_s, n'_s) \in E_s$.
1. let $l = l_s((n_s, n'_s))$
2. $\exists r \in (G - \{s\}).\exists(n_r, n'_r) \in E_r.\ l_r((n_r, n'_r)) = l,$;;; r means receiver
3. if $\exists q \in (G - \{s, r\}).\exists(n_q, n'_q) \in E_q.\ l_q((n_q, n'_q)) = l$ then **false**
 ;;; $\hat{n}$ is not SRC.
4. otherwise let $\hat{n}' = (n_1, \cdots, n'_s, \cdots, n'_r, \cdots, n_k)$
 ;;; replace s-th and r-th nodes to new one.
5. add new edge $(\hat{n}, \hat{n}')$ to $\hat{E}$
6. if $\hat{n}'$ is already included $\hat{N}$ then **true**
7. otherwise add new node $\hat{n}'$ to $\hat{N}$
8. if $match(\hat{n}')$ then **true**

otherwise **false**. ;;; deadlocked

This algorithm has a nondeterminism of selection of sender s. However created MG holds only one possibility. Fortunately, since future communication property and SRC, this nondeterminism is reappeared. For example, when matching asynchronous processes which are $a.\overline{b}$, $\overline{a}.d$, $\overline{c}.b$ and $c.\overline{d}$, this algorithm creates one of four MG which are

$$(a.\overline{b}, \overline{a}.d, \overline{c}.b, c.\overline{d}) \xrightarrow{a} (\overline{b}, d, \overline{c}.b, c.\overline{d}) \xrightarrow{c} (\overline{b}, d, b, \overline{d}) \xrightarrow{b} (0, d, 0, \overline{d}) \xrightarrow{d} (0, 0, 0, 0),$$

$$(a.\overline{b}, \overline{a}.d, \overline{c}.b, c.\overline{d}) \xrightarrow{c} (a.\overline{b}, \overline{a}.d, b, \overline{d}) \xrightarrow{a} (\overline{b}, d, b, \overline{d}) \xrightarrow{b} (0, d, 0, \overline{d}) \xrightarrow{d} (0, 0, 0, 0),$$

$$\cdots .$$

However a partner process of each communication is same in all case.

After successful matching of the graph in Figure 2, the MG becomes as shown in Figure 3, where X in node label $(i,j)/X$ is subset of $\hat{i}((i,j))$, and edge label (l,Y) is $\hat{m}((n,n'))$.

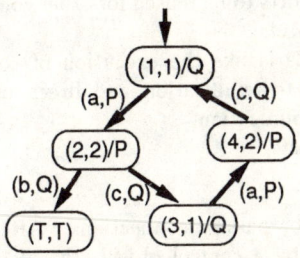

Figure 3: Matching Graph

4 Computational Model

This section describes the basic computational model[HWM92] and discusses its characteristics. The main constituents of this model are objects and ports. Objects are the main execution elements. Ports are used for connection of peer objects.

4.1 Objects

Objects are active components and concurrent operations within them are permitted. Objects have multiple connectors, which are typed by a type graph. At any given time, objects may be connected at multiple ports.

The type graphs can be declared from the main body of the program, or extracted from the main body of the program. For the latter purpose, the compiler executes in the following way.

1. Translate the program to process expression $p \in \mathcal{C}$, in which actions include connector information.

2. For each connectors c,

    (a) change all actions, except actions sent to or received from c, to τ,

    (b) remove sequential τ and connector information,

    (c) if this expression does not include asynchronous communication process $\mathcal{S}$, then a compile error has occurred.

Then, we can get the communication types for each connector. For example, let a process A be $a_x.\overline{b}_y + c_x.\overline{d}_y$, then the connector x type is $a+c$ and the connector y type is $\tau.\overline{b}+\tau.\overline{d}$.

4.2 Ports

The ports connect multiple objects with their connector type type graph, and attempt to match objects by using the type graph of each connected object. When successful, the port makes an MG and that MG is sent to each connected object. Until an MG is received, each object holds execution. Successfully matched objects are then detached from the ports, allowing the ports to be reused for other connections. Then, these objects communicate directly using MG.

The behavior of the ports is like the execution of concurrent logic programs. A matching process corresponds to a unification, and direct communication between objects corresponds to a future communication.

We define two kinds of ports.

1. **Closable Ports**

    These ports are used for passive connections. After several passive objects are connected to one port by a control object, the algorithm is used to test object matching. If all the objects match, the MG is sent to each passive object and a success message is sent to the control object.

2. **Linda TS Ports**

    These ports are used for active connections. In this case, there is no control object.

Instead, a Linda[CG89] TS Port is used to connect two-or-more active object. Each time an object is connected to a port, a search is made by the port for matching objects among the connected objects. The port attempts to find nondeterministically a subset of the connected objects that can be matched. If one is found, an MG is sent to the matched objects, and those objects are then detached. The other unmatched objects stay the port connection, so the port is used continuously.

The port allows the objects to create an active connection among themselves. The connect operation corresponds to the Linda primitive 'in' operation, and the port corresponds to tuple space.

Since the type graph is not concurrent, a single object-port connection is not concurrent. However, since a single object can support two-or-more simultaneous connection to the same port, the object-port connection can express concurrency. In this case, the objects are treated as if they are different objects by the port. Figure 4 shows the relationship between ports and objects.

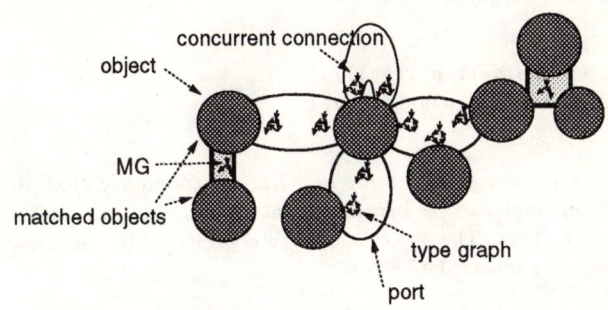

Figure 4: Ports and Objects

5 Language Example

For the purposes of descriptive experimentation and algorithm evaluation, a programming language based on LISP was developed for this model. This language uses the concurrent process functions of LISP and does not use distributed system operation. Ports perform Linda-type matching.

A step-by-step explanation using a concrete example follows.

`(object (self p v) {p ?a !b !!v})`

The above shows the creation of the object template. Since the template itself is passed as the first argument, `self`, the true arguments begin with the second argument. The second argument `p` is assigned to the port and the third argument `v` is assigned to the value. `{p..}` indicates that the communication range for port p. `?a` represents reception of message label 'a', `!b` represents transmission of message label 'b', and `!!v` represents transmission of the message value. Although not shown here, `??x` represents reception of the value, and the received value is substituted for 'x'. Thus, the type for port p is $a.\tau.\bar{b}.\tau.\bar{*}$.

```
(awake (object (..)..) port 10)
```

This is the object created from the template. When the template has been previously described, value of **port** is substituted for **p**, **10** is substituted for **v** and the created object begins operation as an independent thread.

We have two control structures, **cond** and **until**, each one can express internal or external choice.

- (cond (?a ..) (?b ..) ..) is external choice which type is $a.\cdots + b.\cdots + \cdots$.
- (cond (<lisp-condition> ..) (<lisp-condition> ..) ..) is internal choice which type is $\tau.\cdots + \tau.\cdots + \cdots$.
- (until ?a ..) is external choice which type is $\mu x.\cdots + \cdots$.
- (until <lisp-condition> ..) is external choice which type is $\mu x.\cdots + \tau.\cdots$.

Next example is a template of the counter.

```
(object (self p v) {p
  (cond (?inc (awake self p (1+v)))
        (?value !!v (awake self p v)))
})
```

This type is $inc + value.\tau.\overline{*}$. After *inc* or $value.\tau.\overline{*}$ communication, a new object is created in a manner similar to the become operation in the Actor model, and this object is reconnected to the port. The object's identity is preserved by the port.

In order to use this object, let

{p !inc} {p !inc} {p !value ??x} .

The counter increases to 2, and this value is read into x. In this case, three connections have been made and an MG is created each time.

```
(object (self p v) {p
        (until ?quit
               (cond (?inc (incf v))
                     (?value !!v))) })
```

This is the counter for type $\mu A.inc.A + value.\tau.\overline{*}.A + quit$. Unlike with the previously described counter, continuous operation is possible once a connection has been made, and it needs a quit message which shows that the connection has terminated.

{o !inc !inc !value ??x !quit}

This operation is similar to the one previously described. It is type $\tau.\overline{inc}.\tau.\overline{inc}.\tau.\overline{value}.*$ $.\tau.\overline{quit}$. In contrast to the previously described example in which each operation is atomic, here a series of operations is atomic.

Next example is an object which connects to two ports.

```
(object (self in out pattern &aux str)
  {out {in
    (until ?eof ??str }
      (cond ((search str pattern)
              !!str)))
    !eof })
```

It is similar to the grep command in UNIX. The <u>port</u> scope can be assigned without regard for program parentheses. Here $\mu X.eof_{in}.\tau.eof_{out} + *_{in}.(\tau.\overline{*_{out}}.X + \tau.X)$ is the process expression with port information. To get the 'in' type, all actions of other port are changed to τ, and the τ series and port information are deleted. We thus obtain $\mu A.eof + *.A$. Similarly, the 'out' type is $\mu B.\tau.\overline{eof} + \tau.\overline{*}.B + \tau.B = \mu B.\tau.\overline{eof} + \tau.\overline{*}.B$.

Next example is the object which creates ports and objects dynamically.

```
(object (self p &aux q)
  {p (until ?quit ?get-obj
    (setq q (make-port))
    !!q
    (awake (object (self x) ...) q))
  })
```

Whenever an object that is matched to this object sends the message get-obj, it gets a new port that is connected a new object.

Last example is group connected objects.

```
(object (self p &aux x) {p !a !!10 ?b ??x !!(* x 3) })
(object (self p &aux y) {p ?a ??y !c !!(+ y 5) })
(object (self p &aux z) {p ?c ??z !b !!(- z 3) ??z (print z) })
```

These objects can be matching. When they execute, the message sequence is $a, 10, c, 15, b, 12, 36$, and last object print **36**.

6 Discussion

6.1 Matching Cache

In normal operation, objects with the same type are often connected to the same port several times. Let us therefore consider matching caches. These can achieve two kind of cost reductions. One is a graph sending cost, and the other is a matching cost.

When the object send its type graph to the port, the port caches the type graph and return its cache ID (type graph ID), then the object remembers the ID. When matching is successful, the port caches the MG and send its cache ID (MG-ID) to objects, then each object caches the MG and MG-ID. In the next time if the object or the ports going to send a cached graph (type graph or MG) to same receiver, it sends its ID instead of the graph. If the port attempts to match cached same type graphs, it only sends the MG-ID to objects.

It resembles the method search cache mechanism found in several object-oriented languages.

6.2 Indirect Communication

Asynchronous messages without values are only used to indicate external transmission of state transition by internal choice. Also, message causality is ensured in future communication by using matching. Serial communication without values can therefore be deleted. It is not necessary to implement matched object communication in accordance with the given specifications for messages without values. For example, in a serial MG based on the three communication specifications, $a.\tau.\bar{b}$, $\tau.\bar{a}.c$, and $b.\tau.\bar{c}$, branching is not necessary. The three objects need no message and can operate on the basis of the MG alone.

6.3 Message ID

Let us consider implementation of communication based on nondeterminism in the message arrival order and loss of messages. Several distributed programming languages use stream communication in a manner similar to TCP/IP, in which the message arrival order is preserved and messages are not lost. However the communication efficiency of these schemes is poor.

To detect message overtaken and message lost, a message ID jointly established by the sending and receiving sides is required. Stream communication, by numbering the data in order of transmission, is able to create this types of ID. In the model presented here, message IDs are assigned according to the MG edges. When the MG has no loops, it is acceptable to use the edge ID as the message ID. If the MG has loops, the message ID is determined by combining the edge ID and a loop counter value.

When a message does not arrive, the MG indicates the object to which a resend request should be sent. To allow this resend, it is necessary for the object that sends a value message to retain the value until it is confirmed that the message was received.

6.4 Specification with Time and Cost

The timeout interval used for detection of message loss should be chosen rationally. The communication delay can be estimated to some extent from the conditions existing up to that point in time. The processing time of the transmitted object is also needed, but an estimate of this should be included in the specifications. Whether a type graph that includes processing time matches or not can be determined by comparing processing time and request time. The port takes this communication delay into consideration and creates an MG with the timeout interval attached.

The computational cost can also be included in the specifications. Objects which perform the same functions as a port, but which have different computational costs and processing times, can be connected. When a given requirement is included in the specifications and a connection to a port is made, the port will communicate with objects that satisfy that requirement.

6.5 Introduction of Types for Values

Messages with values have no value type. We can express the value type by adding a tag message that indicates the value type. For example, let us consider a generic function 'sin' :

$$\overline{sin.*:real}.\tau.\overline{*:real}$$
$$\overline{sin.*:complex}.\tau.\overline{*:complex},$$

where $*:t$ is a message with a type t value. We can express the same function using tag messages:

$$sin.(real.*.\tau.\overline{real}.\tau.\overline{*} + complex.*.(\tau.\overline{real}.\tau.\overline{*} + \tau.\overline{complex}.\tau.\overline{*})).$$

In the latter, there is no inheritance relation, and a more detailed function type can be expressed. Since we use indirect communications, some tag messages are deletable.

Introducing time or cost information into the type graphs achieves, time[TT92] or cost polymorphism.

7 Conclusion

We presented a method for assigning types to active objects based on a restricted CCS asynchronous communication process (type graph). Objects can be connected to several objects at the same time, and several objects can join to form one connection. Matching of type graphs determines whether communication is successful or not.

The matching graphs (MGs) that are created are state transition graphs that reflect only the nondeterminism of internal selection. An MG shows communication initiative and message causality. Although communications which must be concurrent are expressed serially in the MG, future communications can achieve communication concurrency. As serial massages with no value are not needed, the MG can be reduced, improving communication performance.

Acknowledgments
The author thanks staff of NTT Basic Laboratories (especially Dr. Yoshifumi Manabe and PAM (process algebra meeting) members) and the anonymous referees for their helpful comments on earlier drafts of this paper.

References

[CG89] Carriero, N. and Gelernter, D.: *Linda in context*, Comm.ACM, Vol. 32, No. 4, pp. 444-458, 1989.

[GB83] Goldberg, A. and Robson, D.: *Smalltalk-80 The Language and Its Implementation*, Addison-Wesley, 1983.

[HHWM92] Harada, Y., Hamada, N., Watanabe, S., Miyamoto, E.: *A Type Mechanism for Distributed Computing Environments with Multiple Languages*, Computer Software, Vol. 9, No. 2(1992), pp. 63-74 (In Japanese).

[HWM92] Harada, Y., Watanabe, S. and Miyamoto, E.: *An Agent Model Using Tuples as Communication Sequences (Process Algebra + Tuple Space + Future Variables)*, Multi Agent and Cooperative Computation I, Lecture Notes / Software Engineering 2, Kindai Kagakusha, 1992 (in Japanese).

[Henn88] Hennessy, M.: *Algebraic Theory of Processes,* The MIT Press, 1988.

[HT92] Honda, K. and Tokoro, M: *On Asynchronous Communication Semantics,* Object-Based Concurrent Computing, LNCS 612, 1992.

[KMPS91] Kleinman, A., Moscowitz, Y., Pnueli, A. and Shapiro, E.: *Communication with Directed Logic Variables,* POPL'91, 1991.

[Mil92] Milner, R.: *Calculus of Communication Systems,* LNCS 92, Springer-verlag, 1980.

[MPW89] Milner, R., Parrow, J. and Walker, D. : *A calculus of mobile processes part i,* LFCS, 1989.

[Nier92] Nierstrasz, O.: *Towards an Object Calculus,* Object-Based Concurrent Computing, LNCS 612, 1992.

[NP90] Nierstrasz, O. and Papathomas, M.: *Viewing objects as patterns of communicating agents,* Proc. ECOOP/OOPSLA'90, 1990.

[TT92] Takashio, K. and Tokoro, M.: *DROL: An Object-Oriented Programming Language for Distributed Real-Time Systems,* Proc. OOPSLA'92, 1992.

[Yone90] Yonezawa, A.: *ABCL An Object-Oriented Concurrent System,* The MIT Press, 1990.

[YC88] Yoshida, K. and Chikayama, T.: *A'UM A Stream-Based Concurrent Object-Oriented Language,* Proceedings of the International Conference on Fifth Generation Computer Systems 1988, pp. 638-649.

(Invited Paper)

Adding Implicit Invocation to Languages: Three Approaches*

David Notkin†
David Garlan‡
William G. Griswold††
Kevin Sullivan†

†Department of Computer Science & Engineering, FR-35
University of Washington
Seattle WA 98195 USA
{notkin,sullivan}@cs.washington.edu

‡School of Computer Science
Carnegie Mellon University
Pittsburgh PA 15213 USA
garlan@cs.cmu.edu

††Department of Computer Science & Engineering, 0114
University of California, San Diego
La Jolla, CA 92093-0114 USA
wgg@cs.ucsd.edu

Abstract

Implicit invocation based on event announcement is an increasingly important technique for integrating systems. However, the use of this technique has largely been confined to tool integration systems—in which tools exist as independent processes—and special-purpose languages—in which specialized forms of event broadcast are designed into the language from the start. This paper broadens the class of systems that can benefit from this approach by showing how to augment general-purpose programming languages with facilities for implicit invocation. We illustrate the approach in the context of three different languages, Ada, C++, and Common Lisp. The intent is to highlight the key design considerations that arise in extending such languages with implicit invocation.

1 Introduction

Systems have traditionally been constructed out of components, usually modules, that interact with each other by explicitly invoking procedures provided in their interfaces.

---

*This research was supported in part by the National Science Foundation under Grant Numbers CCR-9112880, CCR-9113367, CCR-8858804, and CCR-9211002, by DARPA Grant MDA 972-92-J-1002, by Siemens Corporate Research, and by SRA (Tokyo Japan). The views and conclusions contained in this document are those of the authors and should not be interpreted as representing the official policies, either expressed or implied, of the U.S. Government, of the Siemens Corporation, or of SRA.

There has recently been considerable interest in an alternative technique, variously referred to as implicit invocation, reactive integration, and selective broadcast. The idea behind implicit invocation is that instead of invoking a procedure directly, a component can announce (or broadcast) one or more events. Other components in the system can register an interest in an event by associating a procedure with the event. When the event is announced the system itself invokes the procedures that have registered interest in the event. Thus an event announcement "implicitly" causes the invocation of procedures in other components without the announcing component needing to know the name of those components.

The advantages of implicit invocation arise because of the separation of the invocation relationship from the "knows about" relationship between components. This makes it easier to add, modify, and integrate components without modifying many (if any) existing components. For example, since components need not explicitly name other components to invoke them it is possible to integrate a collection of components simply by registering their interest in events. Thus, the function of the overall system may be modified without changing any existing components: the new components are invoked based on already-existing event announcements. In contrast, in a system with only explicit invocation, invoking a new component requires that at least one existing component be modified.

Because of properties like these, many systems now use implicit invocation as a key means of composition. Although applications of the technique span many domains, these systems can be grouped into three categories.

The first category is tool integration frameworks. Systems in this category are typically configured as a collection of tools running as separate processes. Event broadcast is handled by a separate dispatcher process that communicates with the tools through communication channels provided by the host operating system (such as sockets in Unix). Examples include Field [Reiss 90], Forest [Garlan & Ilias 91], Softbench [Gerety 89], and several other commercial tool integration frameworks.

The second category is implicit invocation systems based on special-purpose languages and application frameworks. In these systems implicit invocation becomes accessible through specialized notations and run-time support. For example, many database systems now provide notations for defining active data triggers [Hewitt 69] to database applications. Examples include APPL/A [Sutton, Heimbigner & Osterweil 90], Gandalf's daemons [Habermann, Garlan & Notkin 91], AP5's relational constraints [Cohen 89], and "when-updated" methods of some object-oriented languages [Krasner & Pope 88]. Window systems like X [Scheifler and Gettys 86] and Garnet [Myers *et al.* 90] also exploit implicit invocation in a stylized manner. Other specialized applications that can be viewed as exploiting the paradigm include incremental attribute reevaluation, spreadsheet updating, and some blackboard systems [Garlan, Kaiser & Notkin 92].

Despite the successes of systems in these two categories, use of implicit invocation has been relatively limited. In particular, few applications can afford the overhead of separate processes used by tool integration frameworks, and special-purpose languages are limited by their very nature.

This motivates the third category, in which implicit invocation is incorporated into existing, general-purpose programming languages. A limited mechanism of this style is based on wrapper methods in the Common Lisp Object System (CLOS) [Steele 91]. At least two more general mechanisms in this category have been reported on in some depth, one for C++ [Sullivan & Notkin 92] and one for Ada [Garlan & Scott 93]. A third approach has been developed for Common Lisp. In this paper, we compare and contrast the mechanisms employed by these three designs.

In all three categories, implicit invocation is intended to supplement, rather than supplant, explicit invocation. Components may interact either explicitly or implicitly, depending on which mechanism is most appropriate. This property makes it possible to view implicit invocation as a natural complement to an existing explicit invocation system, such as one provided by a standard module-oriented programming language.

This paper has two primary goals. The first is to help make implicit invocation more ubiquitous without further populating the world with special-purpose mechanisms. The second is to identify a variety of design issues that arise when embedding implicit invocation into modern programming languages: these issues are useful in clarifying various approaches to implicit invocation, as well as adding some insights into programming language design itself.

Implicit invocation mechanisms are based on two fundamental concepts. The first is that, in addition to defining procedures that may be invoked in the usual way, a component is permitted to announce *events*. The second is that a component may *register* to receive announced events. This is done by associating a procedure of that component with each event of interest. When one of those events is announced the implicit invocation mechanism is responsible for calling the procedures that have been registered with the event.

Although the basic mechanisms have substantial similarities, the details differ significantly because of the nature of the underlying languages. The paper first introduces the three mechanisms. Then we step back and consider what underlying design decisions were made. We focus on *why* different decisions were made in each language; in most cases programming language issues or "cultural style" caused particular decisions. The three languages—Ada, C++, and Common Lisp—have sufficiently different characteristics to highlight these issues. *How* the basic aspects of implicit invocation are achieved in three diverse programming languages is the central theme in this paper.

2 Ada

Ada is a statically-typed, module-oriented, imperative programming language [Ada 83]. In Ada the basic unit of modularization is the package. Packages have interfaces, which define (among other things) a set of exported procedures. To provide implicit invocation for Ada, we developed a small specification language to augment package interfaces. This language allows users to define events they want the system to support, and to specify which Ada procedures (in which package specifications) should be invoked on announcing the event. This design was strongly influenced both by typing and modularization features of the language and also by the desire to reuse existing Ada compilers and tools for language processing. The following code—which would be part of a complete Ada program—illustrates the declaration of events and the binding of procedures to events.

```
for Package_1
   declare Event_1
      X: Integer; Y: Package_N.My_Type;
   declare Event_2
   when Event_3 => Method_1 B
end for Package_1
for Package_2
   declare Event_3 A,B: Integer;
   when Event_2 => Method_4
   when Event_1 => Method_2 X
end for Package_2
for Package_3
   when Event_2 => Method_3
   when Event_1 => Method_4 Y
end for Package_3
```

In the specification language, **for** clauses identify the package under discussion. The **declare** clauses specify the events that this package will announce and the parameters associated with each event (if any). Each parameter has a type: this may be any legal Ada type. For example, `Package_1` declares two events. The first event, `Event_1`, has two parameters, `X` of type `Integer` and `Y` of type `My_Type`, as defined in `Package_N`.

The **when** clauses indicate which procedures in the package are to be invoked when an event is announced, and what event parameters are to be passed to the procedure. Any of the parameters may be listed and in any order. This list indicates which parameters are to be passed to each procedure. For instance, in the above code fragment, `Package_1` declares its interest in `Event_3`. When `Event_3` is announced (by `Package_2`), `Method_1` should be invoked, passing only the second parameter, `B`.

Before compiling the Ada program the user invokes a preprocessor that translates the specifications into an Ada package called `Event_Manager`. This package provides the run-time support for handling announced events; it is compiled and linked with the rest of the system. Although not illustrated in the example, the preprocessor assumes that the event specification statements are delimited by the special comment mark "--!" so that they can easily be separated from normal Ada code.

The generated interface of `Event_Manager`, illustrated next, provides the list of declared events as an Ada enumerated type, along with a record with a variant part that specifies the parameters for each event. In addition, the generated specification contains the signature of the `Announce_Event` procedure, which allows components to announce events.

```
with Package_N;
package Event_Manager is
  type Event is
    (Event_1,Event_2,Event_3);
  type Argument (The_Event: Event) is
    record
      case The_Event is
        when Event_1 =>
          Event_1_X: Integer;
          Event_1_Y: Package_N.My_Type;
        when Event_2 =>
          null;
        when Event_3 =>
          Event_3_A: Integer;
   Event_3_B: Integer;
        when others =>
          null;
      end case;
    end record;
  procedure Announce_Event(The_Data: Argument);
end Event_Manager;
```

When a component wishes to announce an event, it invokes **Announce_Event**, as follows:

```
Announce_Event(Argument'(Event_1, X_Arg, Y_Arg));
```

The generated body of **Event_Manager** contains the implementation of this procedure, which, as illustrated in the next code fragment, is structured as a **case** statement with one case for every declared event:

```
with Package_1;
with Package_2;
with Package_3;
package body Event_Manager is
procedure Announce_Event(The_Data: Argument) is
  begin
    case The_Data.The_Event is
      when Event_1 =>
        Package_2.Method_2(The_Data.Event_1_X);
        Package_3.Method_4(The_Data.Event_1_Y);
      when Event_2 =>
        Package_2.Method_4;
        Package_3.Method_3;
      when Event_3 =>
        Package_1.Method_1(The_Data.Event_3_B);
      when others =>
        null;
    end case;
  end Announce_Event;
end Event_Manager;
```

3 C++

C++ [Stroustrup 87] is an object-oriented language based on extensions to C. The implicit invocation mechanism added to C++ is statically-typed, with events as objects and with dynamic registration of methods with events. The design of the mechanism was influenced by the object-oriented nature of the language, by the typing structure of the language, and by the original objective of the mechanism, which was to support behavioral entity-relation designs and implementations [Sullivan & Notkin 92].

In the C++ implicit invocation mechanism, events are associated with the interfaces of classes, treating them as equivalents of methods. That is, in addition to exporting methods, classes declare and export a set of events. For example, the interface (encoded in a .h file) for a set class is shown next; a few parts of the actual text are omitted and slightly modified to focus on the important aspects of the example.

```
class Set ...
{
  public:

    Boolean Insert(Object& v);
    Boolean Remove(Object& v);
    stream& PrintOn(ostream& s);

    // PUBLIC EVENT INTERFACE
    VoidEventObject Inserted;
    VoidEventObject Removed;
};
```

This example exports three methods and two events, **Inserted** and **Removed**. As we will show, this allows other classes to register interest in either of these events.[1]

The registration of methods with events—that is, defining the methods to be invoked when an event is announced—is done separately from the event declarations. Suppose that an instance, **this** (the "sending" object in a C++ method invocation), of a class **SetBijectionMediator**, wants to register a method of a class, **UponS1Insert**, to be invoked when an object **s1** announces an event **Inserted**. This is done—usually by the constructor of the object that wants to register with the event—by executing the statement:

```
s1.Inserted.REGISTER(SetBijectionMediator,UponS1Insert);
```

Methods make event announcements by invoking an **Announce** method associated with each event. For example, the implementation of the **Insert** method in the body of the **Set** class includes the statement:

```
Inserted.Announce(v);
```

This causes the **Inserted** event on the set instance to be announced, which in turn causes all methods registered with that event to be invoked. There is a corresponding

---

[1] The **VoidEventObject** type arises because events are implemented as instances of event classes. **VoidEventObject** is an event class, and the **Inserted** and **Deleted** events are instances of that class. The name of the type is chosen by convention: **Void** implies that this event has no return object, **Event** implies that it is defining an event (all event classes have this piece), and **Object** implies that the parameter list of the events of this type include a single element of type **Object**.

UNREGISTER macro that allows an association between a method and an event to be broken.

The details of the C++ mechanism are affected by our desire to handle typing in C++ in a reasonably flexible and uniform way. In the C++ implicit invocation mechanism this is hard because the macros, events, and Announce methods have to be general-purpose and because we want to allow run-time registration.

The heart of the problem is that our event registration method cannot treat pointers to non-static member functions in a uniform manner, since they share no common type. This is because in C++ every non-static member function has an implicit first parameter, this, which is a pointer to its own object; thus non-static member functions from objects of different classes differ in their type signatures. This interferes with our desire to support static type checking.

Our solution is to declare a function type with a first parameter of type void* (a generic pointer), followed by the other parameters. Each client object declares a static member function of this type, which it registers along with a pointer to itself. The static member function is called with the self pointer, which it then type-casts to call the corresponding virtual member function. Passing the object's pointer, in this case, serves a function similar to passing a closure in Lisp.

The STATIC macro—typically used within class declarations in header files—makes it possible to register non-static member functions. The macro takes a non-static member function and creates a corresponding static member function. Reconsidering the use of the REGISTER macro above, we can see that the UponS1Insert method had to be static. But in fact it is a non-static member function declared privately to the SetBijectionMediator class:

```
void* UponS1Insert(Object& o);
```

It is transformed into an "equivalent" static member function by the use of the STATIC macro:

```
STATIC(SetBijectionMediator,void*,UponS1Insert,
              (void* target,Object& o),(o));
```

The first argument indicates the class in which the method resides; that is, which class has the method that may be invoked by the announcement of an event in another class. The second argument indicates the return type of the method; the current mechanism requires this to be void*. The third argument is the name of the non-static member function. The fourth argument is the formal parameter list for the static method being created by the macro. And the final argument is the actual parameter list for the non-static method being transformed.

The STATIC macro creates a new name for the static member function. The REGISTER and UNREGISTER macros use the same name transformation to allow the user of the macros to name the non-static member function while actually registering and unregistering with the generated static member function.

4 Common Lisp/CLOS

Common Lisp, combined with the Common Lisp Object System (CLOS), is an object-oriented dynamically-typed language with substantial run-time flexibility. The implicit invocation mechanism that extends these is a method-based mechanism with dynamic registration. The mechanism was designed to support the construction of a meaning-preserving tool for restructuring software systems [Griswold 91][Griswold & Notkin 93].

Like the Ada and C++ mechanisms, it has support for defining events, registering methods with events, and for announcing events. Common Lisp's flexible nature strongly affected the design of the mechanism. In particular, its dynamic typing, first-class functions, and simple extensible syntax led to a straightforward design and clean syntax.

A `defevent` declaration is used to extend a standard CLOS class definition to allow an object to announce an event. For example, the declarations

```
(defclass world-element ()
  ((value :accessor value :initarg :value :initform nil)))

(defevent delete-object ((obj world-element) &optional reason))
```

create a class `world-element` with a single slot (instance variable) `value`, and then adds an event `delete-object`, which takes a value `obj` of type `world-element` and an optional argument `reason` that defaults to NIL. The first value of an event must be of the type of the class to which the event belongs.[2] The syntax of the `defevent` is similar to that of a method definition, but without a body since the actions of the event are (dynamically) defined by the registrant, not the event announcer. Subclasses of `world-element` inherit the event `delete-object`, and the inherited event may be redefined as long as the event interfaces are consistent according to the method definition rules of CLOS.

Registration for an event is performed using an upon expression (a macro) that creates a structure to wait for a particular event from a particular object. When the object announces the event, the body of the upon is executed. For example, executing the expression

```
(upon ((delete-object the-obj reason) registering-object)    ; 1
  (remhash the-obj object-table)                              ; 2
  (format t "object ~s deleted because ~s~%" the-obj reason)) ; 3
```

creates an obligation for the run-time system to execute the body (lines 2 and 3) of the upon when the value of `the-obj` announces the `delete-object` event. Only the first argument of the upon's event pattern is used in matching an announced event; the remaining arguments of the event pattern are merely bound with the remaining values of the event announcement to allow accessing them in the body of the upon.

An announce expression, when executed, announces that an event has occurred. The expression

```
(announce (delete-object obj "no neighbors"))
```

announces the event `delete-object` with the argument, `obj` (the announcer of the event) with the optional argument provided. If the value of `obj` here and `the-obj` in the upon were the same, this announcement would cause the execution of the upon, causing the value of `the-obj` to be removed from `object-table` and an explanatory message to be printed.

A registration performed with upon can be unregistered using `downoff`, indicating the registrant (`registering-object` in following fragment):

---

[2]CLOS supports multimethod selection, which allows selecting a method to execute based on the type (or value) of any or all the arguments passed to the call, rather than just the first argument, as in C++. Consequently, the first-object convention of event announcement introduces a slight asymmetry with respect to method call.

```
(downoff the-obj 'delete-object registering-object)
```

The event mechanism is implemented in two parts. First, the **defevent** declaration extends the class definition of the announcing object with a new slot (instance variable) so it can keep a list of functions that are to be invoked when the event is announced. This extension is performed using the CLOS metaobject protocol. At the same time, a method with the same signature as the event is created for invoking the registered functions. This method is called by the **announce** expression. For example, the definition of the **delete-object** event causes a **delete-object** slot to be added to the **world-element** class, and defines a method **delete-object** that calls all the functions in the **delete-object** slot of the object announcing the **delete-object** event. Second, the **upon** expression creates an anonymous function (lambda) for the registering object and registers it with the (potentially) announcing object. The signature of the function is the signature of the event it is waiting on, and its body is the body of the **upon**. For example, the **upon** expression above creates a function that is put on the **delete-object** list of the-obj. The function takes two arguments named **the-obj** and **reason**, and the body contains the **remhash** and **format** expressions. Consequently, when **delete-object** is later announced by **the-obj**, the **delete-object** method is called on it and it calls the functions on the list—including the one registered by this **upon**—with the arguments of the announcement.

5 Key Design Questions

These three implementations of implicit invocation in the context of existing programming languages embody sets of design choices that are important to understand, both to see how to use an implicit invocation system, and to observe the limitations of the implementations. The design decisions can be grouped into the following six categories,

- event definition,
- event parameters,
- event bindings,
- event announcement,
- delivery policy, and
- concurrency,

which we now examine in turn.

5.1 Event Definition

The first design issue concerns how events are to be defined. There are several related issues. Is the vocabulary of events extensible? If so, are events explicitly declared? If events are declared, where are they declared? There are four approaches to event extensibility and declaration.

Fixed Event Vocabulary A fixed set of events is built into the implicit invocation system: the user is not allowed to declare new events.

Static Event Declaration The user can introduce new events, but this set is fixed at compile-time.

Dynamic Event Declaration New events can be declared dynamically at run-time, and thus there is no fixed set of events.

No Event Declarations Events are not declared at all; any component can announce arbitrary events.

An example of a system with a fixed event vocabulary is Smalltalk-80 [Goldberg & Robson 83], which provides a small number of events including the **changed** event.[3] Active databases often have a fixed event vocabulary, where events are associated with primitive database operations, such as inserting, removing, or replacing an element in the database. APPL/A is an example of this approach [Sutton, Heimbigner & Osterweil 90].

At the other extreme, tool integration frameworks, such as Field and Softbench, have no explicit event declarations at all. A tool can announce an arbitrary string, although tool builders typically describe the event vocabulary of each tool as externally documented conventions.

For all three mechanisms, we rejected the first alternative as too restrictive. This is because we are embedding largely general-purpose event mechanisms in programming languages: in situations where an implicit invocation mechanism is specially designed for a given task, using a fixed event vocabulary might be a more reasonable decision. All three mechanisms also rejected the fourth alternative as too unpredictable. When it came to selecting among the other approaches, there were arguments on each side. There is no high-level reason that prohibits any of the approaches to be implemented in any of the three mechanisms.

In the Ada mechanism, static event declaration can be implemented efficiently as an Ada enumerated type, also allowing compile-time type checking of event declarations and uses. On the other hand, dynamic event declarations provide more flexibility, since they allow run-time reconfiguration. Thus, a dynamic event system may have an added benefit of reducing recompilation overhead.

In the end, predictability through static checking won out for the Ada mechanism. In particular, we felt that static interface declarations more naturally meshed with the spirit of Ada, led to more comprehensible programs, and better supported large-scale system development, which requires predictable behavior of the components.

In the C++ mechanism, we selected a combination of static and dynamic event declaration. In particular, the event classes are defined statically but instances of the event classes—that is, events themselves—can be defined dynamically. If a new set object is instantiated, for example, it includes new instances of the associated event objects.

The Common Lisp mechanism, in the spirit of run-time flexibility encouraged by the language, allows for dynamic event declaration. That is, creating **defevent** forms at run-time is a relatively straightforward activity.

Where should the declarations of events reside? In particular, since the events represent information shared between (at least) the announcing component and the event

---

[3] By convention, this "event" is announced by invoking the **changed** method on **self**. This causes the **update** method to be invoked on each dependent of the changed object. Other events could similarly be introduced by new methods that had a similar effect, but this is generally not done.

system, it is unclear which component "owns" an event, and thus where events should be declared. There are two obvious choices:

Central Declaration of Events Events are declared at a central point and then used throughout the system.

Distributed Declaration of Events Events are declared by each module (or class), where each module declares the events it expects to announce.

The Ada implementation is neutral on this issue. Since the declarations are embedded within Ada comments, it is possible to declare events in the individual packages. However, an implementor can also place event declarations in a separate file. One drawback to this implementation, however, is that regardless of where the events are declared, they are actually compiled into a central locus of control (the `Event_Manager` package specification). When changes are made to event declarations, all files containing event declarations must be recompiled to correctly rebuild the event manager.

The C++ mechanism requires that events be associated with classes. The primary motivation was that methods and events were to be treated as equals and duals of one another; thus, events should be declared in the interfaces of classes, as are methods. (The equivalent of a centralized event declaration could be defined by convention, designating a special class that holds all the event declarations.)

Note that the Common Lisp mechanism, even with dynamic event declarations, creates a bias with respect to the placement of declarations. In particular, events—like methods in Common Lisp—can be placed anywhere, although they are most naturally placed with their class definition. So, in the same sense as the Ada mechanism, the Common Lisp mechanism is neutral with respect to where the event declarations go, but the practical tendency has been to associate them with class definitions.

5.2 Event Parameters

The next design issue is how events should handle parameters. The question here is, what forms of data passing using event announcements make them easy to use and understand? The choices we considered were:

Simple Names Events are simple names without any parameter information. Data associated with an event (if any) would have to be encoded in the name of the event or passed in global variables.

Fixed Parameter Lists All events have a name and the same fixed list of parameters.

Parameters by Event Type Each event has a fixed list of parameters, but the type and number of parameters can be different for different events.

Parameters by Announcement Whenever a component announces an event, it can specify any list of parameters. For example, the same event name could be announced with no parameters one time and with ten parameters the next.

The use of simple names is found in systems that use events as a kind of interrupt mechanism. In these systems there is typically only a small number of causes for events to be raised. Fixed parameter lists are often used in combination with a fixed set of system-defined events. For example, in an active database events might be required to pass the identity of the data that is being modified. At the other extreme, systems that use strings as events often allow arbitrary parameters: it becomes the job of the receiver to decode the string and extract parameters at run-time.

We considered the first two approaches as being unnecessarily restrictive. We also felt that letting parameters vary for each announcement could lead to undisciplined and unpredictable systems. This led to the decision that the Ada and C++ mechanisms should allow parameters to vary by event type. Allowing parameters to vary by event type over a static list of events also solves a problem of parameter passing in the Ada mechanism: with static events and static parameter lists, a record with a variant part becomes a natural way to represent parameters. The C++ mechanism handles this through the `STATIC` macros.

Technically, the Common Lisp mechanism allows parameters to vary by announcement, since source files can be loaded during execution. However, the actual use of the mechanism is more in the style of the Ada and C++ mechanisms, since an upon expression and an announcement that it is intended to match must agree on the parameter list.

5.3 Event Bindings

Event bindings determine which procedures in which modules will be called when an event is announced. There are two important questions to resolve. First, when are events bound to the procedures? Second, how are the parameters of the event passed to these procedures? Also central to this issue is the granularity of the bindings.

With respect to the first issue, we considered two approaches to event binding:

Static Event Bindings Events are bound to procedures statically when a program is compiled.

Dynamic Event Bindings Event bindings can be created dynamically. Components register for events at run-time when they wish to receive them, and unregister for events when they are no longer interested.

The Ada mechanism uses static event bindings, while the C++ and Common Lisp mechanisms use dynamic event bindings.

The decision to use static event bindings for Ada was largely forced by the language itself. In particular, Ada provides no convenient mechanism for keeping a "pointer" or other reference to a subprogram. It would have been possible to provide an enumerated type representing all procedures that might be bound to any event. Events could be bound to elements of this enumerated type dynamically. Procedures would then be invoked through a large case statement. However, this conflicted with the desire to have a flexible parameter passing mechanism (as described earlier), since the parameters would either have had to be fixed or encoded in the enumerated type.

The C++ and Common Lisp mechanisms allow `REGISTER` and upon statements, respectively, to be executed as part of the basic execution flow, thus adding event-method pairs on-the-fly. In the C++ mechanism we used this feature quite extensively.

For example, in one situation we wanted to keep two sets consistent. To do this we defined a separate component, called a "mediator," which managed consistency of the sets by listening to insert and delete events announced by each set. If an element in one of the sets is modified (rather than inserted or deleted) then modification on its associated element in the other set must be performed. To handle these modifications, whenever we created a new pair of associated elements, one in each set, we also deployed a "submediator" between the elements. The submediator constructor and destructor methods automatically register and unregister with the events of the corresponding elements (which are passed as parameters to the submediator constructor), making it easy for the associated elements to modify one another. With static event binding, this would be impossible since the elements themselves were not even in existence at compile-time.

Despite this use of dynamic event binding, the jury is still out on which approach is better. It may be that the increased flexibility of dynamic event binding is outweighed by the decrease in the predictability of the resulting system. In particular, the behavior of a system is less apparent from its static representation (that is, from the program text) if dynamic event binding is used. Moreover, dynamic event bindings may, depending on how they are realized, introduce race conditions at run-time (see the later subsection on Concurrency).

The three mechanisms represent two different binding granularities. In the Ada mechanism, bindings are between packages (modules); in the C++ and the Common Lisp mechanisms, the bindings are between objects. These decisions are consistent with the nature of the languages (for instance, Ada does not have procedure pointers but C++ and Common Lisp do).

Another design decision is how the parameters from the event are translated into the parameters for the invocation. The choices we considered were:

All Parameters An invocation of a method due to an event announcement passes exactly the same parameters (in number, type and order) as are specified for the event.

Selectable Parameters As part of the event binding, the implementor can specify which parameters of the event are passed in the invocation, and in which order.

Parameter Expressions The invocation passes the results of expressions computed over the parameters of the announced event.

The transmission of all parameters to each procedure bound to an event requires some conspiracy between the designer of the procedure to be invoked and the designer of the events. (Just as is needed between a procedure invocation and a procedure definition for explicit invocation.) We can easily imagine situations in which only some of the information in an event announcement would be useful to a component. It seemed unnecessary to require the component to accept a dummy parameter just for that reason, or, conversely, to require two events to be announced—one with and one without the unneeded data.

In the Ada mechanism, we opted to provide selectable parameters, as this provided a balance between flexibility and ease of implementation. Selectable parameters allows more freedom in matching events to procedures, thereby promoting reusability. Moreover, it is straightforward to build the argument list from the event binding declaration.

We believe that allowing non-side-affecting expressions as parameters to an event system could provide a significant and useful amount of increased flexibility. Sometimes a procedure's parameters do not match those of an event, but some of the procedure's parameters can be made constant to "customize" the procedure invocation to the context of the event. With the ability to construct expressions as part of an event binding, it becomes easier to tailor a procedure to an event without modifying either the announcer or the recipient. The implementation becomes considerably more complex, however. In particular, it is necessary to make sure that operators used in parameter expressions are in scope and have the right type.

In the C++ mechanism, we used the "all parameters" approach. Intermediary components can be interposed to get the same effect as selectable parameters. This simplifies the event mechanism itself, but may complicate the resulting systems built using the mechanism, since there may be more components.

The Common Lisp mechanism technically falls into the "all parameters" category as well. However, since a function gets created each time an **upon** is executed, it has the flexibility of "parameter expressions."

These descriptions point out the central question, which is still open: how should the potential proliferation of components and component interfaces be handled? In explicit invocation, the calling component is usually responsible for understanding all the parameters that the callee component requires; if some are not important to the caller, defaults must be provided. (Some languages, like Ada, allow defaults to be handled by language mechanisms rather than by programming conventions.) In implicit invocation, the same approach can be taken (as we did for C++), with the pressure on the receivers of events rather than on the announcers of events. The Common Lisp mechanism approaches the proliferation problem in a different way. By creating an anonymous function each time an **upon** is executed, the mechanism helps keep the name space trim.

Intermediate approaches, such as selectable parameters, show great potential. Field's mechanism includes a relatively powerful selectable parameter mechanism based on the string scanning functions common to Unix.

5.4 Event Announcement

Although announcing an event is a straightforward concept, there are several ways in which it can be incorporated.

Single Announcement Procedure Provide a single procedure for announcing any event. A closely related variant of this approach is a "language extension" in which an **announce** statement is introduced as a new kind of primitive, with a language preprocessor used to conceal the actual implementation.

Multiple Announcement Procedures Provide one procedure for announcing each event name. For example, a component might call `Announce_Changed` to announce the `Changed` event. The procedure accepts exactly the same parameters (in number, type, order, and name) as the event.

Implicit Announcement Permit events to be announced as a side effect of calling a given procedure. For example, each time procedure `Proc` is invoked, announce event `Event`.

The Ada and Common Lisp mechanisms selected the "single announcement" approach for a number of reasons. First, in comparison to the multiple procedure approach, it is transparent: all event announcements look similar. Second, our users were fairly proficient with the language at hand, and we wanted to stay as close to "pure" Ada and

Common Lisp as possible. This discouraged us from modifying the language. We also wanted to avoid the extra complexity of a preprocessor that would have to process the full Ada or Common Lisp language (and not just specially delimited annotations).

In the Common Lisp mechanism, event announcements are implemented as simple method calls. The announce syntax was added because it is confusing to read Common Lisp code with no knowledge of what is a method call and what is an event announcement.

In the Ada mechanism, we realized that instead of requiring the user to construct an `Event_Manager.Argument` record as a local variable and pass the variable to the procedure, the user could simply pass a record aggregate containing the desired information. This brought the syntax close enough to an **announce** statement to satisfy our desire for promoting events as first-class, without requiring any modification to Ada syntax.

In the C++ mechanism, multiple announcement procedures are used. Specifically, one announcement procedure is defined for each event class. The "similar look" is still achieved by defining special template macros to define these event classes. Thus, this mechanism makes event announcements look different from, but not too different from, method invocations. In C++, the language extension approach was even less attractive, since adding another preprocessor stage would complicate language processing and debugging.

The fourth approach, implicit announcement, has been used as a triggering mechanism for databases [Dayal, Hsu & Ladin 90], for some programming environments [Habermann, Garlan & Notkin 91], and for some language extensions (in particular CLOS's wrapper methods). It is attractive because it permits events to be announced without changing the module that is causing the announcement to happen. Although we could have additionally supported this form of announcement, we chose not to, largely because it would require a preprocessor to transform procedures so that they announce the relevant events.

5.5 Delivery Policy

In most implicit invocation mechanisms, when an event is announced all procedures bound to it are invoked. However, in some mechanisms this is not guaranteed. The design options include:

Full Delivery An announced event causes invocation of all procedures bound to it.

Single Delivery An event is handled by only one of a set of event handlers. For example, this allows such events as "File Ready for Printing" to be announced, with the first free print server receiving the event.

Parameter-Based Selection This approach uses the event announcement's parameters to decide whether a specific invocation should be performed. This is similar to the pattern matching features of Field in that a single event can cause differing sets of subprograms to be invoked depending upon exactly what data is transferred with the event.

State-based Policy Some systems (notably Forest [Garlan & Ilias 91]), associate a "policy" with each event binding. Given an event of interest, the policy determines the actual effect of it. In particular, the policy can choose to ignore the event, generate new events, or call an appropriate procedure. Policies can provide much of the power of a dynamic system without incurring the complexities of a dynamic system.

The single delivery model did not match our general interest in supporting implicit invocation as opposed to indirect explicit invocation,[4] and so was not used in any of the mechanisms. In fact, all three mechanisms use variations of the full delivery model. The only "twist" is that in the C++ and in the Common Lisp mechanisms, which both permit dynamic registration, a given method can be associated with a given event multiple times: that is, the event-method "relation" isn't really a relation because it can have duplicate entries. The implication is that when an event is announced, all *instances* of the methods registered with the event are invoked in these two mechanisms.

It is still unclear what are the benefits of each delivery mechanism. We are beginning to believe that there is a tension between the delivery policy and the independence of the methods that are registered in the same event. In particular, if the methods are independent (that is, whether they are executed in a particular order, or are even executed sequentially is immaterial to the resulting system state), then a full delivery policy seems to lead to the most straightforward analysis by the users. In the face of increasing dependence among the registered methods, it may be that alternative policies or variations on policies are more appropriate. Further, if there is extensive dependence among the registered methods, it is likely that using implicit invocation is inappropriate, and that explicit invocation is more appropriate.

A central question yet to be settled in its entirety is where the desired delivery policies can and should be specified. In language-based approaches, such as the ones described here, placing them in the mechanism itself is important. But more complicated policies may be more effectively placed in the receiving components or in intermediaries situated between the announcing and receiving components.

5.6 Concurrency

The only one of our three languages that has built-in support for concurrency is Ada. (Most Common Lisp implementations have a concurrency mechanism, but there is apparently no standard as yet.) Thus, for Ada's mechanism, we had to consider further whether to or how to handle concurrency. In the Ada design we considered three options.

Package A component is a package, and an invocation is a call on a procedure in the package interface.

Packaged Task A component is a statically-defined task with an interface in a package specification, and an invocation is a call on an entry in the task interface.

Free Task A component is a dynamic task (created, for example, by a task manager). An invocation is a call on an entry in the task interface. However, rather than providing an enclosing package, the task is built inside the `Event_Manager` package.

The first choice leads to a non-concurrent system: events are executed using a single thread of control. The second and third choices would permit concurrent handling of

---

[4] Indirect explicit invocation occurs when passing procedures as parameters or when calling virtual methods in object-oriented languages. In these cases, the specific procedure body that is to be invoked is not known by the invoking procedure, but the fact that such a procedure exists *is* known.

events. Although we do not forbid tasks inside of packages, our implementation adopts the first approach. That is, events are used at the module level, not the task level, and thus the programmer—not the mechanism—is responsible for handling any interactions between the event mechanism and tasks.

Our decision was based primarily on the fact that, given the current understanding of systems built with implicit invocation, it is much easier to develop correct systems using a single thread of control. The central problem is that when you add concurrency, events may return before the actions they initiate are completed, which requires more complex reasoning about the system.

In addition, there are a set of problems in implementing concurrent implicit invocation mechanisms that we could avoid addressing due to this decision. For example, if we had adopted a concurrent approach, it would have either been necessary to require all recipients of an event to be re-entrant, or for the `Event_Manager` task to provide its own internal synchronizing task to ensure that invocations occurred only one at a time. Should a receiving task have attempted to announce another event while in its rendezvous, this could cause a deadlock. Another question might be whether each event spawns a task and returns immediately, or whether they run to completion before returning the thread.

APPL/A is a system that uses an Ada-based event mechanism along with concurrency. Event announcement methods are queued at the recipient. We do not fully understand the consequences of this decision with respect to the use of such an event mechanism.

6 Evaluation

Each of these implicit invocation mechanisms have been fully implemented and have been used in varying degrees.[5]

6.1 Ada

The Ada mechanism was initially developed for use in a masters-level software engineering course [Garlan et al. 92]. The students had an average of five years of industrial experience. Most were familiar with Ada. This early use of the system has resulted in both praise and criticism.

On the positive side, users of the system have had virtually no conceptual problems transferring their abstract understanding of implicit invocation to the use of our implementation. The declarative nature of events apparently fit well with their abstract model. In addition, experienced Ada users found little difficulty adapting their programs to an implicit invocation style. Our attempts to remain close to Ada syntax certainly contributed to this.

On the negative side, there appeared to be two limitations. The first was the common problem of debugging preprocessed source code. Since compiler errors are produced with respect to the preprocessed source, users have to translate between the output of the preprocessor and their initial source input. However, this problem was mitigated by the relative orthogonality of the language extensions since the event-oriented extensions are largely isolated from normal code. The second was the absence of dynamic event declaration and binding. Although Ada programmers are used to strongly typed, static

---

[5] Each of the implementations is available by sending electronic mail to the authors.

system designs, our users were also aware that other implicit invocation systems are more dynamic. (For example, some of them had used Softbench.)

To these drawbacks we would add our own concern with the lack of concurrency supported by our design. As indicated earlier, we believe that it should be possible to exploit the tasking model of Ada, and see this as an opportunity for future work.

6.2 C++

The C++ mechanism was initially developed to support our work in tool integration, with a specific interest in reducing the cost of evolution for integrated environments. We have used the mechanism (and its predecessor) extensively, for efforts in constructing parallel programming environments, computer-aided geometric design environments, etc.

On the whole, programmers seem relatively happy using the mechanism. There are two high-level issues that arise. The first is that the particular style of use that we encourage is non-trivial to learn. We have anecdotal feedback from outside our group, however, that once the approach is learned people tend to produce "cleaner" designs. The second issue is that the typing structure takes some time to learn and understand. This is not a fundamental problem, but it does imply that further work is needed in understanding the relationship between implicit invocation and static typing.

The C++ mechanism has not been used in concurrent applications. Thus we have been able to avoid a collection of issues that will, at some point, be critical. The same is true for issues related to distribution.

6.3 Common Lisp

The Common Lisp mechanism has been used more narrowly than the other two mechanisms. In particular, it has been used almost exclusively to aid in the design and implementation of a program restructuring tool. (One other use has been to implement a facility for tracing events.)

In the restructuring tool, the event mechanism integrates three independently developed subsystems—the core restructuring component, the underlying CFG/PDG representations [Larus 89], and the window system [Rowe *et al.* 91]. To integrate their behavior, intermediary "mediator" components are created and receive events from one subsystem and translate them to direct invocations on another [Sullivan & Notkin 92]. For example, when a program restructuring transformation completes, an announcement of the change is made and all registered restructuring-window mediators are notified of the change, which in turn will update windows containing text or graphics of the program. The separation of these components aids evolution of the system and maintains independence.

Based on this experience, we have noted that programmers who have never used events before usually have some trouble understanding how an **upon** declaration interacts with event announcements. However, we perceive this as part of the natural learning curve associated with implicit invocation, not with this particular mechanism. Another problem is that programmers do not immediately understand that registered objects that are otherwise unreferenceable will continue to receive event announcements unless a **downoff** is executed or the announcing objects themselves become unreferenceable. This problem is a consequence of the fact that Common Lisp supports automatic garbage collection, but event registration references prevent garbage collection of otherwise dead objects.

Although this problem can be solved, it is non-trivial. An event tracing mechanism built into the event mechanism has successfully countered these problems by assisting the programmers in understanding the links between components and the consequent behavior.

7 Related work

A large number of systems have adopted implicit invocation as an integration mechanism. As discussed earlier, most of these tend to fall into the categories of process-oriented tool invocation mechanisms and special-purpose languages. Here we have attempted to broaden the base of applicability by showing how to provide similar functions for standard programming languages.

This work is strongly motivated by others' research, which has demonstrated that implicit invocation is an important new integration mechanism. In particular, Field showed how implicit invocation could be applied to tool integration. Follow-on systems, such as Softbench, have elaborated this style of broadcast-based integration in commercial environments.

Another use of implicit invocation is in the context of some object-oriented systems. One of these is the change propagation mechanism used to support the Model/View/Controller paradigm in Smalltalk-80 [Krasner & Pope 88]. In this system, any object can register as a dependent of another object. When an object "announces" a *changed* event, an *update* method is called on each of the dependent objects. While this use of implicit invocation is limited by the fixed nature of the mechanism (i.e. the events and methods are wired into the Smalltalk environment design), the approach creates problems in conjunction with class inheritance.

We see two significant disadvantages to that approach. First, it forces the event announcer to be aware of the mechanism by which events are being handled. For example, change announcement is actually done by the procedure call "self changed". An alternative would be to perform the announcement on some external entity, as in "dispatcher announce ...": both suffer from the same problem that the announcer must think of the announcement as a procedure call on a specific entity. But a second, and more serious problem, is that one might prefer to think of the events that are to be announced by an object as being part of its interface. Just as procedures determine the functionality of a module (or class) in traditional systems, so, too, are events an integral part of that module's functionality.

CLOS has its own language features for implicit invocation. Specifically, it has a wrapper method mechanism that can be used as an event mechanism. However, it is not as flexible as the mechanism introduced here, which is what led us to introduce the new Common Lisp mechanism. In CLOS, one or more wrapper methods can be defined to augment the behavior of a normal method by executing before, after, or "around" it. When a method is executed, some of its wrapper methods may also be executed, which can be interpreted as the wrapper methods "receiving" the announcement of the call of the main method. Whether one is executed is based on how the types of the arguments match the type signature of the wrapper method, which can deviate from that of the main method by being a sub- or super-class type. However, the selection mechanism can be overridden.

CLOS's mechanism can be characterized as module-based, with implicit declaration of events when methods are defined, and with static event bindings (i.e., declaration of an wrapper method). The delivery policy is based on a match of the wrapper method's type signature with that of the call's arguments (roughly). Event structure is synonymous with method structure, which could be interpreted as "parameters by event type." The parameter passing mode is a combination of passing all parameters and computing parameter expressions.

A primary focus of this paper is better understanding of the design space associated with implicit invocation mechanisms. In that regard it is related to work in formalizing implicit invocation models [Garlan & Notkin 91]. Such efforts are complementary: a formal model makes clear what are the fundamental abstractions necessary to understand implicit invocation, while our concrete application relates these abstractions to the constraints imposed by the real world.

Finally, this work is related to other uses of language extension as a means for enhancing the expressiveness of existing programming languages. One example of language extension is Anna, which augments Ada with specifications [Luckham and won Henke 85]. The primary difference between that kind of work and ours is that we are attempting to change the fundamental mechanisms of interaction in module-oriented languages. That is to say, events are not just additional annotations to permit some tool to perform additional checks, but become an essential part of the computational model for the modules that use them.

8 Conclusion

The contributions of this work are twofold. First, we have shown by example how to add implicit invocation to three quite different programming languages. Some of the design decisions were constrained by the specifics of the languages themselves; but most are more general, based on constraints that are similar to those found in other programming languages (for example, static typing). Therefore, many of our lessons could directly apply to the definition of implicit invocation mechanisms in other programming languages. Second, we have elaborated the design space for this approach and shown how the decisions in this space are affected by the constraints of the programming language that is being enhanced. Ultimately this is the most important thing, since it serves as a checklist for those attempting to apply these techniques to other languages.

References

[Ada 83] Reference Manual for the Ada Programming Language. United States Department of Defense (January 1983).

[Cohen 89] D. Cohen. Compiling Complex Transition Database Triggers. *Proceedings of the 1989 ACM SIGMOD* (1989).

[Dayal, Hsu & Ladin 90] U. Dayal, M. Hsu, and R. Ladin. Organizing Long-Running Activities with Triggers and Transactions. In *Proceedings of the 1990 ACM SIGMOD* (June 1990).

[Garlan & Ilias 91] D. Garlan and E. Ilias. Low-cost, Adaptable Tool Integration Policies for Integrated Environments. *Proceedings of SIGSOFT '90: Fourth Symposium on Software Development Environments.* Irvine, CA (December 1990).

[Garlan, Kaiser & Notkin 92] D. Garlan, G.E. Kaiser, and D. Notkin. Using Tool Abstraction to Compose Systems. *IEEE Computer* (June 1992).

[Garlan & Notkin 91] D. Garlan and D. Notkin. Formalizing Design Spaces: Implicit Invocation Mechanisms. *Proceedings of VDM'91: Formal Software Development Methods*. Springer-Verlag, LNCS 551 (October, 1991).

[Garlan & Scott 93] D. Garlan and C. Scott. Adding Implicit Invocation to Traditional Programming Languages *Proceedings of the 15th International Conference on Software Engineering*. IEEE Computer Society Press, pp. 447-455 (May 1993).

[Garlan *et al.* 92] D. Garlan, M. Shaw, C. Okasaki, C. Scott, and R. Swonger. Experience with a Course on Architectures for Software Systems. *Proceedings of the SEI Conference on Software Engineering Education* (October 1992).

[Gerety 89] C. Gerety. HP SoftBench: A New Generation of Software Development Tools. Technical Report SESD-89-25, Hewlett-Packard Software Engineering Systems Division, Fort Collins, Colorado (November 1989).

[Goldberg & Robson 83] A. Goldberg and D. Robson. *Smalltalk-80: The Language and its Implementation*. Addison-Wesley (1983).

[Griswold 91] W.G. Griswold. *Program Restructuring as an Aid to Software Maintenance*. Department of Computer Science & Engineering, University of Washington (1991).

[Griswold & Notkin 93] W.G. Griswold and D. Notkin. Automated Assistance for Program Restructuring. To appear, *ACM Transactions on Software Engineering and Methodology* (July 1993).

[Habermann, Garlan & Notkin 91] A.N. Habermann, D. Garlan and D. Notkin. Generation of Integrated Task-Specific Software Environments. In *CMU Computer Science: A 25th Commemorative*. ACM Press (1990).

[Hewitt 69] C. Hewitt. PLANNER: A Language for Proving Theorems in Robots. *Proceedings of the First International Joint Conference in Artificial Intelligence.*, Washington DC (1969).

[Krasner & Pope 88] G.E. Krasner and S.T. Pope. A Cookbook for Using the Model-View-Controller User Interface Paradigm in Smalltalk-80. *Journal of Object Oriented Programming 1,3* (August/September 1988), pp. 26-49.

[Larus 89] J.R. Larus. *Restructuring Symbolic Programs for Concurrent Execution on Multiprocessors*. UC Berkeley Computer Science (May 1989).

[Luckham and von Henke 85] D. Luckham and F.W. von Henke. An Overview of Anna, a Specification Language for Ada. *IEEE Software* (March 1985).

[Myers *et al.* 90] B.A. Myers, D.A. Giuse, R.B. Dannenberg, B. Vander Zanden, D.S. Kosbie. E. Pervin, A. Mickish, and P. Marchal. Garnet: Comprehensive Support for Graphical, Highly-Interactive User Interfaces. *IEEE Computer 23*,11, pp. 71-85 (November 1990).

[Reiss 90] S.P. Reiss. Connecting Tools using Message Passing in the Field Environment. *IEEE Software* 7,4 (July 1990).

[Rowe et al. 91] L.A. Rowe, J.A. Konstan, B.C. Smith, S. Seitz, and C. Li. The PICASSO Application Framework. *Proceedings of the 14th ACM Symposium on User Interface Software and Technology* (1991).

[Scheifler and Gettys 86] R.W. Scheifler and J. Gettys. The X Window System. *ACM Transactions on Graphics* 5,2, pp. 79–109 (April 1986).

[Steele 91] G.L. Steele. *COMMON LISP, the Language*, 2nd edition. Digital Press, Burlington MA (1991).

[Stroustrup 87] B. Stroustrup. *The C++ Programming Language*. Addison-Wesley, Reading, MA (1987).

[Sullivan & Notkin 92] K.J. Sullivan and D. Notkin. Reconciling Environment Integration and Software Evolution. *ACM Transactions on Software Engineering and Methodology* 1,3 (July 1992).

[Sutton, Heimbigner & Osterweil 90] S.M. Sutton, Jr., D. Heimbigner, & L.J. Osterweil. Language Constructs for Managing Change in Process-Centered Environments. *Proceedings of ACM SIGSOFT90: Fourth Symposium on Software Development Environments*, pp. 206–217 (December 1990).

Requirements and Early Experiences in the Implementation of the SPADE Repository using Object-Oriented Technology *

Sergio Bandinelli[†] Luciano Baresi Alfonso Fuggetta Luigi Lavazza

CEFRIEL - Politecnico di Milano
Via Emanueli 15
I-20126 Milano (Italy)
e-mail : {bandinelli,lavazza}@mailer.cefriel.it
fuggetta@ipmel2.elet.polimi.it

Abstract

Software development environments (SDEs) pose pressing requirements to the supporting repositories. This paper describes these requirements, as derived within the SPADE project. SPADE is a process centered environment being developed at CEFRIEL and Politecnico di Milano. The aim of the paper is to report the experiences that the authors have gained in building a repository for SPADE using O_2, a "state of the art" object-oriented DBMS.

1 Introduction

In recent years, many researchers in the software engineering area (see for example [Hum89, Ost87]) have identified the software process as the key issue to obtain higher quality products, improved productivity, more controllable projects. By software process we mean the set of activities, rules, methodologies, tools, and roles that participate in the development of software within a given organization.

There is no single process that can be used by any organization, for any kind of product, any development environment, or any software lifecycle. It is necessary to be able to envisage different processes, depending on the characteristics of the product, the market, and the development organization. For this purpose there has been an increasing effort in designing and developing languages and the related support technology to formally describe, assess, and wherever possible, automate software processes.

---

*This work has been partially supported by ESPRIT project 6115 GoodStep - General Object-Oriented Databases for Software Processes

[†]S. Bandinelli is partly supported by DEC, P.za XX Settembre 1, 21100 Varese, Italy.

The degree of automatism of the process enactment[1] depends on the different activities: low-level activities, such as calling a compiler, may be fully automatic, while brain-intensive activities, such as transforming a detailed design into code, are simply guided by the process interpreter, for example producing an agenda for each participant in the development, with reminders of the activities to be still accomplished.

Process centered SDEs (PSDEs) are built around a process interpreter, and in general include a repository for the process data (i.e., the software artifacts plus the process specific information) and a set of integrated tools. Many authors addressed the issue of identifying the requirements for a database system supporting a software engineering environment (see for example the early work by Bernstein [Ber87]). More recently, other works have addressed the issue of the suitability of object-oriented databases as a vehicle to implement software engineering repositories ([ESW92, BBFL93]). Experiences in the usage of object-oriented technology in building software engineering environments (although not process centered) have also been reported [PS91].

SPADE is a process-centered environment that is built around an OODB. The decision of using an Object-Oriented database [AB+89] for building the repository of SPADE descends from the consideration — supported by [ESW92, PS91] among others — that many of the requirements described in [Ber87] have been satisfied — at least partially — by OODBMSs. Other database technologies, like relational databases or structurally object-oriented databases, are clearly inadequate [DEH+91, DEL92].

The work reported here is partially supported by the ESPRIT project GoodStep, that aims at extending the O_2 OODB to support the development of advanced process-centered software engineering environments [Good93].

The paper is organized as follows. Section 2 briefly describes the SLANG software process language. Section 3 gives a conceptual description and classification of data involved in the definition and execution of SLANG models. Section 4 describes the requirements for the database that are posed by the peculiar features of the language and of the whole environment. In Section 5 the O_2 based implementation is described and discussed. Section 6 draws some conclusions and presents future research directions.

2 The SLANG Software Process Language

SPADE (Software Process Analysis, Design and Enactment) is a software process environment, being jointly developed at CEFRIEL and Politecnico di Milano, that provides mechanisms for the definition, analysis, enactment, and evolution of a software development process.

SPADE provides a domain-specific language for modeling and enacting software processes called SLANG (SPADE LANGuage) [BF93, BFG91, BFGG92, BFG93]. SLANG is based on high-level nets and is formally defined in terms of a translation scheme from SLANG into ER nets. ER nets [GMMP91] are a mathematically defined class of high-level Petri nets that provide the designer with powerful means to describe concurrent and real-time systems. In ER nets, it is possible to assign values to tokens and relations to transitions, describing the constraints on tokens consumed and produced by transition firings.

---

[1] "enactment" means execution, in the software process jargon. This word has been introduced to stress the concept that the execution is only partly automatic.

2.1 SLANG Features

A SLANG process model *SLANGSpec* is a pair of sets: (*ProcessTypes, ProcessActivities*). *ProcessTypes* is a set of type specifications which defines the data manipulated by the process; *ProcessActivities* is a set of activity definitions, which specifies the process computations in terms of logical work units using an extended high-level Petri net formalism. These features are now described in more detail.

Process types. In SLANG, all process data are typed, and data with the same properties and characteristics may be grouped as belonging to the same type. Type definitions are organized in a type hierarchy, defined by an "is-a" relationship, whose root is the type `ProcessData`. Types inherit the attributes and operations of their ancestors in an object-oriented style. An example of such type hierarchy is given in Figure 1.

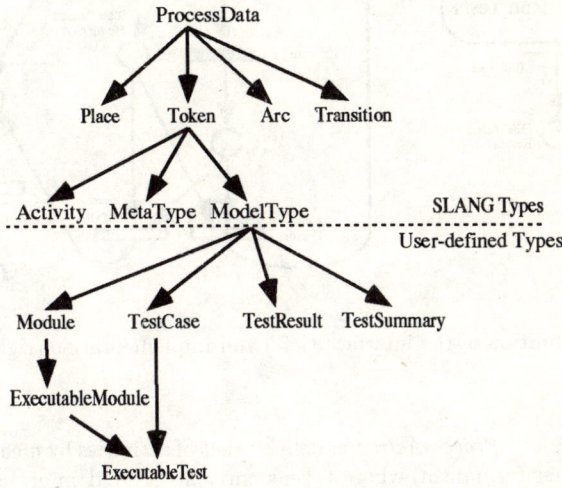

Figure 1: An "is-a" hierarchy of type definitions.

The set of type definitions whose root is "ModelType" varies from one SLANG process model to another, depending on the process to be described. Type descriptions may be added or changed during process enactment. The change of a type requires data instances of that type to change accordingly. Change propagation can be specified within the process definition as being either *lazy* (the changes are visible only when the modified type is used), *eager* (the change has an immediate impact on the process state), or any intermediate strategy.

SLANG offers reflective mechanisms to support process evolution. During process enactment, type definitions and activity definitions can be manipulated as data. Since all process data are typed, two special types are therefore introduced: *Activity* and *Metatype*. *Activity* is the type whose instances are activity definitions; *Metatype* is the type whose instances are type definitions.

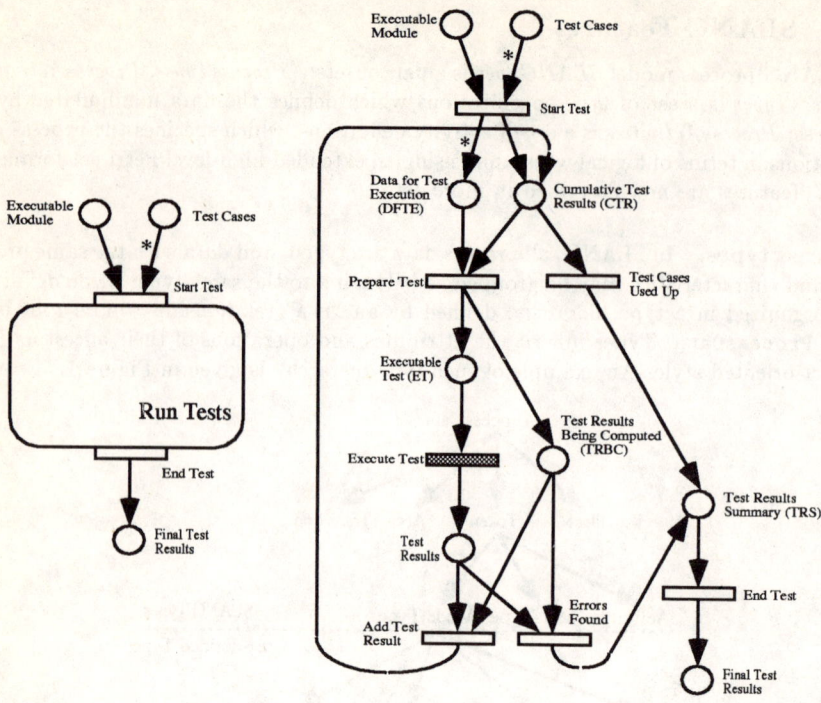

Figure 2: The definition of the interface (left) and implementation (right) of the activity Run tests.

Process activities. *ProcessActivities* defines a set of activities by means of an extended high-level Petri net formalism, where tokens carry structured information of arbitrary complexity. An activity state is given by a net marking, i.e., an assignment of tokens to places. Transitions represent events. The occurrence of an event modifies the activity state. The net topology describes precedence relations, conflicts, and parallelism among events. Each activity corresponds to a logical work unit, that may include invocation of other activities and interaction with the environment (tools and humans).

Activity definition. An *activity definition* is an instance of the special type *activity*: it consists of a net where P is the set of places, T is the set of transitions, and A is the set of arcs. An activity has an *interface* and an *implementation* part. The activity interacts with the rest of the process through its interface, which includes a set of starting events, that may initiate the activity, and a set of ending events, that may end the activity. The implementation part, represented by an high-level Petri net, details how the activity is performed by showing the relationships among the events of interest that may occur during its execution. An activity implementation may also contain invocations to other activities. An example of an activity definition is given in Figure 2.

Places and tokens. Each place has a name and a type. A place behaves as a token repository that may only contain tokens of its type or of any of its subtypes. The only way a place may change its contents is by the firing of an input or output transition. A particular kind of place, called a *user interface* place, may change its content as a consequence of human intervention. User interface places are used to transfer external events caused by humans within the system. The type of a place must be one of the types contained in the *ProcessTypes* set. In particular places can be of type *Activity* (i.e., they may contain tokens whose value is an activity definition), and *Metatype* (i.e., they may contain tokens whose value is a type definition). Consequently, activity and type definitions can be created, manipulated, modified, and deleted as any other values.

Transitions. Transitions represent events whose occurrence takes a negligible amount of time. The occurrence of an event corresponds to the firing of a transition. Each transition has associated with it a guard and an action. The transition's guard is a predicate on input tokens and is used to decide whether an input token tuple enables the transition (an input tuple satisfying a transition guard is called an enabling tuple). The dynamic behavior of a transition is described by the *firing rule*: when a transition fires, tokens satisfying the guard are removed from input places and the transition's action is executed, producing an output tuple that is inserted in the transition's output places.

A software development process involves the activation of a large variety of software tools. Tool invocation is modeled in SLANG by using *black transitions*, i.e., special transitions where the action part has been replaced by a call to a non-SLANG executable routine (e.g., a Unix executable file). When the black transition "fires", the routine is executed *asynchronously*. This means that other transitions may be fired while the black transition is still being executed. It is also possible to fire the black transition itself many times with different input tuples, without waiting for each activation to complete. For example, in Figure 2 the black transition "Execute Test" is used to represent the execution of an external process running the tests.

Arcs. Arcs are weighted with the number of tokens which flow through the arc at each transition firing. Weights can be statically defined (with a default weight of 1), or dynamically computed. In the latter case, the arc weight is indicated by a "*", and it models events consuming *all tokens* that verify a certain property. In addition to "normal" arcs, SLANG provides two special kinds of arc: *read-only* and *overwrite*. A transition can read token values from an input place connected by a read-only arc in order to compute the guard and the action, but no token is actually removed. On the other hand, when an overwrite arc is used to connect a transition to a place, the transition firing causes any previous content of the place to be lost.

2.2 Mechanisms Supporting Process Evolution in SLANG

In process centered environments, process definitions (or models) play the role of the code in regular software systems. The enactment of the process definition causes the automatic execution of computer-based actions and guides the behavior of people involved in the process. In SLANG, the process definition code may include not only the model of the software production process, but also the specification of the software meta-process. Therefore, process enactment involves the execution of activities of both the production process and the meta-process. The meta-process models those actions that do not aim at software production, but concern the management of the process itself: creation/modification of activities, object types, etc.). The reflective nature of SLANG makes it possible to manipulate the process definition (i.e., *ProcessTypes* and *ProcessActivities*) in the same ways other process data are manipulated. Thus process model evolution may be modeled as part of the process itself. This section presents the enaction mechanisms of SLANG, with particular emphasis on process evolution.

The *SLANG interpreter* is responsible for the enaction of SLANG process models. As any other tool, the SLANG interpreter may be called from within the process model, through a black transition. The name *process engine* refers to each running instance of the SLANG interpreter. Whenever the interpreter is called, a new process engine is created. Actually, activity invocation in SLANG may be seen as a derived construct that involves the execution of a call to the SLANG interpreter, via a black transition. Each asynchronous process engine may access shared places during its execution to communicate with other process engines in execution. At the end of execution, the process engine puts the resulting tokens into the places of the invoking activity. Consequently, process engines must be synchronized in order to discipline access to shared and output places in mutual exclusion.

Activity definitions and type definitions used by the activity, are not statically bound to the activity invocation. They are dynamically made available to the process engine at the beginning of the execution of an activity by reading the necessary definitions from places **Activities** and **Types**. This provides the basic interpretive mechanism supporting dynamic evolution.

The mechanisms presented so far provide the ability, within the process model, to manipulate and execute fragments of process definitions. In order to support evolution strategies, it is also necessary to provide mechanisms to manipulate active copies, i.e., the instances of activity definitions that are created during the enactment of the process model.

To manipulate an active copy it is necessary to suspend its execution and make the information about the copy (state, activity and type definitions, etc.) available as a token. SLANG provides a suspension mechanism that forces the termination of the process engine, enables manipulation of the active copy, and later spawns a new process engine to restart execution of the modified active copy.

SPADE supports two main classes of change. It is possible to modify definitions, by modifying tokens whose values are activity and type definitions. It is also possible to modify active copies while they are suspended. In most cases, one first modifies a definition and, at some later instant, the effect of a definition change is made visible in a running active copy. In such a case, it is useful to distinguish between two times: *change definition time* (CDT) and *change instantiation time* (CIT). CDT is the time at which changes are applied to a SLANG definition; CIT is the time at which a change in a definition becomes visible in a running active copy.

The new definition of an activity can be generated by a meta-process that accesses places **Activities** and **Types**, to edit the required definitions. The time at which editing terminates on a set of definitions defines the CDT of such definitions. The corresponding CITs depend on the strategy one wishes to adopt: different strategies may be specified in SPADE in order to reflect the effect of a change to a definition in a running active copy; i.e., different strategies are possible to define CIT, given a CDT. A first strategy (*lazy* *strategy*) does not propagate the modification of activity and type definition to existing active copies. Only when new active copies are created, are the new definitions used. A second strategy (*eager strategy*) is based on the immediate propagation of activity and type definition changes to all existing active copies. Notice that other modification strategies can be envisaged; a whole spectrum of strategies exist from fully lazy to fully eager.

It is also possible to modify a suspended active copy (e.g., its type definitions or its state) without modifying any activity or type definition. This would affect only the changed active copy, with no effect on future creations of active copies of the same or other activities.

3 SPADE Data Description and Classification

This section provides the description and classification of data that will be stored in the SPADE repository. All the information describing a SLANG specification (*ProcessTypes* and *ProcessActivity*) and the process state (all instances of *ProcessData* and its subtypes) are stored in a repository that is shared by all the process engines. The repository is built on top of O_2. The SLANG interpreter uses the database to access both the description of the process model and the process data produced and modified as result of its enactment.

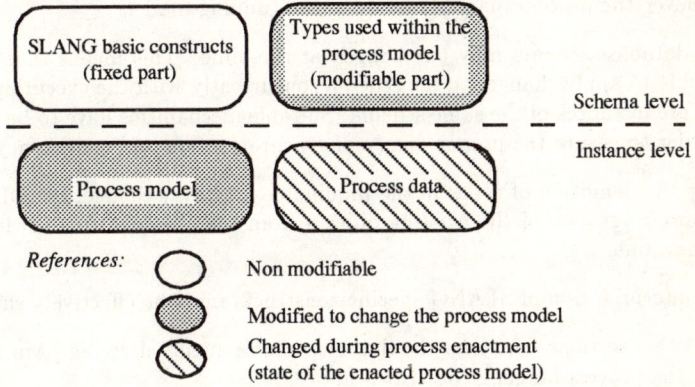

Figure 3: Structure of the SPADE repository.

The SPADE repository is organized according to the following structure.

- The schema of the database is partitioned in two parts: a *fixed part* that contains the types of SLANG basic constructs (including type *Activity* and type *Metatype*), and a *modifiable part* containing the definition of the types used within a specific process model (all subtypes of *ProcessData* type). This modifiable part can change to cope with modification in the modeled process. For example, we may add a type to describe a new class of documents or software items.

- At the instance level, we have two different sets of objects as well. The instances of the types in the fixed part of the schema correspond to a specific process model definition (i.e., a collection of arcs, transitions, and places constituting a SLANG specification). The instances of the modifiable part of the schema correspond to process data (e.g., modules, test results, test cases, etc.) produced or modified during process enactment.

Summing up, we have the scenario described in Figure 3. It is not possible to change the definition of the SLANG language (fixed part of the schema). Changes to the variable part of the schema and to the instances of the fixed part correspond to changes in the process model. Changes to the instances of the modifiable part correspond to changes in the state of the enacted process model.

4 Database Requirements

A first set of SLANG features that poses specific requirements to the OODB is the following:

1. The process engine is a program that depends only on the types in the fixed part of the schema. It must not depend on the types of the modifiable part, because they may be changed both during the process definition and during process enactment (process evolution): it is clearly not feasible to regenerate the process engine whenever the process manager modifies the running model.

2. The database schema may be changed at run-time. This means that it must be possible to apply changes to the schema concurrently with the execution of models that are instances of the same schema. Suitable mechanisms have to be established in order to ensure the proper degree of synchronization and consistency.

3. Since the definition of types in the modifiable part may change, the DBMS has to support migration of the existing objects from the old definition of their type to the new one.

4. The interpretation of SLANG specific constructs must be effectively supported.

The rest of this sections describes the database requirements deriving from the specific features of the process language described above.

The following discussion is based on the class hierarchy described in Figure 4. The graphical convention used is the following: boxes represent classes, where the upper part contains the name, and the bottom part contains relevant properties; arrows represent inheritance relationships.

The given hierarchy is a refinement of the general hierarchy depicted in Figure 1. It is a simplified, although likely, representation of the SLANG class hierarchy: Place and Token are classes belonging to the fixed part of the schema (i.e., to the language definition), while IntToken, StrToken, IntPlace and StrPlace are sample specializations of language elements (i.e., classes used to define the specific process). Note that according to Figure 1 type Place should not originate user defined types. This situation was forced by the features of the typing mechanism of O_2SQL mentioned in Section 5.1.

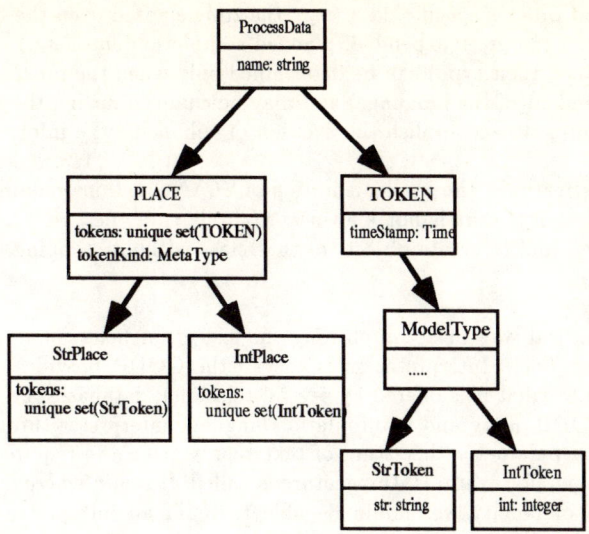

Figure 4: Language constructs class hierarchy.

4.1 Dynamic Interpretation of Queries

The process engine executes the SLANG net specification by computing at each execution cycle the set of transitions that are enabled (i.e., whose guards evaluate to true) and selecting a transition to fire. The firing of a transition involves the execution of the associated action. The guard and action specifications are loaded at run-time from the OODB and then interpreted.

Each process engine must be able to execute queries and update operations on the database. The code to be executed may be changed by the user concurrently with the execution of the model: once a change has been committed, the process engine will use the new definition, when the modified transition has to be fired. In other words, each time the interpreter retrieves a piece of code from the DB (this is done e.g., at each activity initiation) such code may have changed with respect to the previous execution. The process engine must be able to use the last version of such code stored in the database. There are several kinds of changes in the overall model that may be performed during process execution, in particular they may regard:

- the types in the modifiable part;
- the structure of the model (i.e., the topology of the net);
- the text of a guard (or that of an action).

Every time a transition is fired, SLANG executes the action associated with that transition. The effect of the action is the creation of tokens in the output places and the assignment of values to these tokens' attributes. Such values are either taken directly from the input places or computed by the transition action. We remind that tokens represent the artifacts of the software process (e.g., code, specification documents, error reports, etc.) and process specific data (e.g., the time elapsed from the beginning of the project, amount of resources expended, planned completion date, etc.). The description of the artifacts (i.e., their type) can be determined only when the process is instantiated (i.e., it is independent of the language) and may be changed during the execution of the process (for example to accomplish the decision of enhancing the information contained in a report).

Because of these features, the implementation of SLANG actions requires the ability to build objects of a class that is not known at compile time, i.e., we want to be able to define a new class and to create objects of that class without stopping and recompiling the process engine.

The most natural way of accomplishing the execution behavior described above is to interpret the model. Interpretation is easy if the OODB provides a programmatic interface similar to what it is offered by several relational databases, i.e., if it is possible to invoke the OODB query and manipulation language interpreter through a procedure call, passing as a parameter the string of text representing the required operation. In SQL-based systems, for example, this feature is called *dynamic embedded SQL*.

Using this kind of facility we should be able to build an interpreter of dynamically changing code, since we can define at run-time queries implementing transition guards and actions, independently of the process model we are enacting.

Since transition actions may involve the creation of new objects, the interpreter and the language must also be able to accept object creation statements. In fact, the language should be computationally complete, in order to represent transition actions.

4.2 Schema Management

The definitions of types that belong to the modifiable part of the schema (i.e., all types but those defining the elements of the language) may be changed. It must be possible to change these definitions even during process enactment, i.e., when they are used by some process engine.

Moreover, schema updates must be safe: each change must leave the database in a consistent state, avoiding to loose information and, consequently, to cause run-time inconsistency and abortion of transitions. In particular, when a type definition is changed, we must handle the instances of the changed type: we need some mechanism to support migration of the existing objects from the old definition to the new one.

Although it is possible to explicitly convert existing objects, this operation is rather cumbersome, and in general this solution is unfeasible for databases of non trivial size. An automatic mechanism for type migration should support different operating requirements:

- lazy migration: the object is "converted" to the new type only when the object is accessed;

- eager migration: the object is "converted" to the new type as soon as the new type is defined.

- any user-defined migration being an intermediate strategy between fully eager and fully lazy migration.

A complementary approach to type updating consists of providing support for type versioning: both types survive, new objects will be created according to the new type definition, while old objects are accessed according to the corresponding type version.

4.3 Distribution

SPADE supports multi-user project development by allowing the distribution of running activities over a number of workstations. The model of the process that supervises and governs the activities is shared among the workstations. There are, basically, two ways to implement this situation. The first consists in allowing a distributed access from the users' workstations to a DB server. The whole model resides on a server, that is a fundamental component in order to determine the performance of the whole system. This approach appears to be interesting for quite small projects, and for large projects that can be split into quite independent sub-projects. The second idea, suitable for larger projects, is to distribute transparently the process model execution over various workstations. This implies distributing the process data, consisting mainly in the artifacts that are produced locally by each user. The tools used should not need to know anything about the physical distribution of the data used: it should be the responsibility of the database system to manage physical distribution. This approach reduces the client-server traffic on the local area network, while it introduces the need for consistency control mechanisms to preserve the consistency of the distributed databases.

4.4 Other Issues

In this section we briefly describe some features that are frequently mentioned as requirements for a software engineering database, but play a minor part in our environment, at least at the present stage of development. In particular, we describe why at the moment such requirements have not been considered in the first implementation of SPADE.

4.4.1 Concurrency Management

Basic transactional mechanisms (such as two-phase lock) must be available, in order to achieve atomicity of actions. Since transitions deal with tokens — that correspond to database objects — in order to synchronize different process engines accessing the same token it is necessary to provide object-level locking. Locking at a coarser granularity could prevent potentially parallel activities from actually proceed in parallel.

More sophisticated concurrency control mechanisms, such as long or nested transactions, are not needed, since the behavior they provide can be achieved by coding the transaction behavior in the net.

4.4.2 Access Control

Each user has an identity and a role: these attributes can be modeled explicitly in SLANG, and guards may take them into account, so that only users having a specific profile are enabled to perform given actions. In other words, access control is explicitly programmed by the process modeler. The database management system has simply to provide basic mechanisms that prevent unauthorized access to the object base, e.g., from outside the process centered environment.

4.4.3 Versioning

Versioning of artifacts can also be "programmed" in SLANG, thus a specific support by the database is not strictly required. Support from the database could facilitate the process programmer in writing the definition of the versionable artifacts.

5 Using O_2 as a Process Repository

In this section we briefly describe O_2, a "state of the art" object-oriented database management system, and we assess its suitability as the repository supporting a process centered development environment.

The choice of O_2 descended from an evaluation of available OODBMSs with respect to a set of initial requirements (that were then refined into those described in Section 4). Experiments in the development of SPADE repositories using other databases (including GemStone, DEC Object/DB, Ode, PCTE) are currently being carried out at CEFRIEL, in order to assess the variety of features provided by different object-oriented database management systems.

The O_2 OODBMS

The first prototype of O_2 was the result of a research project started in 1986 by the Altaïr consortium; O_2 is now a commercial product of O_2 *Technology*.

O_2 is provided with a complete development environment and a set of user interface tools. Information is organized in *objects* (instances of *classes*), and *values* (instances of *types*). A value has only a type, while an object has an identity, a value and a behavior, determined by the *methods* defined in its class. Methods are coded in O_2C, a fourth generation language, born as a superset of ANSI C, extended to support the object-oriented data model of O_2.

O_2 allows the user to write programs, to manipulate his/her database and to generate an appropriate user interface. However applications written in other languages, like C and C++, have access to the features offered by O_2 by means of an import/export mechanism. The user can also easily design graphic interfaces using O_2Look, built on top of *X Window System* and *Motif*, that provides a set of high-level functions to display and to edit complex objects.

The O_2 system [LRV89, Deu91] offers a declarative query language, called O_2SQL, whose syntax is styled on SQL, the standard query language for relational database. O_2SQL allows the user to query an O_2 database either in an interactive way or under program control.

5.1 The Dynamic Interpretation of SLANG

The basic part of the SLANG interpreter (i.e., the guard evaluation - transition selection - firing loop) has a rather traditional structure, and is therefore written in O_2C.

The dynamic interpretation of guards and actions described in Section 4.1 is achieved by providing the class Transition with two methods, **evaluateGuard** and **executeAction**, that call the O_2SQL interpreter for the evaluation of a query whose text (defined at run-time) represents the guard or the action. The O_2C code of the process engine that calls the O_2SQL interpreter is reported in Figure 5.

```
o2 unique set(list(unique set(Token))) result;
o2 list(Place) parameters;
...
o2query(result, query_code, parameters);
```

Figure 5: Call of the O_2SQL interpreter.

It is quite obvious that the aforementioned methods must be general, i.e., they must be able to deal with any guard or any action.

Therefore, a first requirement is that the call of the query evaluator must not depend on how many places are in input to the transition whose guard we are evaluating. This need is taken into account by declaring the **parameters** of the query as a list of Places, i.e., the **o2query** call will receive any number of instances of any subtype of Place.

It is also required that the result of the query is a general structure (i.e., it is valid for any number of input places, and for any weight of input arcs). The definition of the **result** given in Figure 5 meets this requirement. Its meaning is related to the concept of "enabling tuple", i.e., the set of sets of tokens that satisfies the guard predicate. Each set, whose cardinality depends on the weight of the connecting arc, is taken from a different input place. The inner unique set of **result** represents the set of tokens received from each input place. The enabling tuple is represented by the list of such sets (where the order takes into account the position of the place with respect to the transition). The outer unique set contains all of the enabling tuples.

Although in principle the solution presented in Figure 5 solves the problem of dynamic interpretation of the guards, there are a couple of problems in the implementation of O_2SQL that forced us to modify it.

In O_2SQL any collection (i.e., sets, lists and unique sets) is considered as a value, not as an object: thus it is statically typed, and elements are statically bound to the static type of the collection. For example, in Figure 5 **parameters** is considered as a non-polymorphic list of Places: if the **query_code** refers to any feature of a subtype of Place (as is often the case, since the **query_code** is built knowing the actual type of the Place) it is rejected by the precompiler. In order to overcome this problem, method **evaluateGuard** has to contain an **o2query** call with as many parameters (each one representing an input place) as the maximum fan-in of any transition in the net. Figure 6 reports a piece of code of method **evaluateGuard**. The example refers to the evaluation of the guard of the transition illustrated in Figure 7: note that the guard explicitly mentions attribute int, that is exclusive of type IntToken (see Figure 4).

Since parameters (parameters[0], parameters[1], etc.) are objects, there are no typing problems.

O_2SQL does not support the creation of new objects, as needed by the execution of an action. In order to solve this problem, each token type definition is provided with a template and a duplication method, so that the creation of new objects is performed by "cloning" the template. Such a solution is valid in general, i.e., it is not O_2-specific, since it relies only on the possibility of interpreting queries containing method calls. In

```
o2 list(Place) parameters;              /* the list of input places */
o2 unique set(list(unique set(Token))) result;   /* enabling tuples */

/* let self->Guard be
 "select distinct list(unique set(t11,t12), unique set(t21))\
  from t11 in $1.tokens,\
       t12 in ($1.tokens - unique set(t11)),\
       t21 in $2.tokens\
  where forall t1 in unique set(t11,t12):(t1.name=t21.name and t1.int=3)"
*/
o2query(result, self->Guard,
                parameters[0], parameters[1], parameters[2], ....);
```

Figure 6: Passing many parameters to the O_2SQL interpreter.

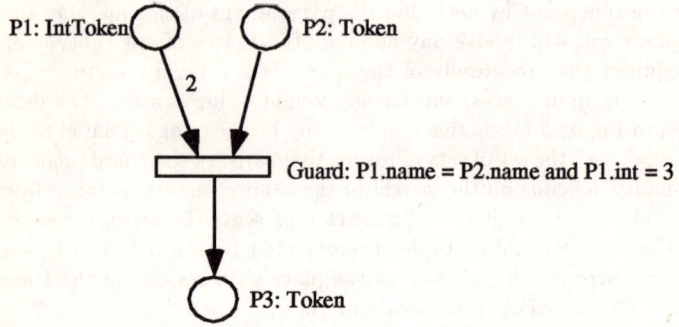

Figure 7: Sample transition and guard

particular the creation of tokens in SLANG is organized as follows:

- The Meta Schema of the SLANG interpreter is explicitly represented by means of the class *MetaType*, whose instances represent types, and in particular token types. The instance of class *MetaType* representing type T has an attribute **prototype** that stores a template instance of type T.

- When a place is created that will store tokens of type T, the attribute **tokenKind** is assigned a reference to the *MetaType* instance that describes type T. For example, when a new place of class *Specifications* is created, the attribute **tokenKind** of that place is associated with the *MetaType* representing class *SpecificationDocument*.

- Class *Token* defines two methods, **duplicate** and **makeAssignments**, that are used to create copies of the prototype token, and to assign its attributes. These methods are redefined in each subclass of *Token*.
  For example, if a new *SpecificationDocument* has to be created in an output place,

a copy of the *SpecificationDocument* prototype referenced by attribute `tokenKind` of the place is produced, by means of the `duplicate` method. The resulting *SpecificationDocument* attributes are then assigned the desired values by means of the (dynamically bound) method `makeAssignments`, that performs assignments by means of the O_2SQL interpreter.

5.2 Run-Time Schema Modification

The version of O_2 that we used to make the experiments reported in this paper (release 4.0) offers the possibility to manipulate the schema only by means of the DB's alphanumeric interface. It is not possible to directly manipulate the schema using O_2's programmatic interface, i.e., it is not possible to invoke the database schema manipulation capabilities at run-time. The only possible way to add new classes to the DB schema is to write the appropriate DDL (Data Definition Language) code and compile it as an independent process. However, the application does not need to be interrupted, because a process could run the application, while another process updates the schema.

Obviously, an extension of the O_2 supporting schema manipulation would greatly facilitate the accomplishment of this task. In order to cope with this requirement the new version of O_2 [O2 93] allows the direct vision and manipulation of the predefined object *Meta Schema*, describing the schema of the used base. This feature facilitates the run-time creation or modification of classes, solving the problem shown above. Furthermore these functions should intercept possible schema inconsistences, letting the programmer avoid many kinds of run-time errors. Another interesting usage of the Meta Schema handling is the ability to build and to use objects of a class that is not known at compile time, as is required by the definition of SLANG actions.

5.3 Type Migration

O_2 does not provide any direct support to type migration. Any change made to the type structure of a class (adding or removal of an attribute, for example) will yield inconsistent objects of that class in each base governed by the schema. This inconsistency will lead to wrong accesses during the execution of a body and abortion of transactions. In order to avoid this problem, the user must *dump* all objects of this class before changing its structure. Dumped information can be later retrieved and associated to instances of the updated type.

The new version of O_2 enables the run-time modification of a type, but this operation is safe only is there are no instances of that type. However, in most cases it is possible to obtain type migration exploiting the mechanisms provided by the O_2 Metaschema. For example, the manual describes a generic function that adds an attribute to any object. Such an effect is obtained by a) creating a subclass of the given object's class that includes the specified attribute, b) creating an object of the latter class, and c) copying the value of each attribute of the old object into the corresponding attribute of the newly created object (the extra attribute is given a default value).

It is interesting to note how point c) is obtained:

1. Using the predefined methods of the Metaschema the definition of the original class is examined, and the name of each of its attributes is retrieved.

2. The text of a function that assigns each attribute of the old object to the corresponding attribute of the new object is composed.

3. Such a function is declared and compiled by means of the predefined method **command** of the predefined object **Schema**.

4. The function is executed by means of a `o2sql` call.

The function described above can be extended to achieve any kind of type migration. However, there is a problem with object identity: the new objects have their own identity, i.e., they are *other* objects then the original ones. This requires a database traversal in order to find out all the existing references to the old objects and transform them into references to the new ones. Such a solution is inefficient but acceptable, since type updates are supposed to be rather unfrequent.

5.4 Distribution

O_2 is based on a client-server architecture: this means that clients (that are responsible for the execution of methods and applications) may run on different machines, while the server (that is responsible for object management) runs on a centralized machine. Although not an ideal situation, this architecture is sufficient to support a distributed SDE with a limited number of people (clients) involved in the process. The number of clients is limited only by the amount of traffic required to move objects to and from the server.

Logical distribution of data (i.e., separate bases having a common schema) will be supported by O_2 in a near future.

5.5 Concurrency Management

O_2 — like many other current implementations of object-oriented databases — provides page-level two-phase locking. This satisfies the requirement for a mechanism allowing atomicity and independence of transition firing; however it can cause logically independent activities to conflict when the involved objects are stored on the same page.

A new version of O_2 to be released shortly should provide a mechanism for manually controlling allocation of objects to pages, in order to prevent the problem. Object-level locking is also planned for a future version.

6 Concluding Remarks

In this paper we have reported our experience in building the repository for a process centered software development environment using O_2. We illustrated the requirements that a PSDE poses to the supporting repository, and we described how O_2 fulfils such requirements.

Our experiment gave encouraging results, that let us undertake the development of an interpreter for SLANG using O_2. However, several goals are still to be met, as discussed in Section 5. Among these, we remind the fully functional embedded query language, support for type migration, and physical distribution of data.

We hope that this paper will contribute to enhance the confidence of the software engineering community in the capabilities of object-oriented databases, as well as to provide some suggestions for the evolution of the object-oriented database technology.

Future activities include:

- Experiments aiming at determining when physical distribution of data is actually necessary (i.e., when it is necessary to store data where it is most frequently needed). This will imply evaluating the limits of the client-server architecture of O_2 and investigating the efficiency issues related with page caching at the clients.

- Integration of tools in the SPADE environment, investigating both the usage of data type-aware tools, and the current development environment tools. It would also be interesting to integrate the process engine and a tool environment such as Field [Rei90], in order to couple the benefits of a PSDE and of a service oriented, message driven tool environment.

- We will also continue to observe the evolution of OODBMS, in order to identify possible features that would allow the construction of more powerful or more efficient repositories for SDEs. It is our will to experiment with such new features, and possibly to use them in the development of the repository for SPADE.

Acknowledgements

People from O_2 Technology provided continuos support and invaluable help.

References

[AB+89]   M. Atkinson, F. Bancilhon, et al. The object-oriented database system manifesto. In *Proceedings of the First DOOD Conference*, Japan, 1989.

[BBFL93] Sergio Bandinelli, Luciano Baresi, Alfonso Fuggetta, and Luigi Lavazza. Requirements and Early Experiences in the Implementation of the SPADE Repository. In *Proceedings of the 8th International Software Process Workshop*, Berlin (Germany), February 1993.

[Ber87]   P.A. Bernstein. Database system support for software engineering - an extended abstract. In *Proceedings of the Ninth International Conference on Software Engineering*, pages 166–178. IEEE, 1987.

[BF93]   Sergio Bandinelli and Alfonso Fuggetta. Computational Reflection in Software Process Modeling: the SLANG Approach. In *Proceedings of the 15th. International Conference on Software Engineering*, Baltimore, Maryland (USA), May 1993.

[BFG91]   Sergio Bandinelli, Alfonso Fuggetta, and Carlo Ghezzi. Software Processes as Real-time Systems: a Case Study Using High-level Petri nets. In Fuggetta, Conradi, and Ambriola, editors, *Proceedings of the First European Workshop on Software Process Modeling*, pages 203–226, Milano (Italy), May 1991. AICA - Italian National Association for Computer Science.

[BFG93]   Sergio Bandinelli, Alfonso Fuggetta, and Sandro Grigolli. Process Modeling-in-the-large with SLANG. In *Proceedings of the 2nd International Conference on the Software Process*, Berlin (Germany), February 1993. IEEE.

[BFGG92]   Sergio Bandinelli, Alfonso Fuggetta, Carlo Ghezzi, and Sandro Grigolli. Process Enactment in SPADE. In J. Derniame, editor, *Proceedings of the Second European Workshop on Software Process Technology*, volume 635 of *LNCS*, Trondheim (Norway), September 1992. Springer-Verlag.

[DEH+91]   S. Dissmann, W. Emmerich, B. Holtkamp, K. Lichtinghagen, and L. Shope. OMSs comparative study. Internal Report D2.4.3-rep-1.0-UDO-EL, ATMOSPHERE, 1991.

[DEL92]   S. Dewal, W. Emmerich, and K. Lichtinghagen. A Decision Support Method for the Selection of OMSs. In *Proceedings of the Second Int. Conference on System Integration*, pages 32–40, Morristown, N.J., 1992. IEEE Computer Society Press.

[Deu91]   O. Deux. The O_2 System. *CACM*, 34(10), October 1991.

[ESW92]   Wolfgang Emmerich, Wilhelm Schäfer, and Jim Welsh. Suitable Databases For Process-centred Environments Do Not Yet Exist. In Jean-Claude Derniame, editor, *Proceedings of the Second European Workshop on Software Process Technology*, volume 635 of *LNCS*, pages 94–98, Trondheim (Norway), September 1992. Springer-Verlag.

[GMMP91]   Carlo Ghezzi, Dino Mandrioli, Sandro Morasca, and Mauro Pezzè. A Unified High-level Petri Net Formalism for Time-critical Systems. *IEEE Transactions on Software Engineering*, February 1991.

[Good93]   GoodStep. Description of software engineering applications and requirements for an object-oriented repository. Deliverable 1, ESPRIT project 6115 GoodStep, March 1993.

[Hum89]   Watts S. Humphrey. *Managing the Software Process*. SEI Series in Software Engineering. Addison-Wesley, 1989.

[LRV89]   C. Lecluse, P. Richard, and F. Velez. O2, an object-oriented data model. In *Proceedings of SIGMOD '89 - Int. Conf. on the Management of Data*, pages 424–433, Portland, OR, 1989. ACM.

[O2 93]   O2 Technology, 7 rue du Parc de Clagny - 78035 Versailles Cedex, France. *The O2 User's Manual*, January 1993. Version 4.2.1 - Chapter 11.

[Ost87]   Leon Osterweil. Software processes are software too. In *Proceedings of the Ninth International Conference on Software Engineering*. IEEE, 1987.

[PS91]   M. H. Penedo and C. Shu. Acquiring experiences with the modelling and implementation of the project life-cycle process: the PMDB work. *Software Engineering Journal*, pages 259–273, September 1991.

[Rei90]   S. Reiss. Connecting Tools using Message Passing in the FIELD Program Development Environment. *IEEE Software*, pages 57–67, July 1990.

Object-Oriented Formal Specification Development using VDM

Amarit Laorakpong   Motoshi Saeki

Tokyo Institute of Technology
Dept. of Electrical & Electronic Engineering
2-12-1 Ookayama, Meguro-ku, Tokyo 152, Japan
e-mail: (amarit,saeki)@cs.titech.ac.jp

Abstract

This paper introduces the Object-Oriented Specification Language, a language based on Formal Description Technique (FDT) in the style of Vienna Development Method (VDM) so called OO_{VDM}, additionally includes its denotational semantics and implementation. Our research contributes to the extension of VDM by an Object-Oriented concept which supports incremental & subtyping inheritance. OO_{VDM} has two types of modules, which are *class* modules and *type* modules. *Class* modules define objects having their internal states. Their states can be changed by the execution of the operations on them. *Type* modules specify objects with no states, i.e. *values*, and denote the domains of the values. OO_{VDM} has two kinds of inheritance mechanisms - *incremental inheritance* and *subtyping inheritance*. Both concepts are useful for overloading existing descriptions and for hierarchical classification of the objects.

Key Word: Vienna Development Method, Object-Oriented Language, Formal Description Technique, Incremental Inheritance, Subtyping Inheritance, Denotational Semantics.

1 Introduction

Object-oriented description style improves methodology not only for programming but also for specifying software [Dahl, 1990] [Booch, 1991]. Its essential concepts are *class* abstraction and *inheritance* based on class hierarchy. The object-oriented methodology enhances the reusability, the extensibility, and the maintainability of the specifications.

To construct verifiable specifications as complete as possible in the early step of software development, efforts of many researchers have been pursued on formal specification languages and their theories. In particular, FDT (Formal Description Technique) [Vissers, 1990] offers great benefits in the design of software systems such as communication systems, reactive systems, and open distributed systems. The languages for FDT such as LOTOS [ISO 8807], Z [Spivey, 1988], and VDM [Bjørner, 1990] [Jones, 1990] etc. are insufficient in term of their writability and comprehensibility. The extension of FDT to facilitate object-oriented description style allows us to more easily construct comprehensive specifications. The extension of Z [Cusack, 1991] [Carrington, 1990] and

LOTOS [Cusack, 1990] [Lee, 1989] has been studied to embed facilities of object-oriented concepts to them. We choose another FDT, Vienna Development Method (VDM), and show its extension to facilitate object-oriented description style. In this paper, we discuss how the two essential concepts — *class* and *inheritance* have been embedded in VDM specification language [BSI, 1991].

Class concepts are used for modularization of software and encapsulation of information into modules. Our language Object-Oriented VDM (shortened to OOVDM) has two types of modules, *class* modules and *type* modules. *Class* modules define objects having their internal states. Their states can be changed by the execution of the operations on them. Each class module is used to encapsulate the definition of an object's state with its operations. *Type* modules specify objects with no states, i.e. *values*, and denote the domains of the values. Each type module is defined as an abstract data type such as one of Algebraic Specification Languages, encapsulating the functions related to the type. For example, non-negative-integers are defined in a type module because it seems to be natural that they have no internal states. OOVDM has a different approach from other FDT in term of its semantics and how things can be defined.

A variety of inheritance concepts have been developed for object-oriented languages. As pointed out in several papers [Wegner, 1988] [America, 1990] [Cusack, 1991], they can be separated into two concepts — *incremental inheritance* and *subtyping inheritance*. Both concepts are useful for their reusability of existing descriptions and for hierarchical classification of the objects. OOVDM has the incremental inheritance concept for class modules, and subtyping inheritance for type modules. Most object-oriented languages have either of the two inheritance mechanisms but not both. OOVDM, however, has been properly implemented with both of these powerful inheritance mechanisms.

In the following section, we will introduce our OOVDM language in conjunction with detailed examples. Section 3 presents the two separated inheritance mechanisms in OOVDM using an example specifying on quadrilaterals system. In section 4, we provide a denotational semantics of these inheritance mechanisms, that is to say, we can formally define them by using VDM itself. On account of spaces in this paper, we cannot show the whole semantics of OOVDM, but only brief sketch on essential parts of the semantics of inheritance mechanism in OOVDM. The denotational semantics of VDM has been discussed in [BSI, 1991], on which semantics of other parts of OOVDM is based.

2 OOVDM

OOVDM presents as a formal specification language, which consists of *class* and *type* modules declaration with both modules expressed in VDM style. In VDM, the values used in a formal specification are defined by the domain equations for the abstract syntax and the semantic domains [Jones, 1990]. VDM insists that the specification of requirements should be formulated from the beginning at the highest possible level of abstract specification, using all the available power of mathematics to describe the desirable, observable and testable properties of the product which is to be implemented. The description of the intended behaviour of a system requires that the meaning of its operations be specified. This is done by recording properties (**pre-** and **post-** condition). OOVDM notation has two modules which are *class* and *type* modules. *Class* module consists of *inherited class, constant, state schema, initial state* and *method*. *Type* module consists of *supertype, value*, and *axiom* declaration (details of both *class* and *type* are discussed in the next sub-section). Each object has *state*, which contains all the properties and can be created, exterminated, or shared. The *state* will change according to the *executed operations*.

2.1 Class & Type Notation

OOVDM can be defined by the following notation. The name of class, *class name*, represents its identity and is defined with parameters which are used when created. The body of class begins from the keyword **class** and ends at the keyword **endclass**. A *subclass* is a class whose properties are inherited from one or more existing classes called *superclasses*. The object can consists of constants and is defined by using the keyword **constant**. State variables are defined by using the keyword **state schema** and written with their attributes. An object will have its initial state as defined in **initial state** when instantiated. Class behaviour is defined in **method** which consists of zero or more *operator schemas*. The *operator schemas* express the relationship of the instances of an object according to **pre-** and **post-** conditions.

Type module allows declaration of compound attributes. The attributes can inherit from existing *types* by using the keyword **supertype**. Furthermore, *type* module may have the declaration of *value* and *axiom* (by using the keyword **value** and **axiom**). *Value* gives the name of value and its type while *axiom* expresses properties of value names [George, 1991].

> **class** *class name*[parameters]
>   **inherited class**
>   **constant**
>   **state schema**
>   **initial state**
>   **method**
>   *operator schema* * *(input, output)*
>   **pre-**
>   **post-**
>   ⋮
> **endclass**

<Class Module>

> **type** *typename*
>   *type declaration*
>   **supertype**
>   **value**
>   *value declaration*
>   **axiom**
>   *axiom declaration*
> **endtype**

<Type Module>

OOVDM Notation

We consider the identifier of an object to differentiate our two OOVDM types of modules, *class* modules and *type* modules. One of the essential characteristics of the object is that each object has its identity which means the object has its identifier to perceive a difference from the other objects. This idea of object identifier can be considered in two ways as an object or anything which is not an object. If we considered it as an object, we will have to deal with an infinite number of identifiers (identifier of identifier of identifier of and so on). It is more natural to identify the object identifier with something that is not an object except for "value". We have many things which can be naturally considered as "value", e.g. integer, character, etc.. Thus we introduced the concept of *type* module to OOVDM in order to define the set of "values" having common properties. From the reasons above, we consider that *class* and *type* concepts should be developed separately.

2.2 Motivational Example of OOVDM

To show the reliance on specification language OOVDM we have defined systems using OOVDM which are library system, stock market system (selling and buying chronological record of companies in stock market), and quadrilateral system [Duke, 1991]. All of the examples defined by our OOVDM have both inheritance mechanisms which are extended from their existing class and type.

In this paper the quadrilateral system will be used as an example. The following section will show how both *incremental* and *subtyping inheritance* mechanisms are used to define and create a new class and a new type from the principle ones.

2.3 Quadrilaterals Example on OOVDM

In this section we will define quadrilateral system by using OOVDM. This example, excerpted and extended from [Duke, 1991], shows the quadrilateral specification and its inheritance. First, we give a definition of each shape and its hierarchy (as shown in Fig.1). A *Quadrilateral* is a figure which represents a general four-sided figure. A figure with both of its opposite sides are parallel is a *Parallelogram*. A *Parallelogram* with all sides of equal length is a *Rhombus* while a *Parallelogram* with perpendicular sides is a *Rectangle*. A figure which has both *Rectangle* and *Rhombus* properties is called a *Square*. The conclusion of the above sentences can be written in a formal way as follow:

- *Quadrilateral* : a general four-sided figure
- *Parallelogram* : a *Quadrilateral* that has parallel opposite sides
- *Rhombus* : a *Parallelogram* with all sides of the same length
- *Rectangle* : a *Parallelogram* with perpendicular sides
- *Square* : both a *Rectangle* and a *Rhombus*

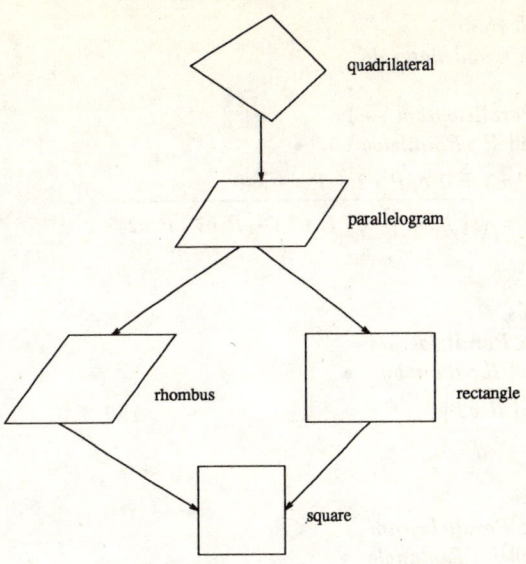

Fig.1 Hierarchy of Quadrilaterals

Since we will define these figures by using vector, we present here the type definition of vector operations:-

- Vector addition $\_+\_ : Vector \times Vector \rightarrow Vector$
- Vector modulus $|\_| : Vector \rightarrow Scalar$
- Vector dot product $\_\cdot\_ : Vector \times Vector \rightarrow Scalar$
- Vector rotation $\_\odot\_ : Vector \times Angle \rightarrow Vector$

From the given definitions, we will define each type by using QOVDM based on their characteristics and hierarchy. All figures are represented by vectors.

    type *Sides*
        $\langle\ v1 : Vector,\ v2 : Vector,\ v3 : Vector,\ v4 : Vector\ \rangle$
    value
        rotate : $Sides \times Angle \mapsto Sides$
    axiom forall $Sd : Sides, \theta : Angle\ \bullet$
        rotate$(Sd, \theta) = \langle Sd.v1 \odot \theta,\ Sd.v2 \odot \theta,\ Sd.v3 \odot \theta,\ Sd.v4 \odot \theta \rangle$
    endtype

    type *Quadrilateral*
    supertype *Sides*
    axiom forall $Q : Quadrilateral\ \bullet$
        $Q.v1 + Q.v2 + Q.v3 + Q.v4 \stackrel{\triangle}{=} 0$
    endtype

type *Parallelogram*
  supertype *Quadrilateral*
  value
    Area : *Parallelogram* ↦ **N**
  axiom forall P : *Parallelogram* •
    $P.v1 + P.v3 \triangleq 0 \land P.v2 + P.v4 \triangleq 0,$
    $\text{Area}(P) = \sqrt{\mid P.v1 \mid^2 \times \mid P.v2 \mid^2 - (P.v1 \cdot P.v2)^2}$
endtype

type *Rhombus*
  supertype *Parallelogram*
  axiom forall R : *Rhombus* •
    $\mid R.v1 \mid \triangleq \mid R.v2 \mid$
endtype

type *Rectangle*
  supertype *Parallelogram*
  axiom forall R : *Rectangle* •
    $R.v1 \cdot R.v2 \triangleq 0$
endtype

type *Square*
  supertype *Rectangle, Rhombus*
endtype

Type Declaration of Quadrilateral System

The type *Parallelogram* has defined function *Area* which computes the area of a *Parallelogram*. Additionally *Rhombus*, *Rectangle* and *Square* inherit its property by **supertype**. The *Area* function in *Parallelogram* and other types which inherit from *Parallelogram* will have the same semantic and cannot be changed in *subtype*. This property and its semantics will be discussed in details in section 3 and 4. From the hierarchy of figures above, we will show an example of writing quadrilateral box figure on the computer display screen by OOVDM. Assuming that the left-bottom of the screen is equal to co-ordinate (0,0) on the x-y axis (see Fig.2), the *QuadrilateralBox* class defines the quadrilateral box figure characteristics by the following definition:

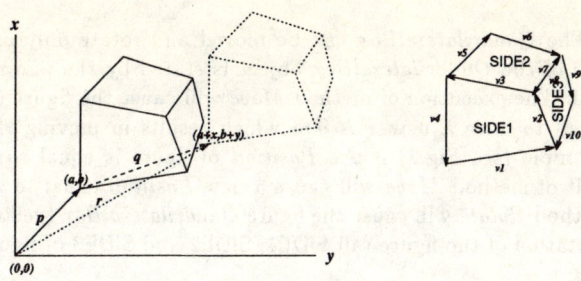

Fig.2 Defined Quadrilateral Box in x-y axis

class $QuadrilateralBox[Side\_v1, Side\_v2, Side\_v3, Side\_v4,$
$Side\_v5, Side\_v6, Side\_v7, Side\_v8,$
$Side\_v9, Side\_v10, Image\_position]$

state schema
$Side1 : Quadrilateral$
$Side2 : Quadrilateral$
$Side3 : Quadrilateral$
$Position : Vector$

initial state
$Side1 = \langle Side\_v1, Side\_v2, Side\_v3, Side\_v4 \rangle \wedge$
$Side2 = \langle Side\_v3, Side\_v5, Side\_v6, Side\_v7 \rangle \wedge$
$Side3 = \langle Side\_v2, Side\_v8, Side\_v9, Side\_v10 \rangle \wedge$
$Position = \{Image\_position\}$

method
$Move(Distance : Vector)$
    pre-
    post- $Position = \overline{Position} + Distance$
$Rotate(Face1 : Quadrilateral, Face2 : Quadrilateral,$
        $Face3 : Quadrilateral, \theta : Angle)$
    pre-
    post- $Face1 = rotate(\overline{Face1}, \theta) \wedge$
            $Face2 = rotate(\overline{Face2}, \theta) \wedge$
            $Face3 = rotate(\overline{Face3}, \theta)$

endclass

QuadrilateralBox Class Declaration

Supposed that the projection of three-dimensional quadrilateral box on x-y plane consists of the definition of three quadrilateral figures which are three *Quadrilateral* and starting origin point (See Fig. 2). Class *QuadrilateralBox* has four state variables which consist of *Side*1, *Side*2, *Side*3 and *Position*. Each of quadrilateral figure represents by vectors, we defined the figure by combine three quadrilateral figures, consequently each quadrilateral box figure has three quadrilateral surfaces (SIDE1, SIDE2 and SIDE3). SIDE1 consists of $v1$, $v2$, $v3$ and $v4$. SIDE2 consists of $v3$, $v5$, $v6$ and $v7$. SIDE3 consists of $v2$, $v8$, $v9$ and $v10$. *Position* holds the starting origin (starting co-ordinate) of figure on x-y plane. The *QuadrilateralBox* can be moved and rotate only on the x-y plane. The initial state of the *QuadrilateralBox* object is stated by the parameters when the object is created. The execution of method *Move* will cause the figure (on this example *QuadrilateralBox*) to have a new *Position* which results in moving the figure on the screen. For example (see Fig.2) if the *Position* of figure is equal to p and *Distance* is q so the result of method *Move* will cause a new *Position* equal to $r(= p + q)$. The execution of method *Rotate* will cause the figure *QuadrilateralBox* (vectors) to move and results in the rotation of the figure (all SIDE1, SIDE2 and SIDE3 of figure are rotated).

3 Inheritance in OOVDM

Inheritance is the technique to create a new class or type by using existing ones. Inheritance concepts in an object-oriented framework can be divided into two basic concepts: *incremental inheritance* and *subtyping inheritance*. *Incremental inheritance* means "adding methods and variables to an existing class to obtain a new class" and *subtyping inheritance* means "hierarchy of instances that instances of subtype are also included in instances of the supertype" [America, 1990] [Cusack, 1991] [Lee, 1989]. We have employed *incremental inheritance* for *class* modules and *subtyping inheritance* for *type* modules in OOVDM based on the concepts of *class* and *type*.

3.1 Incremental Inheritance in OOVDM

We can create a new class module by adding methods and state variable to the existing *class* module. The new class is called *subclass* of the old one (*superclass*). The methods and state variables in the *superclass* can be used in the new *subclass* as far as they are consistent to the newly added descriptions. These inheritance mechanism is called *incremental inheritance*. In case of a method and/or a state variable having the same name as the *superclass* are defined in the *subclass*, the definition of *subclass* will overwrite the old *class* definitions. In OOVDM, *subclass* can refer to *superclass* by using its name (Identity). This means that *inherited subclass* can be derived by modifying recursive instances from *superclasses*. Varieties of incremental inheritance are discussed in [Wegner, 1988]. Clearly, the *operator schemas* which are given in *superclasses* would also exploit the same rules to the instances in inherited *subclass*. From the *QuadrilateralBox* class in the previous section, we will use the *incremental inheritance* mechanism to create a new class called *RectangleBox* which is illustrated by as the following example.

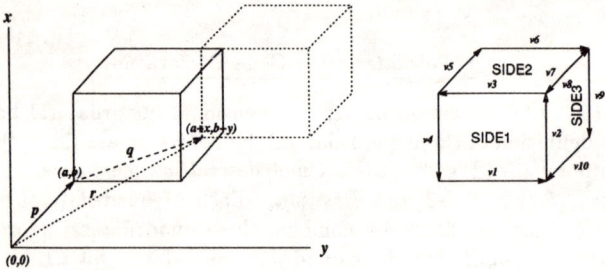

Fig.3 Defined Rectangle Box in x-y axis

```
class RectangleBox[Side_v1, Side_v2, Side_v3, Side_v4,
                  Side_v5, Side_v6, Side_v7, Side_v8,
                  Side_v9, Side_v10, Image_position]
    inherited class QuadrilateralBox
    state schema
        Side1 : Rectangle
        Side2 : Parallelogram
        Side3 : Parallelogram
    method
        RectangleBoxVolume(Face1 : Rectangle, Face2 : Parallelogram,
                          Face3 : Parallelogram, Volume : N)
        pre-
        post- Volume =| Face1.v1 | × | Face1.v2 | × | Face2.v2 |
endclass
```

<u>RectangleBox Class Declaration</u>

We defined three-dimensional rectangle box in the similar way as three-dimensional quadrilateral box. The *RectangleBox* consists of the definition of three quadrilateral figures which are one *Rectangle* and two *Parallelogram* (See Fig. 3). The methods and states of the *RectangleBox* class are inherited from the *QuadrilateralBox* class. From incremental inheritance mechanism, all the methods and states variables possessed by *QuadrilateralBox* (superclass) are also referable from this *RectangleBox* class. The *RectangleBox*'s **state schema** redefined **state schema** in *QuadrilateralBox* (*Side*1, *Side*2 and *Side*3), from the incremental inheritance property all of these three states will overwrite all *Side*1, *Side*2 and *Side*3 which are defined in its superclass (*QuadrilateralBox*). A new method *RectangleBoxVolume* is added to the *QuadrilateralBox* which calculates the volume of rectangle box.

3.2 Subtyping Inheritance in OOVDM

In typed languages such as VDM, a function defined by a type module can not be applied to a value of different type. Assume that we have defined two types *integer* and *real number*. The binary function + should be defined in both of the type modules because the function + is applied to the values of the two separated types — integer and real number. According to our intuition, + should be applied to both integers and real numbers because integers are also real numbers, i.e. the set of integers is a subset of real numbers. The concept of *subtype* results from *compatibility* [Wegner, 1988] or *substitutability* [Cusack, 1991] of application of functions. A subtype can be substituted for its supertype in a description. For example, in the description _+_: *real number* × *real number* → *real number*, we can substitute integer for real number. Let the type σ be the subtype of the type τ. The instance of the subtype σ is also an instance of the supertype τ. The denotation of the type τ is the set of values which is an instance of the type τ, $\mathcal{D}_\tau$. Thus $\mathcal{D}_\sigma \subseteq \mathcal{D}_\tau$ holds. For each function $f_\tau : D_\tau \to R_\tau$ in the supertype τ, a function $f_\sigma : D_\sigma \to R_\sigma$ in the subtype σ is defined to satisfy the following conditions:

1. The name of f_σ is the same as the name of f_τ.

2. **dom** $(D_\sigma \triangleleft f_\tau) \subseteq$ **dom** f_σ : If $x \in D_\sigma$ and $f_\tau(x)$ is defined, then $f_\sigma(x)$ is defined.

3. (**dom** $(D_\sigma \triangleleft f_\tau) \triangleleft f_\sigma) \subseteq (D_\sigma \triangleleft f_\tau)$: If $x \in D_\sigma$, $f_\tau(x)$ is defined, and $f_\sigma(x) = y$, then $f_\tau(x) = y$.

The function f_σ is inherited from the function f_τ from the supertype τ. Note that the subtype σ can have additional functions which are not included in the supertype τ. The $\triangleleft$ denotes domain restriction symbol in VDM.

Let's consider a *Parallelogram* type definition of quadrilateral system which is as follows:

> **type** *Parallelogram*
>   **supertype** *Quadrilateral*
>   **value**
>   Area : *Parallelogram* $\mapsto$ **N**
>   **axiom forall** P : *Parallelogram* •
> $P.v1 + P.v3 \triangleq 0 \wedge P.v2 + P.v4 \triangleq 0,$
> $\text{Area}(P) = \sqrt{|P.v1|^2 \times |P.v2|^2 - (P.v1.P.v2)^2}$
> **endtype**

Parallelogram Type Declaration

Let's consider a *Parallelogram* type definition of quadrilateral system which is defined in section 2.3. This type inherited from *supertype Quadrilateral* by *subtyping inheritance* mechanism, so that all the type declaration, value declaration and axiom declaration in *Quadrilateral* are inherited by the type *Parallelogram*. Furthermore a new value declaration and axiom declaration are added to type *Parallelogram* though which type *Rhombus*, *Rectangle* and *Square* inherit these properties by *subtyping inheritance* mechanism. The hierarchy of class and type on quadrilateral system are shown in Fig.4.

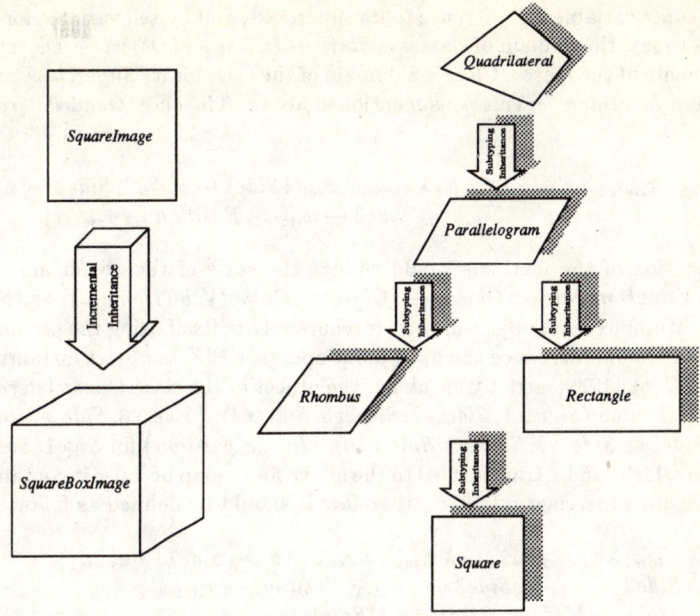

Fig.4 Incremental & Subtyping Inheritance of Quadrilateral System

4 Denotational Semantics of OOVDM

An *object* is a computational entity that can encapsulate both behaviour and state, and interacts by sending and receiving messages [Jones, 1990]. The behaviour of an object is described by its response to a message. For each different sort of message, a *method* is defined. A collection of methods define the behaviour of an object. Having defined the syntax of OOVDM in the previous section, we will specify its semantics in this section.

4.1 Denotation of Class Module

The syntax of VDM which we used to specify the method abstraction is based on [Bjørner, 1990]. Objects which are defined by OOVDM can be considered as finite mapping from state names and method names to values or functions. Referring to state values and invoking methods are *map* applications. For example, an initial object in the class *QuadrilateralBox* is

$$\{ \; Side1 \mapsto \langle Side\_v1, Side\_v2, Side\_v3, Side\_v4 \rangle ,$$
$$Side2 \mapsto \langle Side\_v3, Side\_v5, Side\_v6, Side\_v7 \rangle ,$$
$$Side3 \mapsto \langle Side\_v2, Side\_v8, Side\_v9, Side\_v10 \rangle ,$$
$$Position \mapsto \{ Image\_position \},$$
$$Move \mapsto MMove, Rotate \mapsto MRotate \}$$

where *MMove* and *MRotate* are denotation of the method *Move* and *Rotate* respectively. A class is a function which is an λ abstraction by state variables for object instantiations, by **super** variable for reference to its superclass, and by **self** variable for recursive call. That is to say, the domain of classes is $State \to (Class \to (Object \to Object))$, where $State$ is a domain of the states, $Class$ is a domain of the class for its $Superclass$, and $Object$ is a finite map $Identifier \mapsto Values$ as mentioned above. The class $QuadrilateralBox$ can be expressed as:

$$\lambda\, x_{state1} \lambda\, x_{state2} \lambda\, x_{state3} \lambda\, x_{state4} \lambda\, x_{super} \lambda\, x_{self} \{Side1 \mapsto x_{state1}, Side2 \mapsto x_{state2},$$
$$Side3 \mapsto x_{state3}, Position \mapsto x_{state4}\}$$

The execution of the methods would change the state of the object and cause the result $InputValueDomain \to (Object \to (Object \times OutputValueDomain))$ as the domain of methods. Methods in an object may refer recursively to itself using the pseudo variable x_{self}. Thus we should introduce the fixed point operator FIX to object instantiation. As discussed in [Cook, 1989], strictly speaking, the object of the class $QuadrilateralBox$ will have the initial value $\langle Side\_v1, Side\_v2, Side\_v3, Side\_v4 \rangle$, $\langle Side\_v3, Side\_v5, Side\_v6, Side\_v7 \rangle$, $\langle Side\_v2, Side\_v8, Side\_v9, Side\_v10 \rangle$, $\{Image\_position\}$ for $Side1, Side2, Side3$ and $Position$ which can be transformed to the above finite map because it contains neither self reference nor superclass reference, therefore it should be defined as follow:

$$FIX(\lambda\, x_{state1} \lambda\, x_{state2} \lambda\, x_{state3} \lambda\, x_{state4} \lambda\, x_{super} \lambda\, x_{self} \{Side1 \mapsto x_{state1},$$
$$Side2 \mapsto x_{state2}, Side3 \mapsto x_{state3}, Position \mapsto x_{state4}$$
$$Move \mapsto MMove, Rotate \mapsto MRotate\}$$
$$(\langle Side\_v1, Side\_v2, Side\_v3, Side\_v4 \rangle)$$
$$(\langle Side\_v3, Side\_v5, Side\_v6, Side\_v7 \rangle)$$
$$(\langle Side\_v2, Side\_v8, Side\_v9, Side\_v10 \rangle)(\{Image\_position\})$$

The meaning of OOVDM description is the meaning of class modules and type modules which are included in the description. The denotation of class is roughly shown below:

class classname **inherited class** classname ... **state** ... $Meth\#1$ $Meth\#2$.	$\Longrightarrow$	$\lambda X_{state}\ \lambda Y_{super}\ \lambda Z_{self}$ $\begin{bmatrix} StateName & \mapsto & X_{state} \\ Meth\#1\_Id & \mapsto & MMeth\#1\_Id \\ Meth\#2\_Id & \mapsto & MMeth\#2\_Id \\ & \vdots & \\ Inherited\_Meth & \mapsto & Meth\_Id \end{bmatrix}$

Denotation of Class

Each method (for example $Meth\#1$) is transformed into the map from $Meth\#1\_Id$ to $MMeth\#1\_Id$ which stands for the denotation of the body of $Meth\#1$. The inherited method ($Inherited\_Meth$) holds only method Id ($Meth\_Id$) which refers to the denotation of its *superclass*'s method ($Meth\_Id$).

4.2 Inheritance & Subtyping Semantics

We can define super-subtype relationship in type module which will cause properties inheritance of functions in supertype to functions in subtype. The condition which is mentioned in section 3.2 asserts that the properties of a supertype are preserved in subtype, so the inherited function f_σ should accept at least all the input values that f_τ can accept and return the same value. Now we will show how formal semantics of the inherited functions in a subtype module satisfied this condition. The meaning of the inherited function can be defined by using the meaning of the function f_τ as follows. Let $F_\sigma : D_\sigma \to R_\sigma$ and F_τ be the denotations of the functions f_σ and f_τ respectively.

$$F_\sigma \equiv M[DescriptionsOf\_f_\sigma] \dagger (D_\sigma \triangleleft F_\tau)$$

where M is a meaning function and $DescriptionsOf\_f_\sigma$ is a OOVDM source code of f_σ.

Let's consider an example of type module *Parallelogram* and *Rhombus*. From the definition of function *Area* in type *Parallelogram*, this function is the map function to natural number.

$$Area_{Parallelogram} : \mathcal{D}_{Parallelogram} \mapsto \mathcal{D}_N$$

From the definition of type *Rhombus*, which take *Parallelogram*'s function *Area* by subtyping inheritance mechanism. The meaning of inherited function $Area_{Rhombus}$ is written below:

$$\begin{aligned} Area_{Rhombus} &= \phi \dagger (\mathcal{D}_{Rhombus} \triangleleft Area_{Parallelogram}) \\ &= \mathcal{D}_{Rhombus} \triangleleft Area_{Parallelogram} \end{aligned}$$

$Area_{Rhombus}$ is the same as $Area_{Parallelogram}$ except for its domain, i.e. the domain of $Area_{Rhombus}$ is restricted to the $\mathcal{D}_{Rhombus}$ which is the subset of domain of $\mathcal{D}_{Parallelogram}$ ($\mathcal{D}_{Rhombus} \subset \mathcal{D}_{Parallelogram}$).

The main difference of subtying and incremental inheritance is that in subtying inheritance the descriptions of the supertype override its subtype in case that conflict about output values has occurred.

An *object* is represented by a finite map of VDM, so we can simply define the semantics of incremental inheritance mechanism by using map overwriting operator of VDM. Let Δ be a denotation of a class δ, and $DescriptionsOf\_\sigma$ be an OOVDM source code of a subclass module σ. The denotation Σ of the subclass σ can be defined as :

$$\Sigma \equiv \lambda x_{state} \lambda y_{state} (\Delta(x_{state}) \dagger M[DescriptionsOf\_\sigma](\Delta(x_{state}))(y_{state})).$$

From the *RectangleBox* example, the denotation semantics will be expressed as follow:

$\lambda x_{state1} \lambda x_{state2} \lambda x_{state3} \lambda x_{state4} \lambda y_{state} (\Delta(x_{state1})(x_{state2})(x_{state3})(x_{state4}))$
$\dagger (\lambda y_{state} \lambda y_{super} \{ Side1 \mapsto x_{state1}, Side2 \mapsto x_{state2},$
$\quad Side3 \mapsto x_{state3}, RectangleBoxVolume \mapsto MRectangleBoxVolume \}$
$\quad (\Delta(x_{state1})(x_{state2})(x_{state3})(x_{state4}))(y_{state}))$
$= \lambda x_{state1} \lambda x_{state2} \lambda x_{state3} \lambda x_{state4} \lambda y_{state} \{ Side1 \mapsto x_{state1}, Side2 \mapsto x_{state2},$
$\quad Side3 \mapsto x_{state3}, Position \mapsto x_{state4}, Move \mapsto MMove,$
$\quad Rotate \mapsto MRotate, RectangleBoxVolume \mapsto MRectangleBoxVolume \}$
where $\Delta = \lambda x_{state1} \lambda x_{state2} \lambda x_{state3} \lambda x_{state4} \{ Side1 \mapsto x_{state1}, Side2 \mapsto x_{state2},$
$\quad Side3 \mapsto x_{state3}, Position \mapsto x_{state4},$
$\quad Move \mapsto MMove, Rotate \mapsto MRotate \}$

5 Conclusion & Future Research

This paper contributes to the extension of VDM by an object-oriented concept which supports incremental & subtyping inheritance. Since the concepts and aims of the two inheritance mechanisms should be developed separately, our language OOVDM has two kinds of modules for objects and data, each module has the facility of either of these inheritance mechanisms. We have applied incremental inheritance for class module, and subtyping inheritance for type module. Class concept and its inheritance mechanisms emphasis on reusable of descriptions, while type concept and its inheritance mechanisms are used for hierarchical classification of object's states.

Our future research will focus on improvement of OOVDM with the feature to describe concurrent systems, reactive systems, and real time systems. We will introduce the concurrency of objects, and synchronization mechanisms to OOVDM. Furthermore a technique to provide the denotational semantics for the language will be developed. New feature such as multiple inheritance will be introduced into OOVDM. Since the scope of this paper has been restricted to single inheritance, we will explore multiple inheritance mechanism for both *incremental inheritance* and *subtyping inheritance* in the future.

References

[America, 1990] Pierre America, Frank van der Linden, *"A Parallel Object Oriented Language with Inheritance and Subtyping"* ECOOP/OOPSLA'90 Proceedings, pp.161-168, October 1990.

[Bjørner, 1990] Dines Bjørner, *"Formal Software Development The VDM Approach"*, 1990.

[Booch, 1991] Grady Booch, *"Object-Oriented Design with applications"*, Prentice Hall, 1991.

[BSI, 1991] BSI IST/5/50, *"VDM Specification Language"*, March 1991.

[Carrington, 1990] D. Carrington, D. Duke, R. Duke, P. King, G. Rose, G. Smith, *"Object-Z: An object-oriented extension to Z"*, FORTE89, pp.281-296, 1990.

[Cook, 1989] W. Cook, J. Palsberg, *"A Denotational Semantics of Inheritance and its Correctness"*, OOPSLA'89 Proceedings, pp.433-443, 1989.

[Cusack, 1990] E. Cusack, S. Rudkin, C. Smith, *"An Object Oriented Interpretation of LOTOS"*, FORTE89, Formal Description Technique II, pp.211-226, 1990.

[Cusack, 1991] Elspet Cusack, *"Inheritance In Object Oriented Z"*, ECOOP'91, July 1991.

[Dahl, 1990] Ole-Johan Dahl, *"Object Orientation and Formal Techniques"*, VDM'90 VDM and Z, April 1990.

[Duke, 1991] Roger Duke, Paul King, Gordon Rose, Graeme Smith, *"The Object-Z Specification Language Version 1"*, Technical Report, Queensland 4072, May 1991.

[Freeman, 1989] P.Freeman, *"Strategic Directions in Software Engineering: Past, Present and Future"*, In G.X. Ritter, editor, IFIP 89, pages 205-210, North-Holland, 1989.

[George, 1991] Chris George, *"The RAISE Specification Language, A Tutorial"*, VDM'91 Formal Software Development Methods, October 1991.

[ISO 8807] *"Information processing systems – Open Systems Interconnection – LOTOS – A formal description technique based on the temporal ordering of obsevational behaviour"*, ISO 8007, 1989.

[Jones, 1986] Cliff B. Jones, *"Systematic Software Development Using VDM"*, C.A.R.Hoare series, Prentice-Hall, 1986.

[Jones, 1990] C.B. Jones, R.C. Shaw, *"Case Studies in Systematic Software Development "*, Prentice Hall, 1990.

[Lano, 1992] K. Lano, H. Haughton, *"Reasoning and Refinement in Object-Oriented Specification Languages"*, ECOOP'92, pp.78-97, 1992.

[Ledru, 1991] Yves Ledru, *"Towards the Formal Development of Terminating Reactive Systems"*, Docteur en Sciences Appliquées, Dec. 1991.

[Lee, 1989] K. Lee, J. H. Hur, *"OLOTOS: An Object-Oriented Extension of LOTOS for Distributed Processing"*, KAIST Technical Report, CS-TR-89-41, 1989.

[Meyer, 1988] Bertrand Meyer, *"Object-oriented Software Construction"*, C.A.R.Hoare series, Prentice-Hall, 1988.

[Middelburg, 1988] K. Middelburg, *"The VIP VDM Specification Language"*, VDM'88- The way Ahead, Springer-Verlag, 1988.

[Schmidt, 1990] Uwe Schmidt, Hans-Martin Hörcher, Norsk Data GmbH, *"Programming with VDM Domains"*, VDM'90 VDM and Z, April 1990.

[Spivey, 1988] J.M. Spivey, *"Understanding Z, a Specification Language and its Formal Semantics"*, Cambridge University Press, 1988.

[Stølen, 1991] K. Stølen, *"An Attempt to Reason about Shared-State Concurrency in the style of VDM"*, VDM'91 Formal Software Development Methods, October 1991.

[Wegner, 1988] Peter Wegner & Stanlet B. Zdonik, *"Inheritance as an Incremental Modification Mechanism or What Like Is and Isn't Like"*, ECOOP'88, pp.55-77, 1988.

[Wordsworth, 1988] J.B. Wordsworth, *"Practical experience of formal specification: a programming interface for communications"*, ESEC'89, pages 140-158, Springer-Verlag, 1988.

[Vissers, 1990] C. A. Vissers, *"FDTs for Open Distributed Systems, a Retrospective and a Prospective View"*, Protocol Specification, Testing, and Verification, X, pp.341-362, June 1990.

Springer-Verlag and the Environment

We at Springer-Verlag firmly believe that an international science publisher has a special obligation to the environment, and our corporate policies consistently reflect this conviction.

We also expect our business partners – paper mills, printers, packaging manufacturers, etc. – to commit themselves to using environmentally friendly materials and production processes.

The paper in this book is made from low- or no-chlorine pulp and is acid free, in conformance with international standards for paper permanency.

Lecture Notes in Computer Science

For information about Vols. 1–665
please contact your bookseller or Springer-Verlag

Vol. 666: J. W. de Bakker, W.-P. de Roever, G. Rozenberg (Eds.), Semantics: Foundations and Applications. Proceedings, 1992. VIII, 659 pages. 1993.

Vol. 667: P. B. Brazdil (Ed.), Machine Learning: ECML – 93. Proceedings, 1993. XII, 471 pages. 1993. (Subseries LNAI).

Vol. 668: M.-C. Gaudel, J.-P. Jouannaud (Eds.), TAPSOFT '93: Theory and Practice of Software Development. Proceedings, 1993. XII, 762 pages. 1993.

Vol. 669: R. S. Bird, C. C. Morgan, J. C. P. Woodcock (Eds.), Mathematics of Program Construction. Proceedings, 1992. VIII, 378 pages. 1993.

Vol. 670: J. C. P. Woodcock, P. G. Larsen (Eds.), FME '93: Industrial-Strength Formal Methods. Proceedings, 1993. XI, 689 pages. 1993.

Vol. 671: H. J. Ohlbach (Ed.), GWAI-92: Advances in Artificial Intelligence. Proceedings, 1992. XI, 397 pages. 1993. (Subseries LNAI).

Vol. 672: A. Barak, S. Guday, R. G. Wheeler, The MOSIX Distributed Operating System. X, 221 pages. 1993.

Vol. 673: G. Cohen, T. Mora, O. Moreno (Eds.), Applied Algebra, Algebraic Algorithms and Error-Correcting Codes. Proceedings, 1993. X, 355 pages 1993.

Vol. 674: G. Rozenberg (Ed.), Advances in Petri Nets 1993. VII, 457 pages. 1993.

Vol. 675: A. Mulkers, Live Data Structures in Logic Programs. VIII, 220 pages. 1993.

Vol. 676: Th. H. Reiss, Recognizing Planar Objects Using Invariant Image Features. X, 180 pages. 1993.

Vol. 677: H. Abdulrab, J.-P. Pécuchet (Eds.), Word Equations and Related Topics. Proceedings, 1991. VII, 214 pages. 1993.

Vol. 678: F. Meyer auf der Heide, B. Monien, A. L. Rosenberg (Eds.), Parallel Architectures and Their Efficient Use. Proceedings, 1992. XII, 227 pages. 1993.

Vol. 679: C. Fermüller, A. Leitsch, T. Tammet, N. Zamov, Resolution Methods for the Decision Problem. VIII, 205 pages. 1993. (Subseries LNAI).

Vol. 680: B. Hoffmann, B. Krieg-Brückner (Eds.), Program Development by Specification and Transformation. XV, 623 pages. 1993.

Vol. 681: H. Wansing, The Logic of Information Structures. IX, 163 pages. 1993. (Subseries LNAI).

Vol. 682: B. Bouchon-Meunier, L. Valverde, R. R. Yager (Eds.), IPMU '92 – Advanced Methods in Artificial Intelligence. Proceedings, 1992. IX, 367 pages. 1993.

Vol. 683: G.J. Milne, L. Pierre (Eds.), Correct Hardware Design and Verification Methods. Proceedings, 1993. VIII, 270 Pages. 1993.

Vol. 684: A. Apostolico, M. Crochemore, Z. Galil, U. Manber (Eds.), Combinatorial Pattern Matching. Proceedings, 1993. VIII, 265 pages. 1993.

Vol. 685: C. Rolland, F. Bodart, C. Cauvet (Eds.), Advanced Information Systems Engineering. Proceedings, 1993. XI, 650 pages. 1993.

Vol. 686: J. Mira, J. Cabestany, A. Prieto (Eds.), New Trends in Neural Computation. Proceedings, 1993. XVII, 746 pages. 1993.

Vol. 687: H. H. Barrett, A. F. Gmitro (Eds.), Information Processing in Medical Imaging. Proceedings, 1993. XVI, 567 pages. 1993.

Vol. 688: M. Gauthier (Ed.), Ada-Europe '93. Proceedings, 1993. VIII, 353 pages. 1993.

Vol. 689: J. Komorowski, Z. W. Ras (Eds.), Methodologies for Intelligent Systems. Proceedings, 1993. XI, 653 pages. 1993. (Subseries LNAI).

Vol. 690: C. Kirchner (Ed.), Rewriting Techniques and Applications. Proceedings, 1993. XI, 488 pages. 1993.

Vol. 691: M. Ajmone Marsan (Ed.), Application and Theory of Petri Nets 1993. Proceedings, 1993. IX, 591 pages. 1993.

Vol. 692: D. Abel, B.C. Ooi (Eds.), Advances in Spatial Databases. Proceedings, 1993. XIII, 529 pages. 1993.

Vol. 693: P. E. Lauer (Ed.), Functional Programming, Concurrency, Simulation and Automated Reasoning. Proceedings, 1991/1992. XI, 398 pages. 1993.

Vol. 694: A. Bode, M. Reeve, G. Wolf (Eds.), PARLE '93. Parallel Architectures and Languages Europe. Proceedings, 1993. XVII, 770 pages. 1993.

Vol. 695: E. P. Klement, W. Slany (Eds.), Fuzzy Logic in Artificial Intelligence. Proceedings, 1993. VIII, 192 pages. 1993. (Subseries LNAI).

Vol. 696: M. Worboys, A. F. Grundy (Eds.), Advances in Databases. Proceedings, 1993. X, 276 pages. 1993.

Vol. 697: C. Courcoubetis (Ed.), Computer Aided Verification. Proceedings, 1993. IX, 504 pages. 1993.

Vol. 698: A. Voronkov (Ed.), Logic Programming and Automated Reasoning. Proceedings, 1993. XIII, 386 pages. 1993. (Subseries LNAI).

Vol. 699: G. W. Mineau, B. Moulin, J. F. Sowa (Eds.), Conceptual Graphs for Knowledge Representation. Proceedings, 1993. IX, 451 pages. 1993. (Subseries LNAI).

Vol. 700: A. Lingas, R. Karlsson, S. Carlsson (Eds.), Automata, Languages and Programming. Proceedings, 1993. XII, 697 pages. 1993.

Vol. 701: P. Atzeni (Ed.), LOGIDATA+: Deductive Databases with Complex Objects. VIII, 273 pages. 1993.

Vol. 702: E. Börger, G. Jäger, H. Kleine Büning, S. Martini, M. M. Richter (Eds.), Computer Science Logic. Proceedings, 1992. VIII, 439 pages. 1993.

Vol. 703: M. de Berg, Ray Shooting, Depth Orders and Hidden Surface Removal. X, 201 pages. 1993.

Vol. 704: F. N. Paulisch, The Design of an Extendible Graph Editor. XV, 184 pages. 1993.

Vol. 705: H. Grünbacher, R. W. Hartenstein (Eds.), Field-Programmable Gate Arrays. Proceedings, 1992. VIII, 218 pages. 1993.

Vol. 706: H. D. Rombach, V. R. Basili, R. W. Selby (Eds.), Experimental Software Engineering Issues. Proceedings, 1992. XVIII, 261 pages. 1993.

Vol. 707: O. M. Nierstrasz (Ed.), ECOOP '93 – Object-Oriented Programming. Proceedings, 1993. XI, 531 pages. 1993.

Vol. 708: C. Laugier (Ed.), Geometric Reasoning for Perception and Action. Proceedings, 1991. VIII, 281 pages. 1993.

Vol. 709: F. Dehne, J.-R. Sack, N. Santoro, S. Whitesides (Eds.), Algorithms and Data Structures. Proceedings, 1993. XII, 634 pages. 1993.

Vol. 710: Z. Ésik (Ed.), Fundamentals of Computation Theory. Proceedings, 1993. IX, 471 pages. 1993.

Vol. 711: A. M. Borzyszkowski, S. Sokołowski (Eds.), Mathematical Foundations of Computer Science 1993. Proceedings, 1993. XIII, 782 pages. 1993.

Vol. 712: P. V. Rangan (Ed.), Network and Operating System Support for Digital Audio and Video. Proceedings, 1992. X, 416 pages. 1993.

Vol. 713: G. Gottlob, A. Leitsch, D. Mundici (Eds.), Computational Logic and Proof Theory. Proceedings, 1993. XI, 348 pages. 1993.

Vol. 714: M. Bruynooghe, J. Penjam (Eds.), Programming Language Implementation and Logic Programming. Proceedings, 1993. XI, 421 pages. 1993.

Vol. 715: E. Best (Ed.), CONCUR'93. Proceedings, 1993. IX, 541 pages. 1993.

Vol. 716: A. U. Frank, I. Campari (Eds.), Spatial Information Theory. Proceedings, 1993. XI, 478 pages. 1993.

Vol. 717: I. Sommerville, M. Paul (Eds.), Software Engineering – ESEC '93. Proceedings, 1993. XII, 516 pages. 1993.

Vol. 718: J. Seberry, Y. Zheng (Eds.), Advances in Cryptology – AUSCRYPT '92. Proceedings, 1992. XIII, 543 pages. 1993.

Vol. 719: D. Chetverikov, W.G. Kropatsch (Eds.), Computer Analysis of Images and Patterns. Proceedings, 1993. XVI, 857 pages. 1993.

Vol. 720: V.Mařík, J. Lažanský, R.R. Wagner (Eds.), Database and Expert Systems Applications. Proceedings, 1993. XV, 768 pages. 1993.

Vol. 721: J. Fitch (Ed.), Design and Implementation of Symbolic Computation Systems. Proceedings, 1992. VIII, 215 pages. 1993.

Vol. 722: A. Miola (Ed.), Design and Implementation of Symbolic Computation Systems. Proceedings, 1993. XII, 384 pages. 1993.

Vol. 723: N. Aussenac, G. Boy, B. Gaines, M. Linster, J.-G. Ganascia, Y. Kodratoff (Eds.), Knowledge Acquisition for Knowledge-Based Systems. Proceedings, 1993. XIII, 446 pages. 1993. (Subseries LNAI).

Vol. 724: P. Cousot, M. Falaschi, G. Filè, A. Rauzy (Eds.), Static Analysis. Proceedings, 1993. IX, 283 pages. 1993.

Vol. 725: A. Schiper (Ed.), Distributed Algorithms. Proceedings, 1993. VIII, 325 pages. 1993.

Vol. 726: T. Lengauer (Ed.), Algorithms – ESA '93. Proceedings, 1993. IX, 419 pages. 1993

Vol. 727: M. Filgueiras, L. Damas (Eds.), Progress in Artificial Intelligence. Proceedings, 1993. X, 362 pages. 1993. (Subseries LNAI).

Vol. 728: P. Torasso (Ed.), Advances in Artificial Intelligence. Proceedings, 1993. XI, 336 pages. 1993. (Subseries LNAI).

Vol. 729: L. Donatiello, R. Nelson (Eds.), Performance Evaluation of Computer and Communication Systems. Proceedings, 1993. VIII, 675 pages. 1993.

Vol. 730: D. B. Lomet (Ed.), Foundations of Data Organization and Algorithms. Proceedings, 1993. XII, 412 pages. 1993.

Vol. 731: A. Schill (Ed.), DCE – The OSF Distributed Computing Environment. Proceedings, 1993. VIII, 285 pages. 1993.

Vol. 732: A. Bode, M. Dal Cin (Eds.), Parallel Computer Architectures. IX, 311 pages. 1993.

Vol. 733: Th. Grechenig, M. Tscheligi (Eds.), Human Computer Interaction. Proceedings, 1993. XIV, 450 pages. 1993.

Vol. 734: J. Volkert (Ed.), Parallel Computation. Proceedings, 1993. VIII, 248 pages. 1993.

Vol. 735: D. Bjørner, M. Broy, I. V. Pottosin (Eds.), Formal Methods in Programming and Their Applications. Proceedings, 1993. IX, 434 pages. 1993.

Vol. 736: R. L. Grossman, A. Nerode, A. P. Ravn, H. Rischel (Eds.), Hybrid Systems. VIII, 474 pages. 1993.

Vol. 737: J. Calmet, J. A. Campbell (Eds.), Artificial Intelligence and Symbolic Mathematical Computing. Proceedings, 1992. VIII, 305 pages. 1993.

Vol. 738: M. Weber, M. Simons, Ch. Lafontaine, The Generic Development Language Deva. XIII, 246 pages. 1993.

Vol. 739: H. Imai, R. L. Rivest, T. Matsumoto (Eds.), Advances in Cryptology – ASIACRYPT '91. X, 499 pages. 1993.

Vol. 740: E. F. Brickell (Ed.), Advances in Cryptology – CRYPTO '92. Proceedings, 1992. X, 565 pages. 1993.

Vol. 741: B. Preneel, R. Govaerts, J. Vandewalle (Eds.), Computer Security and Industrial Cryptography. ESAT, 1991. VIII, 274 pages. 1993.

Vol. 742: S. Nishio, A. Yonezawa (Eds.), Object Technologies for Advanced Software. Proceedings, 1993. X, 543 pages. 1993.